Deploying ACI

The complete guide to planning, configuring, and managing Application Centric Infrastructure

Frank Dagenhardt, CCIE No. 42081,

Jose Moreno, CCIE No. 16601,

With contributions from
Bill Dufresne, CCIE No. 4375

Cisco Press

800 East 96th Street

Indianapolis, Indiana 46240 USA

Deploying ACI

The complete guide to planning, configuring, and managing Application Centric Infrastructure

Frank Dagenhardt, Jose Moreno, Bill Dufresne

Copyright © 2018 Cisco Systems, Inc.

Published by:
Cisco Press
800 East 96th Street
Indianapolis, IN 46240 USA

Printed in the United States of America

1   18

Library of Congress Control Number: 2017962494

ISBN-13: 978-1-58714-474-5

ISBN-10: 1-58714-474-3

Warning and Disclaimer

Trademark Acknowledgments

All terms mentioned in this book that are known to be trademarks or service marks have been appropriately capitalized. Cisco Press or Cisco Systems, Inc., cannot attest to the accuracy of this information. Use of a term in this book should not be regarded as affecting the validity of any trademark or service mark.

Special Sales

For information about buying this title in bulk quantities, or for special sales opportunities (which may include electronic versions; custom cover designs; and content particular to your business, training goals, marketing focus, or branding interests), please contact our corporate sales department at corpsales@pearsoned.com or (800) 382-3419.

For government sales inquiries, please contact governmentsales@pearsoned.com.

For questions about sales outside the U.S., please contact intlcs@pearson.com.

Feedback Information

At Cisco Press, our goal is to create in-depth technical books of the highest quality and value. Each book is crafted with care and precision, undergoing rigorous development that involves the unique expertise of members from the professional technical community.

Readers' feedback is a natural continuation of this process. If you have any comments regarding how we could improve the quality of this book, or otherwise alter it to better suit your needs, you can contact us through email at feedback@ciscopress.com. Please make sure to include the book title and ISBN in your message.

We greatly appreciate your assistance.

Editor-in-Chief: Mark Taub

Alliances Manager, Cisco Press: Arezou Gol

Product Line Manager: Brett Bartow

Executive Editor: Mary Beth Ray

Managing Editor: Sandra Schroeder

Development Editor: Christopher Cleveland

Project Editor: Mandie Frank

Copy Editor: Bart Reed

Technical Editors: Lauren Malhoit, Sadiq Hussain Memon

Editorial Assistant: Vanessa Evans

Designer: Chuti Prasertsith

Composition: codemantra

Indexer: Erika Millen

Proofreader: Larry Sulky

Americas Headquarters
Cisco Systems, Inc.
San Jose, CA

Asia Pacific Headquarters
Cisco Systems (USA) Pte. Ltd.
Singapore

Europe Headquarters
Cisco Systems International BV Amsterdam,
The Netherlands

Cisco has more than 200 offices worldwide. Addresses, phone numbers, and fax numbers are listed on the Cisco Website at www.cisco.com/go/offices.

Cisco and the Cisco logo are trademarks or registered trademarks of Cisco and/or its affiliates in the U.S. and other countries. To view a list of Cisco trademarks, go to this URL: www.cisco.com/go/trademarks. Third party trademarks mentioned are the property of their respective owners. The use of the word partner does not imply a partnership relationship between Cisco and any other company. (1110R)

About the Authors

Frank Dagenhardt, CCIE No. 42081, is a technical solutions architect for Cisco focusing on next-generation data center architectures. Frank has over 22 years in Information Technology and holds certifications from HP, Microsoft, Citrix, and Cisco. A Cisco veteran of over 11 years, he works with customers daily, designing, implementing, and supporting end-to-end architectures and solutions. In recent months, he has been focusing on policy, automation, and analytics. Frank has worked on and continues to be involved in publications about Cisco products. He presents regularly at Cisco Live on data center topics. He lives in Michigan with his wife and four wonderful children.

Jose Moreno, CCIE No. 16601 and CCDE No. 20100008, attended the Polytechnic Universities of Madrid and Milan. After he graduated, he started his career as a network architect in a big data center in Germany, at Amadeus Data Processing. In 2007 he moved to Cisco, where he started working as data center systems engineer. Since then he has worked in many different Cisco data center technologies, including Cisco Unified Compute System and the Cisco Nexus switching series. Since 2014 Jose has focused on Cisco Application Centric Infrastructure as a technical solutions architect. Jose has presented multiple times at Cisco Live. He lives with his wife and children in Munich, Germany.

Bill Dufresne is a Distinguished Systems Engineer and member of the Data Center/Cloud Team at Cisco. He regularly works with customers on complex technical designs while leading global teams in various disciplines. He has been with Cisco since 1996 and has more than 31 years of experience in the IT industry. Bill has held several industry certifications, including Cisco CCIE for more than 19 years, VMware VCP, CISSP, Microsoft, and even Banyan Vines. He is an expert in Routing & Switching, Data Center Compute Infrastructure, Software Defined Networking, Virtual Networking, Analytics, and foremost, an expert in Systems, Application, and Cloud Adoption. Bill is a frequent speaker at a multitude of industry conferences including Cisco Live, VMWorld, VMware Partner Exchange, VMware User Groups, EMC World, and various other events. He has worked with many customers of all sizes, across verticals such as Global Financial; Transportation; Retail; Healthcare; State, Local, and National Government; and Higher Education. Bill lives south of Nashville, TN with his wonderful wife, enjoying their 'empty nest' years.

About the Technical Reviewers

Lauren Malhoit has been in the IT industry for over 15 years, starting off as a systems engineer, moving to pre- and post-sales, and finally working at Cisco as a technical marketing engineer for the INSBU for over three years. She's currently the chief technologist and co-host of the Cisco TechWiseTV series.

Sadiq Memon has been with Cisco for 10 years, with 26 years of diversified experience in the IT industry overall. He has been the lead architect from Cisco Advanced Services for many data center projects covering Cisco's Auto & Manufacturing customers globally. Sadiq is one of the few solutions architects from Cisco Advanced Services who started working on ACI technology during its incubation period. He has presented at Cisco Live and participates actively on various blogs and GitHub. Sadiq graduated with a degree in computer systems engineering and possesses several industry certifications, including Cisco's CCIE and CCNA, VMware VCP-DCV, Citrix CCA, and Microsoft MCSE.

Dedications

From Frank:

I would like to dedicate this book to my loving wife Sansi and our four children: Frank, Everett, Cole, and Mia. Sansi, your companionship and encouragement have and always will be the key to any success I enjoy. Thank you for your love and support. Frank, Everett, Cole, and Mia, I thank God for you every day. I can't wait to see where your paths take you. I would also like to further dedicate this book to my parents, Jim and Patty. Your guidance and upbringing made me who I am today and taught me that "you can do anything you put your mind to".

From Jose:

This book is dedicated to Yolanda. Thank you for getting the best out of me.

From Bill:

I would like to thank my family, foremost. Without their support of my work in this challenging space, none of this would have been possible. Especially my lovely and supportive wife, Jill. She always understands the demands of my work, when it takes me time zones away via plane or even a WebEx or Telepresence call. I would also like to thank, posthumously, my maternal grandparents for instilling in me humility and a willingness to help solve challenges that others face. There are too many folks within Cisco to thank individually, but know that if you and I have worked together, you have inspired me in some way. I would also like to thank the myriad of customers over my career. Each interaction has taught me something that I can apply in my future endeavors, and I hope that I have provided value to you likewise - Ancora Imparo.

Acknowledgements

Frank Dagenhardt: I'd like to say thank you to Mark Stanton, who took a chance on me and hired me into Cisco all those years ago.

Thank you to Jim Pisano and James Christopher, for letting me be a part of the best team in Cisco. Without our experiences over the last few years, this book wouldn't have been possible.

Thank you to the INSBU and all of the product managers and TMEs. Thank you for access to information and documentation, as well as all the consultations you have provided over the years—especially Vipul Shah and John Weston.

Mary Beth Ray, thank you for your constant and unwavering support in this endeavor and your infinite patience every time one of my dates slipped.

Chris Cleveland, it was a pleasure to work with you again. Your expertise, professionalism, attention to detail, and follow-up were amazing as always. Thank you for everything.

To our technical editors, Lauren Malhoit and Sadiq Memon: Having been a technical editor in the past, I understand better than most the dedication and effort you put into this book. Thank you for your technical expertise and honest and accurate feedback. We couldn't have done this without you.

Thank-you to the entire production team for this book.

I'd like to thank my co-authors, Jose Moreno and Bill Dufresne. Jose, you are a rock star! I really enjoyed working with you on this project. Even though we were half the world away, we accomplished a lot. You are one of the best engineers I have ever met, and genuinely a great guy. Thanks for everything! Bill, thank you for your contributions to this book. I learn something from you every time we work together. People like you and Jose are the reason why I love my job.

Finally, I want to thank God for the gifts He has given me and the opportunity to do what I love to support my family. I couldn't ask for more.

Jose: I would like to thank Uwe Müller, who made it possible for me, despite a difficult situation, to join the fascinating world of software-defined networking at Cisco. My gratitude also goes to Luciano Pomelli, James Christopher, and Matt Smorto, who gave me the chance to join an ACI-focused team.

I would like to give special recognition to Juan Lage, who has always been a lighthouse for me, providing his expert technical knowledge and nontechnical wisdom—besides sharing a liking for the best soccer team in the world.

A big thank-you goes out to the production team for this book. Mary Beth Ray and Christopher Cleveland have been incredibly professional and a pleasure to work with. I couldn't have asked for a finer team. Huge thanks as well to Bart Reed and Mandie Frank, who went through the pain of correcting my Spanish-influenced English.

A significant part of the work bringing this book to life was done by the technical editors, Lauren Malhoit and Sadiq Memon. It has been great to see how thoroughly you went through every single line.

Lastly, I would like to thank my co-authors, Bill Dufresne and especially Frank Dagenhardt, for their dedication and perseverance in making this book possible, and for offering me the chance to contribute to this project. It has truly been an honor working with you.

Contents at a Glance

Contents

Reader Services

Register your copy at www.ciscopress.com/title/ISBN for convenient access to downloads, updates, and corrections as they become available. To start the registration process, go to www.ciscopress.com/register and log in or create an account*. Enter the product ISBN 9781587144745 and click Submit. When the process is complete, you will find any available bonus content under Registered Products.

*Be sure to check the box that you would like to hear from us to receive exclusive discounts on future editions of this product.

Introduction

It's a whole new world in the data center compared to just a few years ago. Some engineers would question whether we even call it a data center anymore, and whether we should call it a cloud (private) edge instead. New data centers are being built or retrofitted with enhanced capabilities around performance, redundancy, security, visibility, L4-7 service insertion, automation, and operational efficiency. With these goals in mind, Cisco has launched ACI as its premier data center SDN (software-defined networking) platform in order to meet these changes and provide a platform with the scalability, reliability, and comprehensive feature set required in the next-generation data center.

The purpose of this book is to provide a guide for IT professionals who might not be familiar with Application Centric Infrastructure (ACI). It is intended to be used as a "go-to" resource for design considerations and for concise information on the most commonly used aspects of ACI.

Goals and Methods

The goal of this book is to provide a field guide for designing and deploying ACI. This book also tries to bridge the gap between traditional network architectures and ACI by explaining why we do things the way we do. We've tried to bring this information together into one place, with in-depth explanations. Having been network administrators ourselves, we the authors are conscious of the pressures and challenges of finding accurate and relevant information, especially on new technology. We intend this book to be a resource network administrators reach for first. Although there might be more than one way to accomplish a networking requirement, this book focuses on the best way that minimizes operational complexity and maximizes supportability. We realize and respect that there might be corner-case scenarios that call for configurations not described in this book, but we sincerely hope we address the vast majority of common configurations.

Who Should Read This Book?

The target audience for this book is networking engineers in organizations that want to incorporate Cisco data center technologies into their businesses—more specifically, professionals who want to learn about Cisco SDN for next-generation data center fabrics and how Cisco is addressing this trend in the market.

Also, virtualization professionals willing to deepen their networking knowledge will hopefully find this book valuable and easy to follow—especially Chapter 4, which deals with the integration of Cisco ACI with virtualization technologies.

Finally, this book can be very valuable for technicians and operators who desire a solid conceptual background before working with Cisco Nexus 9000 products and solutions.

How This Book Is Organized

This book has been organized in a similar manner to how you might encounter different decision points when deploying a data center network fabric. The initial chapters start with an introduction to ACI and focus on building or designing a fabric. The next step after deciding on a design is bringing up a fabric for the first time and integrating with virtualization platforms. An introduction to networking in ACI and external connectivity are then explored. Next, we examine how to manage an ACI network versus a traditional network. With the drive toward microsegmentation, the need for increased visibility and control arises, which is why we next explore the migration to application-centric networking. Multitenancy is detailed before moving to the next topic, integrating L4-7 services, where any service device can be inserted into an application data flow quickly and easily. Most organizations are concerned with redundancy and high availability, so we examine Multi-Site ACI designs next. This book would be incomplete if we helped you design and implement ACI without exploring how to troubleshoot and monitor an ACI fabric. The last chapter features an overview of programmability and automation. Many organizations are trying to build their own private cloud. We will examine the features and capabilities that ACI has to help you become cloud like or operationally efficient.

In particular, Chapters 1 through 13 cover the following topics:

- **Chapter 1, "You've Purchased ACI. Now What?":** This chapter provides the reader with a foundation for understanding what trends are driving the adoption of ACI in today's data centers. In addition, a high-level overview of ACI and its capabilities is provided.

- **Chapter 2, "Building a Fabric":** This chapter focuses on common decision points when designing and building an ACI fabric.

- **Chapter 3, "Bringing Up a Fabric":** This chapter delves into the basic requirements and how to interface with the devices to bring up a fabric for the first time.

- **Chapter 4, "Integration of Virtualization Technologies with ACI":** This chapter provides the information needed to decide how to integrate with ACI and which virtualization technologies to use.

- **Chapter 5, "Introduction to Networking with ACI":** This chapter focuses on how networking is performed inside the ACI fabric as well as how it differs from how we have done it in the past.

- **Chapter 6, "External Routing with ACI":** This chapter delves into how to connect external networks and devices to ACI from a Layer 2 and Layer 3 standpoint.

- **Chapter 7, "How Life Is Different with ACI":** This chapter provides insight into the differences between managing a traditional network "switch by switch" and managing an ACI network as a single fabric with tenants and application policy.

- **Chapter 8, "Moving to Application-Centric Networking"**: This chapter explores the advantages of configuring more granular policy based on applications and their functions.

- **Chapter 9, "Multi-Tenancy"**: This chapter covers the ability to create separate tenants on an ACI network. It explores some of the use cases for this feature and the effect it may have on your network, security, and services resources.

- **Chapter 10, "Integrating L4-7 Services"**: This chapter delves into the details of integrating services into the ACI fabric. It explores different device types, design scenarios, and how to implement them in ACI.

- **Chapter 11, "Multi-Site Designs"**: This chapter provides an introduction to and overview of the different ways ACI can be configured to meet redundancy or business continuity requirements through the use of separate ACI fabrics.

- **Chapter 12, "Troubleshooting and Monitoring"**: This chapter covers the troubleshooting and monitoring tools built into ACI to help find and resolve issues with the ACI fabric or the devices connected to it.

- **Chapter 13, "ACI Programmability"**: This chapter provides an introduction to and overview of automation programmability and how you can use it to become more operationally efficient with ACI.

Chapter 1

You've Purchased ACI. Now What?

Well, you've decided to walk the Application Centric Infrastructure (ACI) path. You may be asking yourself, "Now what?" or "Where do I start?" Although every new project raises questions like this, ACI takes things to a different level, because, for the first time in the history of networking, you have a truly novel way of building and operating the infrastructure. Let's talk about some of those basic changes you will learn about in this book.

Industry Trends and Transitions

We'll start with why you even considered ACI in the first place. Industry changes are impacting almost every aspect of IT. Applications are changing immensely, and we're seeing their lifecycles being broken into smaller and smaller windows as the applications themselves are becoming less structured. What the network used to control and secure has changed greatly with virtualization via hypervisors. With containers and microservices being deployed more readily, we're seeing change happen at a much faster pace.

Recall what moving application workloads from "physical" to "virtual" meant to traffic flows within the data center. Those long-established north-south flows were significantly disrupted to a more east-west direction. Assume, for a moment, that the collapse ratio of a physical-to-virtual move is 1:30. Now imagine the potential collapse ratio using containers at a factor of 1:300. Consider the impact of this new east-west pattern. As we look at these new traffic flow patterns, consider that many data centers still contain mainframes and other legacy compute elements, as well as physical x86-based bare metal servers, hypervisors, containers, microservices, and whatever may be next. This is where ACI excels: It supports various workload platforms simultaneously and consistently.

This faster pace necessitates change in how the networks are built, maintained, and operated. It also requires a fundamental change to how networks provide security via segmentation. Firewalls alone cannot keep pace, and neither can manual device-by-device configuration. No matter how good you are at copying and pasting, you're eventually going to commit a mistake—a mistake that will impact the stability of the network.

It is time for an evolutionary approach to systems and network availability. It is time to embrace policy.

Next-Generation Data Center Concepts

The days of the static data center ended when x86 virtualization took hold in the 2000s. However, that was not the end of the story for workload agility. Just as our personal communication devices get more powerful and easier to use, so too have application architectures. Yes, containers and microservices are becoming a reality because the agility, comparative availability, and scale of virtualized workloads are not enough for businesses going forward. With that in mind, what customers had called data centers are now being retooled as private clouds. In all, this is a useful change because it enables the infrastructure to provide what the applications need instead of the applications being made to fit a system's model.

Along with new models for applications, the impact on the network has been a change to much more of an east-west traffic flow. The use of hypervisors to host application work-loads began this new traffic paradigm. If you consider the density of workloads per host on a hypervisor, containers as a method of virtualization offer a much higher density, due to the fact that only the application and not the operating system is included in each container. This is the impact we now must build networks to support, spreading the traf-fic patterns between various applications' workload elements. We must also consider the fact that there will continue to be host-, hypervisor-, container-, and microservice-based workloads all coexisting on the same network infrastructure.

This means that the network now needs to be as flexible and scalable (for both increase and decrease) as the applications it supports. This is where a workload-independent network policy really enables IT to provide that private cloud capability for workloads, whether bare metal, virtualized, containers, or microservice based. Without this consis-tent policy, the effect of having to manage different types of workloads, potentially for the same application, becomes a huge administrative burden. If we consider that between 60% and 70% of the cost of an infrastructure is administrative (that is, the people operat-ing it), it's the first area of focus for bringing those costs down. In addition, use of net-work policy enables the eventual movement of workloads between private clouds (includ-ing multiple locations) and public clouds, thus enabling the realization that is the hybrid cloud.

New Application Types

We've briefly touched on new application models. We can follow the change in application design with the change in how we more effectively communicate via smart devices of all types. Whereas applications used to reside exclusively inside the walls of the data center, now the applications (or elements of them) can also reside in the public cloud or on the smart device itself. Let's follow the well-understood model of the smart device application. It must be compact in size and able to be versioned with some regularity. You are certainly well aware of how you see daily updates to certain smart device applications. This is the new model of application development and maintenance that traditional data centers must be able to adapt to in order to become private cloud infrastructures.

So how do we take something like a smart-device application and apply it to something like an Enterprise Resource Planning (ERP) style application? Consider all the moving pieces of an ERP application: There are presentation tier elements, several database elements, and application logic of multiple elements such as customer contacts, projects, products, and so on. Let's take just the most common of these elements: the presentation tier (in essence, the web front end). This can now evolve into a smart-device element, but some level of access from traditional x86-based laptops and desktops also needs to be present. In recent applications (many are called *traditional applications*), these web servers provided content to browsers via multiple ports and protocols, for example including TCP-80, TCP-443, TCP-8080, TCP-8443, and UDP-FTP. Scale was achieved by adding more web servers, all configured identically.

You might think that having 10 or more web servers configured identically would be just fine. However, consider the recent security vulnerabilities on SSL (eventually on multiple TCP ports like 443, 8443, and so on). Now having to patch every server for that vulnerability basically takes the application out of service or leaves critical vulnerabilities in the application. Instead, modern application design breaks those elements down to the very essence of the service they provide—the microservice. Imagine being able to patch the SSL vulnerability by creating new operating elements of the presentation tier that include the SSL fix for ports 443 and 8443 and deploy them without touching the port 80 and 8080 microservices? Think of this when it comes to scale of the application.

Consider the idea of what in the retail industry is known as "looks to books." In other words, someone browsing for information or a product is a "look", whereas a user wanting to perform a secured transaction is a "book." Each of these uses different ports of the application tier. Should you scale the SSL portion of the application tier if you see a spike in look-related traffic? It's not the most efficient use of infrastructure resources. Therefore, microservices design provides the freedom to scale, patch, update, and quiesce elements of any application more effectively than monolithic, traditional applications. However, the infrastructure also needs to be aware of this scale, both up and down, to better support the applications. You'll see how this is achieved as you read through this book.

Automation, Orchestration, and Cloud

We have only briefly mentioned cloud concepts to this point. However, with the changes coming in application models, cloud (in the form of public, private, and hybrid models) is a reality for customers of any size and sophistication. As such, the building blocks of successful cloud deployments and operations begin with a flexible infrastructure that provides some level of policy-based configuration. For private cloud and eventually hybrid cloud to be realized, all infrastructure elements must become pools of resources. Think of how effective Cisco Unified Compute System (UCS) Manager has been at taking a bunch of x86 compute resources and, via policy, creating easy-to-scale, -manage, and -maintain pools of compute for application consumption. The same must now be applied to the network. The Cisco ACI policy provides similar ease of scale, management, and maintenance to that found in UCS Manager. However, those are just the building blocks of cloud.

Automation and orchestration are where we find the tools to provide the flexibility and potential to provide self-service to the business and the applications that operate it. First, let's better define the terms *orchestration* and *automation* because they tend to get used interchangeably. Note that automation, by definition, is the ability to make a process work without (or with very little) human interaction. Can you automate the deployment of a configuration of compute elements, including operating system and patches, via a tool like Puppet or Chef? Absolutely. One could argue that Cisco UCS Manager is automation for compute hardware configuration, and that the ACI policy model is automation for network and L4-7 services within it. I would agree with both of these assertions. However, orchestration means taking those infrastructure elements being automated and tying them together into a more meaningful motion to achieve an end result.

Thus, orchestration tools must address more than one domain of the infrastructure and can also include items within or supplied by the infrastructure. Good examples of orchestration include tools such as Cisco UCS Director, Cisco CloudCenter, Cisco Process Orchestrator, VMware vRealize Orchestrator, Heat for OpenStack, and others. These examples all allow, in varying degrees, the ability to string together tasks and processes that can provide a self-service capability for application deployment, application retirement, user on- and off-boarding, and so on. The key is that automation on its own provides the ability to lower that 60–70% administrative cost to the data center infrastructure, and orchestration provides the tools to realize a flexible and real-time infrastructure for private, public, and hybrid cloud environments. You cannot achieve true cloud operations without automation and orchestration.

End-to-End Security

Do the bad guys ever sleep? That question is best answered when we first understand who the bad guys are. Because we cannot identify all immediate risks to an infrastructure or a company—and, yes, even headlines can be severely impacting to business—we must do our utmost to keep the infrastructure from harm and from harboring harm, both from the outside and within. Even with an unlimited budget, security cannot be considered 100% or ironclad. However, if the infrastructure is flexible enough—perhaps the network even provides scalable and flexible security—your environment can be less hospitable or accommodating to the so-called "bad guys."

To this end, let's focus on the network. Until the advent of ACI, the network mantra had been "Free and Open Access" from its inception. I recall hearing this from several of my university customers, but even they have been forced to change their viewpoint. In legacy networks, we had free and open access, which necessitated the use of firewalls, where we only opened ports and protocols appropriate to allow applications to operate correctly and provide protocol inspections. This is something the firewall was originally designed to do. However, something the firewall was never originally design to do was to act as a route point within the network. Due to the need to secure segment portions of the network and provide bastion or edge security, we have forced firewalls to become rout-ers, and they pose severe limitations on the routing capabilities and options for a legacy network.

Now consider the ACI network, where, as you might have heard already, a whitelist security policy is in place. Nothing can communicate unless the network policy explic-itly allows it. Are you thinking firewall now? Well, not so fast. Although the Cisco ACI whitelist model does change the paradigm, it is more akin to stateful access control lists (ACLs) at the TCP/UDP level within a switch or router—effective, but cumbersome in the legacy or blacklist model sense. However, there is still a need to have deep protocol inspection and monitoring, which is something firewalls and intrusion prevention systems (IPSs) do very well. So let's get those devices back to doing what they do best and let ACI handle the forwarding and ACL-based security. As you will see in the book, IPSs and such network services devices can be automatically inserted in the network with ACI services graph (see Chapter 10 "Integrating L4-7 Services").

Have you ever experienced a completely correct configuration on a firewall? No cruft from legacy configurations or applications long since retired? Probably not, and this is directly due to the fact that most applications and their needed communication protocols and ports are not truly understood. What's the usual outcome of this misunderstanding? A very open firewall policy. Ultimately the thought of security behind a firewall config-ured in such a manner is as hollow and gaping as the open pipe the firewall permits to not impact application communication, thus favoring ease of use over security.

Finally, how do we approach securing different applications from each other or from improper access? Effective segmentation is the answer, and ACI provides the industry-leading option for that. From multi-tenancy and endpoint group (EPG) isolation to individual workload segmentation for remediation or rebuild when an intrusion is found, Cisco ACI can act on these items for any type of workload—bare metal or virtual-ized. Additionally, Cisco ACI can offer enhanced segmentation that starts outside of the data center via TrustSec. This capability, based on a device or user credentials, only allows packet flows to specific segments within the ACI fabric, which effectively allows segmentation of users of, say, a payroll system or sales data from the endpoint to the application elements hosted on an ACI fabric, inclusive of firewall, IPS, and other relevant L4-7 services.

Spine-Leaf Architecture

So how does all this occur? Couldn't we just create new forwarding paradigms for exist-ing network architectures and carry on? In a word, no. One of the great impacts in IT in the last ten or so years has been virtualization. This has caused a huge shift in traffic flows within the data center, and if we project forward to cloud-native applications built using microservices, this impact will increase. Thus, a change in design was necessary and, quite honestly, it's about time for a change. Gone are the days of data center net-works being defined by a "core, distribution, access" model. A new robust model that scales east-west without impact while maintaining reachability can bring new capacities and the required flow-awareness. Spine-leaf is the name of this new model. It simply allows for true accessibility in a deterministic path across the entire data center fabric. This is the basis of Cisco ACI, with a few extras added in.

When we say Cisco ACI has extras, essentially we mean that spine-leaf is the new underlying architecture of any modern data center network design. No matter which data center vendor you talk to (Cisco, Arista, Juniper, or VMware), we are all building our next-generation data centers leveraging this spine-leaf architecture. The control-plane protocols may differ from design to design, but in essence a highly scalable design using the two-stage spine-leaf model is the key base to build from. Cisco ACI's extras include whitelist segmentation, Virtual Extensible LAN (VXLAN) overlay, centralized policy configuration, and more.

Why a VXLAN-based overlay? Overlays are not new in networking; they have existed at least since the days when Multi protocol Label Switching (MPLS) was invented. Let's consider that analogy for a moment. Originally, MPLS was created in order to make service provider networks cheaper (although its current applicability has transcended by far that initial objective). The edge network devices that customers connect to (called in MPLS jargon Provider Edge or PE) would communicate to each other via tunnels. The core network routers (called Provider or P devices) would just provide connectivity between the PE devices, and would be oblivious to whatever the PE devices were transporting inside of their tunnels. Thus, they did not need to learn every single customer route, but just a bunch of internal prefixes. That allowed the use of devices with fewer hardware resources as P routers.

The VXLAN-based overlay in Cisco ACI follows the same primary objective: Leaf switches (think PE devices) establish VXLAN-based tunnels with each other that traverse the spine layer. Spine switches (comparable to P routers) are there to provide massively scalable IP connectivity, but not much more (with one notable exception, as we will see at the end of this section). Consequently, all intelligence needs to be delivered at the tunnel endpoints, the leaf switches. Note that this is a dramatic conceptual difference when comparing VXLAN fabrics with traditional networks: While in traditional networks most of the intelligence resides in (typically) two central, highly critical devices, in VXLAN overlays the intelligence is distributed across the leaf switch layer, making the fabric much more scalable and resilient.

You might ask whether there is an increased price associated with spine-leaf designs: After all, we used to have two intelligent devices in legacy networks at the distribution layer, but now we have possibly tens, if not hundreds, of intelligent (and potentially expensive) devices at the leaf layer. Wouldn't that increase the overall cost of a spine-leaf architecture? The answer to this question is two-fold: On one hand, you can program leaf switch intelligence in relatively cheap application specific integrated circuits (ASICs), a discipline in which the Cisco Nexus 9000 – the hardware basis of Cisco ACI – excels. On the other hand, since the intelligence is now distributed across the network edge and not centrally located, leaf switches do not need to know every single detail of the complete network.

Reflect for a second on the previous sentence. It might sound obvious, but it brings another paradigm shift for networking professionals: The scalability of a network is not determined by the scalability of the individual switches, but depends on the network design. For example, if you have a look at the Verified Scalability Guide for Cisco APIC at cisco.com, you will see that in the main section of the document there are two columns: Per Leaf Scale and Per Fabric Scale. Take, for example, the number of bridge domains, a concept roughly equivalent to that of a VLAN, as we will see later in this chapter. Each Cisco ACI leaf switch supports up to 3500 bridge domains in legacy mode (see more about legacy mode in Chapter 8, "Moving to Application-Centric Networking"), but a single Cisco ACI fabric can support up to 15,000 bridge domains.

In legacy networks you would probably configure every VLAN everywhere, since you could not possibly know in advance where the workloads for that particular VLAN might attach to the network. Now you need to be conscious with resources since you cannot fit 15,000 bridge domains in every leaf switch. Fortunately. Cisco ACI takes care of the efficient configuration of network resources automatically, and it will only deploy configuration wherever it is needed. For example, if a certain ACI leaf switch does not have any workload attached that is connected to a specific bridge domain, it does not make any sense consuming resources for that bridge domain. Therefore the BD will not be programmed in the hardware of that leaf switch.

There is an additional implication of this new scalability design model: You should not put too many workloads on individual leaf switches, since their scalability is limited. For example, if you are thinking about building up a Cisco ACI fabric by connecting a bunch of Fabric Extenders (FEXs) to your leaf switches, and attaching hypervisor hosts to the Fabric Extender ports, think again. How many virtual machines will you be connecting to a single leaf switch? Are you still within the scalability limits of a single leaf switch? Or would it be more economical using multiple leaf switches instead of Fabric Extenders? Obviously, the answers to these questions depend on many parameters, such as the server virtualization ratio, or the average number of virtual machines per VLAN. Chapter 2, "Building a Fabric," will dive deeper into these topics.

The leaf switch is where all the exciting networking happens. Traditional L2 and L3 forwarding operations happen on the leaf. Edge routing with dynamic protocols for reachability, such as Border Gateway Protocol (BGP), Open Shortest Path First (OSPF), and Enhanced Interior Gateway Routing Protocol (EIGRP), on leaf ports will turn a leaf with external access into a border leaf. This is not a special designation or switch hardware model, just the nomenclature to designate that a particular leaf switch plays a border role in the fabric. You will also note that the entire fabric is a routed network. So you might ask, "How do I achieve L2 reachability or proximity for my applications if everything is routed?" Simple: by use of VXLAN encapsulation across that spine-leaf ACI network. VXLAN is a solution to the data center network challenges posed by traditional VLAN technology and the Spanning Tree Protocol. The ACI fabric is built on VXLAN, but its configuration is abstracted and simplified through policy. The Virtual Tunnel Endpoint (VTEP) process and traffic forwarding are already programmed by the Application Policy Infrastructure Controller (APIC) based on the policies configured on it. So, should you understand the basics of VXLAN transport? I would say it's a good idea to do so if you're going to operate an ACI spine-leaf fabric.

Coming back to the spine switches, essentially their main function is to interconnect the leaf switches with each other providing abundant bandwidth. In Cisco ACI they have an additional function though: They have an accurate map of what endpoint is attached to each leaf (both physical and virtual) across the ACI fabric. In this model, outside of some BGP route reflectors and multicast rendezvous points, you can think of the spine as the "master of endpoint reachability." Let's describe the process with an example: When a certain leaf switch receives traffic with the destination of, say, IP address 1.2.3.4, it will look into its own forwarding table. If it does not know to which other leaf switch it should forward the packets, it will just send the first packet to any of the spines (note that this does not imply any extra network hop, since the spines are always between any two given leaf switches). The spine will intercept the packet, look up the destination in its endpoint connectivity directory, and forward it to the leaf switch where the destination endpoint 1.2.3.4 is attached. When return traffic comes back to the originating leaf switch, it will update its forwarding tables with the information on how to reach 1.2.3.4 directly.

Note   The VXLAN solution that ACI uses is VXLAN Ethernet Virtual Private Network (EVPN)

Existing Infrastructure and ACI (Places in the Network)

You might have thought that an ACI fabric is all you need in the data center. That's not entirely true. Actually, if you recall the aforementioned border leaf designation, you can begin to get the idea that ACI is not intended to be the edge of the WAN or Internet in your data center. You still would need WAN and Internet routers, even with Ethernet handoffs from your carriers. This is not only good security design, but it also allows the ACI fabric to have a clearly defined edge and not function as a transit network between the WAN, Internet, campus, and so on.

Consider, for a moment, the need to migrate applications and workloads into the new ACI fabric. For this to be accomplished correctly, with minimal impact to existing or the new ACI infrastructures, clearly defined boundaries for L2 and L3 connectivity and forwarding are required. New routers could be used to achieve this, or existing elements such as the Nexus 7000 or 6000 series of switches could provide all of the requirements needed to achieve such a migration. In addition, the Nexus 7000 series also supports wide-area network technologies such as Multi protocol Label Switching (MPLS), Locator-Identifier Separation Protocol (LISP), L2-over-L3 transport for traditional WAN termination, intelligent forwarding based on workload location, and data center interconnect technologies. Chapter 6, "External Routing with ACI," will cover external connectivity in detail.

You also have multiple options for connecting ACI across on-premise data centers. Multi-Pod and Multi-Site are two different options for this type of interconnect. Both of these options differ from general L2–L3 connectivity by the leaf switches for actually connecting to the spines in the ACI fabric. This connectivity between pods or sites requires only L3 transport to form the proper forwarder to extend the logical VXLAN overlay. The main difference between Multi-Site and Multi-Pod is in the management plane. Multi-Pod logically extends the APIC cluster across the pod fabric locations. Multi-Site uses separate APIC clusters federated by a Multi-Site controller. If you are familiar with the Cisco UCS

Central model for multiple UCS domains, you will understand this model. Chapter 11, "Multi-Site Designs," will further explain these options.

ACI Overview

At its heart, Cisco Application Centric Infrastructure is a software-defined, policy-based network infrastructure. However, it has so many additional capabilities and much more extensibility (via north-southbound Application Programming Interfaces) that it not only exceeds what most customers need today for agility and scale in their network infrastructures, but it will be relevant for many years and system evolutions to come. ACI is no longer the "network providing open access to all." It is now able to provide custom infrastructure, visibility, services, and security constructs to any application design, model, and workload type.

This new infrastructure requires new ways of operating the network fabric and the devices that provide L4-7 services within it. In essence Cisco ACI is software-defined networking (SDN), but with many more capabilities than traditional SDN, as discussed previously. As the business demands to IT continue to evolve with ever-increasing efficiency, agility and scale requirements, traditional device-by-device (perhaps scripted) configuration of network elements simply will not keep pace or scale to meet business needs.

This cultural change for our traditional network subject matter experts can seem daunting at first, but the ease with which configuration and immediate state data are available make the change more than worthwhile. Immediate knowledge of the state of the network for a specific application can be the key to minimizing return-to-service timeframes, performing proactive maintenance, and banishing the phantom of the ever-popular help desk call of "Why is my application response time so slow?" With ACI and the Application Policy Infrastructure Controller (APIC) cluster, IT staff with appropriate access can determine if there is a fault in the fabric, where and what it is, and then either remediate the issue quickly or emphatically state that the issue is not in the ACI fabric.

The benefits for different buying centers are as follows:

- **Cloud Administrator:** The ability to build and consume network infrastructure as part of an application, via APIs or Platform as a Service (PaaS) options.

- **Application Owners:** The agility to lifecycle the network elements supporting the application, in lockstep with the application lifecycle.

- **Security Operations:** Improved control of workload-to-workload or outside-to-application communication via built-in access control lists (contracts). Also, the ability to achieve segmentation/isolation in an automated fashion to protect against the spread of malware/ransomware.

- **Operations Team:** One console to easily understand the health of the data center network fabric and the components that create it: controllers and spine and leaf switches.

- **Server/Systems Team:** Improved integration of physical and virtual networks for improved reliability and enhanced agility. Also, if desired, an improved mechanism for policy enforcement and workload isolation within the native hypervisor.

ACI Functional Components

Application Centric Infrastructure requires only three base components for operation, as described in this section.

Nexus 9500

The flagship modular Nexus switch for the private-cloud data center. Whether based on a policy model like ACI, a programmability model using other tools, or the standard NX-OS CLI, this switch provides scalability not found with off-the-shelf ASICs. The chassis models include 4-, 8-, and 16-slot options, each using the same line cards, chassis controllers, supervisor engines, and 80% efficient power supplies. The individualized parts, based on the particular chassis, are the fan trays and fabric modules (each line card must attach to all fabric modules). What you don't see listed is any sort of mid-plane or backboard. With each line card connecting to each fabric module, there is no need for such a limiting design element. What we have scaled outside of the chassis in a spine-leaf fabric also exists inside the 9500 chassis: You can compare the architecture inside of a single Nexus 9500 chassis with a spine-leaf fabric, where the line cards have the role of a leaf, and the fabric modules the role of a spine.

Line cards include physical ports based on twisted-pair copper for 1/10Gbps and optical Small Form-factor Pluggable (SFP) as well as Quad Small Form-factor Pluggable (QSFP) for 1/10/25/40/50/100Gbps port speeds. All ports are at line rate and have no feature dependencies by card type other than the software under which they will operate. Some are NX-OS only (94xx, 95xx, 96xx series), some are ACI spine only (96xx series), and still others (the latest, as of this writing, of the 97xx-EX series) will run both software operating systems, but not simultaneously. There are also three different models of fabric modules, based on scale: FM, FM-S, and FM-E. Obviously, if your design requires 100Gbps support, the FM-E is the fabric module for your chassis.

Nexus 9300

Remember how all the ACI's "interesting work" happens in the leaf? That means the 9300 series of leaf switches are those devices responsible for the bulk of the network functionality: switching L2/L3 at line rate, supporting VTEP operations for VXLAN, IGP routing protocols such as BGP, OSPF, EIGRP, multicast, anycast gateways, and much more.

They also support a wide range of speeds in order to accommodate both modern and not so modern workloads that can be found in data centers: as low as 100Mbps for legacy components in your data center, and as high as 100Gbps for the uplink connectivity to the rest of the network (depending on switch model, uplink module or uplink ports). Sizes vary from 1 to 3 rack units high, with selectable airflow intakes and exhaust to match placement, cable terminations, and airflows within any data center.

Additionally, the rich functionality and high performance of the Nexus 9300 series comes at an affordable price, since probably the biggest item in the cost structure of a spine-leaf network architecture is due to the leaf switches.

Application Centric Infrastructure Controllers

Finally, we get to "the brains" of the solution: the Application Centric Infrastructure Controllers. These single rack-unit appliances are based on the UCS C-series x86 server and are always installed in odd numbers. Why, you may ask? After all, isn't high availability (HA) based on a model of an even number of elements? Wait, it must be N+1, right? Well, it's a little of both. In the end, all this policy is stored in a database. That database breaks up the elements of a policy into shards and distributes copies of a shard across the odd-numbered elements that are the Application Centric Infrastructure Controllers.

The APIC offers a GUI mechanism for access, along with a fully exposed API set, allowing consumers a rich set of tools with which to configure and operate an ACI fabric. Hint: take a look on GitHub (www/github/com/datacenter) and check out the useful apps being developed that use the APIs of the APIC. You can use and also contribute to this community of APIC API consumers.

The APIC is also how the leaf and spine elements are added to and retired from the fabric. It's also how they get their firmware updates and patches. No more device-by-device operations or scripting. The APIC does all that operations work for you via a few simple mouse clicks or via those exposed APIs.

Have you ever wondered, "How is my network configured right now?" Maybe that only happens when the help desk phone rings. We all know the network is to blame, until proven otherwise. Well, those fantastic Cisco ASICs in the Nexus 9500 and 9300 that make up the fabric also report significant details about the health and configuration of the ACI fabric, to the second. You can throw away those expensive and outdated wall-sized network diagrams and instead use the APIC GUI to see exactly how the network is functioning—and if there are any impacts, you can realize a faster recovery-to-service time than ever before. In essence, the APIC knows all about what the fabric is doing; it is the central "point of truth" for the ACI fabric. This is what a controller-based policy network can provide, operationally speaking. Chapter 7, "How Life is Different with ACI," will dwell on many of the benefits of the centralized policy provided by the APIC.

Protocols Enabling the ACI Fabric

By now you must be thinking that, with all these advanced capabilities, ACI must be based on some magic new set of proprietary Cisco protocols. Well, that would be flawed thinking. Actually, ACI is based entirely on a set of existing and evolving standards that allows for the unique and powerful capabilities that provide a truly flexible, automated, scalable, and modern network to support applications.

Data Plane Protocols

Forwarding across the ACI fabric is entirely encapsulated in VXLAN, as described above in this chapter. Let's face it: It's time to evolve how we segment our network in terms of network policy. VLANs and IP subnets have historically allowed us to segment traffic on a switching infrastructure, but we have not evolved that segmentation to effectively deal with the latest application architectures and security threats. With these requirements in mind, we must begin shrinking those L2 domains, both from a network policy and a security standpoint. Instead of having all the virtual and physical servers inside of a network subnet being able to communicate to each other, the goal is incrementing isolation as much as possible, even up to the point where you can define over which protocols servers can or cannot talk to their neighbors, even if inside of the same subnet.

Clearly VLANs won't scale to meet these needs; plus, 802.1Q between data center locations is fraught with issues using standard protocols. Enter VXLAN. Here is a protocol that allows for minimized fault domains, can stretch across an L3 boundary, and uses a direct-forwarding nonbroadcast control plane (BGP-EVPN). This can provide L3 separation as well as L2 adjacency of elements attached at the leaf that might reside across the fabric on another leaf.

The use of VXLAN is prevalent across the ACI fabric, within the spine and leaf switches, and even within various vSwitch elements attached to the fabric via various hypervisors. However, 802.1Q VLANs are still exposed in the ACI policy model because the actual vNIC of any "hypervised" workload and those of bare-metal servers today do not support VXLAN native encapsulation. Therefore, 802.1Q networks still appear in ACI policy and are valid forwarding methods at the workload NIC.

Control Plane Protocols

Several well-understood and -tested protocols form the ACI control plane. Let's start overall with bringing up of the fabric elements from day one, after unpacking your new ACI switches. Each new leaf or spine attached to the fabric uses a specific type-length value in a Local Link Discovery Protocol (LLDP) signaling flow to connect with the APIC and thus register itself as a potential new addition to the fabric. Admission is not allowed until a human or some automation point adds the new leaf or spine element. This guards against the registration of switches for nefarious purposes.

Forwarding across the fabric and reachability are achieved via a single-area link-state interior gateway protocol, more specifically Intermediate System to Intermediate System (IS-IS). This lends itself to massive scaling, with simplicity at the heart of the design.

Various interior gateway protocols are supported for communicating with external routing devices at the edge of the fabric: I-BGP, OSPF, and EIGRP, along with static routing are options for achieving IP communication to and from the fabric itself. These protocols run only on the border leaf, which physically attaches the adjacent networks to the fabric. Border leaf switches are not a special device configuration, only a notation of the edge of the ACI fabric connecting to adjacent networks.

Because the data plane of the ACI fabric uses VXLAN, the control plane protocol in use, as of version 3.0, is Multi-Protocol BGP with EVPN. This provides an enhancement over the prior use of multicast to deal with control-plane traffic needs around broadcast, unknown unicast, and multicast (BUM) traffic across the VXLAN fabric.

The Council of Oracle Protocol (COOP) is how reachability information is related from the leaf to the spine switches to track elements attached to the fabric via the leaf. COOP uses an MD5-authenticated zero-message queue to achieve this control-plane communication.

OpFlex is another new control-plane protocol used in ACI. Although it is pre-standard, Cisco and a consortium of ecosystem partners have submitted it for ratification. OpFlex is a protocol designed to communicate policy intent, from APIC, and compliance or noncompliance from a policy-enforcement element attached to the ACI fabric. Until the Internet Engineering Task Force (IETF) ratification, the OpFlex protocol is used to communicate policy between the APIC and the Application Virtual Switch (AVS). This not only demonstrates the use of OpFlex, but also allows for ACI policy to reach into server virtualization hypervisor host to enforce policy defined on the APIC, as Chapter 4, "Integration of Virtualization Technologies with ACI," will describe in detail.

Interacting with ACI

At this point you're probably wondering, "How do I work with this amazing new infrastructure?" It's time that we think of products like Cisco ACI as part of a larger puzzle. This means integration is a key factor in how you work with ACI and APIC, namely. You've probably heard phrases like "We've got an API for that" when talking about integration. Yes, ACI exposes 100% of its native capabilities via API. However, that exposed API enables ACI to be integrated in several different ways. Let's review what those mechanisms are.

GUI

ACI enables an HTML 5 user interface on the APIC itself. This interface is most useful to those who may not have an immediate need for automation or programmability of the fabric via external means. It also provides a great tool for operations to see and interpret the health of the overall ACI environment.

The GUI of the APIC is also a great "central source of truth" about how the fabric is configured and performing at any point in time. Also, several troubleshooting tools are offered within the GUI for the fabric itself. However, the entirety of the APIC GUI capabilities and elements is offered via API for consumption through other methods.

You may have heard the terms *network mode* and *application mode* as ways to deploy ACI. Let's be clear: They are simply different ways to create the policy that defines particular ACI constructs across the fabric. Both operate at the same time across the APIC and the same ACI fabric. Most customers begin defining their ACI policies with a network-centric view because it most closely resembles the data center networks they have in place today. Chapter 8, "Moving to Application-Centric Networking," will cover these operation modes in great detail, as well as how to move from a network-centric to an application-centric deployment.

NX-OS CLI

Earlier we discussed how SDN really is the direction in which networks will be built, no matter the controller mechanisms used. This is a major operational change for many network admins and operators. So, how does Cisco address this learning gap? The fully exposed API allows for developing a CLI option that functions much like NX-OS. If you're most comfortable with typing **conf t**, this is a viable interface for you to use with ACI. It also allows for more in-depth troubleshooting, akin to Cisco UCS.

Open REST API

As was mentioned previously, ACI has a very open and exposed set of APIs. This has already allowed for development of interesting ways to interface with the APIC and drive configuration tasks and other functions to be realized within the ACI fabric and policy model. The best examples of some of this work are publicly available via the GitHub repository at www.github/datacenter/aci. You'll find several examples here, but the most long-lived of these is the ACI Toolkit. This project has evolved continuously since ACI was launched, and it has had numerous contributors. The Toolkit is essentially a set of Python scripts used to affect the ACI controller with great success. The Toolkit is an easy way to get used to scripting large configuration elements such as multiple workload groups, EPGs, or tenants within the ACI policy model. It is just one example of the use of the Open API model, which extends the capabilities of ACI.

If you're new to this whole API game, the Toolkit is certainly one way to get started. Another is with the API Inspector that's built into the APIC GUI. This enables anyone with access to it to quickly determine the format of API calls to perform the same functions being created in the GUI. This is not only a great tool for getting familiar with APIs but is also a great tool for troubleshooting API calls into the APIC that may not provide the desired or expected outcome based on format (or that may fail altogether). Refer to Chapter 13, "ACI Programmability," for more information about the REST API or ACI automation in general.

Introduction to the Policy Model

What follows here is a brief overview of the elements of the ACI policy model. These elements will all be covered in much more detail throughout the book; however, consider this a quick study of the basic concepts that make up the ACI fabric configuration.

Application Network Profiles and Endpoint Groups

Application network profiles are the top construct of what defines a policy within ACI. Underneath this construct are all the other items that make up a policy designed to support an application across the ACI fabric using L4-7 services, access outside the fabric, and shared resources such as Active Directory (AD), Domain Name Service (DNS) or Dynamic Host Configuration Protocol (DHCP) servers.

Application Network Profiles contain endpoint group (EPGs), which are used to define elements attached to the fabric with the same characteristic—say, web servers for a particular application, hypervisor guests that use the same port group, or even workloads of any kind attached to the same VLAN/VXLAN. These are all examples of endpoint groups. Whereas tenants are the top construct in an ACI policy, the EPG is the smallest construct. As we've mentioned, the ACI fabric is like a whitelist firewall, and what makes communication possible is another policy construct between each EPG: the contract.

A contract is defined as a level of understanding between two or more parties. In the case of ACI, these parties are the EPGs. The contract between EPGs holds the forwarding behaviors, including ACLs and L4-7 service graphs.

VRFs and Bridge Domains

Virtual routing and forwarding tables (VRFs) have been well established for use in switching platforms. The ACI application policy takes this into account with a VRF construct. There can be multiple VRFs in an application policy, and just like VRFs in other switches, they forward traffic between themselves. Therefore, attention must be paid to the addressing within and across the VRFs of an application profile in Cisco ACI.

Where would a Layer 3 construct like VRF be without a Layer 2 construct? Well, the bridge domain (BD) is that L2 foundation. Thus, each VRF (also called a context) can have multiple BDs associated with it. Once again, IP addressing should be paid attention to here because VRFs will forward between the various BDs connected to them. The absolute top construct in the ACI policy model is the tenant. It is via the VRF(s) contained within each tenant that isolation is achieved across the shared ACI fabric and that L2 and L3 domains and addressing can be duplicated. Thus, VRFs among tenants do not forward traffic among themselves by default. Each tenant would need its own L2 and L3 outside connectivity. Alternatively, if commonly shared border leaf ports are being used, standard forwarding rules apply on the external network devices (namely, respecting IP address overlap, the need for NAT, and other such constructs to maintain reachability and path forwarding).

Fabric Topologies

As with flexible network design, even ACI fabrics have options for scale, forwarding, diversity, and management. The three main options are briefly discussed in this section. There are key differences between the options and how you may choose to operate your ACI fabric(s) with respect to location diversity and the fault domains of the data, control, and management planes.

Single-Site Model

The easiest and most widely deployed ACI fabric is a single-site model, where a single fabric exists in one physical location only. Thus, all the fabric elements, APICs, and devices reside within the reach of short-range fiber pairs. Here, we have scale capacities of up to six spines and 80 leaf switches, still with the same three APICs for control and management. One thing to remember about a single fabric is that every leaf attaches to every spine. There are no cross-connects between spines or between leaf switches. It is a true Clos fabric. A single fabric with great scale and the ability to span extremely large environments with logical separation at the tenant level shows why you have chosen wisely when you decided to deploy ACI in your data center. If you need more than 80 leaf switches in a single location, you can currently scale to 200 leaf switches with the same maximum of six spines, but you will need a five-APIC cluster.

Multi-Pod Model

ACI fabrics can be deployed in pods, where there can be a common management plane of the single APIC cluster, but individual control planes of MP-BGP and COOP, and individual forwarding planes between the spine and leaf switches in each pod. This allows for segmentation of control planes inside very large fabrics or to meet a compliancy requirement. Multi-Pod uses a separate IP transit network using MP-BGP EVPN between the pods. This transit network is actually connected via each spine in each pod. Again, this will occur at 40Gbps or 100Gbps, depending on the leaf-spine fabric in each pod.

You may be wondering how many pods you can connect. There can be more pods than three, but considering the recommended number of APIC in a cluster is three, it suggests that three is the correct answer. There is still the 50 millisecond round trip time (RTT) requirement as well. Inside a single data center, this is not a problem. By the way, the round trip time is measured spine to spine across the transit network.

Multi-Site Model

Beyond the Multi-Pod method of connecting and operating multiple ACI fabrics is the Multi-Site design. Essentially, Multi-Pod and Multi-Site share many attributes for connectivity between the fabrics and locations. The use of the MP-BGP with EVPN-based IP network for interconnecting the spines of each fabric is the same between the two options. The round-trip delay and port speeds of the network connecting the pods and sites with each other are also shared specifications for both of these options. What is strikingly different is that Multi-Site actually uses separate APIC clusters per fabric. In order to achieve consistency among them, we need to employ the use of the ACI multisite controller. This becomes the element that synchronizes the policy configurations between the various ACI fabrics in the Multi-Site deployment. The main difference between Multi-Pod and Multi-Site is the separation of the control and management planes between fabrics: While all pods in a Multi-Pod design share the same Cisco ACI APIC cluster, each site in a Multi-Site architecture has its own set of APICs. If true location and fabric isolation is key to your data center operations, then Multi-Site is your correct design for more than one fabric or location.

Summary

So much for the glancing blows of an introduction to or quick synopsis of ACI, its technology, and elements. Now it's time to delve deeply, chapter by chapter, into mining the gold nuggets of learning that are contained within these elements. It may be best to read this engaging book with an available ACI fabric or simulator such as the one provided at dcloud.cisco.com to build and refine your skills and command of the Cisco Application Centric Infrastructure as you go. Enjoy!

Chapter 2

Building a Fabric

You need to consider many dependencies and requirements when building a new network. If you're like many network engineers, this will be the first time you've implemented a Clos architecture or a software-defined network (SDN) solution. This chapter provides guidance on common decision points you will encounter as you design an Application Centric Infrastructure (ACI) network. The following topics are covered:

- Logical and physical fabric considerations

- Migration strategies for ACI

- Workload types, tenancy, and secure segmentation

- Virtual machine manager (VMM) integration

- Integrating Layer 4-7 (L4-7) services

- Multisite considerations

Building a Better Network

We are in a new era of IT. The ultimate goal of next-generation data center networks is policy-based automation of network management and operations, both virtual and physical. Using and reusing "known-good" policy allows IT to rapidly deploy, change, secure, and troubleshoot any workload—virtualized, containerized, and/or bare-metal. As we discussed in Chapter 1, "You've Purchased ACI. Now What?" this is being driven by application requirements and business needs. IT organizations are being asked to become more "cloud like" or adopt cloud operational models that provide the capabilities to meet these business needs. Networks have also changed from three-tier architectures to two-tier architectures that address application requirements for high-performance, low-latency, and secure east-to-west traffic. In the data center, manufacturers are moving away from designs that rely heavily on big boxes in the center of your network and instead are distributing the redundancy and performance via protocols to many devices across the

network. This allows networks to scale out very easily, moves the performance and security closer to the servers, and takes advantage of the redundancy and efficiency that's built
into modern hardware and protocols. The network is also being treated as a fabric instead
of being managed on an individual switch-by-switch basis. This allows engineers to move
away from managing individual devices and instead manage the network more efficiently
as a whole with policy. In this model, the Application Policy Infrastructure Controller
(APIC) controllers can correlate information from the entire fabric to provide insight and
security, and eliminate remedial tasks in a way that has not been available in the past, all
on open-standards-based protocols. The network can tell you the health of the individual
applications in production. The network can detect applications and apply the correct
configuration and security to a port or workload. The network can automate the configuration of virtual and physical L4-7 devices. In this chapter, we examine some of the
decision points you will encounter as you design and build a better network.

Fabric Considerations

Proper network design requires the network engineer to consider many factors, some
of which include but are not limited to the application requirements, integration points
into existing networks, physical facilities, multiple sites, types of hosts connecting to
the network, security requirements, and the scalability limits of the architecture being
designed. Each of these considerations can affect the design of the network as well as
how many and which types of devices you may use in your design. The information in
this chapter is higher-level design information regarding decision points engineers need
to consider as they properly design a ACI fabric. We will revisit many of the topics in this
chapter in more depth in the following chapters.

Roles of a Leaf

If you're like many engineers, this is your first time working with a spine-and-leaf architecture. With new technologies come new concepts and naming conventions. The ACI
leaf switches in the ACI spine-and-leaf fabric, from a physical standpoint, are mainly used
for connecting to external networks or devices and providing different types of physical
or virtual connectivity and capacity. This is somewhat different from previous architectures. As shown in Figure 2-1, when considering this architecture for the first time, many
engineers try to connect their existing network directly to the spines.

This method of physically connecting devices seems more natural due to the best practices of the past 15 years, but it is incorrect. As a rule, all traffic enters and exits the ACI
fabric through a leaf. The left side of Figure 2-2 shows physical connectivity in a traditional network. The right side of Figure 2-2 shows how this changes with ACI now that
everything enters or exits a leaf.

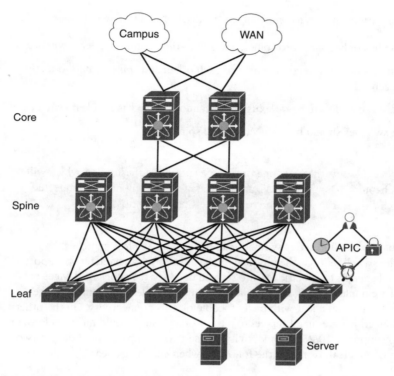

Figure 2-1 *Incorrect ACI Design*

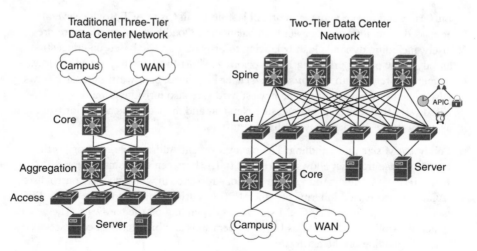

Figure 2-2 *Traditional Two- and Three-Tier Data Center Networks*

Here are several additional points to remember as we discuss ACI leaf switches:

■ ACI leaf switches only connect to spines, and spines only connect to leaf switches.

■ ACI leaf switches do not directly connect to each other, and spines do not directly connect to each other.

■ Modular chassis-based switches (Nexus 9500) cannot be used as ACI leaf switches.

■ All ACI leaf switches should be connected to all spines.

Note   As with any technology, there are one or two exceptions to these rules, which will be covered in later chapters. In some designs, all ACI leaf switches will not be connected to all spines, in which case traffic will not be routed as efficiently as possible.

Several models of Nexus 9000 series switches can be used as ACI leaf switches. You should choose the switch that has the physical media connectivity characteristics, port density, supported speeds, or specific feature set you need for the types of devices or architecture you are implementing. For instance, if I am using a leaf to connect to the data center core, I may want a leaf with ports capable of 40G connectivity. On the other hand, if I am connecting bare-metal servers to a top-of-rack leaf, I would most likely want the capability to support 1/10/25G connectivity. These two examples would dictate two different models of ACI leaf. Consider the following when choosing a leaf:

■ **Port speed and medium type:** The latest Cisco ACI leaf nodes allow connectivity up to 25, 40, and 50Gbps to the server and uplinks of 100Gbps to the spine.

■ **Buffering and queue management:** All leaf nodes in Cisco ACI provide several advanced capabilities for flowlet load balancing to load-balance traffic more precisely, including dynamic load balancing to distribute traffic based on congestion, and dynamic packet prioritization to prioritize short-lived, latency-sensitive flows (sometimes referred to as *mouse flows*) over long-lived, bandwidth-intensive flows (also called *elephant flows*). The newest hardware also introduces more sophisticated ways to keep track and measure elephant and mouse flows and prioritize them, as well as more efficient ways to handle buffers.

■ **Policy CAM size and handling:** The policy Content Addressable Memory is the hardware resource that allows filtering of traffic between endpoint groups (EPGs). It is a Ternary Content Addressable Memory resource in which access control lists (ACLs) are expressed in terms of which EPG (security zone) can talk to which EPG (security zone). The policy CAM size varies depending on the hardware. The way in which the policy CAM handles Layer 4 operations and bidirectional contracts also varies depending on the hardware.

■ **Multicast routing support in the overlay:** A Cisco ACI fabric can perform multicast routing for tenant traffic (multicast routing in the overlay), depending on the leaf model.

- **Support for analytics:** The newest leaf switches and spine line cards provide flow measurement capabilities for the purposes of analytics and application dependency mappings. These capabilities may not be enabled yet in the current software release.

- **Support for link-level encryption:** The newest leaf switches and spine line cards provide line-rate MAC Security (MACsec) encryption. This functionality is not yet enabled with Cisco ACI Release 2.3.

- **Scale for endpoints:** One of the major features of Cisco ACI is the mapping database, which maintains the information about which endpoint is mapped to which Virtual Extensible LAN (VXLAN) tunnel endpoint (VTEP), in which bridge domain, and so on. The newest hardware has bigger TCAM tables. This means that the potential storage capacity for this mapping database is higher, even if the software may not take advantage of this additional capacity yet.

- **Fibre Channel over Ethernet (FCoE):** Depending on the leaf model, you can attach FCoE-capable endpoints and use the leaf node as an FCoE N-Port Virtualization device.

- **Support for Layer 4 through Layer 7 (L4-7) service redirect:** The L4-7 service graph is a feature that has been available since the first release of Cisco ACI, and it works on all leaf nodes. The L4-7 service graph redirect option allows redirection of traffic to L4-7 devices based on protocols. It works on all hardware versions, but it has some restrictions depending on the leaf chosen.

- **Microsegmentation, or EPG classification capabilities:** *Microsegmentation* refers to the capability to isolate traffic within an EPG (a function similar or equivalent to the private VLAN function) and to segment traffic based on virtual machine properties, IP address, MAC address, and so on. The capability for the fabric to provide the second capability depends on both software and hardware. Traffic entering a leaf from a virtualized server running a software switch that supports Cisco OpFlexTM protocol can be classified in different EPGs based on several parameters: IP address, MAC address, virtual machine properties, and so on. Traffic entering a leaf switch from a physical server can be categorized into an EPG based on IP address or MAC address; specific hardware is required to provide this capability. Traffic entering a leaf from a virtualized server not running a software switch that supports the OpFlex protocol also requires the leaf to provide hardware support for microsegmentation.

First-generation Cisco ACI leaf switches are the Cisco Nexus 9332PQ, 9372PX-E, 9372TX-E, 9372PX, 9372TX, 9396PX, 9396TX, 93120TX, and 93128TX switches. Second-generation Cisco ACI leaf switches are Cisco Nexus 9300-EX and 9300-FX platform switches. Table 2-1 summarizes some of the current models to highlight the differences in their characteristics.

Table 2-1 *Sample of Cisco ACI Fabric Hardware Options*

	Port Count	Host Ports Type	Use (Leaf/ Spine)	Policy TCAM	Uplink Module	IP-Based EPGs
9396PX	48 × 1/10G ports and 12 × 40G ports	10G SFP+	Leaf	Regular TCAM with M12PQ	Bigger TCAM with M6PQ or M6PQ-E	Yes, with M6PQ-E
9396TX	48 × 1/10G ports and 12 × 40G ports	10GBase-T	Leaf	Regular TCAM with M12PQ	Bigger TCAM with M6PQ or M6PQ-E	Yes, with M6PQ-E
93128TX	96 × 1/10G ports and 6 × 40G ports	10GBase-T	Leaf	Regular TCAM with M12PQ	Bigger TCAM with M6PQ or M6PQ-E	Yes, with M6PQ-E
9372PX	48 × 1/10G ports and 6 × 40G ports	10G SFP+	Leaf	Bigger TCAM		No
9372TX	48 × 1/10G ports and 6 × 40G ports	10GBase-T	Leaf	Bigger TCAM		No
93120TX	96 × 1/10G ports and 6 × 40G ports	10GBase-T	Leaf	Bigger TCAM		No
9332PQ	32 × 40G ports	40G QSFP+	Leaf	Bigger TCAM		No
9372PX-E	48 × 1/10G ports and 6 × 40G ports	10G SFP+	Leaf	Bigger TCAM		Yes
9372TX-E	48 × 1/10G ports and 6 × 40G ports	10GBase-T	Leaf	Bigger TCAM		Yes
9336PQ	36 × 40G ports	40G QSFP+	Spine	N/A		N/A

	Port Count	Host Ports Type	Use (Leaf/ Spine)	Policy TCAM	Uplink Module	IP-Based EPGs
9504	With 9736PQ: 36 × 40G ports per line card	40G QSFP+	Spine	N/A		N/A
9508	With 9736PQ: 36 × 40G ports per line card	40G QSFP+	Spine	N/A		N/A
9516	With 9736PQ: 36 × 40G ports per line card	40G QSFP+	Spine	N/A		N/A

Note   For more information about the differences between the Cisco Nexus 9000 Series switches, refer to the following resources:

- https://www.cisco.com/c/en/us/products/collateral/switches/nexus-9000-series-switches/datasheet-c78-738259.html

- https://www.cisco.com/c/en/us/products/switches/nexus-9000-series-switches/models-comparison.html

We previously alluded to the fact that ACI leaf switches will be used for different roles based on their physical capabilities or place in the network. This is true both physically and logically. Not only is a Clos fabric separated into spine and leaf, but ACI leaf switches are usually characterized based on their specific role. Here are the most common roles you may encounter:

- **Border leaf:** One or more pairs of redundant leaf switches used for external connectivity to the external network. These connections can be Layer 2 or Layer 3 connections, or both. These leaf switches can be an enforcement point for policy both entering and exiting the fabric. ACI leaf switches are available that support 10G, 40G and 100G connectivity, various routing protocols, and advanced feature sets to gain additional security and visibility into traffic entering and exiting the data center.

■ **Services leaf:** One or more pairs of redundant leaf switches used for connectivity of L4-7 services, either virtual or physical. These leaf switches are optional, unless you are incorporating a new capability only supported in new hardware. In the previous situation, the device would have to be located under the hardware that has the desired capability to use the functionality. In this scenario, to avoid upgrading all switches in a fabric, customers purchase a small number of devices with the functionality needed and then group the services under those ACI leaf switches. In larger networks, some customers find it more operationally efficient to group their devices under services leaf switches, in a given rack. Other customers do not use services leaf switches and allow their virtual L4-7 services to exist on any server (if virtual) in any rack (virtual or physical) at any time.

■ **Transit leaf:** One or more pairs of redundant leaf switches that facilitate the connectivity to spines that exist across multiple geographic locations. These types of ACI designs are called *stretched fabric* or *pseudo-wire* designs. The result is that a single fabric with a single management domain exists across multiple geographically diverse sites. The distance allowed between these sites depends on the technologies, bandwidth, and round-trip times available. We will examine this topic in more depth in later chapters; however, the transit leaf switches perform the critical role of connecting to spines in other locations. Therefore, it is a best practice that they be used for this task alone.

■ **Storage leaf:** One or more pairs of redundant leaf switches used for connectivity of IP or FCoE storage services, either virtual or physical. Similar to the services leaf switches, these leaf switches are optional, unless you are incorporating a new capability only supported in new hardware. Typically, customers use the IP-based endpoint group functionality when applying policy to IP-based storage devices. This functionality allows ACI to focus specifically on the storage traffic for security, priority, and visibility. With the capabilities within ACI, we have the ability to create security zones similarly to how we use zoning on the Fibre Channel storage fabric. Engineers can define policies that specify that only certain hosts or initiators have access to certain storage devices or targets over iSCSI. An additional benefit of designing this policy is that we can now see health and traffic statistics for any of the storage traffic we create policies for. See Figure 2-3 for details.

Fibre Channel over Ethernet (FCoE) is another widely used data center technology. At the time of writing this book, first-hop FCoE is supported in N Port Virtualization mode in the ACI EX hardware. In today's ACI implementation, FCoE is supported over the Ethernet transport, meaning that the FCoE traffic would come from the host to the ACI leaf and then be proxied to another Fibre Channel switch over Ethernet media once again, at which time it could be broken out to native Fibre Channel. This is shown in Figure 2-4.

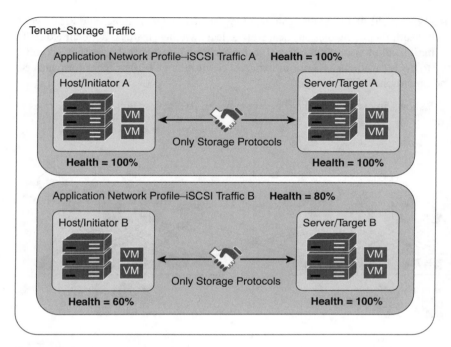

Figure 2-3   *ACI Storage Policy*

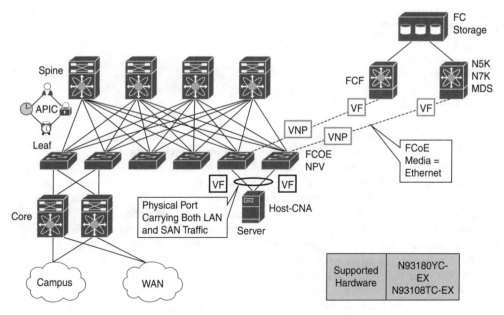

Figure 2-4   *ACI FCoE Topology*

If this is a brownfield ACI upgrade, you may only buy a few EX switches and locate your hosts underneath them, creating physical storage leaf switches. If this is a greenfield ACI implementation, all of your 9300 EX ACI leaf switches will support this feature, so you will need to decide if it makes sense to logically create storage leaf switches for management and operational efficiency.

Figure 2-5 shows an example of the different types of ACI leaf switches and their roles in the fabric.

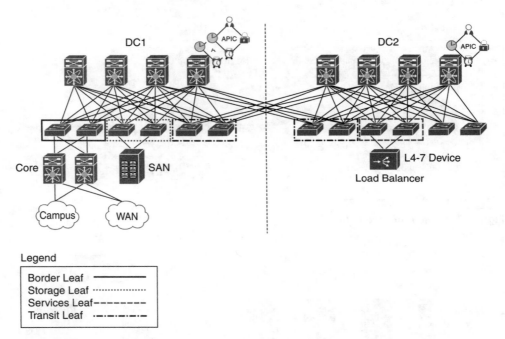

Figure 2-5 *Logical Leaf Names*

Network engineers might not see every type of leaf in every implementation. The type and number of ACI leaf switches can vary based on the architecture, the size of the implementation, or the feature requirements. For example, a stretch fabric is the only architecture that requires transit leaf switches. An engineer may also choose to logically group ACI leaf switches by their function to reduce operational or configuration complexity, even though there is no technical or resource constraint requiring it. The constant innovation of the switch hardware over time may bring new capabilities to the platform that can only be delivered through new hardware. In this case, you may choose to augment your existing fabric with a few new switches and attach hosts to those devices so that they can take advantage of the new capabilities, which effectively creates services leaf switches or storage leaf switches. To summarize, in greenfield installations these roles are mainly logical designations due to the fact that you will most likely be purchasing the newest hardware with all available capabilities at that time, whereas for existing ACI implementations, these roles can evolve to become physical requirements based on new feature sets.

The one leaf role that is always required is the border leaf. It is always a best practice to have designated ACI leaf switches to perform this function no matter the size or complexity of the network.

ACI leaf switches also perform the role of local routing and switching as well as enforcement of policy; they are the place where policies are applied to traffic on the fabric. Besides forwarding traffic, the leaf discovers the endpoints and can map them to destinations on the VXLAN network. The leaf also informs the spine switch of the endpoint discoveries.

Leaf switches are at the edge of the fabric and provide the Virtual Extensible LAN (VXLAN) tunnel endpoint (VTEP) function. They are also responsible for routing or bridging tenant packets and for applying network policies. Leaf devices can map an IP or MAC address to the destination VTEP.

The following are the last two considerations we are going to discuss that pertain to leaf switches:

- Fabric Extenders attached to the fabric

- Licensing and APIC sizing

Fabric Extender (FEX) Technology is based on the emerging standard IEEE 802.1BR. The Cisco FEX Technology solution is composed of a parent switch, which in this case is an ACI leaf but traditionally has been a Cisco Nexus 5000 Series switch, Nexus 6000 Series switch, Nexus 7000 Series switch, Nexus 9000 Series switch, or a Cisco Unified Computing System Fabric Interconnect. In ACI, the parent switch is then extended to connect to the server as a remote line card with some models of the Nexus 2X00 Series Fabric Extenders. In a traditional network, this would add additional network connectivity at a much lower price point without increasing the management footprint.

ACI changes this dynamic somewhat. In ACI, all of the devices are managed with your APIC controllers; therefore, adding additional ACI leaf switches or switches to your network never increases the number of management points. An ACI network is usually less expensive than a traditional Nexus 7/5/2K network, reducing the cost differential between a Fabric Extender and a fully featured leaf that can route and apply policy locally while supporting any device, versus sending the traffic to a parent switch and only supporting end hosts. Attaching a Fabric Extender to an ACI network also requires a license that adds to the cost of the Fabric Extender. Because of these limitations, it is generally recommended to move forward with a leaf instead of a Fabric Extender. Customers may still have a use case for Fabric Extenders, such as lights-out ports for servers, or they may want to migrate existing Fabric Extenders over from a previous network for investment protection, which is also a valid design.

Once you have decided on your ACI leaf design, the last thing you should consider is the licensing and controller size. A license is required for each of the ACI leaf switches and Fabric Extenders. Licensing is also required for the APIC controllers. The APIC controllers are sized based on the number of physical ports in your fabric. At press time, a large APIC controller configuration is used for more than 1000 ports and a medium-sized APIC controller is used for fewer than 1000 ports. The controllers are sold in groups of (at least) three, up to a maximum of five, and are physical appliances that run on the C series UCS server platform. When you purchase a large or medium controller, you are purchasing a server with more or fewer resources to process the information the APIC controller is receiving from the fabric. A reason to purchase more than three controllers is for redundancy or performance reasons in some configurations.

Fixed vs. Modular Spine

A second decision point that network engineers will find themselves faced with early on in the design process is whether to use a fixed or modular chassis for the spine. Spines provide redundancy, bandwidth, and scalability for the spine-and-leaf network. However, the redundancy and bandwidth benefits usually come from adding additional devices to the network, not from augmenting the existing devices. In other words, we scale out horizontally for bandwidth and redundancy instead of scaling up with the existing device. This is a departure from how we have planned for these concerns in the past. Previously when we wanted redundancy between devices we added more links to a port channel and diversified the links across multiple line cards. We did this because the number of devices and/or active paths our protocols could support was limited, so we put the redundancy in the hardware hoping it would never fail. With ACI, we can scale far past our previous limitations and take advantage of advancements in the protocols, so we design our network knowing that parts of it may fail, and when they do, they will fail gracefully with a nominal effect, if any, on production. In ACI, the links between the ACI leaf switches and the spines are active/active links. Because the links used to connect ACI leaf switches to spines are L3 links, we are able to intelligently load-balance or steer traffic for better performance or to avoid issues in the network. It is possible to add additional line cards to a modular switch to increase your bandwidth, or use additional ports on a fixed configuration switch. However, this gives you extra bandwidth without giving you the higher level of additional hardware redundancy that adding an entirely new switch would give you. This method would also limit the scalability of your fabric. You could exhaust all of the ports on your spine before you reach the scalability limits for ACI leaf switches in the fabric.

In the ACI fabric, we track every host on the fabric. The Cisco ACI fabric forwards traffic mainly based on host lookups, and a mapping database stores the information about the leaf switch on which each IP address resides. This information is stored in the fabric cards of the spine switches. As mentioned previously, the spine switches have two form factors: fixed configuration and modular chassis. The models also differ in the number of endpoints they can hold in the mapping database, which can depend on the type of switch or number of fabric modules installed. Here are the hardware scalability numbers (at press time):

- **Fixed form-factor Cisco Nexus 9336PQ:** Up to 200,000 endpoints
- Modular switches equipped with six fabric modules can hold the following numbers of endpoints:
    - **Modular 4-slot switch:** Up to 300,000 endpoints
    - **Modular 8-slot switch:** Up to 600,000 endpoints
    - **Modular 16-slot switch:** Up to 1.2 million endpoints

Note You can mix spine switches of different types, but the total number of endpoints that the fabric supports is the minimum common denominator. You should stay within the maximum tested limits for the software, which are shown in the Capacity Dashboard in the APIC GUI. At the time of this writing, the maximum number of endpoints that can be used in the fabric is 180,000.

At the time of this writing, you can use these fixed-form-factor spine switches:

- Cisco Nexus 9336PQ switch
- Cisco Nexus 9364C switch (which requires Cisco ACI software Release 3.0 or newer)

Note At press time, the connectivity to the leaf nodes is provided by these line cards:

- N9K-X9736PQ line card
- N9K-X9732C-EX line card
- N9K-X9736C-FX line card (which requires Cisco ACI software Release 3.0 or newer)

For more information about the differences between the Cisco Nexus fixed-form-factor spine switches, refer to https://www.cisco.com/c/en/us/products/collateral/switches/nexus-9000-series-switches/datasheet-c78-731792.html.

The differences between these spine switches and line cards are as follows:

- **Port speeds:** The Cisco Nexus 9364C switch and 9732C-EX and 9736C-FX line cards make it possible to connect uplinks at both 40 and 100Gbps speeds.
- **Line-card mode:** Newer line cards have hardware that can be used in either Cisco NX-OS mode or Cisco ACI mode.
- **Support for analytics:** Although this capability is primarily a leaf function and it may not be necessary in the spine, in the future there may be features that use this capability in the spine. The Cisco Nexus 9732C-EX and 9376C-FX line cards offer this hardware feature.

- **Support for link-level encryption:** The Cisco Nexus 9364C switch and the N9K-X9736C-FX line card can support MACsec encryption.

- **Support for Cisco ACI Multi-Pod and Multi-Site:** Cisco ACI Multi-Pod works with all spines in terms of hardware, but at the time of this writing, software support for the Cisco Nexus 9364C switch is not yet available. Cisco ACI Multi-Site (which requires Cisco ACI Release 3.0 or newer) at the time of this writing requires the Cisco Nexus 9700-EX or 9700-FX spine line cards. Refer to the specific documentation on Multi-Pod and Multi-Site as well as the release notes for more details.

Integration Planning and Considerations

Once you have decided on your spine-and-leaf hardware design, we can move on to some of the capabilities that you will need to consider as you plan the different phases of your ACI implementation. The following sections cover the implications of the different security features you can choose to enable in ACI. We also discuss the influence that supporting more than one tenant on the fabric may have on your design. After visiting the topic of security, we examine the easiest way to get started with ACI, as well as the middle and end states many customers are driving toward.

Security Considerations

ACI is designed and built from the ground up with security embedded in the fabric. The entire fabric is a zero-trust architecture. This means, by default, devices that are connected to ACI are not allowed to communicate on the fabric until you have defined a policy and applied that policy to a workload or port. If your traffic does not match the policy, it will be dropped in hardware, at line rate, on ingress or egress at the physical port (virtual machine traffic can be dropped at the virtual switch). This is much different from how traditional networks are configured. In a traditional network, if a port is enabled, the device connected to the port can get anywhere in the configured Layer 2 domain (such as VLAN 1) or anywhere the network device may have a Layer 3 path to. In ACI, the fabric has the capability to act as a Layer 4 firewall, which allows us to be much more thoughtful about which security traffic we let the fabric handle and which traffic we send to a more capable L4-7 device. Any port can be a 10G or 40G firewall, and we can get to any of our resources in two hops or less due to the spine-leaf fabric. As you learn more about defining policies in later chapters, you will be able to specify how open or granular you want your security policies to be. Another decision point is how your L4-7 devices will be connected and leveraged in your data center fabric. Three main modes of integration are supported:

- **Integrating L4-7 devices through the use of a device package or service policy mode:** This is an integration developed and maintained by the device vendor, through the use of ACI's open API, to allow the APIC controller to horizontally orchestrate and manage a given L4-7 device. The device is leveraged through the ACI policy model and the reuse of known-good policy. The device is also automatically decommissioned when the policy or application is removed.

- **Service manager mode:** This integration is similar to the previous one in that it uses a device package. However, in this mode, the firewall or load-balancer administrator defines the L4-7 policy, Cisco ACI configures the fabric and the L4-7 device VLANs, and the APIC administrator associates the L4-7 policy with the networking policy.

- **No device package or network policy mode:** The L4-7 device is connected to the fabric. We send traffic to and from the devices through the use of policy, but do not orchestrate the configuration or decommissioning of the device. The IT or security department would manage the L4-7 device in the same manner they always have. This provides less functionality than using a device package but offers a much easier way to get traffic to the device versus using virtual routing and forwarding (VRF) and VLAN stitching, as we have done in the past. This can also help organizations maintain administrative boundaries between departments.

Another significant security feature that is built into ACI is the concept of multitenancy. A *tenant* is a construct that is similar to a feature that we have in our traditional NXOS products. This feature is called a virtual device context (VDC) and takes a single switch and divides it up into multiple logical switches. ACI does not use VDCs, but with its tenant functionality, it takes this concept to a new level. Instead of virtually dividing up a single device, we can take the same physical network or fabric and divide it up into multiple logical networks and management domains, as illustrated in Figure 2-6. In this scenario, you could have two networks running on the same fabric being managed independently with separate policies that act like ships in the night. A tenant can be used a number of ways. It can be used to logically separate two companies running on the same physical fabric. It can be used to separate business units, security zones, development environments, or even internal production and external DMZ networks. A tenant is a separate data and management plane within the fabric. The management and visibility of resources and policy within a tenant can be controlled with role-based access control and limited to individual users or groups. You could build a fabric with one tenant or multiple tenants—it is completely dependent on the needs of your business. We also have the ability to share known-good policy and resources between tenants, through the use of what is called the *common tenant*. Items that we put in this tenant can be leveraged by any tenant.

As you can see, the tenant construct is very powerful, and we will explore this in greater detail in upcoming chapters. One thing is clear: A network engineer can use ACI as a foundation to architect a more complete security solution in the data center.

Phased ACI Migration

ACI can be implemented as a greenfield solution, but more often than not it is integrated with an existing brownfield network. A large quantity of new capabilities exists in ACI, but most of the time people start with the basics and move to a more complex deployment over time. One of these basic modes is called network-centric mode, which essentially involves taking your current network and bringing it into ACI, VLAN by VLAN.

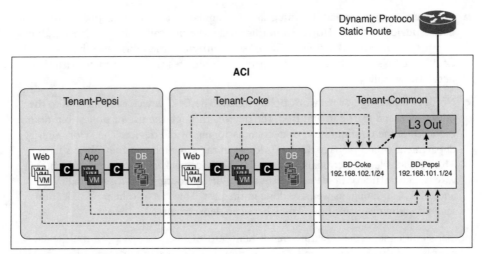

Policies and resources can
be used by other tenants:

• Security Policy
• Network Policy
• L4-7 Resources

Figure 2-6   *Common Tenant*

We will explore the different levels of security with which you can implement network-centric mode. You can implement network-centric mode as a single tenant or you can use the multitenancy feature. You also have the capability to start with one tenant and expand to additional tenants at a later date. Later, we will examine some of the considerations if you intend to do this.

In the following paragraphs, we examine some of the ACI features that allow you to pick and choose which users, resources, and policies can be shared between tenants. Most companies want the capabilities to eventually implement what we call *application-centric mode* or a *microsegmented zero-trust fabric*. In this configuration, instead of applying security or having visibility on a VLAN-by-VLAN basis, we can be much more granular and secure individual devices, applications, or tiers of applications as well as see their associated health scores. Application-centric mode can also manage and automate the insertion of Layer 4-7 services on a tier-by-tier or device-by-device basis, giving you enhanced ability to apply those services. Finally, we use the term *hybrid mode* to describe implementations that mainly use network-centric mode but may weave in some features from application-centric mode, such as L4-7 services control. Figure 2-7 shows these modes and the stages of their progression into production. In the following section, we describe these modes and their considerations in more detail.

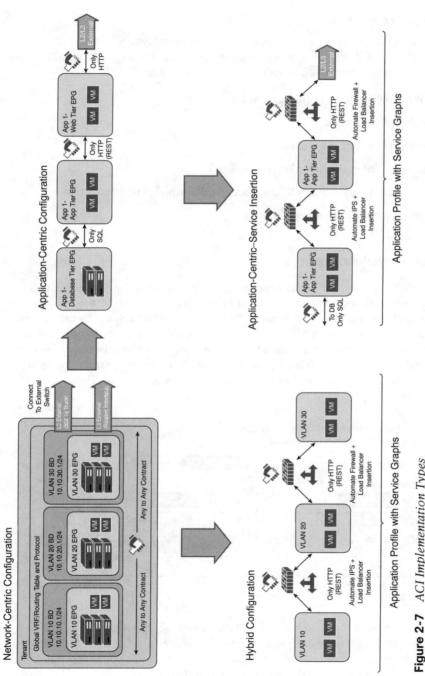

Figure 2-7 *ACI Implementation Types*

Network-Centric Mode: Single Tenant

When you implement network-centric mode in a single tenant, you're taking your network as it exists today (VLAN by VLAN) and replicating it inside of ACI. The benefits for doing this can be great, which include but are not limited to the following:

■ Improved application performance and lower latency

■ Zero-touch provisioning

■ Fabric-wide firmware management

■ Fabric-wide configuration backup and rollback

■ Reduced configuration errors through reuse of known-good configuration

■ Integration into virtualization platforms

■ Health scores

■ Advanced troubleshooting tools

By default, ACI controls how devices communicate on the fabric through policy and contracts. Some customers turn off the security functionality that is inherent in ACI when they deploy in network-centric mode. This is what we call an *unenforced network*. An unenforced network requires less work but gives you the capability to put devices into groups, integrate into existing virtualization platforms, and have health visibility on the independent groups or VLANs. The caveat is that ACI does not enforce any security between devices for the VRF/context the devices are a member of. This is shown in Figure 2-8.

• Policy Enforce: No Communication Without Contracts
• Policy Unenforced: All Communication Allowed

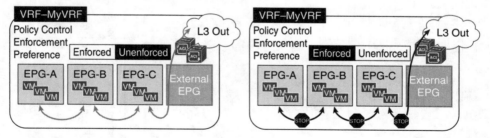

Figure 2-8   *Security: VRF Policy Enforcement*

Other companies leave the default security in place, add the VLAN groups to ACI, and simply configure the security contracts between the devices to allow any traffic between devices. This requires additional work, but it can make it easier for you to move to a zero-trust fabric at a later date. This is due to the fact that you will only be adding more restrictive filters to already existing contracts if and when you decide to do so at a later date. This method also allows for less disruption because you are affecting a smaller portion of the fabric when you make the individual security changes between groups or VLANs (see Figure 2-9).

• Left: Policy Enforced With ANY to ANY Contracts
• Right: Policy Enforced With Mixed Granularity

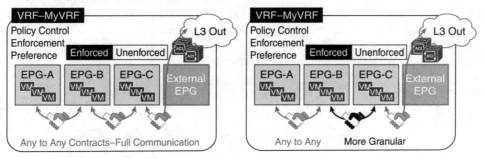

Figure 2-9   *Security: Policy Enforcement*

When you design the fabric based on a single tenant, you will have what we call Layer 3 and/or Layer 2 outbound connections from the fabric to the existing or core network. These connections provide the ability for Layer 2 connectivity to be brought into or shared out of the fabric, or the ability to advertise and route traffic in and out of the fabric over the Layer 3 connection. These connections will normally exist inside the single tenant you have created. You also have the ability to create more than one of each type of connection and control which connections can be used by which VLANs or groups. You may consider putting the L2 Out and/or L3 Out in the common tenant if there is a chance for the creation of additional tenants in the future. This could help avoid additional redesign and reconfiguration at a later date. Figure 2-10 shows these configurations. Please note WAN Integration will be examined in depth in later chapters.

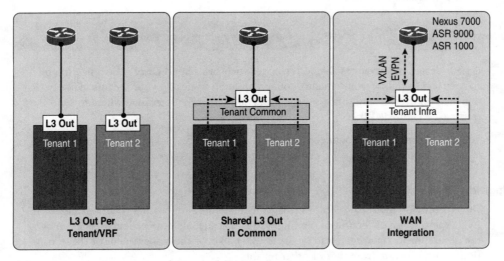

Figure 2-10   *External Connectivity/Tenant Design Considerations*

Network-Centric Mode: Multiple Tenant

Often when engineers hear the word *multitenancy*, they immediately think of hosting multiple companies on the same network. That is certainly a valid use case. What can be even more exciting is to think of the multitenancy use cases inside of an individual company or business. For instance, you could have separate networks for your production and development environments, or separate networks for production and the DMZ. You could have separate networks for individual business units or separate services on the network, such as virtualization vendor traffic or IP-based storage. Figure 2-11 shows some different examples of multitenancy scenarios.

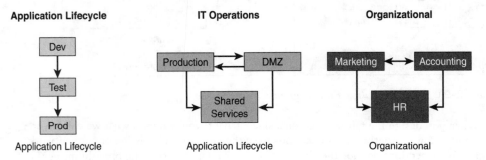

Figure 2-11 *Multitenant Approach*

When you are planning multitenancy scenarios, you have the option of keeping tenants completely separate or allowing them to communicate and share resources. If the tenants will be operating as ships in the night, you have fewer constraints. You have the opportunity to do things like reuse IP addressing schemes or replicate networks. This provides flexibility for testing acquisition strategies or research groups, but the networks would never be able to communicate on the fabric without the use of some type of network address translation device.

Note   At press time, ACI does not support network address translation (NAT) natively.

If your design incorporates shared resources such as a shared L3 or L2 connection to the network for all of your tenants, you are required to design your tenants in a way that there are no overlapping subnets so ACI can appropriately determine where to send the traffic (see Figure 2-12).

You can optimize traffic between tenants as you see fit by picking and choosing which tenants can communicate with devices in other tenants, as shown in Figure 2-12.

Individual Tenant Resources

Tenants provide the separation of management and data-processing functions inside of ACI. A tenant is a collection of configurations that belong to a particular entity, such as the development environment in Figure 2-13, and keeps the management of those configurations separate from that of other tenants.

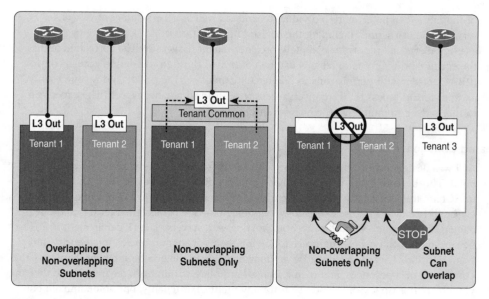

Figure 2-12   *Tenant IP Address Considerations*

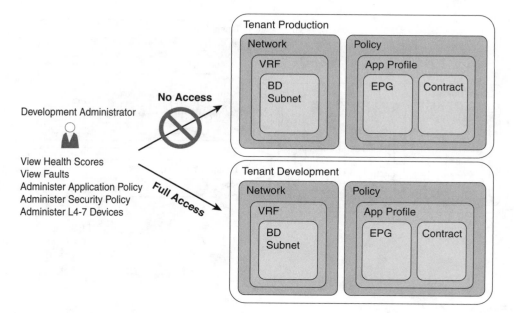

Figure 2-13   *Tenant Administration*

The tenant also provides a data-plane isolation function using VRF instances (private networks) and bridge domains. Resources such as L3 and L2 connections in and out of the fabric can be given to individual tenants, as well as access and control to L4-7 services. Health scores, including the health of application policies and groups as well as event alerts, are reported separately on a per-tenant basis as well as correlated across the entire fabric. Access to tenants can be controlled through role-based access control (RBAC). Users with permissions to one tenant cannot see the policy and resources in another tenant unless they are given access to additional tenants as well. The exception to this is the common tenant, which we discuss next.

Shared Common Resources

ACI was designed from the ground up with security, multitenancy, and efficiency in mind. This becomes very apparent when you start defining policy in ACI. The policies in ACI are foundationally built on the idea of reusing known-good configurations, policies, and resources. Figure 2-14 shows two tenants—one named "marketing" and one named "accounting"—and they're both hosting web servers. The IT department needs to be sure that both business units are following their corporate policies for security and configuration. This can be done by defining a policy in the common tenant, based on the company's best practices, and then reusing that policy within both tenants. Not only can you create this policy once and use it for any number of tenants, but you eliminate configuration drift and the potential for human error because of the reuse of a known-good configuration.

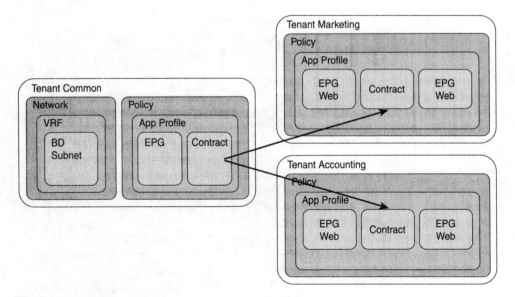

Figure 2-14 *Policy Re-Use*

ACI has three default tenants:

- **Infra tenant:** The infra tenant is the infrastructure tenant and is used for all internal fabric communications, such as tunnels and policy deployment. This includes switch-to-switch (leaf, spine, Application Virtual Switch [AVS]) and switch-to-APIC communications. The infra tenant is not exposed to the user space (tenants), and it has its own private network space and bridge domains. Fabric discovery, image management, and Dynamic Host Configuration Protocol (DHCP) for fabric functions are all handled within this tenant.

- **MGMT tenant:** The management tenant provides convenient means to configure access policies for fabric nodes. Although fabric nodes are accessible and configurable through the APIC, they can also be accessed directly using in-band and out-of-band connections.

- **Common tenant:** A special tenant with the purpose of providing "common" services to other tenants in the ACI fabric. Global reuse is a core principle in the common tenant. Here are some examples of common services:

  - Shared L3 out

  - Shared private networks

  - Shared bridge domains

  - Shared application services such as DNS, DHCP, and Active Directory

  - Shared L4-7 services

Evolution to Application-Centric Mode

Now that you are familiar with network-centric mode, we can dig deeper into secure segmentation and application-level visibility. As we explored previously, customers often start with network-centric mode and then, once they are comfortable with managing and supporting the network on a day-to-day basis, move to more granular visibility and security. As with network-centric mode, there are multiple ways to implement segmentation in your network. The easiest way to get started is to look at segmenting the servers by application versus the VLAN or IP address with which they are currently associated. We start here, because the hardest part about creating a zero-trust network is understanding your application dependencies. If you think about it, creating a zero-trust network is basically inserting a firewall between every server. If we start by segmenting whole applications, it can be much easier to realize the value of additional security and visibility without having to know all the dependencies of every server.

In the example that follows, the customer traditionally puts all of their servers in VLAN 10. This customer does not differentiate between the type or function of servers; all servers are placed in VLAN 10. Customer A recently moved to ACI in network-centric mode, which means they created a bridge domain using the subnet and default gateway for VLAN 10 as well as an endpoint group called "VLAN 10." When the customer is ready, they can now create additional groups associated with that same bridge domain but name these new groups based on the application to which these servers belong. These servers will then be moved from the group called VLAN 10 and placed into the group called "Exchange servers" without any IP addressing information being changed. All the Exchange servers are being put into the same group so they can, by default, communicate with each other freely. This removes the burden of the customer having to know the dependencies of how every Exchange server talks to every other Exchange server. However, the customer can still control how other servers and end users talk to the Exchange servers as a group. The customer can also see the health of the Exchange servers versus the servers that currently exist in the VLAN 10. This example is depicted in Figure 2-15.

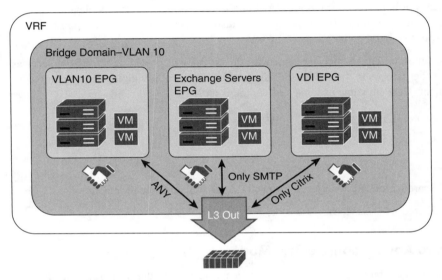

Figure 2-15   *Basic App Segmentation*

This method allows the customer to slowly migrate some or many applications into a more secure environment, meanwhile leaving other devices in the "VLAN 10" group untouched. This practice also paves the way to move into a more granular zero-trust environment, or microsegmentation as most customers visualize it. We discuss this next.

Microsegmentation

Microsegmentation is one of the hottest buzzwords in the data center today. Many companies are trying to reduce their attack surface and exposure of critical assets to threats inside and outside of the data center. Although we've had the ability to create very secure networks in the past, as the level of security increased, so did the complexity; meanwhile, the ability to respond to changes as well as the user experience generally deteriorated. With ACI, all of that is in the past. The APIC controller has the ability to see across the entire fabric, correlate configurations, and integrate with devices to help manage and maintain the security policy you define. We see every device on the fabric, physical or virtual, and can maintain consistency of policy and recognize when policy needs to be enforced. The fabric itself acts as a Layer 4 firewall that is zero trust (all traffic is denied by default), unlike a traditional trust-based network (where all traffic is allowed by default). This means devices cannot talk on the network without a policy being defined and applied. We have gone from being very open in our network-centric mode to more restrictive as we start to define and gain visibility into independent applications on the network. Now we will discuss the highest level of visibility and the most restrictive security capabilities, where we not only can identify individual applications but also identify functional roles or tiers within the individual applications and the unique security requirements of each of those roles or tiers. We call these *application profiles*. In Figure 2-16, we have defined a vanilla web application profile. This application is composed of three functional tiers: web, application, and database. We have been instructed to secure this application based on the individual tiers or roles within the application.

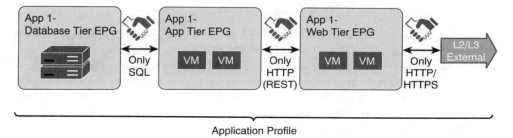

Figure 2-16 *Application Centric Configuration*

Note   A contract is the ACI policy that defines the allowed communication between two groups of devices.

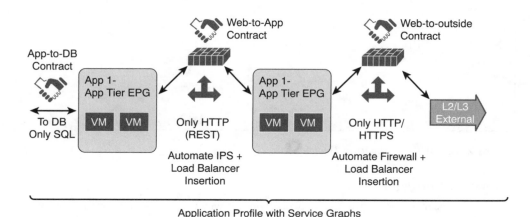

Figure 2-17 *Application Centric: Service Insertion*

The web tier is the only tier that should be able to communicate with external devices or users, and only do so on ports 80 and 443. Our company policy also requires that all communication between external devices and/or users must go through a firewall to mitigate security concerns as well as a load balancer to address redundancy issues. In Figure 2-17, from right to left you can see that our policy allows outside users or devices to only talk to the web server group over port 80 or 443 after traversing the firewall and load balancer. This configuration is defined in the web-to-outside contract or policy. The communication is only allowed between the objects that are using this policy; therefore, outside users or devices will not be able to communicate with the application and database tiers. Next, we will define the policy or contract between the web and application tiers. In this contract, we only allow communication between the two groups over port 80 for REST calls to the application tier, and we still require the traffic to be sent to an intrusion prevention system (IPS) and load balancer. Finally, we define a policy or contract between the application and database tiers allowing port 1433 or SQL communication with no services inserted.

Remember, the web tier will not be able to talk directly to the database tier because communication has not been allowed with a contract. Also, because there are no Layer 4-7 services integrated between the app and DB tiers, the fabric itself will act as a stateless Layer 4 firewall enforcing security at line rate. As you can see from this example, this application is now very secure on a tier-by-tier basis, where we can control security and services integration at every level. Now that we have defined this policy, we are now tracking the health of that individual application across the fabric. If the application were to experience an issue, specifically with our database group, we would see the health score of that individual group go down as well as the health score of the top-level application profile. This allows us to quickly determine and remediate issues when they arise, as shown in Figure 2-18.

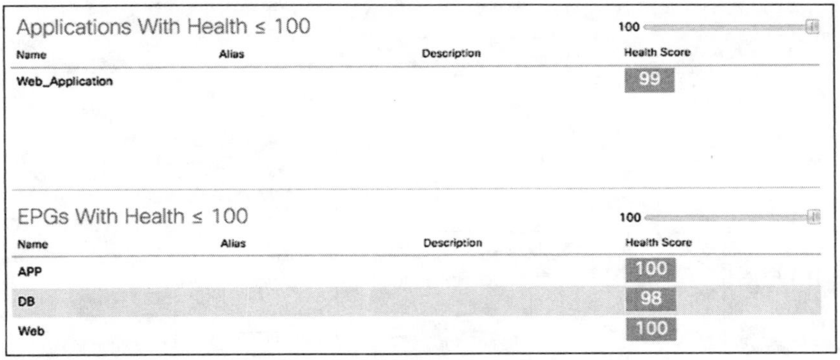

Figure 2-18   *Web Application Health Score*

Bare-Metal Workloads

ACI is designed to simplify your network, which is why it is very important to create a policy once and enforce it on any workload, virtual or physical. To create or apply policy, we first need to put devices into groups. We can do this in ACI for bare-metal or physical workloads based on VLAN ID, VXLAN, NVGRE (Network Virtualization using Generic Routing Encapsulation), IP address, MAC address, and/or the physical switch or port the device is plugged into. It is important to remember that policy is applied based on how the device is connected to the network. So, a single physical server could have multiple policies applied to different physical or virtual adapters as they connect to the network. Traffic from multiple IP addresses on the same physical network connection can have different policies applied as well. This allows us to apply policy to multiple logical unit numbers (LUNs) represented by multiple IP addresses on the same storage device, or multiple applications (that is, websites) using multiple IP addresses to consolidate on the same physical NIC. Depending on the type of bare-metal workload you are interfacing with, you may have to replicate some of the policy that is defined in ACI in the individual physical device. The bare-metal workloads need to be configured to use the parameters that ACI is expecting in its policies (VLANs, Link Aggregation Control Protocol, and so on). With certain servers, these configurations can be automated. In the case of Cisco Unified Computing System (UCS), a tool called ACI Better Together (B2G) tool looks at policy in ACI and replicates needed configurations in UCS Manager. This policy can then be applied to both B (blade) and C (rack mounted) series servers, because they can both be managed by the fabric interconnects and UCS Manager. This is a major benefit of open and programmable devices, where Cisco has already done the integration for enterprises.

Note   More information for the B2G tool can be found at https://communities.cisco.com/docs/DOC-62569.

Virtualized Workloads

The following sections of this chapter will describe at a high level how Cisco ACI integrates with different server virtualization and Linux container platforms, since this is often one of the first considerations when designing and building an ACI Fabric. Chapter 4 "Integration of Virtualization Technologies with ACI" will offer more comprehensive and in-depth details on this aspect."

Virtualization platforms have become a critical component of the data center. Some companies have settled on a single virtualization vendor. Other companies support multiple virtualization platforms for best-of-breed features, cost, application requirements, or to avoid vendor lock-in. Either way, it is important that you be able to accommodate whichever virtualization strategy your company decides on today or integrates with in the future. It is also critical that you be able to enforce your company's policies across these platforms in a consistent manner. ACI allows you to do this with its integrations into platforms such as Microsoft, VMware, OpenStack, and KVM. These integrations not only allow you to enforce consistent policy, but they also automate the configuration of the network policies inside the virtualization platforms.

Containers

Containers have gained and are continuing to gain momentum in many IT application environments. The same challenges exist with containers that have existed in the past with traditional virtual workloads. If you thought applying policy to ~100 virtual machines on the same physical machine might be tough, imagine applying policy to any number of containers running on a single physical or virtual machine or across multiple physical or virtual machines. Fortunately, ACI gives you the capability to do this. In ACI, with the help of Contiv, we are able to identify individual containers and apply and enforce policy on a container-by-container basis using endpoint groups in ACI, as illustrated in Figure 2-19.

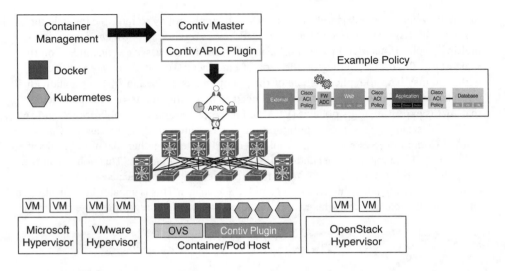

Unified Policy Automation and Enforcement Across Physical, Virtual, and Container Resources

Figure 2-19   *Cisco ACI + Contiv (ACI Mode)*

Note   For more information on Contiv, see chapter 4 or visit http://contiv.github.io/

Virtual Machine Manager (VMM) Integration

In this section, we explore at a high level how the virtualization concepts we previously discussed in this chapter are implemented in Cisco ACI. Specifically, we examine the integration options available for ACI and virtualization technologies so that you can make informed decisions based on your environment as you design and get ready to deploy your new ACI network.

It is also worth noting that if you chose not to integrate ACI with your virtualization platform or do not meet the minimum requirements for the integration, ACI can still support virtualization platforms on the network. Without integration, you would continue to interact with these servers much like you do today, trunking VLANs down to the hosts individually. A virtual server without integration is treated similarly to a bare-metal workload on the fabric.

AVS

Cisco Application Virtual Switch (AVS) is a hypervisor-resident distributed virtual switch that is specifically designed for the Cisco Application Centric Infrastructure and managed by Cisco APIC. Cisco AVS software is included when you purchase ACI. There are no additional license or support costs to use this capability.

The Cisco AVS is integrated with the Cisco Application Centric Infrastructure. It is based on the highly successful Cisco Nexus 1000V switch, which is the industry's first and leading multihypervisor virtual switch. The Nexus1000V is managed similar to a modular-based switch, and the management is done by a dedicated Virtual Supervisor Module. Cisco AVS uses the same vSphere Installation Bundle as the Nexus 1000V Virtual Ethernet Module but uses APIC as the controller instead of Virtual Supervisor Module. Cisco AVS implements the OpFlex protocol for control-plane communication. OpFlex, the southbound API, is an open and extensible policy protocol used to transfer abstract policy in XML or JavaScript Object Notation (JSON) between Cisco APIC and AVS. Once AVS is configured, there are no additional steps to utilize AVS. You simply define and apply policy the same way you would to any virtualized device with the benefit of added functionality. AVS installation and upgrades can be managed with the use of a free tool available on the Cisco website called Virtual Switch Update Manager (VSUM). VSUM allows you to easily manage the software upkeep of your virtual switching environment across hundreds or even thousands of servers. You also have the option to use vSphere Update Manager or the ESXi CLI to perform the installations and upgrades.

AVS provides enhanced capabilities for virtualized devices, including local switching and policy enforcement at the hypervisor level. Table 2-2 summarizes some of these enhanced capabilities.

Table 2-2   *AVS Enhanced Capabilities*

Feature	Cisco AVS	VMware VDS	Comments
Attribute-based EPGs (microsegmentation)	Supported	Supported with EX hardware and later	Granular EPG definition using VM or networking attributes.
TCP connection tracking (DFW)	Supported	Not Supported	Helps prevent TCP-based attacks.
FTP traffic handling (DFW)	Supported	Not Supported	Helps prevent FTP-based attacks.
Centralized troubleshooting using familiar tools	Supported	Not Supported	Better troubleshooting right from APIC.
VXLAN encapsulation mode with no local switching	Supported	Not Supported	Fabric visibility to all VM traffic for better telemetry.
VXLAN encapsulation mode with local switching	Supported	Not Supported	Simplified configuration for blade servers, IPv6 tenants, and large-scale environments.
Multiple Layer 2 hops between host and leaf	Supported	Not Supported	Investment protection by extending ACI to existing virtual and physical networks.

Feature	Cisco AVS	VMware VDS	Comments
Independent of CDP/ LLDP support	Supported	Not Supported	Useful when the blade switch does not support Cisco Discovery Protocol / Link Layer Discovery Protocol.
Telemetry reporting of VM traffic statistics	Supported	Not Supported	OpFlex is used for telemetry reporting.

In previous versions of ACI software and hardware, AVS was needed to perform attribute-based microsegmentation with VMware virtualized workloads. Although AVS still provides many additional benefits, we now have the ability to perform microsegmentation of VMware workloads without AVS. Some of the features and dependencies regarding AVS follow:

■ APICs is installed.

■ All switches are registered.

■ For VXLAN encapsulation, set the maximum transmission unit (MTU) greater than or equal to 1600 on all intermediate devices on the path between the Cisco ACI fabric and the Cisco AVS, including blade switches. To optimize performance, the MTU should be set to the maximum supported size that all intermediate devices on the path between the Cisco ACI fabric and the Cisco AVS support.

■ When adding additional VMware ESXi hosts to the VMM domain with the Cisco AVS, ensure that the version of the ESXi host is compatible with the distributed virtual switch (DVS) version already deployed in the vCenter.

During the design and planning process, it will be important to review any requirements for microsegmentation, performance, and reliability. Based on these requirements, assess the minimum version of ACI and the need for AVS. If an enterprise has EX hardware, it may not need AVS for microsegmentation. However, if an enterprise has a requirement for local switching in the hypervisor or stateful Layer 4 firewalling, AVS will need to be used.

VMware

The APIC integrates with VMware vCenter instances to transparently incorporate the Cisco ACI policy framework to vSphere workloads. The APIC creates a distributed virtual switch (DVS) mapped to the Cisco ACI environment, and uplinks (physical network interface cards [pNICs]) are added to the DVS. The APIC manages all application infrastructure components and constructs on the DVS. The network administrator creates Application Network Profiles that contain one or more EPGs in the APIC, and the APIC pushes them to vCenter as port groups on the DVS. Server administrators can then provide virtual machine connectivity by assigning the virtual NICs (vNICs) to a specific port group. If you are microsegmenting devices, the system can also automatically place the devices in groups based on a number of attributes.

Customers can choose between two options: VMware vSphere Distributed Switch (VDS) and Cisco Application Virtual Switch (AVS). Although Cisco ACI can function with the native VMware VDS, Cisco AVS provides additional benefits, including greater flexibility to attach to the fabric, greater link redundancy, and enhanced security features, all at no additional cost to the user.

This integration offers significant operational benefits to the day-to-day administration of your virtualization infrastructure. The day-to-day work of configuring and trunking VLANs down to servers from the switch is eliminated and handled with policy. In ACI, you assign a dynamic pool of VLANs which ACI uses to automatically create these configurations and do the work for you. If you choose to use AVS, you also have the option of extending the VXLAN network down to the host further simplifying the configuration burden and reducing VLAN sprawl on third-party devices such as blade servers and their switches.

The ability to provide full physical and virtual policy enforcement means that ACI can truly provide you with a holistic approach to managing your virtual environment traffic. ACI not only focuses on how virtual machines communicate to devices on the network (virtual or physical), but also on the security, performance, and redundancy of the physical host that the virtual machines reside on. For instance, when using vCenter the system can be configured to apply security and performance guarantees on a cluster-by-cluster basis. Using this model, enterprises can define and enforce service level agreements (SLAs) on management, vMotion traffic, and NFS or storage traffic individually, while maintaining visibility and performance metrics on a cluster-by-cluster basis. You can then apply microsegmentation policies to your virtual machines based on any number of attributes, as shown in Figure 2-20.

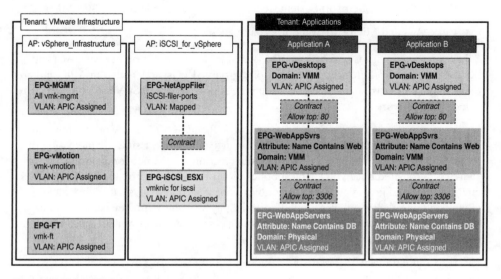

Figure 2-20   *VMware Example*

ACI also has the capability to integrate northbound into your existing orchestration platforms, such as VMware vRealize. This integration can be leveraged at any time and uses predefined blueprints to build in to your vRealize Orchestrator workflows that interact with ACI to automate and orchestrate network policy.

Here's a summary of some of the items you will want to plan for as you architect how ACI will interact with your VMware environment:

- Do you want to integrate with your VMware environment? Do you have the correct VMware licensing to support distributed virtual switching?

- Will you be using out-of-band management (recommended) or in-band (across-the-fabric) management to interact with vCenter? APIC will need permissions to interact with vCenter.

- Will you be using AVS or default VDS integration? If AVS, what will you use to manage the install and upgrade of AVS? Will you be using VLAN mode or VXLAN (AVS-only) mode. In VLAN mode, you will need an unused pool of VLANs (we recommend around 200). In VXLAN mode, you will need to consider MTU and VXLAN hardware support on your servers or any intermediary switching.

Microsoft

The Application Policy Infrastructure Controller integrates with Microsoft VM management systems and enhances the network management capabilities of the platform. The Cisco Application Centric Infrastructure integrates in one of two modes, and you can choose either one based on your deployments:

- Cisco ACI with Microsoft System Center Virtual Machine Manager (SCVMM)
- Cisco ACI and Microsoft Windows Azure Pack

When integrated with Cisco ACI, SCVMM enables communication between ACI and SCVMM for network management. Endpoint groups (EPGs) are created in APIC and are created as VM networks in SCVMM. Compute is provisioned in SCVMM and can consume these networks.

Similar to the vCenter integration, we can allow ACI and SCVMM to work together to eliminate day-to-day provisioning tasks for the virtual network. Using a combination of dynamic VLANs and the OpFlex protocol, the creation of VM networks on the logical switch is automated once you enable a policy to flow into your virtualized Microsoft environment. ACI gives you total control over your virtual and physical environment, allowing you to define policies around both the physical and virtual machines. You have the ability to define policies for your supporting control traffic as well as your virtual workload data traffic.

Cisco ACI integrates with Microsoft Windows Azure Pack to provide a self-service experience for the tenant. The ACI resource provider in Windows Azure Pack drives the APIC for network management. Networks are created in SCVMM and are available in Windows Azure Pack for the respective tenants. ACI Layer 4-7 capabilities for F5 and Citrix load balancers and stateless firewall are provided for tenants.

Windows Azure Pack for Windows Server is a collection of Microsoft Azure technologies, available to Microsoft customers at no additional cost for installation into their data centers. It runs on top of Windows Server 2012 R2 and System Center 2012 R2 and, through the use of the Windows Azure technologies, enables you to offer a rich, self-service, multitenant cloud, consistent with the public Windows Azure experience.

Windows Azure Pack includes the following capabilities:

- **Management portal for tenants:** A customizable self-service portal for provisioning, monitoring, and managing services such as networks, bridge domains, VMs, firewalls, load balancers, and shared services.

- **Management portal for administrators:** A portal for administrators to configure and manage resource clouds, user accounts, and tenant offers, quotas, pricing, website clouds, virtual machine clouds, and service bus clouds.

- **Service management API:** A REST API that helps enable a range of integration scenarios, including custom portal and billing systems.

OpenStack

ACI is designed to be programmatically managed through an API interface that can be directly integrated into multiple orchestration, automation, and management tools, including OpenStack. Integrating ACI with OpenStack allows dynamic creation of networking constructs to be driven directly from OpenStack requirements, while providing additional visibility within the ACI Application Policy Infrastructure Controller down to the level of the individual VM instance.

OpenStack defines a flexible software architecture for creating cloud-computing environments. The reference software-based implementation of OpenStack allows for multiple Layer 2 transports, including VLAN, GRE, and VXLAN. The Neutron project within OpenStack can also provide software-based Layer 3 forwarding. When utilized with ACI, the ACI fabric provides an integrated Layer 2 and Layer 3 VXLAN-based overlay networking capability that can offload network encapsulation processing from the compute nodes onto the top-of-rack or ACI leaf switches. This architecture provides the flexibility of software overlay networking in conjunction with the performance and operational benefits of hardware-based networking.

Layer 4-7 Services

As discussed throughout this book, for years network engineers have had to be very resourceful when integrating Layer 4-7 devices into the network. We used features like ACLs, VLAN ACLs, policy-based routing, and VRF stitching to get traffic where we wanted it to go. Many times, the end result was successful, but the delivery was inefficient. All of the traffic for a VLAN had to be sent to the firewall when we only wanted to inspect or block a few servers. When virtualization hit the scene, everything became even more complex. Traffic may flow between two virtual servers on a physical host but still need to conform to security policies. In ACI, all of that has changed. We can now apply security on a case-by-case basis to any flow across the fabric. We can leverage the fabric for Layer 4 inspection when it makes sense, or we can selectively send traffic to a higher-level Layer 4-7 device when needed. Any port can be a high-speed firewall, load balancer, or IDS/IPS device. These devices can be physical or virtual on any vendor's virtualization platform. Another benefit of ACI is that it gives you operational simplicity by providing horizontal integration in managed mode with ecosystem partner devices. This integration allows ACI to automatically negotiate and configure connectivity for a device, program the policy on the device, send traffic to the device, and monitor the policy as long as it is valid inside of ACI. When you remove or delete the policy, the configuration will be removed and the resources will be decommissioned automatically for you. This integration may require operational changes inside of a company and is not a fit for every customer, or the device you have might not be one of the 60 different horizontal integrations supported. In this case, unmanaged mode can be used, where you can continue to manage the device the way you always have, and ACI just sends the traffic there, much more easily. Let's explore each of these modes in more detail.

Note   An ecosystem partner is a partner that is collaborating with Cisco and ACIs open architecture to develop solutions to help customers use, customize and extend their existing IT investments into ACI. Some of these ecosystem partners include Check Point, Palo Alto, Citrix and F5 to name a few.

Managed Mode

Managed mode for ACI L4-7 devices is a game-changing feature available in ACI that addresses service integration and operational issues in your data center environment. By allowing the APIC to integrate with these L4-7 devices, you can create "known-good" policy based on your company's requirements and reuse the policy over and over again to eliminate human error and configuration drift. Changes can be made to the environment quickly through use of predefined templates and resources such as your Adaptive Security Appliance (ASA), Palo Alto, and Check Point firewalls. This allows you to install a firewall once and deploy it multiple times to different logical topologies. These virtual or physical devices can exist anywhere on the fabric and be leveraged without penalty due to the fact that any device can reach any other device in two hops or less. The benefits of managed device integration follow:

- A configuration template that can be reused multiple times.

- A more logical/application-related view of services.

- You can provision a device that is shared across multiple departments.

- ACI manages VLAN assignments.

- ACI collects health scores from the device.

- ACI collects statistics from the device.

- ACI can update ACLs and pools automatically with endpoint discovery.

Today, over 65 different ecosystem partners have integrations with ACI. Before you can leverage a device in managed mode, an ecosystem partner has to develop a device package. A device package is a .zip file that contains two items:

- An XML file that defines the capabilities of the device.

- Python scripts telling the APIC how to interact with the device.

These device packages are updated and maintained by the individual vendors. Because the individual vendors have full control over the device packages, these packages can be developed in a way that allows them to leverage the features in the vendor devices that make them unique.

As you are designing your fabric, you will have to decide if your IT operational or organizational model supports managed device integration. An example would be a security department that wants to continue using their existing tools and does not want ACI orchestrating the firewalls they are responsible for. Typically, we see customers using managed devices for insertion of services in east-to-west flows inside the data center, whereas devices like edge firewalls remain unmanaged. Another item to consider is that the APIC monitors the configuration of policy on the devices that it is managing. The APIC will connect to the device and make sure the correct configuration is in place as long as the policy is in place. If the L4-7 device has virtualization features, it is recommended that you provide the ACI with its own slice or context of the device to administer. This provides a clear demarcation point for control and mitigates the possibility of an administrator logging in to the device and making changes, just to have the APIC overwrite them. Many companies also use virtual devices in this instance instead of larger physical devices to avoid resource contention. Engineers may want to consider the decision flow in Figure 2-21 when deciding which devices should be used in managed or unmanaged mode.

Unmanaged Mode

ACI supports in-depth integration with over 60 ecosystem partners. Some of these integrations are through device packages and some of these integrations are control-plane integrations with partners such as Infoblox or solutions like Firepower and Identity Services Engine. Whatever services you are using, ACI is able to integrate with any device in your environment. Some customers have requirements that ACI should only do network automation for service devices. The customer may have an existing orchestrator or tool for configuring L4-7 service appliances, or perhaps the device package is not available for L4-7 devices. In this situation, you would use unmanaged mode or network-only switching. Unmanaged mode provides the following benefits:

- The network-only switching feature adds the flexibility for the customer to use only network automation for service appliances. The configuration of the L4-7 device is done by the customer, who can keep current L4-7 device configuration and administration tools.

- A device package is not required.

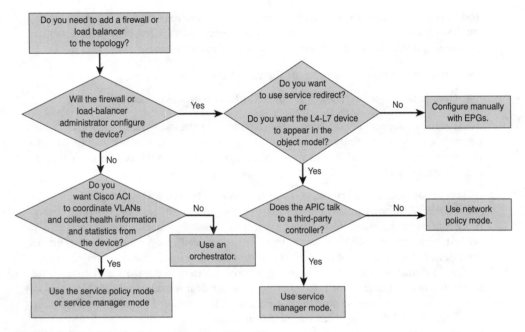

Figure 2-21 *Service Integration Decision Tree*

Customers also leverage unmanaged mode as a first step into ACI. As mentioned previously, you get the benefit of easy and optimized traffic flow to the device without changes to your organization's workflow, tools, or responsibilities. If, at a later date, you decide to leverage the full power of device packages or other integrations, you can turn those capabilities on at any time.

Additional Multisite Configurations

We have explored many of the decision points that need to be considered when designing an ACI fabric within the walls of a single data center. Many customers must provide a data center environment that is continuously available. Customers expect applications to always be available, even if the entire data center experiences a failure.

Companies also commonly need to be able to place workloads in any data center where computing capacity exists, and they often need to distribute members of the same cluster across multiple data center locations to provide continuous availability in the event of a data center failure. To achieve such a continuously available and highly flexible data center environment, enterprises and service providers are seeking an active/active architecture.

When planning an active/active architecture, you need to consider both active/active data centers and active/active applications. To have active/active applications, you must first have active/active data centers. When you have both, you have the capability to deliver new service levels by providing a continuously available environment. A continuously available, active/active, flexible environment provides several benefits to the business:

- **Increased uptime:** A fault in a single location does not affect the capability of the application to continue to perform in another location.

- **Disaster avoidance:** Shift away from disaster recovery and prevent outages from affecting the business in the first place.

- **Easier maintenance:** Taking down a site (or a part of the computing infrastructure at a site) for maintenance should be easier, because virtual or container-based workloads can be migrated to other sites while the business continues to deliver undisrupted service during the migration and while the site is down.

- **Flexible workload placement:** All the computing resources on the sites are treated as a resource pool, allowing automation, orchestration, and cloud management platforms to place workloads anywhere, thus more fully utilizing resources. Affinity rules can be set up on the orchestration platforms so that the workloads are co-located on the same site or forced to exist on different sites.

- **Extremely low recovery time objective (RTO):** A zero or nearly zero RTO reduces or eliminates unacceptable impact on the business of any failure that occurs.

When deploying Cisco ACI in two (or more) data centers, you can choose between four main deployment model options for interconnecting them (see Figure 2-22):

- Stretch a single Cisco ACI fabric between the two locations.

- Use the Multi-Pod architecture.

- Use independent fabrics, one per site, and interconnect them.

- Use the Multi-Site architecture.

ACI has evolved the stretch fabric and independent fabric designs to new architectures called Multi-Pod and Multi-Site. We will cover these designs in depth in later chapters. Because they are evolutions of the listed designs, the following design considerations apply to them as well.

Cisco ACI Stretched Fabric

A Cisco ACI stretched fabric is a partially meshed design that connects Cisco ACI leaf and spine switches distributed in separate locations (see Figure 2-22, top left). The stretched fabric is functionally a single Cisco ACI fabric. The interconnected sites are one administrative domain and one availability zone with shared fabric control planes, using the Intermediate System to Intermediate System (IS-IS) protocol, Cooperative Key Server Protocol (COOP), and Multiprotocol Border Gateway Protocol (MP-BGP). Administrators can manage up to three sites as one entity; configuration changes made on any APIC node are applied to devices across the sites.

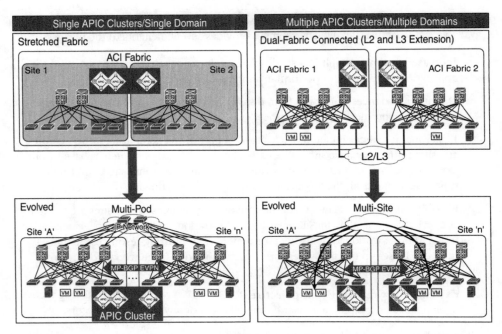

Figure 2-22   *Interconnecting ACI Fabrics: Design Options*

The stretched fabric is managed by a single APIC cluster, consisting of three APIC controllers, with two APIC controllers deployed at one site and the third deployed at the other site. The use of a single APIC cluster stretched across all sites, a shared endpoint database synchronized between spines at both sites, and a shared control plane (IS-IS, COOP, and MP-BGP) defines and characterizes a Cisco ACI stretched fabric deployment.

Cisco ACI Multi-Pod

Multi-Pod enables provisioning a more fault-tolerant fabric composed of multiple pods with isolated control-plane protocols. Also, Multi-Pod provides more flexibility with regard to the full mesh cabling between leaf and spine switches. For example, if leaf switches are spread across different floors or different buildings, Multi-Pod enables provisioning multiple pods per floor or building and providing connectivity between pods through spine switches.

Multi-Pod uses MP-BGP Ethernet Virtual Private Network as the control-plane communication protocol between the ACI spines in different pods. The communications between the pods are transported over a network called the *inter-pod network.*

Multi-Pod gives you full ACI functionality across an entire multipod fabric. This configuration creates a single availability zone with one APIC cluster for an entire multipod fabric that provides a central point of management. Live VM migration is supported within and across pods. Scalability limits are similar to that of a single fabric, and L4-7 services are fully supported across pods.

Cisco ACI Multi-Site

A Multi-Site design is the architecture interconnecting multiple APIC cluster domains with their associated pods. A Multi-Site design could also be called a "multi-fabric" design, because it interconnects separate availability zones (fabrics), each deployed either as a single pod or multiple pods (a Multi-Pod design). Tenants, applications, VRFs, Bridge Domains, subnets, EPGs (including μSeg), and policies can be stretched across these availability zones. Live VM migration within and across sites is supported (vSphere 6 and above) with support for IP mobility across sites. Multi-Site can selectively push configuration changes to specified sites, enabling staging/validating while preserving tenant isolation. This configuration supports site-local L4-7 stitching. Multi-Site adds full-site active/active or active/standby deployment with end-to-end policy definition and enforcement even across continents.

The Cisco ACI Multi-Pod and Multi-Site architectures can be combined to meet two different requirements. You can create a group of flexible Cisco ACI islands that can be seen and operated as a single logical entity (fabric) and function using the classic active/active model. You then can also reliably interconnect and scale those fabrics.

Cisco ACI Dual-Fabric Design

In a Cisco ACI dual-fabric design, each site has its own Cisco ACI fabric, independent from each other, with separate control planes, data planes, and management planes (refer to Figure 2-22, top right). The sites consist of two (or more) administration domains and two (or more) availability zones with independent control planes (using IS-IS, COOP, and MP-BGP). As a consequence, administrators need to manage the sites individually, and configuration changes made on the APIC at one site are not automatically propagated to the APIC at the other sites. You can deploy an external tool or orchestration system to synchronize policy between the sites.

A dual-fabric design has an APIC cluster per site, and each cluster includes three (or more) APIC controllers. The APIC controllers at one site have no direct relationship or communication with the others at other sites. The use of an APIC cluster at each site, independent from other APIC clusters, with an independent endpoint database and independent control plane (using IS-IS, COOP, and MP-BGP) per site, defines a Cisco ACI dual-fabric design.

Pervasive Gateway

The dual-fabric design raises a question, however: If endpoints that are part of the same IP subnet can be deployed across separate Cisco ACI fabrics, where is the default gateway used when traffic needs to be routed to endpoints that belong to different IP subnets?

Cisco ACI uses the concept of an *anycast gateway*—that is, every Cisco ACI leaf node can function as the default gateway for the locally connected devices. When you deploy a dual-fabric design, you will want to use the anycast gateway function across the entire system (pervasive gateway) independent of the specific fabric to which an endpoint connects.

The goal is to help ensure that a given endpoint always can use the local default gateway function on the Cisco ACI leaf node to which it is connected. To support this model, each Cisco ACI fabric must offer the same default gateway, with the same IP address (common virtual IP address 100.1.1.1 in Figure 2-23) and the same MAC address (common virtual MAC address). The latter is specifically required to support live mobility of endpoints across different Cisco ACI fabrics, because with this approach the moving virtual machine preserves in its local cache the MAC and IP address information for the default gateway.

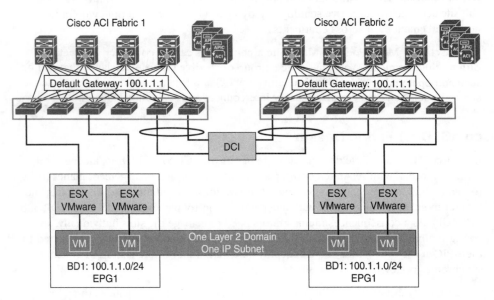

Figure 2-23 *ACI Pervasive Gateway*

Note The capability to have the default gateway active on multiple sites requires ACI software release 1.2(1i) or later.

VMM Considerations

To provide tight integration between physical infrastructure and virtual endpoints, Cisco ACI can integrate with hypervisor management servers (VMware vCenter, Microsoft SCVMM, KVM and OpenStack are available options at press time). These hypervisor management stations are usually referred to as *virtual machine managers*, or *VMMs*. You can create one or more VMM domains by establishing a relationship between the VMM and the APIC controller.

In a single-fabric or Multi-Pod design, VMM integration becomes a non-issue. In a single-fabric design, a single APIC cluster is leveraged because the multiple sites are actually a single fabric. The individual VMM integrations can be leveraged via policy equally in any of the data centers where the fabric is stretched. This is due to the fact that you are providing a single control and data plane across the stretched fabrics. Therefore, if the same VMM environment exists in multiple data centers, it can be leveraged. You can also leverage technologies such as cross-vCenter migration, which is available in VMware vSphere Release 6.0 if you choose to create more than one vCenter cluster.

In the dual-fabric or Multi-Site solution, separate APIC clusters are deployed to manage different Cisco ACI fabrics; hence, different VMM domains are created in separate sites. Depending on the specific deployment use case, you may want to allow endpoint mobility across data center sites, which requires moving workloads across VMM domains. At the time of this writing, the only possible solution is to integrate the APIC with VMware vSphere Release 6.0, because this release introduces support for live migration between VMware ESXi hosts managed by different vCenter servers.

Cisco ACI Release 1.2 introduces support for integration with vCenter 6.0, so it is the minimum recommended release needed to support live migration across the dual-fabric deployment. Note that Cisco ACI Release 11.2 supports live mobility only when the native VMware vSphere Distributed Virtual Switch (DVS) is used. Starting with the next Cisco ACI release, support will be extended to deployments using the Cisco Application Virtual Switch (AVS) on top of vSphere.

Summary

The many capabilities of ACI provide a scalable, resilient foundation for your data center. Once it is decided which features the enterprise would like to use, migrations to ACI can be performed in a step-by-step fashion. ACI also has the capability to grow with your businesses' data center needs, whether that is a single data center or multiple data centers. This chapter covered the following topics:

- Leaf and spine networks are purpose-built for today's applications. ACI leaf switches provide capacity, features, and connectivity. Spines provide redundancy and bandwidth.

- A leaf can perform many functions, such as a storage, services, transit, and border functionality. ACI leaf switches are often grouped based on their functionality.

- Licensing is based on the controllers and the number of ACI leaf switches and Fabric Extenders (FEXs). Controllers are sized based on the number of ACI leaf switches and ports in your fabric.

- ACI is built with security in mind, from the ground up. ACI uses features such as RBAC, tenants, zero-trust fabric, and services integration to enforce security.

- Many enterprises use a phased approach, starting with network-centric mode, then hybrid mode, and finally application-centric mode.

- Policy and resources created in the common tenant can be created once and reused many times across multiple tenants.

- ACI can provide application-level visibility and monitoring with health scores.

- Policy created for applications can be applied to physical, virtual, and container resources.

- L4-7 services can be administered and integrated into ACI with device packages or in network-only mode.

- ACI is a flexible architecture that can adjust to any single or multiple data center needs.

- ACI can also accommodate active/active and active/passive data center environments, while enabling a cloud operational model.

With ACI on the Nexus 9000, Cisco provides a highly available implementation of standards-based spine-leaf technology and builds on it with new innovation required to meet the specific demands within today's data centers.

Chapter 3

Bringing Up a Fabric

Setting up a network for the first time can be daunting. Although ACI simplifies your network deployment, it is still different from what you have done in the past. This chapter guides you through the information needed as well as what to expect as you are setting up ACI for the first time. We will cover the following topics:

- Logical and physical fabric considerations

- Interacting with the GUI

- Fabric setup

- Advanced mode

- Firmware management

- Configuration management

Out of the Box

Before you can take advantage of the new network you have designed, you first need to take it out of the box and set it up. In this chapter, we explore the basic requirements needed for setup and to enable the most common services. We examine decision points you will have to consider for management communication with ACI. As with traditional Cisco switches, setup scripts are available to help you get things going quickly. After configuring the controllers with the correct information, we examine the modes used to interact with the GUI and look at any differences they have. Two of the most important yet tedious tasks in traditional network management revolve around managing firmware and backing up device configurations. There is finally a better way—with the APIC controller. We examine how to enable these features so that your maintenance windows take less time and your network is always backed up.

Suggested Services

ACI can run as an autonomous data center fabric. ACI can also integrate into the existing services that are available in your data center. These services can provide ACI with information to enforce your security policies in the form of role-based access control (RBAC). ACI can also use services such as Network Time Protocol (NTP) to provide accurate timestamps on events that may occur on your network and/or correlate events across multiple devices in the fabric. Many customers have investments in existing tools they want to pull information from, or send information to, from within ACI. In this section, we examine some of the suggested services to be used in conjunction with ACI.

Enterprises will need to make a decision on how they want to integrate with these services through the use of the in-band or out-of-band management network. An *in-band network* creates a management network using the existing ACI fabric to carry the management traffic. An *out-of-band network* relies on a completely separate network to carry the management traffic. We cover the two types of management network in more depth later in this chapter, but it is generally a best practice to support a full out-of-band network. The benefit of an out-of-band (OOB) network is access to the devices in the event that the fabric is experiencing production issues and is unavailable. To use the OOB network, all of the ACI devices (controllers and switches) will need OOB network connectivity through their management 0 ports. The Application Policy Infrastructure Controllers (APICs) also have Cisco Integrated Management Controllers (CIMCs) for lights-out management that will need to be cabled, configured, and given an IP address on the management network. The services we discuss in the following list also need to be reachable on the OOB network:

- **DNS:** If you plan to use Domain Name System (DNS) names to specify devices in your ACI configuration, you will need to configure DNS services for ACI to be able to resolve those names to IP addresses. DNS services can be very helpful, because you are resolving to a name and not an IP address. Changes can then be made to the IP address of a referenced device without affecting your configuration. This service is also something to consider if you are experiencing issues. You may think you have an issue with your NTP server, when in reality the DNS name of the NTP server isn't being resolved, so ACI will not know how to contact the server even though it is up and running.

- **NTP:** One of the most valuable services we will examine is Network Time Protocol (NTP). NTP is not new to the data center environment. Network devices have used NTP for years to sync their internal system clocks with a device or "server" that is considered a time reference. Using an NTP server helps eliminate time drift across fabric devices, which can occur when they are being manually set. It also allows the devices to periodically reach out to the server to re-sync, when devices gain or lose time naturally. When the time is in sync across the fabric, the APIC can then correlate the information that is collected across the entire fabric to determine the health of the fabric. The ACI fabric will also use this information for timestamping of events and audit logs.

An offset present on one or more devices can hamper the ability to properly diagnose and resolve many common operational issues. In addition, clock synchronization allows for the full utilization of the atomic counter capability built in to the ACI, upon which the application health scores depend. You should configure time synchronization before deploying a full fabric or applications so as to enable proper usage of these features. For these reasons, even though it is possible to configure a fabric without NTP, it is a best practice to treat it as a required service.

- **SNMP:** Enterprises have used Simple Network Management Protocol (SNMP) for years to manage their infrastructure environments. ACI provides extensive SNMPv1, v2, and v3 support, including management information bases (MIBs) and notifications (traps). The SNMP standard allows any third-party applications that support the different MIBs to manage and monitor the ACI fabric. The management and monitoring of the fabric includes the spine and ACI leaf switches as well as the APICs. This functionality exists mainly to integrate into existing monitoring systems that engineers may already be using to monitor their environments. Going forward, enterprises and ecosystem partners are looking to leverage the ACI application programming interface (API) to monitor and interact with an ACI fabric.

- **RBAC:** Role-based access control (RBAC) is a necessity in most of today's data center environments. Enterprises generally create a user ID and password in a centralized directory for an individual user. This allows IT to create, maintain, and destroy the user IDs in one place. In the context of a network device, it also allows for auditing individual user interactions with a device as well as the assigning of specific roles to users—the opposite of which is that everyone uses the default usernames and or passwords to access the fabric. In this scenario, it is impossible to audit changes if everyone appears identical to the system. It is also more challenging to restrict access when every user is using the admin ID and password.

The APIC uses policies to manage the access, authentication, and accounting (AAA) functions of the Cisco ACI fabric. The combination of user privileges, roles, and domains with access rights inheritance enables administrators to configure AAA functions at the managed object level in a very granular fashion. A core APIC internal data access control system provides multitenant isolation and prevents information privacy from being compromised across tenants. Read/write restrictions prevent any tenant from seeing any other tenant's configuration, statistics, faults, or event data. Unless the administrator assigns permissions to do so, tenants are restricted from reading fabric configuration, policies, statistics, faults, or events. RBAC allows the APIC to use external authentication that may already exist in the environment, such as RADIUS, TACACS+, or LDAP/Active Directory servers for authentication. Once the user is authenticated, we rely on the Cisco AV-Pair that is defined in the external authentication server to define the scope and roles to which the user belongs. The security scope and role will define the privileges the user has to manage the ACI network. It is also imperative to leave the internal database as a backup authentication method just in case the external authentication server is not reachable.

■ **Email / Call Home:** Cisco Call Home is a feature in many Cisco products that will provide email or web-based notification alerts in several different formats for critical events. This allows administrators to resolve issues before they turn into outages. Call Home provides an email-based notification for critical system policies. A range of message formats is available for compatibility with pager services and XML-based automated parsing applications. You can use this feature to page a network support engineer, email a Network Operations Center (NOC), or use Cisco Smart Call Home services to generate a case with the Technical Assistance Center (TAC). The Call Home feature can be used in the following way:

■ The Call Home feature can deliver alert messages containing information about diagnostics and environmental faults and events.

■ The Call Home feature can deliver alerts to multiple recipients, referred to as Call Home *destination profiles*. Each profile includes configurable message formats and content categories. A predefined destination profile is provided for sending alerts to the Cisco TAC, but you also can define your own destination profiles.

To use the Call Home service for email messages, you need to have an email server that is reachable via the management network you choose. Outbound mail servers often require that email destined for external domains originate from a valid email address in the local domain. Ensure the From address you use for Call Home is a valid local email address; otherwise, the mail server may refuse to forward Call Home messages to Cisco. You may also have to allow email relaying on the email server from the APICs. If you plan to have Cisco TAC as one of your Call Home destinations for automatic case generation, you will also need to meet the following requirements:

■ A Cisco.com ID associated with an active support contract for your company.

■ An active support contract that includes the device(s) to be registered.

■ **Syslog:** Cisco ACI sends system log (syslog) messages to the console. Many enterprises choose to send syslog messages to an external logging server. Sending syslog to an external destination allows you to archive and retain the syslog messages for greater lengths of time. Retaining copies of the messages on an external server allows an engineer to examine important system messages in the cases where they are no longer available on the APIC, either due to technical issues or aging policies. Not all system messages indicate problems with your system. Some messages are purely informational, while others may help diagnose problems with communications lines, internal hardware, or the system software. The syslog servers will need to be reachable via the management network. In many cases, the syslog server itself will need to be configured to accept messages from any of the APICs in your ACI fabric.

Management Network

In any IT environment, the management network is a critical consideration. Enterprises that treat the management network with the thoughtfulness it deserves often find themselves in a better position to face any challenge that presents itself. Challenges can come in the form of network outages or misconfigurations due to human error. If the enterprise overlooks the management network, they might find that they are not able to remotely access key devices in the face of hardware, software, or human errors. We explore both types of management networks in the sections that follow.

Out-of-Band Network

Using an out-of-band network is a best practice recommendation. An OOB network increases the odds that you will be able to access the devices in the event that the fabric is experiencing production issues and is unavailable. When you use the initial setup script on the APICs, you will be configuring an OOB address on each of the controllers. Once the fabric is up and running, you will have the chance to perform additional management network tasks, such as changing addressing or assigning OOB network addresses to the spines and leaf switches. When you decide on a subnet and address range, you will also need to decide if you would like to assign the addresses statically or dynamically. Static assignment can be quick and easy for a small network; however, it is a best practice to create a pool of addresses and allow the controller to automatically assign the addresses for devices from the pool. This automates the addition of future devices so that when they come online, they can take advantage of any policies you have already created (such as DNS and NTP) without the need for human intervention. As you configure external services, Layer 4-7 device integrations, and/or virtual machine manager (VMM) integrations in ACI, you will pick which management network the APIC controllers will use to interact with these devices. The fabric policy can also be used to define which management network (in band or out of band) should be treated as the default. It is a best practice to restrict the IP addresses and protocols that are able to interact with your ACI devices over the OOB management interfaces to only the necessary subnets and devices.

In-Band Network

Circumstances may present themselves when you will want to communicate directly with services or devices that are directly attached to or communicating through the fabric. Using the fabric for management communication is called "using an in-band management network." This management network can be used in parallel to or in place of an OOB management configuration. In other words, they are not mutually exclusive. The in-band management network can only be configured after the initial setup of the APICs. A subnet range will need to be determined and IP addresses will need to be defined for the controllers, spines, and leaf switches. You have three ways to communicate with devices attached to the fabric from the in-band network:

■ Directly attach devices to the in-band network using the subnet and IP addressing you have defined.

■ Use an external router outside of the fabric to route between the in-band network and the devices you want to communicate with.

■ Use ACI policy to allow communication between the in-band network and other networks that exist in ACI.

Note   Previous to ACI release 2.0(1), a bug (CSCuz69394) prevented the third option from working. If you want to use the third option, make sure you are on a recent version of the code.

No matter which method you choose for in-band communication, it is still a best practice to restrict the IP addresses and protocols that are able to interact with your ACI devices over the in-band management interfaces to only the necessary subnets and devices.

What to Expect when You Configure a Controller

Whether this is your first time setting up ACI or your tenth, the first task you will undertake is getting the controllers up and running with a base configuration. The Cisco Application Policy Infrastructure Controller is an appliance that is built on the Cisco Unified Computing Systems (UCS) C-Series server platform. After you rack, stack, and provide redundant power to the APIC, you will want to cable the device appropriately. You will need a total of five connections. As shown in Figure 3-1, two 10G ports connect to the ACI leaf, and three connect to the management network (CIMC and OOB management).

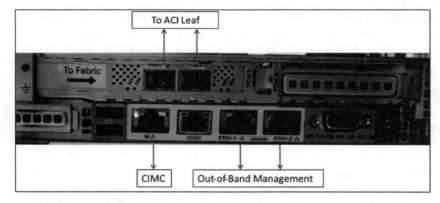

Figure 3-1   *APIC Controller Connections*

Note   The unlabeled port is the RJ-45 console port that can be used for console connections to the APIC after initial setup via the setup dialog shown later in this section in Example 3-1.

Once everything is cabled correctly, connect a VGA monitor and USB keyboard to the appliance and power cycle/reboot the appliance. During the startup or power-on self-test (POST), press **F8** to enter the CIMC configuration utility. Enter the information in Table 3-1 and then press **F10** to save the configuration. Then press **Esc** to exit.

Table 3-1 *CIMC Configuration Values*

Field	Value
NIC Mode	Dedicated
DHCP Enabled	Unchecked
CIMC IP	IP address as per assignment
Prefix/Subnet	Subnet mask
Gateway	IP default gateway
Pref DNS Server	(Optional) DNS server

Once this is complete, you can now access the CIMC via web browser with the management IP address you assigned. The default username is **admin** and the password is **password**. It is recommended that you change the default CIMC and BIOS passwords. The CIMC can now be used to remotely troubleshoot or configure the APICs. This configuration will have to be performed on every APIC appliance. After the CIMC is configured, in the CIMC GUI, verify that you have set the parameters outlined in Table 3-2.

Parameters	Settings
LLDP	Disabled on the VIC
TPM Support	Enabled on the BIOS
TPM Enabled Status	Enabled
TPM Ownership	Owned

Once the configuration is complete, you can now choose to continue the configuration via direct connection (monitor and keyboard) or remotely through the CIMC virtual console.

When the APIC reboots, you will be brought to a setup script. Example 3-1 demonstrates the setup dialog. This configuration will need to be performed on every controller. In most ACI designs, the setup of the clustered controllers will be completed in sequence (one after the other) within a few minutes of each other. The exception to this would be a Multi-Pod or Multi-Site architecture. Controllers that will be physically located at another site or in another pod will be brought up when the additional site or pod is brought up.

Example 3-1   *Sample Initial Setup Dialog as Displayed on the Console*

```
Cluster configuration
  Enter the fabric name [ACI Fabric1 #1]:
  Enter the number of controllers in the fabric (1-16) [3]:
  Enter the controller ID (1-3) [2]:
  Enter the controller name [apic2]:
  Enter address pool for TEP addresses [10.0.0.0/16]:
  Enter the VLAN ID for infra network (1-4094)[] <<< This is for the physical APIC
                          Enter address pool for BD multicast addresses (GIPO)
  [255.0.0.0/15]:

Out-of-band management configuration...
  Enter the IP address for out-of-band management: 192.168.10.2/24
  Enter the IP address of the default gateway [None]: 192.168.10.254
            Enter the interface speed/duplex mode [auto]:

Administrator user configuration...
  Enable strong passwords? [Y]
  Enter the password for admin:
```

Let's examine some of the aspects of the initial controller setup dialog, as outlined in Table 3-2.

Table 3-2   *Setup for Active APIC*

Name	Description	Default Value
Fabric Name	Fabric domain name.	ACI Fabric1
Fabric ID	Fabric ID.	1
Number of active controllers	Cluster size.	3 **Note:** When setting up APIC in an active-standby mode, you must have at least three active APICs in a cluster.
POD ID	Pod ID.	1
Standby Controller	Setup standby controller.	NO
Controller ID	Unique ID number for the active APIC instance.	Valid range: 1–19
Controller name	Active controller name.	apic1
IP address pool for tunnel endpoint addresses	Tunnel endpoint address pool.	10.0.0.0/16

Name	Description	Default Value
		This value is for the infrastructure virtual routing and forwarding (VRF) only.
		This subnet should not overlap with any other routed subnets in your network. If this subnet does overlap with another subnet, change this subnet to a different /16 subnet. The minimum supported subnet for a three-APIC cluster is /23. If you are using Release 2.0(1), the minimum is /22.
VLAN ID for infrastructure network	Infrastructure VLAN for the APIC to switch communication, including virtual switches.	Experience has shown that VLAN 3967 is a good choice.
	Note: Reserve this VLAN for APIC use only. The infrastructure VLAN ID must not be used elsewhere in your environment and must not overlap with any other reserved VLANs on other platforms.	
IP address pool for bridge domain multicast address (GIPO)	IP addresses used for fabric multicast.	225.0.0.0/15
		Valid range: 225.0.0.0/15 to 231.254.0.0/15 (prefix length must be a /15 for 128k IP addresses).
IPv4/IPv6 addresses for the out-of-band management	IP address that you use to access the APIC through the GUI, CLI, or API.	This is dependent on the individual environment.
	Note: This address must be a reserved address from the VRF of a customer.	
IPv4/IPv6 addresses of the default gateway	Gateway address for communication to external networks using out-of-band management.	This is dependent on the individual environment.

Name	Description	Default Value
Management interface speed/ duplex mode	Interface speed and duplex mode for the out-of-band management interface.	auto
		Valid values are as follows: auto, 10BaseT/Half, 10BaseT/Full, 100BaseT/Half, 100BaseTFull, 1000BaseT/Full.
Strong password check	Check for a strong password.	[Y]
Password	Password of the system administrator.	
	Note: This password must be at least eight characters long, with at least one special character.	

Note   To change the VLAN ID after the initial APIC setup, export your configurations, rebuild the fabric with a new infrastructure VLAN ID, and import the configurations so that the fabric does not revert to the old infrastructure VLAN ID. See the KB article about using export and import to recover configuration state (https://tinyurl.com/APICtrPRF).

Note   IPv6 management addresses can be provisioned on the APIC at setup time or through a policy once the controller is operational.

Fabric Infrastructure IP Range Recommendations

When you're provisioning an APIC, one of the required inputs during the setup stage is an IP range for infrastructure addressing inside the fabric, primarily for the purposes of allocating tunnel endpoint (TEP) addresses. The default value for this range is 10.0.0.0/16. Although technically it is possible to select a range that overlaps with other subnets in the network, it is highly recommended that you select a unique range for this.

It is often a requirement that the infrastructure IP range needs to be extended beyond the ACI fabric; for example, when the Application Virtual Switch (AVS) is used, a Virtual Machine Kernel interface is automatically created using an address from the infrastructure range, as shown in Figure 3-2. If this range overlaps with other subnets elsewhere in the network, routing problems may occur.

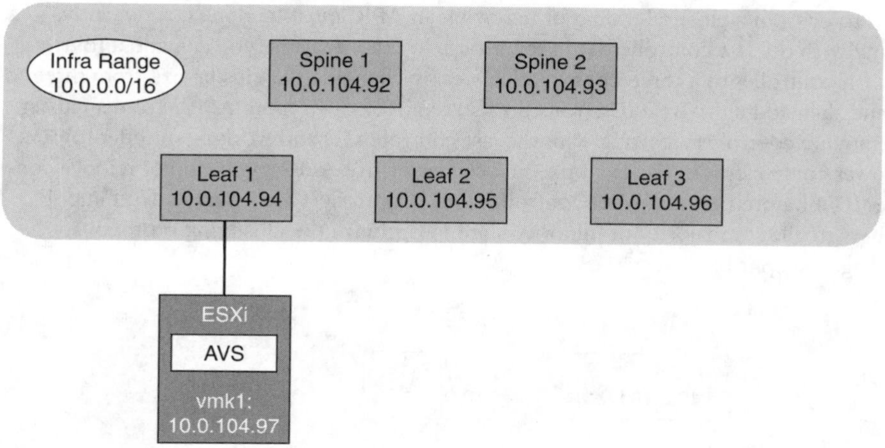

Figure 3-2 *Extending the Infrastructure IP Range Beyond the Fabric*

The minimum recommended subnet size in a three-APIC scenario is /22. The number of addresses required depends on a variety of factors, including the number of APICs, the number of leaf/spine nodes, the number of AVS instances, and the number of virtual port channels (VPCs) required. To avoid issues with address exhaustion in the future, it is recommended that customers consider allocating a /16 or /17 range, if possible.

When considering the IP range, bear in mind that changing either the infrastructure IP range or VLAN after initial provisioning is not generally possible without a fabric rebuild.

Fabric Infrastructure VLAN Recommendations

During fabric provisioning, the system will also ask for a VLAN number to be used as the infrastructure VLAN. This VLAN is used for control communication between fabric nodes (leaf, spine, and APICs). It is important for this VLAN number to be unique within the network, if possible. In a scenario where the infrastructure VLAN is extended outside of the ACI fabric (for example, if you're using Cisco AVS or OpenStack integration with OpFlex), it may be a requirement for this VLAN to traverse other (non-ACI) devices. In that case, be sure that the infrastructure VLAN does not fall within a range that is prohibited on the non-ACI device (for example, the reserved VLAN range within a Nexus 7000, as shown in Figure 3-3).

Experience has shown VLAN 3967 to be a good choice for the ACI infrastructure VLAN to avoid the issue just outlined.

Cluster Size and APIC Controller ID

It is required that you build ACI controller clusters with a minimum of three controllers. If the needs of your enterprise change over time, you have the ability to add or remove

72
Chapter 3: Bringing Up a Fabric

APICs to or from a cluster. Adding or removing an APIC must be done concurrently, starting with the last controller ID in the group. In this situation, you can add a fourth and fifth controller to a three-controller cluster by changing the cluster size from three to five and then adding two APICs. You can also remove one or more APICs from a cluster by removing controllers starting with the last controller ID and working in order toward the lower controller IDs. For example, in a cluster of five APICs, you cannot remove controller ID 4 before first removing controller ID 5. Controllers are usually added in odd numbers to allow a majority or minority state to optimize the clustering protocol and guard against split-brain scenarios.

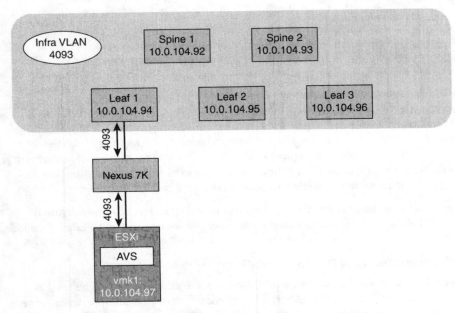

Figure 3-3 *Extending the Infrastructure VLAN Beyond the Fabric*

About High Availability for APIC Cluster

The high availability (HA) functionality for an APIC cluster enables you to operate the APICs in a cluster in an active/standby mode. In an APIC cluster, the designated active APICs share the load, and the designated standby APICs can act as a replacement for any of the APICs in an active cluster.

An admin user can set up the HA functionality when the APIC is launched for the first time. It is recommended that you have at least three active APICs in a cluster, and one or more standby APICs. An admin user will have to initiate the switch over to replace an active APIC with a standby APIC.

Logging In to the GUI for the First Time

Now that you have completed the initial setup of all the controllers, the rest of the configuration will be completed through one of three interfaces:

- Two graphical user interface (GUI) modes (Advanced and Basic) that guide you through the tasks of managing fabrics of various sizes

- NX-OS-style command-line interface (CLI)

- REST API

Unless you are already very familiar with ACI, you will most likely be continuing your setup and configuration through the GUI. To get to the graphical user interface, you will first need one of these supported web browsers:

- Chrome version 35 (at minimum)

- Firefox version 26 (at minimum)

- Internet Explorer version 11 (at minimum)

- Safari version 7.0.3 (at minimum)

Once you have opened your selected browser, enter the following URL: **https:// mgmt_ip-address**. The management IP address will be the management address you entered during the setup script. A page will appear that is similar to the page in Figure 3-4.

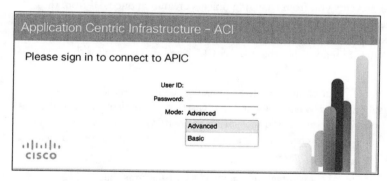

Figure 3-4   *ACI Login Screen*

At the login screen, you will be asked for the username and password you entered during the setup script. Before you click the login button, you will notice at the bottom of the screen that you are given the ability to pick a mode. We explore these modes in the following section.

Basic Mode vs. Advanced Mode

The APIC GUI has two operating modes:

- Basic GUI
- Advanced GUI

The Basic GUI is simplified in comparison to the more powerful Advanced GUI. The Basic GUI provides for easier and faster configuration of ACI constructs. The Basic GUI has intelligence embedded that enables the APIC to create some of the ACI model constructs automatically for you. The Basic GUI provides validations to ensure consistency in the configuration, which reduces and prevents faults.

The Basic GUI enables network administrators to configure leaf ports, tenants, and application profiles without the need to fully understand and configure the ACI policy model. The Advanced GUI instead has a 1:1 mapping with the complete object model. The main differences between the Advanced GUI and the Basic GUI are in the workflows that need to be performed to achieve the same configuration. For instance, with the Basic GUI, the user configures one port at a time, as was the case prior to Cisco ACI; hence, the GUI creates one object for each port. If you want to configure many ports simultaneously and identically, the preferred tool is the Advanced GUI.

You should also use the Advanced GUI if you want to create configurations using interface profiles, selectors, policy groups, and so on, or if you plan to automate the fabric. Changes made through the Basic GUI can be seen, but cannot be modified, in the Advanced GUI, and changes made in the Advanced GUI cannot be rendered in the Basic GUI. The GUI also prevents you from changing objects created in one GUI from the other GUI. The Basic GUI is kept synchronized with the NX-OS CLI, so if you make a change from the NX-OS CLI, these changes are rendered in the Basic GUI, and changes made in the Basic GIU are rendered in the NX-OS CLI. The same is true for the Advanced GUI.

To further simplify configuration and day-to-day management, the Basic GUI also streamlines the dashboard and available menu tabs. The Basic GUI also favors configuration of default policies versus giving you the option to create your own. You also have the option to configure the switches visually and to click port configurations to enable and disable them.

Some enterprises want to take advantage of the majority of features that ACI has to offer, but not all of them. For example, some customers might not want to automate, orchestrate, and use managed L4-7 services in ACI. Some customers might have smaller networks with just a single tenant. In such cases, the Basic GUI is the way to go. For everyone else, it is recommended that they learn the policy model and use the Advanced GUI. Table 3-3 outlines the Basic and Advanced GUI considerations.

Table 3-3   *Basic and Advanced GUI Considerations*

Feature	Basic GUI	Advanced GUI
Port configurations from the topology view	Yes	No
Use of switch and port selectors	No	Yes
Reuse of the same policy	No	Yes
L4-7 device package based	No	Yes
L4-7 network-only stitching	Yes	Yes

Note   You should use the Advanced GUI to manage any policy you've created prior to Release 1.2. It is recommended that you choose a GUI style and stick with it. It is *not* recommended that they switch back and forth between Basic and Advanced GUI configurations.

Basic mode will be deprecated after Cisco APIC Release 3.0(1). We realize that customers may already be using Basic mode or may not upgrade to 3.0(1) immediately, which is why it is covered in this book. Cisco does not recommend using Basic mode for configuration with 3.0(1) and later. However, if you want to use Basic mode, use the following URL: *APIC URL*/indexSimple.html

Whichever GUI you choose to use, you will need to become familiar with the menu and submenu bars. The menu bar is displayed across the top of the APIC GUI (see Figure 3-5). It provides access to the main tabs.

Figure 3-5   *Menu Bar*

You can navigate to the submenu bar (see Figure 3-6) by clicking one of the tabs in the menu bar. When you click a menu bar tab, the submenu bar for that tab is displayed. The submenu bar is different for each menu bar tab and might also differ depending on your specific configurations.

Figure 3-6   *Submenu Bar*

Each of the items in the menu bar represents a discrete area of configuration and monitoring. Some or all of these items may be visible depending on the GUI mode you are logged in to. The menu and submenu items are organized as described in the sections that follow.

System Tab

Use the System tab to collect and display a summary of the overall system health, its history, and a table of system-level faults.

Tenants Tab

Use the Tenants tab in the menu bar to perform tenant management. In the submenu bar, you see an Add Tenant link as well as a drop-down list that contains all the tenants. Up to five of the most recently used tenants are also displayed on the submenu bar.

A tenant contains policies that enable qualified users domain-based access control. Qualified users can access privileges such as tenant administration and networking administration.

A user requires read/write privileges for accessing and configuring policies in a domain. A tenant user can have specific privileges into one or more domains.

In a multitenancy environment, a tenant provides group user access privileges so that resources are isolated from one another (such as for endpoint groups and networking). These privileges also enable different users to manage different tenants.

Fabric Tab

The Fabric tab contains the following sections in the submenu bar:

- **Inventory:** Displays the individual components of the fabric.

- **Fabric Policies:** Displays the monitoring and troubleshooting policies and fabric protocol settings or fabric maximum transmission unit (MTU) settings.

- **Access Policies:** Displays the access policies that apply to the edge ports of the system. These ports are on the leaf switches that communicate externally.

VM Networking Tab

Use the VM Networking tab to view and configure the inventory of the various virtual machine managers (VMMs). You can configure and create various management domains under which connections to individual management systems (such as VMware vCenter and VMware vShield) can be configured. Use the Inventory section in the submenu bar to view the hypervisors and VMs that are managed by these VM management systems (also referred to as *controllers* in API).

L4-L7 Services Tab

Use the L4-L7 Services tab to perform services such as importing packages that define devices on Layers 4 to 7. You can view existing service nodes in the Inventory submenu.

Admin Tab

Use the Admin tab to perform administrative functions such as authentication, authorization, and accounting (AAA) functions, scheduling policies, retaining and purging records, upgrading firmware, and controlling features such as syslog, Call Home, and SNMP.

Operations Tab

Use the Operations tab to perform day-to-day operational functions. Administrators can troubleshoot fabric issues with visibility and troubleshooting tool, or plan for capacity with ACI optimizer. ACI can monitor fabric resources with the capacity dashboard, and track an endpoint anywhere in the fabric with endpoint tracker. The visualization tool helps you see fabric usage to avoid issues like hot spots.

Apps Tab

The Apps tab allows enterprises to upload and install applications that allow customers to better align their network with their business needs. Applications are available from ecosystem partners to augment current IT department investments. A common example of this is the Splunk app that sends log information from the APIC to the Splunk application for processing.

Discovering the Fabric

The APIC is a central point of automated provisioning and management for all the switches that are part of the ACI fabric. A single data center might include multiple ACI fabrics; each data center might have its own APIC cluster and Cisco Nexus 9000 Series switches that are part of the fabric. To ensure that a switch is managed only by a single APIC cluster, each switch must be registered with that specific APIC cluster that manages the fabric.

The APIC discovers new switches that are directly connected to any switch it currently manages. Each APIC instance in the cluster first discovers only the leaf switch to which it is directly connected. After the leaf switch is registered with the APIC, the APIC discovers all spine switches that are directly connected to the leaf switch. As each spine switch is registered, that APIC discovers all the leaf switches that are connected to that spine switch. This cascaded discovery allows the APIC to discover the entire fabric topology in a few simple steps.

After a switch is registered with the APIC, it is part of the APIC-managed fabric inventory. Within the Application Centric Infrastructure fabric (ACI fabric), the APIC is the single point of provisioning, management, and monitoring for switches in the infrastructure.

Note Before you begin registering a switch, make sure that all switches in the fabric are physically connected and booted in the desired configuration.

Step 1.   On the menu bar, choose **Fabric > Inventory**.

Step 2.   In the navigation pane, click **Fabric Membership**. In the work pane, in the Fabric Membership table, a single leaf switch is displayed with an ID of 0. It is the leaf switch that is connected to apic1.

Step 3.   Configure the ID by double-clicking the leaf switch row and performing the following actions:

    a. In the **ID** field, add the appropriate ID (leaf1 is ID 101, and leaf2 is ID 102). The ID must be a number that is greater than 100 because the first 100 IDs are for APIC appliance nodes.

    b. In the **Switch Name** field, add the name of the switch and click **Update**.

Note   After an ID is assigned, it cannot be updated. The switch name can be updated by double-clicking the name and updating the **Switch Name** field.

An IP address gets assigned to the switch, and in the navigation pane, the switch is displayed under the pod.

Step 4.   Monitor the work pane until one or more spine switches appear.

Step 5.   Configure the ID by double-clicking the spine switch row and performing the following actions:

    a. In the **ID** field, add the appropriate ID (spine1 is ID 203, and spine2 is ID 204).

Note   It is recommended that leaf nodes and spine nodes be numbered differently. For example, you can number spines in the 200 range and number leaf switches in the 100 range.

    b. In the **Switch Name** field, add the name of the switch and click **Update**.

An IP address gets assigned to the switch, and in the navigation pane, the switch is displayed under the pod. Wait until all remaining switches appear in the Node Configurations table before you go to the next step.

Step 6.   For each switch listed in the Fabric Membership table, perform the following steps:

    a. Double-click the switch, enter an ID and a name, and click **Update**.

    b. Repeat this step for the next switch in the list.

Fabric Extenders

Fabric Extenders (FEXs) may be part of your ACI design. Similar to other Nexus products, Fabric Extenders in ACI must be configured after the parent switch is provisioned and fully functional. Fabric Extenders are not included in the ACI fabric zero-touch provisioning. At press time the following is supported when using a FEX with the ACI fabric:

- Only straight-through attachment of a Fabric Extender to a leaf is supported.

- A license is required for each FEX device being used in ACI.

- Current scalability is 18 FEXs per leaf / 200 per fabric.

- Some FEX models can support both Fibre Channel over Ethernet (FCoE) and data connectivity.

- The following FEX models are supported:

  - N2K-C2232PP-10GE

  - N2K-C2232TM-E-10GE

  - N2K-C2348UPQ

  - N2K-C2348TQ

  - N2K-C2332TQ

  - N2K-C2248TP-E-1GE

  - N2K-C2248TP-1GE

  - N2K-C2248PQ-10GE

  - N2K-B22IBM-P

  - N2K-B22DELL-P

However, because this list can be frequently updated, refer to the release notes of the Nexus 9000 switch for the ACI software you use for an accurate and updated list.

A Fabric Extender in ACI can only be attached to a single leaf with one or more ports. The ports that connect the FEX to a leaf are able to be part of a port channel. The following is a link to a configuration example displaying the policy required to configure a Fabric Extender in ACI: https://tinyurl.com/FEXACI.

Required Services

At the beginning of the chapter, we reviewed suggested services. Within those services, NTP was listed as a required service due to the dependence of time synchronization in the visibility, management, and troubleshooting functionalities that exist within ACI. Many enterprises have moved to ACI to leverage these features, which require NTP. In the following sections, we explore the three minimal tasks required to prepare a fabric to be production-ready, to accept policy, and to accept applications. We examine these steps in the Basic GUI and Advanced GUI separately due to differences in their configuration. In each GUI, the tasks are the same:

1. Configure the management network.

2. Configure NTP.

3. Configure the route reflectors.

Settings can be verified as tasks are completed. Advanced mode requires policies for correct operation. We explore the hierarchy and relationship of access policies in depth. Policies will also be used to configure the aforementioned required services.

Basic Mode Initial Setup

The Basic GUI has been streamlined to allow enterprises to use the most common features within ACI without learning and using the policy model. Following this same approach, the initial setup of the fabric has been streamlined as well. Once the following sections have been completed, your fabric will be ready to accept policy, devices, and applications.

Management Network

Configuring the management network in the Basic GUI is quick and easy. The items you need to configure can be found under the System menu and the In Band and Out of Band submenus. In this section, we assume you are going to use out-of-band (OOB) management. When you highlight **Out of Band Management Configuration** in the left navigation pane, you will see configuration options to the right in the work pane. Using the work pane, you have the following options available:

- Configure a node (switch/controller) with the OOB management IP address and gateway.

- Configure an access restriction for which subnets can be used to interact with the previously configured management addresses.

- Configure an access restriction for which protocols can be used to interact with the previously configured management addresses.

The only item that is required is to configure a node. If you do not configure additional restrictions, all communications will be allowed. It is a best practice to configure additional access restrictions. You can find step-by-step configuration information in the document "Cisco APIC Basic Configuration Guide, Release 2.x" at Cisco.com.

Note   Be careful when adding nodes and restrictions that you don't accidently prevent yourself from accessing the devices remotely.

If you want to configure in-band management, follow these steps:

Step 1.   Log in to the Basic mode in the APIC GUI, and on the menu bar, click **System > In Band & Out of Band.**

Step 2.   In the navigation pane, choose **In-Band Management Configuration.**

Step 3.   (Optional) In the **Encap** field, enter a new value to change the default VLAN that is used for in-band management.

Step 4.   Expand **Nodes** and perform the following actions:

   a. In the **Nodes** field, choose the appropriate node to associate with the in-band address.

   b. In the **IP address** field, enter the desired IPv4 or IPv6 address.

   c. In the **Gateway** field, enter the desired IPv4 or IPv6 gateway address. Click **Submit.**

Note   The default gateway IP address will be the pervasive gateway of the ACI fabric on the VRF for the in-band management.

Step 5.   Click the **L2 Connectivity** tab, expand **Ports**, and perform the following actions:

   a. In the **Path** field, from the drop-down list, choose the port that is connected to a server for management or to the outside.

   b. In the **Encap** field, specify a VLAN to use on this port.

Step 6.   Expand **Gateway IP Address for External Connectivity** and in the **IP address** fields, list the desired gateway IPv4 and IPv6 addresses for external connectivity.

Step 7.   Expand **ACLs** and add the desired ports you want to connect to the in-band management network. Click **Submit.**

NTP

We have covered the value of NTP in detail. To configure NTP, navigate to the **System** menu and then to the **System Settings** submenu. Highlight **NTP** in the left navigation pane. In the work pane on the right you will see NTP configuration options. You have the ability to modify these four items:

■ **Description**

■ **Administrative State:** Enable/Disable

■ **Authentication:** Enable/Disable

■ **Add an NTP Server or Provider**

First enable the administrative state. Next, add an NTP server using the plus sign on the middle-right. A new window will open where you can add details regarding the NTP server. You have the ability to modify these items:

- **Name:** IP or hostname (requires DNS configuration)

- **Description**

- **Preferred:** If you have more than one server, which is the primary?

- **Minimum Polling Intervals and Maximum Polling Intervals**

- **Management Network:** Which management network will you use to communicate with the NTP server?

Enter the IP address for the NTP server. Next, check the **Preferred** check box. Select the default OOB management network. Click **Submit** and then **Submit** again to save your settings.

Verifying your configuration is easy. Highlight **NTP** in the left navigation pane. In the work pane on the right, double-click the NTP server you have configured. A new window will open up. Click the **Operational** tab in the upper-right. In the **Deployed Servers** tab, you should now see the management IP addresses listed with their sync status.

Note   You may also want to explore the date-time settings to adjust the time offset for your time zone.

Route Reflectors

Cisco ACI uses MP-BGP (Multiprotocol–Border Gateway Protocol) to distribute external routing information across the leaf switches in the fabric. Therefore, the infrastructure administrator needs to define the spine switches that are used as route reflectors and the autonomous system number (ASN) that is used in the fabric.

The Cisco ACI fabric supports one ASN. The same ASN is used for internal MP-BGP and for the internal BGP (iBGP) session between the border leaf switches and external routers. Given that the same ASN is used in both cases when using iBGP, the user needs to find the ASN on the router to which the Cisco ACI border leaf connects and to use it as the BGP ASN for the Cisco ACI fabric.

To summarize, in order to perform Layer 3 routing in the fabric and connect externally from the fabric over Layer 3, you need to configure route reflectors. You should configure at least two spines per pod as route reflectors for redundancy.

You can make the spine switches the route reflectors by configuring them as such under **System > Systems Settings**, as shown in Figure 3-7. Highlight **BGP Route Reflector** in the navigation pane on the left side. In the work pane on the right side, you will be able to configure the following:

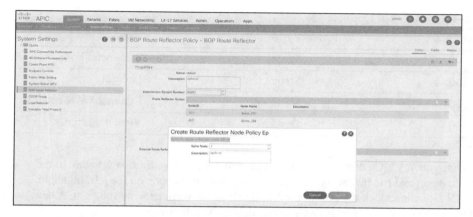

Figure 3-7 *Configuring Spine Switches as Route Reflectors*

- **Description**

- **Autonomous System Number:** This should be unique in your environment (for example, 65001).

- **Route Reflector Nodes:** Choose the spine nodes you want to be the route reflectors.

- **External Route Reflector Nodes:** Used for Multi-Pod or WAN integration.

Enter the autonomous system number. Add the route reflector nodes by clicking the plus to the right of the Route Reflector Node window. Enter the device number of the spine you want to configure as the route reflector. Click **Submit**. Repeat these actions for the next spine node. Click **Submit** at the bottom-right of the page to save your changes.

VLAN Domains

In spanning-tree networks, the user must specify which VLANs belong to which ports by using the **switchport trunk allowed VLAN** command. In the Cisco ACI fabric, a VLAN pool is used to define a range of VLAN numbers that will ultimately be applied on specific ports (for hosts or network devices) on one or more leaf nodes. A VLAN pool can be configured either as a static or a dynamic pool. Static pools are generally used for hosts and devices that will be manually configured in the fabric (for example, bare-metal hosts or L4-7 devices attached using traditional services insertion). Dynamic pools are used when the APIC needs to allocate VLANs automatically—for instance, when using VMM integration or automated services insertion (service graphs).

It is a common practice to divide VLAN pools into functional groups, as shown in Table 3-4. It is a best practice to assign specific domains and pools to individual tenants.

Table 3-4   *VLAN Pool Example*

VLAN Range	Type	Use
1000–1100	Static	Bare-metal hosts
1101–1200	Static	Firewalls
1201–1300	Static	External WAN routers
1301–1400	Dynamic	Virtual machines

To configure a VLAN domain and pool in Basic mode, you would first navigate to the **Fabric** menu and the **Inventory** submenu. In the navigation pane on the left, highlight **VLAN Domains**. Click the plus in the **VLAN Domains** work pane on the right. A new window will open. In this window, you can define the following:

- **Name:** Name for the group of VLANs or VLAN domain you are configuring (for example, Tenant1_Vmware_VDS, Tenant1_Physical, Tenant2_CheckpointFW, and so on).

- **Allocation Mode:** Static or dynamic. Dynamic is normally used for automating Layer 4-7 services and virtualization. Static is normally used for physical devices or connectivity.

- **VLAN Range:** The range of VLANs you would like to include in this domain. You can specify one or more.

Define the name (use underscores for spaces). Your allocation mode will most likely be static to start with. Then click the plus sign to define a VLAN range. In the middle of the window, under **VLAN Ranges,** you will see the **To and From** field highlighted. Populate that field with the appropriate VLAN range for the devices you will be connecting. The allocation mode can be left to **Inherit from parent.** Click **Update** and then **Submit.** Repeat as necessary.

Advanced Mode Initial Setup

The Advanced GUI can sound intimidating at first. In reality, it is not harder to use or learn than the Basic GUI; it just takes a little more time to learn how all the policy objects relate to each other. Once you are familiar with the relationships and order of operations, it will become like second nature. When using the Advanced GUI, you do everything with a policy. It is a best practice to leave the default policies in place and create new policies with names that make sense for your company and environment. A byproduct of creating new policies is the ability to look at them and reference default configurations.

The naming convention you use for policies in the Advanced GUI is very important. You want it to be standardized, modular, and meaningful. How you name your policies will make the difference between a streamlined administrative experience and a cluttered one. Table 3-5 shows best-practice recommendations regarding policy-naming conventions in ACI.

Table 3-5 *ACI Policy-Naming Conventions (Best Practices)*

Policy Name	Examples
VRFs	
*[Function]*_VRF	Production_VRF
Bridge Domains	
*[Function]*_BD	Main_BD
Endpoint Groups	
*[Function]*_EPG	Web_EPG
Subnets	
*[Function]*_SBNT	App1_SBNT
Attachable Access Entity Profiles	
*[Function]*_AEP	VMM_AEP
	L3Out_AEP
VLAN Pools	
*[Function]*_VLP	VMM_VLP
	L3Out_VLP
Domains	
*[Functionality]*_PHY	BareMetal_PHY
*[Functionality]*_VMM	vCenter1_VMM
*[Functionality]*_L2O	L2DCI_L2O
*[Functionality]*_L3O	L3DCI_L3O
Contracts, Subjects, and Filters	
*[Tenant]_[Prov]_to_[cons]*_CON	Prod_Web_to_App_CON
*[Rulegroup]*_SUBJ	WebTraffic_SUBJ
*[Resource-Name]*_FLT	HTTP_FLT
Application Profiles	
*[Function]*_ANP	Prod_SAP_ANP
Interface Policies	
*[Type][Enable|Disable]*_INTPOL	CDP_Enable_INTPOL
	LLDP_Disable_INTPOL
Interface Policy Groups	

Policy Name	Examples
*[Type]_[Functionality]_*IPG	vPC_ESXi-Host1_IPG
	PC_ESXi-Host1_IPG
	PORT_ESXi-Host1_IPG
Interface Profiles	
*[Node1]_[Node2]_*IPR	101_102_IPR

In Table 3-5, the policies are mainly named based on function. The policies also include a suffix that helps the administrator easily determine what type of policy they are working with. This becomes vital as you start to leverage other forms of management, such as the API.

ACI was designed as a stateless architecture. The network devices have no application-specific configuration until a policy is defined stating how that application or traffic should be treated on the network. Even then, the policy or configuration is not implemented until you see interesting traffic that matches the policy, meaning that the individual hardware, capabilities, and configuration are abstracted and what really matters is the intent of the policy. The two most frequent types of policy you will be configuring in ACI are access policies and tenant policies. These ACI policies can be thought of in two distinct ways: The *access policies* control the physical configuration of the individual switch ports. The *tenant policies* control the logical configuration of the fabric. An analogy can be made to a house. Think of the access policies like the exterior walls and foundation of the house, and the tenant policies like the interior walls of a house. The walls and foundation are the support structure for the house, which need to be configured correctly to build a solid structure, and they don't often change. The interior walls can and often do get changed and remodeled over the life of the house. The ACI fabric depends on the access policies to define how physical configuration should be implemented on a port or group of ports once a tenant policy is applied. A tenant policy defines how that application or traffic should be treated once it hits the network. You need to have both the physical and logical policies for the system to work correctly. This also makes it easy to leave physical connectivity, IP addressing, and VLANs in place, but dynamically change the tenant or logical policy at any time, as shown in Figure 3-8.

The policies we are exploring are also very modular. The planning that's done up-front will quickly pay off in the future when, instead of re-creating a configuration over and over again, we are instead adding a port to a known-good policy. It takes time at the beginning to learn this new way of doing things, but once you do, you will quickly see the efficiencies (such as when you add a device to the fabric and it inherits the correct configuration).

Fabric policies are another type of policy that applies to the fabric (or fabrics) as a whole. These policies are usually configured once and then modified infrequently after that. The initial setup for services like NTP and the route reflectors will be configured through these policies. Later, you can use these policies to change the settings across that entire fabric (or fabrics) at a global level.

We explore these policy types further in the following sections.

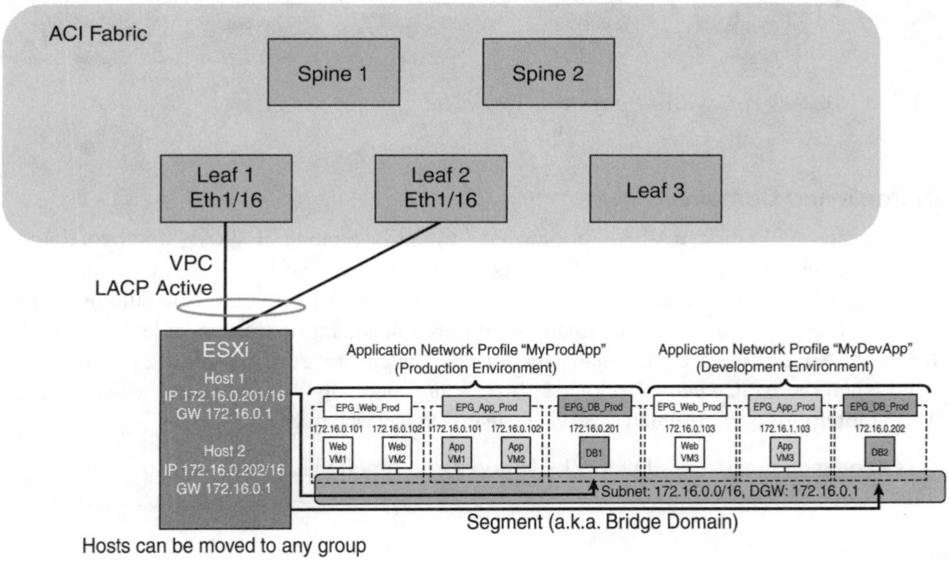

Figure 3-8 *Static Physical Configuration Mapping to Dynamic Policy*

Access Policies

Gaining mastery over access policies is a crucial part of becoming proficient at configuring, managing, and troubleshooting ACI in Advanced mode. Access policies are responsible for the physical configuration of the ports to which devices are attached. Access policies are configured in a hierarchical manner and built to be modular so that you can change isolated details without having to modify or re-create the entire policy. Once access policies are defined, the configuration stays dormant until a tenant policy is triggered. When the tenant policy is applied, the port is configured with the physical characteristics defined in the access policy. Both policies are needed for ACI to function correctly.

Access policies are also created to simplify configuration and reduce human error through the reuse of known-good policy. An engineer might create a single policy to use on all of their lights-out management ports, blade server connections, or rack-mounted ESX servers. When you need to add a new server, you can just add a port to the existing best-practice policy, thus eliminating configuration drift. You can also pre-stage policies on ports. For example, ports 1–5 on every switch may have access policies configured for server management, just waiting for devices to be attached.

The hierarchical access policy relationships are defined in Figure 3-9. In the information that follows, we will be referencing the figure from left to right.

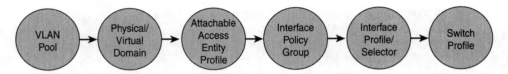

Figure 3-9   *Access Policy Configuration Workflow*

VLAN Pools and Domains

In the Cisco ACI fabric, a VLAN pool is used to define a range of VLAN numbers that will ultimately be applied on specific ports on one or more leaf nodes. A VLAN pool can be configured either as a static or a dynamic pool. Static pools are generally used for hosts and devices that will be manually configured in the fabric (for example, bare-metal hosts or L4-7 devices attached using traditional services insertion). Dynamic pools are used when the APIC needs to allocate VLANs automatically—for instance, when using VMM integration or automated services insertion (service graphs).

It is a common practice to divide VLAN pools into functional groups, as shown in Table 3-6.

Table 3-6   *VLAN Pool Example*

VLAN Range	Type	Use
1000–1100	Static	Bare-metal hosts
1101–1200	Static	Firewalls
1201–1300	Static	External WAN routers
1301–1400	Dynamic	Virtual machines

A domain is used to define the scope of VLANs in the Cisco ACI fabric—in other words, where and how a VLAN pool will be used. There are a number of domain types: physical, virtual (VMM domains), external Layer 2, and external Layer 3. It is common practice to have a 1:1 mapping between a VLAN pool and a domain. It is also common practice to have separate VLAN pools and domains per tenant.

Attachable Access Entity Profiles

The Attachable Access Entity Profile (AAEP) is used to map domains (physical or virtual) to interface policies, with the end goal of mapping VLANs to interfaces. Configuring an AAEP is roughly analogous to configuring **switchport access vlan** *x* on an interface in a traditional NX-OS configuration. In addition, AAEPs allow a one-to-many relationship (if desired) to be formed between interface policy groups and domains, as shown in Figure 3-10.

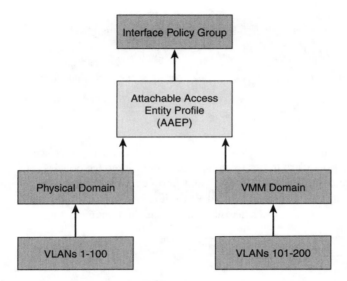

Figure 3-10 *AAEP Relationships*

In the example in Figure 3-10, an administrator needs to have both a VMM domain and a physical domain (that is, using static path bindings) on a single port or port channel. To achieve this, the administrator can map both domains (physical and virtual) to a single AAEP, which can then be associated with a single interface policy group representing the interface and port channel.

Interface Policies

Interface policies are responsible for the configuration of interface-level parameters, such as LLDP, Cisco Discovery Protocol, LACP, port speed, storm control, and Miscabling Protocol (MCP). Interface policies are brought together as part of an interface policy group (described in the next section).

Each type of interface policy is preconfigured with a default policy. In most cases, the feature or parameter in question is set to "disabled" as part of the default policy.

It is highly recommended that you create explicit policies for each configuration item rather than relying on and modifying the default policy. For example, for LLDP configuration, it is highly recommended that you configure two policies—LLDP_Enabled and LLDP_Disabled (or similar)—and use these policies when either enabling or disabling LLDP. This helps prevent accidental modification of the default policy, which may have a wide impact.

Note   You should not modify the Interface Policy for "LLDP Interface" named "default" because this policy is used by spines and leaf nodes for bootup and to look for an image to run. If you need to create a different default configuration for the servers, you can create a new LLDP policy and give it a name, and then use this one instead of the policy called "default."

Interface Policy Groups

In a Cisco ACI fabric, access ports, port channels, and VPCs are created using interface policy groups. The interface policy group ties together a number of interface policies, such as Cisco Discovery Protocol, LLDP, LACP, MCP, and storm control. When you're creating interface policy groups for port channels and VPCs, it is important to understand how policies can and cannot be reused. Consider the example shown in Figure 3-11.

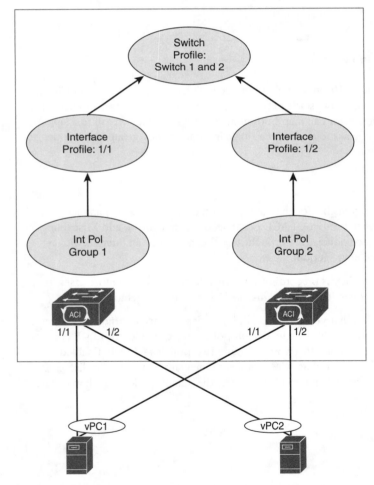

Figure 3-11   *vPC Interface Policy Groups*

In this example, two servers are attached to the Cisco ACI leaf pair using VPCs. In this case, two separate interface policy groups must be configured, associated with the appropriate interface profiles (used to specify which ports will be used) and assigned to a switch profile. A common mistake is to configure a single interface policy group and attempt to reuse it for multiple port channels or VPCs on a single leaf node. However, using a single interface policy group and referencing it from multiple interface profiles will result in additional interfaces being added to the same port channel or VPC, which may not be the desired outcome.

A general rule is that a port channel or VPC interface policy group should have a 1:1 mapping to a port channel or VPC. Administrators should not try to reuse port channel and VPC interface policy groups for more than one port channel or VPC. Note that this rule applies only to port channels and VPCs. For access port interface policy groups, these policies can be reusable.

It may be tempting for administrators to use a numbering scheme for port channels and VPCs (such as PC1, PC2, vPC1, and so on). However, this is not recommended because Cisco ACI allocates an arbitrary number to the port channel or VPC when it is created, and it is unlikely that the numbering will match, which could lead to confusion. Instead, it is recommended that you use a descriptive naming scheme (for example, Firewall_Prod_A).

Interface Profile

Interface profiles exist in the ACI fabric to marry a port or a range of ports to a specific interface policy group. As a best practice for configuration and troubleshooting, you should name your interface profile the same as the switch with which you will be associating the interface profile. An interface/leaf profile would then be created for every leaf and every VPC pair in your ACI fabric, as shown in Figure 3-12.

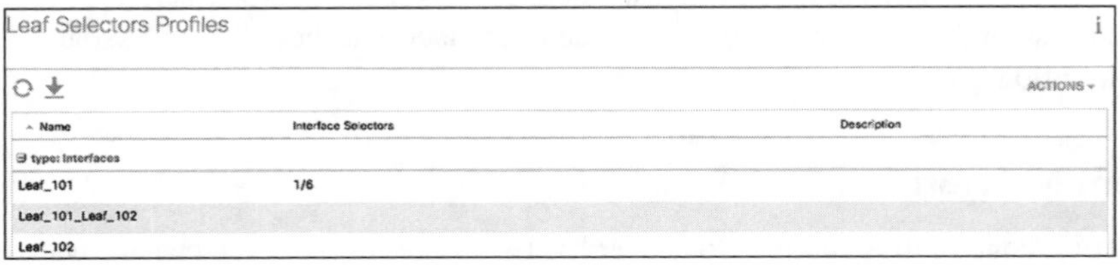

Figure 3-12 *Leaf Selector Profile*

It is also a best practice to name your interface selectors the same as the port you are selecting. For instance, if you are selecting port 1/6, you would name the selector 1_6, as shown in Figure 3-13.

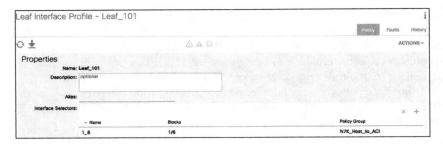

Figure 3-13 *Interface Selectors*

Once all of your policies are defined, configuring a port should be as simple as adding an interface selector to the interface profile and selecting which policy group to consume.

Switch Profile

Switch profiles specify from which ACI leaf your interface profiles will be selecting interfaces. As with interface profiles, it is a best practice to define a switch profile for each individual leaf and VPC pair in your fabric, as demonstrated in Figure 3-14.

Profiles – Leaf Profiles		i
		ACTIONS ⁓
⌃ Name	Leaf Selectors	Description
Leaf_101_102_VPC	101–102(Common_Leaf_Pol)	GUI Interface Selector Generated Profile: Leaf_...
Leaf_101_Profile	101(Common_Leaf_Pol)	
Leaf_102_Profile	102(Common_Leaf_Pol)	

Figure 3-14 *Leaf Profiles*

When a switch profile is defined, you will also choose to associate interface selector profiles, which should be very straightforward due to the fact that they share the same naming convention.

Management Network

An Application Policy Infrastructure Controller has two routes to reach the management network: One is by using the in-band management interface, and the other is by using the out-of-band management interface.

The in-band management network allows the APIC to communicate with the leaf switches and with the outside using the ACI fabric, and it makes it possible for external management devices to communicate with the APIC or the leaf switches and spine switches using the fabric itself.

The out-of-band management network configuration defines the configuration of the management port on the controllers, the leaf switches, and the spine switches.

To configure the management networks in the Advanced GUI, you will need to navigate to the **Tenants** menu item. The mgmt (management) tenant contains all the configuration details for both the in-band and out of band networks. To enter the mgmt tenant, double-click it. For this example, we are going to configure an out-of-band network. In the Advanced GUI, you have the ability to assign static addresses or use a pool of addresses that are automatically assigned. It is a best practice to use the pool of addresses. When you use a pool, a new switch that is added to the fabric is automatically assigned an address and can utilize existing policies that are in place, with no user intervention. To configure the out-of-band network, follow these steps:

Step 1. In the navigation pane, expand the tenant **mgmt**.

Step 2. Right-click **Node Management Addresses** and click **Create Node Management Addresses**.

Step 3. In the Create Node Management Addresses dialog, perform the following actions:

a. In the **Policy Name** field, enter a policy name (**switchOob**).

b. In the **Nodes** field, check the boxes next to the appropriate leaf and spine switches (**leaf1**, **leaf2**, and **spine1**).

c. In the **Config** field, check the box next to **Out-of-Band Addresses**.

Note   The Out-of-Band IP Addresses area is displayed.

d. In the **Out-of-Band Management EPG** field, choose the EPG from the drop-down list (**default**).

e. In the **Out-of-Band IP Addresses** and **Out-of-Band Gateway** fields, enter the desired IPv4 or IPv6 addresses that will be assigned to the switches. Click **OK**.

The node management IP addresses are configured. You must configure out-of-band management access addresses for the leaf and spine switches as well as for APIC.

Step 4. In the navigation pane, expand **Node Management Addresses** and click the policy you created. In the work pane, the out-of-band management addresses are displayed against the switches.

Step 5. In the navigation pane, expand **Security Policies > Out-of-Band Contracts**.

Step 6. Right-click **Out-of-Band Contracts** and click **Create Out-of-Band Contract**.

Step 7. In the Create Out-of-Band Contract dialog, perform the following tasks:

a. In the **Name** field, enter a name for the contract (**oob-default**).

b. Expand **Subjects**. In the Create Contract Subject dialog, in the **Name** field, enter a subject name (**oob-default**).

    c. Expand **Filters**, and in the **Name** field, from the drop-down list, choose the name of the filter (**default**). Click **Update** and then click **OK**.

    d. In the Create Out-of-Band Contract dialog, click **Submit**.

An out-of-band contract that can be applied to the out-of-band EPG is created.

Step 8. In the navigation pane, expand **Node Management EPGs > Out-of-Band EPG-default**.

Step 9. In the work pane, expand **Provided Out-of-Band Contracts**.

Step 10. In the OOB Contract column, from the drop-down list, choose the out-of-band contract you created (**oob-default**). Click **Update** and then click **Submit**. The contract is associated with the node management EPG.

Step 11. In the navigation pane, right-click **External Network Instance Profile** and click **Create External Management Entity Instance**.

Step 12. In the Create External Management Entity Instance dialog, perform the following actions:

    a. In the **Name** field, enter a name (**oob-mgmt-ext**).

    b. Expand the **Consumed Out-of-Band Contracts** field. From the **Out-of-Band Contracts** drop-down list, choose the contract that you created (**oob-default**). Click **Update**. Choose the same contract that was provided by the out-of-band management.

    c. In the **Subnets** field, enter the subnet address. Click **Submit**. Only the subnet addresses you choose here will be used to manage the switches. The subnet addresses that are not included cannot be used to manage the switches.

The node management EPG is attached to the external network instance profile. The out-of-band management connectivity is configured.

Note   You can make out-of-band management access the default management connectivity mode for the APIC server by clicking **Fabric > Fabric Policies > Global Policies > Connectivity Preferences**. Then, on the Connectivity Preferences page, click **ooband**.

Note   The APIC out-of-band management connection link must be 1Gbps.

Fabric Policies

Fabric policies are found on the main **Fabric** tab in the APIC GUI and are concerned with configuration of the fabric itself (for example, IS-IS, management access, MP-BGP, and fabric MTU). Many of the policies found in this section should not be modified under normal circumstances, and the recommendation is to not change them. However, there are a number of policies that deserve consideration and are therefore covered in this section.

NTP

Within the Cisco Application Centric Infrastructure (ACI) fabric, time synchronization is a crucial capability upon which many of the monitoring, operational, and troubleshooting tasks depend. Clock synchronization is important for proper analysis of traffic flows as well as for correlating debug and fault timestamps across multiple fabric nodes.

An offset present on one or more devices can hamper the ability to properly diagnose and resolve many common operational issues. In addition, clock synchronization allows for the full utilization of the atomic counter capability that is built in to the ACI, upon which the application health scores depend.

The procedure for configuring NTP in the Advanced GUI is as follows:

Step 1. On the menu bar, choose **Fabric > Fabric Policies**.

Step 2. In the navigation pane, choose **Pod Policies > Policies**.

Step 3. In the work pane, choose **Actions > Create Date and Time Policy**.

Step 4. In the Create Date and Time Policy dialog, perform the following actions:

   a. Enter a name for the policy to distinguish between the different NTP configurations in your environment. Click **Next**.

   b. Click the plus sign to specify the NTP server information (provider) to be used.

   c. In the Create Providers dialog, enter all relevant information, including the following fields: **Name**, **Description**, **Minimum Polling Intervals**, and **Maximum Polling Intervals**.

   If you are creating multiple providers, check the **Preferred** check box for the most reliable NTP source.

   In the **Management EPG** drop-down list, if the NTP server is reachable by all nodes on the fabric through out-of-band management, choose **Out-of-Band**. If you have deployed in-band management, see the details about In-Band Management NTP. Click **OK**.

   Repeat the steps for each provider you want to create.

Step 5. In the navigation pane, choose **Pod Policies > Policy Groups**.

Step 6. In the work pane, choose **Actions > Create Pod Policy Group**.

Step 7.   In the Create Pod Policy Group dialog, perform the following actions:

   a. Enter a name for the policy group.

   b. In the **Date Time Policy** field, from the drop-down list, choose the NTP policy that you created earlier. Click **Submit**. The pod policy group is created. Alternatively, you can use the default pod policy group.

Step 8.   In the navigation pane, choose **Pod Policies > Profiles**.

Step 9.   In the work pane, double-click the desired pod selector name.

Step 10.   In the **Properties** area, from the **Fabric Policy Group** drop-down list, choose the pod policy group you created. Click **Submit**.

Route Reflectors

The BGP route reflector policy controls whether MP-BGP runs within the fabric and which spine nodes should operate as BGP reflectors. When a Cisco ACI fabric is initially provisioned, MP-BGP is not enabled inside the fabric. However, in the majority of cases, MP-BGP must be enabled to allow the distribution of external routing information throughout the fabric.

It is important to note that the BGP autonomous system number (ASN) is a fabric-wide configuration setting that applies across all Cisco ACI pods that are managed by the same APIC cluster and should be unique in your environment (Multi-Pod).

To enable and configure MP-BGP within the fabric, modify the BGP Route Reflector default policy under **Pod Policies** on the **Fabric Policies** tab. The default BGP route reflector policy should then be added to a pod policy group and pod profile to make the policy take effect.

Managing Software Versions

Many hours have been spent during maintenance windows upgrading individual switches one by one. Cisco ACI makes the traditional method of managing device firmware a thing of the past. The Cisco APICs are looking at the network as a single entity or fabric and not as a bunch of individual devices. ACI has consolidated the software image management for the entire fabric, as well as the controllers, and wrapped it in a process that is easy to administer. We examine each of the parts of the firmware management process separately in the sections that follow. At a high level, the steps to upgrade or downgrade the ACI fabric are as follows:

Note   The procedure/steps for upgrading and downgrading are the same unless stated otherwise in the release notes of a specific release.

Step 1.   Download the ACI Controller image (APIC image) into the repository.

Step 2.   Download the ACI switch image into the repository.

Step 3. Upgrade the ACI controller cluster (APICs).

Step 4. Verify the fabric is operational.

Step 5. Divide the switches into multiple groups (for example, divide into two groups: red and blue).

Step 6. Upgrade the red group of switches.

Step 7. Verify the fabric is operational.

Step 8. Upgrade the blue group of switches.

Step 9. Verify the fabric is operational.

Additionally, here are some general guidelines regarding ACI fabric upgrade/downgrade:

- Divide switches into two or more groups. Upgrade one group at a time. That way, you will maintain connectivity for your redundant servers and not lose fabric bandwidth entirely during the upgrade window.

- Do not upgrade or downgrade nodes that are part of a disabled configuration zone.

- Unless specified otherwise in release notes of a specific release, you can upgrade (or downgrade) controllers before switches, and vice versa (switches before controllers).

- A specific release, or a combination of releases, may have some limitations and recommendations for the upgrade or downgrade procedure. Double-check the release notes for the release before upgrading or downgrading your ACI fabric. If no such limitations or recommendations are specified in the release notes, the aforementioned steps should be followed to upgrade or downgrade your ACI fabric.

Firmware Repository

The ACI firmware repository is a distributed store that houses firmware images required to upgrade or downgrade the ACI fabric. The firmware repository is synced to every controller in the cluster. A firmware image is downloaded into the firmware repository from an external server (HTTP or SCP) when a download task is configured. Another option is to upload the firmware from a folder on your local machine via an upload task. Three types of firmware images can be stored in the repository:

- **Controller/APIC image:** This image consists of software that runs on ACI controllers (APICs).

- **Switch image:** This image consists of software that runs on ACI switches.

- **Catalog image:** This image consists of Cisco-created internal policies. These internal policies contain information about the capabilities of different models of hardware, the compatibility across different versions of software, and the hardware and diagnostic tests. This image is usually bundled and upgraded along with the controller image. Unless specifically instructed by the release notes of a specific release, an administrator should never have to individually upgrade a catalog image.

The firmware will be added to the repository in two separate tasks. The first task is for the controller software to be added to the repository and replicated across the controllers. Second, the switch image will be uploaded to the repository and replicated across the controllers. The catalog image is a part of the controller image and will be added to the repository when the controller image is added.

To check the status of your tasks, perform the following steps:

Step 1.   In the navigation pane, click **Download Tasks**.

Step 2.   In the work pane, click **Operational** to view the download status of the images.

Step 3.   Once the download reaches 100% in the navigation pane, click **Firmware Repository**. In the work pane, the downloaded version numbers and image sizes are displayed.

Controller Firmware and Maintenance Policy

The controller firmware policy specifies the desired version of software for controllers. Once the controller software is in the firmware repository, the controller software policy can be modified to reflect the target software version to which you would like to upgrade or downgrade. The controller maintenance policy specifies when the upgrade of controllers should start. The controller firmware policy and the controller maintenance policy apply to all the controllers in the cluster. The steps to perform a software upgrade are as follows:

Step 1.   In the navigation pane, click **Controller Firmware**. In the work pane, choose **Actions > Upgrade Controller Firmware Policy**. In the Upgrade Controller Firmware Policy dialog, perform the actions specified in step 2.

Step 2.   In the **Target Firmware Version** field, from the drop-down list, choose the image version to which you want to upgrade. In the **Apply Policy** field, click the radio button for **Apply now**. Click **Submit**. The Status dialog displays the "Changes Saved Successfully" message, and the upgrade process begins. The APICs are upgraded serially so that the controller cluster is available during the upgrade.

Step 3.   Verify the status of the upgrade in the work pane by clicking **Controller Firmware** in the navigation pane.

Note   The controllers upgrade in random order. Each APIC takes at least 10 minutes to upgrade. Once a controller image is upgraded, it drops from the cluster, and it reboots with the newer version while the other APICs in the cluster are still operational. Once the controller reboots, it joins the cluster again. Then the cluster converges, and the next controller image starts to upgrade. If the cluster does not immediately converge and is not fully fit, the upgrade will wait until the cluster converges and is fully fit. During this period, a "Waiting for Cluster Convergence" message is displayed in the Status column for each APIC as it upgrades.

Note   When the APIC that the browser is connected to is upgraded and it reboots, the browser displays an error message.

Step 4.   In the browser's **URL** field, enter the URL for the APIC that has already been upgraded and then sign in to the controller as prompted.

Firmware Groups and Policy

A *firmware group* is how ACI groups the switches in the fabric to which you configure a firmware policy. A *firmware policy* specifies the desired firmware version for switches in the group. In other words, we are declaring all of these switches belong at this firmware level. Typically, all of the switches in a single fabric will belong to the same firmware group. However, these policies give you the capability to create multiple groups of switches that have different firmware policies or target firmware versions. These policies are merely responsible for determining software versions. Making changes to these policies will not trigger an upgrade.

Maintenance Group and Maintenance Policy

A *maintenance group* is a group of switches on which you would configure a maintenance policy. A *maintenance policy* specifies a schedule for upgrade. The maintenance policy acts on the previously defined firmware groups and policies. Maintenance groups allow enterprises to perform upgrades across the fabric in manageable portions on an ad-hoc or scheduled basis. Furthermore, if the devices that are connected to your fabric are done so redundantly, maintenance groups give you the ability to perform upgrades with little to no disruption to production data. Most customers use the *two-group method*, as follows:

Step 1.   Divide your switches into two groups: a red group and a blue group. Put one half of the spines in the red group and the other half in the blue group. Also, put one half of the leaf switches in the red group and the other half in the blue group.

Step 2.   Upgrade the red group.

Step 3.   After the red group upgrade is complete, confirm the fabric is healthy.

Step 4.   Upgrade the blue group.

Customers that are very risk adverse might opt for the *four-group method*:

Step 1.   Divide your switches into four groups: a red spines group, a blue spines group, a red leaf switches group, and a blue leaf switches group. Put one half of the spines in the red spines group and the other half of the spines in the blue spines group. Then, place half the leaf switches in the red leaf switches group and the other half in the blue leaf switches group.

Step 2.   Upgrade the red leaf switches group.

Step 3.   After the red leaf switches group upgrade is complete, confirm the fabric is healthy.

Step 4.   Upgrade the blue leaf switches group.

Step 5.   After the blue leaf switches group upgrade is complete, confirm the fabric is healthy.

Step 6.   Upgrade the red spines group.

Step 7.   After the red spines group upgrade is complete, confirm the fabric is healthy.

Step 8.   Upgrade the blue spines group.

As you can see, the four-group method lengthens the procedure and time to perform the upgrade. Enterprises will have to make their own decisions on which upgrade process best fits their environment.

Using the Scheduler

The scheduler enables you to specify a window of time for operations such as upgrading APIC clusters and switches. The windows of time can be "one time only" or recur at a specified time and day each week. This section explains how the scheduler works for upgrades. For more information about the scheduler, see the "Cisco Application Centric Infrastructure Fundamentals" document.

Note   When you're performing a cluster upgrade, the APICs must all be the same version for them to join the cluster. There is no automatic upgrade when joining the fabric.

Maintenance windows are a common event in most IT organizations. The scheduler can automatically start both cluster upgrades and switch upgrades. The following discusses each of these processes in more detail:

■ **APIC cluster upgrade:** There is a default scheduler object for APIC upgrades. Although the generic scheduler object has several properties, only the start time property is configurable for the APIC cluster upgrade. If you specify a start time, the APIC upgrade scheduler is active from the specified start time for the duration of 1 day. Any time during this active one-day window, if **runningVersion != desiredVersion** for the controllers, the cluster upgrade will begin. None of the other parameters of the scheduler are configurable for APIC upgrades. Note that you can also perform an APIC upgrade by using a one-time trigger, which does not use the scheduler. This one-time trigger is also called *upgrade-now*.

■ **Switch upgrades:** A scheduler may be attached to a maintenance group. A scheduler attached to a switch maintenance group has several configurable parameters, such as the following:

- **startTime:** The start of an active window

- **concurCap:** The number of nodes to upgrade simultaneously

- **Duration:** The length of an active window

Any time during an active window, if **runningVersion != desiredVersion** for any switch in that group, the switch will be eligible for an upgrade. Among nodes eligible for an upgrade, the following constraints are applied to picking upgrade candidates:

- No more than the **concurCap** nodes should currently be upgrading.

- Only one node in a VPC pair is upgraded at a time.

- The APIC cluster should be healthy before starting a node upgrade.

Configuration Management

ACI provides significant benefits over traditional architectures in the realm of configuration management. It has never been easier to back up and maintain configuration across all of the devices in your data center. A feature in ACI called *Configuration Snapshots* allows snapshots of configurations to be taken on an ad-hoc or scheduled basis in a matter of seconds. These known-good configurations can be compared and rolled back just as fast. Imagine that before a maintenance window, a snapshot is taken. During the maintenance window, it is decided that the changes need to be rolled back, and this process is executed with just a couple clicks. This can be done in just seconds. If you are using this chapter to configure or deploy your first ACI fabric, now would be a great time to perform a backup, so you have a clean slate to revert back to in case of a configuration issue. In the sections that follow, we examine configuration management in greater detail.

Configuration Snapshots

Configuration snapshots are configuration backup archives, stored (and replicated) in a controller managed folder. ACI has the ability to take snapshots of the fabric configuration at two levels:

- Fabric

- Individual tenants

These snapshots are grouped independently of each other and can be compared for configuration differences or rolled back at any time. Here are some of the actions the system will take when a snapshot is rolled back:

- Deleted managed objects are re-created.

- Created managed objects are deleted.

- Modified managed objects are reverted to their prior state.

Snapshots can be stored either on the APICs or sent to a remote location. Once the snapshots are sent off box, you can then re-import the configurations at any time. Import and export security settings using AES-256 encryption can be configured via a 16-to-32 character passphrase to safeguard your information. ACI also has the capability to schedule reoccurring snapshots on a schedule set by the administrator, as shown in Figure 3-15.

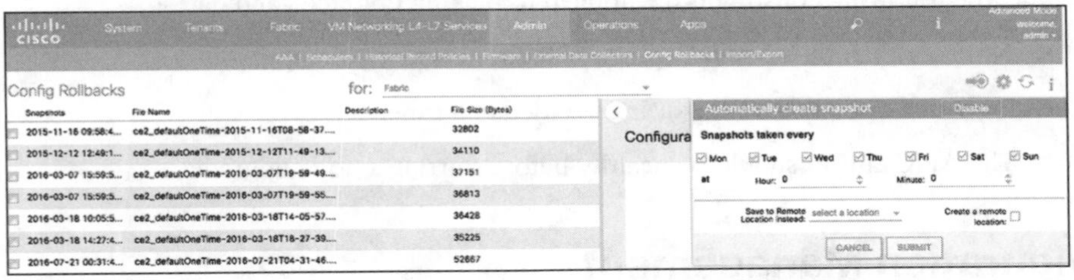

Figure 3-15   *Automatically Create Snapshots on a scheduled basis*

Configuration snapshots are available in both the Basic and Advanced GUI. Snapshots do not back up the entire APIC configuration. To back up the entire configuration, we need to look at configuration backups.

Configuration Backup

All APIC policies and configuration data can be exported to create backups. This is configurable via an export policy that allows either scheduled or immediate backups to a remote server. Scheduled backups can be configured to execute periodic or recurring backup jobs. By default, all policies and tenants are backed up, but the administrator can optionally specify only a specific subtree of the management information tree. Backups can be imported into the APIC through an import policy, which allows the system to be restored to a previous configuration.

Figure 3-16 shows how the process works for configuring an export policy.

The APIC applies this policy in the following way:

   1. A complete system configuration backup is performed once a month.

   2. The backup is stored in XML format on the BigBackup FTP site.

   3. The policy is triggered (it is active).

Note   To manage your configuration backup, navigate to **Admin > Import/Export**. In the navigation pane on the left you will find **Export Policies**. It is here that you will also find policies to export information for TAC if the need arises.

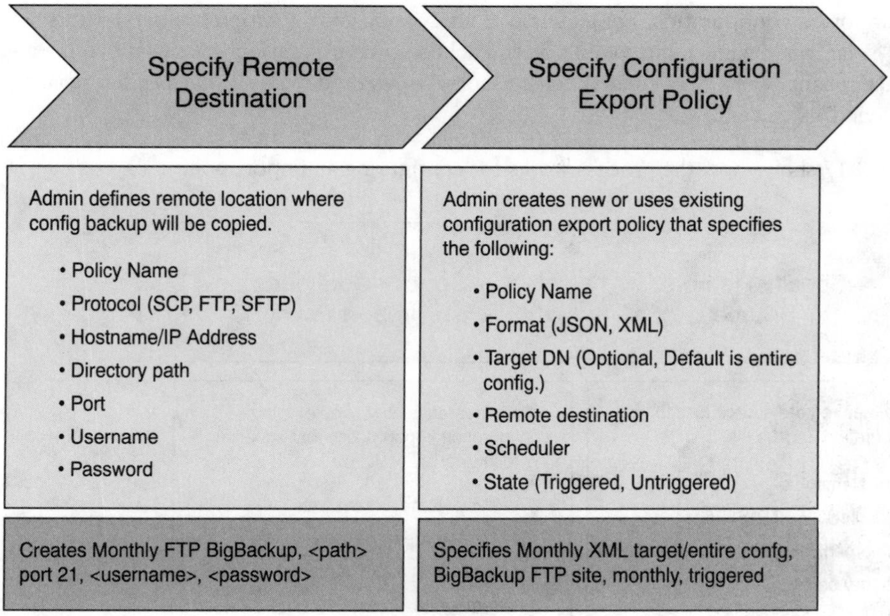

Figure 3-16   *Configuring an Export Policy*

Being able to restore your configuration is as important as backing it up. An administrator can create an import policy that performs the import in one of the following two modes:

- **Best-effort:** Ignores objects within a database shard (partition of data) that cannot be imported. If the version of the incoming configuration is incompatible with the existing system, the database shards that are incompatible are not imported while the import proceeds with those that can be imported.

- **Atomic:** Ignores database shards (partition of data) that contain objects that cannot be imported while proceeding with shards that can be imported. If the version of the incoming configuration is incompatible with the existing system, the import terminates.

An import policy supports the following combinations of mode and type:

- **Best-effort merge:** The imported configuration is merged with the existing configuration, and objects that cannot be imported are ignored.

- **Atomic merge:** The imported configuration is merged with the existing configuration, and shards that contain objects that cannot be imported are ignored.

- **Atomic replace:** Overwrites the existing configuration with imported configuration data. Any objects in the existing configuration that do not exist in the imported configuration are deleted. Objects are deleted from the existing configuration that have children in the existing configuration but do not have children in the incoming imported configuration. For example, if an existing configuration has two tenants ("solar" and "wind"), but the imported backed-up configuration was saved before the tenant "wind" was created, tenant "solar" is restored from the backup but tenant "wind" is deleted.

Figure 3-17 shows how the process works for configuring an import policy.

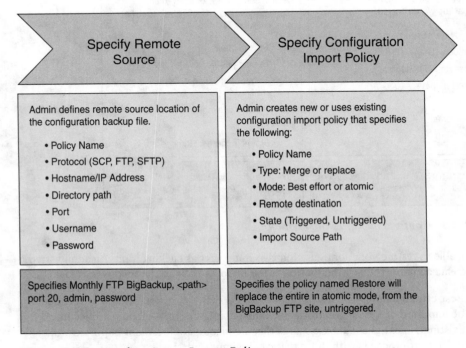

Figure 3-17   *Configuring an Import Policy*

The APIC applies this policy in the following way:

1. A policy is created to perform a complete system configuration restore from monthly backup.

2. The atomic replace mode does the following:

   a. Overwrites the existing configuration.

   b. Deletes any existing configuration objects that do not exist in the imported file.

   c. Deletes children objects that do not exist in the imported file.

3. The policy is untriggered (it is available but has not been activated).

Summary

ACI is a full-featured and scalable data center fabric that enables security and performance for applications and services. Delivering the critical features for next-generation data center networks, ACI is designed with the following requirements: resiliency, virtualization, efficiency, and extensibility. When the fabric was built is important to understand in order to enable foundational features and requirements.

This chapter covered the following topics:

■ The services that are suggested and required for a production ACI fabric.

■ Management networks are needed for the support of a production network. ACI supports both in-band and out-of-band management networks.

■ Application Policy Infrastructure Controllers (APICs) use a quick-and-easy setup script. It is important to choose the right input for the infrastructure network and VLAN.

■ ACI supports multiple interfaces for configuration. When using the GUI, you will have the option of Basic or Advanced.

■ How to configure required services in both Basic and Advanced mode.

■ Becoming an expert in ACI requires understanding the policy that drives the configuration. Advanced mode access and fabric policies were explained.

■ Production networks require software and configuration management. This chapter explored firmware maintenance policies as well as configuration archival and rollback.

■ Controlling and managing access to network resources is critical for a production network. ACI supports in depth role-based access control (RBAC).

With this information, you'll find it easy to get started building and exploring an ACI fabric.

Chapter 4

Integration of Virtualization Technologies with ACI

In this chapter, you will learn the following:

- The benefits for virtualization and network professionals of integrating Cisco ACI and virtualization technologies

- Deep dive into the integration with VMware vSphere, Microsoft System Center Virtual Machine Manager, OpenStack, Docker containers, and Kubernetes

- Design recommendations and caveats when integrating Cisco ACI with virtualization technologies

Why Integrate Cisco ACI with Virtualization Technologies?

Unless you have been living under a rock for the last 15 years, your organization has most likely adopted server virtualization in your data center. This means that some of your servers have virtualization software installed, and the virtual machines (VMs) running there are not directly connected to a traditional physical switch, but to the virtual switch inside of the hypervisor.

In the last few years, an additional technology has strongly emerged that also makes use of virtual switches: Linux containers (often called "Docker" containers, after the company that created a simplified way of managing Linux containers), favored by other industry trends such as micro-services application architectures and the DevOps paradigm.

Integrating Cisco ACI with virtualization technologies will bring the following significant benefits for the virtualization administrator:

- Network virtualization, or the possibility of programmatically deploying and configuring networking policies for virtual machines.

- Additional network functionality, such as inter–data center connectivity, multi-tenancy, and micro-segmentation.

- No need to learn networking. Cisco ACI makes sure that virtual workloads have consistent network policies with the rest of the data center.

- Quicker resolution of network issues. Because the management and troubleshooting of the entire network is done centrally, identifying network problems and fixing them is much easier, as opposed to having to deal with different consoles for the virtual and physical networks.

- Network management processes (such as adding new virtual switches and backing up virtual switch configurations) are taken care of by the network administrator, using Cisco ACI tools.

- Virtualization admins also have the possibility of deploying virtual networks without involving the network team, directly from their virtualization console (such as vCenter in the case of VMware vSphere or Horizon in the case of OpenStack).

Similarly, the network administrator can also greatly benefit from the integration of Cisco ACI with virtual networking environments:

- Cisco ACI is significantly augmented with information about all endpoints in the data center, including virtual machines and Docker containers. This dramatically improves available network insights.

- This additional information is very relevant, for example, when troubleshooting network issues whose root cause may lie in the virtual or physical parts of the network. Using Cisco ACI's native tools, such as the Troubleshooting Wizard and the Endpoint Tracker, for all workloads in a data center can help to shorten the time it takes to fix networking problems.

- It is now much easier to deploy consistent network policies across the whole data center, independent of the form factor of the application workloads.

- Bandwidth management is more accurate because the network is aware of all traffic flows, including those involving virtual machines and Docker containers.

The following sections go into much more detail about these benefits.

Networking for Virtual Machines and Containers

Server virtualization and Linux containers are very important technologies that can increase efficiencies for the data center, but at the same time they can pose challenges for the network administrator. The main reason is that both server virtualization and Linux containers are not purely compute technologies, but they have an important networking aspect to them that needs to be operated and managed.

Essentially, the network architecture of virtual machines and containers is similar: Both are entities that live inside of a physical host (ignoring for a moment the possibility of nested virtualization), and both have their own MAC and IPv4 or IPv6 addresses. The underlying operating system has a fixed set of physical network interfaces that need to be shared across all the existing virtual machines.

Note that we are somewhat oversimplifying here because there are fundamental differences between container and virtual machine networking. For example, containers do not have their own TCP stack but use just a namespace in the host networking stack, comparable to virtual routing and forwarding (VRF) in a router, whereas virtual machines bring their own Transmission Control Protocol (TCP) stack, completely separate from the one in the hypervisor. However, these differences do not affect the essence of the discussion in this section.

Most virtualization and container technologies provide networking to logical compute instances (virtual machines or containers) by means of virtual switches that exist inside the operating system, as Figure 4-1 shows. Whereas the physical network interface cards (NICs) of the physical host are connected to traditional switches over real cables (represented by the black lines in the figure), connectivity to the virtual switch (represented by the gray lines) is typically controlled by the virtualization software and can be dynamically modified.

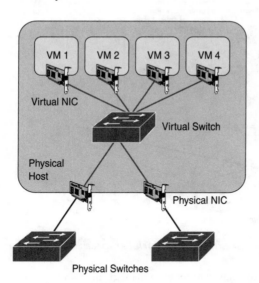

Figure 4-1 *Overall Network Architecture in a Hypervisor*

This setup presents some challenges:

- Who should manage the virtual switch inside the physical host? Some virtualization administrators might be equally capable of managing networks as well. However, in many cases, complex network configurations, including concepts such as sophisticated network security and quality of service (QoS), are not their core field of expertise.

- Is the network policy for virtual and physical machines consistent? Virtual switches embedded in the hypervisor might have different functionality than purpose-built Ethernet switches, whose software and hardware have evolved over the last two decades. However, from a network and security standpoint, all workloads in the data center should have consistent policies. How does one achieve this consistency with different software capabilities and management concepts?

- How does one manage and troubleshoot the network holistically? The network is often the first point where people tend to look for culprits upon any incident in the data center. However, having two (or more) different sets of tools to manage and troubleshoot different parts of the network does not necessarily make finding the root cause of a network problem easier.

Additionally, the situation might grow even more complex when additional virtualization vendors and technologies are introduced. For example, Figure 4-2 depicts an example with diverse technologies such as network virtualization, Linux containers, and bare-metal servers coexisting in the same network.

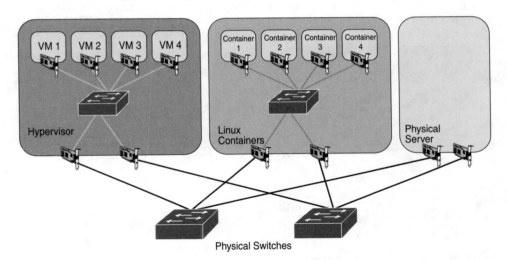

Figure 4-2 *Coexistence of Different Technologies from a Network Perspective*

In this case, you would have at least three different networks to manage and troubleshoot individually: the physical switches, the virtual switches inside of your hypervisors, and the virtual switches inside of your Linux container hosts. If on top of that you have multiple hypervisor vendors (most companies out there have a dual-hypervisor strategy) and multiple container frameworks (because containers are still a nascent technology, chances are that your IT departments will be using more than one container framework as they mature), the situation becomes really challenging.

In the worst case, you would have to individually assess the capabilities of each virtual switch, have different processes for network management, depending on the workload, and have different network and security policies for applications that are deployed in bare-metal servers, in virtual machines, and in containers.

Benefits of Cisco ACI Integration with Virtual Switches

Cisco ACI can alleviate the problems described above. As previous chapters have explained, the Cisco ACI concept is based on a centralized repository, located in the Application Policy Infrastructure Controllers (APICs), that distributes network policy to individual switches.

It is only natural extending this concept so that network policy is not only deployed to physical switches but to virtual ones located in hypervisors or Linux container hosts as well. This way, network and security policy for a workload is independent of its form factor (bare metal, virtual machine, or Linux container), and the network can be managed holistically:

- If an application workload is migrated to a different form factor (for example, from a virtual machine to a container, or from one hypervisor to another), the system administrator does not need to reinvent the proverbial "network wheel" in the new platform because the previous network policy will consistently apply in the new hypervisor as well.

- Network troubleshooting is greatly improved, by providing a single pane of glass for all workloads. Locating the root cause for problems is easier because network administrators can look at network flows, end to end, and not only in siloes.

- Network management becomes much simpler because all network information for all workloads in a data center is contained in a single repository, with consistent application programming interfaces (APIs) and software development kits (SDKs).

- Should the network configuration change for a certain workload—for example, because of new regulatory requirements—the corresponding policy only needs to be changed once. This single policy repository makes finding policy inconsistencies easier, in case virtual and physical switches have conflicting configurations, such as the allowed VLANs and the Etherchannel mode.

Note that one key element of the Cisco ACI architecture that enables configuring disparate data planes (physical switches and virtual switches for different hypervisors) with the same policy is the declarative character of the OpFlex protocol, the mechanism used to distribute policy to the switches in the ACI fabric. Other networking frameworks that use imperative models to configure the individual fabric elements are more difficult to integrate with heterogeneous data planes. Refer to the section "OpFlex," later in this chapter, for more details on this aspect of the ACI architecture.

To illustrate the power of combining a single network policy across multiple workload form factors, Figure 4-3 shows an example of an application profile in a Cisco ACI fabric, where the Database instances are bare-metal servers (represented by the letter B in the lower part of the canvas), and the Web instances can be either VMware or Microsoft virtual machines (represented by the letters V and M, respectively). Note that this is only an example, and many other combinations are possible, including Kubernetes containers (letter K), OpenStack instances (letter O), and Red Hat Virtualization virtual machines (letter R).

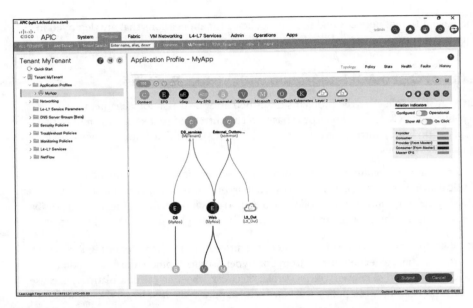

Figure 4-3 *A Sample Application Profile with Multiple Integrations*

In this example, the network policy was decided independently of the workload types, at application design time. ACI contracts, application tiers, and external connectivity are specified for an architecture without you having to know in advance details such as on which hypervisor the architecture will be deployed.

Thus, the decision of whether to use physical servers, virtual machines, or even Docker containers can be taken up at a later stage, with the assurance that the previously defined network policies will be respected.

Comparing ACI Integration to Software Network Overlays

The same way that the management plane in traditional networks has evolved from a distributed approach into a modern centralized concept like Cisco ACI, hypervisor vendors have developed concepts to centrally manage virtual switches.

For virtual switches that work only at Layer 2 of the ISO/OSI model (that is, without any IP functionality), hypervisor vendors came across a fundamental problem: how to create network segments across multiple hypervisors, without having to manage the physical network? And this is where some of those vendors turned to encapsulation technologies such as Virtual Extensible LAN (VXLAN).

Encapsulation technologies are not new in the network industry. For example, Multiprotocol Label Switching (MPLS) is an encapsulation protocol that many network administrators have been using for years to create network overlays. The main difference here is that the tunnel endpoints (TEPs) of the overlay tunnels in this case are not tradi-tional network devices but rather virtual switches inside of hypervisor hosts—hence, the name *software network overlay*.

Figure 4-4 shows the basic concept: network segments (broadcast domains) are created in virtual switches and are made available to virtual machines in other hypervisors as well. Virtual switches are interconnected to each other using VXLAN tunnels, essen-tially encapsulating the VM traffic in a UDP packet sourced from one hypervisor and addressed to another. Therefore, the physical network only sees the IP addresses of the physical hosts (that is, the tunnel endpoints), and not those of the virtual machines (in the payload of the VXLAN packet inside of the tunnel). When connectivity with other workloads outside of the overlay is required, a gateway will bridge or route traffic from the VXLAN-based overlay to the physical network connected to the outer world.

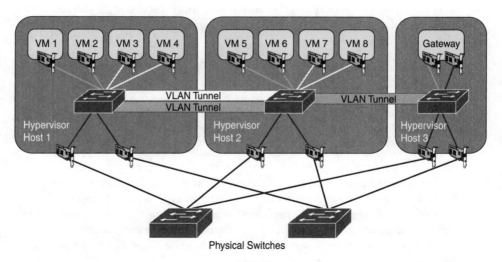

Figure 4-4   *Generic Architecture of Software Network Overlays*

As the previous discussion made apparent, software-based overlays solve a specific prob-lem for a specific platform. If you are using, say, VMware vSphere ESXi as a hypervisor, you can have consistent management for your VMware virtual switches using one of VMware's software network overlays, such as NSX for vSphere. However, you will be using a different management plane for the rest of the network, including your physical hosts, your Linux containers, other hypervisors such as Microsoft Hyper-V or Red Hat Virtualization, or even with different versions of the vSphere hypervisor that support other incompatible software overlays (such as NSX for Multi-Hypervisor or the recently announced NSX-T).

A centralized network policy that covers all the workloads in a data center has many advantages over software network overlays:

- The hypervisor admin does not need to learn networking. Most software network overlays need to replicate complex network structures such as routing protocols, load balancing, and network security inside of the hypervisor. This, in turn, demands from the hypervisor administrator that they be an expert on these fields too.

- Management and troubleshooting consistency, as explained earlier in this chapter.

- Bandwidth can be consistently managed. If an organization is using two overlays (for example, due to a dual-hypervisor strategy), it is impossible to make sure that critical applications have access to bandwidth in the event of network congestion, because each hypervisor is not aware of the other one, and the physical network is oblivious to the traffic inside of the tunnels.

In data centers where most of the workloads run on a specific technology, this approach might be deemed as adequate, but even in those situations there are some caveats to consider:

- A hypervisor-centric network overlay brings a VXLAN-based network overlay that is designed to operate completely independent to the rest of the network. In contrast, Cisco ACI can obtain the same benefits by extending VXLAN to both physical and virtual switches (in the case of AVS for vSphere or OVS for OpenStack, for example), without breaking the network operations model.

- Software-based gateways between the virtual and physical world are typically required when running hypervisor-centric overlays, which often represent chokepoints that need to be carefully sized so that they do not degenerate into bottlenecks. Even though some software-based overlays sometimes support hardware-based gateways, their functionality tends to be pretty low as compared to what is offered by the virtual switches. In contrast, the distributed architecture of Cisco ACI makes gateways utterly unnecessary, because the VXLAN overlays are integrated with physical network hardware.

- Typically, the few hosts running on bare metal are the most critical ones, such as mainframes or big databases. Even if these servers represent a small percentage of the overall server number, they should be carefully included in the network strategy.

- Even if modern CPUs can cope with traffic on the order of 10Gbps or more, certain network operations require deterministic performance that usually can only be achieved with purpose-built ASICs, such as higher bandwidths (50Gbps or 100Gbps are common in modern data centers), encryption, or complex quality of service (QoS) operations.

- Even if the general-purpose CPU of a hypervisor could cope with the network bandwidth, every CPU cycle spent in a network operation is not available for the virtual machines. Therefore, you might be paying for expensive hardware and hypervisor licenses just to move packets in your data center. Hyperscale cloud providers such as Microsoft Azure have recognized this and usually offload network operations from the host to field-programmable gate arrays (FPGAs) to have more CPU cycles available to the VMs.

This book does not aim to offer a detailed comparison between ACI and different software network overlays, because much literature exists around this topic. Instead, the next sections explain in detail how the integration with different virtualization technologies works.

Virtual Machine Manager Domains

Before going into details about integration with different hypervisors and their virtual switches, it is worth considering some generic aspects about virtual networking in Cisco ACI.

The first critical concept to understand is the virtual machine manager domain, or VMM domain. A *virtual machine manager* is the entity that controls a virtualization cluster, such as the Microsoft System Center VMM, the VMware vCenter server, the Red Hat Virtualization Manager, the OpenStack control nodes, and the Kubernetes or Openshift master nodes. A VMM domain in ACI represents a bidirectional integration between the APIC cluster and one or more of these VMMs. When you define a VMM domain in ACI, the APIC will in turn create a virtual switch in the virtualization hosts.

Strictly speaking, you could create the virtual switch in advance, and by creating the VMM domain, you allow Cisco ACI to assume control over it. However, it is practical letting the APIC create the virtual switch, because it will define it with the right attributes, such as the correct maximum transmit unit (MTU) and Neighbor Discovery Protocol, among many other things.

Additionally, in integrations such as Kubernetes, the virtual switch is never created or even managed by Cisco ACI, but the relationship here is rather unidirectional: In these cases, the virtual switch sends information that is used by Cisco ACI to properly configure the physical fabric.

On the Cisco ACI side, the VMM domain contains all the relevant information extracted out of the virtual environment. For example, Figure 4-5 shows how a VMware VMM domain displays details such as the number of hosts in the vSphere cluster and the virtual machines running inside each host.

Besides, VMM domains contain information relative to the data-plane integration with the virtualization environment, for VMware and Microsoft integrations. Figure 4-5 shows the required configuration to create a VMM domain for Microsoft System Center VMM.

It is noteworthy that you can configure (in a single place) how the links between the hypervisor physical NICs and Cisco ACI leaf switches are to be configured. In the past, a common source of problems was link misconfiguration, where the virtualization and network admins inadvertently introduced discrepancies such as configuring the hypervisor with standalone links, but the physical network with Etherchannel. As you can imagine, such situations (which required comparing configurations deployed by different administrators on different consoles) were not easy to troubleshoot.

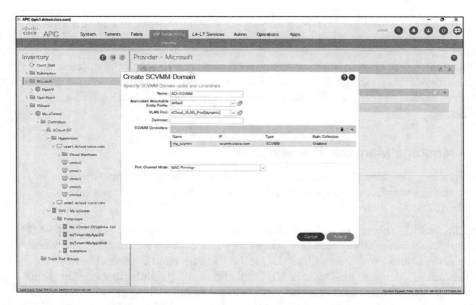

Figure 4-5 *VMM Domains Show Information about the Virtual Environments*

For example, the Port Channel Mode defines how Cisco ACI will configure the physical NICs of the hypervisor hosts as well as the ports of the physical switch to which they are attached. Here are the options available:

- **Static Channel - Mode On:** This option is to be used when the hypervisor hosts are not directly connected to an ACI leaf switch, but to another Layer 2 device such as a blade switch that does not support Link Aggregation Control Protocol (LACP). In the past this option was used as well for virtual switches that did not support LACP, but nowadays most virtual switches include support for dynamically negotiated port channels.

- **LACP Active:** This is normally the recommended option for most deployments. If the hypervisor is connected to two different physical leaf switches, a virtual port channel (VPC) must be enabled for them.

- **LACP Passive:** LACP in passive mode is only recommended when there is an intermediate switch (such as a blade switch) between the hypervisors and the ACI leaf switches, and this blade switch requires LACP Passive.

- **MAC Pinning+:** This mechanism selects a physical NIC in the host for every virtual NIC (MAC), and it will stick to it unless that physical NIC fails. Consequently, this is equivalent to not having Etherchannel enabled, because the upstream switches will always see individual MAC addresses coming from the same physical port.

- **MAC Pinning-Physical-NIC-Load:** This is similar to MAC Pinning, but the load of the physical NICs is taken into consideration before an interface for a new virtual machine is selected. This Etherchannel mode is not supported with the Cisco Application Virtual Switch for VMware vSphere.

It is not strictly required that you fill the **Port Channel Mode** field. If it is left empty, APIC will configure the physical ports of the host matching the Port Channel policy defined for the ACI leaf ports in the ACI access policies.

As you can see, there are other options to specify, such as from which VLAN pool the integration will pick up the encapsulation identifiers and with which Attachable Entity Profile the VMM domain will be associated (VMM domains are associated with Attachable Entity Profiles the same way as physical domains, which tells Cisco ACI on which ports to look for virtualization hosts belonging to this environment).

When a virtualization installation with one or multiple clusters is associated with a VMM domain, the APIC automatically sets the right port channel configuration on all the ports connecting to the cluster or clusters, as well as validates that settings for VLAN/VXLAN always come from the right pool. In addition, EPGs that allow end-user VM connectivity and policy will be deployed to the virtual switch and the connected ACI leaf(s) for any host under the vCenter or SCVMM servers associated with the VMM domain, thus accomplishing virtual and physical automation.

After you create the new VMM domain, it will contain information relative to the virtualization environment. For example, Figure 4-6 shows a VMM domain configured for VMware vSphere showing the virtual machines running on a particular virtualization host.

In order to be able to configure virtual machines into any given endpoint group (EPG), you need to extend that EPG to the VMM domain. The act of associating an EPG with a VMM domain will trigger the creation of a network object in the virtual switch. For example, in the case of VMware, a port group would be created in the virtual switch with the same name as the EPG.

After you have created the VMM domain, the next step in the process is associating EPGs with it, so that port groups are created in the virtual switch in the hypervisor. Figure 4-7 describes this concept.

The same way that EPGs need to be associated with one or more physical domains to be deployed on a certain set of physical ports, EPGs can be associated with one or more VMM domains (for example, if virtual machines out of multiple virtualization clusters are to be placed in the same EPG). And obviously, multiple EPGs can be associated with a single VMM domain. This simple act of associating an EPG with a VMM domain triggers the creation of a virtual network segment in the virtualization environment that can be used to provide connectivity to virtual machines. Figure 4-8 shows an example of the Cisco ACI GUI to add a VMM domain association to an EPG.

Figure 4-6 *Sample Screen for VMM Domain Creation in Cisco ACI*

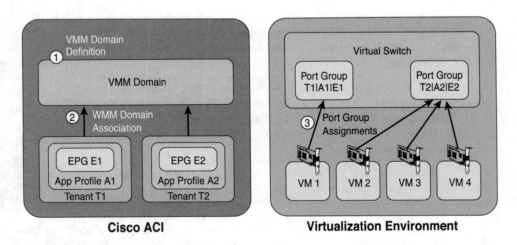

Figure 4-7 *Overall Process for Configuring Virtual Networking in Cisco ACI*

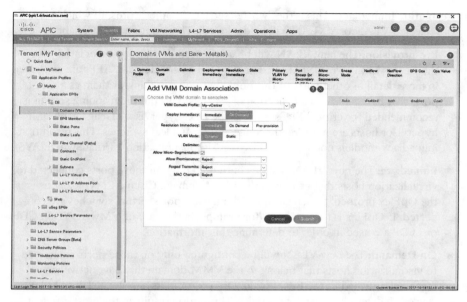

Figure 4-8 *Associating an EPG with a VMM Domain*

VLANs or VXLANs can be used for date-plane communication between the hypervisor and the Cisco ACI physical leaf switch. These VLANs or VXLANs do not need to be explicitly configured by the network administrator, but are selected out of a dynamic VLAN or VXLAN pool assigned to the VMM domain. Only one VLAN or VXLAN pool can be associated with a VMM domain.

If you want to manually assign a specific VLAN or VXLAN ID out of the pool to a certain EPG, you can certainly do so, but the overall recommendation is to let ACI pick up one dynamically, for simplicity and consistency reasons. Note that Cisco ACI will configure the assigned VLAN automatically in the virtual switch, and if the virtualization administrator changes it, the APIC will flag this mismatch and will flag it as an alert.

Note that because VLAN IDs are locally significant in Cisco ACI (to the leaf switch or even to the port where they are used), you could reuse the same VLAN IDs on two different VMM domains. For example, if you have two vSphere clusters, A and B, you could reuse the same VLAN IDs in the VLAN pools allocated to both VMM domains. This greatly enhances the VLAN scalability of virtual data centers.

However, using this approach is not recommended if you are not close to the theoretical limit of 4096 VLANs in a data center (the actual number is slightly lower), because having multiple distinct virtual networks with the same VLAN ID might be confusing for professionals not familiar with Cisco ACI.

As Figure 4-8 shows, when associating a VMM domain with an EPG, there are some settings that control where and when VLAN and VXLAN IDs will be deployed:

■ **Resolution immediacy:** This is the "where" setting (in other words, to which ports the selected VLAN or VXLAN will be deployed). Three options are available:

   ■ **Pre-provision:** The new VLAN will be configured on all ports associated with the Access Entity Profile (AEP) containing the VMM domain. AEPs are explained in more detail in other parts of this book, but you can think of them as a set of ports that have allocated a collection of VLANs. This pre-provisioning setting is recommended for critical EPGs, such as the EPG hypervisor management, or if hypervisor hosts are not directly connected to ACI leaf switches. This resolution immediacy mode is not supported by the Cisco Application Virtual Switch (AVS).

   ■ **Immediate:** The new VLAN will be configured only on those ports connected to virtualization hosts that belong to the VMM domain. Cisco ACI typically uses the OpFlex protocol to detect on which physical ports virtual switches are connected. If OpFlex is not available (for example in the case of VMware VDS), CDP or LLDP are used in order to determine this information.

   ■ **On Demand:** The new VLAN will be configured only on those ports connected to virtualization hosts that belong to the VMM domain that have active virtual machines attached to the EPG. Again, OpFlex (or in its absence, CDP or LLDP) is used to determine host connectivity. This option results in the most efficient usage of hardware resources in the ACI leaf nodes, and supports live migration of virtual machines (in VMware speech called vMotion) across the virtualization cluster.

■ **Deployment immediacy:** This is the "when" setting (or more specifically, when the policy will be programmed into the hardware). Here you can choose from two options:

   ■ **Immediate:** The new policy (VLAN, VXLAN, contract, and so on) is programmed into the hardware immediately after the policy has been downloaded by the leaf switch. As you can imagine, there are important resource implications when using this option, because the hardware resources in any switch are finite.

   ■ **On Demand:** The new policy is deployed into the hardware only after the first packet is received on an ACI leaf port. This option preserves leaf resources, especially when not all virtualization hosts have virtual machines in every single EPG, thus making it the overall recommendation.

Which option you use highly depends on your environment and whether you are close to the maximum scalability numbers. The following examples should give you a good indication of what is the best combination of resolution and deployment immediacy in your case:

■ If you have fewer than 1000 EPGs in your environment, you are well below the scalability limits of EPGs per leaf (3500 EPGs + BDs). That means you can safely deploy every VLAN everywhere. Even if it is not the most efficient option, this will give you additional stability because your integration will not depend on CDP/LLDP working correctly.

- Even if you have started reaching the EPG+BD scalability limits in your environment, you might stick to pre-provisioning VLANs by carefully assigning only those leaf ports where hosts from a specific VMM domain are connected to its corresponding AAEP.

- Pre-provisioning can also be very helpful in bringing up hypervisor infrastructure virtual interfaces as quickly as possible (for example, management, NFS, storage, Live Migration/vMotion), because Cisco ACI does not need any signaling to take place before a VLAN is configured.

- Pre-provisioning might be your only choice if no CDP/LLDP communication with the virtualization host is possible (for example, if the hosts are not directly attached to an ACI leaf but to another Layer 2 device such as a blade switch).

- For environments with high scalability requirements, with only a few virtual machines per EPG, you will achieve greater VLAN densities by using On Demand Resolution because a certain VLAN ID will only be configured on the hosts with virtual machines attached to the corresponding EPG.

At the time of this writing, there are different scalability limits regarding the number and size of virtual environments that can be associated with Cisco ACI 3.0(1):

- Two hundred vSphere vCenter servers with the VMware vSphere Distributed Switch

- Fifty vSphere vCenter servers with the Cisco Application Virtual Switch (AVS)

- Five Microsoft System Center Virtual Machine Manager instances

Please refer to the scalability limits for additional details such as the number of hosts per virtualization environment, the maximum number of EPGs, or other scalability metrics.

EPG Segmentation and Micro-Segmentation

Once you have assigned certain EPGs to your VMM domain, you can configure them with any other Cisco ACI functionality. A very important example is traffic filtering and isolation, which in Cisco ACI is defined by consuming and providing contracts in the EPGs. Although this functionality is not exclusive to EPGs associated with virtual machines, there are some details on EPG segmentation specific to virtualization environments.

More specifically, micro-segmentation allows Cisco ACI to dynamically allocate virtual machines to EPGs based not only on static assignments and networking information (IP and MAC address), but on virtual machine metadata as well (its name, operating system, and associated tags, for example), thus automating the assignment of security policies to virtual machines.

The way that micro-segmentation works in Cisco ACI is by defining "micro-segmentation" EPGs (also called "micro-segment," "μSeg," "uSeg," or just "micro" EPGs) inside of Application EPGs, with the **Allow Micro-Segmentation** option enabled, and then using contracts between those micro-segment EPGs to filter traffic. Additionally, whether or not an endpoint belongs to a micro-segment EPG is not statically defined, but is dynamically configured based on rules that look at certain attributes or metadata of that endpoint.

Micro-segmentation is not a feature exclusive to virtual machines because it can be configured for physical endpoints, too. However, whereas the criteria used to allocate physical machines to micro-segment EPGs depend only on their MAC or IP addresses, virtual machines offer a richer set of attributes that can be used for this configuration, such as the virtual machine's name, its operating system, and even custom attributes or tags.

For example, imagine that inside of your EPG "Web" you find out that you have a combination of Windows and Linux virtual machines, and you would like to apply different security policies to each of those, such as allowing SSH TCP port 22 for Linux, and RDP TCP port 3389 for Windows. Although you could define static EPGs, and ask your virtualization admin to manually map the VMs to the correct port group, a more automated approach would be defining two micro-segment EPGs—"Web-Linux" and "Web-Windows"—and allocating VMs to each EPG dynamically, depending on their reported operating system.

A similar situation might arise where you want to differentiate across production and development virtual machines inside of one single EPG based on their names, so that the mere act of changing the name of a virtual machine—say, from "DEV-web-server" to "PRD-web-server"—would change the assigned EPG and consequently its network policy.

The first thing you need to do is to create the micro EPG. There is a specific folder inside of your application profile that contains µSeg EPGs. It is important to notice that these micro-segmentation EPGs are not associated with individual EPGs in particular, but to all the EPGs in the application profile. Figure 4-9 shows the first step of the micro-segmentation EPG Wizard, where a µSeg EPG is created for development machines.

Here are some important items of note concerning this first step of creating micro-segmentation EPGs:

- Although technically µSeg EPGs could be associated with a different bridge domain than the Application EPGs, this option is not supported by Cisco anymore. The strong recommendation is that you have both the µSeg EPG and the Base EPG in the same bridge domain.

- QoS settings can be different than the Application EPGs. For example, in the use case described previously with micro-segments for development and production workloads, you could assign a limited bandwidth to the Development EPG to make sure that development machines do not impact production traffic.

- As in Application EPGs, the default setting for **Preferred Group Membership** is **Exclude,** which means that policies defined in the vzAny EPG would not apply to endpoints included in the micro-segmentation EPG (if the vzAny EPG is marked to be included in the preferred group membership).

■ Notice the **Match Precedence** attribute; this will be used to break micro-segmentation EPG attribute rules, as explained later in the chapter.

■ When VMM integration is used, the μSeg EPGs will not create additional port groups or networks in the virtual environment. Instead, the VMs will connect to the Base EPG port group or network, and ACI will reclassify and apply the right policy at the leaf. This fact can be surprising, or even confusing at first, because in vCenter the VMs appear as assigned to a port group, but in reality μSeg EPG rules in ACI can change that assignment without any apparent notification in vCenter. The reason for this discrepancy is simply that vCenter does not support ACI micro-segmentation logic natively. There is a solution for this problem though: The VMware admin can check μSeg EPGs assignments at any time using the Cisco ACI plug-in for vCenter, explained later in this chapter.

■ The VMM association with the EPG must be marked as **Allow Micro-Segmentation** if VMware's VDS are used so that virtual machines assigned to them are eligible to be allocated with μSeg EPGs (refer to Figure 4-8 earlier in this chapter for an example of enabling this option).

Figure 4-9 *First Step in the Creation of a Micro-Segmentation EPG*

Figure 4-10   *Second Step in the Creation of a Micro-Segmentation EPG*

The second step to create a micro-segmentation EPG is very simple, but equally important: You need to associate the micro-segmentation EPG with the VMM domain, as Figure 4-10 shows. The VMM domain association here is identical to the process for Application EPGs, with one difference: Micro-segmentation EPGs require the **Resolution Immediacy** setting to be **Immediate**, as Figure 4-10 shows.

After creating the EPG, you are now ready to consume and provide contracts, as required by the security policy you want to implement, and to define attribute rules that control which endpoints will be associated with this micro-segmentation EPG. To define these rules, you can proceed to the µSeg Attributes screen of the micro-segmentation EPG, as Figure 4-11 illustrates. Coming back to our example, here you would define a rule such as "VM Name starts with DEV," so that all VMs whose names begin with the string "DEV" are assigned to the Development micro-segmentation EPG.

As a side note, it is recommended that you permit all traffic between the micro-segmentation EPGs until you are sure that the configured rules have the desired effect. Otherwise, if you wrongly allocate a virtual machine to a certain micro-segmentation EPG, that VM will get the wrong network policy.

Contract inheritance can very useful with micro EPGs because they can inherit the contracts from the Application EPG (if the Application EPG does not inherit contracts because multi-level inheritance is not supported) and you can just add additional rules for the micro-segmentation EPGs.

Figure 4-11 *Defining Attributes for Micro-Segmentation EPGs*

Figure 4-12 *Micro-Segmentation Example Using a "Quarantine" Micro-Segmentation EPG*

For example, if you have an Application EPG called "Web" and two micro EPGs called "Web-Windows" and "Web-Linux," both micro EPGs could inherit the contracts from the Web EPG, and you could just add additional contracts for Remote Desktop Protocol in the Web-Windows EPG and for SSH in the Web-Linux EPG. Note that this approach is only valid if you would like to add new connectivity in the micro-segmentation EPGs.

Another interesting application of micro-segmentation EPGs is the use of external tools to dynamically change the network and security posture of a virtual machine by "marking" it in a certain way. For example, consider the situation where a malware detection tool should be able to place a VM in a quarantine group. You could just have the malware detection software set a custom attribute or a tag in a virtual machine and have a "Quarantine" micro-segmentation EPG that matches on it. Figure 4-12 illustrates a sample micro-segmentation EPG matching on a vSphere tag.

You can use different logical schemes when matching μSeg rules. For example, if you are using rules in a *match-any* block, VMs will be assigned to this μSeg EPG as soon as one of the rules is matched. The *match-all* operator, on the other hand, demands that all rules be matched before a VM is assigned to a certain μSeg EPG. As Figure 4-13 shows (later in this section), you can combine match-any and match-all blocks, as required by your logic.

If you're using a match-any scheme, it might happen that VMs match rules in two distinct micro-segmentation EPGs. In this case, a predefined precedence order will be used to break the tie. Here is the precedence order for the VMware DVS, as documented in the "Cisco ACI Virtualization Guide" (the precedence order for the AVS swaps the first and second items):

1. IP address

2. MAC address

3. vNIC domain name

4. VM identifier

5. VM name

6. Hypervisor identifier

7. VMM domain

8. vCenter data center

9. Custom attribute

10. Operating system

11. Tag

It is important to understand this, because otherwise you will not be able to predict the results of your rules. To illustrate this, let's consolidate the previous two examples with three micro-segmentation EPGs and match-any rules:

1. **Micro-segmentation EPG "Production":** Assign to this EPG all VMs whose names begin with the string "PRD."

2. **Micro-segmentation EPG "Development":** Assign to this EPG all VMs whose names begin with the string "DEV."

3. **Micro-segmentation EPG "Quarantine":** Assign to this EPG all VMs with tag "MALWARE."

When you set the MALWARE tag on a VM, you will observe that it is not placed in the Quarantine micro-segmentation EPG, as might have been expected. The reason is that the VM name attribute has a higher priority (5) than the VM tag attribute (11), and therefore after matching on the name, the APIC looks no further.

The way to modify this default behavior is through the use of the micro-segmentation EPG **Match Precedence** setting, shown back in Figure 4-9. If you set **Match Precedence** for the micro-segmentation EPG "Quarantine" to a higher value (say 10, for example, because the default is 0), now you will observe that the VMs with the MALWARE tag are correctly mapped to it.

In order to fulfill more sophisticated requirements, you can configure additional nested rules, combining match-all and match-any. For example, Figure 4-13 describes how to configure a micro-segmentation EPG for development virtual machines (whose name starts with "DEV") that have either a Red Hat or a CentOS operating system.

Figure 4-13 *Using Complex Attribute Rules in Micro-Segmentation EPGs*

On the other hand, you might be wondering how filtering packets between VMs that are assigned to the same port group is possible in the first place: Both Microsoft's vSwitch and VMware's vSphere Distributed Switch leverage VLANs as broadcast domains without any packet filtering functionality. If two virtual machines are assigned to a port group (corresponding to an EPG), wouldn't the virtual switch just forward the packet, without the Cisco ACI fabric even knowing? How can Cisco ACI filter the traffic between micro-segmentation EPGs?

When configuring µSeg EPGs, Cisco ACI deploys this integration in the background using different VLANs between the physical leaf switch port and the hypervisor. This essentially forces the vSphere VDS and Microsoft's vSwitch to send packets that normally would be switched locally upstream to the Cisco ACI leaf switch. Whereas Cisco ACI can reconfigure Microsoft's vSwitch using OpFlex, private VLAN technology is used with VMware's VDS to force this behavior, as Figure 4-14 illustrates.

The Cisco ACI leaf switch will then evaluate the µSeg EPG policies and, if required, forward the packet to the destination virtualization host. Otherwise, the packet will be dropped.

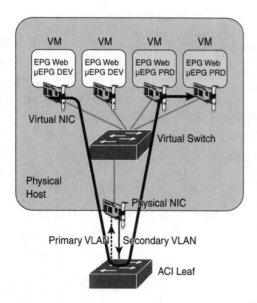

Figure 4-14 *Using Private VLAN Technology for Micro-Segmentation EPGs*

You might argue that this architecture seems to be suboptimal for two VMs in the same host that otherwise would directly send traffic to each other without having to hit the physical network. However, this situation is usually not that common. For example, if you take a 32-host cluster, the probability that the destination VM is in the same host as the source VM is roughly 1/32 (that is, 3%).

Additionally, if you are using features such as VMware Dynamic Resource Scheduling (DRS), you have no control (and that is a good thing) over which host each virtual machine runs on because this decision is made by the cluster itself, to use resources as efficiently as possible.

But even if the probability of two VMs being in the same host were higher (for example, because you have smaller clusters, or because you are using affinity rules to make sure that certain VMs absolutely reside on the same host), the additional latency introduced by the extra hop would typically be negligible, and you would have difficulties just measuring it. Remember that the latency of the Nexus 9000 portfolio switches is on the order of magnitude of 1 microsecond; plus, for a typical 7-meter cable in a rack, you would have around 50 additional nanoseconds of transmission delay each way (very conservative, taking less than 50% the speed of light). Compared to latencies introduced by software processing in the virtual switch itself (running on CPUs that ideally are already busy serving applications on virtual machines), you might even find out that in certain cases going up to the top-of-rack switch and doing the heavy lifting there (in this case, applying packet-filtering rules) is more performant than software switching inside of the hypervisor.

Intra-EPG Isolation and Intra-EPG Contracts

All endpoints connected to a Cisco ACI EPG can communicate with each other by default, but in some situations this is not desired. For example, you might not want management ports of IT devices in the data center to speak to each other, but instead only to the management station. This way, you increase security by preventing lateral movements by attackers who have compromised some assets in your infrastructure.

This feature is supported for physical servers as well as for the native virtual switches in VMware vSphere (the vSphere Distributed Switch) and Microsoft SCVMM (the Microsoft vSwitch), but it is not supported for the integration with Cisco Application Virtual Switch for VMware.

But what about if you don't want to drop all traffic, but only part of it? For example, you might want to allow Internet Control Message Protocol (ICMP) traffic for troubleshooting purposes, but forbid anything else. In that case, you can leverage intra-EPG contracts, a feature introduced in the Cisco ACI Version 3.0(1) supporting VMware vSphere Distributed Switch (VDS), OpenStack's Open vSwitch (OVS) and bare-metal servers. Intra-EPG contracts are supported on both standard Application EPGs and microsegment (µSeg) EPGs. Lastly, you need some hardware features for intra-EPG contract support: Cisco ACI leaf switches of the -EX and -FX series (or later) will support intra-EPG contracts.

Figure 4-15 shows how easy it is to associate an intra-EPG contract with an EPG. You just need to right-click the name of an EPG in the left panel of Cisco ACI and select **Intra-EPG Contract**. After that, you have to choose which contract to use, click **Submit**, and you are done—no need to specify whether the contract is consumed or provided.

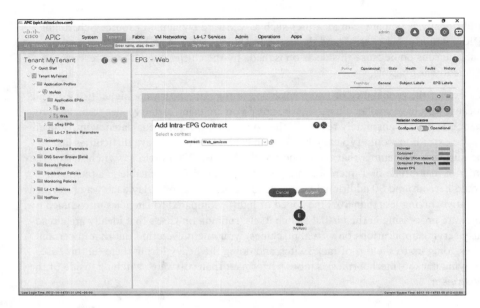

Figure 4-15   *Associating an Intra-EPG Contract with an EPG*

At the time of this writing, intra-EPG contracts are only supported for the integration with the VMware vSphere Distributed Switch and bare-metal servers, and you will see a warning in the GUI reminding you of this fact, as Figure 4-16 shows.

The implementation of both features (intra-EPG isolation and intra-EPG contracts) is based on the same creative usage of VLAN technology between the virtual switch and the Cisco ACI leaf switch described earlier. You do not need to be aware of this fact when configuring the fabric, though, because Cisco ACI will take care of all the implementation details for you.

As you have seen, Cisco ACI offers a rich set of options for traffic filtering between EPGs and inside of EPGs, both for bare-metal servers and virtual machines (Figure 4-17 summarizes the different concepts explained in this chapter):

■ Contracts can be used to filter traffic between EPGs.

■ Endpoints inside of a given EPG can communicate with each other by default, unless intra-EPG contracts or isolation enforcement are configured.

■ Intra-EPG isolation enforcement prevents all communication between endpoints inside a given EPG.

■ Intra-EPG contracts restrict the communication between endpoints inside a given EPG to specific traffic, as defined in the contract.

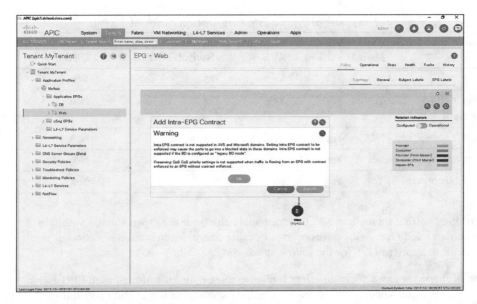

Figure 4-16 *Warning on Intra-EPG Contract Virtual Switch Support*

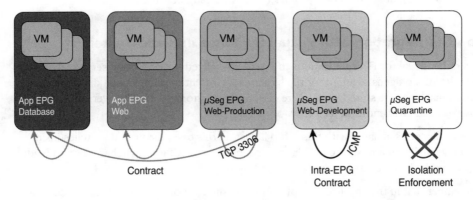

Figure 4-17 *Summary of EPG Traffic-Filtering Options*

Lastly, to complete the picture, Table 4-1 summarizes which hypervisors support each one of these traffic-filtering options for ACI Release 3.0(1). Note that support might (and probably will) be enhanced in future Cisco ACI releases, so referring to the release notes is probably a good idea.

Table 4-1   *Summary of Support of Traffic Filtering Options with ACI 3.0(1)*

Feature	Bare Metal	VMware VDS	VMware AVS	Microsoft vSwitch	OpenStack OVS	Kubernetes OVS
EPGs	Yes	Yes	Yes	Yes	Yes	Yes
μSeg EPGs (IP/MAC-based)	Yes	Yes	Yes	Yes	N/A	N/A
μSeg EPGs (other)	N/A	Yes	Yes	Yes	N/A	N/A
Isolation Enforcement	Yes	Yes	No	Yes	No	No
Intra-EPG Contract	Yes	Yes	No	No	No	Yes

The μSeg entries are marked N/A (for "not applicable") for the Open Virtual Switch in Kubernetes and OpenStack environments because micro-segmentation is a concept that's difficult to apply to OVS for the following reasons:

■ Kubernetes can achieve an effect similar to μSeg by means of tag-based EPG assignments using Kubernetes annotations, as later sections in this chapter will show.

■ OpenStack security groups can be enforced directly at the host, programmed by APIC using host protection profiles if the ML2 plug-in is used.

Cisco ACI Integration with Virtual Switches in Blade Systems

It is rather usual for IT organizations to install virtualized hosts in blade servers. Because not a lot of storage is required for the hypervisors (oftentimes the virtual disks for the virtual machines are stored somewhere else, in shared storage), blade servers offer a very compact and efficient form factor.

One challenge associated with this setup is that, in this case, the virtual switches inside of the virtualization hosts are not directly connected to ACI leaf switches, but to a blade switch in the blade chassis.

Remember that in the absence of OpFlex (like in the case of VMware VDS), Cisco ACI tries to find out on which physical network ports hypervisors are connected using Local Link Discovery Protocol (LLDP, enabled per default) or Cisco Discovery Protocol (CDP, disabled per default). If you have an additional switch in between, Cisco ACI will not be able to determine where each hypervisor is connected, because the only visible LLDP or CDP neighbors seen by the Cisco ACI leaf switches are the blade switches, as Figure 4-18 depicts.

With certain blade systems such as Cisco UCS, the Cisco APIC uses a simple trick to overcome the existence of this additional L2 device between the host and the ACI leaf switch: The LLDP/CDP neighbor seen by the leaf switch should be the UCS fabric interconnect, and the LLDP/CDP neighbor seen by the virtual switch over its physical interfaces should be the UCS fabric interconnect, too. By comparing the neighbors found on both the ACI leaf ports and the virtual switch, Cisco ACI can indirectly determine whether the ports to which the UCS fabric interconnects are attached lead to a certain virtualization host, thus enabling "Immediate" and "On-Demand" resolution immediacy when associating an EPG with a VMM domain. Otherwise, as indicated earlier in this chapter, the only option left is using "Pre-Provision" resolution immediacy so that ACI configures the new VLAN on all ports associated with the AAEP containing the VMM domain.

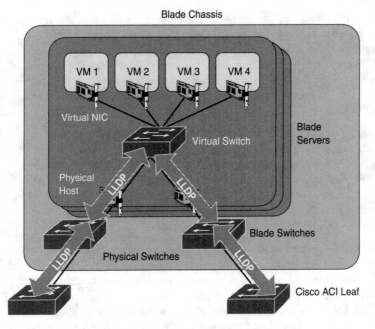

Figure 4-18 *Blade Switches and CDP/LLDP Signaling*

Note that this construct requires the existence of a single Layer 2 hop between the ESX host and the Cisco ACI leaf switch (typically the blade switch). If you had two or more distinct Layer 2 hops, the reported LLDP/CDP neighbors by the virtual switch in the hypervisor and the physical port in the ACI leaf would not match any more.

Another problem when using VLANs is the fact that the VLAN picked up for a certain EPG needs to exist in the blade switch. Otherwise, even if APIC configures the new VLAN in the virtual switch and the ACI leaf switch, the blade switch in the middle does not know anything about this new VLAN, and will drop the packets. An alternative here is creating in the blade switches all VLANs contained in the VLAN pool associated with the VMM domain. You might have a limitation here on the number of VLANs that certain blade switches support, so make sure you select a blade system that supports the full VLAN range, such as Cisco UCS.

As you will see later, Cisco AVS can optionally use VXLAN to communicate with the ACI leaf switch, so it is not affected by this problem, and is therefore ideal for integration with blade switches. However, VXLAN packets do flow over the ACI infrastructure VLAN, so you need to create this single infrastructure VLAN in the blade switches. After that, associating an EPG with a VMM domain configured for the AVS in VXLAN mode will create a new VXLAN network ID (VNID) and will be transported over the infrastructure VLAN as well.

One additional point to take into consideration when using blade switches is whether you can bond (or in Cisco terminology, "channel") multiple physical interfaces in the host for redundancy purposes. Some blade architectures such as Cisco Unified Compute System will not support this, so when you specify the load-balancing mode for traffic from the virtual switch (configured in the AAEP), make sure you select MAC Pinning as your channeling protocol (in other words, no channeling). Essentially, MAC Pinning means that for any given virtual NIC, traffic will be load-balanced to a physical NIC and will stay there (unless it fails, in which case it will be failed over to a working physical NIC in the same virtual switch).

Finally, some blade server vendors such as HP make creative usage of VLANs in order to achieve results such as optimization of hardware resources. Virtual Connect is one of the HP offerings for blade switching in its popular c7000 blade chassis, with a switching mode called "Tunnel Mode," where the Virtual Connect switch will consolidate MAC tables for multiple VLANs into a single table, making the assumption that the same MAC address cannot appear in two different VLANs. However, when using Cisco ACI, you could have multiple EPGs mapped to the same bridge domain.

As shown in Figure 4-19, if you have multiple EPGs (marked in the figure with solid and dotted lines) mapped to the same bridge domain, you will have different VLANs for each EPG. When a dotted-line virtual machine sends multi-destination traffic (multicast or broadcast, such as ARP traffic), the ACI leaf will replicate the packets from the dotted-line to the solid-line VLAN, as shown in the figure. Now if Virtual Connect has a single MAC learning table for both VLANs, the MAC address of the dotted-line VM will be coming from both the virtual switch on the dotted-line VLAN and the physical ACI fabric on the solid-line VLAN, which will cause connectivity issues.

Note that this is a specific behavior of the HP Virtual Connect blade switches operating in Tunnel Mode. The workaround is either disabling Tunnel Mode in Virtual Connect or having one single EPG per bridge domain in the application profiles with EPGs mapped to the VMM domain.

OpFlex

As explained in the introduction of this book, OpFlex is the declarative policy distribution protocol that Cisco ACI uses to disseminate network configuration from the Application Policy Infrastructure Controller to the physical and virtual switches connected to the ACI fabric. *Declarative* means that OpFlex does not distribute configuration per se, but rather policy. In other words, it does not instruct the switches on how to perform a certain operation, but just describes (declares) the operation that needs to be performed.

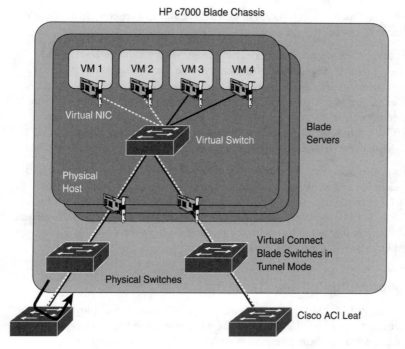

Figure 4-19 *Connectivity Issue with HP Virtual Connect Blade Switches in Tunnel Mode and Multiple EPGs per BD*

Imagine a control tower at an airport instructing the pilots in each aircraft which buttons to press and which levers to pull to land their planes. Obviously, this "imperative" approach does not scale, so the airport controllers instead follow a "declarative" strategy: They just tell the pilots where and when they should land, but not how to fly their machines.

Declarative policy distribution is essential in complex systems at scale, such as the public cloud. Examples of declarative policies are Quickstart ARM templates in Microsoft Azure and CloudFormation templates in Amazon Web Services (AWS), two of the most popular public cloud vendors.

Cisco ACI OpFlex leverages declarative policy distribution to physical and virtual switches, which in the context of virtualization integration is critical. One essential advantage of this model is that the policy distributed to physical switches and virtual switches of different types (VMware, Microsoft, Red Hat Virtualization, OpenStack) remains exactly the same and is then interpreted locally at the switch layer.

Therefore, when Cisco ACI integrates with a virtual switch, the desired model is augmenting the virtual switch so that it understands OpFlex policies, and thus it is able to receive network policy as any other switch in the Cisco ACI fabric. Most virtual switch integrations work like this: Virtual switch extensions for the Microsoft vSwitch or

OpFlex agents for the Open vSwitch (OVS) in OpenStack and Kubernetes clusters implement the OpFlex protocol for this purpose.

There is one notable exception to this architecture: the VMware vSphere Distributed Switch (VDS). Being that the vSphere VDS implementation is closed, it is not possible for Cisco or any other organization other than VMware to enhance or modify the native VDS with OpFlex in any way. This is very different from other virtual switches that are extensible in nature, such as Microsoft's Hyper-V vSwitch and, of course, the Open Virtual Switch (OVS). Consequently, Cisco ACI needs to use traditional imperative APIs (as opposed to the declarative character of OpFlex) in order to configure the vSwitch.

The OpFlex protocol works over the Cisco ACI infrastructure VLAN for all virtual and physical switches in the fabric. When a virtual switch supports the OpFlex protocol, the infrastructure VLAN needs to be extended out of the physical fabric. You do this by enabling the check box **Infrastructure VLAN** in the Attachable Entity Profile associated with the VMM domain. If you fail to do so, the integration between Cisco ACI and the OpFlex-enabled virtual switch will not work.

Deployments over Multiple Data Centers

As discussed in Chapter 11, "Multi-Site Designs," Cisco ACI supports deployments over multiple data centers through a variety of options. There are some basic concepts we can consider now in the context of the integration with virtual machine managers:

- **Site (sometimes called "fabric"):** This is a set of Cisco ACI nodes (spines and leaf switches) managed by a single cluster of Cisco APICs.

- **Pod:** Sites can be optionally divided in pods, which can be server rooms or data center cells. You still have a single cluster of Cisco APICs managing all the pods in a site. Pods are interconnected to each other using VXLAN.

- **Multi-Site:** Cisco ACI capability, introduced with the 3.0(1) version, that allows you to connect multiple sites (each one with its own cluster of APICs) to each other over VXLAN and to manage them cohesively. These sites can be different rooms in one location, or separate data centers distributed around the world. VRFs, bridge domains, and endpoint groups can be optionally stretched over all the sites.

It is important to note that these concepts do not necessarily equate to physical locations, but to ACI logical design units: You could have multiple ACI "sites" (fabrics) inside of the same data center, and you could stretch a pod over multiple physical locations (as long as the latency between the locations does not exceed 50 milliseconds).

Also note that the integration between Cisco ACI and a virtualization platform is configured at the site level: between a cluster of APICs and one or more VMware, Microsoft, OpenStack, Red Hat Virtualization, Openshift or Kubernetes clusters.

Ideally, from a business continuity perspective, you should align your networking and compute HA (high availability) designs: If you have multiple virtualization clusters in a single location for redundancy reasons, you should probably match that design in the network with multiple Cisco ACI sites, effectively building in your data center what the public cloud industry has dubbed "availability zones."

If, on the contrary, your business continuity requirements allow having single virtualization clusters per application in a certain data center, a sensible design would be building ACI with a single cluster of APICs as well. In other words, you might not require control-plane redundancy in one region, because you provide disaster recovery with a data center in a different region.

Live migrations (vMotion in VMware language) can take place across pods, and even across sites. The limitation is rather whether the virtualization domain supports cross-cluster live migration. At the time of this writing, only VMware vSphere supports cross-vCenter vMotion. However, even in this case, you should consider that live migration only makes actual sense in metro environments with low latency and high bandwidth.

Refer to Chapter 11 for more details on Multi-Pod and Multi-Site deployments.

VMware vSphere

The following sections describe some of the particulars of the different virtualization integrations that exist in Cisco ACI. Note that this book will not cover the integration with Red Hat Virtualization (formerly known Red Hat Enterprise Virtualization) introduced in ACI version 3.1, since it is still rather new.

VMware has been the prevalent hypervisor for server virtualization for the last few years. As a matter of fact, VMware was the first company that heavily bet on server virtualization and pioneered it worldwide, which gave the company a considerable head start and market advantage. Even now that server virtualization is mostly a commodity feature present in almost every operating system, VMware is still the most common hypervisor found in many organizations.

The network architecture for vSphere corresponds to the patterns explained in the previous sections, but the nomenclature for the different components varies when compared to other hypervisors. The following terms are used in VMware documentation:

- Virtual machines have *virtual network interface cards* (vNICs)

- vNICs are logically attached to *port groups* configured in a virtual switch (called vSwitch, VSS, or VDS; see the paragraphs that follow for more information on these switch types).

- Port groups contain important information such as the VLAN ID encapsulation to use.

- vSwitches can be logically attached to the physical NICs of the host (called *vmnics*) to provide external connectivity.

VMware differentiates between the vSphere Standard Switch (VSS) and the vSphere Distributed Switch (VDS). The VDS was introduced some years ago in the Enterprise Plus level of the vSphere licensing model, and it offers the possibility of centrally managing the configuration for all virtual switches in a vSphere cluster from the vSphere vCenter server, the management console for the vSphere hypervisor.

In other words, if you can manage each host individually, you just need the VSS. But if you want centralized administration of your virtualization hosts and the virtual switches inside, and you have the money to invest in the vSphere Enterprise Plus license, the Virtualized Distributed Switch is your friend.

Cisco ACI Coexistence with the vSphere Standard Switch

Note that this section's title uses the term *coexistence* instead of *integration*. If you are not using the Distributed Virtual Switch from VMware (probably for cost reasons), then introducing Cisco ACI does not force you out of this path. However, there will be no management integration between ACI and the vSphere ESX hosts.

That is to say, you can configure your virtual and physical switches using separate mechanisms the same way you have been doing up until now, as Figure 4-20 illustrates. The main advantage of using Cisco ACI is having a centralized management point for the physical network instead of having to configure multiple distinct network devices.

In Cisco ACI, you would use static bindings (at the port or leaf level) in the corresponding EPGs to explicitly allocate packets coming from each ESXi port on specific VLANs to certain EPGs. Virtual machines would then appear to Cisco ACI as if they were physical hosts.

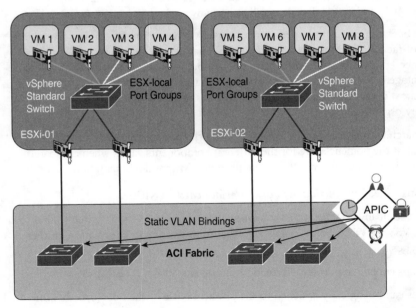

Figure 4-20   *Coexistence of Cisco ACI and VMware vSphere Standard Switch*

Cisco ACI Coexistence with the vSphere Distributed Switch

Typically, if you have the Virtual Distributed Switch, you would want to integrate it with Cisco ACI. However, if you choose not to do so, they can obviously coexist. This section covers this possibility for the sake of completeness.

In a way similar to configuring vSphere Standard Switch coexistence, you would configure on one side the vSphere Distributed Switch (or Switches) on the vSphere vCenter server, and on the other side you would configure the physical ports on ACI, taking care that the VLAN IDs are the same, as illustrated by Figure 4-21.

However, as the next section articulates, integrating the vSphere Distributed Switch with Cisco ACI will result in considerable advantages at no additional cost.

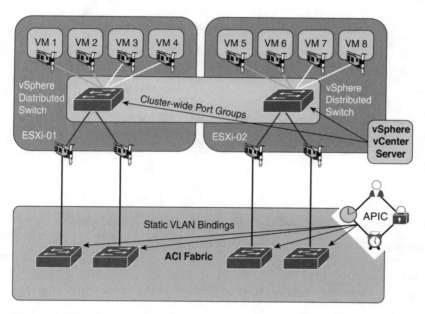

Figure 4-21   *Coexistence of Cisco ACI and VMware vSphere Distributed Switch*

Cisco ACI Integration with the vSphere Distributed Switch

If you already have the required vSphere license to run the vSphere Distributed Switch in your environment, the integration with Cisco ACI offers a great deal of advantage in terms of simplification and additional functionality.

The first thing you should verify is that your vSphere VDS version is supported for integration with your version of Cisco ACI. At the time of this writing, VDS versions 5.1 through 6.5 are supported. For additional information, you can visit the latest Cisco ACI Virtualization Compatibility List (https://www.cisco.com/c/en/us/solutions/collateral/data-center-virtualization/application-centric-infrastructure/solution-overview-c22-734588.html).

When you integrate ACI with one or more vCenter clusters, a folder will be created in each vCenter server containing a Distributed Virtual Switch. Both the folder and the Distributed Virtual Switch itself will be named after the VMM domain, so choose the name of the VMM domain carefully. Choose a name meaningful for the VMware administrator, so that she can tell at first sight that that specific Virtual Switch is managed by ACI (such as "ACI_VDS1," for example). Figure 4-22 shows the different attributes you can specify when creating a VMM domain for the vSphere Distributed Switch.

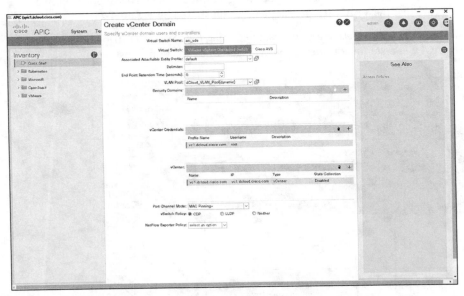

Figure 4-22   *Creating a VMM for the vSphere Distributed Switch*

In addition to the Attachable Entity Profile, the VLAN pool, and information about the vCenter server, here are some properties shown in Figure 4-22 that are worth mentioning:

- **End Point Retention Time:** The time (in seconds, between 0 and 600) that endpoints will be retained in memory after a VM is detached from the virtual switch (for example, because it is shut down or has been deleted).

- **Delimiter:** The port groups created in vCenter upon associating an EPG with a VMM domain have by default the naming convention Tenant|Application|EPG. If you want to use a delimiter other than "|", you can specify it here.

- **Port Channel Mode:** This is the port channel policy (or "bonding" in server administration parlance) that will be configured on the physical interfaces of each ESX host. This parameter is critical, because some blade switches do not support channeling, and therefore MAC Pinning needs to be selected (as Figure 4-22 shows).

- **vSwitch Policy:** Indicates which protocol to use so that Cisco ACI can discover to which physical leaf ports the ESX hosts are connected. With the VDS, you need to configure one, because ACI relays on either CDP or LLDP to discover where the ESX hosts are attached, because the VDS does not support the OpFlex protocol. Furthermore, VMware's native VDS supports either CDP or LLDP, which is why you cannot choose both in the GUI. When you select one or the other, APIC will configure the new VDS in VMware accordingly. You can verify this setting in vCenter in the properties of the VDS, after the APIC has created it.

- **NetFlow Exporter Policy:** Indicates whether NetFlow should be configured in the virtual switch.

One reason you might want to specify a delimiter different from the default one ("|") is because you might have systems such as configuration management databases or monitoring software that need to contain information regarding the virtual port groups created by Cisco ACI. Some of these systems might have limitations regarding the characters they can support. In case they do not support the vertical bar character ("|"), you can configure Cisco ACI to create the port groups with another delimiter.

ACI will automatically configure certain parameters of the VDS such as the maximum transmit unit (MTU) to values matching those in the rest of the fabric (9000 bytes, in the case of the MTU), so that you do not need to take care of that yourself.

After you have configured the integration (by creating the VMM domain), Cisco ACI can communicate with the vCenter server and will configure port groups as EPGs are associated with the VMM domain. Similarly, port groups will be deleted from the virtual switch when the association between a certain EPG and the VMM domain is deleted, provided there are no existing VMs configured on that port group.

After the port group is created in the virtual switch by ACI, the virtualization admin can allocate virtual machines to that port group, as with any other port group in the environment, using vCenter's GUI or APIs.

vCenter administrators should refrain from deleting or modifying APIC-created port groups in vCenter, or changing the configuration of the APIC-managed DVS. If they do so, alerts will be triggered in Cisco ACI, warning of an inconsistent configuration.

vCenter User Requirements

As the previous section described, a vCenter username is required so that Cisco ACI can create some objects in vCenter and can retrieve information to be displayed and leveraged in Cisco ACI. Even though in a lab environment giving Cisco ACI root access to the vCenter server might be just fine, in production it is recommended that you configure a dedicated user who has just enough privileges to perform the required actions for the integration.

Here is the minimum set of privileges given to the user assigned to Cisco ACI for the VMM integration:

- Alarms

- Distributed Switch

- dvPort Group

- Folder

- Host:

  - Host.Configuration.Advanced settings

  - Host.Local operations.Reconfigure virtual machine

  - Host.Configuration.Network configuration

- Network

- Virtual machine

  - Virtual machine.Configuration.Modify device settings

  - Virtual machine.Configuration.Settings

Micro-Segmentation with the VDS

Other than the general concepts of micro-segmentation discussed earlier in this chapter, there are some noteworthy specifics concerning integration with the VMware VDS.

The main highlight is that vSphere custom attributes and tags can be used as micro-segmentation EPG criteria. Custom attributes and tags are metadata that can be attached to a VM. Custom attributes were used by VMware in early vSphere versions and have been mostly deprecated in favor of tags. Custom attributes are key-value pairs such as **"MALWARE"="YES"** or **"DEPARTMENT"="FINANCE"**. Tags are single strings that are grouped in categories and that can be associated with objects such as virtual machines. For example, the tag "MALWARE FOUND" could belong to the category "Security." Cisco ACI can use VM tags as criteria for micro-segmentation EPG association if the vSphere hosts are running version 6.0 or later.

Blade Servers and VDS Integration

Because the VDS integration relies on VLANs and CDP/LLDP between the VDS and the Cisco ACI leaf (because OpFlex isn't supported due to the closed nature of the VDS), you need to observe the following points:

- If you are not using Cisco UCS, you want to select **Pre-Deploy** as your **Deployment Immediacy** option when associating an EPG with the VMM domain.

- You need to make sure that the VLAN IDs contained in the VLAN pool are configured in advance in the blade switches, because Cisco ACI will not manage those components.

- If your blade switches do not support bonding the vmnics of the ESX together (such as Cisco UCS), make sure you select MAC Pinning as the load-balancing algorithm in your Attachable Access Entity Profile.

Cisco ACI Integration with Cisco Application Virtual Switch

As the previous sections have explained, VMware's vSphere Distributed Switch has some limitations:

- It is a Layer 2 switch, so it is still based in VLANs. The lack of Layer 3 support prevents additional functionality such as VXLAN integration with ACI.

- Its control protocols are very rudimentary and are essentially reduced to LLDP/CDP (other than the management API of vCenter). These Layer 2 protocols do not interoperate well when the virtualization hosts are not directly attached to an ACI leaf, but there are additional Layer 2 bridges in between (such as blade switches).

- It is lacking functionality such as packet filtering, which must be compensated for using ACI hardware.

VMware does actually have a more advanced switch that addresses the VDS limitations just described, but unfortunately it is only sold as part of the NSX for vSphere product, and thus at a significant cost increase.

Additionally, the vSphere Distributed Switch software is not open or extendable in any shape or form, which consequently has left network vendors such as Cisco with only one possibility: develop a new switch for VMware vSphere that addresses the limitations of the VDS.

Cisco was in the lucky situation of already having the Nexus 1000v, a mature virtual switch with rich functionality and supported by vSphere, so it did not have to start from scratch. Building on that basis, the Application Virtual Switch was developed, which offers a much richer set of networking functions as compared to the native vSphere VDS:

- It is a L2/L3 switch and has VXLAN functionality.

- It has packet-filtering functionality, so the complete packet-forwarding decision can take place inside of the hypervisor, without leveraging ACI leaf hardware, as the "Distributed Firewall" section will further explain.

- It supports the OpFlex protocol, which allows for a richer integration with Cisco ACI.

Note that VMware has publicly announced its intention of not supporting third-party switches anymore in vSphere environments starting with version 6.5U2, which would put AVS in an unsupported status. To help AVS users navigate the consequences of VMware's decision, Cisco has introduced in Cisco ACI version 3.1 a sort of second-generation AVS switch called ACI Virtual Edge (AVE), which will eventually replace AVS. Note that Cisco will still support AVS, so that organizations can migrate from AVS to AVE at their own convenience.

AVE uses a different switching mechanism than AVS. Instead of interacting with the native virtual switch of the hypervisor, AVE is a virtual machine that performs all switching and routing functions. One of the most important benefits of this architecture is that, being a virtual machine, AVE is hypervisor-independent, although in its first release it is only supported with the VMware vSphere ESXi hypervisor.

Since AVS is still leveraged by many organizations, and AVE has only been recently introduced, this chapter will focus on AVS.

When you create a VMM domain in Cisco ACI for integration with AVS, the parameters to be configured are slightly different from the ones for the VDS. In addition, the options to be configured depend on the deployment mode for AVS. For example, Figure 4-23 illustrates the required information if you're configuring AVS without local switching (also known as "FEX mode"). In this switching mode, AVS behaves as a sort of Nexus Fabric Extender, sending every packet up to the physical ACI leaf, even those between virtual machines in the same EPG.

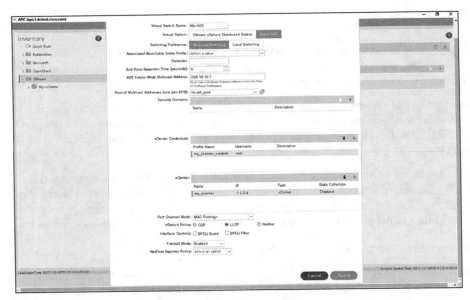

Figure 4-23   *Configuring a VMM Domain for Cisco AVS in "No Local Switching" Mode*

As you can see, in No Local Switching mode, there are really few options to configure. For example, there is no VLAN pool to define. However, the recommended deployment options for Cisco Application Virtual Switch is in Local Switching mode, so that packets are locally processed in the hypervisor. Figures 4-24 and 4-25 show the configuration screens for the AVS in Local Switching mode, with VLAN and VXLAN encapsulation, respectively. In Local Switching mode, the AVS will only send up to the physical ACI nodes any packets that traverse EPG boundaries (that is, traffic between virtual machines that belong to different EPGs).

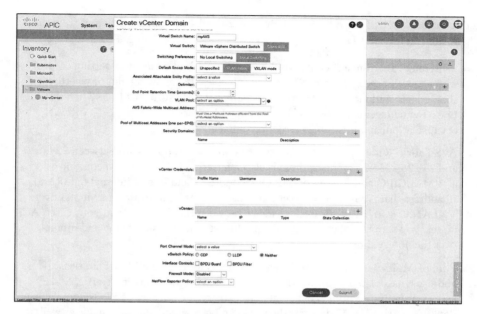

Figure 4-24 *Configuring a VMM Domain for Cisco AVS in Local Switching Mode with VLAN Encapsulation*

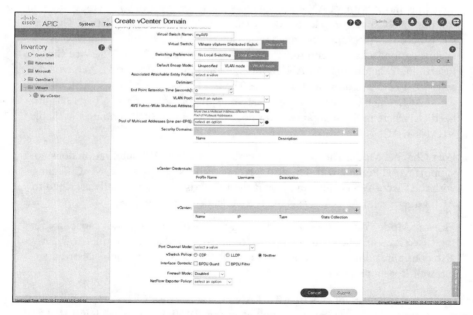

Figure 4-25 *Configuring a VMM Domain for Cisco AVS in Local Switching Mode with VXLAN/Mixed Encapsulation*

Let's consider some of the options in Figures 4-24 and 4-25 that are different from the VMM domain for the VDS:

- **Switching Preference (Local Switching):** As described earlier, this setting controls whether AVS processes intra-EPG packets locally (Local Switching) or whether it should also send intra-EPG traffic upstream to the physical ACI leaf switch (No Local Switching, also known as FEX mode). FEX mode only supports VXLAN encapsulation, and it is typically not recommended.

- **AVS Fabric-Wide Multicast Address:** Valid multicast address are between 224.0.0.0 and 239.255.255.255. This address is also referred to in some documentation as a "VMM GIPO address" (Group IP Outer address), and it is an internal multicast IP address that AVS will use to send traffic to the ACI physical leaf switches over VXLAN. If you have additional switches between the ESX host and your Cisco ACI nodes, you should make sure that this multicast IP address is unique and routable over the non-ACI network.

- **Pool of Multicast Addresses:** When VXLAN is used, an additional multicast IP address is associated with each EPG to deal with multidestination traffic. Make sure your multicast pool is big enough to cater to the number of EPGs you plan to deploy over this VMM domain (the pool can be enlarged at a later stage, as well, if required).

- **VLAN Pool:** A VLAN pool is obviously required if you deploy AVS in Local Switching mode with VLAN encapsulation. However, it is not so obvious why you can optionally specify a VLAN pool when using VXLAN encapsulation. The reason is because AVS supports mixed encapsulation—for example, when VXLAN encapsulation lacks a certain functionality (most prominently L4-7 Service Graph Insertion). If the optional VLAN pool is specified in VXLAN mode, AVS would revert to VLANs to provide this feature. These VLANs have a local significance for Cisco ACI, which essentially means that you can potentially reuse VLAN IDs utilized elsewhere in the ACI fabric, thus not impacting the total amount of available VLANs in ACI.

- **Port Channel Mode:** The only remark here is that Cisco AVS integration does not support MAC Pinning with Physical NIC Load checking. However, MAC Pinning with the Cisco AVS is only advisable if the ESX hosts are not directly attached to ACI. Otherwise, LACP Active is the recommended option.

- **Firewall Mode:** You can configure whether the Distributed Firewall capability for the Cisco AVS instance will be enabled, disabled, or in Learning mode. You can also configure a logging destination for firewall logs. Se the section "Distributed Firewall" for more details.

The reason why you cannot specify a VXLAN pool is because Cisco ACI already has a reserved range of VXLAN virtual network identifiers (VNIDs) to be used with AVS.

In summary, the recommended deployment mode for Cisco AVS is Local Switching with default VXLAN encapsulation; optionally, you can define an additional VLAN pool to enable mixed encapsulation when required.

Cisco AVS Installation

The Cisco AVS has a software component that needs to be installed on every virtualization host. Some virtualization admins might have some concerns about the eventual increased complexity of managing this extra agent. To answer those concerns, Cisco has enhanced the mature Cisco Virtual Switch Update Manager (VSUM) to support the Application Virtual Switch (AVS). Cisco VSUM is a software product originally developed to integrate the software management experience of the Cisco Nexus 1000v into vCenter, and now Cisco ACI users can benefit from its functionality at no cost.

This installation process of the Cisco AVS is very easy and smooth and can be performed using the Cisco Virtual Switch Update Manager. Alternatively, you could use VMware Virtual Update Manager (VUM), the Cisco ACI plug-in for vCenter, or even the ESX command-line interface to install it. However, because the VSUM is the most comfortable and resilient way to install Cisco AVS, this is what this section will focus on. For further details on these alternative installation procedures, refer to the AVS installation guides at Cisco.com.

Cisco VSUM is a tool that you can easily deploy into your vCenter cluster in the form of a virtual appliance. After you install VSUM and register it with vCenter, the VSUM icon will appear in the Home screen of the vCenter server, and the virtualization admin can use it to install and configure AVS. Figure 4-26 shows how the graphical user interface (GUI) of Cisco VSUM integrates into vCenter.

Blade Servers and AVS Integration

Cisco ACI does not rely on CDP or LLDP as a control protocol to communicate with AVS, but rather it relies on OpFlex. This protocol runs over the infrastructure VLAN, so it is imperative that you check the box **Enable Infrastructure VLAN** in the AAEP and that the infrastructure VLAN exist in the blade switches.

The additional ease of integration of AVS with VXLAN makes it a very convenient choice as compared to the VDS in blade server environments, because you do not need to create VLANs in advance in the blade switches.

As discussed in the design sections, it is recommended that you use a combination of AVS for VM traffic and VDS for management traffic. In this case, the VDS VLANs for infrastructure (management, vMotion, NFS, and so on) would have to be pre-populated in the blade switch, but the rest of the port groups will work over VXLAN without requiring additional configuration.

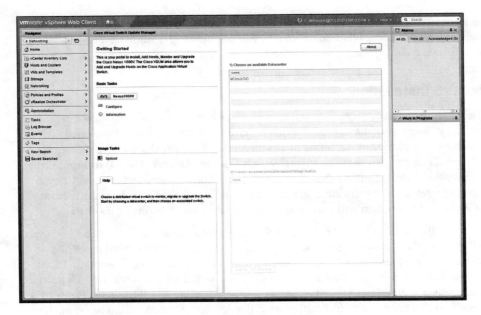

Figure 4-26 *Home Screen of VSUM for AVS Installation*

Distributed Firewall

Cisco AVS Distributed Firewall is a hardware-assisted functionality of Cisco AVS that improves security for virtual machines. AVS is aware of traffic flows and tracks the state of TCP and FTP connections, so that only packets that belong to legitimate TCP connections are allowed. Cisco AVS Distributed Firewall functionality works in conjunction with Cisco ACI leaf switch hardware to reduce the possibility of distributed denial of service (DDoS) attacks and to improve the overall network security posture.

The "distributed" character of this feature implies that the TCP and FTP state information is maintained even after vMotion events. When a virtual machine is migrated over vMotion to a different ESXi host, the state of the existing connections to and from that virtual machine is moved as well, so that the firewall functionality provided by AVS continues to work in the destination ESXi host.

When a consumer establishes a TCP connection to a provider (for example, a Web connection to TCP port 80), Cisco ACI will open up TCP source port 80 in the opposite direction so that the provider can send return traffic to the consumer. However, malicious software in the provider server might try to leverage this fact by sending TCP attacks sourced on TCP port 80. Cisco ACI Distributed Firewall will prevent these attacks, restricting communication to only TCP flows initiated by the consumer.

The state of the TCP flows tracked by the Distributed Firewall supports aging with a default of 5 minutes, so that idle TCP connections will not consume resources in the hypervisor.

When creating the VMM domain for AVS, you can specify the administrative state for the Distributed Firewall as follows:

- **Disabled:** Cisco AVS will not inspect packets.

- **Learning:** Cisco AVS will inspect packets and create flow tables, but it will not drop any packets. This is the default mode.

- **Enabled:** Cisco AVS will inspect packets, create flow tables, and drop any packets not allowed by the Cisco ACI security policy specified with EPGs and contracts.

The Distributed Firewall works in both Local Switching and No Local Switching modes, as well as with VLAN, VXLAN, or mixed encapsulation.

If after creating the VMM domain you want to change the administrative state of the Distributed Firewall, you can change it in the Firewall policy that Cisco ACI created when you configured the VMM domain. You can find that policy in the Fabric Access Policies, as Figure 4-27 shows.

Last but not least, as Figures 4-24 and 4-25 show, note the option at the very bottom of the screen where you can enable sending syslog messages to an external syslog server. This would protocol the activity of the AVS Distributed Firewall, logging both permitted and denied flows.

Figure 4-27 *Changing Firewall Policy for an Existing AVS VMM Domain*

You have the possibility to control for which contracts the Distributed Firewall functionality in AVS will be used. Figure 4-28 shows the options that Cisco ACI offers you
when configuring a filter for a contract (notice the **Stateful** check box). If you enable the
Stateful option for a contract used between EPGs associated with an AVS-based VMM
domain, the firewall functionality will be used and state information will be tracked by
Cisco AVS.

By having information about which clients have initiated TCP connections to the servers
using which source TCP ports, AVS will allow exactly the reverse flow for the return
traffic from the server to the client, but not to any other destination or TCP port.

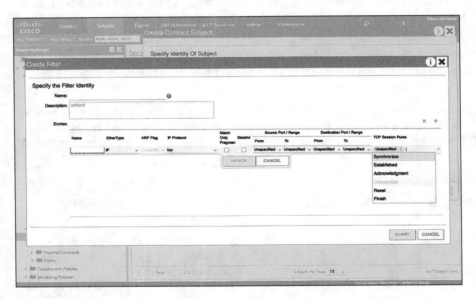

Figure 4-28   *Options when Configuring Filters in Cisco ACI, Including the*
Stateful *Check Box*

Regarding the File Transfer Protocol, you do not need any additional configuration to
enable AVS to snoop into the FTP traffic in order to allow traffic on dynamically negotiated FTP ports. Note that only active FTP is supported by the Distributed Firewall in
AVS because passive FTP does not dynamically negotiate TCP ports.

You can refer to Chapter 8, "Moving to Application-Centric Networking," for further
details on other filtering options for traffic isolation.

Virtual Network Designs with VDS and AVS

The most obvious networking design for a VMware cluster would be with a single virtual
switch (AVS or VDS), like Figure 4-29 illustrates. In this case, traffic from VMs and infrastructure traffic flows coming from virtual interfaces of the ESXi host itself (from virtual

NICs called "VM Kernel NICs" or just "vmknics") are combined into the same physical cables connecting to the ACI leaf switches.

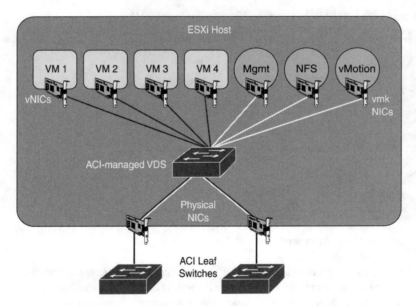

Figure 4-29 *Sample Configuration with a Single VDS*

In this design, using quality of service (QoS) is a must, because otherwise you could have management traffic draining out VM traffic (vMotion traffic is well known for grabbing as much bandwidth as it can), or the other way around.

Another important aspect of this design is how the Management vmknic comes up, because in some situations there could exist a race condition: the Management vmknic needs ACI to configure the relevant VLANs, but ACI needs the Management vmknic to be up before accessing the hypervisor host. To break this chicken-and-egg situation, you can configure the VMM domain assignment to the Management EPG with Pre-Provision as the Resolution Immediacy policy, so that the management VLANs will be deployed in the ports connected to ESX hypervisors under all circumstances. Note that the Cisco AVS does not support Pre-Provision, so this design is only recommended when you're using integration with the native vSphere Distributed Switch.

An alternative design would be to create two ACI-managed vSphere Distributed Switches—that is, two distinct VMM domains associated with the same vSphere cluster. You would use one VDS for VM traffic and the other one for infrastructure traffic. Such a setup would look like the scenario represented in Figure 4-30. Note that this is only an option with the VDS integration, as only one AVS is supported per ESX host.

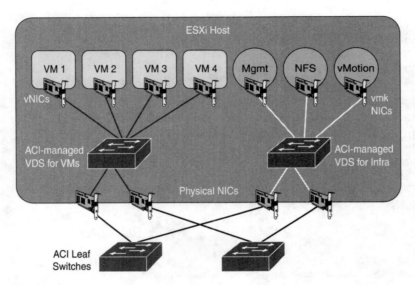

Figure 4-30 *Sample Configuration with Two ACI-managed VDSs*

The advantage of such a design is a clear delimitation between VM traffic and infrastructure traffic (for example, for legacy ESXi hosts that do not have 10GbE connections). Having QoS would still be recommended to guarantee that no traffic category gets drained out by the others. For example, you want to guarantee that storage traffic always has enough bandwidth.

If you are using VLAN encapsulation, remember to allocate non-overlapping VLAN pools to each VMM domain. Even if VLAN IDs are locally relevant to the physical ports in Cisco ACI, VMware ESX hosts do not have the concept of "VLAN local relevance": The VLAN IDs for VMs and infrastructure need to be unique.

Another situation where this design is recommended is when you're using Cisco AVS. The reason is that Cisco AVS does not support Pre-Provision as the Resolution Immediacy policy, which is required by the management vmknic to come up correctly (besides being recommended for other infrastructure traffic categories such as vMotion, NFS, and iSCSI). Having AVS for VM traffic and VDS for infrastructure traffic is a great solution in this case, if you have enough physical NICs in your ESX hosts. Note that with server solutions such as Cisco UCS, where physical NICs can be created in software, this last point should not be an obstacle.

A variant of this design is using VDS not to separate VM traffic from infrastructure traffic but to separate traffic from two different groups of virtual machines. If, for example, you have demilitarized zone (DMZ) virtual machines and Intranet virtual machines running on the same ESX host, some organizations would like to separate DMZ and Intranet traffic into different physical ACI leaf switches. This objective can be achieved by having two ACI-managed VDS instances in a vCenter cluster, each connected to a different set of ACI leaf switches. Note that this is not possible with the AVS because you can only have one AVS instance per ESX host.

Another possibility of separating outgoing traffic on different physical interfaces with a single VDS is using the Trunk Port Groups functionality to create two sets of port groups in the VDS, each transporting a different set of VLANs.

The setup with two vSphere Distributed Switches has an important variation: when one of the VDSs is not managed by Cisco ACI but is controlled by vCenter. This is actually a fairly typical migration scenario, where in the same EPG you combine static port bindings (for VMs attached to the vCenter-controlled VDS) and VMM integration (for VMs attached to the ACI-controlled VDS), as Figure 4-31 describes.

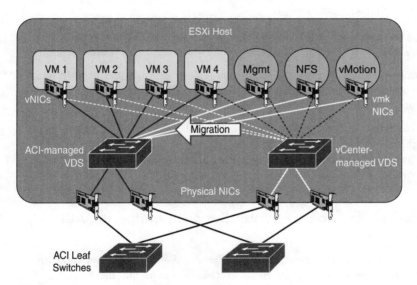

Figure 4-31   *Sample Migration Scenario to an ACI-Managed VDS/AVS*

The migration to an ACI-managed switch such as VDS or AVS would roughly follow these guidelines:

1. All VMs and vmknics are connected to the vCenter-managed VDS, with static port bindings configured in the Cisco ACI EPGs.

2. Each of those EPGs will be associated with a VMM domain. This will create corresponding groups in the ACI-managed VDS/AVS.

3. The virtualization admin can migrate the single virtual machines and vmknics at their own pace, without any outage.

One downside of this approach is that it requires two extra physical NICs in the host (once again, note that this is not a problem with Cisco UCS virtual interface cards, because physical NICs are created on demand). If you have the extra hardware, this process offers the smoothest migration to an ACI-integrated environment.

If you do not have the extra vmnics in your ESX host, the migration looks similar, but instead you move one of the physical NICs from the vCenter-managed VDS to the ACI-managed VDS/AVS. Consequently, there is no network redundancy during the migration window, which should therefore be kept as short as possible.

Independent of whether you have one or more virtual switches, or even whether you leverage Cisco ACI VMM domains or just use static bindings, it is important that you configure separate EPGs for vSphere infrastructure traffic (management, vMotion, NFS, and so on) for the following reasons:

- Your vSphere infrastructure EPGs should be in a tenant separated from the tenant where you have your VMs. See Chapter 9, "Multi-Tenancy," for a detailed example.

- The vMotion vmknics are typically silent, so you need to configure the vMotion EPG in a bridge domain with either Unknown Unicast Flooding or with a subnet (which automatically enables MAC gleaning).

- It is critical that you configure the right security policy for the vmknics interfaces, to protect your virtualization infrastructure. Make sure you follow a whitelist policy in this regard, and configure only the necessary access (especially for the management vmknics).

Cisco ACI Plug-in for vSphere vCenter Server: Configuring ACI from vCenter

In some organizations, the management flow just described—having the network admin creating the port groups (by associating EPGs to VMM domains) and the virtualization admin associating the VMs with the corresponding port groups—is not desirable. Instead, the virtualization admin should control the full configuration flow end to end, including the management of the port groups.

One possibility for achieving this workflow would be to have the virtualization admins using Cisco ACI to associate EPGs with VMM domains, but there are two main disadvantages with this approach:

- The main administrative tool of a VMware administrator is the vCenter server. Having to access a different management tool would imply an additional learning effort.

- The nomenclature in Cisco ACI has been designed for network administrators, and VMware administrators would have to learn new terms (for example, "EPG" instead of "port group").

The Cisco ACI plug-in for vCenter addresses both issues: The virtualization admin is able to access, manage, and configure many relevant attributes of Cisco ACI right from inside vCenter, using familiar terminology and thus reducing the required learning curve. Figure 4-32 depicts the home screen of the Cisco ACI plug-in for vCenter.

Additionally, this plug-in gives the virtualization administrator further information about the network, such as other endpoints that are present in the EPGs (port groups) where vSphere virtual machines are attached.

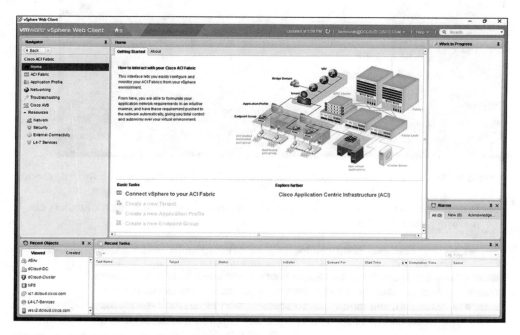

Figure 4-32   *Cisco ACI Plug-in for vSphere vCenter*

Besides, tasks such as reconfiguring the network whenever a new port group is con-figured are automatically performed by ACI. For example, creating a new port group with this plug-in is a very simple task, as Figure 4-33 shows. The plug-in will perform all required network changes at both the virtual and physical levels.

This plug-in enables the virtualization administrator to configure new port groups with-out needing to involve the network team, which eventually results in a better process agil-ity and implementation velocity. Advanced Cisco ACI features such as L4-7 service graph insertion is also available in the Cisco ACI plug-in for vCenter, which gives unprecedented control and agility to the virtualization professional.

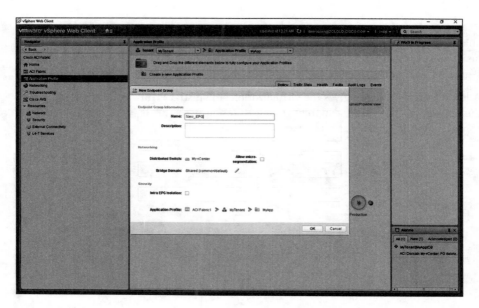

Figure 4-33   *Port Group (EPG) Creation with the Cisco ACI Plug-in for vSphere vCenter*

For example, here are some of the network operations that VMware administrators can perform right from vCenter:

- Create, edit, and modify endpoint groups (EPGs) and VMM associations. This will result in creating, editing, and modifying the associated port groups in the VDS or AVS.

- Create, edit, and modify micro-segmentation EPGs, for dynamic assignment of virtual machines to EPGs. This is especially important, because otherwise there are no other vCenter notifications when Cisco ACI changes the EPG assignment for virtual machines based on micro-segmentation EPG rules.

- Read operational information such as which endpoints (not only vSphere virtual machines, but also bare-metal servers as well as virtual machines from other hypervisors) are allocated to which EPG.

- Create, edit, and modify virtual routing and forwarding (VRF) tables, bridge domains, ACI tenants, and application profiles (for example, for creating the required networking constructs for new applications right from within vCenter).

- Create, edit, and modify contracts provided and consumed by EPGs and micro-segmentation EPGs, as well as create, edit, and modify contracts, subjects, and filters, to be able to change the security posture for any virtual machine without having to involve the networking team.

- Insert L4-7 service graphs in contracts that have a single provider, to dynamically insert into (or remove from) the data path physical or virtual appliances such as firewalls or load balancers.

- Conduct endpoint-to-endpoint troubleshooting sessions, including information related to faults, packets dropped, recent policy changes, network events, and Cisco ACI Traceroute (see Chapter 12, "Troubleshooting and Monitoring," for more details on troubleshooting sessions). This troubleshooting information is extremely helpful because it empowers the virtualization admin with the required tools to identify (and in many cases, resolve) network issues without requiring an ACI expert.

However, some ACI tasks require deeper networking expertise. Consequently, they are not available in the vCenter plug-in but must be performed directly on the APIC. Here are a couple examples:

- Managing external connectivity over L2 or L3 to the ACI fabric over external networks, because this operation typically involves knowledge of routing and Layer 2 protocols.

- Creating L4-7 service graph templates, because expertise in the network service domains (such as from firewall or load balancer specialists) is typically required for this task.

As you can see, the Cisco ACI plug-in augments vCenter with comprehensive network functionality that can be leveraged by the VMware administrator. The plug-in not only empowers the VMware administrator with a tool for advanced virtual network troubleshooting and deployment, but it also provides exhaustive networking information on the complete fabric, including bare-metal workloads and virtual machines in other hypervisors as well as integration with L4-7 physical/virtual network services.

Cisco ACI Coexistence with VMware NSX

In some situations, the virtualization administrator might decide to implement VMware NSX, a hypervisor-based network overlay using VXLAN tunnels between vSphere hosts. Typically, the reasons for doing so are more political than technical, because Cisco ACI addresses most of the challenges that NSX seeks to solve at a much lower cost. Here are some examples:

- Virtual network configuration (without having to involve the network team) through the use of the Cisco ACI plug-in for vCenter

- Additional network security with micro-segmentation

- Dynamic EPG associations for VMs based on attributes such as their names, the operating system running inside, and even custom attributes or tags

- Easy and performant interconnection of data centers over VXLAN, through the ACI Multi-Pod technology.

If even in the light of these facts the virtualization administrator decides to implement NSX, it should be noted that NSX can run on top of ACI as it does on any other physical network infrastructure, because the independence of the underlying network is one of the premises behind the design of NSX. However, you need to be aware that no integration between both technologies is possible. Nevertheless, Cisco ACI's functionality helps to overcome some of the limitations of VMware NSX. Here are some examples:

■ Pervasive Layer 2 domains across the whole data center allow the virtualization administrator to place NSX gateways in any ESX host, instead of dedicating specific ESX clusters for gateway functions. ESX hardware utilization and placement becomes much easier with Cisco ACI.

■ The usage of port profiles guarantees the correct operation and easier management of all necessary ports for different vSphere functions, including VXLAN, VMware vSAN (VMware's storage virtualization solution), and NFS storage and management, allocating the desired amount of bandwidth to each of these functions through the usage of Cisco ACI QoS functionality.

■ Advanced troubleshooting capabilities such as the Troubleshooting Wizard (discussed in Chapter 12) will help the virtualization administrator to quickly locate and fix communication problems between ESX hosts. Unfortunately, Cisco ACI cannot troubleshoot or manage VM-to-VM communication when using NSX, because this traffic is encapsulated inside of VXLAN packets, and therefore the VMs' addresses are in effect obfuscated from ACI.

Regarding the virtual network design, the most efficient option would be having two VDS switches in each ESX host: one ACI-managed VDS or AVS for infrastructure traffic (management, vMotion, NFS, iSCSI, vSAN, and most notably VXLAN), and a second NSX-managed VDS for VM traffic.

Cisco ACI's goal is to make every application in the data center to be deployed quicker, to perform better, and to be managed more efficiently. In this case, NSX is like any other application for Cisco ACI, and thus it can equally benefit from Cisco ACI's improvements over legacy networks.

Microsoft

Cisco ACI can integrate with Microsoft virtualization in two deployment modes:

■ System Center Virtual Machine Manager (SCVMM)

■ Azure Pack

Because Microsoft Azure Pack has recently been superseded by Microsoft Azure Stack, and Azure Stack does not support any network integration other than BGP neighbor adjacencies (which could be configured as "external routed connections" in ACI, but those will be discussed in a separate chapter), this section will focus on SCVMM integration.

Introduction to Microsoft Hyper-V and SCVMM

Microsoft has a hypervisor embedded in Windows Server called Hyper-V. Organizations can use this hypervisor free of charge because it is included in the Windows Server licensing. In order to operate Hyper-V clusters, no actual central management plane is required, but when clusters reach a certain size, it is highly recommended.

System Center Virtual Machine Manager (or SCVMM for short) is the component of the System Center suite that centralizes management of Hyper-V clusters, and it is a required component for the integration with Cisco ACI. In other words, Hyper-V clusters without SCVMM are not supported for this integration.

SCVMM can be installed in standalone mode or in a highly available (HA) mode; Cisco ACI supports both modes for integration.

Naming conventions in SCVMM might not be straightforward for an APIC administrator, so here's a quick cheat sheet with the most important SCVMM networking concepts you should understand:

- **Cloud:** A cloud contains logical networks, and integration with ACI creates resources inside of an existing cloud in SCVMM.

- **Tenant cloud:** SCVMM has the concept of "tenant," which can leverage certain central resources. You can add logical networks to tenant clouds to make them accessible to specific users of the Hyper-V environment.

- **Logical network:** This is an abstract concept that represents a network partition. Equivalent to a VMM domain, a logical network contains logical switches and Hyper-V hosts.

- **Host group:** For ease of management, Hyper-V hosts can be grouped so that when you're adding or removing hosts from a cloud, you can use the host groups rather than the individual hosts.

- **Logical switch:** This is the main component of a logical network.

- **VM Network:** This concept roughly corresponds to a subnet, and in ACI it matches the idea of EPGs.

Preparing for the Integration

Overall, two pieces of software enable integration:

- **APIC SCVMM agent:** This is an application that needs to be installed on the server with SCVMM, and it runs as a Windows service. On one side, it interacts with SCVMM via PowerShell, on the other it exposes a REST API to communicate with Cisco APIC.

- **APIC Hyper-V agent:** This software needs to be installed on every Hyper-V host, and it enhances the capabilities of Microsoft Hyper-V vSwitch and communicates with Cisco ACI leaf switches over the OpFlex protocol.

These two software pieces can be downloaded in a single .zip file from the Cisco website; they require that SCVMM be at least 2012 R2 or later, with Update Rollup 5 or later installed. In addition to installing these two packages, you need to generate and install digital certificates. Refer to the "Cisco ACI Virtualization Guide" at Cisco.com for the latest information about how software versions are supported or how to install the agents and the digital certificates.

After installing the required packages, you can proceed with the creation of the VMM domain in Cisco ACI. The screen for creating a Microsoft-based VMM domain is depicted by Figure 4-34. Once the VMM domain is created in the APIC, the following will be created inside of the cloud specified in the VMM domain:

- A logical network

- A logical switch

- A logical port profile for the Hyper-V host uplinks

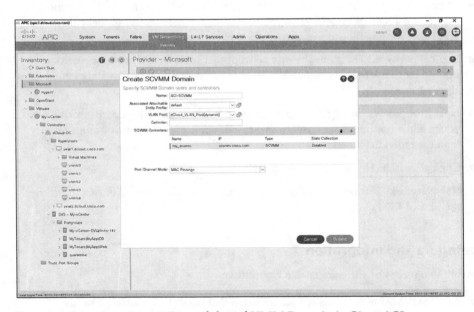

Figure 4-34 *Creating a Microsoft-based VMM Domain in Cisco ACI*

The options you see in this screen have the same meaning as for the VMware-based VMM domains, so they will not be described in this section.

Because the software agent installed in the Hyper-V hosts supports the OpFlex protocol, the APIC can communicate with the agent over the infrastructure VLAN. If you look into the VM networks in SCVMM, you will recognize the infrastructure subnet configured there, which has the name "apicInfra."

Now, the next configuration task involves adding the Hyper-V hosts to the logical switch created by the APIC. You can do this in SCVMM in the Fabric panel. In the properties of a Hyper-V host, you can add the logical switch and specify which physical adapters in the host to use for external connectivity.

After this, you only need to add the logical network to any tenant cloud that you want to integrate with ACI, and the VM networks created by associating the VMM domain with EPGs will be available for those tenants to use. Note that the SCVMM tenant and the ACI tenant concepts are not related to each other. The created VM networks will pick one VLAN out of the VLAN pool associated with the VMM domain to encapsulate the traffic between the Hyper-V host and the Cisco ACI leaf switch.

Micro-Segmentation

Micro-segmentation works in a similar way to the VMware integration. You need to ensure that your Hyper-V hosts are running at least Windows Server 2012 R2 or later with Update Rollup 9 or later installed.

Here are a few remarks regarding how micro-segmentation works concerning the ACI integration with SCVMM:

- As with the VMware integration, the micro-segmentation EPGs will not reflect in SCVMM as a VM network.

- The "custom attribute" and "tag" criteria are not available in rules inside of SCVMM-associated micro-segmentation EPGs, because these concepts do not exist in SCVMM.

- The default attribute precedence order is the same as in AVS (that is, MAC address, then IP address, and so on).

At press time, Cisco ACI 3.0(1) supports intra-EPG isolation enforcement for Microsoft's vSwitch, but not intra-EPG contracts.

Blade Servers and SCVMM Integration

At press time, the integration with SCVMM leverages VLAN technology (VXLAN is not supported) between the Hyper-V hosts and the ACI leaf switches; therefore, you need to observe the guidelines:

- If you are not using Cisco UCS, you want to select **Pre-Deploy** as your **Deployment Immediacy** option when associating an EPG with the VMM domain.

- You need to make sure that the VLANs contained in the VLAN pool are configured in advance in the blade switches, because Cisco ACI will not manage those components.

- If your blade switches do not support bonding together the physical NICs of the Hyper-V hosts (such as Cisco UCS), make sure you select MAC Pinning as the load-balancing algorithm in your Attachable Access Entity Profile.

OpenStack

OpenStack emerged in 2010 as a common project between the company Rackspace and NASA, with the goal of creating an open-source software architecture that enables organizations to deploy private cloud environments.

Initially, OpenStack consisted of a small number of open-source components, each providing a specific functionality required for private cloud. For example, the Nova project was the OpenStack component responsible for compute virtualization, Swift was responsible for object storage, and Quantum (later renamed Neutron) delivered the required networking components.

There were other projects in the initial OpenStack installments, and additional ones have been included with every new release. OpenStack has been managed since 2012 by the OpenStack Foundation, and software releases happen twice a year and are codenamed alphabetically. For example, the 2016 Fall release was named Newton, the 2017 Spring release Ocata, and the 2017 Fall release Pike. From the initial two projects of the Austin release in 2010 (Nova and Swift), the Pike release in 2017 officially consisted of 32 projects. That should give you an idea of the current level of functionality (and complexity) that OpenStack has reached.

To cope with this complexity, a number of companies have created OpenStack distributions with the goal of simplifying the deployment, maintenance, and operations of OpenStack. Although these distributions mostly use the standard upstream open-source components of OpenStack, they might remove elements that are not stable enough or even add new functionality that enhances it (such as installer software, for example).

Additionally, OpenStack's inherent modularity has made possible the appearance of architectures that replace this or that component of OpenStack with something equivalent, such as storage, the hypervisor, or the network. As a consequence, there is not one single OpenStack out there, but many different flavors of it. At the time of this writing, Cisco ACI integrates with, among others, the following OpenStack options:

- Mirantis OpenStack

- OpenStack with an external router

- OpenStack with a VMware hypervisor

- Red Hat OpenStack with OSP (OpenStack Platform) Director

- Red Hat with Ubuntu

As mentioned earlier, OpenStack is a highly modular architecture, and most hypervisors in the market support the Nova APIs so that they can be used in an OpenStack environment. However, with the notable exception of VMware ESX, the Cisco ACI integration with OpenStack supports only KVM (Kernel Virtual Machine) as the hypervisor providing server virtualization in OpenStack compute nodes.

ML2 and Group-Based Policy

Regardless of the OpenStack distribution, the main OpenStack component with which Cisco ACI integrates is, unsurprisingly, OpenStack Networking (also known as Neutron).

Neutron is the component responsible for managing the networking between virtual machines in OpenStack, plus other functions such as IP addressing, DHCP, and routing traffic in and out of the OpenStack environment.

The main networking component in Neutron is the ML2 (Modular Layer 2) plug-in. This is the framework that allows OpenStack to use a variety of L2 options for virtual machine connectivity, including the following:

- Flat network
- VLAN
- VXLAN
- GRE

Out of these options, Cisco ACI supports VLAN and VXLAN encapsulations in ML2.

OpenStack ML2 models the network using some primitives such as "networks" (Layer 2), "subnets," and "routers" (layer 3). Besides, more recently added functionality such as QoS and Layer 4-7 network services are configured outside of ML2.

This fragmentation of network policy, added to the fact that developers using OpenStack are not necessarily networking experts, motivated the creation of the Group-Based Policy (GBP). GBP aims to abstract network policy into concepts more easily understood by non-networking experts, and to consolidate network attributes in a single repository. The OpenStack GBP network policy model matches nicely with Cisco ACI concepts such as endpoint groups and contracts, so it is a great option for integrating Cisco ACI with OpenStack.

It used to be required to pick up either the ML2 or the GBP mode of operation of the Cisco ACI plug-in for OpenStack. However, later versions of the plug-in work in the so-called "universal" mode, meaning that the ML2 and GBP operation modes can coexist in the same OpenStack environment. This makes it much easier for the administrator, because you can install the plug-in, test both modes of operations, and decide which one you like best.

Installing Cisco ACI Integration with OpenStack

Because different OpenStack distributions have different ways of installing and upgrading OpenStack components, a single consolidated installation method for the Cisco ACI plug-in for OpenStack does not exist. For example, the Mirantis OpenStack distribution uses an open-source project called Fuel that's specifically developed to maintain software versions in OpenStack. The Red Hat distribution utilizes its own software distribution package for OpenStack called OpenStack Platform Director (or OSP Director for short), and the installation for the Ubuntu distribution leverages a custom repository server that can be accessed with the **apt-get** command.

However, without going into details of each specific distribution, the installation process roughly looks like this:

- Configure Cisco ACI to enable basic IP communication for the different OpenStack nodes, including the transport of the infrastructure VLAN that will be used for OpFlex communication.

- Basic configuration of the OpenStack nodes, enabling LLDP (this will allow Cisco ACI to learn to which leaf switch ports each compute node is physically connected).

- Install and configure the software in the Neutron network nodes and configure Neutron appropriately.

- Install and configure the OpFlex agent in the Nova compute nodes.

- Start agent services.

- Initialize the ACI OpFlex tenant and create the VMM domain for OpenStack in Cisco ACI.

As you can see, creating the VMM domain is part of the installation process. This is a very important difference when comparing the OpenStack integration with VMware or Microsoft. In OpenStack, the VMM domain is not created from the ACI GUI, API or CLI, but from OpenStack itself. You will actually find no option in the GUI to create an OpenStack VMM domain. And, by the way, this is the same approach that the Contiv and Kubernetes integrations adhere to.

The following sections describe in more detail how these moving parts interact with one another, clarifying their role in the integration between Cisco ACI and OpenStack.

Cisco ACI ML2 Plug-in for OpenStack Basic Operations

The following are some of the functions offered by the Cisco ACI ML2 plug-in for OpenStack:

- Distributed switching

- Distributed routing

- Distributed DHCP

- External connectivity

- Source NAT (SNAT)

- Floating IP addresses

The most prominent characteristic of the Cisco ACI ML2 plug-in is that the original network constructs of OpenStack Neutron remain constant, so "translating" them into Cisco ACI policies is required:

- OpenStack "projects" are equivalent to ACI "tenants." When a project is created in OpenStack, the ML2 plug-in will create a corresponding tenant in Cisco ACI. The name of this tenant will be the concatenation of the OpenStack VMM domain's name and the OpenStack project's name.

- A VRF in the tenant will be created at the same time.

- After the project is created, the next step for the OpenStack administrator is creating OpenStack networks and subnets for the new project. This will create corresponding bridge domains inside the ACI tenant, with the subnets definitions. Additionally, one EPG per each bridge domain (and hence one per each OpenStack network) will be created. As you can see, the ML2 plug-in implies a 1:1 relationship between BDs and EPGs.

- The application network profile encompassing the EPGs in an ACI tenant will be named after the VMM domain.

- Attaching a subnet to a router in OpenStack has the effect of enabling connectivity to that subnet from the others. The effect in ACI is the creation of a permit-all contract that will be applied to the corresponding EPGs.

The Cisco ACI plug-in for OpenStack will replace the functionality of the Open vSwitch agent (otherwise running in the compute nodes) and the L3 agent (otherwise running in the network nodes). If you inspect the Neutron software processes (with the command **neutron agent-list**), you will see that those two process are not started, and in their place the OpFlex Open vSwitch agent will be running in the compute nodes.

Upon a new instance launching (which is typically how virtual machines are referred to in OpenStack), one of the first operations involves providing the instance with an IP address. As mentioned at the beginning of this section, the Cisco ACI ML2 plug-in for OpenStack includes a distributed DHCP function that works in two stages:

1. At instance creation time, the Neutron network nodes will decide different configuration details for the new instance, including its IP address. This information will be published to the corresponding compute nodes with a file named /var/lib/OpFlex-agent-ovs/endpoints.

2. When the new instance issues its DHCP request, the compute node where the instance starts already knows the IP address it is going to get (via the aforementioned file). Therefore, it does not need to forward the DHCP request to the network nodes but instead will answer the request directly.

The distributed nature of DHCP is an important scalability feature of the Cisco ACI integration with OpenStack, which provides a great deal of performance in cases where many instances are started simultaneously.

Cisco ACI ML2 Plug-in for OpenStack Security

As you would assume, there is a virtual bridge inside of each OpenStack compute host where instances are connected, typically called br-int (which stands for "bridge-integration," because it is where instance traffic comes together). However, instances are not directly connected to this bridge but rather indirectly, as Figure 4-35 shows.

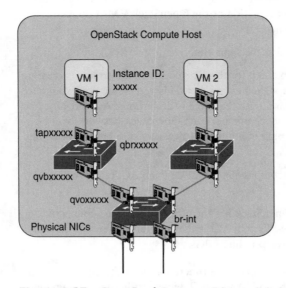

Figure 4-35   *OpenStack Instance Connectivity to the br-int Bridge*

As you can see, there is an additional Linux bridge between the instance and the br-int bridge. This additional virtual switch (prefixed with the string "qbr") is a dedicated bridge per virtual machine, and it serves multiple purposes, such as the following:

■ You can inspect traffic to and from the OpenStack instance because you can run tcpdump in the OpenStack compute node on the "tap" interface, which is visible to the host operating system.

■ Similarly, you can apply network filters on the "tap" interface, typically using the Linux software-based firewall iptables.

Neutron ML2 does not support sophisticated concepts such as contracts, subjects, and filters, and network security is provided in the form of "security groups." As explained in previous sections, when two subnets are connected to a router, Cisco ACI allows all traffic between them with permit-all contracts. If the OpenStack administrator restricts traffic between two subnets using security groups, these network security filters will be deployed by the OpFlex Agent in the compute nodes using iptables rules applied to the tap interfaces of the corresponding instances.

These rules can be inspected in the compute nodes using the iptables commands, but they are not visible from Cisco ACI.

Cisco ACI ML2 Plug-in for OpenStack and Network Address Translation

Network address translation (NAT) is a critical functionality for OpenStack that enables on one hand egress communication from all instances to the outside world (actually, to the outside of the OpenStack project) and on the other hand ingress connectivity externally to specific instances.

A critical component in order for both ingress and egress communication to occur is an external routed network (also known as "L3out"), which can be either shared by multiple OpenStack projects (ACI tenants) or dedicated to specific projects. A shared L3out can be created by the plug-in installation process or manually by the Cisco ACI administrator in the common tenant, usually using the default VRF.

If a project is using this shared external routed network connection, a "shadow" L3out will be created inside of the corresponding tenant.

Egress communication is performed with source NAT (SNAT). A specific public IP address is assigned to each Nova compute node out of a subnet specified in the configuration file for the Cisco ACI plug-in (etc/neutron/plugins/ml2/ml2_config/ml2_conf_cisco_apic.ini) with the option host_pool_cidr. An additional bridge domain (with a corresponding associated EPG) is created in the common tenant. Figure 4-36 shows this setup distributed across a project-specific tenant and the common tenant.

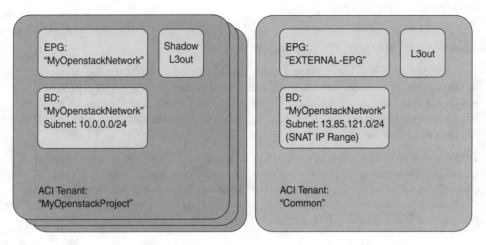

Figure 4-36 *External Routed Network and SNAT Architecture for the ML2 Plug-In*

The SNAT address range is configured in the bridge domain and set to be advertised externally over the external routed network. In the EPG, you can see the IP address assignments out of the SNAT address block to the specific compute nodes.

When traffic leaves an instance for an IP address not known inside of its tenant, a default route will point it to the shadow L3out. However, the compute node will first "source NAT" the traffic to its allocated IP address, and the traffic will be classified by ACI as in the SNAT EPG in the common tenant. Return traffic will follow the inverse path.

The second function of network address translation in OpenStack is allowing ingress connectivity to specific instances. This is known in OpenStack as a "floating IP address." Essentially, public IP addresses are assigned to instances (and not to compute nodes, as in the case of SNAT), and traffic addressed to those public addresses from outside the OpenStack cloud is sent to those instances. Additionally, this public IP address will be used for egress connectivity, instead of the SNAT IP address allocated to the compute node that would be used in the absence of a floating IP address.

The IP address range used for floating IP addresses will be configured in the bridge domain in the common tenant, next to the SNAT IP address range, and also needs to be set to "advertised externally." You can define a single IP address range to be shared across all OpenStack projects, which will be allocated to a single EPG, or you can use different ranges (and therefore EPGs) for different tenants so that you can control traffic between EPGs with contracts.

For example, if you have a "common services" OpenStack project as well as other individual OpenStack projects, and you have allocated different floating IP address ranges to each project, you can control which projects can access the common services tenant through contracts between the EPGs mapped to different floating IP address ranges.

You can inspect the floating IP address ranges from OpenStack with the command **neutron net-list**, and in ACI you can look at the bridge domain created in the common tenant for the Cisco ACI ML2 plug-in.

Cisco ACI GBP Plug-in for OpenStack

As the previous section has explained, the Cisco ML2 plug-in offers some performance optimizations to OpenStack (such as the distributed nature of forwarding, DHCP, and NAT), and above all, it offers a simplification of the management of OpenStack networking constructs. However, it does not add any functionality that is not present in the native Neutron ML2 plug-in.

That is the main reason why the Group-Based Policy was developed, in order to enhance OpenStack networking functionality with a rich declarative model, which happens to closely resemble that of Cisco ACI. The Group-Based Policy (GBP) was introduced with the Juno OpenStack release, so it has already gone through a considerable maturation process and has reached a good degree of stability.

GBP is not by any means specific to Cisco ACI, and it supports many networking technologies. Given its declarative nature, GBP drivers translate intent-based statements to any GBP-based network plug-in. Actually, a Neutron plug-in has been developed for GBP that translates GBP policy to Neutron/ML2 primitives.

GBP consists of the following objects:

- **Policy Target:** Typically the NIC of an OpenStack instance.

- **Policy Group (or Policy Target Group):** Comparable to an EPG in Cisco ACI. It contains policy targets.

- **Policy Filter:** Comparable to a filter in Cisco ACI. It defines traffic-matching rules.

- **Policy Action:** A set of possible actions to be carried out with traffic (such as allow or redirect).

- **Policy Rule:** Comparable to a subject in Cisco ACI. It contains sets of filters and actions.

- **Policy Rule Set:** Comparable to a contract in Cisco ACI. It contains policy rules.

GBP also contemplates the option of inserting (and removing) network services in the traffic flow, which is commonly known as *network service chaining* or *network service insertion*, and is equivalent to a Cisco ACI service graph. Objects used for chaining include service chain nodes, service chain specs, and service chain instances.

There are other GBP networking primitives that specify forwarding characteristics:

- **Layer 2 Policy:** Comparable to a BD in Cisco ACI. it is a set of policy groups associated with a single Layer 3 policy.

- **Layer 3 Policy:** Comparable to a VRF in Cisco ACI.

- **Network Service Policy:** Specific parameters required for service chains.

As you can see, the GBP object model is very close to the ACI model. The Neutron driver for GBP performs a task that can be considered the opposite to the translation model of the Cisco ACI ML2 plug-in: It translates GBP objects to Neutron ML2 concepts.

Another interesting aspect of GBP is the concept of "sharing." This is especially useful when sharing services such as external routed connections, which is simplified by setting the **shared** attribute of an object to **True** at creation time.

GBP can be used, like the rest of the OpenStack components, from the command line (unsurprisingly using the command **gbp**), from the OpenStack Horizon GUI, or from the OpenStack orchestration tool Heat. You can find in Cisco.com a "GBP User Guide," but to give you a glimpse of the way it works, here are some of the commands that manage GBP objects in OpenStack (and simultaneously in Cisco ACI as well):

- **gbp policy-classifier-create:** Creates a policy classifier (a filter in ACI)

- **gbp policy-rule-create:** Creates a policy rule (a subject in ACI)

- **gbp policy-rule-set-create:** Creates a policy rule set (a contract in ACI)

- **gbp group-create:** Creates a policy group (an EPG in ACI)

- **gbp update-group** *group_name* **--consumed-policy-rule-sets** *rule_set_name*: Consumes a ruleset (contract) in a group (EPG)

- **gbp update-group** *group_name* **--provided-policy-rule-sets** *rule_set_name*: Provides a ruleset (contract) from a group (EPG)

- **gbp nat-pool-create:** Creates an IP address range for floating IP addresses

The list goes on and on, but you get the point: Managing OpenStack networking with the Cisco ACI plug-in is mostly identical to managing Cisco ACI itself.

Docker: Project Contiv

Linux containers have taken the IT industry by storm during the last 5 years, mostly fueled by the innovation and simplification brought by a company called Docker.

Essentially, Linux containers enable the possibility of running applications on a Linux operating system without having to install any library, module, or dependency. It is sort of like a virtual machine, but much lighter, because it does not include a full operating system. That makes Linux containers easier to distribute, and makes them the perfect platform for encapsulating applications throughout their full lifecycle, from development through testing and staging until production.

Docker Networking

When you install Docker on a Linux system, one of the objects that's created is a network bridge called "docker0" and a private network range. In other words, a virtual switch.

When creating a container, you have a variety of network options, the default being allocating a private IP address to the Linux container out of the private IP range and connecting it to a Linux bridge called docker0 (created when Docker is installed). To achieve communication with the outside network, the bridge will translate the container's private IP address to the actual IP address of a physical network adapter of the host, not too different from how your home router enables Internet connectivity for the systems in your private network, as Figure 4-37 illustrates.

Each container has its own Ethernet interface isolated in a dedicated network namespace. The namespace is a fundamental concept for Linux containers, which are a sort of walled garden that limit the visibility of certain objects. For example, Container 1 can see its own Ethernet interface, but no other.

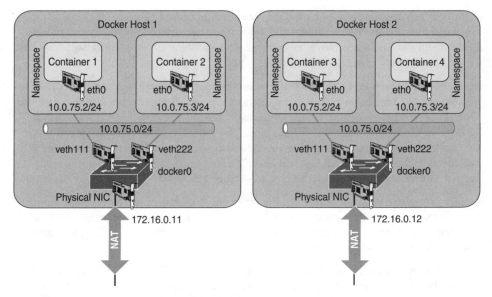

Figure 4-37   *Default Docker Networking in a Single Host*

This setup, although very simple to implement for individual hosts, has some drawbacks when implemented in clusters that include multiple Docker servers:

- When two Docker containers in different hosts communicate (say, for example, Containers 1 and 3), they do not see their real IP addresses, but their translated IP addresses (the host IP addresses 172.16.0.11 and 172.16.0.12 in the figure). This has adverse effects, for example, when implementing security policies.

- Docker containers accessible from outside the host need to expose specific ports so that the docker0 bridge will perform port address translation (PAT) for incoming traffic. This means that two containers in the same host cannot expose the same port, which imposes additional coordination to make sure that this type of conflict does not happen.

- A way to avoid this coordination would be dynamic port allocation, but this in turn brings its own challenges, such as letting all others containers know on which port a certain container is listening.

As a consequence of these challenges, Docker developed in 2015 the Container Networking Model (CNM), a framework that aimed to simplify creating alternative networking stacks for Docker containers. Docker even refactored the docker0 implementation and built it on top of CNM, to make it equal to other CNM-based network plug-ins. This is what Docker refers to as "batteries included but swappable." Docker comes with a default implementation (in this case, networking), but if you don't like it, you can easily replace it with a custom one.

A number of network plug-ins have been developed in order to change Docker's networking behavior, and on the other hand Docker's native networking implementation has evolved and now includes an overlay concept. This proliferation of network solutions has created confusion in some situations.

Project Contiv has been created in order to bring clarity into the Docker network plug-in ecosystem. The idea is having a single plug-in to support all popular networking options. One of the main ideas behind Contiv is getting rid of the network address translation inherent in Docker's default networking model, by replicating the networking concept that has been successful in the server virtualization arena and supporting pure Layer 3 networks, overlays using VXLAN, and Layer 2 networks using VLANs. You can find further information about Contiv at http://contiv.github.io.

Contiv centralizes network policy in a highly available cluster of master nodes (running the "netmaster" Contiv function). Policy is then distributed to each container host (running the "netplugin" Contiv agent). In order to change the networking policy, you interact with the netmaster function over its API.

The integration between Contiv and Cisco ACI supports both VLAN and VXLAN encapsulation, and it essentially maps a VLAN or a VXLAN segment to an EPG in Cisco ACI, as Figure 4-38 shows.

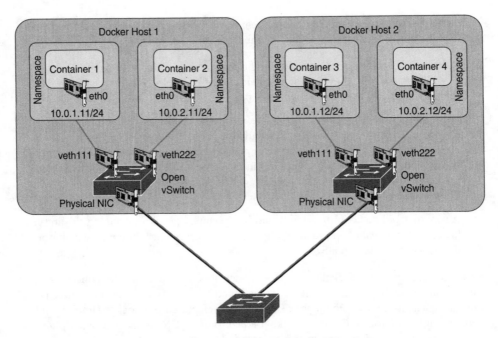

Figure 4-38   *VLAN/VXLAN Encapsulation Using Contiv*

The integration with Contiv, however, follows a different pattern than other ACI integrations such as VMware, Microsoft, OpenStack, and Kubernetes, because it is not based in the VMM concept. Instead, the Contiv administrator will create objects that result in similar constructs in Cisco ACI.

For example, without going into the details of Contiv syntax (you can get the full commands from http://contiv.github.io/documents/networking/aci_ug.html), a possible sequence of commands might be the following:

1. Create external contracts (referring to ACI contracts).

2. Create a network (matching the IP address space and gateway of the BD, or a subset).

3. Create a(n) (empty) policy for internal traffic filtering between the containers.

4. Add rules to the policy.

5. Create groups, associated with the policy and/or the external contracts.

6. Create an application policy containing the groups. In this moment, the application policy will be deployed to Cisco ACI in the form of an application network profile, and the groups will be translated into EPGs.

Cisco ACI integrates with Contiv so that the policies created in Contiv are actually deployed in Cisco ACI, and networking in the Docker hosts is configured so that traffic flows through ACI in order for network policies to be enforced correctly. For example, Figure 4-39 shows what a network policy looks like in the Contiv interface.

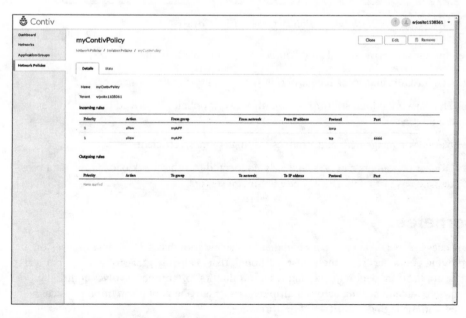

Figure 4-39 *Network Policy in Contiv GUI*

And Figure 4-40 illustrates how Contiv has deployed that policy to Cisco ACI in the form of EPGs and contracts. Notice that all relevant objects match in both GUIs: EPG name, contract name, port numbers, and so on.

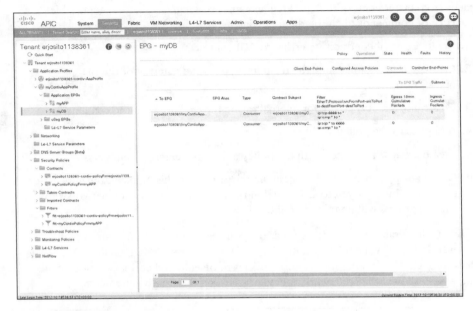

Figure 4-40 *Cisco ACI Network Policy Created by Contiv*

The integration between ACI and Contiv brings multiple benefits:

- Cisco ACI brings its rich networking functionality to Docker networking.

- The network administrator is aware of network policies deployed by the Docker administrator.

- Network management and troubleshooting are more efficient.

- Docker containers can be seamlessly connected to other workloads in the data center, such as virtual machines and bare-metal servers.

Kubernetes

As successful as Docker's initial container implementation has been, it just focuses on deploying containers to a single host. Although that is already great for a developer testing an application, deploying containers in production oftentimes involves additional operations such as scaling across multiple hosts, restarting containers upon physical issues, and managing security and performance.

To address these challenges, a number of so-called container orchestration frameworks have emerged, such as Docker Swarm, Mesosphere DC/OS, and Kubernetes. Even though the jury is still out as to whether one of these is on its way to becoming a de facto standard, the industry seems to be rallying around Kubernetes. For example, both Mesosphere and Docker have announced additional support for Kubernetes in their orchestrators, and a number of enterprise-grade container platforms such as Pivotal Cloud Foundry and Red Hat OpenShift have chosen Kubernetes as their underlying technology.

The rise of the public cloud has also contributed to the popularity of Linux containers in general, and Kubernetes in particular. Due to their portability, containers are a popular option for making sure that an application can be deployed to on-premises infrastructure or to the public cloud, without any code changes. All major cloud vendors (Amazon Web Services, Google Cloud Platform, and Microsoft Azure) support some form of Kubernetes cluster. Consequently, having an application containerized in Kubernetes immediately grants you the possibility of moving it to the public cloud.

Cisco ACI not only integrates with multiple server virtualization technologies, as previous sections in this chapter have shown, but with the leading container orchestration frameworks, including Kubernetes. Additional Cisco ACI has introduced in its version 3.1 integration with Red Hat Openshift Container Platform and Cloud Foundry (the latter as beta feature) as additional container platforms. This chapter will focus on Kubernetes, since Openshift and Cloud Foundry can be considered as derivatives from Kubernetes.

Another interesting functionality included in Cisco ACI 3.1 is the support for Kubernetes deployments on VMware vSphere virtual machines. The difficulty of this type of deployments is that there are two virtual switches (the vSphere virtual switch and the Kubernetes virtual switch) between the Cisco ACI leaf switch and the container itself.

Kubernetes Networking Model

Kubernetes' networking model drastically differs from Docker's. Much like Docker created the Container Networking Model (CNM) as a network plug-in framework, the Cloud Native Computing Foundation (CNCF, the organization governing the development of Kubernetes) has developed the Container Networking Interface (CNI) to make possible network plug-ins for Kubernetes.

Kubernetes' smallest network unit is the pod, which is a group of containers that are handled as a single entity. Containers inside of a pod share some of their Linux namespaces, which means they can communicate with each other easier. Pods are sometimes defined with a single container, in which case you can think of a pod as just a wrapper for a container. Each pod gets an IP address, and network policies are defined at the pod level. Kubernetes is very adamant about one general rule that every CNI-based network plug-in should adhere to: no network address translation (NAT), both for the communication between pods and between Kubernetes nodes (hosts).

Cisco ACI integrates with Kubernetes using the CNI framework without requiring any NAT, as mandated by Kubernetes. This integration supports at the time of this writing Kubernetes version 1.6, and it requires Cisco ACI 3.0(1) or greater.

The integration model is similar to OpenStack: installing the components required for the integration with Cisco ACI on the Kubernetes master nodes will create (among other things) a Kubernetes VMM domain in Cisco ACI, where ACI admins can keep track of the physical nodes in a Kubernetes cluster, or the different nodes that have been deployed.

When integrating Cisco ACI with Kubernetes, you need four distinct subnets:

■ **Pod subnet:** Pods will receive an IP address out of this range, independent of the node in which they are instantiated.

■ **Node subnet:** Kubernetes nodes will have IP addresses out of this subnet.

■ **Node Service subnet:** Pods can internally expose services using IP addresses out of this subnet. It is a sort of embedded load balancer in Kubernetes, where nodes are aware of exposed services and can further send traffic to the corresponding pods.

■ **External Service subnet:** This is the only subnet that is required to be advertised to the external world. Services that are to be externally available become an IP address and TCP port out of the External Service subnet. Cisco ACI will load-balance the traffic to the corresponding Node Service subnet IP addresses, and after that Kubernetes internal mechanisms will redirect the traffic to the individual pods.

Figure 4-41 describes this setup (except the Node subnet, which is not visible to the pods or the users).

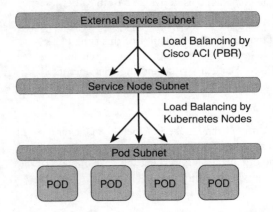

Figure 4-41 *Load-Balancing Layers in Kubernetes with Cisco ACI*

These two layers of load balancing exist because of the Kubernetes architecture. Kubernetes only defines load balancing at the Service Node tier, which is required so that groups of pods can internally expose services. Kubernetes does not define how to perform external load-balancing to groups of pods exposed to the external world, and this is where Cisco ACI can load-balance external traffic using Policy-Based Routing (PBR) to the corresponding service node IP addresses and ports.

Isolation Models

One fundamental premise that has determined what the integration between Cisco ACI and Kubernetes looks like is to not impose any burden on Kubernetes users (application developers), because that would negatively impact its adoption. Linux containers in general and Kubernetes containers in particular are technologies that have been created and made popular by developers. If creating applications with Cisco ACI and Kubernetes were too complicated for developers, they would just use something else.

Consequently, here are the different isolation models that will be described in this section and the following ones:

- **Cluster isolation:** All deployments in all namespaces (except for the kube-system namespace) are assigned to a single EPG. This is the default isolation mode that mimics Kubernetes operation without Cisco ACI if no additional option is specified when deploying an application on a Kubernetes cluster.

- **Namespace isolation:** Kubernetes namespaces are sort of like logical folders where applications are deployed (not to be confused with Linux namespaces, an operating system technology that enables Linux containers). You can optionally assign specific Kubernetes namespaces and all applications contained in them to separate EPGs. This kind of isolation is similar to a per-department isolation, assuming that each Kubernetes namespace represents something like a department or a division in an organization.

- **Deployment isolation:** Kubernetes deployments are a group of pods responsible for a single application and can be managed as a single entity. Developers can also map individual deployments to separate EPGs, in order to isolate applications from each other.

Any Kubernetes deployment that does not specify any network policy will work as well with Cisco ACI integration in the cluster isolation mode. However, developers will have the option to configure additional security policies if they want to assign a namespace or a deployment to an EPG different from the default one.

When you install the Cisco ACI integration in a Kubernetes cluster, three EPGs will be created in ACI (in a configurable tenant and application profile):

- **kube-nodes:** Kubernetes nodes will be assigned to this EPG.

- **kube-system:** Special pods running in the kube-system namespace will be assigned to this EPG.

- **kube-default:** Any pod created in a namespace other than kube-system will be assigned to this EPG.

When you install a Kubernetes cluster, a number of services for the cluster are provided using Kubernetes pods. Some prominent examples of these services are DNS and etcd (a distributed key-value store that acts as the configuration database for Kubernetes). These special pods are deployed in a special namespace called kube-system, to differentiate them from the rest. To honor this status, Cisco ACI assigns system pods by default to the kube-system EPG and preconfigures some contracts that control which other EPGs can access services such as ARP, DNS, kube-API, and Healthcheck.

When you deploy pods to Kubernetes without any additional options, they will be placed in the kube-default EPG, thus mimicking Kubernetes behavior without segmentation. However, you can optionally deploy specific pods to a separate EPG if you desire to have additional security. Here are the steps for doing so:

1. Create a new EPG in the Kubernetes tenant in Cisco ACI.

2. Create the new pods/deployments/namespaces in Kubernetes associated with the new EPG using annotations.

The next sections include additional details about these two steps.

Creating a New EPG for Kubernetes Pods

As described in the previous section, by default all non-system pods are assigned to the kube-default EPG. If you want to override this behavior, you first need to create a new EPG in the Kubernetes tenant (created when the software for ACI integration was installed in Kubernetes).

After creating the new EPG, you need to make sure it will have connectivity to the system pods and to the external network by providing or consuming contracts:

■ If the pods in the new EPG are to have external connectivity, consume the kube-l3out-allow-all contract from the common tenant.

■ Consume the arp and dns contracts from the Kubernetes tenant.

■ Provide the arp and health-check contracts from the Kubernetes tenant.

Figure 4-42 describes the contracts that need to be consumed and provided by custom Kubernetes EPGs.

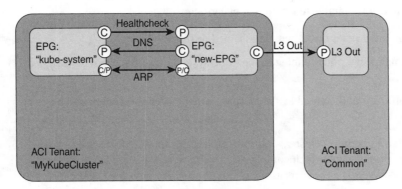

Figure 4-42   *Contract Design for Custom Kubernetes EPGs*

Assigning a Deployment or a Namespace to an EPG with Annotations

Two concepts still need to be defined before we begin this section. The first one is a Kubernetes *deployment*. Essentially, a deployment is a set of Kubernetes pods where you define important attributes such as the containers to be placed inside of each pod, the image of the individual containers, and how many replicas of the pods are required for scalability reasons.

Deployments are an important concept in Kubernetes because they allow the administrator not to have to work with individual pods. For example, if you want to increase the number of pods for a certain application tier, you would just modify the **replicas** property of the corresponding deployment.

Similarly, you do not want to assign individual pods to an EPG, but to deployments. This would have the effect of assigning all replicas (pods) immediately to the EPG.

You can optionally decide to assign all deployments (not just individual deployments) that are created in a certain Kubernetes namespace. As explained previously, Kubernetes namespaces are typically created for specific development teams or projects, so it makes sense to have a certain degree of network isolation based on Kubernetes namespaces.

Kubernetes uses a sophisticated system of metadata to signal user-defined properties of individual objects. This metadata is called an *annotation*, which is essentially a key-value pair. If you are familiar with VMware vSphere, annotations are very similar to vSphere custom attributes or tags. For example, the way to assign pods to a service is by configuring a tag in a deployment and then matching that tag in the service.

When Kubernetes is integrated with Cisco ACI, deployments and namespaces are allocated to EPGs using this Kubernetes philosophy as well. For example, in order to assign a deployment to a certain EPG, you would add the annotation "OpFlex.cisco.com/endpoint-group" to the deployment with the value you can see in the following **kubectl** command:

```
kubectl annotate deployment myDeployment OpFlex.cisco.com/endpoint-
group='{"tenant":"tenant","app-profile":"app-profile","name":"epg"}'
```

Kubernetes users and administrators can use the **kubectl** command to manage the Kubernetes clusters and deploy applications. It can run in any host or even from the user's desktop, and it connects to the Kubernetes API remotely and securely.

There are other possibilities for assigning an annotation, such as using the **acikubectl** command (specific to the integration with Cisco ACI) or specifying the annotation directly in the YAML file that is used to create a deployment.

The process for assigning a complete Kubernetes namespace to an EPG (and therefore all objects that are created in the namespace) is exactly the same: Add a Kubernetes annotation to the namespace using either the **kubectl** or **acikubectl** command.

Note the flexibility of this scheme. By using annotations, you can assign any deployment or any namespace (including all containing deployments) to any given EPG in Cisco ACI.

Visibility in ACI for Kubernetes Objects

One of the most remarkable added values of Cisco ACI for Kubernetes clusters is the consolidated visibility that the network administrator has over networking in the container layer, matching the network functionality for other workload types:

■ Pods will be displayed in the Operational panels of the corresponding EPGs as endpoints. Consequently, other endpoint-based tools such as the Endpoint Tracker and the Troubleshooting Wizard can be used as well.

■ The VMM domain for a Kubernetes cluster will show the physical Kubernetes nodes, the namespaces configured in a cluster, and the services, deployments, replica sets, and pods defined in each namespace.

■ The L4-7 configuration in the common tenant will show information about how many Kubernetes nodes have existing pods in which to load-balance external traffic to specific services that are externally exposed.

■ Traffic counters and statistics for flows that are allowed or dropped by the contracts governing the communication between Kubernetes EPGs are very useful when troubleshooting connectivity problems.

The integration with Cisco ACI not only provides automated creation of load-balancing and isolation policies for Kubernetes workloads, but it also enables the Cisco ACI administrator to manage the Kubernetes network exactly the same way as the virtual or physical fabric in the data center.

Public Cloud Integration

This chapter would not be complete without a reference to public cloud environments. With the advent of public cloud computing, more and more customers are shifting their applications to environments such as Amazon Web Services, Google Cloud Platform, and Microsoft Azure.

Cisco has publicly announced a new extension to ACI called the ACI Virtual Edge (AVE) that will make possible new scenarios for hybrid clouds, such as extending network policy by configuring security objects in the cloud from the APIC, or integrating Cisco ACI with software-based networking services running in the public cloud.

Although AVE is not available in the market at press time, its announcement has the potential to dramatically change the way organizations look at hybrid scenarios with the public cloud.

Summary

Modern data centers have many workloads deployed as virtual machines in different hypervisors, and increasingly as Docker containers using orchestration frameworks such as Kubernetes. Server virtualization and containers have increased data center efficiency and enabled concepts such as DevOps. However, they have brought along some challenges as well, such as an increasing complexity and heterogeneity, especially in the connectivity area.

Cisco ACI is the only technology on the market that provides a consistent network policy across bare-metal servers as well as server virtualization technologies such as VMware, Microsoft, Red Hat Virtualization and OpenStack, and Linux container frameworks including Kubernetes, Red Hat Openshift and Cloud Foundry containers. It offers the following benefits:

- Consistent security policies and micro-segmentation for all applications, no matter where they run. This enables hybrid applications as well, where different tiers are deployed using different technologies or even different orchestrators. For example, while the web tier could use Linux containers, the application servers might be virtualized, and the database might stay on a bare-metal server.

- Agile network configuration, because network deployments can be programmatically rolled out using modern REST APIs and software development kits (SDK). VMware professionals can configure the network right from vCenter.

- Integration with a solution such as OpenStack, Kubernetes or Openshift does not impose any constraint on developers, and allows them to use the constructs they know while leveraging enterprise-grade networking with additional security.

- Cisco ACI's embedded data center interconnection technology enables deploying applications across availability zones, or even across geographically separated regions.

- With the upcoming integration between Cisco ACI and public cloud providers such as AWS, Google, and Microsoft Azure with the Cisco ACI Virtual Edge, Cisco ACI truly becomes the only data center network that can provide network policy to every workload on every cloud.

Chapter 5

Introduction to Networking with ACI

Networking in ACI is different. It's a good different: a step forward. It's not different in the manner in which the protocols work. ACI uses standards-based protocols. It's different because the networking exists only to support the policy. The networking constructs inside of ACI exist because the devices we attach to the network talk in this language. Our goal is to attach devices to the network in a way that they can understand in order to communicate with them and then control them with policy.

The underlying ACI network is the highest-performing, most robust network that can be built using today's protocols. It is truly a next-generation data center network. For example, Cisco has eliminated risk by removing Spanning Tree inside of the ACI fabric. ACI is a zero-trust network. ACI uses Virtual Extensible LAN (VXLAN) over a stable Layer 3 network for Layer 2 connectivity and resilience. ACI has increased availability and performance with anycast gateways. The list goes on and on. Setting up and maintaining this type of network on your own would be very complex—and for most, it would be unsupportable. In ACI, the controllers do the majority of the work for you with policy.

The policy in ACI also helps remove barriers that have existed in the past—barriers in the form of limitations due to IP address, subnet, and virtual local area network (VLAN). In this new way of networking with policy, we separate the workloads from those constraints and put them in groups. We then control how one group can talk to another with a contract. These groups and contracts allow us the flexibility of changing how one device talks to another without having to change the IP address, subnet, or VLAN. This type of flexibility was not realistic in previous network designs, and certainly not as a single point of control for all of your devices, both virtual, or physical. We will examine these and other concepts, as listed here:

- Groups and contracts
- Network constructs in ACI
- Connecting devices to the fabric
- Network-centric mode
- Migrating workloads to the fabric

It is important to keep an open mind in this and the following chapters and to revisit topics for additional clarification. As your journey to learn and leverage the concepts of ACI progresses, you will recognize the enhanced capabilities of ACI versus what is available with other network designs.

Exploring Networking in ACI

Networking in ACI has both similarities with and distinctions from the traditional networks many enterprises have in place today. A Layer 3 gateway in ACI is synonymous with a Layer 3 gateway in a traditional network. Link Layer Discovery Protocol in ACI works the same as it would in a traditional network.

The traditional networking functions have also been improved upon in many ways. The Layer 3 gateway is now an anycast gateway, where every member is active, and instances can exist on one or many leafs in the fabric. ACI also introduces new features such as groups, contracts, and bridge domains. In this chapter, we will be examining how to use all of these features together to create a data center network.

Groups and Contracts

Groups or endpoint groups (EPGs) and contracts are the heart of ACI. The statement can be made that groups and contracts are the most important concept you will learn about in ACI. When Cisco created ACI, it was looking for a better way to build and manage a network. Examining other areas of IT, Cisco found that the easiest way to manage devices was to put them into groups and control how one group is allowed to talk to another group. The construct we use to control this communication is called a contract. With contracts, we control security, routing, switching, quality of service (QoS), and Layer 4 through Layer 7 device insertion. Nothing happens in ACI without groups and contracts. Because this is a zero-trust network by default, communication is blocked in hardware until a policy consisting of groups and contracts is defined. Over time we have given names to the different levels of granularity with which you can apply policy with groups and contracts in ACI. For review, the levels of granularity are as follows:

- **Network-centric mode:** A starting point for many customers, where groups and contracts are applied in a very open and basic way to replicate their current networking environment. Groups are implemented such that an EPG equals a VLAN. The network can be made to operate in trust-based mode, meaning you will not need to use contracts because security will be disabled. Or, if the network is left in zero-trust mode, the contracts used will be very open, allowing all communication between two groups. This allows customers to become familiar with ACI before consuming more advanced features. Customers also do not usually use service insertion in this mode. When enterprises are ready to move forward with more advanced features, they can pick individual devices or applications to apply advanced levels of security or features such as service insertion.

- **Hybrid mode:** A mode that borrows features from network-centric and application-centric modes. Enterprises running in this mode are using additional features and levels of security. Your ACI network may be running in network-centric mode with the addition of integrated services and/or more granular contracts. You may be running some of your network in network-centric mode, and other parts where groups and contracts are defined on an application-by-application basis.

- **Application-centric mode:** Application-centric mode gives ACI users the highest level of visibility and security. In this mode, we define groups and contracts based on the individual applications they service. In this mode, groups may contain an entire application, or we may break the applications up into tiers based on function. We can then secure communications by only allowing the traffic that should be allowed between certain tiers or devices. We also have the ability to insert services on a hop-by-hop or tier-by-tier basis. This is the zero-trust model that most enterprises are trying to take advantage of for some or all of their applications. This mode also offers us the ability to track application health and performance on an application-by-application basis.

The point of the preceding explanations is that each of these modes uses the group and contract model. Sometimes there is confusion when we say mode X, Y, or Z. It sounds like we are flipping a switch to change ACI into something different. In reality, it's a friendly name given to the amount of configuration and work effort that is required when you choose to implement one configuration type/mode or the other.

Note   One of the wonderful things about ACI is its dynamic nature. If you are considering adding additional features, you have the ability to spin up a tenant on the fly and test proposed changes without affecting production. This is a great way test configuration elements when moving from network-centric mode to hybrid mode to application-centric mode. It is always prudent to reference the scalability guide for the software release you are working with when designing or making changes to your ACI network. It is recommended that you use ACI Optimizer to examine the resource requirements of your specific design or proposed changes. We will explore ACI Optimizer in chapter 12. Additional information on ACI Optimizer can also be found here: https://www.cisco.com/c/en/us/td/docs/switches/datacenter/aci/apic/sw/kb/b_KB_Using_ACI_Optimizer.html.

Let's explore groups in more detail. Cisco ACI can classify three types of endpoints:

- Physical endpoints
- Virtual endpoints
- External endpoints (endpoints that send traffic to the Cisco ACI fabric from the outside)

The administrator determines how the hardware and software classifies the traffic. Some versions of hardware and software have different classification capabilities, which we will discuss later. A group can contain one device or many devices. A single device can be a member of one or more groups based on its connectivity to the network. A server with two network interface cards may have its production-facing interface in a group called "web servers" and another interface dedicated to backups in a group called "backup." You can then control the communication of these groups individually through the use of contracts. By default, all devices inside of the same group can talk to each other freely. This behavior can be modified with a feature called *intra*-EPG isolation, which is similar to a private VLAN where communication between the members of a group is not allowed. Or, intra-EPG contracts can be used to only allow specific communications between devices in an EPG. In all configurations, members are always allowed to talk to the Switchted Virtual Interfaces or gateways that exist within their associated bridge domains. A group can only be associated with one bridge domain at a time. Multiple EPGs can exist in the same bridge domain.

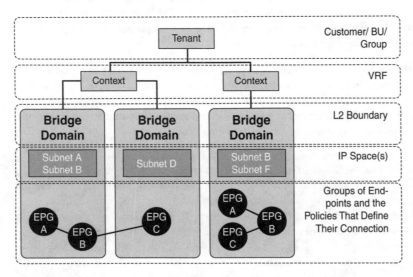

Figure 5-1 *ACI Policy Hierarchy*

Notice the groups depicted in Figure 5-1. EPGs A and B will only be able to use the SVIs for subnets A and B. You will also be able to add a device from either subnet to either group. This highlights the flexibility of having more than one subnet associated with a bridge domain. EPG C will only be able to use the SVI for subnet D, and therefore you can only add devices from subnet D to EPG C. Another, less frequently used option is to associate the subnet with the EPG. Only devices from that group would be able to use that SVI versus every group in the bridge domain having access to the SVI. From the group standpoint, this association of bridge domains to groups only influences which devices can be put into which groups. It does not have any effect on the capability for groups to communicate with one another. We will cover the network implications of the bridge domain with which a group is associated in the next section.

Three different types of groups are available within ACI. The first group is a traditional end point group (EPG). The second is a microsegmented EPG. The third is an external EPG that is created when we connect to an external network, outside of the fabric.

When you create an external routed connection (L3 Out) or an external bridged connection (L2 Out), you also create a new EPG associated with that connection. The devices that are reachable via these external connections become associated with the newly created EPG. Communication to these devices will be controlled based on the configuration of the external EPG and the contracts between it and other devices on the network.

Using traditional and microsegmented EPGs, you can assign a workload to an EPG as follows:

- Map an EPG statically to a port and VLAN.

- Map an EPG statically to a VLAN switchwide on a leaf.

- Map an EPG to a virtual machine manager (VMM) domain (followed by the assignment of vNICs to the associated port group).

- Map a base EPG to a VMM domain and create microsegments based on virtual machine attributes (followed by the assignment of vNICs to the base EPG).

- Map a base EPG to a bare-metal domain or a VMM domain and create microsegments based on the IP address (followed by the assignment of vNICs to the base EPG).

Note If you configure EPG mapping to a VLAN switchwide (using a static leaf binding), Cisco ACI configures all leaf ports as Layer 2 ports. If you then need to configure an L3 Out connection on this same leaf, these ports cannot then be configured as Layer 3 ports. This means that if a leaf is both a computing leaf and a border leaf, you should use EPG mapping to a port and VLAN, not switchwide to a VLAN.

The administrator may configure classification based on virtual machine attributes, and, depending on the combination of software and hardware, that may translate into a VLAN-based classification or MAC-based classification.

Hardware-based switches (depending on the ASIC model) can classify traffic as follows:

- Based on VLAN or VXLAN encapsulation

- Based on port and VLAN or port and VXLAN

- Based on network and mask or IP address for traffic originated outside the fabric (that is, traffic that is considered part of the Layer 3 external traffic)

- Based on source IP address or subnet (with Cisco Nexus E platform leaf nodes and EX platform leaf nodes)

- Based on source MAC address (Cisco Nexus EX platform leaf nodes)

It is possible to configure classification of the incoming traffic to the leaf as follows:

- Based on VLAN encapsulation.

- Based on port and VLAN.

- Based on network and mask or IP address for traffic originating outside the fabric (that is, traffic that is considered part of the Layer 3 external traffic).

- Based on explicit virtual NIC (vNIC) assignment to a port group. At the hardware level, this translates into a classification based on a dynamic VLAN or VXLAN negotiated between Cisco ACI and the VMM.

- Based on source IP address or subnet. For virtual machines, this function does not require any specific hardware if you are using Application Virtual Switch (AVS). For physical machines, this function requires the hardware to support source IP address classification (Cisco Nexus E platform leaf nodes and later platforms).

- Based on source MAC address. For virtual machines, this function does not require specific hardware if you are using AVS. For physical machines, this requires the hardware to support MAC-based classification and ACI version 2.1 or higher.

- Based on virtual machine attributes. This option assigns virtual machines to an EPG based on attributes associated with the virtual machine. At the hardware level, this translates into a classification based on VLAN or VXLAN (if using AVS software on the virtualized host or, more generally, if using software that supports the OpFlex protocol on the virtualized host) or based on MAC addresses (Cisco Nexus 9000 EX platform with VMware vDS).

Note   Each tenant can include multiple EPGs. The current number of supported EPGs per tenant is documented in the Verified Scalability Guide at Cisco.com (https://www.cisco.com/c/en/us/support/cloud-systems-management/application-policy-infrastructure-controller-apic/tsd-products-support-series-home.html).

An EPG provides or consumes a contract (or provides and consumes multiple contracts). For example, the NFS EPG in Figure 5-2 provides a contract that the External EPG consumes. However, this does not prevent the NFS EPG from providing the same or different contracts to other groups, or consuming contracts from others.

The use of contracts in Cisco ACI has the following goals:

- Define an ACL to allow communications between security zones.

- Define route leaking between VRFs or tenants.

Figure 5-2 shows how contracts are configured between EPGs (for instance, between internal EPGs and external EPGs).

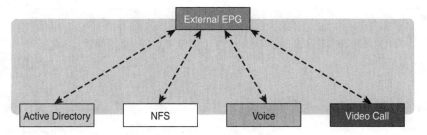

Figure 5-2 *External EPG Contract Example*

Contracts Are ACLs Without IP Addresses

You can think of contracts as ACLs between EPGs. As Figure 5-3 illustrates, the forwarding between endpoints is based on routing and switching as defined by the configuration of VRF instances and bridge domains. Whether the endpoints in the EPGs can communicate depends on the filtering rules defined by contracts.

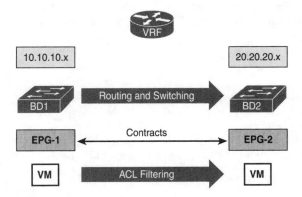

Figure 5-3 *Contracts Are ACLs*

Note   Contracts can also control more than just the filtering. If contracts are used between EPGs in different VRF instances, they are also used to define the VRF route-leaking configuration.

Filters and Subjects

A *filter* is a rule specifying fields such as the TCP port and protocol type, and it is referenced within a contract to define the communication allowed between EPGs in the fabric.

A filter contains one or more filter entries that specify the rule. The example in Figure 5-4 shows how filters and filter entries are configured in the APIC GUI.

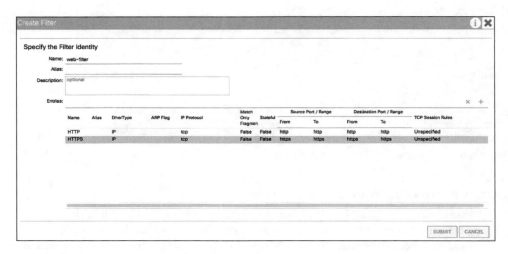

Figure 5-4   *Filters and Filter Entries*

A *subject* is a construct contained within a contract and typically references a filter. For example, the contract Web might contain a subject named Web-Subj that references a filter named Web-Filter.

Concept of Direction in Contracts

As you can see from the previous section, filter rules have a direction, similar to ACLs in a traditional router. ACLs are normally applied to router interfaces. In the case of Cisco ACI, the ACLs (contract filters) differ from classic ACLs in the following ways:

- The interface to which they are applied is the connection line of two EPGs.

- The directions in which filters are applied are "consumer-to-provider" and "provider-to-consumer."

- The ACLs do not include IP addresses because traffic is filtered based on EPG (or source group or class ID, which are synonymous).

Understanding the Bidirectional and Reverse Filter Options

When you create a contract, two options are typically selected by default:

- **Apply Both Directions**
- **Reverse Filter Ports**

The **Reverse Filter Ports** option is available only if the **Apply Both Directions** option is selected (see Figure 5-5).

Figure 5-5 *Apply Both Directions and Reverse Filter Ports Option Combinations*

An example clarifies the meaning of these options. If you require client-EPG (the consumer) to consume web services from port 80 on server-EPG (the provider), you must create a contract that allows source Layer 4 port "any" ("unspecified" in Cisco ACI terminology) to talk to destination Layer 4 port 80. You must then consume the contract from the client EPG and provide the same contract from the server EPG (see Figure 5-6).

Figure 5-6 *The Filter Chain of a Contract Is Defined in the Consumer-to-Provider Direction*

The effect of enabling the **Apply Both Directions** option is to program two Ternary Content-Addressable Memory entries: one that allows source port "unspecified" to talk to destination port 80 in the consumer-to-provider direction, and one for the provider-to-consumer direction that allows source port "unspecified" to talk to destination port 80 (see Figure 5-7).

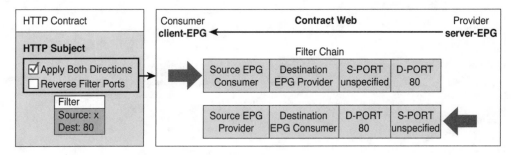

Figure 5-7 *Apply Both Directions Option and the Filter Chain*

As you can see, this configuration is not useful because the provider (server) would generate traffic from port 80 and not to port 80.

If you enable the option **Reverse Filter Ports**, Cisco ACI reverses the source and destination ports on the second TCAM entry, thus installing an entry that allows traffic from the provider to the consumer from Layer 4 port 80 to destination port "unspecified" (see Figure 5-8).

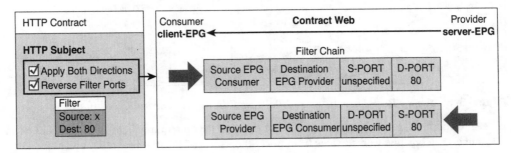

Figure 5-8 *Apply Both Directions and Reverse Filter Ports Options*

Cisco ACI by default selects both options: **Apply Both Directions** and **Reverse Filter Ports.**

Configuring a Single Contract Between EPGs

An alternative method for configuring filtering rules on a contract is to manually create filters in both directions: consumer-to-provider and provider-to-consumer.

With this configuration approach, you do not use **Apply Both Directions** or **Reverse Filter Ports,** as you can see in Figure 5-9.

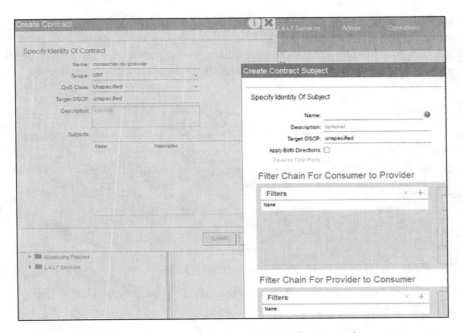

Figure 5-9 *Configuring Contract Filters at the Subject Level*

The configuration of the contract in this case consists of entering filter rules for each direction of the contract. Figure 5-10 provides a graphical representation of the contract and the interface between consumer and provider.

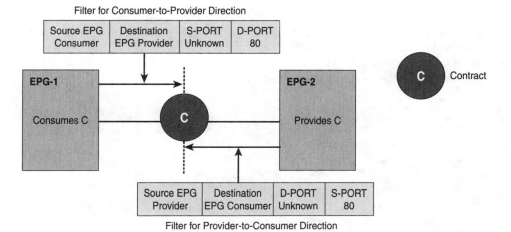

Figure 5-10 *Configuring Filters for Consumer-to-Provider and Provider-to-Consumer Directions*

Note As you can see from this example, more than one contract between any two EPGs is not generally required. Instead, edit one contract and enter additional rules as needed.

Using vzAny

A third option and best practice for reducing the amount of configuration resources contracts consume in the fabric is described in the following examples. In Figure 5-11, we are reusing a single contract and EPG to provide shared services to many groups.

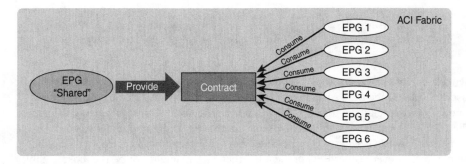

Figure 5-11 *Multiple EPGs Consuming the Same Contract*

In this scenario, a single EPG named "Shared" is providing a contract, with multiple EPGs consuming that contract. This works, but it has some drawbacks. First, the administrative burden is high because each EPG must be configured separately to consume the contract. Second, the number of hardware resources increases each time an EPG associates with a contract.

To overcome these issues, the "vzAny" object may be used—vzAny is simply a managed object within ACI that represents all EPGs within a VRF. This object can be used to provide or consume contracts, so in the preceding example, we can consume the contract from vzAny with the same results, as shown in Figure 5-12.

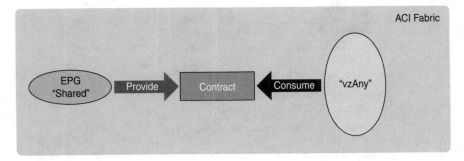

Figure 5-12   *Using vzAny to Consume Shared Services for All EPGs in a VRF*

This is not only easier to configure (although automation or orchestration may render that point moot), but it also represents the most efficient use of fabric hardware resources, so it's recommended for use in cases where every EPG within a VRF must consume or provide a given contract.

You may be wondering what happens if you want to allow shared services to all EPGs in a VRF except for one? This would call for a *Taboo contract*, which is a special type of contract that an ACI administrator can use to deny specific traffic that would otherwise be allowed by another contract. Taboos can be used to drop traffic matching a pattern (any EPG, a specific EPG, matching a filter, and so forth). Taboo rules are applied in the hardware before the rules of regular contracts are applied. Even with the addition of a Taboo contract, vzAny saves a considerable amount of time in manual contract configuration.

Note   For more information on Taboo contracts, see https://tinyurl.com/vzanyrestrict.

Whenever use of the vzAny object is being considered, the administrator must plan for its use carefully. Once the vzAny object is configured to provide or consume a contract, any new EPGs associated with the VRF will inherit the policy—that is, a new EPG added to the VRF will provide or consume the same contract(s) configured under vzAny. If it is likely that new EPGs will need to be added later that might not need to consume the same contract as every other EPG in the VRF, then vzAny might not be the most suitable choice.

For more details about vzAny restrictions, refer to the document, "Use vzAny to Automatically Apply Communication Rules to all EPGs in a VRF," at Cisco.com (http://tinyurl.com/vzany).

> **Note** When vzAny is used with shared services contracts, vzAny is supported only as a shared services consumer, not as a shared services provider.

An additional example of using the vzAny policy to reduce resource consumption is to use it in conjunction with the "established" flag. By doing so, it is possible to configure contracts as unidirectional in nature, which further reduces hardware resource consumption.

In Figure 5-13, two contracts are configured (for SSH and HTTP); both contracts are provided by EPG2 and consumed by EPG1. The **Apply Both Directions** and **Reverse Filter Ports** options are checked, resulting in the four TCAM entries.

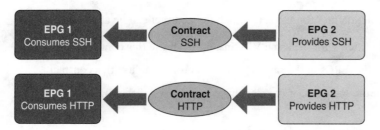

Figure 5-13 *Bidirectional Contract with a Traditional Configuration*

It is possible to reduce the TCAM utilization by half by making the contract unidirectional. However, this scenario presents a problem—return traffic is not allowed in the contracts; therefore, the connections cannot be completed, and traffic fails. In order to allow return traffic to pass, we can configure a rule that allows traffic between all ports with the "established" flag. We can take advantage of vzAny in this case to configure a single contract for the "established" traffic and apply it to the entire VRF, as shown in Figure 5-14.

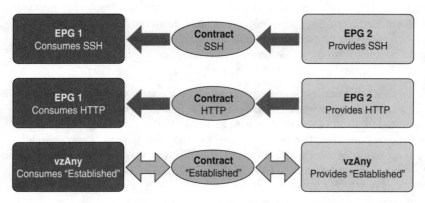

Figure 5-14 *Using vzAny with the "Established" Flag*

In an environment with a large number of contracts being consumed and provided, this can reduce the number of TCAM entries significantly and is recommended as a best practice.

To apply a contract to the vzAny group, navigate to the VRF in question under the tenant in the APIC GUI. Under the VRF object, you will see "EPG Collection for Context"—this is the vzAny object and contracts can be applied here.

Note   TCAM is a fabric resource that should be monitored. There is a systemwide view of available TCAM resources. To view the TCAM resources, on the menu bar, choose **Operations > Capacity Dashboard.** The work pane displays a table that summarizes the capacity for all nodes. We will examine the Capacity Dashboard in chapter 12. More information can also be found at https://tinyurl.com/tcamop.

Contract Scope

The scope of a contract defines the EPGs to which the contract can be applied:

- **VRF:** EPGs associated with the same VRF instance can use this contract.

- **Application profile:** EPGs in the same application profile can use this contract.

- **Tenant:** EPGs in the same tenant can use this contract even if the EPGs are in different VRFs.

- **Global:** EPGs throughout the fabric can use this contract.

This setting ensures the contract will not be applied to any consumer endpoint group outside the scope (application profile, VRF, tenant, and so on) of the provider endpoint group.

Contracts and Filters in the Common Tenant

In Cisco ACI, the common tenant provides resources that are visible and can be used from other tenants. This may mean not having to define the same filter multiple times for the same protocol. Although it is convenient to use filters from the common tenant, the scope of the contract must be taken into account. If multiple tenants provide and consume the same contract from the common tenant, if the scope is set incorrectly, you are effectively establishing a relationship with other tenants.

For instance, imagine that in the common tenant you have a contract called "web-to-app" and you want to reuse it in Tenant A and in Tenant B. In Tenant A, the contract is used to allow EPG-web to talk to EPG-app of Tenant A. In Tenant B, this configuration is replicated, allowing communication between EPG-web and EPG-app with the same contract. If the scope is set to global and the contract is used in this way, you are likely to also enable EPG-web of Tenant A to talk to EPG-app of Tenant B. This is by design, because you are telling Cisco ACI that EPGs in both tenants are providing and consuming the same contract, and the scope of the contract is set to extend outside of the tenant.

To configure this example as intended, verify that you set the scope of the contract correctly at the time of creation. In this example, the contract scope in the common tenant should be set to Tenant. Cisco ACI will then limit the scope or effect of the contract to each individual tenant where it would be used as if the contract had been defined in the individual tenant.

This scoping example can apply within a tenant as well. If you want to reuse a contract across multiple VRFs inside of a tenant, the scope should be set to VRF, not Tenant. If the scope is set to Tenant, you could be enabling cross-VRF communication.

VRFs and Bridge Domains

In this section, we will be discussing two technologies. The first is virtual routing and forwarding (VRF). Cisco has been using this technology for many years to virtualize routing domains on its network devices. The Nexus switch product line comes with a management VRF and a default VRF enabled out of the box. ACI is no different. You have to have at least one VRF, and ACI has the capability to scale out based on your organization's needs. We will discuss design considerations in the subsections that follow.

Bridge domains are a new concept to most engineers. In ACI, a bridge domain defines the unique Layer 2 MAC address space and a Layer 2 flood domain if such flooding is enabled. You can also think of a bridge domain as a container for subnets. It's where our default gateways live. After examining VRFs, we will turn our attention to bridge domains and learn how they affect multicast and Layer 2, as well as which devices have access to which gateways.

VRF Design Considerations

A virtual routing and forwarding (VRF) or context is a tenant's network. A tenant can have one or multiple VRFs. A VRF is a unique Layer 3 forwarding and application policy domain. The VRF is the data-plane segmentation element for traffic within or between tenants. A VRF defines a Layer 3 address domain. One or more bridge domains are associated with a VRF. All of the endpoints within the Layer 3 domain must have unique IP addresses because it is possible to forward packets directly between these devices if the policy allows it. Routed traffic uses the VRF as the VXLAN network identifier, or VNID. Even if Layer 2 traffic uses the bridge domain identifier, the VRF is always necessary in the object tree for a bridge domain to be instantiated.

Therefore, you either need to create a VRF in the tenant or refer to a VRF in the common tenant.

There is no 1:1 relationship between tenants and VRFs:

- A tenant can rely on a VRF from the common tenant.

- A tenant can contain multiple VRFs.

A popular design approach in multitenant environments where you need to share an L3 Out connection is to configure bridge domains and EPGs in individual user tenants, while referring to a VRF residing in the common tenant.

Shared L3 Out connections can be simple or complex configurations, depending on the options you choose. This section covers the simple and recommended options of using a VRF from the common tenant. The use of VRF leaking is a more advanced option that is covered in the section "Shared Layer 3 Outside Connection" in Chapter 6.

When creating a VRF, you must consider the following choices:

- Whether you want the traffic for all bridge domains and EPGs related to a VRF to be filtered according to contracts (enforced versus unenforced mode)

- The policy control enforcement direction (ingress or egress) for all EPGs to outside filtering

Note   Each tenant can include multiple VRFs. The current number of supported VRFs per tenant is documented in "Verified Scalability Guide for Cisco APIC, Release 2.0(1m) and Cisco Nexus 9000 Series ACI-Mode Switches, Release 12.0(1)" at Cisco.com (http:// tinyurl.com/scaleapic). Regardless of the published limits, it is good practice to distribute VRFs across different tenants to have better control-plane distribution on different APICs. Please refer to the scalability document at the following link: https:// www.cisco.com/c/en/us/support/cloud-systems-management/application-policy- infrastructure-controller-apic/tsd-products-support-series-home.html.

Bridge Domain Design Considerations

A bridge domain must be linked to a VRF (also known as a context or private network). The bridge domain defines the unique Layer 2 MAC address space and a Layer 2 flood domain if such flooding is enabled. Although a VRF defines a unique IP address space, that address space can consist of multiple subnets. Those subnets are defined in one or more bridge domains that reference the corresponding VRF.

Bridge domains can span multiple switches. A bridge domain can contain multiple sub- nets, but a subnet is contained within a single bridge domain. Subnets can span multiple EPGs; one or more EPGs can be associated with one bridge domain or subnet. An exam- ple of this is shown in Figure 5-1 at the beginning of this chapter.

The main bridge domain configuration options that should be considered to tune the bridge domain behavior are as follows:

- Whether to use hardware proxy or unknown unicast flooding

- Whether to enable or disable ARP flooding

- Whether to enable or disable unicast routing

- Whether to define a subnet

- Whether to define additional subnets in the same bridge domain

- Whether to constrain the learning of the endpoints to the subnet address space

- Whether to configure the endpoint retention policy

You can configure the bridge domain forwarding characteristics as optimized or as custom, as follows:

- If ARP flooding is enabled, ARP traffic will be flooded inside the fabric as per regular ARP handling in traditional networks. If this option is disabled, the fabric will attempt to use unicast to send the ARP traffic to the destination. Note that this option applies only if unicast routing is enabled on the bridge domain. If unicast routing is disabled, ARP traffic is always flooded.

- Hardware proxy for unknown unicast traffic is the default option. This forwarding behavior uses the mapping database to forward unknown unicast traffic to the destination port without relying on flood-and-learn behavior, as long as the MAC address is known to the spine (which means that the host is not a silent host).

- With Layer 2 unknown unicast flooding (that is, if hardware proxy is not selected), the mapping database and spine proxy are still populated with the MAC-to-VTEP information. However, the forwarding does not use the spine-proxy database. Layer 2 unknown unicast packets are flooded in the bridge domain using one of the multicast trees rooted in the spine that is scoped to the bridge domain. The **Layer 3 Configurations** tab allows the administrator to configure the following parameters:

- **Unicast Routing:** If this setting is enabled and a subnet address is configured, the fabric provides the default gateway function and routes the traffic. Enabling unicast routing also instructs the mapping database to learn the endpoint IP-to-VTEP mapping for this bridge domain. The IP learning is not dependent upon having a subnet configured under the bridge domain.

- **Subnet Address:** This option configures the SVI IP addresses (default gateway) for the bridge domain.

- **Limit IP Learning to Subnet:** This option is similar to a unicast reverse-forwarding-path check. If this option is selected, the fabric will not learn IP addresses from a subnet other than the one configured on the bridge domain. On a Layer 2–only bridge domain, you can still have unicast routing enabled to allow IP learning and to take advantage of the additional troubleshooting features that Cisco ACI offers. It is possible for unicast routing to be enabled under a Layer 2–only bridge domain because traffic forwarding in Cisco ACI operates as follows:

  - Cisco ACI routes traffic destined for the router MAC address.

  - Cisco ACI bridges traffic that is not destined for the router MAC address.

Operating a Bridge Domain in Flood-and-Learn Mode

Deploying a bridge domain in flood-and-learn mode means enabling flooding for unknown unicast traffic and ARP flooding. You should choose this design in the following situations:

- If the bridge domain is connecting two endpoints only; for example, when a bridge domain is used to provide connectivity between two interfaces of a service chain, such as the inside interface of a firewall and the outside interface of a load balancer. (In this case, the optimized bridge domain configuration does not provide any major advantages because the traffic flooded by one port is received by only the other port.)

- If there are silent hosts and ARP gleaning is not sufficient; that is, if a host is silent and will not answer ARP requests to an IP address.

- If there is a requirement not to lose a single packet during the initial conversations between two hosts.

Optimizing a Bridge Domain for Flooding Reduction of Layer 2 Unknown Unicast

If you want to reduce flooding in the bridge domain that is caused by Layer 2 unknown unicast frames, you should configure the following options:

- Configure a hardware proxy to remove unknown unicast flooding.

- Configure unicast routing to enable the learning of endpoint IP addresses (regardless of whether you need to route traffic).

- Configure a subnet to enable the bridge domain to use ARP to resolve endpoints when the endpoint retention policy expires, and also to enable the bridge domain to perform ARP gleaning for silent hosts.

- Define an endpoint retention policy. This is important if the ARP cache of hosts is longer than the default timers for MAC entries on the leaf and spine switches. With an endpoint retention policy defined, you can tune the timers to last longer than the ARP cache on the servers, or if you have defined a subnet IP address and IP routing on the bridge domain, Cisco ACI will send ARP requests to the hosts before the timer has expired, in which case the tuning may not be required.

ARP flooding

If ARP flooding is disabled, a Layer 3 lookup occurs for the target IP address of the ARP packet. ARP behaves like a Layer 3 unicast packet until it reaches the destination leaf switch.

ARP flooding is required when you need Gratuitous ARP (GARP) requests to update host ARP caches or router ARP caches. This is the case when an IP address may have a different MAC address (for example, with clustering or failover of load balancers and firewalls).

Endpoint Learning Considerations

Endpoint learning in the mapping database can be used by Cisco ACI to optimize traffic forwarding (in the case of Layer 2 entries), to implement routing of the traffic (for Layer 3 entries), and to perform advanced troubleshooting for applications (for example, using iTraceroute, the Troubleshooting Wizard, and the Endpoint Tracker).

If routing is disabled under the bridge domain, then the following occurs:

- Cisco ACI learns the MAC addresses of the endpoints in the mapping database.

- Cisco ACI floods ARP requests (regardless of whether ARP flooding is selected).

If routing is enabled under the bridge domain:

- Cisco ACI learns MAC addresses for Layer 2 traffic in the mapping database (this happens with or without IP routing).

- Cisco ACI learns MAC and IP addresses for Layer 3 traffic in the mapping database.

Make sure to use the **Limit IP Learning to Subnet** option to help ensure that only endpoints that belong to the bridge domain subnet are learned.

Note: Warning at the time of this writing, enabling **Limit IP Learning to Subnet** is disruptive to the traffic in the bridge domain

Given these options, it may not be immediately obvious how a bridge domain should be configured. The following sections attempt to explain when and why particular options should be selected.

The recommended bridge domain configuration that works in most scenarios consists of the following settings:

- **Bridge domain configured for hardware-proxy:** Not only does this reduce the flooding due to Layer 2 unknown unicast, but it is also more scalable because the fabric leverages more of the spine-proxy table capacity instead of just relying on the Global Station Table (GST) on the leafs.

- **ARP flooding:** Because of the variety of teaming implementations and the potential presence of floating IP addresses, ARP flooding is required often.

- **IP routing enabled:** It is good to keep IP routing on even for purely bridged traffic, for the reasons previously described related to maintaining an up-to-date mapping database.

- **Subnet and subnet check configured:** It is good to have a subnet defined even if the BD is used for L2 forwarding, for the reasons previously described related to maintaining an up-to-date mapping database.

- **Endpoint retention policy configured:** This ensures that the forwarding tables are up to date even if the ARP cache on the servers may have expired.

You should take caution if you change the BD configuration from unknown unicast flooding to hardware-proxy because of the reasons described previously: The ARP cache on the servers may take a long time to expire and the forwarding tables might not yet be populated in the presence of silent hosts. Table 5-1 summarizes the recommendations for bridge domains with more detailed scenarios.

Table 5-1 *Bridge Domain Recommendations*

Requirements	Hardware Proxy	No ARP Flooding	IP Routing	Subnet	Endpoint Retention Policy	Data Plane Learning of Endpoint IP Address
Routed and bridged traffic, no floating IP addresses, and vPC NIC teaming or no NIC teaming	Yes	No ARP flooding	Yes	Yes	Default endpoint retention policy	On (default)
Routed and bridged traffic and hosts or devices with floating IP addresses or NIC teaming other than vPC	Yes	No ARP flooding	Yes	Yes	Default endpoint retention policy	Off
Non-IP switched traffic and silent hosts	No	—	No	No	Tune local endpoint retention policy	—
Non-IP switched traffic and no silent hosts	Yes	—	No	No	Tune local endpoint retention policy	—
IP Layer 2 switched traffic	Yes	No ARP flooding	Yes (for advanced functions and aging)	Yes (for aging and ARP gleaning)	Default endpoint retention policy	On (default)
IP Layer 2 switched traffic and floating IP addresses (for example, clusters)	Yes	ARP flooding	Yes (for advanced functions and aging)	Yes (for aging and ARP gleaning)	Default endpoint retention policy	Off

In addition to the recommendations in Table 5-1, you may need to disable data-plane-based endpoint IP address learning in bridge domains where you host clustering implementations with floating IP addresses.

Bridge domain legacy mode allows only one VLAN per bridge domain. When bridge domain legacy mode is specified, bridge domain encapsulation is used for all EPGs that reference the bridge domain; EPG encapsulation, if defined, is ignored. Also, unicast routing does not apply for bridge domain legacy mode.

Changing Bridge Domain Settings in a Production Network

When changing bridge domain settings in a production network, use caution because endpoints that had been learned in the mapping database may be then flushed after the change. This is because in the current implementation the VNID used by the same bridge domain configured for unknown unicast flooding or for hardware-proxy is different. When changing bridge domain settings from unknown unicast flooding to hardware-proxy mode, use caution because hardware-proxy mode relies on the mapping database for forwarding unknown unicast MAC addresses. Consider an example where the hosts in the bridge domain are not sending traffic periodically but only when an event requires it: for example, a VMware kernel (VMkernel) interface for vMotion. Such hosts may have a cached ARP entry. If you change the bridge domain settings to hardware proxy and the ARP entry on the hosts doesn't expire immediately afterward, when the host tries to send traffic to another host, that host will effectively be generating unknown unicast MAC address traffic. This traffic in hardware-proxy mode is not flooded, but sent to the spine proxy. The spine proxy does not have an updated mapping database unless the destination host has spoken after you changed the bridge domain settings. As a result, this traffic will be dropped.

Because of this, if you change the settings of a bridge domain from unknown unicast flooding to hardware-proxy mode, you should help ensure either that the hosts in the bridge domain are not silent or that their ARP caches are refreshed after the change.

VRFs and Bridge Domains in the Common Tenant

In this scenario, you create the VRF instance and bridge domains in the common tenant and create EPGs in the individual user tenants. You then associate the EPGs with the bridge domains of the common tenant. This configuration can use static or dynamic routing (see Figure 5-15).

The configuration process in the common tenant is as follows:

Step 1.   Configure a VRF under the common tenant.

Step 2.   Configure an L3 Out connection under the common tenant and associate it with the VRF.

Step 3.   Configure the bridge domains and subnets under the common tenant.

Step 4.   Associate the bridge domains with the VRF instance and L3 Out connection.

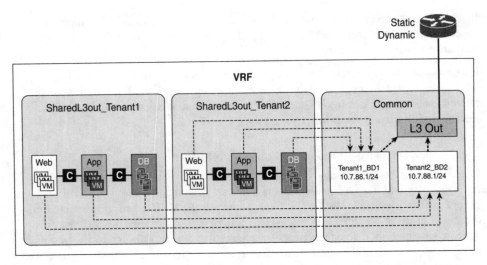

Figure 5-15 *Shared L3 Out Connection Through the Common Tenant with a VRF Instance and Bridge Domains in the Common Tenant*

The configuration process in each tenant is as follows:

Step 1.   Under each tenant, configure EPGs and associate the EPGs with the bridge domain in the common tenant.

Step 2.   Configure a contract and application profile under each tenant.

This approach has the following advantages:

■ The L3 Out connection can be configured as dynamic or static.

■ Each tenant has its own EPGs and contracts.

This approach has the following disadvantages:

■ Each bridge domain and subnet is visible to all tenants.

■ All tenants use the same VRF instance. Hence, they cannot use overlapping IP addresses.

VRFs in the Common Tenant and Bridge Domains in User Tenants

In this configuration, you create a VRF in the common tenant and create bridge domains and EPGs in the individual user tenants. Then you associate the bridge domain of each tenant with the VRF instance in the common tenant (see Figure 5-16). This configuration can use static or dynamic routing.

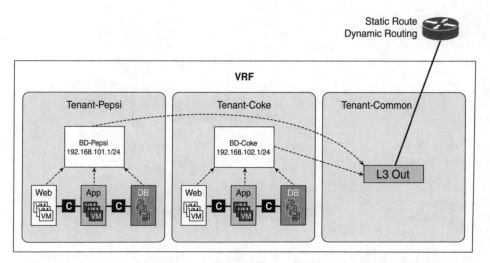

Figure 5-16   *Shared L3 Out Connection with the VRF Instance in the Common Tenant*

Configure the common tenant as follows:

Step 1.   Configure a VRF instance under the common tenant.

Step 2.   Configure an L3 Out connection under the common tenant and associate it with the VRF instance.

Configure the individual tenants as follows:

Step 1.   Configure a bridge domain and subnet under each customer tenant.

Step 2.   Associate the bridge domain with the VRF in the common tenant and the L3 Out connection.

Step 3.   Under each tenant, configure EPGs and associate the EPGs with the bridge domain in the tenant itself.

Step 4.   Configure contracts and application profiles under each tenant.

The advantage of this approach is that each tenant can see only its own bridge domain and subnet; however, there is still no support for overlapping IP addresses.

Layer 3 External Connection in the Common Tenant with VRFs and Bridge Domains in User Tenants

In this configuration, you create a VRF and L3 Out in the common tenant and create a VRF, bridge domains, and EPGs in the individual user tenants. Then you associate the bridge domain of each tenant with the VRF instance in each user tenant, but when you choose the L3 Out connection, you will choose the L3 Out in the common tenant (see Figure 5-17). This configuration can use static or dynamic routing.

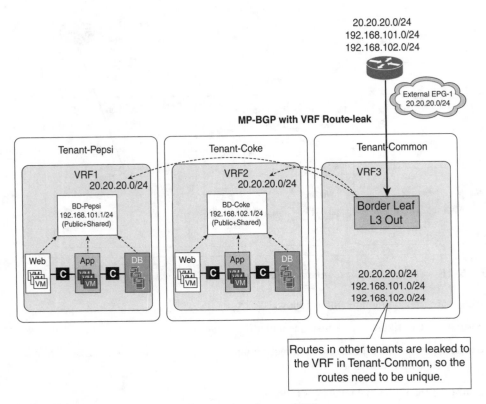

Figure 5-17 *Sharing L3 Out Connection Across VRFs*

Configure the common tenant as follows:

Step 1. Configure a VRF instance under the common tenant.

Step 2. Configure an L3 Out connection under the common tenant and associate it
with the VRF instance.

Configure the individual tenants as follows:

Step 1. Configure a VRF instance under each customer tenant.

Step 2. Configure a bridge domain and subnet under each customer tenant.

Step 3. Associate the bridge domain (public and shared) with the VRF in the customer tenant and the L3 Out connection in the common tenant.

Step 4. Under each tenant, configure EPGs and associate the EPGs with the bridge
domain in the tenant itself.

Step 5. Configure contracts and application profiles under each tenant.

Step 6.   Export the global contract for connectivity to the L3 Out connection from the common tenant to the customer tenants.

Step 7.   Import the contract into the customer tenants and assign the contract to the correct EPGs.

The advantage of this approach is that each tenant has its own L3 forwarding space and can see only its own bridge domains and subnets. However, there is still no support for overlapping IP addresses. The routes need to be unique because they are leaked to the common tenant.

Ingress Versus Egress Filtering Design Recommendations

Whether to apply policy enforcement at ingress or egress (in relation to the L3 Out connection and border leaf) is covered in a later chapter of this book. This section provides a simpler guide to making the choice at the time of VRF deployment.

The ingress policy enforcement feature improves policy CAM utilization on the border leaf nodes by distributing the filtering function across all regular leaf nodes. At the time of this writing, there are some caveats about ingress policy enforcement related to VMware vMotion, where individual endpoints are located on the border leaf nodes.

Therefore, the decision to use ingress policy enforcement depends upon whether or not you use dedicated border leaf nodes.

If you deploy a topology that connects to the outside through a border leaf, you have the following choices:

- Use a pair of leaf nodes as both computing and border leaf nodes. This border leaf is used to connect endpoints and to connect to the outside routing domain.

- Use a dedicated pair of border leaf nodes with VRF-lite L3 Out (that is, per tenant and VRF L3 Out connection). In this case, no hosts connect to the border leaf—only external routing devices.

- Use Layer 3 EVPN services through the spine.

If you are using Cisco Nexus 9300 and 9300 E leaf nodes, the following recommendations apply:

- If you are using a dedicated pair of border leaf nodes, you should enable ingress policy enforcement at the VRF level.

- If you are using leaf nodes that are both border leaf nodes and computing leaf nodes, you should enable egress policy enforcement at the VRF level.

- With Cisco Nexus 9300 EX leaf nodes, you should use ingress policy enforcement, regardless of the location of border and host ports.

Connecting External Networks to the Fabric

It is easy to integrate ACI into your current network design or build a new data center network with ACI. In either circumstance, because ACI acts as a combined aggregation and access layer, it is a best practice for enterprises to connect ACI to the core of their data center. The most common type of connections between ACI and an external network are defined as external routed networks (L3 Out) and/or external bridged networks (L2 Out). The leafs on which these connections reside are logically called *border leafs*. Due to the critical nature of this connectivity, it is a best practice to maintain redundant and separate leafs as the border leafs. It is also a best practice to maintain diversity in the L2 and L3 connectivity when possible, as shown in Figure 5-18. A third type of connection often used for L2 connectivity is called a *static binding*. In the sections that follow, we examine the configuration options for external connections to the fabric and the scenarios to which they apply.

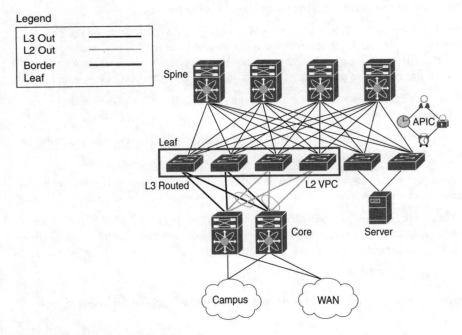

Figure 5-18   *L3/L2 Out Diversity*

L2 Connections

Many data center networks in production today use the aggregation layer, or collapsed core, in the data center for routing or as the Layer 3/Layer 2 boundaries in the data center. These traditional designs rely on Layer 2 connectivity to the server access layer, as shown in Figure 5-19.

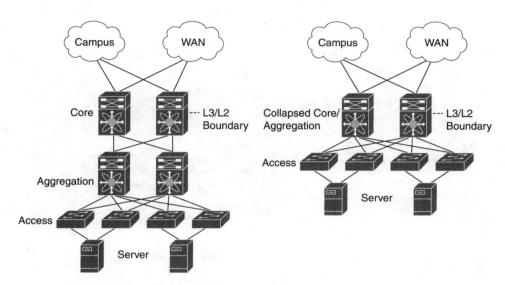

Figure 5-19 *Traditional Data Center Network*

Many enterprises first integrate ACI with their network when the need arises to expand their current access layer. The addition of ACI to the current enterprise network mirrors the addition of a Nexus switch running in NX-OS mode or a traditional L2 switch. The ACI border leaf is connected to the existing network with a Layer 2 connection, and VLANs are trunked into ACI as shown in Figure 5-20.

This type of connectivity allows enterprises to bring VLANs into ACI in a controlled manner without changing how their L3 network behaves. Layer 2 communication from and to hosts that reside inside of ACI would be switched locally. Layer 2 communication to hosts outside of ACI or Layer 3 traffic that needs to be routed would be sent out the L2 links to the existing network to be processed as shown in Figure 5-20.

Individual servers and network service devices also use L2 connections to connect to the fabric on an individual basis.

Two considerations must be made when connecting ACI to an existing network or device: the physical configuration of the links, and how policy will be applied to devices and communications external to the ACI network. The physical configuration or access policies control some of the following attributes:

- VLANs used on the links

- Type of link (Access, Port Channel, Virtual Port Channel)

- Protocols (CDP, LLDP, LACP) to be used on the links

- Speed of the link

- Ports used in the link

- Switches used in the link

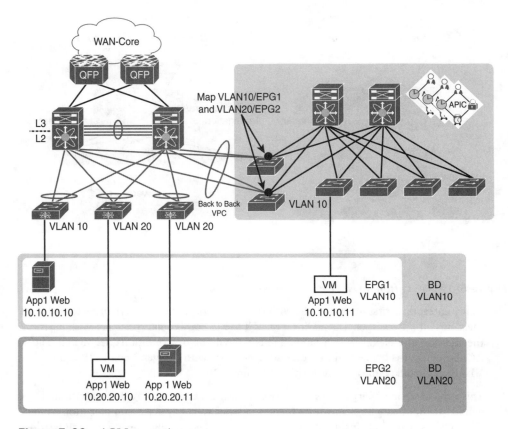

Figure 5-20   *ACI Integration*

How physical links are bound in the ACI logical policy controls the level of security that is applied on the zero-trust fabric and the communication allowed by default. You can choose to insert devices into existing groups on the fabric or create new groups, which will then require contracts for communication by default. Both policies (physical and logical) must be defined before communication can occur.

Note   Access policy or physical configuration of a link does not take effect until logical policy is applied. If logical policy is applied without an access policy configuration, errors will occur.

In the following sections, we examine the logical and physical policies in more depth.

Static Binding

One of the easiest and most commonly used methods for bringing external L2 networks or L2 connected devices into the fabric is a static binding. A static binding involves manually inserting a device or traffic from outside devices into a group or policy within ACI. Because this device (or devices) is inserted directly into the group or EPG, ACI will assume that this device or communication is allowed to interact with any of the other devices in that group or EPG without restriction. By default, security will only be applied when communication is attempted with devices outside of the group to which this device (or devices) is bound. An example of this would be every device in VLAN10 should be allowed to talk to every other device in VLAN10, or a group of web servers should be allowed to talk to other web servers. However, security will be applied if they attempt to talk outside of their group to the application or database servers. A static binding effectively extends the endpoint group outside of the fabric, as shown in Figure 5-21.

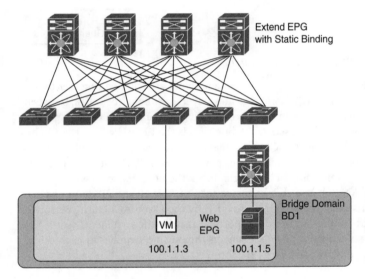

Figure 5-21   *EPG Static Binding*

Note   The feature intra-EPG isolation allows you to prevent all devices inside of a group from communicating with each other. If you wish to isolate some devices but not others, you will need to create additional groups. *Intra*-EPG contracts can also be used to control how devices communicate with each other inside of an EPG.

Connecting EPGs to External Switches

If two external switches are connected to two different EPGs within the fabric, you must ensure that those external switches are not directly connected outside the fabric. It is strongly recommended in this case that you enable Bridge Protocol Data Unit guard on the access ports of the external switches to help ensure that any accidental direct physical connections are blocked immediately.

Consider Figure 5-22 as an example.

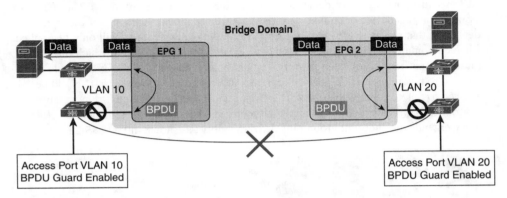

Figure 5-22   *Connecting EPGs to External Switches*

In this example, VLANs 10 and 20 from the outside network are stitched together by the Cisco ACI fabric. The Cisco ACI fabric provides Layer 2 bridging for traffic between these two VLANs. These VLANs are in the same flooding domain. From the perspective of the Spanning Tree Protocol, the Cisco ACI fabric floods the BPDUs within the EPG (within the same VLAN ID). When the Cisco ACI leaf receives the BPDUs on EPG 1, it floods them to all leaf ports in EPG 1, and it does not send the BPDU frames to ports in other EPGs. As a result, this flooding behavior can break the potential loop within the EPG (VLAN 10 and VLAN 20). You should ensure that VLANs 10 and 20 do not have any physical connections other than the one provided by the Cisco ACI fabric. Be sure to turn on the BPDU guard feature on the access ports of the outside switches. By doing so, you help ensure that if someone mistakenly connects the outside switches to each other, BPDU guard can disable the port and break the loop.

Working with Multiple Spanning Tree

Additional configuration is required to help ensure that Multiple Spanning Tree (MST) BPDUs flood properly. BPDU frames for Per-VLAN Spanning Tree (PVST) and Rapid Per-VLAN Spanning Tree (RPVST) have a VLAN tag. The Cisco ACI leaf can identify the EPG on which the BPDUs need to be flooded based on the VLAN tag in the frame.

However, for MST (IEEE 802.1s), BPDU frames don't carry a VLAN tag, and the BPDUs are sent over the native VLAN. Typically, the native VLAN is not used to carry data traffic, and the native VLAN may not be configured for data traffic on the Cisco ACI fabric. As a result, to help ensure that MST BPDUs are flooded to the desired ports, the user must create an EPG (an "MST" EPG) for VLAN 1 as the native VLAN to carry the BPDUs. This EPG connects to the external switches that run MST.

In addition, the administrator must configure the mapping of MST instances to VLANs to define which MAC address table must be flushed when a topology change notification occurs. When a topology change notification event occurs on the external Layer 2 network, this TCN reaches the leafs to which it connects via the "MST" EPG, and it flushes the local endpoint information associated with these VLANs on these leafs, and as result these entries are removed from the spine-proxy mapping database.

Configuring Trunk and Access Ports

In Cisco ACI, you can configure ports that are used by EPGs in one of these ways:

- **Tagged (classic IEEE 802.1Q trunk):** Traffic for the EPG is sourced by the leaf with the specified VLAN tag. The leaf also expects to receive traffic tagged with that VLAN to be able to associate it with the EPG. Traffic received untagged is discarded.

- **Untagged:** Traffic for the EPG is sourced by the leaf as untagged. Traffic received by the leaf as untagged or with the tag specified during the static binding configuration is associated with the EPG.

- **IEEE 802.1p:** If only one EPG is bound to that interface, the behavior is identical to that in the untagged case. If other EPGs are associated with the same interface, then traffic for the EPG is sourced with an IEEE 802.1Q tag using VLAN 0 (IEEE 802.1p tag).

You cannot have different interfaces on the same leaf bound to a given EPG in both the tagged and untagged modes at the same time. Therefore, it is a good practice to select the IEEE 802.1p option to connect an EPG to a bare-metal host.

If a port on a leaf node is configured with multiple EPGs, where one of those EPGs is in IEEE 802.1p mode and the others are tagged, the behavior is different, depending on the switch hardware in use:

- If Cisco Nexus 93180YC-EX or 93108TC-EX switches are used, traffic from the EPG in IEEE 802.1p mode will exit the port untagged.

- If switches other than Cisco Nexus 9000 EX platform switches are used, traffic from the EPG in IEEE 802.1p mode will exit the port tagged as VLAN 0. It is possible in rare cases that certain hosts using the preboot execution environment (PXE) will not understand traffic with a VLAN tag of 0.

Note When an EPG is deployed with the access (untagged) option, you cannot deploy that EPG as a trunk port (tagged) on other ports of the same switch. You can have one EPG, with both tagged and access (IEEE 802.1p) interfaces. The tagged interface allows trunked devices to attach to the EPG, and the access interface (IEEE 802.1p) allows devices that do not support IEEE 802.1Q to be attached to the fabric.

The preferred option for configuring ports as access ports is the access (IEEE 802.1p) option.

You can also define an EPG binding to a VLAN on a leaf without specifying a port. This option is convenient, but it has the disadvantage that if the same leaf is also a border leaf, you cannot configure Layer 3 interfaces because this option changes all the leaf ports into trunks. Therefore, if you have an L3 Out connection, you will then have to use SVI interfaces.

Layer 2 Out

Creating a Layer 2 Outside connection or an external bridged connection incorporates an extra layer of security and control over devices that will be interacting with the fabric. This configuration effectively extends the bridge domain instead of the EPG. Instead of inserting devices into a particular group, a new group in a selected bridge domain is created and a contract is used to control communication and security. Security can then be applied with a single contract as a whole or with individual contracts on a group-by-group basis, as the administrator sees fit. Figure 5-23 shows an example of this.

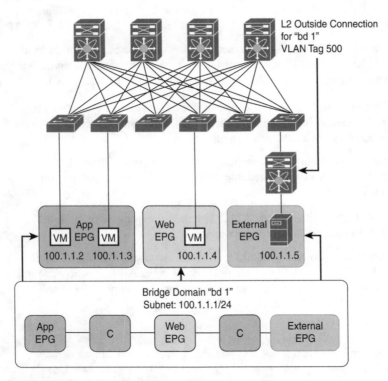

Figure 5-23 *Example of a Layer 2 Outside Connection*

Basic Mode GUI

The basic mode GUI streamlines the process of attaching devices to the fabric. The basic mode GUI was developed in such a way that the user does not have to understand the full ACI policy model to add devices into groups. Once the user has navigated to **Fabric > Inventory > Topology > Configure**, a device can be attached to the fabric in a very fast and intuitive manner. The **Configure** tab allows a switch or switches to be selected, with the port(s) that will be configured outlined in blue, as shown in Figure 5-24.

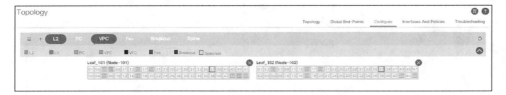

Figure 5-24 *Switch Configuration and Port Type*

The manner in which ports are selected will dictate the options available for configuration. In this example, Configure VPC is available because I have selected ports on two different switches. Ports can be configured in the following manner:

- Clear selected port configuration
- L2/L3 access port
- Create or delete port channel
- Create or delete a virtual port channel
- Connect or delete a fabric extender

Once the port configuration type has been selected, a new screen with configuration details appears. In this screen, you provide input and click the options required for port configuration, as shown in Figure 5-25.

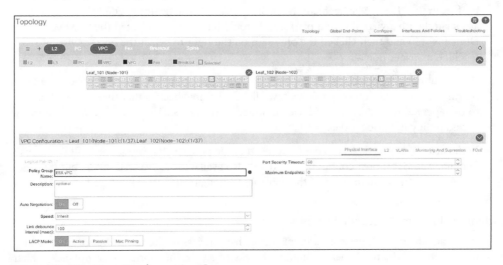

Figure 5-25 *Port Configuration Screen*

When the configuration of the physical settings of the port has been completed, you can then manually map the device into a specific EPG (bare-metal server) or associate it as a virtualization device, as shown in Figure 5-26.

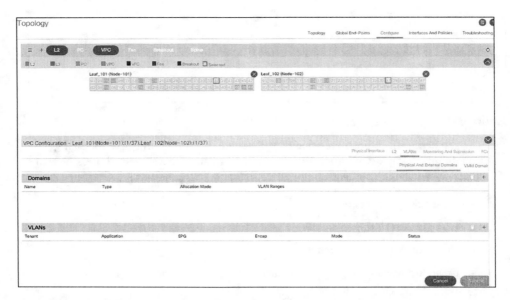

Figure 5-26   *Mapping Devices and VLANs to EPGs*

In Figure 5-26, ACI has been configured to take any data on this port that belongs to VLAN 1000 and to put it into the "VDI_Clients" EPG, in the "VDI_App" application profile, in the "Prod_Management_Network" tenant. If the device needed to be associated with a virtualization platform, I would have simply selected the "VMM Domains" tab and then clicked the plus sign on the right to select the correct virtual machine manager domain.

When **Submit** is selected, ACI completes the necessary configuration and policy changes. Setting up a connection only takes a few clicks. The drawback is that the steps will have to be repeated whenever a new device is added to the fabric. There is no reuse of fabric access policy in basic mode.

In the next section, you learn about advanced mode policies that should be built with reuse in mind. The visual port configuration GUI is also available in advanced mode, but it relies on policies you create (instead of the controller automatically creating them for you).

Advanced Mode Access Policies

In the advanced GUI, network administrators have access to the full power of the policy model. One of the fundamental building blocks of ACI is the fabric access policies, which take the individual parts of configuring physical ports and divide the configuration up into reusable policy. This allows enterprises to develop standard configuration for devices that are attached to the fabric, thus reducing the risk of human error in production environments. This also lends itself to the dynamic nature of ACI.

For example, when you build a house, you plan the foundation, roof, and outer and inner wall layout. As time goes on, sometimes you change the decorations or colors within a room, or even remodel the inside of the house, potentially changing the interior walls and their layout. Typically, you do all of this without changing the exterior walls or the foundation. ACI can be thought of the same way. You can physically cable devices and define the access policies for the physical configuration. Access policies are similar to the foundation, roof, and exterior walls of your house. Once they are complete, you can change the logical or tenant policy as much as you want, without having to change the physical configuration of the devices. The logical tenant policies are like the inside walls of the house.

Fabric Access Policy Configuration

The following three subsections include some review from Chapter 3, "Bringing Up a Fabric." This review is present due to the importance of fabric access policies. Fabric access polices define how resources and configuration relate to devices accessing the fabric. The order in which an access policy is configured is important. If a step is missed and a relationship is not formed between objects, the configuration might not work or will result in an error. Remember, both fabric access policies and logical policies are needed for devices to use the fabric. The workflow for creating an access policy generally follows the flow shown in Figure 5-27.

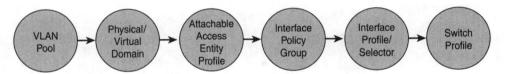

Figure 5-27 *Access Policy Configuration Workflow*

VLAN Pools and Domains

If you recall from the previous chapter, a VLAN pool is a way to logically group VLAN resources so they can be applied to physical and virtual devices. Static pools are used for physical workloads or manual configurations. Dynamic pools are generally used for virtualization integration and horizontal orchestration of L4-7 devices.

It is a common practice to divide VLAN pools into functional groups, as shown in Table 5-2.

Table 5-2 *VLAN Pool Example*

VLAN Range	Type	Use
1000–1100	Static	Bare-metal hosts
1101–1200	Static	Firewalls
1201–1300	Static	External WAN routers
1301–1400	Dynamic	Virtual machines

A domain is used to define the scope of VLANs in the Cisco ACI fabric: in other words, where and how a VLAN pool will be used. There are a number of domain types: physical, virtual (VMM domains), external Layer 2, and external Layer 3. It is common practice to have a 1:1 mapping between a VLAN pool and a domain.

Best practices are as follows:

- Build one physical domain per tenant for bare-metal servers or servers without hypervisor integration requiring similar treatment.

- Build one physical domain per tenant for external connectivity.

- If a VMM domain needs to be leveraged across multiple tenants, a single VMM domain can be created and associated with all leaf ports where VMware ESXi servers are connected.

Attachable Access Entity Profiles

An Attachable Access Entity Profile (AAEP) is the lynchpin of fabric access policies. It is used to map domains (physical or virtual) and VLANS to interface policies. An AAEP represents a group of external entities with similar infrastructure policy requirements. Examine Figure 5-28 to refresh your memory regarding AAEPs and their relationship to other parts of the fabric access policies.

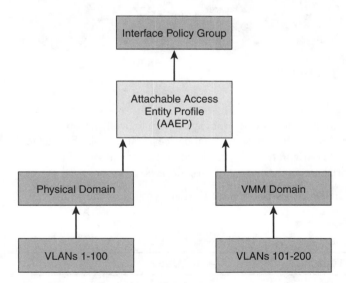

Figure 5-28 *AAEP Relationships*

For best practice purposes, multiple domains can be associated with a single AAEP for simplicity's sake. There are some cases where multiple AAEPs may need to be configured to enable the infrastructure VLAN, such as overlapping VLAN pools, or to limit the scope of the presence of VLANs across the fabric.

Interface Policies

Interface policies are responsible for the configuration of interface-level parameters. Interface policies along with the AAEP are brought together as part of an interface policy group. These policies are then linked to interface profiles and finally to switch profiles.

Each type of interface policy is preconfigured with a default policy. In most cases, the feature or parameter in question is set to "disabled" as part of the default policy.

It is highly recommended that you create explicit policies for each configuration item rather than relying on and modifying the default policy. This helps prevent accidental modification of the default policy, which may have a wide impact.

Best practices are as follows:

- Reuse policies whenever possible. For example, there should be policies for Link Aggregation Control Protocol active/passive/off, 1GE port speed, and 10GE port speed.

- When you're naming policies, use names that clearly describe the setting. For example, a policy that enables LACP in active mode could be called "Link Aggregation Control P-Active." There are many "default" policies out of the box. However, it can be hard to remember what all the defaults are, which is why policies should be clearly named to avoid making a mistake when you're adding new devices to the fabric.

Port Channels and Virtual Port Channels

Configuration of the member ports in port channels and virtual port channels (vPCs) was covered in depth in Chapter 3. However, to form a vPC pair, the virtual port channel default policy will have to be modified. This is where you will configure your vPC protection groups. You have the option to perform this configuration in the following ways:

- **Explicit:** This is the default. In this mode, you manually configure which switches will be vPC pairs.

- **Consecutive:** Automatically provisions vPC pairs 101+102, 103+104.

- **Reciprocal:** Automatically provisions vPC pairs 101+103, 102+104.

Note   The most common deployment type is Explicit, which is the default.

A leaf profile including both switches in the vPC pair will have to be created. The leaf profile will reference the vPC pair and be integrated into the workflow like any other leaf profile, as shown in Figure 5-29.

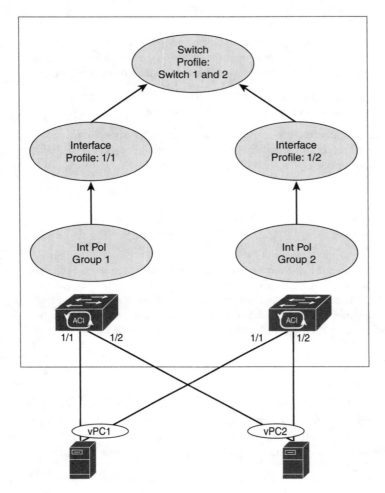

Figure 5-29 *vPC Interface Policy Groups*

Note Be sure to review access policies in Chapter 3 if you need a more in-depth explanation before proceeding.

Interface Overrides

Consider an example where an interface policy group is configured with a certain policy, such as a policy to enable Local Link Discovery Protocol (LLDP). This interface policy group is associated with a range of interfaces (for example, 1/1-2), which is then applied to a set of switches (for example, 101 to 104). The administrator now decides that interface 1/2 on a specific switch only (104) must run Cisco Discovery Protocol (CDP) rather than LLDP. To achieve this, interface override policies can be used.

An *interface override policy* refers to a port on a specific switch (for example, port 1/2 on leaf node 104) and is associated with an interface policy group. In this example, an interface override policy for interface 1/2 on the leaf node in question can be configured and then associated with an interface policy group that has Cisco Discovery Protocol configured, as shown in Figure 5-30.

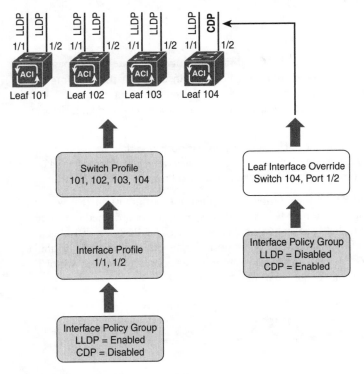

Figure 5-30   *Interface Overrides*

Interface overrides are configured in the Interface Policies section under Fabric Access Policies. An example of creating an interface override is shown in Figure 5-31.

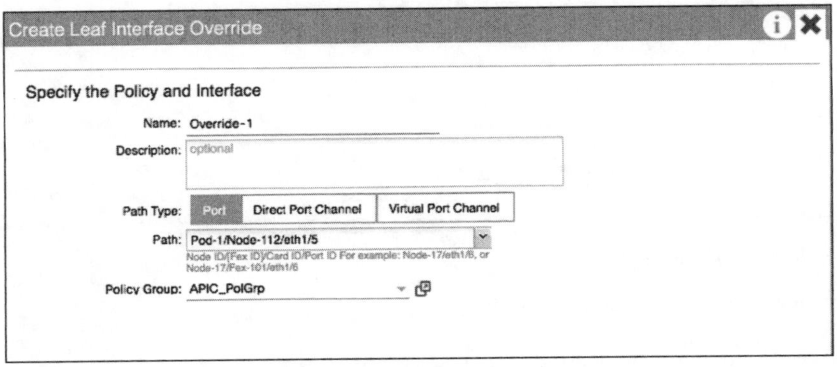

Figure 5-31   *Interface Override Configuration*

> **Note** If the interface override refers to a port channel or vPC, a corresponding port channel or vPC override policy must be configured and then referenced from the interface override.

Miscabling Protocol

Unlike traditional networks, the Cisco ACI fabric does not participate in the Spanning Tree Protocol and does not generate BPDUs. BPDUs are instead transparently forwarded through the fabric between ports mapped to the same EPG on the same VLAN. Therefore, Cisco ACI relies to a certain degree on the loop-prevention capabilities of external devices.

Some scenarios, such as the accidental cabling of two leaf ports together, are handled directly using LLDP in the fabric. However, there are some situations where an additional level of protection is necessary. In those cases, enabling the Miscabling Protocol (MCP) can help.

MCP, if enabled, provides additional protection against misconfigurations that would otherwise result in loop situations. MCP is a lightweight protocol designed to protect against loops that cannot be discovered by either Spanning Tree Protocol or LLDP. It is recommended that you enable MCP on all ports facing external switches or similar devices. MCP must first be enabled globally through the **Global Policies** section of the **Fabric > Access Policies** tab, as shown in Figure 5-32.

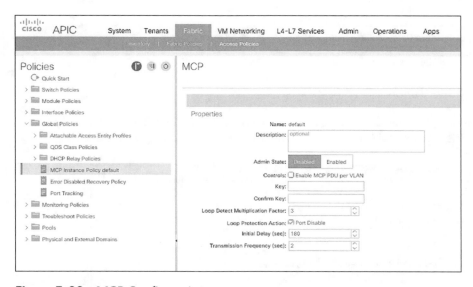

Figure 5-32 *MCP Configuration*

The following parameters can be changed here:

- **Key:** The key to uniquely identify MCP packets within the fabric
- **Initial Delay:** The delay time before MCP begins taking action

■ **Loop Detect Multiplication Factor:** The number of continuous packets that a port must receive before declaring a loop. Note that the action to disable the port upon loop detection can also be enabled here. MCP must also be enabled on individual ports and port channels through the interface policy group configuration, as shown in Figure 5-33. Note that prior to Cisco ACI Release 2.0(2f), MCP detects loops in the native VLAN only. Software Release 2.0(2f) adds support for Per-VLAN MCP and therefore can be used to detect loops in nonnative VLANs.

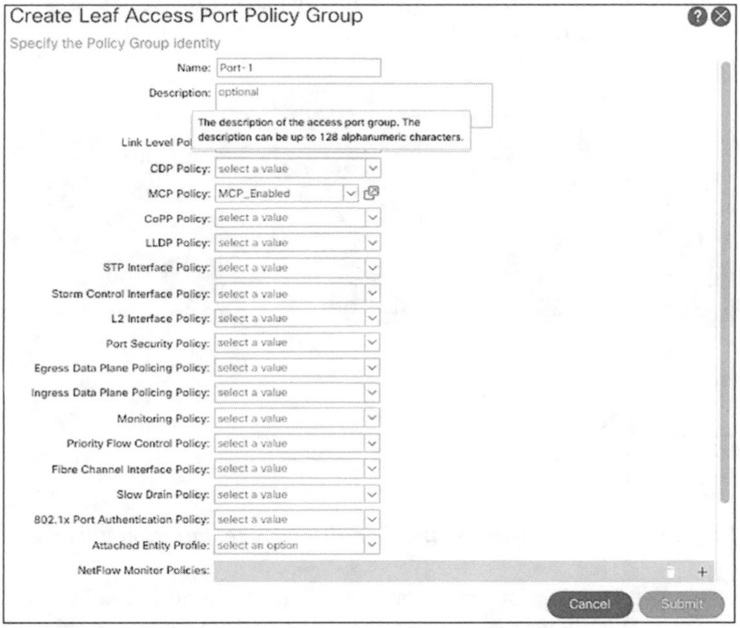

Figure 5-33 *Associating MCP with the Policy Group Storm Control*

■ **Storm control:** A feature used to monitor the levels of broadcast, multicast, and unknown unicast traffic and to suppress this traffic if a user-configured threshold is reached. Storm control on the Cisco ACI fabric is configured by opening the **Fabric > Access Policies** menu and choosing **Interface Policies**. Storm control takes two values as configuration input:

■ **Rate:** Defines a rate level against which traffic will be compared during a 1-second interval. The rate can be defined as a percentage or as the number of packets per second.

■ **Max Burst Rate:** Specifies the maximum traffic rate before storm control begins to drop traffic. This rate can be defined as a percentage or the number of packets per second. Storm control can behave differently depending on the flood settings configured at the bridge domain level. If a bridge domain is set to use hardware proxy for unknown unicast traffic, the storm control policy will apply to broadcast and multicast traffic. If, however, the bridge domain is set to flood unknown unicast traffic, storm control will apply to broadcast, multicast, and unknown unicast traffic.

Port Tracking

The port-tracking feature, first available in Release 1.2(2g), addresses a scenario where a leaf node may lose connectivity to all spine nodes in the Cisco ACI fabric and where hosts connected to the affected leaf node in an active-standby manner might not be aware of the failure for a period of time (see Figure 5-34).

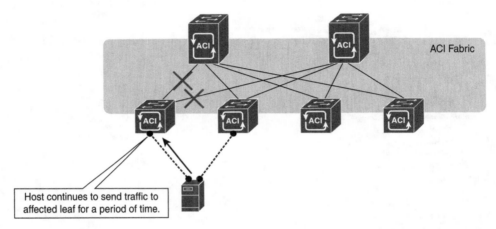

Figure 5-34 *Loss of Leaf Connectivity in an Active-Standby NIC Teaming Scenario*

The port-tracking feature detects a loss of fabric connectivity on a leaf node and brings down the host-facing ports. This allows the host to fail over to the second link, as shown in Figure 5-35.

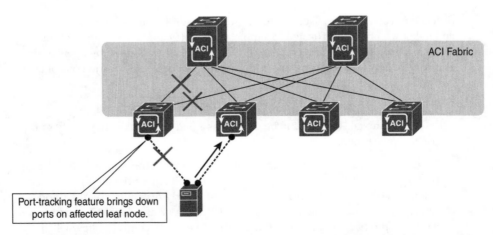

Figure 5-35 *Active-Standby NIC Teaming with Port Tracking Enabled*

Except for very specific server deployments, servers should be dual-homed, and port tracking should always be enabled.

Endpoint Loop Protection

Endpoint loop protection is a feature that takes action if the Cisco ACI fabric detects an endpoint moving more than a specified number of times during a given time interval. Endpoint loop protection can take one of two actions if the number of endpoint moves exceeds the configured threshold:

- Disable endpoint learning within the bridge domain.
- Disable the port to which the endpoint is connected.

The recommendation is to enable endpoint loop protection using the default parameters:

- **Loop detection interval:** 60
- **Loop detection multiplication factor:** 4
- **Action:** Port Disable

These parameters state that if an endpoint moves more than four times within a 60-second period, the endpoint loop-protection feature will take the specified action (disable the port). The endpoint loop-protection feature is enabled by choosing **Fabric > Access Policies > Global Policies**, as shown in Figure 5-36.

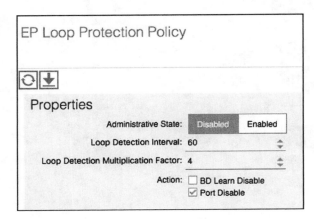

Figure 5-36   *Enabling Endpoint Loop Protection*

If the action taken during an endpoint loop-protection event is to disable the port, the administrator may wish to configure automatic error disabled recovery; in other words, the Cisco ACI fabric will bring the disabled port back up after a specified period of time. This option is configured by choosing **Fabric > Access Policies > Global Policies** and choosing the **Frequent EP move** option, as shown in Figure 5-37.

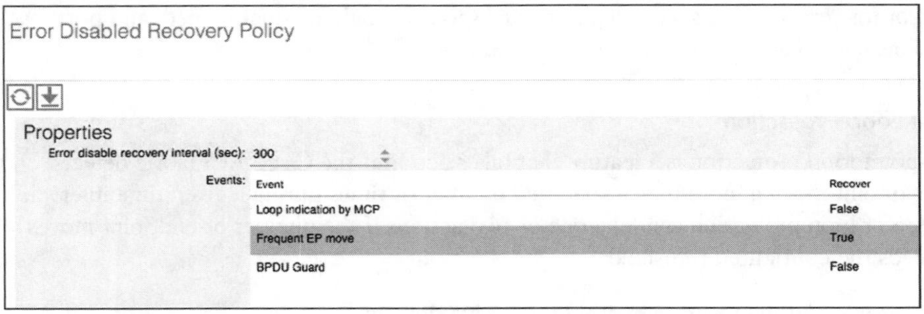

Error Disabled Recovery Policy

Properties

Error disable recovery interval (sec): 300

Events: Event	Recover
Loop indication by MCP	False
Frequent EP move	True
BPDU Guard	False

Figure 5-37   *Error Disabled Recovery Configuration*

Spanning-Tree Considerations

The Cisco ACI fabric does not run Spanning Tree Protocol natively. The flooding scope
for BPDUs is different from the flooding scope for data traffic. The unknown unicast
traffic and broadcast traffic are flooded within the bridge domain; spanning-tree BPDUs
are flooded within a specific VLAN encapsulation (in many cases, an EPG corresponds
to a VLAN, but that's not necessarily the case). Figure 5-38 shows an example in which
external switches connect to the fabric.

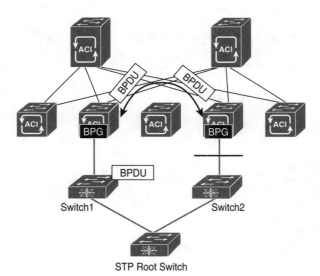

Figure 5-38   *Fabric BPDU Flooding Behavior*

The interactions between the Cisco ACI fabric and the Spanning Tree Protocol are controlled by the EPG configuration.

STP Topology Change Notification (TCN) Snooping

Although the ACI fabric control plane doesn't run STP, it does intercept the STP TCN frame so that it can flush out MAC address entries to avoid blackholing traffic when there is an STP topology change on the outside Layer 2 network. Upon receiving an STP BPDU TCN frame, the APIC flushes the MAC addresses for the corresponding EPG that experienced the STP topology change. This does have an impact on the choice of how the ACI fabric forwards Layer 2 unknown unicast. By default, the ACI leaf forwards the Layer 2 unknown unicast traffic to a spine proxy for further lookup. The spine node will drop the packet if the MAC address doesn't exist in the proxy database. This option is called *hardware proxy*, and it is the default option. Another option is a flood node, like a standard Layer 2 switch. When the hardware proxy option is selected and the fabric detects an STP topology change, the MAC addresses for the EPG will be flushed in the fabric. The Layer 2 traffic will disappear until the MAC addresses are learned again. To prevent this from happening as much as possible, it is recommended that you use a vPC to connect to the ACI leaf and also that you turn on the "peer-switch" feature to avoid a root-bridge change.

Alternatively, you can turn on the unknown unicast flooding to reduce the traffic disruption during an STP topology change.

Network-Centric VLAN=BD=EPG

Network-centric deployment is typically used as a starting point for initially migrating from a legacy network to the ACI fabric. Typically, the legacy infrastructure is segmented by VLANs, and creating the VLAN=EPG=BD mappings in ACI helps to reduce the learning curve of ACI concepts and creates a 1:1 mapping with the legacy environment. Thus, helping to reduce the learning curve, increases comfort levels, and accelerating the migration of applications into ACI.

Using this approach does not require any changes to the existing infrastructure or processes, and the following benefits offered by ACI can still be leveraged:

- A next-generation data center network with high-speed 10Gbps and 40Gbps access and an aggregation network.

- East-west data center traffic optimization for supporting virtualized, dynamic environments as well as nonvirtualized workloads.

- Support for workload mobility and flexibility, with placement of computing and storage resources anywhere in the data center.

- Capability to manage the fabric as a whole instead of using device-centric operations.

- Capability to monitor the network as a whole using the APIC in addition to the existing operation monitoring tools; the APIC offers new monitoring and troubleshooting tools, such as health scores and atomic counters.

- Lower total cost of ownership (TCO) and a common network that can be shared securely across multiple tenants in the data center.

- Rapid network deployment and agility through programmability and integrated automation.

- Centralized auditing of configuration changes.

- Direct visibility into the health of the application infrastructure.

Data centers built prior to ACI use VLANs for the purpose of isolation. VLANs are broadcast domains that allow frames to be sent out all ports of a switch tagged with that VLAN, if the frame has no awareness of the destination. This is called *flooding*. VLANs are generally mapped to one subnet. For example, you may have VLAN 10, which contains all of your database servers. It is likely that these servers will only be assigned to one subnet (perhaps 192.168.10.0/24). Usually a blacklist model is used, meaning traffic is allowed by default within subnets. Security rules are typically assigned at the Layer 3 boundary or default gateway using access control lists (ACLs) or firewall rules.

ACI uses Layer 2 and Layer 3 constructs called bridge domains and endpoint groups (EPGs). You can think of bridge domains as being the same as VLANs in network-centric mode. The bridge domain contains a gateway, or SVI. The SVI acts as a pervasive gateway for our endpoints. In network-centric mode, you have only one SVI, or subnet, contained within a bridge domain.

Endpoint groups are just that—groups of endpoints. They're simply containers for virtual and physical servers. In network-centric mode, you specify endpoints all belonging to the same VLAN, contained within an EPG. There is a one-to-one-to-one-to-one mapping between the bridge domain, EPG, subnet, and VLAN. You may see this described as VLAN=BD=EPG. The ACI configuration of this approach will look similar to Figure 5-39.

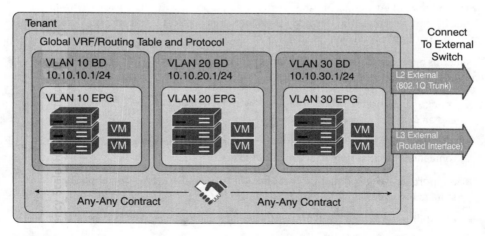

Figure 5-39   *ACI Policy Model—Network-Centric Configuration*

In the network-centric approach, it's not necessary to know which applications, or application tiers, exist on a given VLAN. It is necessary to know which VLANs should be allowed to communicate.

We use contracts to control how VLANs in network-centric mode should communicate. In this mode, because an EPG, subnet, and VLAN are basically all the same, contracts can be set up to behave the same as traditional ACLs. You have an option, when configuring a contract, to allow any traffic to traverse between EPGs. Because a traditional network trusts by default, most enterprises start with these any-any bidirectional contracts, unless extensive ACLs are currently used in their environment. Once these contracts are in place, it is easy to revisit the contracts at a later date and make them more restrictive, as shown in Figure 5-40.

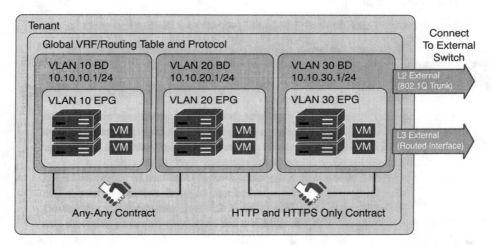

Figure 5-40   *ACI Policy Model—Network-Centric Configuration with Enhanced Security*

It is also possible to use what are called *Taboo contracts*, which are filters within contracts that allow you to deny particular types of traffic. For example, you could create a Taboo contract, alongside a contract permitting everything, that would deny Telnet traffic from your end-user devices to your management devices. In this case, end-user devices are contained within a VLAN (or even different VLANs) that equates to an EPG, and the same would happen for the management servers. A Taboo filter within a contract is applied between the two EPGs (or VLANs) and would deny users from using Telnet to connect to the management devices.

One benefit, with either the application-centric or network-centric approach, is that both contracts and filters are reusable. For example, you can create a contract once and then copy it again between two other EPGs. In the case of the filter, you can create a filter that allows SSH specifically within a contract. Then you can reuse that filter again in another contract. This means you are saving administrative time in configuration, and you are eliminating any human error that could occur. Note that contracts can contain any mix or range of ports and protocols defined in filters.

Applying Policy to Physical and Virtual Workloads

Once an application profile has been created using groups and contracts, devices may be added to the groups so they may consume the policy. Here are three of the most common ways this is accomplished:

- Manually adding the domain and binding in the left navigation pane under each EPG.

- Highlighting the application profile in the left navigation pane and using the drag-and-drop + submit functionality in the right display pane.

- Leveraging the API with POSTMAN or Python.

Note   Prior to adding devices into groups in advanced mode, be sure that your access policies and/or virtual integration have been completed.

Applying policy to a virtual device via a virtual domain is straightforward. The virtual domain should be added in the domains folder under the EPG. At this time, you will need to select the deploy and resolution immediacy. Resolution immediacy controls when policy is pushed from the APIC and programmed into the leaf's object model. The following options are available for resolution immediacy:

- **Pre-Provision:** Pushes policy to the leaf immediately, before a hypervisor is connected to the distributed virtual switch in a VMM domain.

- **Immediate:** Pushes policy to the leaf as soon as a hypervisor is attached to the distributed virtual switch.

- **On-Demand:** Pushes policy to the leaf when a hypervisor is attached to the distributed virtual switch and when a virtual machine is placed into a port group/EPG.

Note   Resolution immediacy has no impact for physical domains.

Deployment immediacy is used to specify when a policy is programmed into the policy CAM on the leaf node. The following options are available for deployment immediacy:

- **Immediate:** Specifies that hardware is programmed as soon as the policy is downloaded to the leaf node.

- **On-Demand:** Specifies that hardware is programmed only when the first packet is received on the data plane.

It is generally recommended that you use the **Pre-Provision** option for resolution immediacy and **On-Demand** for deployment immediacy to ensure that resources are managed appropriately. Users can use the **Immediate** option where necessary to lock in resources for critical services. The **Pre-Provision** option allows policies to be programmed on a leaf switch with no dependency on LLDP or CDP. Use of this option guarantees that the host will be able to communicate through the fabric without having to rely upon an

LLDP/CDP adjacency. It is therefore a recommended option where ESXi management VMkernel interfaces are connected to the ACI VMM domain. It is also recommended for other connected devices that cannot use LLDP or CDP.

For a physical or bare-metal device, you should first specify the domain in which the resource exists in the domains folder under the EPG. The domain that you select will reference the type of physical connection (end host, virtual, storage, L4-7 device, L3 Out, L2 Out) as well as the VLAN resources you will be using. Multiple tenants can also affect how you will assign domains (certain domains could belong to certain tenants). VLAN usage cannot be determined based on the port mapping alone due to the ability to assign multiple domains to a single AAEP. Next, you should select the method in which you will be mapping the EPG to the port(s) and VLAN. An EPG can be mapped to a VLAN on a single port, or to an entire switch or group of switches. By default, a given encapsulation maps to only a single EPG on a leaf switch.

Starting with the v1.1 release, multiple EPGs with the same VLAN encapsulation can be deployed on a given leaf switch (or Fabric Extender), as long as the EPGs are associated with different bridge domains and on different ports. This configuration is not valid when the EPGs belong to the same bridge domain. This does not apply to ports configured for Layer 3 external outside connectivity.

EPGs associated with different bridge domains having the same VLAN encapsulation need to be associated with different physical domains and different NameSpace (VLAN) pools. Two EPGs belonging to a single bridge domain cannot share the same encapsulation value on a given leaf switch.

Only ports that have the **vlanScope** set to **portlocal** allow allocation of separate (port, VLAN) translation entries in both ingress and egress directions. For a given port with the **vlanScope** set to **portlocal**, each VLAN must be unique; given a port P1 and a VLAN V1, a second P1V1 configuration will fail.

Ports that have the **vlanScope** set to **portglobal** configure the VLAN encapsulation value to map only to a single EPG per leaf.

Alternatively, you can highlight the application profile in the left navigation pane and use the drag-and-drop feature to associate bare-metal or virtual workloads (VMware, Microsoft, OpenStack, etc..) with groups. When you do so, a window will open asking for the domain and port mapping where applicable.

The rules of EPG-to-VLAN mapping with a VLAN scope set to global are as follows:

- You can map an EPG to a VLAN that is not yet mapped to another EPG on that leaf.

- Regardless of whether two EPGs belong to the same or different bridge domains, on a single leaf you cannot reuse the same VLAN used on a port for two different EPGs.

- The same VLAN number can be used by one EPG on one leaf and by another EPG on a different leaf. If the two EPGs are in the same bridge domain, they share the same flood domain VLAN for BPDUs and they share the broadcast domain.

The rules of EPG-to-VLAN mapping with the VLAN scope set to local are as follows:

■ You can map two EPGs of different bridge domains to the same VLAN on different ports of the same leaf, if the two ports are configured for different physical domains.

■ You cannot map two EPGs of the same bridge domain to the same VLAN on different ports of the same leaf.

Figure 5-41 shows the EPG-to-VLAN mapping rules described previously.

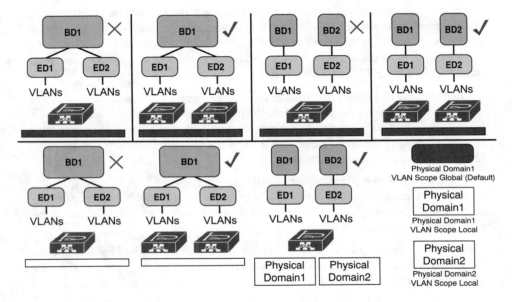

Figure 5-41 *EPG-to-VLAN Mapping Rules*

Moving Devices to the Fabric, VLAN by VLAN

Once an approach to deploying ACI has been finalized, ACI will need connectivity to your current network in order to migrate resources. For the purpose of this book, we are going to assume starting with the network-centric approach and later moving to an application-centric approach. Following what we have already discussed in previous sections of this book, the steps that will be taken are as follows:

Step 1.   Decide on a deployment mode: **network-centric now, application-centric later.**

Step 2.   Set up the fabric and discover the switches.

Step 3.   Configure the required services: OOB MGMT, NTP, RR.

Step 4.   Create fabric access policies for connectivity to the existing network (VPC to Core \ Aggregation), as shown in Figure 5-42.

   a. Configure Loop Protection, Miscabling Protocol (see Figure 5-43).

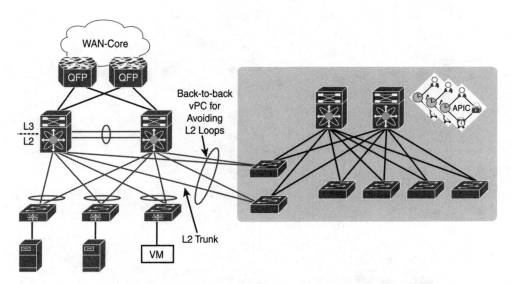

Figure 5-42   *Layer 2 Connectivity Between ACI and the Existing Network*

- Multiple protection mechanisms against external loops.

- LLDP detects direct loopback cables between any two switches in the same fabric.

- Miscabling Protocol (MCP) is a new link level loopback packet that detects an external L2 forwarding loop.

  MCP frame sent on all VLANs on all Ports.

  If any switch detects MCP packet arriving on a port that originated from the same fabric, the port is err-disabled.

- External devices can leverage STP/BPDU.

- MAC/IP move detection and learning throttling and err-disable.

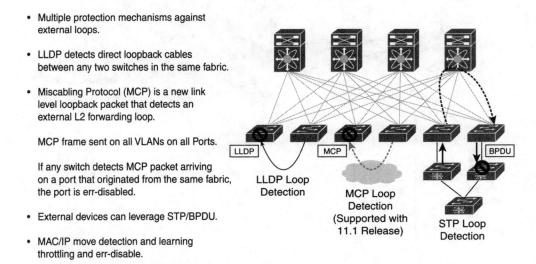

Figure 5-43   *Loop Protection with ACI*

Step 5.   Create a tenant with VLAN=BD=EPG: L2-only bridge domain.

   a.   BD settings: Forwarding = Custom, ARP Flooding = Enabled (due to external gateway; see Figure 5-44).

Figure 5-44   *Temporary Bridge Domain Settings*

Step 6.   L2 statically map VLANs to EPG from external trunk (see Figure 5-45).

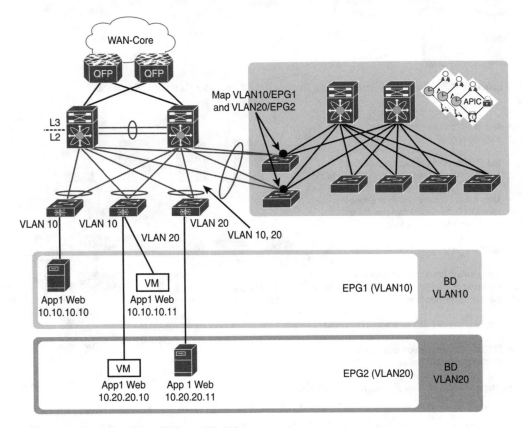

Figure 5-45   *Mapping EPGs to VLANs*

Step 7.   Create fabric access policies for new servers.

    a. On virtual servers, integrate to existing VMware cluster/VDS.

    b. Migrate virtual hosts to new servers on the fabric.

Step 8. Create APIC integration to existing vCenter cluster (OOB MGMT). Create APIC-managed DVS.

Step 9. Connect migrated VMs' vNICs to new port groups (associated to EPGs; see Figure 5-46).

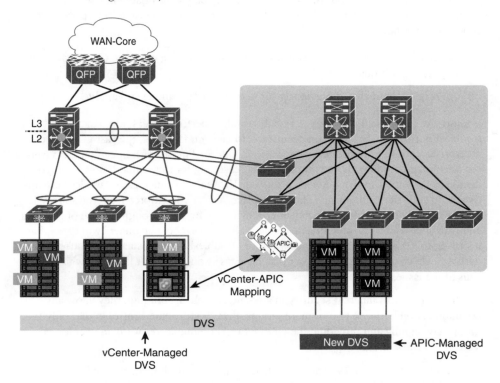

Figure 5-46 *Migrating Existing Hosts to APIC-Managed Distributed Virtual Switch*

Step 10. Remove non-APIC-managed DVS from servers on the fabric if no longer needed.

Note Optionally, you can use L2 external connections to apply more security through contracts in this scenario. Also, you could stand up a new vCenter cluster inside the fabric, leveraging Cross-vCenter vMotion supported with vSphere 6.0 and the ACI 11.2 release.

ACI is now up and running in network-centric mode. This configuration allows enterprises to get used to using and managing ACI with little to no disruption to their existing environment. The servers and devices are integrated with the existing fabric at Layer 2. There has been no change to routing. This configuration gives enterprises the ability to explore and become comfortable with managing ACI. As more and more devices are added to ACI over time, additional steps should be taken to migrate Layer 3 into the fabric. We will examine these steps in the following sections.

Unenforced vs. Enforced VRF

Enterprises have the ability to turn off the fundamental "zero-trust" nature of ACI on a VRF-by-VRF basis. In other words, they can allow resources that exist under a particular VRF to communicate without the use of contracts. Some enterprises choose to use this feature in a network-centric deployment. Here are some of the reasons enterprises may choose this method:

■ No change in security enforcement or operational model; continue to enforce security with traditional methods.

■ All other benefits listed previously for network-centric mode still apply.

In short, ACI retains all of the operational, visibility, performance, redundancy, and troubleshooting benefits, without security enforcement. However, the vast majority of enterprises choose to implement their VRFs in enforced mode with open contracts (versus unenforced mode with no contracts). The reasoning for this is that if and when you decide to increase security between groups or VLANs, it is much easier and less disruptive to do so if the contracts are already in place. When you enforce from the start, you have the ability to modify independent contracts one by one through the use of subjects and filters, instead of making drastic changes all at once. Most engineers will agree that it's easier to get a maintenance window for and troubleshoot an issue when you're dealing with a single change, versus making many changes at once and not knowing which one caused the issue.

Finally, there is also inherent security in any-any contracts. Although they allow any communication between two or more groups, there is still some control in that only the groups consuming and providing the contract can communicate. With an unenforced VRF, it is a free-for-all.

Engineers use VRF *unenforcement* as a troubleshooting tool. If there is an issue on your test ACI fabric, and it is unclear if it is a route/switch- or security-related issue, you can unenforce the VRF. With the VRF unenforced, if traffic passes, you know it's a contract issue. If traffic still does not pass, it is a configuration issue related to connectivity or a route/switch.

L3 Connections to the Core

Until now we have been using ACI as an L2 switch. Although this gives the enterprise a chance to get used to ACI with minimal risk and disruption, the true power of ACI comes when you distribute the performance closer to the hosts. Enabling anycast gateways inside the fabric and allowing ACI to provide high-speed, low-latency services on a policy basis for your servers can provide major benefits. To allow traffic in and out of the fabric at Layer 3, we will need to take advantage of a construct called a *Layer 3 Out*. In most cases, ACI is providing enhanced aggregation and access layer services for your data center. It is best practice to connect ACI to the core of your data center. The core of your data center acts as a barrier between the rest of your network and the data center. It's where services aggregate into, such as your WAN block, campus, and DCI connectivity. ACI also connects to the core and provides L3 connectivity between the devices that reside in the fabric and the rest of the enterprise network. This connectivity is called a *Layer 3 Outside connection* or an *external routed network.*

Figure 5-47 provides a sample diagram of connectivity. In this example, the OSPF neighbor adjacency is between a data center edge firewall and the first leaf node. The other nodes do not have any neighbor relationship. In order for the OSPF leaf to tell the rest of the fabric about any routes it learns, it will have to use route redistribution. Because ACI is multitenant, the protocol of choice is Border Gateway Protocol (BGP) because it carries more information than just routes. We can share information about tenants/VRFs too.

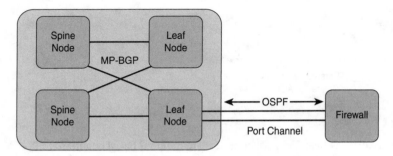

Figure 5-47   *OSPF Neighbor Adjacency Between Leaf Node and Firewall*

In a regular configuration, route peering and static routing are performed on a per-VRF basis, in a manner similar to the use of VRF-lite on traditional routing platforms. External prefixes that are learned on a per-VRF basis are redistributed to the leaf nodes where the tenant endpoints reside. Routes are installed in the forwarding tables of the leaf nodes only if the specific VRF is deployed on that leaf.

Alternatively, shared Layer 3 connectivity can be provided in one of two ways: using shared L3 Out connections or using an MP-BGP and EVPN plus VXLAN connection to an external device (such as a Cisco Nexus 7000 Series switch with appropriate hardware and software). This has the advantage of not requiring separate L3 Out policies for each individual tenant and VRF.

Layer 3 Out and External Routed Networks

In a Cisco ACI fabric, an L3 Out policy is used to configure interfaces, protocols, and protocol parameters necessary to provide IP connectivity to external routing devices. An L3 Out connection is always associated with a VRF. L3 Out connections are configured using the **External Routed Networks** option on the **Networking** menu for a tenant.

Part of the L3 Out configuration involves defining an external network (also known as an *external EPG*). The external network is used to define which subnets are potentially accessible through the Layer 3–routed connection. In Figure 5-48, the networks 50.1.0.0/16 and 50.2.0.0/16 are accessible outside the fabric through an L3 Out connection. As part of the L3 Out configuration, these subnets should be defined as external networks. Alternatively, an external network could be defined as 0.0.0.0/0 to cover all possible destinations.

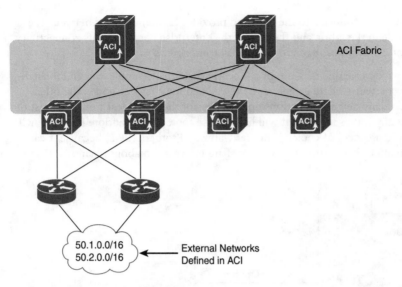

Figure 5-48   *L3 Out Connections*

After an external network has been defined, contracts are required between internal EPGs and the external networks in order for traffic to flow. When defining an external network, check the box **External Subnets for the External EPG**, as shown in Figure 5-49. The other check boxes are relevant for transit and shared services scenarios and are described later in this section.

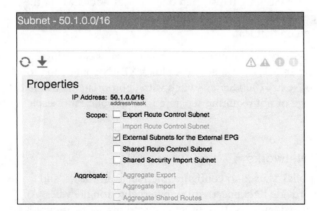

Figure 5-49   *Defining Traffic Filtering for Outside Traffic*

L3 Out Simplified Object Model

Figure 5-50 shows the object model for L3 Out. This helps in understanding the main building blocks of the L3 Out model.

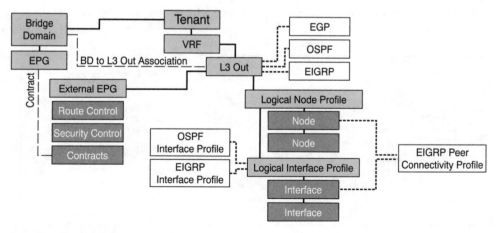

Figure 5-50 *Object Model for L3 Out*

The L3 Out policy is associated with a VRF and consists of the following:

■ **Logical node profile:** This is the leafwide VRF routing configuration, whether it is dynamic or static routing. For example, if you have two border leaf nodes, the logical node profile consists of two leaf nodes.

■ **Logical interface profile:** This is the configuration of Layer 3 interfaces or SVIs on the leaf defined by the logical node profile. The interface selected by the logical interface profile must have been configured with a routed domain in the fabric access policy. This routed domain may also include VLANs if the logical interface profile defines SVIs.

■ **External network and EPG:** This the configuration object that classifies traffic from the outside into a security zone.

The L3 Out connection must be referenced by the bridge domain whose subnets need to be advertised to the outside.

L3 Out policies, or external routed networks, provide IP connectivity between a VRF and an external IP network. Each L3 Out connection is associated with one VRF instance only. A VRF might not have an L3 Out connection if IP connectivity to the outside is not required.

For subnets defined in the bridge domain to be announced to the outside router, the following conditions must be met:

■ The subnets need to be defined as advertised externally.

■ The bridge domain must have a relationship with the L3 Out connection (in addition to its association with the VRF instance).

■ A contract must exist between the Layer 3 external EPG (external subnets for the external EPG) and the EPG associated with the bridge domain. If this contract is not in place, the announcement of the subnets cannot occur.

Figure 5-51 shows the bridge domain and subnet configuration, with the relationship to an L3 Out connection shown.

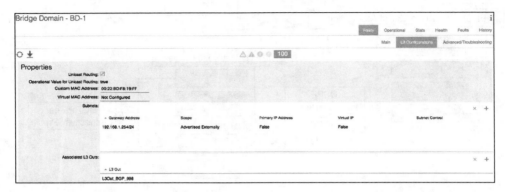

Figure 5-51 *Bridge Domain Relationship to L3 Out Connections*

When specifying subnets under a bridge domain or an EPG for a given tenant, the user can specify the scope of the subnet:

- **Advertised Externally:** This subnet is advertised to the external router by the border leaf.

- **Private to VRF:** This subnet is contained within the Cisco ACI fabric and is not advertised to external routers by the border leaf.

- **Shared Between VRF Instances:** This option is for shared services. It indicates that this subnet needs to be leaked to one or more private networks. The shared-subnet attribute applies to both public and private subnets.

- **External Network (External EPG) Configuration Options:** The external endpoints are assigned to an external EPG (which the GUI calls an external network). For the L3 Out connections, the external endpoints can be mapped to an external EPG based on IP prefixes or host addresses. Note that EPGs for external or outside endpoints are sometimes referred to as *prefix-based EPGs* if defined as networks and masks, or IP-based EPGs if defined as /32. IP-based EPG is also the terminology used to define EPG classification based on the IP address for hosts directly attached to the leaf nodes.

For each L3 Out connection, the user has the option to create one or multiple external EPGs based on whether different policy treatments are needed for different groups of external endpoints.

Under the Layer 3 external EPG configurations, the user can map external endpoints to this EPG by adding IP prefixes and network masks. The network prefix and mask don't need to be the same as the ones in the routing table. When only one external EPG is required, simply use 0.0.0.0/0 to assign all external endpoints to this external EPG.

After the external EPG has been created, the proper contract can be applied between the external EPG and other EPGs.

The main function of the external network configuration (part of the overall L3 Out configuration) is to classify traffic from the outside to an EPG to establish which outside and inside endpoints can talk. However, it also controls a number of other functions such as import and export of routes to and from the fabric.

Here is a summary of the options for the external network configuration and the functions they perform:

- **Subnet:** This is the subnet that is primarily used to define the external EPG classification.

- **Export Route Control Subnet:** This configuration controls which of the transit routes (routes learned from another L3 Out) should be advertised. This is an exact prefix and length match. This item is covered in more detail in the "Transit Routing" section of Chapter 6.

- **Import Route Control Subnet:** This configuration controls which of the outside routes learned through BGP should be imported into the fabric. This is an exact prefix and length match.

- **External Subnets for the External EPG:** This defines which subnets belong to this external EPG for the purpose of defining a contract between EPGs. This is the same semantics as for an ACL in terms of prefix and mask.

- **Shared Route Control Subnet:** This indicates that this network, if learned from the outside through this VRF, can be leaked to the other VRFs (if they have a contract with this external EPG).

- **Shared Security Import Subnets:** This defines which subnets learned from a shared VRF belong to this external EPG for the purpose of contract filtering when establishing a cross-VRF contract. This configuration matches the external subnet and masks out the VRF to which this external EPG and L3 Out belong.

- **Aggregate Export:** This option is used in conjunction with **Export Route Control Subnet** and allows the user to export all routes from one L3 Out to another without having to list each individual prefix and length. This item is covered in more detail in the "Transit Routing" section in Chapter 6.

- **Aggregate Import:** This allows the user to import all the BGP routes without having to list each individual prefix and length. You achieve the same result by not selecting **Route Control Enforcement Input** in the L3 Out (which is the default). This option is useful if you have to select **Route Control Enforcement Input** to then configure action rule profiles (to set BGP options for instance), in which case you would then have to explicitly allow BGP routes by listing each one of them with **Import Route Control Subnet**. With **Aggregate Import**, you can simply allow all BGP routes. The only option that can be configured at the time of this writing is 0.0.0.0/0.

Border Leafs

Border leaf switches are Cisco ACI leaf switches that provide Layer 3 connections to out-side networks. Any Cisco ACI leaf switch can be a border leaf, and there is no limitation on the number of leaf switches that can be used as border leaf switches. The border leaf can also be used to connect to computing, IP storage, and service appliances. In large-scale design scenarios, for greater scalability, it may be beneficial to separate border leaf switches from the leaf switches that connect to computing and service appliances.

Border leaf switches support three types of interfaces to connect to an external router:

- Layer 3 (routed) interface.

- Subinterface with IEEE 802.1Q tagging. With this option, multiple subinterfaces can be configured on the main physical interface, each with its own VLAN identifier.

- Switched virtual interface. With an SVI, the same physical interface that supports Layer 2 and Layer 3 can be used for Layer 2 connections as well as an L3 Out connection.

In addition to supporting routing protocols to exchange routes with external routers, the border leaf applies and enforces policy for traffic between internal and external end-points. As of Release 2.0, Cisco ACI supports the following routing mechanisms:

- Static routing (supported for IPv4 and IPv6)

- OSPFv2 for regular, stub, and not-so-stubby-area (NSSA) areas (IPv4)

- OSPFv3 for regular, stub, and NSSA areas (IPv6)

- EIGRP (IPv4 only)

- iBGP (IPv4 and IPv6)

- eBGP (IPv4 and IPv6)

Through the use of subinterfaces or SVIs, border leaf switches can provide L3 Out con-nectivity for multiple tenants with one physical interface.

We will examine Layer 3 routing in great detail in the following chapter.

Migrating the Default Gateway to the Fabric

The Layer 2 network-centric ACI fabric, which we discussed previously, has been grow-ing over time. In certain VLANs, we now have more hosts inside of the fabric than outside. The enterprise application owners want the added benefit of local routing and switching at the leaf, because they feel it would improve application response time. Now that you have an understanding of L3 external connectivity and ACI, let's explore how to move a gateway into the fabric. Figure 5-52 shows the current environment as it sits today.

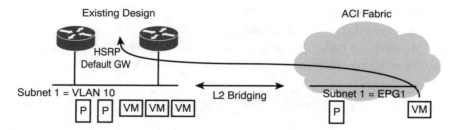

- Default gateway up to this point is still deployed in the brownfield network.
- ACI initially provides only L2 connectivity services.
- L2 path between the two networks leveraged by migrated endpoints to reach the default gateway.

Figure 5-52 *Default Gateway Considerations*

The steps to migrate the L3 gateways into the fabric are as follows:

Step 1. Create fabric access policies for connectivity to the existing network (L3 link to core), as shown in Figure 5-53.

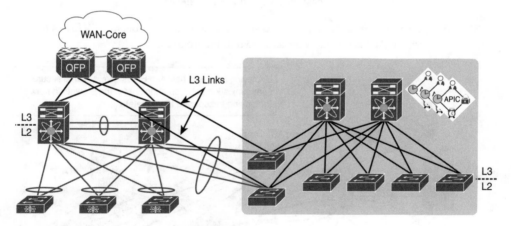

Figure 5-53 *L3 Connectivity to Existing Network*

Step 2. Create an L3 external routed connection in ACI.

Step 3. Add the L3 Out to the bridge domain.

    a. Add the L3 Out to the associated L3 Outs under the BD.

    b. Recommended option: Create Test BD and Groups (to advertise outside of the fabric).

Step 4.   Add the subnet to the bridge domain.

    a. Check that the bridge domain subnet is advertised externally.

    b. Optional: Change the MAC address to match the HSRP vMAC previously used in the brownfield network (see Figure 5-54).

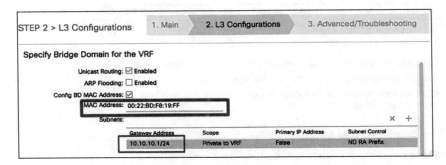

Figure 5-54 *Change MAC to Previous HSRP vMAC (Optional)*

    c. Simultaneously shut down the brownfield interface and click **Submit** to enable the anycast gateway on the ACI network.

Step 5.   Deploy contracts as needed to secure communication between VLANs for which ACI is the gateway, as shown in Figure 5-55.

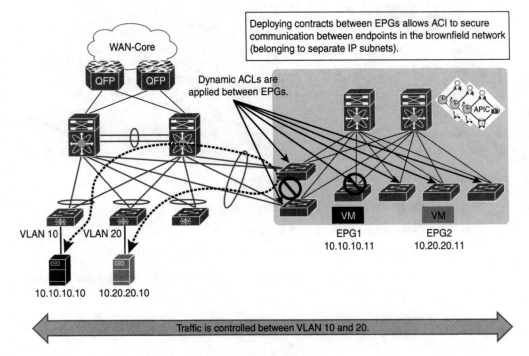

Figure 5-55 *Deploy Contracts to Secure Communication*

Step 6.   Modify the bridge domain to use the default or optimized setting, now that the gateways exist in the fabric (see Figure 5-56).

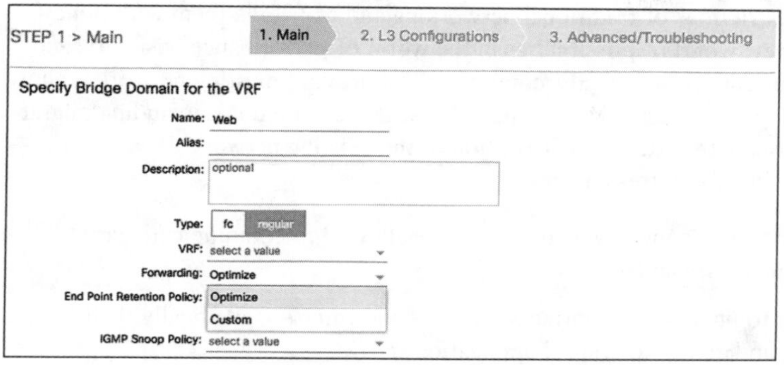

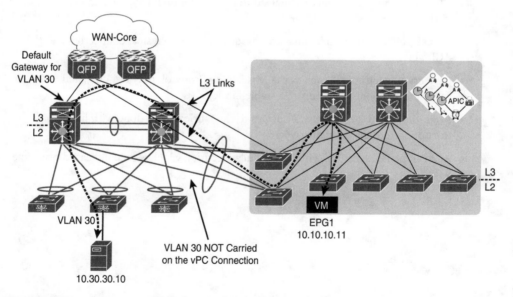

Figure 5-56   *Setting the Bridge Domain to Optimize*

Step 7.   Traffic for VLANs that exist outside of ACI will have to traverse the L3 links, as shown in Figure 5-57.

Figure 5-57   *Layer 3 Traffic Flow Between ACI and Traditional Network*

Summary

The networking capabilities of ACI are flexible, dynamic, and powerful. Decoupling devices from the restrictions of traditional networking and managing them with policy opens up a whole new world of possibilities in the world of performance, visibility, and security. When your enterprise is ready, connecting ACI to your existing network is similar to connecting any other access layer switch. All of this can be done, including migrating host to the fabric, with little to no disruption to the existing network. Here are the key items to remember about this chapter:

- Groups and contracts control which devices are allowed to communicate with each other, not IP addresses and VLANs.

- It is important to understand contracts, subjects and filters—specifically their scope, directionality, and ability to control application traffic.

- Contracts in the common tenant can be reused by any other tenant, assuming the correct scope is set.

- It is recommended that you use vzAny whenever possible.

- VRFs and bridge domains can be used to control routing, Layer 2, and multicast traffic.

- Access policies are used in advanced mode to control physical connectivity to the ACI fabric.

- Protection mechanisms such as the Miscabling Protocol, port tracking, and STP snooping can be used to ensure a stable fabric.

- Migrating Layer 2 and Layer 3 devices to the fabric can be done with little to no disruption to the existing network.

- ACI can be implemented with less-granular security, which is then increased over time.

Chapter 6

External Routing with ACI

Connecting ACI to your existing network is a very important step. The connectivity choices that are made can affect the scalability, redundancy, and complexity of your design. In previous chapters, we discussed connectivity for Layer 2 communication. In this chapter, we discuss how to enable Layer 3 communication and integrate with routing protocols you may already be using in your environment. Specifically, we cover the following topics:

- Physical connectivity options

- Routing protocols

- External EPGs and contracts

- Multitenant routing considerations

- Transit routing

- WAN integration

- Quality of Service

- Multicast

Layer 3 Physical Connectivity Considerations

Getting the most out of ACI means moving Layer 3 routing into the fabric. To move routing into the fabric, we have to have a way to advertise these hosted networks to the rest of the world as well as allow communication to and from the fabric and networks via Layer 3. A data center fabric is home to many critical applications, and these L3 outside links are their lifelines to the outside world. When you're considering your Layer 3 design, it is important to review some of the following items:

■ North/south bandwidth requirements

■ Expected level of redundancy

■ Media types

■ Neighbor devices such as routers, switches, and firewalls

■ Routing protocol or static routes

These decision points will lead you to select the correct physical device for your border leaf, such as a Nexus 9K that supports copper or fiber host-facing ports at 10G, 40G, or 100G, or, as we will discuss later in this chapter, the capability to integrate with other technologies such as the Nexus 7K or ASR platform. Once the physical platform is decided upon, the next decision points will be how many links, which technologies to use, and whether you will use a routing protocol or static routes. Figure 6-1 shows some of these options.

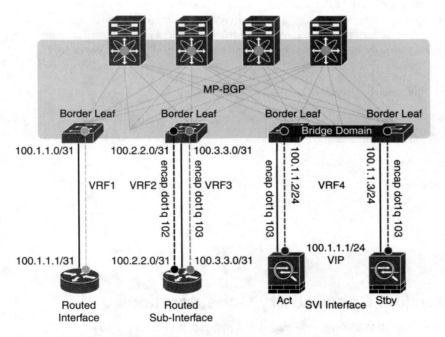

Figure 6-1   *L3 Out Routed Interface Options for Border Leafs*

We will discuss the major decision points in the following sections.

Routed Ports Versus Switched Virtual Interfaces

ACI has the capability to use routed ports, subinterfaces, and switched virtual interfaces (SVIs) for its Layer 3 external connections. The port configuration you choose (Access, Port Channel, VPC) will restrict the features you have the ability to deploy. An example is that ACI supports routed access ports, but not routed port channels. In general, it is a best practice to deploy routed ports when possible instead of SVIs for external routed connections for the following reasons:

- SVIs require you to run the port as an L2 port.

- L2 ports require spanning tree on the neighboring switch. Spanning tree ports traditionally have to transition through listening and learning states.

- BPDUs will be sent from the neighboring switch towards ACI.

- If the VLAN is reused on other ports on the neighboring switch, or even additional ACI leafs or ports, it can expose the network to risk (see the "Outside Bridge Domains" section, next).

Given these factors, routed ports have less risk and converge faster than ports using SVIs. In traditional networking, recommended practice dictates that you use routed port channels if possible. ACI does not currently support this configuration. ACI does support the configuration of multiple routed access ports for a single L3 Out, creating equal-cost multipath and redundancy through multiple links, as shown in Figure 6-2. You will generally find that routing protocols and static routes support at least four equal-cost multipath links.

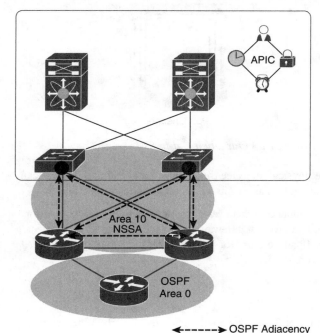

◀------▶ OSPF Adjacency

Figure 6-2 *Using Multiple Routed Access Ports for Redundancy*

Your architecture may dictate the use of subinterfaces and/or switched virtual interfaces. This type of configuration is usually found in the scenarios listed below:

■ Connection to legacy devices.

■ Migration from your existing network.

■ Integration of L4-7 devices.

■ Single interface to host multiple L3 Outs for multiple tenants. Routing relationships could be established for different private networks (VRFs) or tenants on the same physical interface

Figure 6-3 shows supported configurations for L3 Out using SVI.

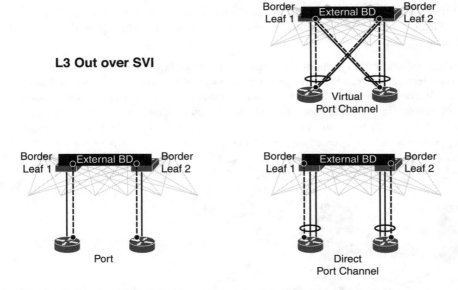

Figure 6-3   *Supported Configurations for L3 Out when Using SVIs*

With an SVI interface, the same physical interface that supports Layer 2 and Layer 3 can be used for a Layer 2 outside connection as well as a Layer 3 outside connection.

It is best practice to use a port channel or (whenever possible) a virtual port channel for increased redundancy. If a shared gateway or gateway redundancy is also a requirement, it is possible to use a secondary IP address or Hot Standby Routing Protocol (HSRP), which is supported in ACI software release 2.2.

Outside Bridge Domains

L3 Out can be configured with Layer 3 interfaces, subinterfaces, or SVIs. When configuring an SVI on L3 Out, you can specify a VLAN encapsulation. Specifying the same VLAN encapsulation on multiple border leaf nodes in the same L3 Out results in the configuration of an external bridge domain. Compared to a bridge domain inside the fabric, there is no mapping database for the L3 Out, and the forwarding of traffic at Layer 2 is based on "flood and learn" over VXLAN. It is recommended that you limit the use of the same SVI encapsulation to two leafs configured in vPC mode. At press time, it is not supported to have an L3 Out made of non-EX (first-generation) leafs consisting of two or more vPC pairs (four or more leafs, two vPC domains) with SVIs, all with the same VLAN encapsulation. If the destination MAC is the SVI MAC address, the traffic is routed in the fabric as already described.

Bidirectional Forwarding Detection

Cisco ACI Software Release 1.2(2g) added support for bidirectional forwarding detection (BFD), which is a software feature used to provide fast failure detection and notification to decrease the convergence times experienced in a failure scenario. BFD is particularly useful in environments where Layer 3 routing protocols are running over shared Layer 2 connections, or where the physical media does not provide reliable failure detection mechanisms. Some of the benefits of using BFD are as follows:

- It provides subsecond Layer 3 failure detection.

- It supports multiple client protocols (for example, OSFP, BGP, EIGRP).

- It is less CPU-intensive than routing protocol hello messages (the BFD echo function uses the data-plane).

- The client protocol is notified when BFD detects a failure. The client protocol does not need to run low hello timers.

In Cisco ACI, BFD is supported on L3 Out interfaces only, where BGP, OSPF, EIGRP, or static routes are in use. BFD is not supported for fabric interfaces (that is, interfaces used to connect leaf and spine nodes together). BFD in Cisco ACI has the following characteristics:

- BFD Version 1 is used.

- Cisco ACI BFD uses asynchronous mode (that is, both endpoints send hello packets to each other).

- BFD is not supported for multihop BGP. By default, a BGP global policy exists for both IPv4 and IPv6 sessions. The default timers specified in this policy have a 50-millisecond interval with a multiplier of 3, as shown in Figure 6-4.

Figure 6-4   *BFD Configuration*

This global default policy can be overridden if required by creating a new nondefault policy and assigning it to a switch policy group and then a switch profile. BFD is also configurable on a per-tenant basis (under **Networking > Protocol Policies**) and will override the global BFD policy.

It is recommended that you enable BFD on L3 Out SVIs wherever possible to help ensure fast failure detection (assuming that the connected device supports it). For routed interfaces and subinterfaces, BFD may still be enabled, although physical interface mechanisms should ensure fast failure detection in most circumstances. In summary, here are some common uses for BFD or instances where BFD is needed:

- L3 hop over an intermediate L2 connection

- Protocol software failures

- Unidirectional link

- When physical media does not provide reliable failure detection

- When the routing protocol is running over an interface type that does not provide link failure notification, such as SVI

BFD may not be needed with directly connected point-to-point L3 links. A link-down event is typically detected faster than BFD.

Access Port

An access port is a single port used for connectivity in an ACI network. You have the capability to use an access port for Layer 3 external network connectivity as well. It is a best practice to use multiple access ports running as routed ports for an external Layer 3 network connection. Figure 6-5 shows an example of this configuration.

Port Channel

A port channel bundles individual interfaces into a group to provide increased bandwidth and redundancy. Port channeling also load-balances traffic across these physical interfaces. For this reason, the recommended practice is to deploy port channels in even numbers. The port channel stays operational as long as at least one physical interface within the port channel is operational. In ACI, you will be creating the port channel using multiple leaf ports on a fixed configuration switch. It is a best practice to diversify port channels across different physical line cards and/or ASIC port groups on the neighboring switch for physical diversity, if possible, as shown in Figure 6-6.

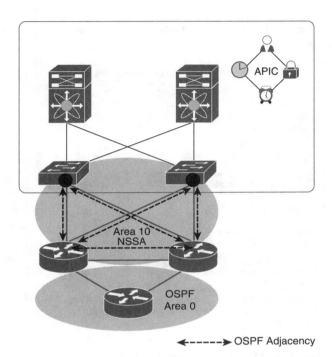

Figure 6-5   *Using Multiple Routed Access Ports for Redundancy*

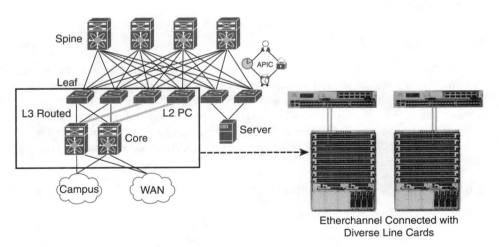

Figure 6-6   *Port Channel Diversity*

You create a port channel by bundling compatible interfaces. You can configure and run either static port channels or port channels running the Link Aggregation Control Protocol (LACP). These settings are implemented in ACI based on the configuration of your fabric access policy. It is important that the settings on both sides of your port channel match, as shown in Figure 6-7.

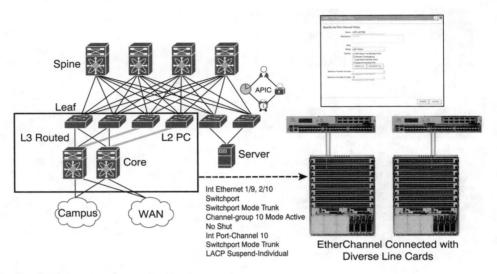

Figure 6-7   *Configuration Parity*

Once the port channel is up and running at Layer 2, ACI will create an outside bridge domain and bring up the SVIs or subinterfaces as configured in your external routed network configuration.

Virtual Port Channel

Virtual Port Channel (vPC) is a virtualization technology that presents paired devices as a unique Layer 2 logical node to access layer devices or endpoints. In the past, you may have heard this technology referred to as *Multichassis EtherChannel*. A virtual port channel allows links that are physically connected to two different devices to appear as a single port channel to a third device. The third device can be a switch, server, or any other networking device that supports link aggregation technology. vPC provides the following technical benefits:

- Eliminates Spanning Tree Protocol (STP) blocked ports

- Uses all available uplink bandwidth

- Allows dual-homed servers to operate in active/active mode

- Provides fast convergence upon link or device failure

- Offers dual active/active default gateways for servers

vPC also leverages native split-horizon/loop management provided by port-channeling technology: a packet entering a port channel cannot immediately exit that same port channel.

By using vPC, users get the following immediate operational and architectural advantages:

- Simplified network design
- Building a highly resilient and robust Layer 2 network
- Scaling available Layer 2 bandwidth, increasing bisectional bandwidth

vPC leverages both hardware and software redundancy aspects:

- vPC uses all port channel member links available so that in case an individual link fails, a hashing algorithm will redirect all flows to the remaining links.
- A vPC domain is composed of two peer devices. Each peer device processes half of the traffic coming from the access layer. In case a peer device fails, the other peer device will absorb all the traffic with minimal convergence time impact.
- Each peer device in the vPC domain runs its own control plane, and both devices work independently. Any potential control plane issues stay local to the peer device and do not propagate or impact the other peer devices.

You can configure dynamic routing protocol peering over a vPC for an L3 Out connection by specifying the same SVI encapsulation on both vPC peers, as illustrated in Figure 6-8. The SVI configuration instantiates an outside bridge domain. The external router peers with the SVI on each leaf device. In addition, the SVIs on the two leaf devices peer with each other. Failure of a vPC port channel to one leaf will not bring down the neighbor adjacency.

If static routing is required toward the fabric, you must specify the same secondary IP address on both vPC peer devices' SVIs. This configuration is not supported when using a dynamic routing protocol.

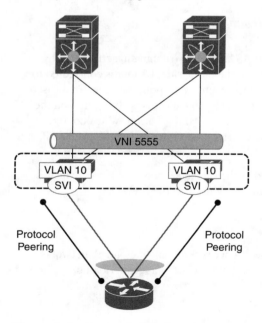

Figure 6-8 *Dynamic Routing: Peering over vPC*

> **Note**   When vPC is used with an ACI fabric, a peer link is not required between the leaf switches that make up a vPC pair.

Gateway Resiliency with L3 Out

Some design scenarios may require gateway resiliency: for example, where external services devices (such as firewalls) require static routing to subnets inside the Cisco ACI fabric, as shown in Figure 6-9.

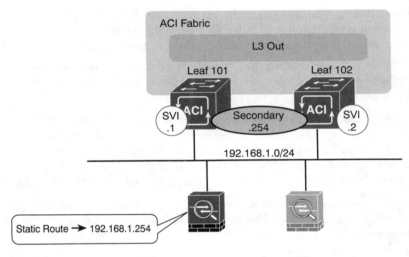

Figure 6-9   *L3 Out Secondary Address Configuration*

In the example in Figure 6-9, a pair of Cisco ASA firewalls (running in active-standby mode) are attached to the Cisco ACI fabric. On the fabric side, L3 Out is configured to connect to the firewalls. On the firewalls, a static route exists pointing to internal Cisco ACI subnets through the 192.168.1.254 address. This .254 address is configured on the fabric as a shared secondary address under the L3 Out configuration. When configuring the interface profile under L3 Out, you have configuration options for Side A, Side B, and secondary addresses, as shown in Figure 6-10.

In this example, 192.168.1.254 is configured as the shared secondary address, which is then used as the next hop for the static route configured on the firewall.

Hot Standby Routing Protocol

Hot Standby Routing Protocol (HSRP) provides network redundancy for IP networks, ensuring that user traffic immediately and transparently recovers from first-hop failures in network edge devices.

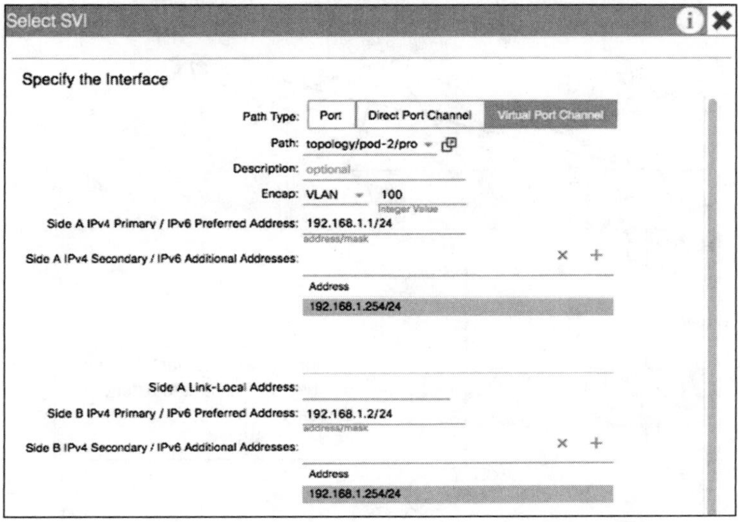

Figure 6-10 *SVI Configuration*

By sharing an IP address and a MAC (Layer 2) address, two or more routers can act as a single virtual router. The members of the virtual router group continually exchange status (hello) messages. This way, one router can assume the routing responsibility of another, should it go out of commission for either planned or unplanned reasons. Hosts continue to forward IP packets to a consistent IP and MAC address, and the changeover of devices doing the routing is transparent.

Using HSRP, a set of routers works in concert to present the illusion of a single virtual router to the hosts on the LAN. This set is known as an *HSRP group* or a *standby group*. A single router elected from the group is responsible for forwarding the packets that hosts send to the virtual router. This router is known as the *active* router. Another router is elected as the *standby* router. In the event that the active router fails, the standby assumes the packet-forwarding duties of the active router. Although an arbitrary number of routers may run HSRP, only the active router forwards the packets sent to the virtual router.

ACI supports HSRP on L3 Out routed interfaces and routed subinterfaces, specifically where customers may connect an external L2 network to ACI, but do not want to extend the L2 network in question into ACI using traditional means. In this configuration, the HSRP hello messages are exchanged via the external L2 network, and do not go over the fabric links within the fabric. Currently, HSRP is not supported on SVIs. Figure 6-11 demonstrates an example of this.

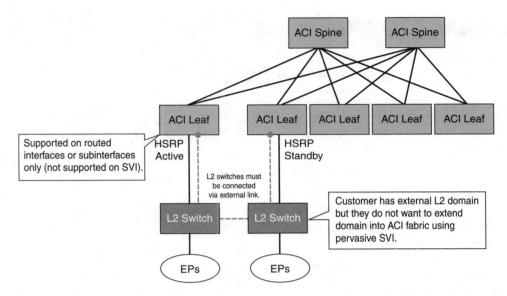

Figure 6-11   *HSRP Example in ACI*

Here are the current HSRP features supported in ACI:

- Version 1 and 2

- Support for IPv4 and IPv6

- Supports BFD

- Authentication (MD5 and simple authentication)

- Configurable timers (min 250 msec hello timer)

- Configurable vMAC or option to use burnt-in-MAC address

- Priority/preemption

With that in mind, the current guidelines and limitations are as follows:

- The HSRP state must be the same for both HSRP IPv4 and IPv6. The priority and preemption must be configured to result in the same state after failovers.

- Currently, only one IPv4 and one IPv6 group are supported on the same subinterface in Cisco ACI.

- Users must configure the same MAC address for IPv4 and IPv6 HSRP groups for dual-stack configurations.

- HSRP VIP must be in the same subnet as the interface IP.

- It is recommended that you configure interface delay for HSRP configurations.

- Object tracking on HSRP is not supported.

- HSRP is not supported on SVI; therefore, no VPC support for HSRP is available.

- Multiple group optimization (MGO) is not supported with HSRP.

- ICMP IPv4 and IPv6 redirects are not supported.

- High availability and Non-Stop Forwarding (NSF) are not supported because HSRP is not restartable in the Cisco ACI environment.

- There is no extended hold-down timer support because HSRP is supported only on leaf switches. HSRP is not supported on spine switches.

- HSRP version change is not supported in APIC. You must remove the configuration and reconfigure.

- HSRP Version 2 does not interoperate with HSRP Version 1. An interface cannot operate both Version 1 and Version 2 because both versions are mutually exclusive. However, the different versions can be run on different physical interfaces of the same router.

Routing Protocols

As of Release 2.0, Cisco ACI supports the following routing mechanisms:

- Static routing (supported for IPv4 and IPv6)

- OSPFv2 for regular, stub, and not-so-stubby-area (NSSA) areas (IPv4)

- OSPFv3 for regular, stub, and NSSA areas (IPv6)

- EIGRP (IPv4 only)

- iBGP (IPv4 and IPv6)

- eBGP (IPv4 and IPv6)

Through the use of subinterfaces or SVIs, border leaf switches can provide L3 Out connectivity for multiple tenants with one physical interface.

Static Routing

Routers forward packets using either route information from route table entries that you manually configure or the route information that is calculated using dynamic routing algorithms.

Static routes, which define explicit paths between two routers, cannot be automatically updated; you must manually reconfigure static routes when network changes occur. Static routes use less bandwidth than dynamic routes. No CPU cycles are used to calculate and analyze routing updates.

Static routes should be used in environments where network traffic is predictable and where the network design is simple. Static routes should not be used in large, constantly changing networks because static routes cannot react to network changes.

Static routes are very easy to configure in ACI. When you configure your L3 Out, a routing protocol will not be selected. Later in the process when a node is defined, you will also define the static routes. When you define the static route, you will be able to modify the following parameters:

- Prefix

- Priority for the static route

- Next hop and next hop priority (the absence of a next hop adds a null route)

- Enable BFD

As you would expect, the configuration is very straightforward. This configuration does not exchange routes with neighboring devices. Static routes will need to be added on the neighboring devices as well, so that traffic has a return path.

Enhanced Interior Gateway Routing Protocol

Enhanced Interior Gateway Routing Protocol (EIGRP) was Cisco's proprietary routing protocol, based on IGRP, but it's now an open standard. EIGRP is a distance vector routing protocol, with optimizations to minimize routing instability incurred after topology changes and the use of bandwidth and processing power in the router. Most of the routing optimizations are based on the Diffusing Update Algorithm (DUAL), which guarantees loop-free operation and provides fast router convergence.

The EIGRP routing protocol is very easy to configure and manage. For this reason, EIGRP is widely deployed across Cisco customers and is supported in ACI. To become an EIGRP neighbor, three essential configuration values must be matched: active hello packets, autonomous system number (ASN), and K values. EIGRP may use five K values or metric components to select the best route for the routing table. These are Bandwidth, Load, Delay, Reliability, and MTU. By default, EIGRP uses only two components: Bandwidth and Delay. When you configure a routing protocol on the L3 Out connection, you will select EIGRP. It is at this point that the AS number is able to be configured, as shown in Figure 6-12.

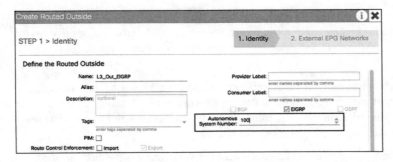

Figure 6-12   *Configuring EIGRP on a Routed Outside Connection or L3 Out*

During the configuration, you will add a node and interface profile. When the node and router ID are configured, avoid using the loopback. Loopbacks should be used only in BGP routing protocol configuration.

When the EIGRP interface profile is added, and the protocol profile is configured, ACI will ask for an EIGRP interface policy. It is here where the final K values (Bandwidth and Delay) will be configured. The EIGRP interface policy will then be applied to the interface that you choose in the next screens.

Note If the K value related to MTU size is used as an enabled metric, the default MTU size of an ACI leaf is 9000. Change the MTU size on one neighbor or the other so that the MTU sizes match.

Open Shortest Path First

Open Shortest Path First (OSPF) is a routing protocol developed for IP networks by the Interior Gateway Protocol working group of the Internet Engineering Task Force (IETF). It was derived from several research efforts, including a version of OSI's IS-IS routing protocol.

OSPF has two primary characteristics:

- It is an open protocol. Its specification is in the public domain (RFC 1247).

- It is based on the Shortest Path First (SPF) algorithm, sometimes known as the Dijkstra algorithm.

OSPF is a link-state routing protocol that calls for the sending of link-state advertisements (LSAs) to all other routers within the same hierarchical area. Information on attached interfaces, metrics used, and other variables are included in OSPF LSAs. As OSPF routers accumulate link-state information, they use the SPF algorithm to calculate the shortest path to each node.

OSPF is widely deployed in enterprises and is a go-to standard for open routing protocols. ACI supports external connectivity to external OSPF routers on OSPF normal areas, NSSA areas, and stub areas, including Area 0 (backbone area). Keep the following points in mind as you are configuring and using OSPF with ACI:

- ACI border leafs running OSPF are always autonomous system boundary routers (ASBRs).

- All external routes learned in OSPF are redistributed into MP-BGP.

- MP-BGP routes are redistributed into OSPF as external Type-2 routes.

- OSPF areas on different border leafs (border leaf pairs) are different OSPF areas, even if area IDs match, as shown in Figure 6-13.

- Supports IPv4 (OSPFv2) and IPv6 (OSPFv3).

- ACI border leaf switches follow OSPF protocol rules, as shown in Figure 6-14.

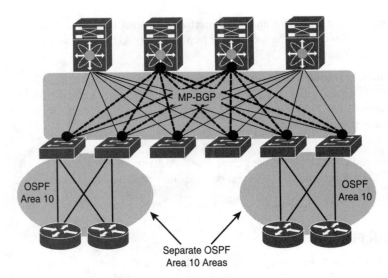

Figure 6-13 *OSPF Areas on Different Border Leaf Switches Are Different OSPF Areas*

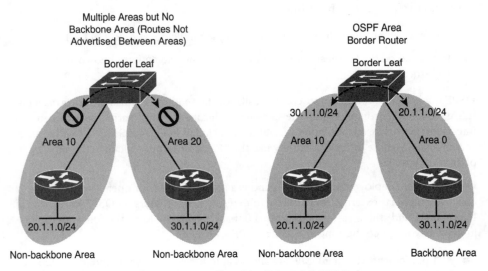

Figure 6-14 *ACI Border Routers Follow Traditional OSPF Rules*

When you configure a routing protocol on the L3 Out connection, you will select OSPF. It is at this point that the particulars of your OSPF area and the area number are configured, as shown in Figure 6-15.

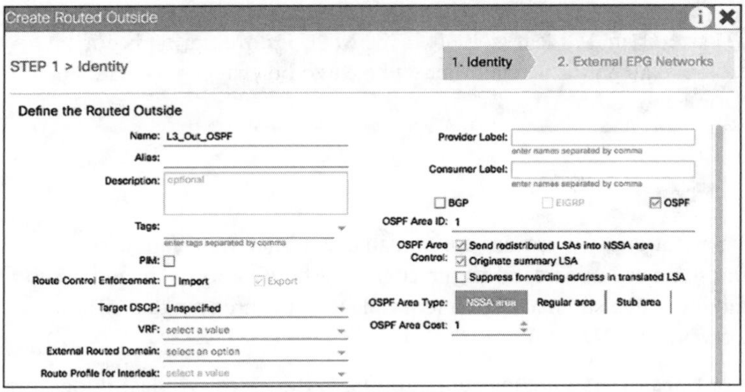

Figure 6-15 *Configuring the OSPF Area and Area ID for a Routed Outside or L3 Out*

During the configuration, you will add a node and interface profile. When the node and router ID are configured, avoid using the loopback. Loopbacks should only be used in a BGP routing protocol configuration. When the OSPF interface profile is added, and the protocol profile is configured, ACI will ask for authentication information as well as an OSPF policy. The OSPF policy (see Figure 6-16) is where you can manage parameters such as the type of link (broadcast or point-to-point), passive participation, BFD, and MTU ignore. The OSPF interface policy will then be applied to the interface(s) you choose in the next screens.

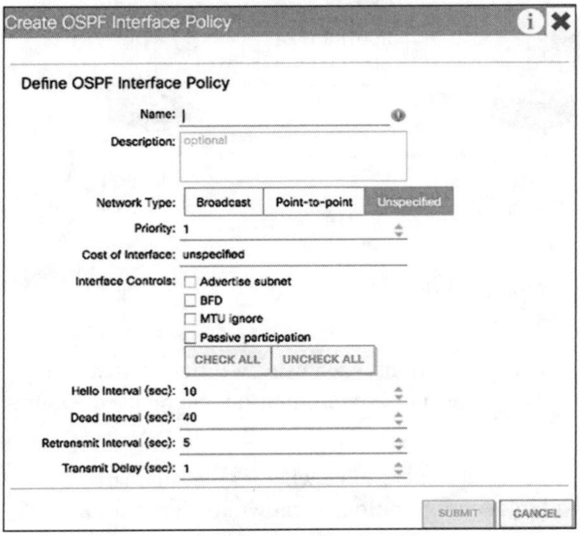

Figure 6-16 *OSPF Interface Policy*

> **Note** The default MTU size of an ACI leaf is 9000. If the **MTU ignore** option is not selected, the MTU size on one neighbor or the other will have to be changed to match in order for a neighbor relationship to form.

OSPF Summarization

For OSPF route summarization, two options are available: external route summarization (equivalent to the summary-address configuration in Cisco IOS Software and Cisco NX-OS Software) and inter-area summarization (equivalent to the area range configuration in Cisco IOS Software and NX-OS).

When tenant routes or transit routes are injected into OSPF, the Cisco ACI leaf node where the L3 Out connection resides is acting as an OSPF autonomous system boundary router (ASBR). In this case, the summary-address configuration (that is, external route summarization) should be used. Figure 6-17 illustrates this concept.

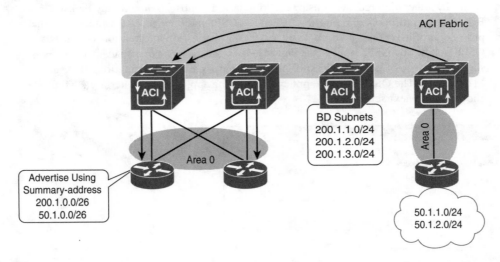

Figure 6-17 *OSPF Summary-Address Operation*

For scenarios where there are two L3 Out connections, each using a different area and attached to the same border leaf switch, the area range configuration will be used to summarize, as shown in Figure 6-18.

The OSPF route summarization policy is used to determine whether the summarization will use the area range or summary-address configuration, as shown in Figure 6-19.

In this example, checking the **Inter-Area Enabled** box means that area range will be used for the summary configuration. If this box is unchecked, summary address will be used.

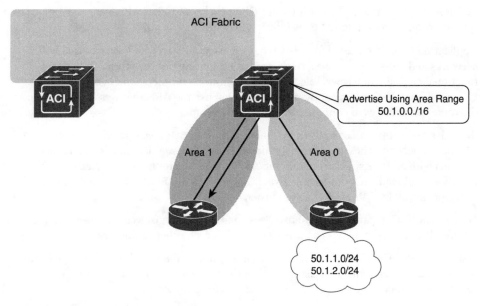

Figure 6-18 *OSPF Area Range Operation*

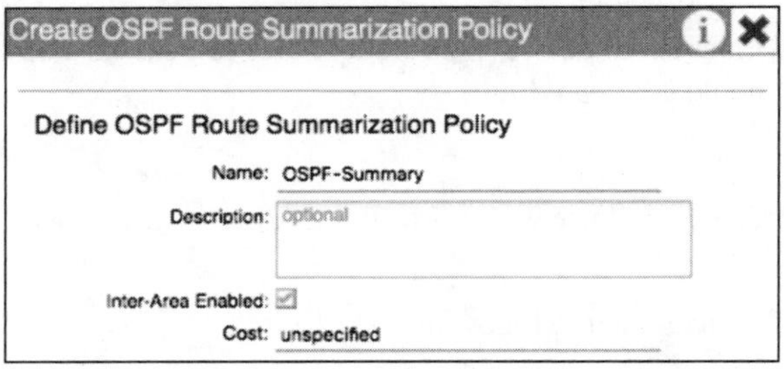

Figure 6-19 *OSPF Route Summarization*

Border Gateway Protocol

The Border Gateway Protocol (BGP) is an inter-autonomous system routing protocol. An autonomous system (AS) is a network or group of networks under common administration using common routing policies. BGP is used to exchange routing information for the Internet and is the protocol used between ISPs. Customer networks, such as universities and corporations, usually employ an interior gateway protocol (IGP) such as Routing Information Protocol (RIP), Enhanced Interior Gateway Routing Protocol (EIGRP), or Open Shortest Path First (OSPF) for the exchange of routing information within their networks. Customers connect to ISPs, and ISPs use BGP to exchange customer and ISP routes. When BGP is used between autonomous systems, the protocol is referred to as *external*

BGP (eBGP). If a service provider is using BGP to exchange routes within an autonomous system, the protocol is referred to as *interior* BGP (iBGP).

Application Centric Infrastructure (ACI) has the capability to peer with external BGP networks and redistribute the routing information throughout the fabric. To use this functionality, you will have to select BGP as the routing protocol when you create the L3 routed outside connection. By default, ACI will use the ASN that was defined when the route reflectors were configured during fabric setup.

iBGP design best practices need to be followed for the iBGP deployment between the ACI border leaf switches and external routers. The ACI border leaf needs to have iBGP sessions with all BGP speakers within the AS. In cases where the route reflector technology is deployed, ACI border leaf switches need to have iBGP sessions with all route reflectors in the BGP Route Reflector cluster.

Notice that border leafs don't have iBGP sessions among themselves. This is not required because border leaf switches can learn routes from each other through MP-BGP.

Unless you are using WAN integration, be sure to follow the VRF-lite best practices for the multitenant deployment scenarios. When the Layer 3 outside connection is required for each tenant, configure separate iBGP sessions for each tenant.

When you are configuring the routed outside connection, the BGP-specific configuration requires you to create a node profile with the following information:

- Router IDs (for iBGP peering with external device) with static routes to the next-hop address. Note that a loopback should be created.

- BGP peering details, such as the Neighbor IP.

- The interface and interface profile you will use with port, IP, and VLAN encapsulation details.

- A BGP peer connectivity profile, including the following:

  - Peer address

  - Authentication

Next you will create an external endpoint group. This group will represent all the devices (or a subset of devices) that are reachable through this L3 Out and BGP connection. Many enterprises use the subnet 0.0.0.0/0 to assign all external endpoints reachable via this link to the EPG that is being crafted.

Finally, in order to advertise prefixes from the fabric (leaf) to its neighbor, you need to associate the Layer 3 outside network with the bridge domain (which will create a route map) that contains the subnets you want to advertise. The subnets must be marked as *advertised externally*, and an application profile with an EPG linked to this bridge domain must be created. The public routes will then be advertised to all peers of the associated Layer 3 outside network.

BGP Route Profile

A route profile provides a control mechanism for routes with BGP peers. This can be viewed as a standard route map in the classic BGP configuration.

A route profile can be associated with any of the following:

- Prefix
- Bridge domain
- Layer 3 outside network

When a route profile is associated with a bridge domain, all of the subnets under the bridge domain will be advertised with the same BGP community value. The software also allows the user to associate a route profile with a subnet of a bridge domain; this capability provides the flexibility to mark different BGP community values for different subnets. When a route profile is specified under both the bridge domain and the subnets of a bridge domain, the route profile under the subnet takes precedence.

A route profile with the name "default-export" can be configured and will be applied automatically to the Layer 3 outside network.

Outbound BGP Policy

The ACI border leaf switches support outbound BGP policy to set community or extended community values for tenant routes. The BGP community attributes (standard and extended) are commonly used by network architects to group together certain BGP routes and apply route policy by matching community values.

The following two types of communities are supported:

- **Standard community**: regular:as2-nn2:<community_value>
  - regular:as2-nn2 is a keyword for the standard community.
  - Add a standard community value (for example 666:1001).
- **Extended community**: extended:as4-nn2:<community_value>
  - extended:as4-nn2 is a keyword for the extended community.
  - Add a extended community value.

BGP Protocol Statistics

BGP protocol statistics can be viewed under **Fabric > Inventory** (see Figure 6-20). Investigate them by following these steps:

1. In the navigation pane, expand **Pod ID > Leaf Switch ID > Protocols > BGP** and click the corresponding tenant and private network.

2. Click various options, such as **Neighbors, Interfaces, Routes**, and **Traffic** to check different statistics related to BGP.

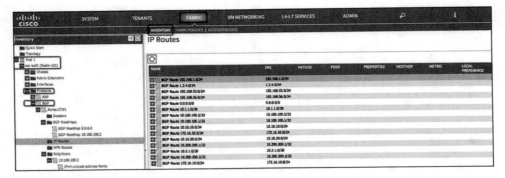

Figure 6-20   *Validating Statistics*

External Endpoint Groups and Contracts

It should be no surprise by now that communication with devices and networks outside the fabric is enabled through the use of groups and contracts. In the following subsection, we explore the flexibility of using these groups to provide external connectivity to devices inside the fabric.

External Endpoint Groups

An external endpoint group (EPG) carries the external network/prefix information. The ACI fabric maps external Layer 3 endpoints to the external EPG by using the IP prefix and mask. One or more external EPGs can be supported for each Layer 3 outside connection, depending on whether the user wants to apply a different policy for different groups of external endpoints. Figure 6-21 shows an example of this.

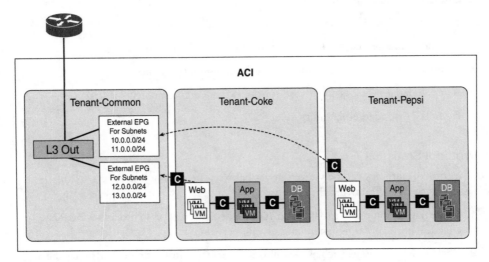

Figure 6-21   *Multiple EPGs Associated with a Single L3 Out Connection*

Most enterprises treat all outside endpoints equally for a given L3 outside link and create only one external EPG per L3 Out. This EPG will then be used when defining contracts between internal endpoint groups and the external L3 connection. This configuration still allows for a significant amount of control due to the contracts that are required between the traditional EPGs and the L3 Out EPGs. These contracts can be individually tailored per group or in a one-size-fits-all fashion.

Contracts Between L3 Out EPGs and Internal EPGs

An L3 Out connection is configured, and ACI interfaces are up. Neighbor relationships to external routers are formed and routes are being advertised. However, the cardinal rule of ACI is "zero trust," and without a contract between the external EPG and the groups you would like to use it, no data shall pass. To enable end-to-end data connectivity, you need to create a contract between the internal EPG(s) and the external EPG. After you apply a contract between the L3 Out EPG and at least one internal EPG, data will be able to pass between the groups in the manner you specified in the contract.

Multitenant Routing Consideration

A common requirement of multitenant cloud infrastructures is the capability to provide shared services to hosted tenants. Such services include Active Directory, DNS, and storage. Figure 6-22 illustrates this requirement.

In Figure 6-22, Tenants 1, 2, and 3 have locally connected servers, respectively part of EPGs A, B, and C. Each tenant has an L3 Out connection linking remote branch offices to this data center partition. Remote clients for Tenant 1 need to establish communication with servers connected to EPG A. Servers hosted in EPG A need access to shared services hosted in EPG D in a different tenant. EPG D provides shared services to the servers hosted in EPGs A and B and to the remote users of Tenant 3.

In this design, each tenant has a dedicated L3 Out connection to the remote offices. The subnets of EPG A are announced to the remote offices for Tenant 1, the subnets in EPG B are announced to the remote offices of Tenant 2, and so on. In addition, some of the shared services may be used from the remote offices, as in the case of Tenant 3. In this case, the subnets of EPG D are announced to the remote offices of Tenant 3.

Another common requirement is shared access to the Internet, as shown in Figure 6-23. In the figure, the L3 Out connection of the Shared Services tenant (shown in the figure as "L3Out4") is shared across Tenants 1, 2, and 3. Remote users may also need to use this L3 Out connection, as in the case of Tenant 3. In this case, remote users can access L3Out4 through Tenant 3.

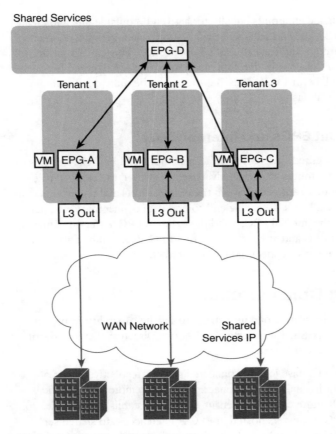

Figure 6-22 *Shared Services Tenant*

These requirements can be implemented in several ways:

- Use the VRF instance from the common tenant and the bridge domains from each specific tenant.

- Use the equivalent of VRF leaking (which in Cisco ACI means configuring the subnet as shared).

- Provide shared services with outside routers connected to all tenants.

- Provide shared services from the Shared Services tenant by connecting it with external cables to other tenants in the fabric.

The first two options don't require any additional hardware beyond the Cisco ACI fabric itself. The third option requires external routing devices such as additional Cisco Nexus 9000 Series switches that are not part of the Cisco ACI fabric. If you need to put shared services in a physically separate device, you are likely to use the third option. The fourth option, which is logically equivalent to the third one, uses a tenant as if it were an external router and connects it to the other tenants through loopback cables.

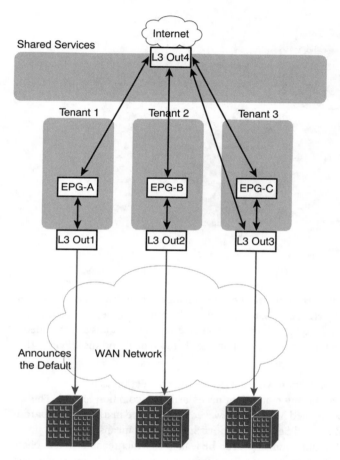

Figure 6-23   *Shared L3 Out Connection for Internet Access*

Shared Layer 3 Outside Connection

It is a common approach for each tenant and VRF residing in the Cisco ACI fabric to have its own dedicated L3 Out connection; however, an administrator may want to use a single L3 Out connection that can be shared by multiple tenants within the Cisco ACI fabric. This allows a single L3 Out connection to be configured in a single, shared tenant (such as the common tenant), along with other tenants on the system sharing this single connection, as shown in Figure 6-24.

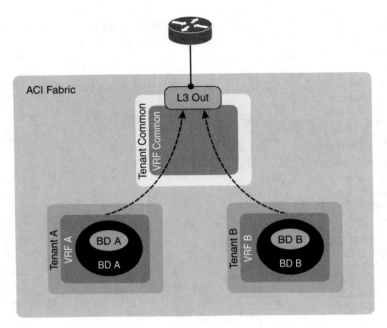

Figure 6-24 *Shared L3 Out Connections*

A shared L3 Out configuration is similar to the inter-tenant communication discussed in the previous section. The difference is that in this case, the routes are being leaked from the L3 Out connection to the individual tenants, and vice versa. Contracts are provided and consumed between the L3 Out connection in the shared tenant and the EPGs in the individual tenants.

To set up a shared L3 Out connection, you can define the connection as usual in the shared tenant (this tenant can be any tenant, not necessarily the common tenant). The external network should be defined as usual. However, it should be marked with **Shared Route Control Subnet** and **Shared Security Import Subnet**. This means that the routing information from this L3 Out connection can be leaked to other tenants, and subnets accessible through this L3 Out connection will be treated as external EPGs for the other tenants sharing the connection (see Figure 6-25).

Further information about these options follows:

- **Shared Route Control Subnet:** This option indicates that this network, if learned from the outside through this VRF, can be leaked to other VRFs (assuming that they have a contract with the external EPG).

- **Shared Security Import Subnets:** This option defines which subnets learned from a shared VRF belong to this external EPG for the purpose of contract filtering when establishing a cross-VRF contract. This configuration matches the external subnet and masks out the VRF to which this external EPG and L3 Out connection belong. This configuration requires that the contract filtering be applied at the border leaf.

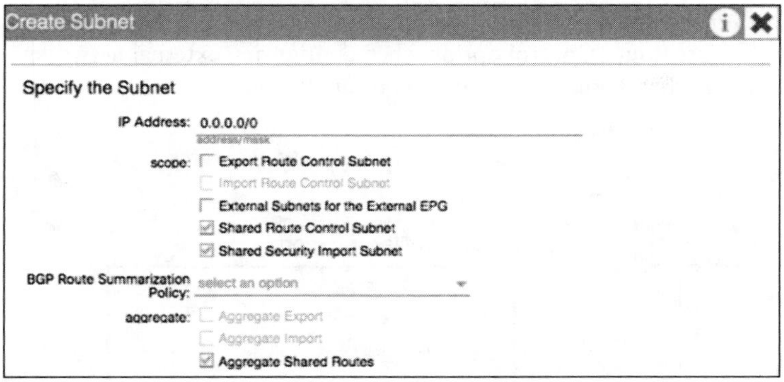

Figure 6-25 *Shared Route Control and Shared Security Import Subnet Configuration*

In the example in Figure 6-25, the **Aggregate Shared Routes** option is checked. This means that all routes will be marked as *shared route control* (in other words, all routes will be eligible for advertisement through this shared L3 Out connection).

At the individual tenant level, subnets defined under bridge domains should be marked as both **Advertised Externally** and **Shared Between VRFs**, as shown in Figure 6-26.

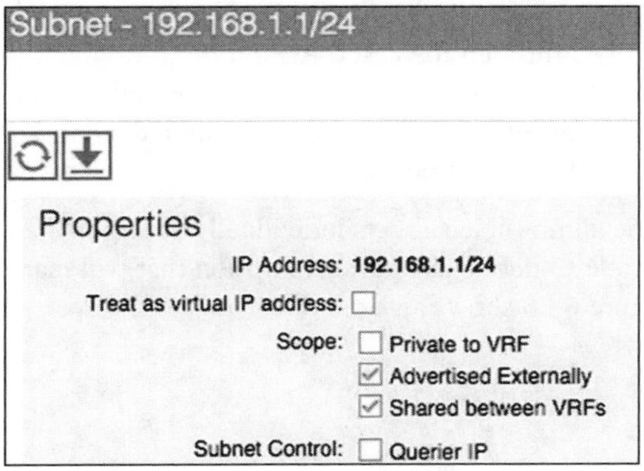

Figure 6-26 *Subnet Scope Options*

Note If you use vzAny on a VRF (for example, VRF1) to reduce the policy CAM consumption, be aware that vzAny also includes the Layer 3 external EPG of the L3 Out connection of VRF1. As a result, if the vzAny of a VRF (VRF1) is a consumer of an EPG of a different VRF (VRF2), the EPG subnets of the second VRF (VRF2) are also announced to the L3 Out connection of VRF1.

Transit Routing

The transit routing function in the Cisco ACI fabric enables the advertisement of routing information from one L3 Out connection to another, allowing full IP connectivity between routing domains through the Cisco ACI fabric.

To configure transit routing through the Cisco ACI fabric, you must mark the subnets in question with the **Export Route Control** option when configuring external networks under the L3 Out configuration. Figure 6-27 shows an example.

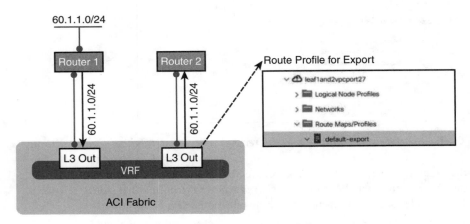

Figure 6-27   *Export Route Control Operation*

In the example in Figure 6-27, the desired outcome is for subnet 60.1.1.0/24 (which has been received from Router 1) to be advertised through the Cisco ACI fabric to Router 2. To achieve this, the 60.1.1.0/24 subnet must be defined on the second L3 Out and marked as an export route control subnet. This will cause the subnet to be redistributed from MP-BGP to the routing protocol in use between the fabric and Router 2.

It may not be feasible or scalable to define all possible subnets individually as export route control subnets. It is therefore possible to define an aggregate option that will mark all subnets with export route control. Figure 6-28 shows an example.

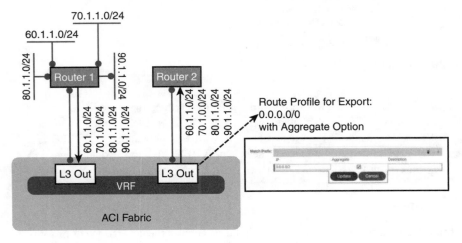

Figure 6-28   *Aggregate Export Option*

In the example in Figure 6-28, there are a number of subnets received from Router 1 that should be advertised to Router 2. Rather than defining each subnet individually, the administrator can define the 0.0.0.0/0 subnet and mark it with both export route control and the **Aggregate** export option. This option instructs the fabric that all transit routes should be advertised from this L3 Out. Note that the **Aggregate** export option does not actually configure route aggregation or summarization; it is simply a method to specify all possible subnets as exported routes. Note also that this option works only when the subnet is 0.0.0.0/0; the option will not be available when you're configuring any subnets other than 0.0.0.0/0.

In some scenarios, you may need to export static routes between L3 Out connections, as shown in Figure 6-29.

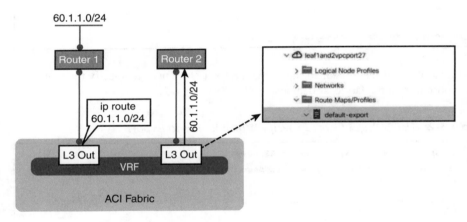

Figure 6-29 *Exporting Static Routes*

In the example in Figure 6-29, a static route to 60.1.1.0 is configured on the left L3 Out. If you need to advertise the static route through the right L3 Out, the exact subnet must be configured and marked with export route control. A 0.0.0.0/0 aggregate export subnet will not match the static route.

Finally, note that route export control affects only routes that have been advertised to the Cisco ACI fabric from outside. It has no effect on subnets that exist on internal bridge domains.

Route maps are used on the leaf nodes to control the redistribution from BGP to the L3 Out routing protocol. For example, in the output in Example 6-1, a route map is used for controlling the redistribution between BGP and OSPF.

Example 6-1   *Controlling Redistribution with a Route Map*

```
Leaf-101# show ip ospf vrf tenant-1:vrf-1
Routing Process default with ID 6.6.6.6 VRF tenant-1:vrf-1
Stateful High Availability enabled
Supports only single TOS(TOS0) routes
Supports opaque LSA
Table-map using route-map exp-ctx-2818049-deny-external-tag
Redistributing External Routes from
static route-map exp-ctx-st-2818049

direct route-map exp-ctx-st-2818049

bgp route-map exp-ctx-proto-2818049

eigrp route-map exp-ctx-proto-2818049
```

Further analysis of the route map shows that prefix lists are used to specify the routes to be exported from the fabric, as demonstrated in Example 6-2.

Example 6-2   *Using Prefix Lists to Specify Which Routes to Export*

```
Leaf-101# show route-map exp-ctx-proto-2818049
route-map exp-ctx-proto-2818049, permit, sequence 7801
Match clauses:
ip address prefix-lists: IPv6-deny-all IPv4-proto16389-2818049-exc-ext-inferred-
  exportDST
  Set clauses:
    tag 4294967295
route-map exp-ctx-proto-2818049, permit, sequence 9801
Match clauses:
ip address prefix-lists: IPv6-deny-all IPv4-proto49160-2818049-agg-ext-inferred-
  exportDST
  Set clauses:
    tag 4294967295
```

Finally, analysis of the prefix list shows the exact routes that were marked as *export route control* in the L3 Out connection, as demonstrated in Example 6-3.

Example 6-3   *Routes Marked as Export Route*

```
Leaf-101# show ip prefix-list IPv4-proto16389-2818049-exc-ext-inferred-exportDST ip
  prefix-list IPv4-proto16389-2818049-exc-ext-inferred-exportDST: 1 entries
seq 1 permit 70.1.1.0/24
```

Supported Combinations for Transit Routing

Some limitations exist on the supported transit routing combinations through the fabric. In other words, transit routing is not possible between all the available routing protocols. For example, at the time of this writing, transit routing is not supported between two connections if one is running EIGRP and the other is running BGP.

The latest matrix showing supported transit routing combinations is available at the following link:

> http://www.cisco.com/c/en/us/td/docs/switches/datacenter/aci/apic/sw/kb/b_KB_Transit_Routing.html

Loop Prevention in Transit Routing Scenarios

When the Cisco ACI fabric advertises routes to an external routing device using OSPF or EIGRP, all advertised routes are tagged with the number 4294967295 by default. For loop-prevention purposes, the fabric will not accept routes inbound with the 4294967295 tag. This may cause issues in some scenarios where tenants and VRFs are connected together through external routing devices, or in some transit routing scenarios such as the example shown in Figure 6-30.

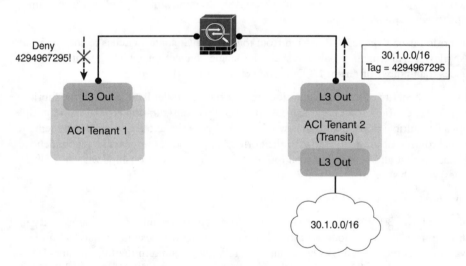

Figure 6-30 *Loop Prevention with Transit Routing*

In the example in Figure 6-30, an external route (30.1.0.0/16) is advertised in Cisco ACI Tenant 2, which is acting as a transit route. This route is advertised to the firewall through the second L3 Out, but with a route tag of 4294967295. When this route advertisement reaches Cisco ACI Tenant 1, it is dropped due to the tag.

To avoid this situation, the default route tag value should be changed under the tenant VRF, as shown in Figure 6-31.

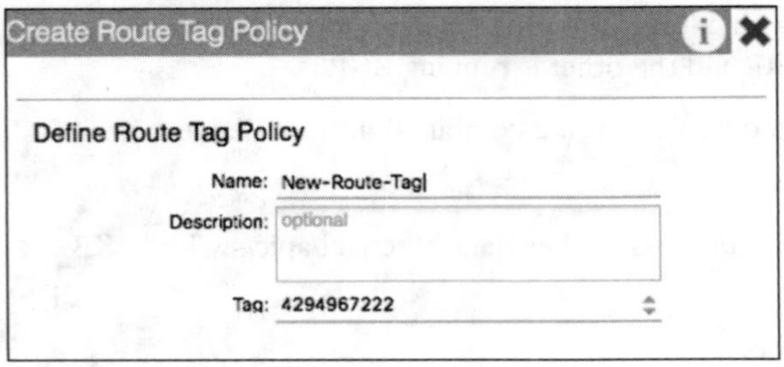

Figure 6-31   *Changing Route Tags*

WAN Integration

In Release 2.0 of the Cisco ACI software, a new option for external Layer 3 connectivity is available, known as Layer 3 Ethernet Virtual Private Network over Fabric WAN (for more information, see the document "Cisco ACI Fabric and WAN Integration with Cisco Nexus 7000 Series Switches and Cisco ASR Routers White Paper" at Cisco.com [http://tinyurl.com/ACIFabNex]).

This option uses a single BGP session from the Cisco ACI spine switches to the external WAN device. All tenants are able to share this single connection, which dramatically reduces the number of tenant L3 Out connections required.

Additional benefits of this configuration are that the controller handles all of the fabric-facing WAN configuration per tenant. Also, when this configuration is used with multiple fabrics or multiple pods, host routes will be shared with the external network to facilitate optimal routing of inbound traffic to the correct fabric and resources. The recommended approach is that all WAN integration routers have neighbor relationships with ACI fabrics (spines) at each site.

Figure 6-32 shows Layer 3 EVPN over fabric WAN.

Note that Layer 3 EVPN connectivity differs from regular tenant L3 Out connectivity in that the physical connections are formed from the spine switches rather than leaf nodes. Layer 3 EVPN requires an L3 Out connection to be configured in the Infra tenant. This L3 Out connection will be configured to use BGP and to peer with the external WAN device. The BGP peer will be configured for WAN connectivity under the BGP peer profile, as shown in Figure 6-33.

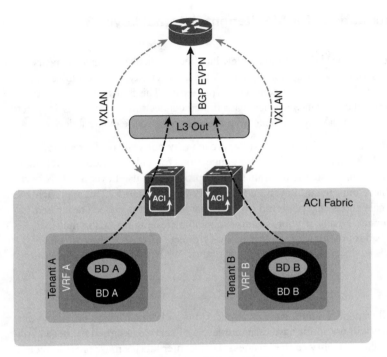

Figure 6-32 *Layer 3 EVPN over Fabric WAN*

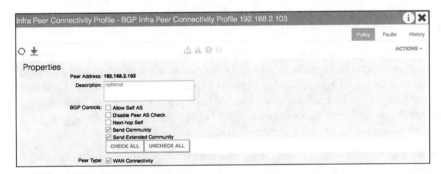

Figure 6-33 *BGP WAN Connectivity Configuration*

The L3 Out connection must also be configured with a provider label. Each individual tenant will then be configured with a local L3 Out connection configured with a consumer label, which will match the provider label configured on the Infra L3 Out connection.

Note   At press time, this capability is only available on three platforms: the Cisco Nexus 7000 Series switch with F3 line card, and the ASR 9K and 1K routers.

Design Recommendations for Multitenant External Layer 3 Connectivity

In a small-to-medium-size environment (up to a few hundred tenants) and in environments where the external routing devices do not support EVPN connectivity, it is acceptable and recommended to use individual L3 Out connections per tenant. This is analogous to the use of VRF-lite in traditional environments, where each routed connection is trunked as a separate VLAN and subinterface on the physical links from the leaf nodes to the external device.

In a larger environment, the L3 Out per-tenant approach may not scale to the required level. For example, the total number of L3 Out connections for a given Cisco ACI fabric is 400 at press time. In that case, the recommended approach is to use Layer 3 EVPN over fabric WAN to achieve multitenant Layer 3 connectivity from the fabric. This approach will provide a greater scale and is also preferred over the shared L3 Out approach described earlier in this document. Finally, if your organization will be leveraging ACI in multiple fabric or multiple pod topologies for disaster recovery or active/active scenarios, where path optimization is a concern, Layer 3 EVPN over fabric WAN should be a consideration.

Quality of Service

The ACI fabric will transport a multitude of applications and data. The applications your data center supports will no doubt have different levels of service assigned to these applications based on their criticality to the business. Data center fabrics must provide secure, predictable, measurable, and sometimes guaranteed services. Achieving the required Quality of Service (QoS) by effectively managing the priority of your organization's applications on the fabric is important when deploying a successful end-to-end business solution. Thus, QoS is the set of techniques to manage data center fabric resources.

As with normal QoS, QoS within ACI deals with classes and markings to place traffic into these classes. Each QoS class represents a Class of Service, and is equivalent to "qos-group" in traditional NXOS. Each Class of Service maps to a Queue or set of Queues in Hardware. Each Class of Service can be configured with various options, including a scheduling policy (Weighted Round Robin or Strict Priority, WRR being default), min buffer (guaranteed buffer), and/or a max buffer (static or dynamic, dynamic being default).

These classes are configured at a system level, and are therefore called system classes. At the system level, there are six supported classes, including three user-defined classes and three reserved classes which are not configurable by the user.

User-Defined Classes

As mentioned above, there is a maximum of three user-defined classes within ACI. The three classes are:

- Level1
- Level2
- Level3 (always enabled & equivalent to best-effort class in traditional NXOS)

All of the QoS classes are configured for all ports in the fabric. This includes both the host-facing ports and the fabric or uplink ports. There is no per-port configuration of QoS classes in ACI as with some of the other Cisco technologies. Only one of these user-defined classes can be set as a strict priority class at any time.

Reserved Classes

As mentioned above, there are three reserved classes that are not configurable by the user:

- Insieme Fabric Controller (IFC) Class — All APIC-originated or -destined traffic is classified into this class. This class has the following characteristics. It is a strict priority class. When Flowlet prioritization mode is enabled, prioritized packets use this class.

- Control Class (Supervisor Class) — This class has the following characteristics. It is a strict priority class. All supervisor-generated traffic is classified into this class. All control traffic, such as protocol packets, uses this class.

- SPAN Class — All SPAN and ERSPAN traffic is classified into this class. This class has the following characteristics. It is a best effort class. This class uses a congestion algorithm of Deficit Weighted Round Robin (DWRR) and least possible weight parameters. This class can be starved.

Classification and Marking

When Quality of Service is being used in ACI to classify packets, packets are classified using layer 2 Dot1p Policy, layer 3 Differentiated Services Code Point (DSCP) policy, or Contracts. The policies used to configure and apply DSCP and Dot1p are configured at the EPG level using a "Custom QoS Policy". In the "Custom QoS Policy" a range of DSCP or Dot1p values will be used to create a rule and map these values to a DSCP target. If both Dot1p and DSCP policy are configured within an EPG, the DSCP policy takes precedence. The order in which one QoS policy takes precedence over another is based on the following list starting with the highest priority and ending with the lowest:

1. Zone rule

2. EPG-based DSCP policy

3. EPG-based Dot1p Policy

4. EPG-based default qos-grp

A second example of this hierarchy would be if a packet matches both a zone rule with a QoS action and an EPG-based policy. The zone rule action will take presidence. If there is no QoS policy configured for an EPG, all traffic will fall into the default QoS group (qos-grp).

QoS Configuration in ACI

Once you understand classification and marking, configuration of QoS in ACI is straightforward. Within the APIC GUI, there are three main steps to configure your EPG to use QoS:

1. Configure Global QoS Class parameters — The configuration performed here allows administrators to set the properties for the individual class.

2. Configure Custom QoS Policy within the EPG (if necessary) — This configuration lets administrators specify what traffic to look for and what to do with that traffic.

3. Assign QoS Class and/or Custom QoS Class (if applicable) to your EPG.

Contracts can also be used to classify and mark traffic between EPGs. For instance, your organization may have the requirement to have traffic marked specifically with DSCP values within the ACI fabric so these markings are seen at egress of the ACI fabric, allowing appropriate treatment on data center edge devices. The high-level steps to configure QoS marking using contracts are as follows:

1. ACI Global QoS policies should be enabled.

2. Create filters — Any TCP/UDP port can be used in the filter for later classification in the contract subject. The filters that are defined will allow for separate marking and classification of traffic based on traffic type. For example, SSH traffic can be assigned higher priority than other traffic. Two filters would have to be defined, one matching SSH, and one matching all IP traffic.

3. Define a Contract to be provided and consumed.

4. Add subjects to the contract.

   1. Specify the directionality (bidirectional or one-way) of the subject and filters

   2. Add filters to the subject

   3. Assign a QoS class

   4. Assign a target DSCP

5. Repeat as necessary for additional subjects and filters.

Traffic matching on the filter will now be marked with the specified DSCP value per subject.

Multicast

Many enterprise data center applications require IP multicast support and rely on multicast packet delivery across Layer 3 boundaries to provide necessary services and functions.

Previous versions of the ACI fabric were limited to constraining IPv4 multicast at Layer 2 within each bridge domain based on the Internet Group Management Protocol (IGMP) snooping state. Any inter–bridge domain multicast routing, as well as multicast routing in to or out of the Cisco ACI fabric, requires a Protocol-Independent Multicast (PIM) router external to the fabric to perform those functions.

With the introduction of APIC 2.0(1), along with the Cisco Nexus 9300 EX leaf-switch platforms based on the leaf-and-spine engine (LSE) application-specific integrated circuit (ASIC), the Cisco ACI fabric itself provides distributed Layer 3 IP multicast routing between bridge domains, reducing or eliminating the need for external multicast routers.

The following multicast protocols are now supported with the 2.0(1) release:

- PIM any-source multicast (PIM-ASM)

- PIM source-specific multicast (PIM-SSM)

- Static rendezvous point (RP), Auto-RP, and bootstrap router (BSR) for RP-to-group mapping

Note   Bidirectional PIM (PIM-bidir), IPv6 multicast (PIM6 and multicast listener discovery [MLD]), and PIM rendezvous point functions are not supported in the Cisco ACI fabric in APIC 2.0(1). In addition, Layer 3 multicast routing is not supported with fabric extenders or in conjunction with the Multi-Pod function, also introduced in APIC 2.0(1).

Native Layer 3 IP multicast forwarding between bridge domains in the Cisco ACI fabric requires Cisco Nexus 9300 EX platform leaf switches, built with the LSE ASIC. Earlier leaf-switch platforms do not have the hardware capability to perform inter–bridge domain multicast routing and require an external multicast router to perform this function.

Multicast Best-Practice Recommendations

This section describes recommended best practices for three possible Cisco ACI fabric deployment scenarios. The scenarios differ in the capabilities of the leaf-switch platforms (see Figure 6-34):

- All leaf switches are first-generation switches that do not use the Cisco Nexus EX platform. They are based on the application leaf engine (ALE) ASICs and require external multicast routers to perform inter–bridge domain and entry and exit multicast routing.

- All leaf switches are second-generation Cisco Nexus EX platform switches. They are based on the LSE ASIC and support native inter–bridge domain Layer 3 multicast routing as well as entry and exit multicast routing at the border leaf.

- The leaf switches are a hybrid of some Cisco Nexus EX platform leaf switches and some leaf switches that do not use the EX platform.

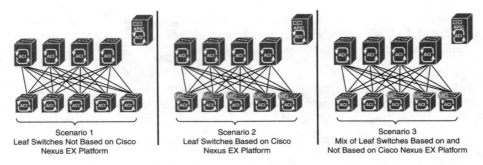

Figure 6-34   *Three Possible Multicast Deployment Scenarios*

Scenario 1: Leaf Switches Not Based on Cisco Nexus EX Platform

The best-practice recommendation is integration of external multicast routers with the Cisco ACI fabric to support inter–bridge domain and entry and exit IP multicast routing, as shown in Figure 6-35.

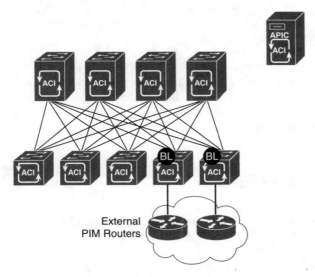

Figure 6-35   *Scenario 1: External PIM Router*

Scenario 2: Leaf Switches Based on Cisco Nexus EX Platform

For Cisco ACI fabrics in which all leaf switches are based on the EX platform (see Figure 6-36), the best-practice recommendation is to enable native IP multicast routing in the Cisco ACI fabric. This configuration uses the latest technology generation, simplifies the network design, and simplifies IP multicast routing configuration and management. Documentation outlining how to enable multicast in the ACI fabric can be found in "Cisco ACI and Layer 3 Multicast" at Cisco.com (http://tinyurl.com/ACIL3Multi).

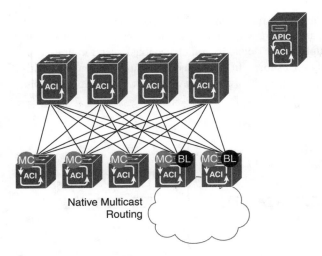

Figure 6-36   *Scenario 2: Native Layer 3 Multicast*

Scenario 3: Hybrid Fabric with Leaf Switches Both Based on and Not Based on Cisco Nexus EX Platform

In a hybrid environment (see Figure 6-37), in which some of the leaf switches are not based on the EX platform and others are based on the EX platform, the best-practice recommendation is to continue to use an external router to perform multicast routing. Although it is technically possible to combine native multicast routing on EX platform leaf switches for some bridge domains with external multicast routing, for other bridge domains, design, configuration, and management become increasingly complex and error-prone.

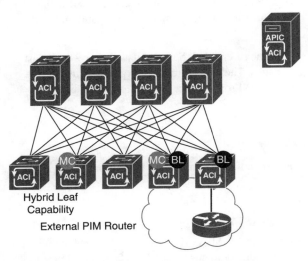

Figure 6-37   *Scenario 3: Hybrid Leaf Capability*

Furthermore, when you enable multicast routing in the APIC, you enable it at the tenant VRF level and then, optionally, at the bridge domain level. For example, if you have a tenant VRF instance with multiple bridge domains, you can enable Layer 3 multicast on all those bridge domains or only on a subset. In either case, you must first enable multicast at the VRF level in order to enable multicast routing on one or more bridge domains within that VRF instance (see Figure 6-38).

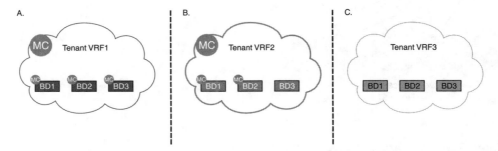

Figure 6-38   *Layer 2 Versus Layer 3 Multicast for Tenant VRF Instances and Bridge Domains*

As shown in Figure 6-38, Tenant VRF1 has Layer 3 multicast enabled for the VRF instance and for all the bridge domains in that VRF instance. Leaf switches can route multicast traffic between any of those bridge domains, and border leaf switches can route traffic in to and out of the Cisco ACI fabric for those bridge domains.

Tenant VRF2 has Layer 3 multicast enabled for the VRF instance, but not all the bridge domains have Layer 3 multicast enabled. Leaf switches can route multicast traffic between BD1 and BD2, but not into BD3. BD3 may or may not have Layer 2 multicast enabled (Layer 2 multicast with IGMP snooping in the bridge domain is enabled by default but can be disabled). If it does, IP multicast traffic can be constrained within the bridge domain, but it cannot be routed to other bridge domains or in to and out of the fabric.

Tenant VRF3 does not have Layer 3 multicast enabled, but may have Layer 2 multicast enabled for some or all the bridge domains. The leaf switches perform no inter–bridge domain routing in this case. An external PIM router must provide any inter–bridge domain multicast routing.

Multicast Configuration Overview

In this section we examine the minimum configuration needed to support both PIM-ASM and PIM-SSM.

Minimum Multicast Configuration: PIM-ASM

The minimum configuration for basic Layer 3 PIM-ASM requires you to enable multicast for the VRF instance, add one or more bridge domains on the **Interfaces** configuration subtab, and define a static rendezvous point address in the **Rendezvous Points** subtab. The PIM rendezvous point must be located outside the Cisco ACI fabric. Verify that the rendezvous point IP address is reachable from inside the fabric.

The industry best practice for rendezvous point configuration is AnycastRP using Multicast Source Discovery Protocol (MSDP), with static rendezvous point address configuration. The Layer 3 multicast configuration in the Cisco ACI fabric provides support for specifying a static rendezvous point address for PIM-ASM, as well as dynamic options for disseminating rendezvous point information such as BSR and Auto-RP.

Minimum Multicast Configuration: PIM-SSM

The minimum configuration for basic Layer 3 PIM-SSM requires you to enable multicast for the VRF instance, add one or more bridge domains on the **Interfaces** configuration subtab, and enable IGMPv3 processing on those bridge domains (PIM-SSM does not require a rendezvous point).

Summary

The Cisco ACI solution allows you to use standard Layer 3 technologies to connect to external networks. These external networks can be Layer 3 connections to an existing network, WAN routers, firewalls, mainframes, or any other Layer 3 device.

This chapter covered the following topics:

- L3 physical connectivity considerations

- Static and supported routing protocols

- Access control in and out of the fabric through the use of contracts

- Multitenant routing considerations

- WAN integration

- Quality of Service

- Multicast best-practice recommendations

No matter what you are connecting to, ACI has the ability to provide reliable and high-performance connectivity to meet simple or complex application and data center needs.

Chapter 7

How Life Is Different with ACI

In this chapter, you will learn the following:

- How Cisco ACI makes network administrators' lives easier
- How dashboards simplify network operations
- How to snapshot and restore configurations
- How to use the software management functionality in Cisco ACI for firmware upgrades and downgrades
- How to use the topology tools in Cisco ACI in order to obtain valuable information
- How to leverage the centralized CLI in Cisco ACI
- How to do some typical verifications such as routing table and MAC table checks

As you probably have figured out already, Cisco Application Centric Infrastructure (ACI) can be used as any other network, if you choose to do so. You could configure it using the command-line interface, without introducing any automation or integration into other system hypervisors or Layer 4–Layer 7 network services such as firewalls and application delivery controllers.

Actually, many organizations that introduce Cisco ACI start like this, using just a bunch of ACI's features and extending ACI's functionality, step by step. Introducing a new technology should not force you into a new path, just for the sake of it and deploying Cisco ACI certainly does not force you into using features that you do not need.

However, Cisco ACI's different approach to networking introduces new possibilities that can make the life of network professionals much easier. This chapter describes how Cisco ACI can make many of the daily tasks of IT administrators easier.

Managing Fabrics versus Managing Devices

The first noticeable difference between Cisco ACI and a traditional network is the centralized management approach. A Cisco ACI fabric is still a distributed system from the data-plane and control-plane perspectives: Each switch knows what it needs to do, and if something unexpected happens, it does not need to ask the Application Policy Infrastructure Controller (APIC), as previous chapters have explained.

That is actually one main difference as compared to the first approaches to software-defined networking (SDN) that tried to centralize the control plane. As experience has proven over and over again, distributed systems scale better and are far more resilient than centralized ones. Why break something that works really well?

However, the management concept of a network does not need to be distributed, too, and that is one of the weaknesses of network architectures that Cisco ACI does solve. This section describes multiple advantages that network professionals get out of Cisco ACI's centralized management architecture.

Centralized CLI

Cisco ACI does have a NX-OS-like command-line interface (CLI) to offer. Cisco ACI's CLI is implemented on top of Cisco ACI's REST API. The graphical user interface (GUI) is also based on the same REST API, as well as ACI's automation and integration frameworks, as later chapters in the book will show. As a consequence, the functionality that Cisco ACI's CLI offers is consistent with the rest of the ways of interacting with ACI, such as the GUI or other automation tools that leverage its API.

Obviously, some new concepts are introduced in Cisco ACI that do not have an NX-OS counterpart (tenants and external networks, for example). However, for the rest of the commands, Cisco ACI's CLI is very similar to what network engineers know from other Cisco Nexus products. Showing the MAC address table at the switches, a list of the *virtual routing and forwarding (VRF)* tables, and the state of the interfaces are some activities that network operators often do on a daily basis.

However, if the network contains a lot of switches, sometimes it can be tricky to know on which switch to run the command. Where should you start looking for a MAC address? Where exactly is the routing adjacency being established? With Cisco ACI's centralized CLI, you can run a certain CLI command on one switch, on a subset of switches, or on all of them to be able to quickly find the information you're searching for.

Have you ever executed a network change that requires having four Secure Shell (SSH) windows open at the same time, and you need to switch from one to the next? With Cisco ACI, this operational burden is greatly reduced, as you have seen throughout this book. Not only are **show** commands centralized, but network administrators can go into **config t** mode to configure simple or complex ACI policies through the APIC CLI.

Just to mention one example, think of how you would find where a certain IP address is attached to the network. In a traditional network, you would first try to figure out its

MAC address at the default gateway. Then you would try to find that MAC in the distribution switches, and finally you would track it down to the (hopefully) right access switch. By the time you are done, that information might already be stale, because those IP and MAC addresses might belong to a virtual machine (VM) that has been moved to a different hypervisor.

As opposed to that complex process, you could just issue a single command at the Cisco ACI controller, and that would tell you exactly on which port (or ports) a certain IP address is connected, as demonstrated in Example 7-1.

Example 7-1 *Using Cisco ACI's Centralized CLI to Find MAC and IP Addresses of Endpoints Connected to Any Switch in the Fabric*

```
apic# show endpoints ip 192.168.20.11

Dynamic Endpoints:
Tenant      : Pod2
Application : Pod2
AEPg        : EPG1

 End Point MAC     IP Address                Node    Interface          Encap
 ---------------   ----------------------    ------  ---------------    --------
 00:50:56:AC:D1:71  192.168.20.11            202     eth102/1/1         vlan-12

Total Dynamic Endpoints: 1
Total Static Endpoints: 0
apic#
```

Example 7-1 demonstrates the power of a centralized CLI; more examples of useful commands are provided throughout this book.

Nevertheless, the overall recommendation is to use the GUI for complex changes, because the GUI offers multiple support tools when configuring policies: immediate feedback in case the network configuration provokes faults in the system, wizards that facilitate common tasks, and contextual help that offers additional information about what is being configured.

System Dashboard

Dashboards are another manifestation of the centralized management character of Cisco ACI. Dashboards are useful not only for non-networking people in order to understand the overall state of the fabric, but they can be extremely useful for network professionals as well. Imagine you are a network operator, you come in for your work shift, and you want to get a sense of how your switches are performing today. Where do you start? Most likely your organization has built some kind of fault-overview system that will show network devices in green, yellow, or red ("traffic light" monitoring tools) so that a glimpse into that tool will suffice to see whether anything unusual is going on.

This is the main concept of a dashboard—to deliver a quick summary of the state of a complex system, with the possibility of drilling down if additional details are required.

You could argue that the network itself should actually give this functionality out of the box. If you think about it, why should you buy yet another tool just to know what your network is doing? Shouldn't the network be able to tell? Or are networks today incomplete systems that leave it up to the user to define how they should be managed?

Another problem of the traditional approach is the lack of application centricity. One of the main limitations of traditional networking is that application and customer knowledge gets lost. What does it mean that a certain device shows as yellow or even red in the monitoring system? Is there any impact for any customer? If so, to which one? To which of the applications of that customer? Putting the application and customer knowledge back into the network is not an easy task to do, and Chapter 8, "Moving to Application-Centric Networking," will lay out different strategies for doing that.

Furthermore, imagine the situation where not one but two devices go red. On which problem should the network operator focus next? Knowing the application and customer impact of each of the problems would help the person troubleshooting the network determine which one of the two problems is more urgent, and where to focus first.

This information and much more is what can be rendered available in ACI in an easy-to-consume fashion, without having to acquire additional tools to do so. When you log in to ACI, the first page you see is actually the overall system dashboard, and from there you can decide what to do next.

For example, Figure 7-1 depicts something similar to the usual traffic-light-based monitoring system that network operators are used to working with today, but enriched with the concept of tenants, which is discussed in the next section.

Tenant Dashboards

The concept of tenants has already appeared multiple times in this book, and Chapter 9, "Multi-Tenancy," explains it in depth. For this section, you only need to know that Cisco ACI can optionally divide the physical network into different sections, which are managed independently from each other. This is what is generally referred to as *multi-tenancy*. If you are not using multi-tenancy in your system, though, you probably have configured your network objects under the default tenant that comes preconfigured in ACI, called "common."

In any case, if you see in the network dashboard that the health of a tenant is not 100%, you will probably want to gather additional information in order to identify and fix the problem. Intuitively, most people will double-click the tenant name, and that will take you from the overall system dashboard to the tenant page showing the tenant dashboard. Here, you can run multiple verifications and find out more detailed information about the objects that are grouped below this specific tenant.

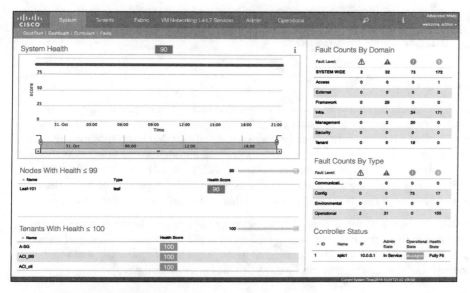

Figure 7-1   *Cisco ACI System Dashboard*

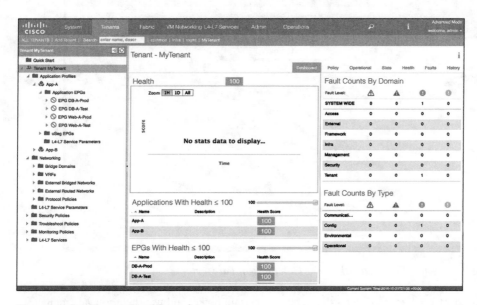

Figure 7-2   *Tenant Dashboard*

As you can see in Figure 7-2, the tenant dashboard gives detailed information about the applications and the endpoint groups (EPGs) inside of those applications that are impacted by the problem—or maybe, as in Figure 7-2, the *absence* of problems for all applications and EPGs. This is a very intuitive way of locating network problems from the top down, starting with the most critical applications in the network and working down to the problems impacting them, instead of trying to figure out the impact of specific network issues.

Health Scores

Health scores are offered in ACI as a visual summary of the operational state of any object. Instead of just three possible states (green, yellow, and red), Cisco ACI calculates what is called a *health score:* a number between 0 and 100 that not only shows whether a certain object is healthy but also provides an accurate evaluation of how close or how far that object is to the state of perfect health. A health score of 100% means that the specific object is operating as it should in every way. On the other side of the scale, as you can imagine, a health score of 0% means that that object is completely inoperative.

Health scores are calculated depending on whether there are active alerts in the system associated with a certain object, taking into account the number and severity of those alerts. How this is calculated is documented in the APIC in the Fabric tab, and some parameters of that calculation can be modified, as Figure 7-3 shows.

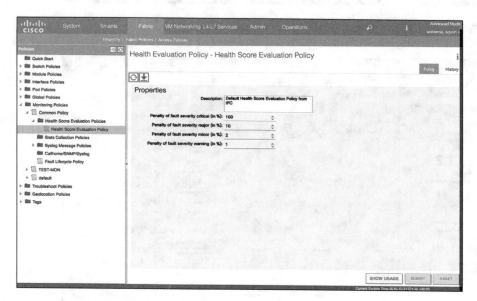

Figure 7-3   *Modifying Health Score Calculation Parameters*

Cisco ACI will take all alerts that refer to a certain object and use them to evaluate its health score. As you can imagine, not every alert is treated the same, because more severe ones should more greatly impact the health score. You can see the weight with which different alert types (critical, major, minor, and warning) are considered in order to calculate the health score.

Because most people are visual, Cisco ACI associates the health score scale with colors: the range 0 to 100 is divided in three parts, each associated with a color. Here are the default settings:

- 0% to 32%: red

- 33% to 65%: yellow

- 66% to 100%: green

These thresholds affect only the color in which health scores are shown in the GUI; they do not have any other effect in the system. Cisco ACI will not do anything special just because a certain object has changed from green to yellow, for example.

Physical and Logical Objects

The previous section discussed how Cisco ACI calculates health scores for most objects in the system. But what is an object? An object can be anything in Cisco ACI, such as a network segment, a broadcast domain, a switch, an Ethernet port—the list goes on and on.

As you may have realized, some of the objects in ACI are physical (for example, a switch and Ethernet port) and others are logical (for example, a network segment and broadcast domain).

Logical objects are typically groupings of physical objects. For example, an EPG is associated to a list of ports. Assume that one EPG is configured on four different physical ports; if one of those goes down, the health score of the EPG will go down from 100% to 75%.

Logical objects are abstractions that greatly simplify network management. If you think about it, the network industry has always used logical object groupings in order to manage IT systems, but ACI now incorporates new sophisticated ways of grouping objects. The ultimate object groupings in ACI are tenants and applications, and this is what gives Cisco ACI its name. Logical groups and the Cisco ACI object model are the true secret behind Cisco ACI's success.

Health scores are calculated from the bottom up: Failures in the physical objects are weighted and reflected in the logical groups. In the preceding example, a port failure will reduce the health score of one or more EPGs. This will result in bringing down the health score of the application network profile that contains those EPGs, and as a consequence, the health score of the tenant containing that application network profile. This will be reflected in the overall system dashboard so that the network operator can quickly view in the tenant (the top logical object grouping) any faults that can happen in individual physical objects.

By default, Cisco ACI dashboards show only objects that do not have a health score of 100%. In other words, objects that have an anomaly, even a small one. Most dashboard widgets contain a sliding bar with which you can specify the objects to be shown. If you move it to the far right end, all objects will be shown, even those with 100% health. If, on the other hand, you move it to the left, you can set a threshold so that only objects with a lower health score will be shown.

More importantly, health scores are calculated globally, regardless of whether the servers for a certain application are localized in a single rack or spread all across the data center. This is the power of application centricity, as opposed to the device centricity of legacy networks.

Network Policies

The concept of *policies* is central to Cisco Application Centric Infrastructure. But what is a policy? This section defines a policy as a sort of configuration template that can be applied to one or multiple objects of a certain type. For example, if you are familiar with the way in which ports are configured in many Cisco devices, you might be familiar with the concept of a *port profile*, which is a configuration template (or policy) that can be applied to one or multiple ports. If you modify the original port profile, all ports that refer to it will inherit that modification: You make one single change and it affects multiple objects.

Fabric-wide Policies

Cisco ACI takes this concept of a policy or configuration template to a whole new dimension. In fact, virtually all configuration parameters of the network are managed via policies, which makes ACI very flexible and easier to operate.

For example, think of Network Time Protocol (NTP) configuration. In traditional networks, you need to log in to every single switch and configure the appropriate NTP servers. If you want to add a new NTP server, you need to log back in again to every single switch to make the change. Other than the obvious overhead and inefficient usage of the network administrators' time, this process is error prone and difficult to audit. How can you be sure that all your switches are compliant with your standards and have the right NTP servers configured? Again, through logging in to every single switch and verifying.

In ACI, you would configure NTP differently. You would configure an NTP policy once, with the NTP servers that you want every switch to have, as Figure 7-4 shows. The controller will take care of configuring every single switch. If you want to add a new NTP server, you add it once to your fabric-wide policy, regardless of whether you have four switches in the fabric or 100. If you want to check what the NTP configuration of your fabric is, you just need to verify this single fabric-wide NTP policy, period. This is a much more efficient and effective way of configuring this particular feature, but the same applies to many other global configuration settings—SNMP, Call Home, QoS, or anything else.

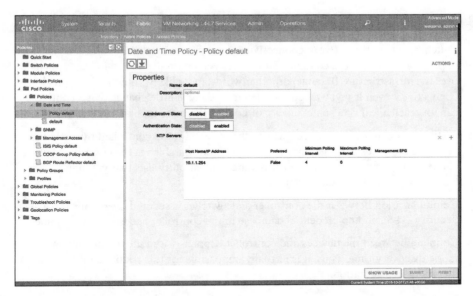

Figure 7-4   *NTP as an Example of a Single Policy That Applies to Multiple Switches*

You will find most fabric-wide network policies in the Fabric Policies section of the Fabric tab of the GUI, although some policies might appear in other, more intuitive places. For example, you can find QoS policies in the Access Policies section of the Fabric tab.

Comparing the ACI Controller to Traditional Network Management Systems

If you've had some experience with network management software, you might have the following question: How can I be sure that the controller deployed the policies correctly to the switches? The answer to that question is two-fold: First, the APIC is much more tightly coupled to the switches than traditional network management systems. Second, ACI's declarative model is a much more robust architecture. In the next few paragraphs we look at these two characteristics of ACI more in detail.

ACI's controller-based architecture is not to be mistaken with legacy network management software, which is normally loosely coupled to network devices. That is to say, there are many factors that can break the integration between the controller (say, a traditional network management tool) and the controlled devices. For example, the management software might not support the hardware of the software of a specific device, network connectivity might be broken, or you could simply have stored the wrong Simple Network Management Protocol (SNMP) credentials in the management station.

In ACI, the controller and the switches are very tightly coupled. Here are some aspects that illustrate this integration, but bear in mind this list is by no means exhaustive:

- There is a very specific network topology that has been thoroughly tested and vali-dated (the APICs attached to leaf switches, and the leaf switches attached to spine switches), where the network connectivity parameters are self-maintained, as you saw in previous sections (the communication between controller and switches happens over the infrastructure IP range). In other words, most likely you could not break the connectivity even if you wanted to. Therefore, there is little chance that a controller cannot reach a leaf or a spine, unless, of course, there are cabling problems.

- ACI hardware and software are specifically designed to be controlled by an APIC. That is, all features without any exception are configurable via the controller. Forget about interoperability matrixes or hardware compatibility lists that you might know from legacy network management systems.

- Communication between the controller and switches is secured over Transport Layer Security (TLS), and no credential database in the controller needs to be maintained.

- Coupling between the devices and controller happens without user interaction at fabric discovery time. Thus, it is virtually impossible for this coupling to be broken due to misconfiguration.

So, an event in which a policy is not properly deployed to the switches is highly unlikely. If you are a CLI person and have ever evaluated network management software, you've probably found yourself investigating in the CLI what the heck that strange software did when you clicked something, or whether the intended changes were actually deployed to the switches. I can assure you that with ACI, you will find soon enough that in most cases this is a futile task, because every single policy you define in the controller GUI (or over the controller REST API, or over the CLI) is reliably and consistently deployed across the network on all switches that belong to the fabric.

A second big difference when comparing legacy network management systems (NMSs) with Cisco ACI is that ACI uses a declarative model, as opposed to an imperative model. What does this mean? The ACI controller will not send configuration commands to the switches, but just a "description" (a declaration) of what those switches should be doing. The switches will then answer with a positive or a negative answer, depending on whether or not they can fulfill that desire (if they have hardware resources, if they support that functionality, and so on).

If you compare that to legacy NMSs, you'll find they typically function following an imperative model: They need to understand all the capabilities of the underlying devices as well as send the exact commands the managed switches understand. Any software upgrade that brings a syntax change to those commands will break that integration.

In order to better understand the importance of this concept, you can think of another type of controlling system that manages complex devices: an airport control tower. If the tower tried to tell every pilot exactly what they needed to do in order to land their plane in an "imperative" fashion (press this button, pull that lever, turn that switch, and so on), there would be two consequences: The system would not scale, and it would be very fragile (what if the pilot cannot find the button they need to press?). However, if the tower limits itself to giving "declarative" instructions to the pilot (such as "you are the next one to land on Runway 2"), trusting that the pilot knows how to fly their plane, then that system will be much more scalable and robust.

This discussion might appear to be too philosophical, but it is one of the core reasons why Cisco ACI is so stable, even when dealing with huge networks and different devices, where classical network management approaches tend to collapse.

Troubleshooting the Deployment of Global Policies

Note that earlier we said "in most cases," because in our universe there are very few rules without exceptions. Theoretically, there might be some extremely unlikely situations in which policies are not correctly applied to the switches. Therefore, we need a way of verifying whether policies have been applied to the switches, no matter how unlikely this situation might be.

This is one of the use cases for the ACI device-centric CLI. As previously stated, there are two ways to access it: connecting directly to either the in-band or out-of-band manage-ment IP address of the switch, and connecting via the APIC controller. Coming back to the NTP example, the only task you need to do is to connect to a device over its CLI and issue the command **show ntp peer-status**, for example. It's as easy as that. Alternatively, you can even run that command from the controller on all switches in the network, so that you don't need to check switch after switch. Chapter 12, "Troubleshooting and Monitoring," includes additional details about multiple ways to use Cisco ACI's CLI.

Configuring Multiple Ports at the Same Time

Many network administrators are familiar with port profiles, a concept of NX-OS and IOS that allows you to configure multiple ports in a switch at the same time. You prob-ably noticed the critical phrase in the previous sentence: "in a switch." Because Cisco ACI is a fabric-centric system, rather than a device-centric system, is it possible to define port ranges that apply to multiple switches?

If you read the previous chapters in this book, you already know the answer—yes, abso-lutely. This section will not dwell on the details of access policies because they have been explained elsewhere in this book. Suffice it to say that through the proper use of ACI access policies, you can solve very elegantly the following tasks:

- If you have standards in your data center such as "the first 20 ports of every switch in every rack are used for server management purposes," you could configure those 20 ports in every single switch with a single interface policy covering ports 1 through 20 that is applied to all your ACI leaf switches.

- If you configure both switches in a rack symmetrically (if a server connects to port 15 in switch A, it will connect to port 15 in switch B as well), you can use a single interface profile that applies to both leaf switches A and B.

- If you want to manage each switch individually to have maximum flexibility, you can still do so by having interface profiles that apply to single switches.

And of course, you can use a combination of these three possibilities: configuring some port ranges over all the switches in the fabric, other ports over a subset of the switches (such as the two switches inside of a certain rack), and the rest of the ports individually in each switch.

Maintaining the Network

You can look at ACI as a network that brings all the required maintenance tools along with it. If you think about it, a network is much more than a bunch of switches and routers connected to each other. You need network management tools that help you to make sure those routers and switches are working as they should. And guess what? Those tools are not included with traditional networks—you need to buy them separately, and the integration between the tool and the devices is on you.

Cisco ACI is changing the game rules: It brings everything you need in order to operate the network. The next sections introduce some of the tools, other than packet forwarding, that are a part of Cisco ACI.

Fault Management

How are faults managed in a traditional switch? Simple answer: They're not. Syslog messages are generated, SNMP traps are sent out, but no fault management concept exists where the operator can acknowledge faults or where faulty states are tracked and cleared when they disappear. At best, the fault management is very rudimentary, which is what forces organization(s) to buy expensive monitoring tools that include fault management as part of their network operations.

Faults Across the Network

Cisco has built many fault management functions natively into Cisco ACI. For example, a system-wide fault view in the System tab, as displayed in Figure 7-5, can quickly show a summary of all the issues happening at a current state in the network.

Having this centralized fault view is extremely useful, and it is something that legacy networks cannot offer without the help of external tools. Ideally, you should have zero faults in your ACI fabric, so any time you see a fault popping up in this panel, it is an indication that some action needs to be taken.

As a good practice, it is recommended that you verify in this section of the GUI whether additional faults have been generated after executing network configuration changes.

Faults are grouped into categories so that the operator can easily browse over the problems that are being seen. For example, the last fault in Figure 7-5 indicates that thresholds have been exceeded. There are exactly two occurrences. Instead of showing two different faults, this view aggregates identical faults into a single line. If you double-click this line, you would see the two individual faults that make up that table row, as Figure 7-6 shows.

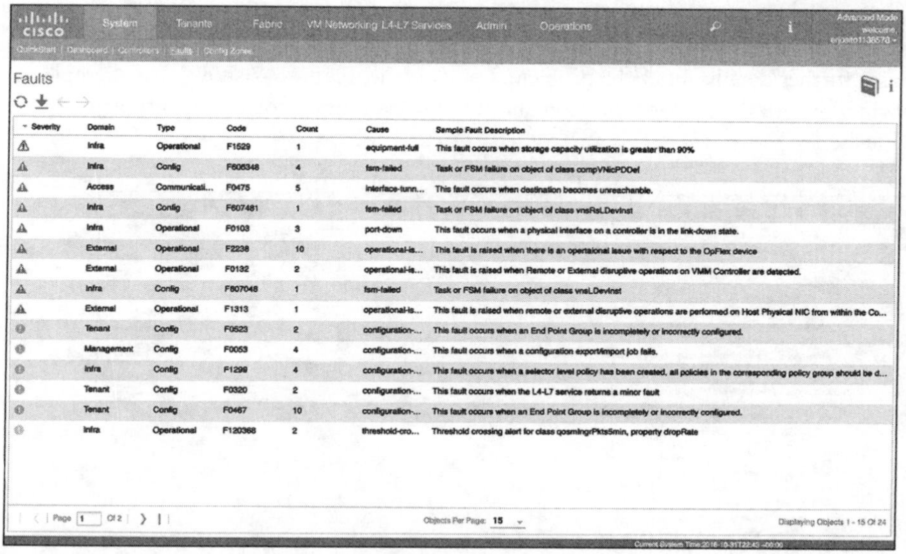

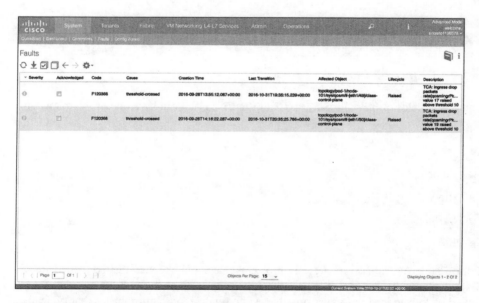

Figure 7-5 *Centralized View for Fabric-wide Fault Management*

Figure 7-6 *Showing Individual Faults*

Aggregating two faults into a single line might not sound like a great achievement, but this hierarchy offers a consolidated view of the state of the network without too much noise. Coming back to Figure 7-5, a single screen of information has aggregated more than 50 faults (if you add up the individual faults that make up each line).

When the details of a single fault are shown, rich information can be displayed to the user, such as recommended actions to clear the fault or more descriptive text that explains further details about the problem. For example, Figure 7-7 shows one example of a window with detailed information about the packet drop problems mentioned previously.

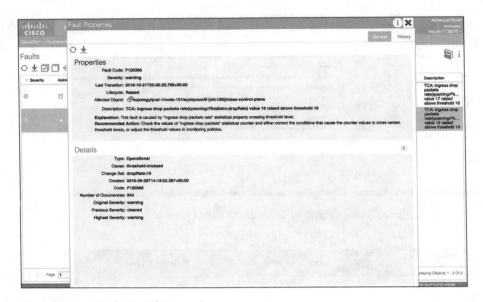

Figure 7-7   *Fault Detail Example*

One of the fields displayed is Severity. Faults in Cisco ACI can have one of the following severity levels:

- Critical
- Major
- Minor
- Warning
- Info

Critical faults indicate severe network problems that should be investigated immediately. Major faults are problems that impact the correct function of the network and therefore should be looked into as soon as possible. Minor faults represent problems that typically do not impair the network, but represent a certain risk for the system integrity. Warnings have no negative impact to the network service, but they should be diagnosed before they degenerate in higher-severity issues. Finally, informational messages do not represent any risk to network operation.

Fault Lifecycle

Faults follow a predetermined lifecycle during which they can optionally be acknowledged by operators. Faults go through the following phases:

- **Soaking:** The fault has been identified, but in order to avoid sharing faults for transient conditions, the system waits an interval of time before raising it.

- **Soaking-Clearing:** This state happens if the fault gets cleared while it is in the soaking state.

- **Raised:** If the fault persists after soaking, it enters the raised state.

- **Raised-Clearing:** This state happens if the fault gets cleared while it is in the raised state.

- **Retaining:** After either Soaking-Clearing or Raised-Clearing, a clearing interval starts. If after that interval the fault is still inactive, it goes into the Retaining state. After a retaining interval, the fault would be deleted.

If a fault is acknowledged by a user, it gets deleted.

Here are the default values for the intervals associated with fault lifecycle management:

- **Soaking interval:** From 0 to 3600 seconds. The default is 120 seconds.

- **Clearing interval:** From 0 to 3600 seconds. The default is 120 seconds.

- **Retaining interval:** From 0 to 31,536,000 seconds (one year). The default is 3600 (one hour).

These timers can be verified and adjusted under the Fabric tab in APIC, as Figure 7-8 shows.

Immediate Fault Reporting for Change Validation

An interesting use of faults is the immediate feedback of whether or not configuration changes trigger any faulty conditions in the system. This is one reason to use the GUI for network changes, because you can see right away whether your change has successfully gone through the system or if it has triggered any faults.

To that purpose, in most configuration sections of the APIC, you can see a summary of the faults related to the objects you are configuring. Figure 7-9, for example, indicates that a minor fault has occurred. The four icons represent the four possible fault severities (critical, major, minor, and warning), and the number is the object's health score.

Note that this fault summary reflects just the state of the object being configured. Therefore, if somebody else is wreaking havoc on a different object in ACI, you will not see it reflected in the object you are working on (unless some dependencies exist between both objects, of course).

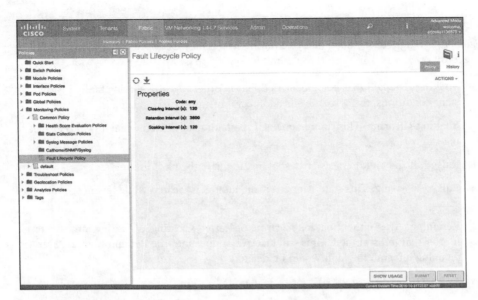

Figure 7-8 *Fault Lifecycle Management Configurable Parameters*

If a network engineer is in the middle of some configuration and this kind of notification pops up, it is a hint that the deployed configuration is either incorrect or incomplete. Figure 7-9 shows this immediate fault indication, displaying the existence of major faults for the currently selected object in the GUI (notice the four icons at the left of the health score, denoting the existence of one major fault).

This is a great help in order to identify problems in the middle of a complex action. Compare this with the approach in traditional networks—after pasting a big chunk of CLI commands into an SSH session, you find that several alerts are thrown back at you, without any possibility of seeing which one of the commands actually triggered the problem.

Configuration Management

Configuration management is one of the major disciplines of operating a network. In a static network, you would not need configuration management, because the configuration of every device would always look exactly the same. Real life, however, looks different. For example, think about network changes—sooner or later you will need to modify the network configuration to accommodate new applications or scale existing ones. You need to evaluate the potential impact of those changes, just in case they go wrong. Although most will not, some of those changes will inevitably cause an outage. You need to minimize application impact and be able to roll back to a valid configuration as soon as possible. These are all examples of configuration management tasks.

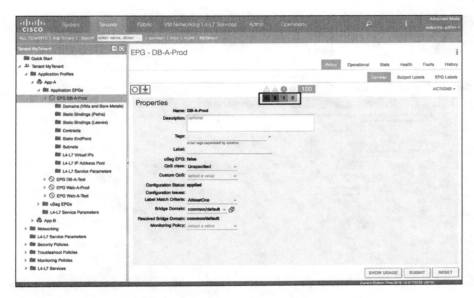

Figure 7-9 *Immediate Fault Reporting in the EPG Dashboard*

The next few sections discuss how ACI alleviates the burden traditionally associated with configuration management of legacy networks.

Evaluating Change Impact

Have you ever found yourself, before you press Enter after typing a command into a CLI-driven network, mentally going over all the dependencies and implications your action might have? Have you ever overlooked one of them, and pressing that Enter key results in undesired implications? Most network administrators have been in that situation, and that is because evaluating the impact of network changes is not an easy thing to do.

Cisco ACI introduces certain tools for making that evaluation easier. One of these tools is the Policy Usage tool, which can inform you about dependencies that might not be apparent, before a change is pushed to the system.

Figure 7-10 shows an example of the Policy Usage information—in this case describing the potential impact of a change to a Link Layer Discovery Protocol (LLDP) interface policy. Imagine that you feel the urge to modify this specific default policy for LLDP, and you are wondering whether that change could have any impact. By clicking the **Policy Usage** button on the LLDP policy, you can see, for example, how many virtual machines could be impacted if you deploy the wrong default LLDP policy. Having this kind of visibility might be very useful in order to prevent accidental changes within a big network impact.

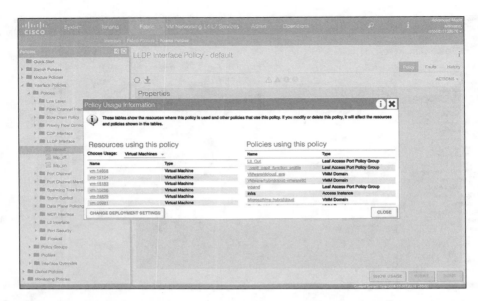

Figure 7-10   *Evaluating Change Impact with the Policy Usage Tool*

Configuration Zones: Running Changes Gradually

So we have a single system. Does that mean any network administrator can bring it down with a single wrong policy that is deployed to all switches? Actually, yes, but that's the case as well with traditional networks, where, for example, the wrong Spanning Tree or VTP Pruning setting one switch can bring down the whole network.

However, Cisco ACI has a mechanism to partition the network so that system-wide changes can be deployed gradually throughout the system. This offers network administrators much more granular control when they are introducing critical changes into the system.

Cisco ACI is based on policies, as other chapters in this book have already discussed. You can potentially have a certain policy to which many objects refer. Traditional networks also have a concept of policies (for example, port profiles in NX-OS), but they are limited to individual switches. In ACI, you have network-wide policies.

Is this a bad thing? Absolutely not. It means you can change network behavior very easily, which is an important attribute of ACI. But this also means you can introduce severe problems if you are not careful. To control the impact of modifying network-wide policies, Cisco ACI introduces the concept of *configuration zones*. You can think of these zones as a way to execute network changes in a gradual fashion. Even if the policy you are modifying is network-wide, it will be changed only in one part of the network—that is, in one configuration zone. When you are satisfied with the change, and it works as expected, you can proceed with the rest of the configuration zones.

You can define configuration zones in the System panel, and you assign leaf switches to each configuration zone (remember that in Cisco ACI, most policies are deployed in leaf switches). Once you have done that, you can enable or disable the deployment of configuration changes for any given configuration zone. If deployment mode is disabled, policy modifications will not be propagated for that given zone, so no changes will be performed on the corresponding switches.

If any change has been scheduled but not yet deployed, you will be able to see it, along with all pending changes, as Figure 7-11 shows. A network administrator can deploy these changes manually, once there is certainty that they entail no risk.

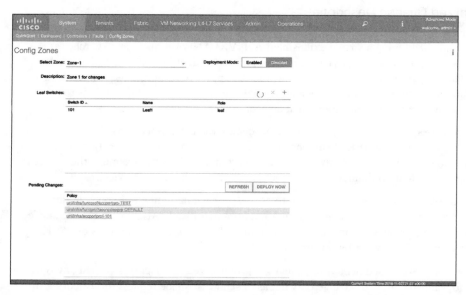

Figure 7-11 *Config Zone with Deployment Mode Disabled and Pending Changes*

An interesting use case is the combination of configuration zones and stretched fabric designs (with or without Multi-Pod technology), where each configuration zone might be mapped to one location. As you might remember from previous chapters, a stretched fabric design is one where your ACI switches are deployed across multiple physical locations. Multi-Pod is a design variant where you connect the spines in different locations to each other over an IP network, instead of direct spine-to-leaf connections, as is the case with stretched designs.

However, chances are that these physical locations exist in the first place in order to achieve higher resiliency and availability levels. So you might argue that creating a single big management domain, where human error can bring down everything at the same time, is not something necessarily desirable. An option would be deploying one individual ACI fabric in each location, but that would increase the cost and the management overhead. Alternatively, you could have the best of both worlds by having one single ACI fabric and shaping configuration zones to match the physical locations that Cisco ACI is stretched upon, to reduce the impact of human error. Or you could have a small section of your network configured as a test area with deployment mode enabled, and the production area would have deployment mode disabled. This way, network changes would always be run immediately in the test part of your network, but should be manually deployed in production.

This simple feature of configuration zones allows for having at the same time both centralized configuration management and multiple deployment areas, thus greatly reducing the risk of change deployment

Centralized Change Description

Have you ever had a network change that involves multiple devices at the same time—for example, deploying a virtual extensible LAN (VXLAN) over many leaf switches at the same time, or modifying dynamic routing protocol redistribution over multiple edge devices? Typically, you would document in the appropriate change request all steps required to run the change in each individual device, as well as all the actions to roll back the change, again for each individual device.

As a consequence, anybody who wants to deploy the change needs to copy your documented actions and paste them, one at a time, in every involved device. This manual process dramatically increases the chance for misconfigurations (for example, the operator copies the right configuration chunk but pastes it into the wrong device).

Cisco ACI's centralized architecture fixes this problem naturally: only one configuration for any change, and only one configuration for any rollback. Also, you have one single point of management that is based on a modern REST API, which reduces dramatically the chances for any configuration errors.

You could even document your changes in group-based REST clients so that any operator who wants to run your change only needs to send that single request for executing the change, thus eliminating the possibility of copy-and-paste errors.

Atomicity of Network Changes

Even though we now have a single point of management, a single configuration to send, and have eliminated the chance for manual mistakes when copying and pasting in a CLI, you could still introduce a mistake in the change definition. This brings into play a very important concept of Cisco ACI—its *atomicity*.

Imagine you have a very complex change, possibly involving creating multiple VRFs, subnets, and packet filters across many switches. But you made a mistake when writing the required configuration, and as a consequence, part of the change is syntactically or semantically wrong (for example, you could be trying to configure the IP address 10.20.30.357 on an interface, which will obviously generate an error).

In a traditional CLI-based network, parts of your change would be successfully implemented, and those parts that aren't correct would not be implemented. This results in a partially incorrect configuration, which has neither the new state nor the old one. What's more, rolling back this partial change can be particularly complex because you need to check which configuration items have been deployed and which ones have not.

If you have ever pasted a big chunk of configuration into an SSH session, you know the feeling: praying for all the lines to be correct as they are taken by the CLI. Otherwise, rolling back individual lines might be challenging.

In ACI, when you execute a configuration change—either through the GUI, with the CLI, or from an external orchestrator—it will be validated before being implemented, and either it will be completely deployed or it will not be deployed at all. In other words, Cisco ACI's API REST calls are atomically executed. And remember that every change in ACI goes through the API, including the CLI and the GUI. For example, if you send hundreds of lines of JSON code, but a minuscule error is buried somewhere in those lines, you do not need to worry—your change will be completely rejected, so there's no need to roll back anything.

This atomicity has very important consequences and greatly simplifies deployment of complex changes, on top of the architectural benefits of the single point of management that Cisco ACI offers.

Configuration Snapshots

Now suppose our configuration change has gone through, and it has been deployed on multiple zones; however, some hours later, customers report problems. Unfortunately, no rollback action was documented, and after troubleshooting, we decide that the best possible action is to roll back that change.

Cisco ACI offers the possibility of centralized configuration snapshots and rollback operations. You can export the complete network configuration in a single file to an external server, and you can import a configuration file to restore the network to a previous state. Compare that to the manual process of rolling back each switch individually. Even if you're using network management tools that support configuration saving and rollback, you would need to schedule as many rollback operations as switches you have in the network.

Cisco ACI goes one step further and does not even require that you export these configuration snapshots to an external server. You can store them locally in the controller nodes, which greatly simplifies the operation of taking the snapshot, thus eliminating interference of network problems or temporary outages of the external configuration server. All that's required is one single click or REST API call in order to snapshot the configuration, and one single click or REST API call in order to revert the active configuration to a snapshot—and that's network-wide.

The configuration management engine offers you the possibility to compare multiple snapshots with each other, as Figure 7-12 illustrates. In this case, the XML code being shown indicates that a new tenant has been created. Note the button **Undo these changes**, which allows you to roll back the change immediately.

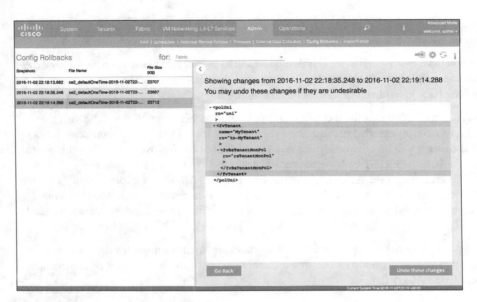

Figure 7-12 *Comparing Fabric-Wide Configuration Snapshots*

What if you don't want to snapshot all of the configuration but only a part of it? You can run configuration snapshots of specific objects, or of specific tenants, and restore them as easily. Considering the previous example, you might want to restore the snapshot taken for the specific tenant a few hours ago, without affecting other changes that have been introduced for other tenants in the meantime.

This is the scenario illustrated by Figure 7-13, where only snapshots for one specific tenant have been taken (note the "for:" text box at the top of the figure).

Is this important? It's critical, because some organizations purposely reduce the speed at which they deploy network changes so that changes can be rolled back one at a time. For example, a certain change for a specific customer could be rejected, because another change is being run in the same maintenance window. This organization is reducing its agility when coping with changes, because of its inability to properly perform configuration management when changes are parallelized.

And moreover, that organization is increasing the space between changes, and therefore changes are bigger, more complex, and entail more risk. Cisco ACI's embedded configuration management can help an organization to increase its agility, and at the same time decrease configuration change risks.

Network Audit Trails

Have you ever faced a problem where the cause was an undocumented configuration mistake? In this case, being able to inspect the network for changes is of paramount importance. Configuration change accounting tools that leverage protocols such as TACACS+ are an integral part of most critical networks.

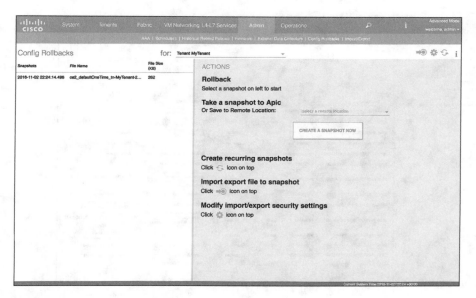

Figure 7-13   *Tenant-Specific Snapshots*

Although Cisco ACI supports TACACS+ integration for authentication and authorization, it does not need external network auditing tools because it incorporates this functionality natively in the APIC controller. You can certainly export network changes to centralized accounting tools if you wish, but if you're wanting to find out about changes in ACI, the GUI or the API offer all you need.

You have multiple ways you can access these audit trail logs. First of all, in the Fabric section of the GUI you can find all changes performed to the system across all tenants and objects. If you don't know what you are looking for, this is the place to start. Figure 7-14 shows a screenshot of the audit log for the whole fabric.

However, you might have some context information that filters the logs you want to search. For example, if you are troubleshooting a problem related to a certain tenant, you might want to start looking for changes that have been made for that tenant. To that purpose, you can access these tenant-specific audit trail logs from each tenant. As Chapter 9 explains in detail, you can even make this audit trail information available to application owners by granting them access to the tenant so that they can see network actions that could potentially impact their applications, thus greatly enhancing their visibility, as Figure 7-15 describes.

But this audit trail is not just network-wide or tenant-wide. Besides tenants, many other objects have a history tab where you can search for changes performed for a specific object. Or you can even let Cisco ACI show you the relevant audit logs for a specific issue in the Troubleshooting Wizard, which makes configuration accounting extremely easy to use. For more details about the Troubleshooting Wizard, refer to Chapter 12, where it is discussed at depth.

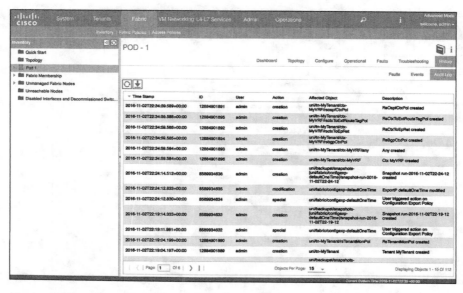

Figure 7-14 *Network-wide Audit Trail*

Figure 7-15 *Tenant-Specific Audit Log*

Again, embedded change accounting and audit logs comprise an extremely powerful network management function of Cisco ACI that can greatly help you pinpoint what changes have taken place in any environment. This is useful when troubleshooting problems, because experience shows that most problems originate from incorrect network changes.

Upgrading the Software

Software runs in every switch in every network. Every piece of software has features, and along with those features comes software caveats and security vulnerabilities. It is not a matter of whether the software versions you are using have bugs or security holes. They have them—you can be sure about it. Instead, it is a matter of when you hit one of them, how easy and efficient is it to upgrade the software to a new level that fixes the problem.

There are other not-so-dramatic reasons why you would want to upgrade the software, such as to get new functionality or support for new hardware. In any case, it is a healthy practice to upgrade the software running on your switches on a regular basis. Whether the time interval between upgrades should be one month or two years is open to debate, but most organizations upgrade at least once a year, if not more often.

However, not everybody is doing so. The reason is that network software upgrades have traditionally been a pain in the neck. This process can involve selecting the right image on the right switch or router, copying over the image to the device, configuring the device so that it takes the image in the next reload, rebooting the device, and checking that the new software has loaded accordingly—and that's for each individual switch or router in your network. Most importantly, you want to avoid any service disruption during software upgrades. If you have a couple dozen switches in your data center, no wonder your organization might be reluctant to embark on software upgrade tasks.

Cisco ACI has embedded software management tools in the controller that alleviate most of the challenges just described. First and foremost, the controller can assume the functionality of a software repository, from which you can effortlessly orchestrate software upgrades and downgrades.

You only need to load two images to the software repository for a software upgrade: one for the controller and one for the switches. The controller images are the same for all controller generations and sizes (at the time of this writing, four controller models exist—M1, M2, L1, and L2—and all of them share the same image). Similarly, there is a single switch image for all Nexus 9000 ACI switches, regardless of whether they are leaf or spine switches and on which hardware generation they are based. Two images are needed—no more, no less.

The software upgrade (or downgrade) is a three-step process:

Step 1.   Upload both software images (for the controller and for the switches).

Step 2.   Upgrade the controller cluster.

Step 3.   Upgrade the switches.

The first thing you want to do is to upload the images for the new version to ACI's firmware repository. After you have the images in the firmware repository, the next step is upgrading the APIC controller so that it recognizes the switches with the new software when they come up. Remember that in Cisco ACI, the controller is not in the data plane, so this upgrade is does not have any impact on production traffic. All controller nodes will be upgraded when you initiate the controller upgrade, as Figure 7-16 illustrates, one APIC node after the other. After some minutes of unattended activities, your controller cluster will be running on the new software.

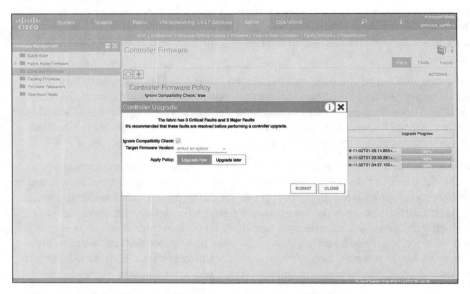

Figure 7-16   *Controller Firmware Upgrade*

After you verify that all APIC nodes have been correctly upgraded, you can proceed with the second phase—upgrading the switches. You could certainly do it the same way as with the controller, and upgrade all in one go (in parallel or sequentially). However, chances are that you want to do this upgrade in stages: First upgrade one switch, see whether it works, then a couple of more, and then eventually all the rest.

Most customers divide the upgrade into multiple stages, depending on the criticality of the network, but you could take the following approach as a good compromise:

1. Upgrade the even spine switches.

2. Upgrade the odd spine switches.

3. Upgrade the even leaf switches.

4. Upgrade the odd leaf switches.

For example, Figure 7-17 shows a use case where switches have been divided in four groups: leaf and spine switches, even and odd. The network admin has chosen to upgrade each group manually and independently of the others. Other possibilities might be automated upgrades in maintenance windows defined in schedulers.

Figure 7-17 *Manual Firmware Upgrade of a Subset of Switches*

Upgrading the spines does not have any impact for applications, as long as there is at least one spine up. Leaf switches will redirect traffic to the remaining spine or spines, and applications will not notice any downtime. Similarly, upgrading the leaf switches does not have any application impact, as long as the servers are dual-homed to two individual switches, as is normally the case in most environments. That is why separating leaf and spine switches in odd and even groups might make sense in many designs.

Obviously, in big environments, you'll probably want to segment this process even more. At press time, Cisco ACI supports up to 200 leaf switches, and you probably do not want to upgrade half of them simultaneously, so you would reduce the size of the groups of switches that are upgraded at a time. These are called *maintenance groups* in ACI, and you can handle them separately. For example, you could manually upgrade some of them, and when you are sure about the software upgrade, let the system upgrade the other maintenance groups in scheduled maintenance windows.

In case you decide to postpone the software upgrade to a later time, you can use either one-time triggers or recurring triggers. You would use recurring triggers if you have pre-defined maintenance windows (say, once a month) when you can reboot your network. In either case, you have the following options that allow you to further tune how the upgrade process will be performed, as Figure 7-18 shows:

■ When the upgrade process should be started

■ How many nodes are allowed to be upgraded concurrently

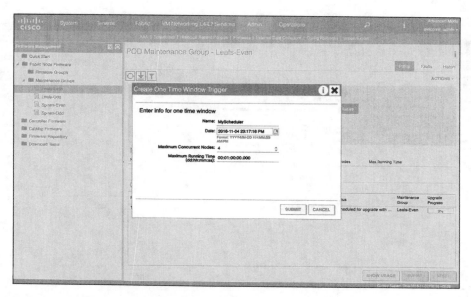

Figure 7-18 *Always Configure a Maximum Running Time When Using Triggers*

A very important remark here: Be sure you always configure a maximum running time. Otherwise, you could find yourself with unexpected behaviors, such as a trigger that initiates a firmware upgrade days or even weeks after it has been defined. If the trigger is active, and its maximum running time is unlimited, every change in the target firmware policy of a maintenance group using that trigger will immediately unleash the firmware upgrade.

Note that when you're upgrading the network in phases, a question arises concerning how long you should have a network running with mixed firmware versions in the switches and/or the controllers. You need to consider that having different firmware versions poses a risk, because you might run into a combination of different versions and features that have not been thoroughly tested by Cisco.

The core of the issue involves reducing two risks at the same time:

- On one hand, you want to reduce the risk of software problems and device downtime by rolling out new software to switches and controllers in chunks of devices, not all at the same time.

- On the other hand, you want to reduce the risk of running a combination of multiple software versions in the same ACI fabric for a long time.

Cisco's recommendation is therefore to run software upgrades in phases to minimize outages and to verify that the new software does not bring any major bugs that impact your operation, but to complete the software upgrade in the whole fabric sooner rather than later, ideally within a few hours.

Breaking the Shackles of IP Design

Traditional networks are slaves of the underlying IP design. This means that network administrators for years have designed their security and network policies based on the border between IP segments on networks.

Access Control Lists Without IP Addresses

As other chapters in this book have already described, security in Cisco ACI is based on the concept of *contracts*, which can be considered a way to define communication rules between multiple zones or EPGs. Therefore, contract definitions do not include any IP addresses but rather the UDP or TCP ports over which two or more zones can communicate with each other (or the IP protocol or the Ethertype).

As a consequence, network administrators defining a security policy do not need to be concerned with IP addresses. When contracts are consumed or provided by a certain EPG, the IP addresses of the endpoints in that EPG will be used to configure the security policy.

This fact has very important implications: for example, the network administrator could define the contracts for a certain application, and the same contracts (or multiple copies from the same contract) could be used for different application instances, such as development, staging, and production environments. Even if the endpoints for each application instance have different IP addresses, the contracts can stay the same.

QoS Rules Without IP Addresses

As you have already seen, contracts are a way of define which security zones can speak to each other, without having to type a single IP address. Security is not the only attribute defined by contracts, however—the quality of service (QoS) level can be specified too, in order to indicate how the traffic controlled by the contract should be prioritized by Cisco ACI.

As with the security policies, the network administrator can now define policies (contracts) that can be reused across many applications or application instances, regardless of whether or not the endpoints providing those applications have the same IP addresses.

QoS Rules Without TCP or UDP Ports

But there is more to it: What if no policy is required to prioritize certain traffic? You might think this is not possible, because somebody needs to tell the network which traffic is sensitive to latency and which one is sensitive to bandwidth. But what if the network could discern the two traffic categories from each other?

This is where dynamic packet prioritization comes into play, a technology that at press time was only available in Cisco ACI. For example, for a long time, network administrators needed to know on which ports certain latency-sensitive traffic runs, such as VoIP control packets. With this information, QoS rules were configured to prioritize traffic on this port over other packets. However, with dynamic packet prioritization, this is not required anymore: The network admin can leave to the network itself the job of deciding which packets should be prioritized over which other packets, in order to maximize application throughput for both bandwidth-intensive and latency-sensitive traffic types.

And the best thing about advanced QoS in Cisco ACI is the considerable ease with which it can be configured. For example, dynamic packet prioritization can be enabled with a single click across the fabric, as Figure 7-19 illustrates.

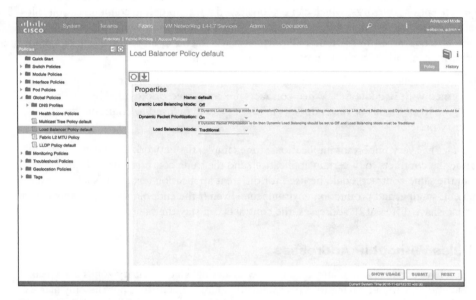

Figure 7-19   *Enabling Dynamic Packet Prioritization*

Physical Network Topology

Many chapters of this book describe policies and other logical objects that are an integral part of Cisco ACI. However, network operators will most likely want to have a look now and then at the physical objects in Cisco ACI, such as network switches and ports. As in any other network, switches are interconnected within a certain topology, servers are connected to switches, and Cisco Fabric Extenders might be used in order to extend the reach of ACI leaf switches.

ACI as a Clos Fabric and Design Implications

As you know by now, Cisco ACI is a Clos fabric—in other words, a spine-and-leaf architecture. This architecture is by no means something specific to ACI, and it is implemented by many other network technologies from both Cisco and the network industry overall, such as FabricPath or VXLAN, to name just two.

However, some issues specific to Cisco ACI might influence the way in which administrators deal with network problems that differs from how they did so in the past, as the following sections discuss.

Connecting Endpoints to Leaf Switches

Nothing can be connected to ACI spines other than ACI leaf switches (multipod designs and WAN router integration in ACI being two notable exceptions). This is not a recommendation, but a strict requirement. However, for network administrators used to legacy distribution/access designs, this might come as a surprise, because many of these designs used to have critical devices such as firewalls, load balancers, and uplinks to the network core connected directly to distribution switches.

In Cisco ACI, you cannot do this, so you would probably want to deploy dedicated leaf switches with higher-bandwidth ports in order to connect these devices. At press time, the Nexus 9332PQ is an example of this kind of leaf switch, offering 40Gbps ports where external devices can be attached. The Cisco Nexus 9000 EX switches introduced support for 25Gbps server-facing ports at scale with 100Gbps uplinks.

Scaling an ACI Fabric Means Adding More Leaf Switches

But why does ACI have the aforementioned restriction? In other technologies such as FabricPath and VXLAN, you can certainly attach external systems to the spines. However, you need to bear in mind that the moment you do so, you are running two functions simultaneously on the same device: the spine function and the leaf function.

On one hand, this gives you more flexibility, but it breaks many of the design principles of spine/leaf designs. One of these principles is scalability, because in legacy networks, scalability is essentially a scale-up problem at the distribution layer, whereas Clos fabrics transform scalability into a scale-out issue at the leaf layer. In other words, in order to increase network scalability, you just need to add more leaf switches to your fabric. However, if you are using your spines to connect to your network core (which is possible in FabricPath and VXLAN), for example, you are back into the scale-up issue of legacy networks.

Because Cisco ACI strictly enforces the orthodox Clos design rules, scaling an ACI fabric is extremely easy:

- If you need more bandwidth or redundancy inside of the fabric, you just need to add more spines.

- If you need more scalability in any other dimension (such as the supported number of VLANs, VRFs, or endpoints, for example), you just need to add more leaf switches.

- If you have a combination of leaf switches of different hardware generations (and therefore most likely with different scalability limits), each of them can scale up independently without having to go down to the minimum common denominator.

In order for this concept to work (especially the last two items), it is of paramount importance that leaf switches only consume those resources that are required. For example, if a certain leaf does not have any endpoint attached to a given EPG, no hardware resources should be consumed by that EPG. In the case that a locally attached endpoint pops up that does belong to that EPG, only then will that EPG configuration consume hardware resources. In other words, spreading your endpoints over multiple leaf switches equally distributes the consumption of hardware resources.

Obviously, this depends on the endpoint distribution. For example, in the case of EPGs, if you have many endpoints per EPG, chances are that all EPGs exist in all leaf switches. In this case, all leaf switches need to consume hardware resources for each EPG. However, in this situation, you would probably not have that many EPGs. In the opposite case, if you have just a few endpoints per EPG on average, chances are that many leaf switches do not have any endpoint for many of those EPGs. In this scenario, the per-leaf scalability concept of Clos fabrics applies best.

Note how different this is from legacy networks, where if you need to scale up any dimension, it usually involves replacing the whole network (or at least the distribution switches, where most functionality is condensed).

Fabric Topology and Links

In traditional networks, additional tools are required in order to show the network topology to the network admin. Cisco ACI includes a graphical tool for this purpose, again making the usage of external network management software unnecessary, as Figure 7-20 shows. Once more, if external tools need access to the topology, all information is accessible over Cisco ACI's REST API.

Individual Device View

As you have noticed before, the physical topology does not display the full network topology, but only the controllers, and the spine and leaf switches. More detailed information such as attached Fabric Extenders or connected servers is left out of the overall topology for simplicity reasons, but you can see this when moving to the individual device view by double-clicking a device from the global topology. Figure 7-21 shows an example of this device topology.

The device topology will show a graphical representation of the switch and the state of its physical ports, as well as external systems connected to it. For simplicity reasons, external systems connected to server-facing ports are not displayed initially (as in Figure 7-21), but you can display them by clicking the particular port they are attached to. This way, the screen is not unnecessarily crowded.

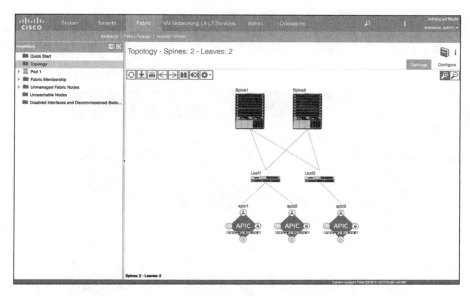

Figure 7-20 *Embedded Topology Visualization in Cisco ACI*

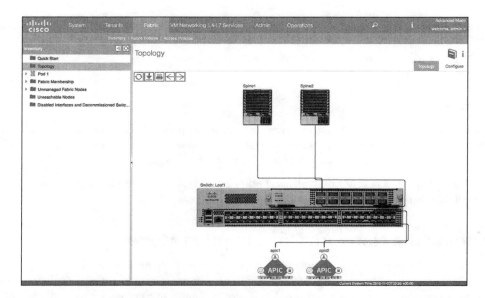

Figure 7-21 *Embedded Device Visualization in Cisco ACI*

The topology view also offers access to more detailed information, such as port-specific tasks (accessed by right-clicking any port).

Additionally, the Configure tab in the device visualization displays a port configuration wizard that makes port configuration a walk in the park. For example, Figure 7-22 shows how to configure a virtual port channel (VPC) just by clicking two ports on two different switches.

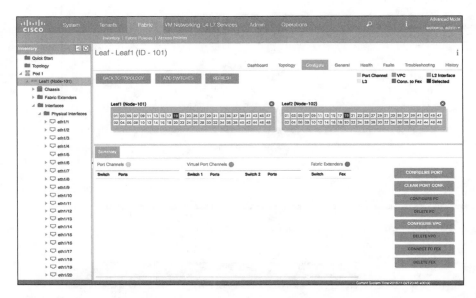

Figure 7-22   *Configuring a VPC with the Port Configuration Wizard*

Port View

As with any other network, you can look at the individual ports, check their state, shut them down, enable them again, check their statistics, browse the history of related configuration changes (as previous sections in this chapter have explained), and other actions.

Note that you can access not only physical ports in Cisco ACI switches but logical ports as well, like port channels or virtual port channels.

Changing the Network Consumption Model

Changing the network consumption model is a fancy way of saying "giving your work to others and getting away with it." Has anybody in your organization complained that the network team is too slow when asked to deploy a change, or to provide a piece of information? The best possible answer to such complaints is to enable those individuals outside the network organization to achieve their objectives on their own, without having to even pick up the phone to call their favorite network administrator.

This is an extremely important aspect of Cisco ACI. Not only does the network admin reduce some load, through externalizing routine operations such as checking the state of the network or a switch port, but the network becomes more agile and more relevant than ever, because it gets into the hands of the people who are actually using it.

Let's look at an example: You go a restaurant and want to order some food, but no waiter is available. You wait, and wait, and wait, but no waiter comes; they seem to be extremely busy with other tables. Maybe a waiter will eventually take your order, or maybe you will leave that restaurant frustrated. No matter how good the food is, chances are you will never come back to that restaurant again. But now imagine you can order using your mobile phone, and your food gets to your table a few minutes later. By changing the consumption model, the customer experience has been dramatically improved.

But wait a second; in this example the waiters are replaced by an ordering mobile app. Are we saying that network admins are doomed to disappear? By no means—the point is that routine activities that deliver no added value to an organization will be automated, so that network administrators will have more time to concentrate in other high-touch activities such as architecture design and troubleshooting.

Depending on the network activity you want to externalize (that is, give to others to run on their own), you might use different techniques:

- For virtualization administrators, you might want to leverage ACI's VMM integration. For example, through the integration with OpenStack, Horizon users can create applications and EPGs in ACI directly from the tool they are used to working with, without having to reach out to the network admin. Similar effects can be achieved with the VMware vCenter plug-in or integration with Microsoft System Center VMM, for other hypervisors. Refer to Chapter 4, "Integration of Virtualization Technologies with ACI," for more information.

- Another possibility for giving more direct network consumption to other groups in your organization is through the management multi-tenancy and role-based access control (RBAC), as Chapter 9 describes in detail. You can grant access to the Cisco ACI GUI to people interested in certain applications so that they can quickly check the state of the network (for example, by looking at the dashboards, as described in this chapter). Through RBAC, you can make sure those individuals are not able to execute operations that they shouldn't, such as modifying the network configuration. For example, think about storage administrators being able to verify on their own whether the network or something else is the reason for a storage performance issue, without having to talk to the networking team.

- Finally, for more complex tasks, you might want to leverage Cisco ACI's programmability, in order to integrate other people's tools within the network, so that network configuration is integrated into their existing processes. Chapter 13, "ACI Programmability," goes into this area in greater detail and includes practical examples.

All in all, Cisco ACI enables for the first time in networking history an easy way to enable your internal and external customers to directly consume some aspects of the network, thus improving their experience and satisfaction, which is crucial for the success of any organization.

Summary

This chapter described multiple additional tools that Cisco ACI introduces to make the life of a network administrator easier. Cisco ACI embeds in the APIC controller functions for change, fault, and performance management, to name a few, thus making Cisco ACI a self-sufficient system. In this aspect, Cisco ACI is very different from legacy networks, which always require additional network management tools to be operated properly.

Security is an integral component of Cisco ACI, and many organizations decide to leverage ACI's security functionality in order to increase the level of protection in their data centers. Cisco ACI contracts offer a very easy-to-maintain way of managing security, with a concept similar to that of zone-based firewalls, where the ruleset (ACI contracts) does not need to be updated every time new servers connect to the fabric or leave it.

Additionally, the centralized aspect of Cisco ACI enables efficiencies that are not possible with a device-centric management model, such as system-wide health scores, simplified configuration snapshots, and automated software upgrades. This central management point can be leveraged over a command-line interface, a graphical user interface, or an application programming interface in order to perform a network administrator's daily tasks.

The centralized management in Cisco ACI offers additional advantages, such as having a single view for all logs, audit trails, faults, and events in the system. This centralized repository for network and state information not only makes the job of network admins easier, but integration with other applications is greatly simplified.

Finally, Cisco ACI offers multiple ways to improve your customers' experience (both internal and external). You can grant them the ability to get what they need from the network when they need it. Other chapters in this book describe how to achieve this objective in detail, either through multi-tenancy or automation. Thus, you can change the way in which network services are consumed in your organization.

Chapter 8

Moving to Application-Centric Networking

In this chapter, you will learn:

- Why application-centricity is required by many organizations
- Operational benefits of application-centric models
- How to move from a network-centric model to an application-centric model
- How to increase the level of security in an application-centric model
- How to find out application dependencies

The previous chapters have explained the multiple operative benefits Cisco ACI can bring to an organization, even without pouring application knowledge into the network configuration. Traditionally, network administrators have separated servers into VLANs and subnets, and therefore most application knowledge is lost. When an application person says "Our Microsoft Exchange has a problem," they need to translate that phrase to "VLAN 13 has a problem."

Is a certain VLAN or subnet used for the email application? Or for enterprise resource planning? Which databases do the web servers in the ecommerce platforms need to have access to? Can a staging server speak to production workloads? These are important questions that often need to be answered—for example, when troubleshooting an application problem, when evaluating the application impact of a network change, or when going through a security audit. In traditional networks, however, the only way to answer them is by looking at external documentation, such as a network diagram depicting the network implementation for a certain application. The network itself does not store application-level information (other than VLAN descriptions, which tend not to be too reliable and do not contain an awful lot of metadata).

Other than the lack of application knowledge in the network, another problem is the fact that security and network designs are tightly coupled together. We'll illustrate this with an example: Imagine a certain two-tier application composed of web servers and databases. When it is deployed for the first time, the network admin might place the servers into two different subnets: one for the web servers and another for the databases. Doing so allows for separating web servers from databases with access control lists (ACLs) or even firewalls, if required.

Now suppose that after some time the application needs to be partitioned into two zones, to separate one group of web servers serving critical customers from another web server group serving noncritical customers. Both web server groups (critical and noncritical) should be isolated from each other, so that if a security incident affects the noncritical customers, it will not propagate to the critical ones.

This is an example of a typical application security requirement that the network admin might use different options to achieve, each with its own limitations: Implementing private VLANs (PVLANs) would isolate server groups inside of one subnet, but the application owner needs to be sure that no communication whatsoever will be required between critical and noncritical servers because PVLANs are essentially an all-or-nothing isolation technology. Alternatively, the noncritical web servers might be moved to a different subnet, thus making the use of ACLs or firewalls possible. However, the application owner would have to reconfigure the IP addresses on those servers, thus incurring downtime for the application.

You are probably visualizing the application admin frowning and wondering why network folks need to complicate things so much. At the end of the day, it is a simple request, separating servers from each other, right? However, what the application admin does not realize is that the security design and the network design are very tightly coupled to each other, so every additional security requirement potentially forces the network admin to redesign the network.

With Cisco ACI, that tight coupling is removed. In the preceding example, the network admin could configure a security policy in ACI without having to force the application admin to change a single IP address. The next sections explain how.

"Network-Centric" Deployments

You might have heard the terms *network-centric* and *application-centric* as two different ways of deploying Cisco ACI. They refer to different configuration styles, and they differ basically in the amount of application-related information you inject into the network policy. Note that these two forms of configuring Cisco ACI do not require different licenses, different GUIs, or even different hardware. They are just different ways of defining the policy model that defines the way an ACI network will work.

At this point, you should make sure you understand the concepts of virtual routing and forwarding (VRF) tables, bridge domains (BDs), and endpoint groups (EPGs), explained previously in this book, before proceeding further, because a basic understanding of these constructs is assumed in the following example.

Imagine you're an administer of a non-ACI network, and you do not have the slightest idea of the applications that run on top of it. However, you would still like to deploy

Cisco ACI in order to improve network agility and to simplify network operations. You can certainly "translate" your traditional network configuration into an ACI policy, without having to increase your application knowledge. This is what some people refer to as the network-centric deployment mode.

Essentially, you have a one-to-one mapping between VLANs, subnets, and broadcast domains. In Cisco ACI jargon, you would define a one-to-one correspondence between BDs and EPGs, and each of those BD-EPG combinations would correspond to what you would call a virtual local area network (VLAN). That is why this deployment model is sometimes called the "VLAN=EPG=BD" model or "VLAN-centric."

Figure 8-1 shows a configuration example where three EPGs and three BDs have been defined in a dedicated tenant, representing a configuration for three VLANs. Alternatively, you could define these objects under the common tenant (the next chapter explores some of the advantages of Cisco ACI's multi-tenancy model). For now, let's concentrate on the BD and EPG definitions.

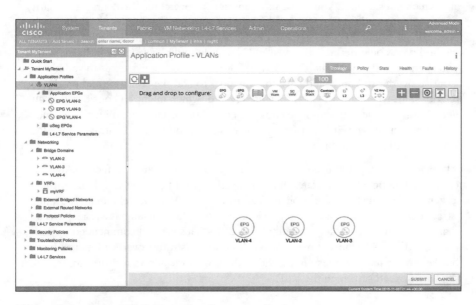

Figure 8-1 *Network-Centric Configuration Style*

As you can see, EPGs have been named with VLAN numbers, and their descriptions match the VLAN descriptions configured in the non-ACI configuration. This is the configuration style usually referred to as network-centric or network mode.

At this early stage, you should be aware of the two important aspects of this design:

■ How to design traffic isolation between VLANs

■ Whether to implement your BDs and EPGs in legacy mode

Removing Packet Filtering in Network-Centric Deployments

Oftentimes, traditional networks do not impose any traffic isolation between VLANs, and the Cisco ACI administrator might want to design an ACI network mimicking this behavior. Remember that ACI is a whitelist system, as explained in previous chapters, so if you want to override this concept into a blacklist system (all communications are allowed per default), you have some configuration changes to make. You have the following options for doing so:

- Enabling the **Unenforced** check box of the VRF containing the BDs. This option eliminates all filters between EPGs. That is, Cisco ACI behaves as a traditional network where administrators have defined no security in the form of access control lists (ACLs). This is the easiest way to eliminate traffic isolation, but it is quite coarse in which the feature operates at the VRF level for all EPGs contained in it.

- In order to have more granularity over which EPGs can freely speak to each other and which ones cannot, you could use contracts to overcome the coarse granularity of the **Unenforced** option. You would define a contract that allows all traffic, and both consume it and produce it in all EPGs. Although you gain flexibility with this method (you could define individual EPGs that do underlie security policies, which you cannot achieve with the **Unenforced** VRF setting), a drawback is the administrative overhead: You would have to remember to add the consume and produce relationships to all new EPGs as they are created, which might be considered as an unnecessary burden and possible cause of error. For example, if an inexperienced ACI admin creates an EPG but forgets to consume/produce the contract, that EPG would be isolated from the rest.

- Alternatively, you could use vzAny contracts to achieve a similar effect. vzAny contracts will be explained later in this chapter, but for now you can think of them as generic contracts that are applied to all EPGs in a VRF. They eliminate the administrative burden mentioned in the previous section, plus consume fewer resources than associating a contract manually to all EPGs. This is the recommended option for most designs because it means a very low administrative overhead, puts a lower burden on the hardware resources, and at the same time allows for finer control than the **Unenforced** setting in the VRF.

Increasing Per-Leaf VLAN Scalability

Traditional networks do not put that much focus on per-leaf scalability because most legacy concepts can scale only as much as the individual switches. As Chapter 7, "How Life Is Different with ACI," discussed, spine/leaf fabrics like Cisco ACI can scale well beyond the 4000 VLANs of traditional fabrics (15,000 EPGs at this time). However, there is a limit in the number of EPGs and BDs that can be supported in a single individual leaf switch. In order to address this per-leaf limit, it is necessary to understand the technical reasons behind it.

Cisco ACI uses in each leaf switch internally unique VLAN IDs to represent both EPGs and BDs. The standard 12-bit VLAN namespace supports theoretically 4094 VLANs (VLANs 0 and 4095 have a special meaning and cannot be used), out of which Cisco ACI reserves some additional VLAN IDs (594 to be accurate) for internal purposes. That leaves 3500 VLAN IDs that a given leaf switch can use to identify either EPGs or BDs.

If you have a single EPG in every BD (remember that in these network-centric designs, each VLAN equates to an EPG and its corresponding BD), you could have a maximum of 1750 EPGs and 1750 BDs (which would consume the total 3500 VLAN IDs available at a certain leaf switch). As a side note, remember that this allocation of VLAN IDs to BDs and EPGs is local to each leaf, so the overall fabric would scale well over this limit, as long as EPGs and BDs do not need to be present in every leaf switch.

If you are wondering why there's this apparently wasteful consumption of VLAN IDs, it is to uniquely identify EPGs that belong to the same BD. What if you do not have that requirement? After all, in network-centric approaches, you only have one EPG per each BD.

In those cases, you might consider enabling the so-called *legacy mode* in your bridge domains. The legacy-mode setting for bridge domains will limit the supported number of EPGs to just one; the advantage to this is that it will double the scalability of ACI per leaf switch to 3500 EPGs and BDs.

Essentially, this setting is telling Cisco ACI to use a single identifier for the EPG and the BD that contains it. As a logical consequence, no more than one EPG can be addressed per BD.

Before you jump to reconfigure all your BDs to legacy mode in order to increase scalability, consider that legacy mode imposes heavy constraints on the EPG design (the one EPG-per-BD rule), so it is not recommended unless you really need to increase EPG scalability per leaf switch over the standard 1750. With legacy mode, you are basically negating some of the logical grouping flexibility of Cisco ACI.

For example, imagine you have configured your bridge domains in legacy mode, but now you would like to add a second EPG to one of your BDs. In this case, you would get an error message, as Figure 8-2 shows.

This example illustrates the flexibility that is lost with bridge domains in legacy mode. Although it is a very interesting setting that doubles the per-leaf scalability of Cisco ACI in terms of EPGs, you should use it with care because it reduces the flexibility of ACI when it comes to workload policies such as micro-segmentation. If you need more than 1750 VLANs in a single leaf switch, you would typically try to localize your VLANs in leaf switches as much as possible so that you do not run into this issue—although that might not be possible in all situations. This is where legacy mode comes into play.

Looking at the Configuration of a Network-Centric Design

You could check the configuration of your network-centric BDs and EPGs with the CLI, and it should look very familiar to you (other than the concept of bridge domains, which does not exist in VLAN-centric configurations), as shown in Example 8-1.

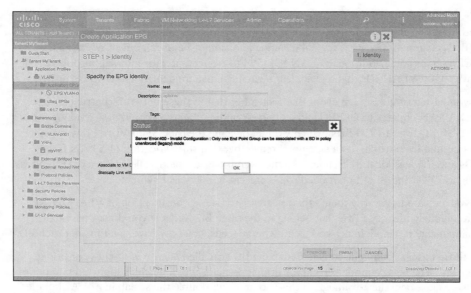

Figure 8-2   *Error Message when Associating a Second EPG with a Legacy BD*

Example 8-1   *CLI Configuration of a Basic ACI Design in Network Mode (VLAN=EPG=BD)*

```
apic1# show running-config tenant MyTenant
 tenant MyTenant
    vrf context myVRF
      no contract enforce
      exit
    application VLANs
      epg VLAN-1
        bridge-domain member VLAN-2
        exit
      epg VLAN-2
        bridge-domain member VLAN-3
        exit
      epg VLAN-3
        bridge-domain member VLAN-4
        exit
      exit
    bridge-domain VLAN-1
      vrf member myVRF
      exit
    bridge-domain VLAN-2
      vrf member myVRF
      exit
```

```
    bridge-domain VLAN-3
      vrf member myVRF
      exit
    interface bridge-domain VLAN-2
      ip address 10.0.1.1/24 scope public
      exit
    interface bridge-domain VLAN-3
      ip address 10.0.2.1/24 scope public
      exit
    interface bridge-domain VLAN-4
      ip address 10.0.3.1/24 scope public
      exit
    exit
apic1#
```

You might have observed that in this particular example, the **Unenforced** option has been configured at the VRF level, so no contracts will be used between EPGs—and as a consequence, every EPG can speak to every other EPG in this VRF.

This configuration is very similar to standard NX-OS-based configurations, and it is extremely simple, as compared to the configuration of legacy networks. Remember that this is the configuration for the whole network, not for a single switch. For example, defining a subnet in a bridge domain would deploy that IP address to every single switch that requires it. Compare this to the configuration effort required to deploy a similar functionality on a VXLAN fabric, for example.

Alternatively, you could look at this design from a REST API perspective. Although we delve into the REST API and programmability concepts in Chapter 13, "ACI Programmability," having a look at it now makes sense from a migration perspective. Should you want to deploy a network-centric configuration over the REST API of Cisco ACI, Example 8-2 shows the JSON payload you would be using (the other option would use XML; refer to Chapter 13 for more information on this topic).

This piece of configuration is a bit harder to understand for humans, but it has a very interesting advantage—it is easy to generate for machines. For example, imagine that you want to connect a legacy network to Cisco ACI, and you want to create in ACI all VLANs present in the other non-ACI network. You could write some code in Python (or any other programming language for that matter) that looks at the text-based configuration of one of the non-ACI switches, extracts the VLANs to be created, and generates JSON code to import into ACI so that the same VLANs are created in the Cisco ACI fabric.

Example 8-2 *JSON Configuration of a Basic ACI Design in "Network Mode" (VLAN = EPG/BD)*

```json
{"fvTenant": {"attributes": {"dn": "uni/tn-MyTenant"}, "children": [
  {"fvBD": {"attributes": {"descr": "This is my VLAN 2 BD", "name": "VLAN-2"},
  "children": [{"fvRsCtx": {"attributes": {"tnFvCtxName": "myVRF"}}},
    {"fvAccP": {"attributes": {"encap": "vlan-2"}}},
    {"fvSubnet": {"attributes": {"ip": "10.0.2.1/24", "preferred": "yes",
    "scope": "public"}}}]}},
  {"fvBD": {"attributes": {"descr": "This is my VLAN 3 BD", "name": "VLAN-3"},
  "children": [{"fvRsCtx": {"attributes": {"tnFvCtxName": "myVRF"}}},
    {"fvAccP": {"attributes": {"encap": "vlan-3"}}},
    {"fvSubnet": {"attributes": {"ip": "10.0.3.1/24", "preferred": "yes",
    "scope": "public"}}}]}},
  {"fvBD": {"attributes": {"descr": "This is my VLAN 4 BD", "name": "VLAN-4"},
  "children": [{"fvRsCtx": {"attributes": {"tnFvCtxName": "myVRF"}}},
    {"fvAccP": {"attributes": {"encap": "vlan-4"}}},
    {"fvSubnet": {"attributes": {"ip": "10.0.4.1/24", "preferred": "yes",
    "scope": "public"}}}]}},
  {"fvAp": {"attributes": {"name": "VLANs"}, "children": [
    {"fvAEPg": {"attributes": {"descr": "vlan-2 EPG", "name": "VLAN-2"},
    "children": [{"fvRsBd": {"attributes": {"tnFvBDName": "VLAN-2"}}}]}},
    {"fvAEPg": {"attributes": {"descr": "vlan-3 EPG", "name": "VLAN-3"},
    "children": [{"fvRsBd": {"attributes": {"tnFvBDName": "VLAN-3"}}}]}},
    {"fvAEPg": {"attributes": {"descr": "vlan-4 EPG", "name": "VLAN-4"},
    "children": [{"fvRsBd": {"attributes": {"tnFvBDName": "VLAN-4"}}}]}}
]}}]}}
```

"Application-Centric" Deployment: Security Use Case

Even if you decide to start your ACI fabric with a configuration similar to the one described in the previous section (sometimes called network-centric), sooner or later you'll likely want to make use of the additional network policies that Cisco ACI provides and refine your network configuration to include additional application-related details. The rest of this section describes the main two use cases for doing so: security and operations.

As the example at the beginning of the chapter highlighted, changes in the application often translate into new network security requirements, such as establishing security controls independently of the network boundaries.

Implementing a richer security model than what legacy networks support is what some people refer to a Cisco ACI "application-centric" design. Being able to deviate from the VLAN=EPG=BD design described in the previous section allows for additional flexibility when you're defining network and security policies for the endpoints connecting to the network.

This is where concepts like micro-segmentation come into play. Micro-segmentation usually refers to the possibility of implementing network filters between any two given server groups in the data center, independently of the underlying IP design—even if those servers are inside of the same subnet. Taking this concept to the limit, these server groups might contain a single server, so micro-segmentation includes the use case of isolating a single server from the rest (for example, because it has been compromised as a result of a hacking attack).

Whitelist vs. Blacklist Models

Cisco ACI implements what the security industry has dubbed a "whitelist model," which means that IT administrators must explicitly allow traffic so that it is permitted to transit through the network. If a certain traffic category has not been allowed, it will be dropped.

Compare this to the "blacklist model" in legacy networks: The network allows everything to flow per default, unless an administrator configures security rules to block certain traffic types. This model is more lenient, because if no application knowledge exists, the default network configuration will let everything through. From a security perspective, it is very dangerous though—every time you allow a protocol that the application does not need, you are unnecessarily increasing your attack surface, and therefore compromising the overall application security.

Whitelist models tend to be more accurate, and the reason is quite clear: If a certain required protocol is not allowed between two servers, rest assured that somebody will pick up the phone and initiate the action so that the security policy gets modified accordingly. However, when was the last time somebody called you to ask to remove a security rule that wasn't required anymore?

However, understandably not every IT administrator has information at hand about all protocols the application components need in order to operate correctly. Trying to deploy a whitelist security model comprehensively will probably lead to network problems, because chances are that administrators forget to allow some important protocol required for an application to function correctly. Therefore, a transition phase is required so that organizations that do not have knowledge about their application dependencies have time to acquire it, and thus move toward the goal of a whitelist policy.

Enforced vs. Unenforced: ACI Without Contracts

Organizations typically implement whitelist models gradually. This is where an important security setting in ACI comes into play: If you want to allow all traffic inside of a certain VRF to be forwarded, regardless of filters that may have been configured in the network, you can set the VRF to **Unenforced**.

The first use case is the gradual implementation of security policies between subnets or even inside of subnets (micro-segmentation). You can start with all VRFs set to **Unenforced** and implement additional security policies one VRF after the other, as you gather more detailed information about the application component dependencies.

The second use case is troubleshooting. In the case of a network problem, you will find yourself wondering whether you set the correct filters for the application. Setting the VRF to **Unenforced** temporarily and trying to reproduce the problem will quickly tell you whether this is the case. Once you are satisfied with the test result, you can modify the filters and reset the VRF to **Enforced**, making the ACI switches reprogram the security filters. Realize that for the time you have your VRF "unenforced," you will be vulnerable to attacks.

Endpoint Groups as a Zone-Based Firewall

Normally you don't implement packet filters using individual IP addresses but rather configure groups of servers in your access control lists—be it in firewalls or routers. Otherwise, the ruleset would quickly grow to unacceptable levels if you used individual IP addresses without any summarization.

However, as previous sections in this chapter have described, this is not sufficient to support the dynamic character of today's applications. Micro-segmentation requirements force the security administrator to cope with ever-changing security filters and server groupings, without having to change the servers' IP addresses.

That brings us to the concept of endpoint groups (EPGs). Remember that an EPG is a flexible grouping of servers inside of one bridge domain (BD), which in turn is associated with one or more subnets. It is therefore a more granular concept than the subnet level, and a more flexible one, because you can move servers across EPGs without changing the servers' IP addresses (as long as those EPGs are associated with the same BD, which is where the subnet definition is configured, including the default gateway).

As other sections in this chapter have explained, you could look at EPGs as zones in a zone-based security concept. First, you define endpoint zone membership, and then you define the communication rules between zones, bearing in mind that a zone can correspond with one complete subnet, but not necessarily.

Dynamic EPG Relationships: Micro-Segmentation EPGs

In the first Cisco ACI versions, assigning a server to an EPG was a strictly manual process. In the case of bare-metal servers, the network admin would configure a physical network port in a certain EPG. For virtual machines, the virtualization administrator would associate the virtual NIC of the VM to a given EPG—which is exactly how legacy networks work today: configuring a certain VLAN on a switch port or assigning a virtual machine's virtual network interface card (vNIC) to a certain port group.

However, it might be desirable that bare-metal and virtual machines be automatically associated with EPGs, depending on some attributes. For example, you might want to automatically assign all Windows web servers to an EPG called "Web-Windows," and all Linux web servers to another one called "Web-Linux." The Web-Windows EPG would let through ports that are required for Windows management, and the Web-Linux EPG would let through the ports needed in Linux. Thus, no unnecessary TCP or UDP ports would be open for any server.

Another use case is the automatic segregation of servers by external tools. Take, for example, a DNS-based security application such as Cisco OpenDNS. If OpenDNS detects suspicious Domain Name Service (DNS) requests coming from a certain server, it might ask the network to put that IP address in quarantine. Instead of having to locate to which physical or virtual port that server is attached, it might be easier just inserting a rule that tells ACI to move the server with that IP to a "Quarantine" EPG.

Let's examine a last use case: automatic EPG selection for preboot execution environments (PXEs). With modern server systems like Cisco Unified Computing System (UCS), you can predefine the MAC address of the server network interface cards (NICs), so you know in advance (even before ordering the physical hardware) which MAC address you need to configure in your PXE server. You would need to configure the network accordingly, however, so that the DHCP request generated by the newly connected server is sent over to the right PXE server. This way, the server gets its operative system and configuration parameters and therefore can boot. This means you need to know on which ports the servers with PXE requirements are connected, so that somebody maps the physical network ports to the EPG with connectivity to the PXE server.

Alternatively, with Cisco ACI, you could configure MAC-based EPG assignments so that whenever a new server with PXE requirements is connected, its MAC address is recognized independent of the physical port to which the new server is attached. As a consequence, the server interface will be placed into the correct EPG. This effectively allows for a better process in order to streamline server installations in PXE boot environments, where server MAC addresses can be configured via software like in Cisco UCS.

Multiple EPGs in the Same Subnet

As previous sections have explained, EPGs are sets of endpoints that belong to one bridge domain, where subnet definitions exist. For the sake of simplicity, let's assume a single subnet is configured in a bridge domain (you could have more, the same way that you can configure secondary IP addresses in VLANs in legacy networks today).

In this case, each EPG in a BD contains a subset of the endpoints associated with a subnet. That is, EPGs allow for a more granular segregation technique than filtering at the subnet demarcation point (router or firewall), as has been already mentioned in this chapter.

You could compare this technology to a private VLAN (PVLAN), in that it provides intra-subnet segmentation. However, EPGs are much more flexible because they enable the possibility of filtering at Layer 4 (TCP or UDP) instead of at Layer 2 (like PVLANs do). You could call EPGs "PVLANs on steroids."

This is the main concept behind micro-segmentation: The smaller your endpoint groups are, the more granular your security policy is. You can start with big endpoint groups (one EPG per BD, as in the VLAN=EPG=BD designs described earlier in this chapter) and then make your policy more and more granular, as new security requirements come into the picture.

As explained before, this design is not compatible with the legacy mode of bridge domains, so before creating a second EPG associated with a bridge domain, you would have to disable legacy mode on that bridge domain.

Contract Security Model

EPGs are only one half of the solution, however. Were the security concept of ACI implemented just as source-destination rules that allow traffic between two specific EPGs, the problem of the ruleset complexity would not have been addressed. Actually, most firewall systems support the logical grouping of endpoints into object groups (the naming varies depending on the firewall vendor), but this has not helped to reduce complexity significantly.

Here is where the innovation of the Cisco ACI object model comes into play. The key concept here is the "contract" that you can view as a "service." You can define multiple contracts in your system that correspond to IT services supplied by servers in your data center: database services, web services, SSH services, and so on.

Let's take, for example, a database service. If you have databases inside of one EPG (called "DB," for example), that EPG will be a "provider"—that is, you will configure that EPG to provide the database contract. If nobody is accessing those databases, no access control list needs to be configured. But as soon as there is another EPG (say, "Web") that needs to access those databases, that EPG will become a "consumer." In other words, the web servers are clients of the database servers, because they consume the services that the database servers provide.

When you configure the Web EPG to consume the contract that the DB EPG provides, you will have established the full contract relationship. Now ACI knows which servers must access which other servers on which ports, and will program access control lists accordingly, on all the virtual and physical ports where "Web" and "DB" servers are connected.

Does this really help to solve the ruleset complexity problem? Absolutely. Imagine you are troubleshooting the connection between your web and database servers, and you want to have a look at the security settings. Instead of browsing throughout the entire ruleset, which may include hundreds of other entries, you only need to look at the contracts that those EPGs provide and consume. That is, the complexity does not get higher as your system grows bigger or your application dependencies become more complex.

Inter-EPG Communication

So you have two EPGs—Web and DB—and you want to define what communication should happen between them. First, you probably want to check whether you have VRF-wide policies:

- If the VRF is working in unenforced mode, communication between EPGs is not restricted, even if no contract is configured.

- If contracts are provided or consumed by the "Any" EPG at the VRF level, those contracts apply automatically to the individual EPGs inside of that VRF. See the section "Any EPG," later in this chapter, for an explanation of the Any EPG, also called "vzAny" (that is the internal name in Cisco ACI's data model).

Let's assume for the sake of simplicity that both EPGs are mapped (over their bridge domain) to a single VRF, that VRF is working in enforced mode, and that no contracts are provided or consumed by the Any EPG in the VRF. Because Cisco ACI follows a whitelist security model, if no contract has been created, the default setting does not allow any traffic between EPGs A and B.

If, for example, you want to allow for the Web endpoints to access the databases over MySQL TCP port 3306, you would define a contract called something like "DB Services," where you configure a subject called "MySQL," and inside that subject you define a filter containing TCP port 3306. Subjects are comparable to folders inside of contracts grouping multiple filter rules together. One contract can have multiple subjects, but many customers decide to implement a single subject in each contract for simplicity reasons.

You have defined the contract, and now you need to apply it. This means that the DB EPG will provide the contract (the databases provide the "database service") and the Web EPG will consume it. After you apply the contract, all web servers will be able to open TCP connections on port 3306 on databases.

If you add new web servers or databases to these EPGs, Cisco ACI will automatically adjust its policy to incorporate the new endpoints. Notice how this is radically different from traditional ACL management, where the security admin needs to manually update the ACLs or the object-groups on which those ACLs are based.

Contract Scope

A very important characteristic of contracts is their *scope*, and that's for two reasons: resource consumption and security. Figure 8-3 shows the existing options available in Cisco ACI to define the scope of a newly created contract.

Think of two instances of an application—TST and PRD (for test and production). You could have two application profiles in the same tenant, each with two EPGs for Web and DB. You would therefore have two Web EPGs (Web-TST and Web-PRD) and two DB EPGs (DB-TST and DB-PRD). Web-PRD should be able to access DB-PRD but not Web-TST or DB-TST.

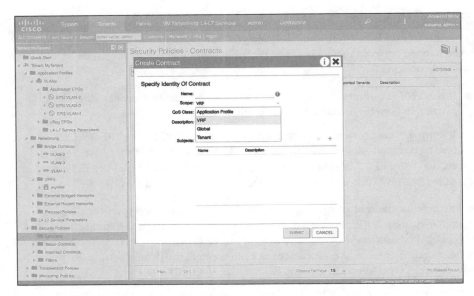

Figure 8-3   *Possible Options for the Scope of a Contract*

Now you have your "Database" contract. Both DB-TST and DB-PRD provide the contract, and both Web-TST and Web-PRD consume it. The question is, with this setup, would Web-PRD be able to access DB-TST?

The answer is, "it depends," as is often the case in the IT world. It depends on the contract scope: If the scope was defined as "Application Profile," Web-PRD will not be able to talk to DB-TST. If the scope was defined as VRF, Tenant, or Global (assuming all EPGs are in the same VRF), Web-PRD will be able to talk to DB-TST, because the production web servers are consuming the same contract that the test databases are providing.

Another way to look at this is to think of contracts as an abstraction that generates ACLs and access control entries (ACEs). The scope of a contract will determine when an ACL is modified, and ACEs will be added or deleted. For example, if the scope is "Application Profile," new ACEs will be added with each endpoint that attaches to the EPGs in the same application profile, but not for endpoints that attach to EPGs in a different application profile.

This way, it becomes obvious why if the contract scope is "Application Profile"—Web-PRD servers would not be able to speak to DB-TST servers. Their ACL would not contain the ACEs related to the DB-TST endpoints, being those in a different application profile.

This comparison illustrates another very important aspect of contracts. Imagine you are already using that contract in a high number of EPGs. For every additional EPG that also uses the contract, all ACLs for the endpoints in the previous EPGs will have to be updated—even if those endpoints are in different VRFs, without any routing in place to communicate to each other. In this case, you would be wasting quite a bit of the policy content-addressable memory (CAM) of your switches. Reducing the scope of the contracts to something like VRF, Tenant, or Application Profile would greatly reduce the amount of consumed policy CAM.

You should realize that the contract implementation in Cisco ACI is more complex than the preceding simplified example suggests, and contracts do not explode in access control entries as the previous paragraph might seem to suggest. However, that comparison is usually helpful in understanding the way in which contract scope works.

Contract Subject Settings

Settings in contract subjects control how filters are deployed in the network. Remember that contracts contain one or more subjects, and subjects contain one or more filters. This section explains the most important subject variables.

Let's focus first on the second check box shown in Figure 8-4 when creating a subject: the option "Reverse Filter Ports" (we will come back to "Apply Both Directions" further down).

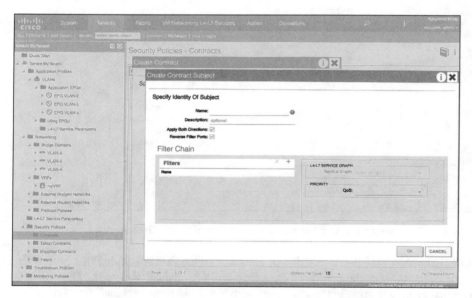

Figure 8-4 *Creating a Contract Subject with* **Apply Both Directions** *and* **Reverse Filter Ports**

As Figure 8-4 shows, the default setting is to reverse the filter ports. This essentially means that return traffic should be allowed. In order for a TCP connection to work, the client (consumer) would send a SYN request with a destination port of, say, TCP 80, and the server (provider) would return a SYN ACK with that source port, TCP 80. "Reverse filter ports" means that if you allow destination TCP port 80 from consumer to provider, the source TCP port (port 80) will also be allowed from provider to consumer.

So you might be wondering why you wouldn't want to set this option in a contract. A common situation is when you have unidirectional flows where you do not expect the provider to answer to the consumer (for example, in many UDP traffic flows).

Now, let's move back to the first one of the options shown in Figure 8-4: whether a subject should be applied in both directions. If you deselect this check box, the GUI will change in certain ways. The previously discussed option **Reverse Filter Ports** is now grayed out, and two filter sections are shown. The first one specifies the filters for traffic going from the consumer to the provider (client to server), and the second one specifies the filters for traffic going the opposite direction (server to client).

This allows you to define asymmetric filters for both directions in the communication, as Figure 8-5 illustrates.

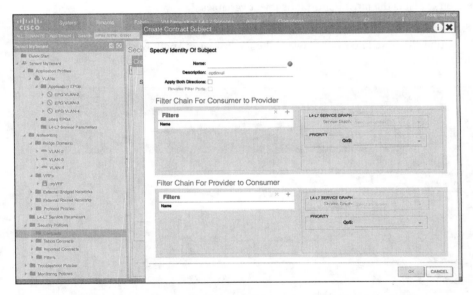

Figure 8-5 *Creating a Contract Subject Without* **Apply Both Directions**

Note that none of the previously discussed options allows for specifying that both sides of the contract are at the same time consumers and providers. If you want to have bidirectional communication in the sense that both EPGs can be servers and clients for a certain service (a frequent use case would be so you can connect from any server to any other server over SSH), you would need to apply the contract as both a provider and consumer to both EPGs.

If you have this kind of situation, consider using the Any EPG, as described later in this chapter.

Filter Settings

Contract subjects can contain one or more filters that can contain one or more rules. There are some important options when creating filters, as Figure 8-6 shows.

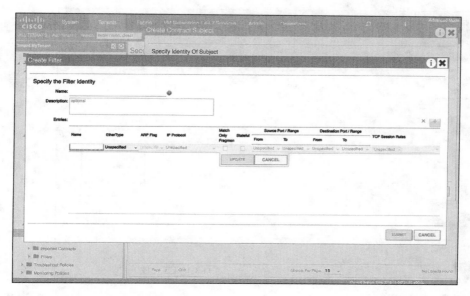

Figure 8-6 *Filter Options*

You would only specify fields where you want your filter to act. Every text box you leave "unspecified" means that ACI will not verify that part of the packet. For example, if you did not fill any field at all (except the compulsory **Name** box for the rule), the rule would match every single packet.

Experienced network administrators will recognize most of the options in this dialog:

- You can assign a name to the filter, and to each one of the rules in the filter.

- You can filter down to the EtherType level (for example, to discard FCoE frames or only allow ARP and IP packets).

- The **IP Protocol** field allows you to specify which IP protocols will be dropped or forwarded, such as TCP, UDP, ICMP, and OSPF, to name a few.

- You can match on fragments.

- The **Stateful** flag is specific to the Application Virtual Switch, and it will be explained in the next section.

- Last but not least you can see the source and destination TCP/UDP port ranges, as you would expect in the definition of an Access Control List. If you want to define a rule for a single port, you would configure the same number in the **From** and **To** fields.

Additionally, you can configure the packet filter to match traffic only if specific TCP flags are present in the packet, as Figure 8-7 illustrates (note that unless you have configured the filter to match on TCP packets, the TCP options will not be configurable).

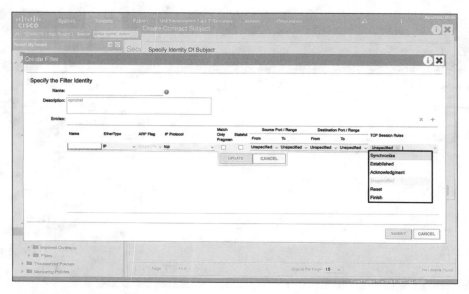

Figure 8-7   *TCP Flag-based Filtering*

Contract Subject Labels

What if the databases are not just running MySQL, but PostgreSQL too? (Whether this is a good or bad idea is not debated in this chapter.) PostgreSQL uses a different TCP port (5432), so a possibility would be adding a second filter to our contract subject including this port. Automatically, all web servers would be able to access the databases over TCP port 5432 as well.

But what if only some servers should be able to access the databases over MySQL (TCP port 3306) and others over PostgreSQL (TCP port 5432)? Normally you would solve this by providing two different contracts out of the DB EPG and consuming only one of them at each individual Web EPG. However, in some environments, having multiple contracts is not desirable—for example, in order to keep the overall amount of contracts low (the maximum limit to the number of contracts is 1000 at press time). Cisco ACI offers the concept of *subject labels* to achieve this function over one single contract and multiple subjects.

Instead of adding a filter to the contract subject, you would define a second subject to the DB Services contract. Similar to the "MySQL" subject, you would add a "PostgreSQL" subject, where you would configure a filter including TCP port 5432.

Now you have two EPGs: Web-MySQL and Web-PostgreSQL. As you have probably guessed, the task is that the servers in Web-MySQL can only open TCP connections to the databases on the MySQL port, and not on the PostgreSQL TCP port. Similarly, the Web-PostgreSQL servers should only be able to use the PostgreSQL port.

Both Web EPGs will consume the DB Services contract, but with labels you can configure whether all subjects are part of the relationship or only some of them. Essentially, when using labels, you are restricting the subjects that an EPG is providing or consuming (if you're not using labels, all subjects in a contract are provided or consumed).

For example, you would define in the contract subject MySQL a consume label "mysql" (with match type AtLeastOne). That means if the subject needs to be consumed, the consumer needs to match at least one of the labels defined in the subject. You would do the same in the subject PostgreSQL, defining the consume label "postgresql" with the same match type.

At this point, the contracts would be broken, because no web server is consuming the subjects (because none of them specifies any label). What obviously comes next is defining the appropriate consumption label in each one of the EPGs: If you look in the GUI at the Contracts section of each EPG's policy, you will be able to add the corresponding label to the contract.

The use of multiple contracts instead of subject labels is typically preferred because of its simplicity, but subject labels can help in reducing the overall number of contracts used (for example, if a certain organization is getting close to the maximum number of contracts supported in ACI). Figure 8-8 shows the section of the GUI where you would configure contract subject labels.

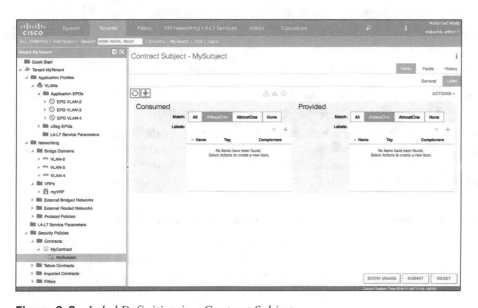

Figure 8-8 *Label Definition in a Contract Subject*

As a last remark, bear in mind that labels are checked before filters. If there is no label match, no filter will be even considered. Therefore, you need to take special care when designing a label policy. Refer to the "Cisco ACI Best Practices Guide" whitepaper at Cisco.com for further information about recommendations when defining contracts.

Contract Inheritance

Introduced in Cisco ACI 2.3, *contract inheritance* alleviates the administrative burden when configuring multiple EPGs with similar contract configurations. When creating a new EPG, one or more "EPG Contract Masters" can be defined. When doing so, the newly created EPG will be configured with the same consumed and provided contracts as its contract masters, hence the term "inheritance".

In order to get the most out of this powerful and flexible feature, you should be aware of its main characteristics:

- The inheritance is dynamic: If after creating an EPG you change the contract policy of its contract masters, the changes will be propagated to the inheriting EPG.

- Contract inheritance is supported by application EPGs, micro-segmentation EPGs and EPGs applied to external Layer-2 and Layer-3 connections.

- An EPG and its contract masters must be in the same tenant.

- If an EPG has multiple contract masters, it will inherit provided and consumed contracts from all of them.

- You can configure contracts in an EPG with contract masters. The locally defined contracts will not replace the inherited contracts, but they will be added to the inherited contracts.

- vzAny, taboo and intra-EPG contracts are not supported by contract inheritance.

- Only one level of contract inheritance is supported. In other words, contract masters of a certain EPG cannot have contract masters themselves.

After configuring contract inheritance, make sure to check in the Topology view of your EPG that the contract policy is correct. The Topology view will reflect both locally configured and inherited contracts with different colors. Additionally, you can see the effective contract rules in the EPG Operational view, under the tab "Contracts".

Stateful Firewalling with Cisco Application Virtual Switch

The previous sections have shown how packet filtering at Layers 3 and 4 in Cisco ACI hardware is semi-stateful: that is, return traffic is allowed only for existing TCP connections, but other aspects of the TCP sessions (sequence numbers, for example) are not tracked.

The reason for this is the incredible amount of hardware resources required in a platform that needs to support that many TCP connections. If Cisco ACI hardware is extended to the hypervisor with the Cisco Application Virtual Switch (AVS), however, it can leverage server resources to maintain the state of existing TCP sessions.

This is sometimes referred to as the *connection-tracking capability* of Cisco AVS. Not only does AVS keep track of TCP sequence numbers and TCP handshake state, but it is able to inspect the workload in order to open dynamically negotiated TCP ports, as in the case of FTP, for example.

You might have noticed the **Stateful** check box in Figure 8-6, which enables more granular filtering for virtual machines connected to the Cisco ACI AVS. As a previous section has explained, Cisco ACI gives you the option of statically configuring filters for the return traffic from the server back to the client. If the server is listening on TCP port 80, the network will allow all packets with the source TCP port 80 going from the server back to the client.

This might not be desirable, however, because all destination ports are allowed and not just the TCP port from which the client initiated the connection to port 80. In other words, somebody who gains access to the server could freely communicate with other systems, as long as the source TCP port of the packets were 80.

For that reason, Cisco ACI implements the option of configuring the filters for return traffic only after having seen traffic from client to server (from the consumer to the provider). This is what has been traditionally called "reflexive ACLs" in other Cisco network products.

When you set the **Stateful** flag in the filter, traffic initiated from the server side (provider) will be allowed only if a previous client-to-server flow was already seen on a certain source/destination TCP port combination.

Even if the server initiated a SYN attack on a valid port combination, the fabric will identify that the connection has already been established, so no SYN packets should be coming from that server. As a consequence, the SYN attack will be dropped.

For more information on the distributed firewall functionalities of the Application Virtual Switch, you can refer to the corresponding chapter in the "Cisco Application Centric Infrastructure Best Practices Guide" at Cisco.com (http://www.cisco.com/c/en/us/td/docs/switches/datacenter/aci/apic/sw/1-x/ACI_Best_Practices/b_ACI_Best_Practices/b_ACI_Best_Practices_chapter_01010.html).

This TCP state information is not static to a single VMware vSphere ESXi hypervisor host, but it would move along a virtual machine if it were to be migrated to a different host.

As with any other stateful packet filter, you need to consider some limits in this area if you use this functionality in Cisco AVS. Here are the limits at press time:

- 250,000 flows per ESX host

- 10,000 flows per endpoint

This firewalling functionality in Cisco AVS is enabled once you configure the AVS-based virtual machine manager (VMM) integration in APIC. After that, all ESX hosts that are added to the VMM integration will have the firewall configured consistently.

As Figure 8-9 shows (at the very bottom of the screen), you have three possibilities for configuring the firewall, as defined in the list that follows:

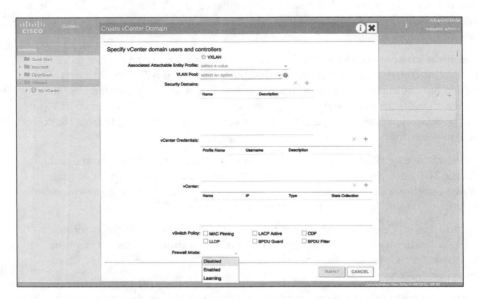

Figure 8-9 *Available Firewall Modes when Adding AVS-based VMM Integration*

- **Disabled:** AVS will not track TCP state.

- **Enabled:** AVS will track TCP state and will drop deviations from the expected behavior.

- **Learning:** AVS will track TCP state and create dynamic connections, but will not drop packets. If you plan on enabling the AVS Distributed Firewall, it is recommended that you start in Learning Mode at least some hours before moving it to Enabled Mode, so that AVS has some time to create the connection database.

Note Please note that as explained in Chapter 4 "Integration of Virtualization Technologies with ACI", VMware has publicly announced its intention of not supporting third-party switches any more in vSphere environments starting with version 6.5U2. As a consequence, Cisco has created a second-generation AVS switch that will be called ACI Virtual Edge (AVE), which would eventually replace AVS and is not affected by VMware's strategy change.

Intra-EPG Communication

In initial versions of Cisco ACI, all endpoints inside an EPG could communicate with each other without any restriction. Essentially, this meant that all endpoints inside an EPG were at the same security level. Still, were any endpoint in an EPG to become compromised (that is, its security level changed), it could be dynamically moved to another quarantined EPG with a different security policy that restricted its access to the rest of the IT infrastructure.

However, in some situations, you might want to restrict communications inside of one EPG. For example, think of lights-out management server ports like Cisco Integrated Management Controller (CIMC) or HP's Integrated Lights-Out (ILO) Management. Those management ports are to be accessed from management stations, but under no circumstances should they communicate with each other.

Another example would be using dedicated ports over which backup clients communicate to their servers. Each client port talks to a server port, but no two client ports should speak to each other. Essentially, it is the same example as the previous one with CIMC interfaces.

Cisco ACI offers an extremely easy way to accomplish this function via the **Intra EPG Isolation** option in each EPG, as you can see in Figure 8-10. Per default, it is set to **Unenforced**, which means that all endpoints in that EPG can freely talk to each other. With this setting, you can make sure that all endpoints in that EPG can only speak to other endpoints belonging to other EPGs, but not to each other.

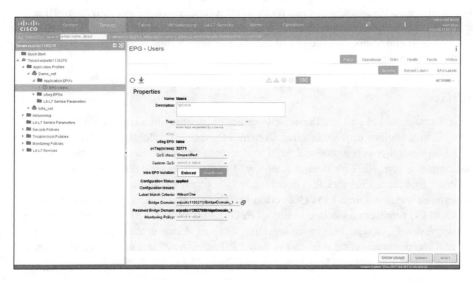

Figure 8-10 *EPG Policy with* **Intra EPG Isolation** *Option Set to* **Unenforced**

Before we dig further into the topic of intra-EPG isolation enforcement, take into account that this is not the only mechanism of intra-subnet traffic filtering in ACI, as the section "Dynamic EPG Relationships: Micro-Segmentation EPGs" previously in this chapter highlighted. Additionally, since version 3.0 Cisco ACI supports Intra-EPG Contracts for physical and virtual workloads. Chapter 4 "Integration of Virtualization Technologies with ACI" described how to configure Intra-EPG Contracts in the section "Intra-EPG Isolation and Intra-EPG Contracts". Think of intra-EPG isolation as an additional tool in your toolbox for traffic segmentation design. Use intra-EPG isolation for simple, all-or-nothing type traffic filtering, and contracts (either contracts between micro-segmentation EPGs or intra-EPG contracts) for contracts for more dynamic and sophisticated workload segregation.

As you might be thinking, intra-EPG isolation is a very similar feature to what in legacy networks is offered with the private VLAN (PVLAN) functionality. Actually, this *is* PVLAN functionality, only it's much easier to implement because you do not have to bother about primary, community, or isolated VLAN IDs (the API will configure that for you).

One use case for intra-EPG communication policies is preventing server-to-server communication in purpose-specific NICs, such as NICs dedicated for backup, management, or storage connectivity. In these situations, you typically want to connect those NICs with something else (a backup server, a management station, or a storage subsystem), but you want to prevent those servers from speaking to each other.

This strict, all-or-nothing segmentation allows you to increase security in client-server communication patterns, where the clients, often with dedicated interfaces, do not need to see each other. Examples of this pattern include backup designs (there is no need for servers to speak to each other over their backup NICs, only to the backup server), remote storage (using a protocol such as NAS or iSCSI), or even management connections. For example, imagine that you have an out-of-band (OOB) management network. You typically only need to access your servers and switches from your jump server or management stations; servers should not reach out to each other on those ports. By activating intra-EPG segmentation enforcement, you are drastically reducing the possibility that compromised endpoints execute lateral moves over the OOB management networks to attack other servers.

Any EPG

What if you would like to use the same contract everywhere in a certain VRF? For example, you want to provide Internet Control Message Protocol (ICMP) services from all EPGs (remember you would still need to consume those services so that the contract relationship is formed). This is what the "Any" EPG is for. Essentially, this is a logical construct that represents all EPGs contained inside of a VRF. In the VRF configuration, you can see the menu item **EPG Collection for This Context**. And that is exactly what the Any EPG represents: a collection of all EPGs inside of this VRF (you might remember that in previous Cisco ACI software versions, VRFs were called "contexts"). Sometimes you will see documentation refer to the Any EPG as "vzAny," because this is the internal name of this EPG when you look directly into Cisco ACI's object model.

Coming back to the previous example, you could define a contract that permits only ICMP traffic and then provide it in the VRF, as Figure 8-11 shows. This will automatically provide the contract for all EPGs inside of that VRF. You can then go to another EPG (say, the Management EPG) and consume the "ICMP" contract. Endpoints in the Management EPG will be able to ping every single endpoint in the VRF.

The overall configuration steps would look something like this:

Step 1.   Configure your filter, subject, and contract in the Security Policies section (**PermitICMP** in this example). This step is optional; you could use a pre-defined contract such as the "default" contract in the common tenant to allow all traffic.

Step 2.   Go to **EPG Collection for This Context** in your VRF.

Step 3.   Add the provided and/or consumed contracts.

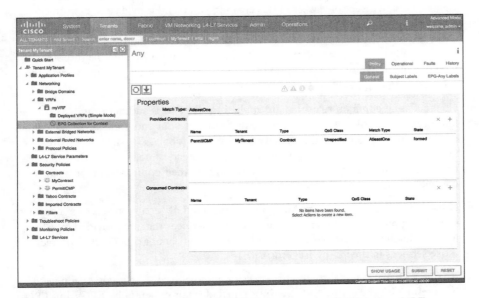

Figure 8-11   *vzAny Used to Provide ICMP Services in all EPGs in a VRF*

Note that other endpoints in other EPGs other than Management will not be able to reach other EPGs via ICMP, unless they consume the ICMP contract, too. If you now wanted all endpoints inside of the VRF to be able to ping each other, you could both provide and consume the ICMP contract in the Any EPG.

But what if you would like to add some exceptions to this rule, and maybe have some specific EPG that does not provide the ICMP service? Since ACI version 2.1(1h), vzAny contracts support the option of not being applied to every single EPG in a certain VRF, but just to a subset of them. This function is called "Preferred Group Member," and it can be very useful in order to migrate from a network-centric to an application-centric policy model, as later sections in this chapter describe. This is yet another example on how flexible Cisco ACI's object model is, because you do not need to change the security policy when adding new endpoints or new EPGs into the VRF, as they will automatically inherit the defined policy.

Furthermore, this way of applying contracts to the whole VRF is very efficient. Therefore, if you have protocols that are provided or consumed by all EPGs in a VRF, you would probably want to use the Any EPG in order to use the hardware resources in your ACI leaf switches as efficiently as possible.

Let's look at some use cases for contracts applied to the Any EPG:

■ You might want to disable traffic filtering in a VRF. As described in the "Network-Centric Designs" section earlier in this chapter, you could provide and consume a "permit any" contract from the vzAny EPG, and that would be equivalent to disabling contract enforcement in the VRF (although with the additional flexibility of optionally defining exceptions over the Preferred Group Member feature). This would come in handy for configuring Cisco ACI to work as a legacy network with no traffic filtering functionality whatsoever.

■ Consolidating common rules that are applied to all EPGs is another example of a fairly typical use of vzAny. Chances are that most of your endpoints require a couple of management protocols: ICMP, Network Time Protocol (NTP), maybe Secure Shell (SSH) or Remote Desktop Protocol (RDP). Instead of configuring the same set of protocols in every contract, you could centralize their configuration on a single contract consumed by vzAny.

■ Note that one restriction of vzAny prevents this kind of "common services" contract from being provided, so that if you have central services that are provided by EPGs in VRF1 and consumed by other EPGs in VRF2, you cannot provide the contract for those services in the vzAny EPG for VRF1.

■ If your VRF has external routed networks or external bridged networks, you need to be careful with the vzAny EPG because it includes not only regular EPGs, but EPGs associated with these connections too.

For more details about the usage and constraints of contracts consumed and provided by the vzAny EPG, refer to the document "Use vzAny to Automatically Apply Communication Rules to all EPGs in a VRF" at Cisco.com (http://www.cisco.com/c/en/us/td/docs/switches/datacenter/aci/apic/sw/kb/b_KB_Use_vzAny_to_AutomaticallyApplyCommunicationRules_toEPGs.html).

Contract Definition Best Practices to Efficiently Use Resources

Policy content-addressable memory (CAM) is a scarce resource in any network switch. As you probably know, CAM is required in order to be able to make the extremely high amount of lookup operations per second in switches.

For an idea of why CAM is required, consider that new switch models offer 48 × 25Gbps server-facing ports and 6 × 100Gbps uplinks. That makes a total of 1.8Tbps full-duplex, which means 3.6Tbps (tera*bits* per second) is flowing in any given direction through the switch, which translates to 450GBps (giga*bytes* per second). Assuming a conservative packet size of 450 bytes (to make numbers easy), you would have one billion packets traversing the switch at peak condition. That is one billion memory lookups per second, which explains the high performance (and high cost) delivered by CAM.

Due to that fact, CAM resources are not unlimited in switches, if they are to be affordable. Therefore, putting some thought into how to preserve those resources is probably something valuable to do.

First, Cisco ACI already incorporates technologies to optimize CAM consumption. For example, by default, a certain EPG (and associated contracts) will be programmed in a leaf switch only if endpoints associated with that EPG are locally attached; otherwise, no CAM resources will be consumed.

Even with those embedded optimizations, however, there are some best practices related to contract configuration that should be observed, especially in organizations deploying ACI with an elevated number of EPGs, contracts, and filters per switch:

- Define contract scope as small as possible. Use "Application Profile" scopes by default, and increase to VRF, Tenant, or Global only when needed.

- Use the Any EPG (also known as vzAny) whenever you have some services (ICMP or SSH, for example) that are commonly consumed by all EPGs in a VRF.

- The really important factor for scalability is not necessarily the amount of contracts, but the amount of filters. Unidirectional subjects with "reflexive" filters (matching on the TCP flag "established") are more secure and efficient than bidirectional subjects (which automatically create two filters, one for each direction—provider-to-consumer and consumer-to-provider), if used along with vzAny designs.

- If you're coming close to the 1000-contract limit, use subject labels instead of having multiple contracts in one single EPG.

If you are interested in these topics, you should refer to the latest version of the "Cisco ACI Best Practices Guide" at Cisco.com.

"Application-Centric" Deployment: Operations Use Case

If *security* is one of the main drivers of application-centric deployments with ACI, *operations* is the other big reason to refine a VLAN-based network policy. As explained at the beginning of this chapter, one of the goals of having an application-centric network is to bridge the language gap between application and network administrators. That is to say, even if an organization does not have the knowledge to deploy a whitelist policy model as described in the previous section, it might still introduce application information in the network.

The following sections describe different ways of doing so, along with the associated benefits.

Application-Centric Monitoring

As Chapter 12, "Troubleshooting and Monitoring," explains in detail, health scores in ACI give a very good indication of whether or not certain objects are working as they should. The more granular EPGs are defined in Cisco ACI, the more information their associated health scores will deliver to an operator.

If a network operator sees that the EPG "Web-PROD" is having an unexpectedly low health score, they would immediately know whom to call. If, on the other hand, the EPG had been called something like "VLAN-17," that process might be more complicated.

There is another equally important aspect to this: The health scores are now meaningful not only for network operators, but for application operations team members as well. Application experts can now have a look at Cisco ACI and extract meaningful information out of it. Network folks not only speak about VLANs and subnets now but also about the applications running on the network.

Quality of Service

The previous sections dealing with the security use case explained in depth the contract model and how contracts can be used in order to control which EPGs can speak to which other ones, as well as which protocols are used.

However, packet filters are not the only functionality that can be controlled using contracts. Quality of service (QoS) is another important feature of contracts. In traditional networks, it is very difficult to determine which applications fall into which QoS class; however, in ACI, this is straightforward. As you might have realized, QoS can be configured directly in the contract (or more accurately, in its subject) controlling the communication between any given pair of EPGs, by allocating traffic matched by the contract to one of three QoS classes, called Level1, Level2 and Level3, as Figure 8-12 depicts. As you can see in this figure, you could leave the class assignment "unspecified," which actually assigns the traffic to Level3. What these three classes actually do can be customized in the **Fabric** tab of the GUI, under **Global Policies**, as Chapter 9, "Multi-Tenancy," describes in more detail.

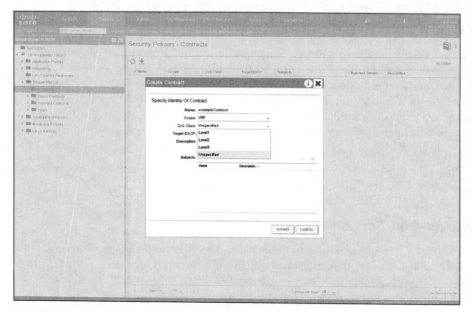

Figure 8-12 *Configuring QoS Class for a Contract*

Obviously, one prerequisite so that contracts define a QoS policy meaningful to the network administrator is that the EPGs being connected through contracts have a meaningful correspondence with applications, from a naming convention perspective.

We'll explain this with two examples. Imagine a network-centric ACI configuration. You have EPGs called VLAN-2, VLAN-3, VLAN-4, and so on. You might have contracts between those EPGs, called VLAN2-to-VLAN3 and VLAN3-to-VLAN4, for example. One of those contracts is associated with QoS class Level1, the other contract to QoS class Level2. Now picture an operator that needs to find out whether that configuration is correct. They will probably have a hard time trying to figure out whether VLAN3 should be a higher or a lower priority than VLAN4, for example.

Life could look much simpler if the EPGs and contracts had meaningful names such as Web, App, and DB for the EPGs, and App-Services and DB-Services for the contracts. Now this is a scenario much easier to troubleshoot for an operator from a QoS perspective. You would only need to talk to an app specialist and ask whether database traffic is more critical than web traffic, for example.

If you think about it, the previous example is yet another situation where Cisco ACI is bridging the language gap that exists between network and application administration teams, which has been one of the biggest IT barriers in recent years.

Impact Analysis

One of the most feared tasks of every network administrator is to evaluate the application impact of network failures. The reason is again the lack of application knowledge in the network. Confronted with this question, the network admin will have to go and recollect that knowledge again. For example, imagine that you need to evaluate the application impact of an access switch upgrade. For the sake of simplicity, let's assume the switch has no routing functionality (it does only Layer 2), so you will need to figure out which systems are directly connected and to which applications those systems belong. In order to do that, you would typically go through these steps:

Step 1. Gather all MAC addresses connected to the switch.

Step 2. From ARP tables in other Layer 3 devices, correlate those MAC addresses to IP addresses.

Step 3. Get virtual IP addresses configured in application delivery controllers that refer to those IP addresses.

Step 4. Get DNS names for the physical and virtual IP addresses out of DNS servers that support reverse lookups.

Step 5. Contact application teams or dig out application documentation from diagrams, documents, or (in the best case) a configuration management database (CMDB), and find out which applications those servers are part of.

And that was only a Layer 2 switch; you can probably think of a more critical network component in your system where evaluating its impact would be nothing short of a nightmare, where you would have to similarly evaluate routing, access control lists, firewall rules, and other more complex constructs.

If you think about it, Steps 1 to 4 are required in order to bridge the language gap between application and network people. Network administrators think in IP and MAC addresses, VLANs and subnets. Application people typically think in application layers and, eventually, maybe in server names. In many organizations, that's the only common term between network and application departments.

However, Steps 1 through 4 are the easy ones. There are off-the-shelf tools that can retrieve that information dynamically, but step 5 is the trickiest one, because it is extremely difficult discovering those application dependencies dynamically in the IT infrastructure.

Chapter 7 described the "Policy Usage" function in ACI. This offers a very quick way for network administrators to find out what applications can potentially be impacted when a certain policy is changed, provided the EPGs are defined in an application-centric fashion.

Asset Allocation

Here's a similar use case to the impact analysis that goes in the opposite direction: Instead of evaluating which tenants and applications use a certain infrastructure, you might be interested in knowing which infrastructure a certain tenant or application is using.

Most service providers, and an increasing number of enterprises, need this information for a variety of reasons. It could be charging money for the usage of that infrastructure, or as simple as justifying IT spending by showing which applications leverage which portion of the data center.

For other IT elements, such as servers, this allocation has been uncomplicated in the past. When a certain server is purchased, it used to be dedicated to a single application. Server virtualization changed that demography, and for that purpose most hypervisors incorporate resource monitoring measures that allow you to elucidate which part of the server a specific virtual machine is using. This is insufficient, though. The reason is that the mapping between application and IT infrastructure is still external. As has already been discussed, this is a very hard problem to solve.

With Cisco ACI, you can follow the application dependency relationships from the top down: If you are interested in how much infrastructure a certain tenant is using, you could first find out which application network profiles are configured on that tenant. And then you could find out which EPGs are in every application, and which ports in which EPG.

For example, Figure 8-13 shows the Health panel for an application using two EPGs connected to six ports across two physical leaf switches, as well as the health of all objects involved (application, EPG, ACI leaf switch and physical ports).

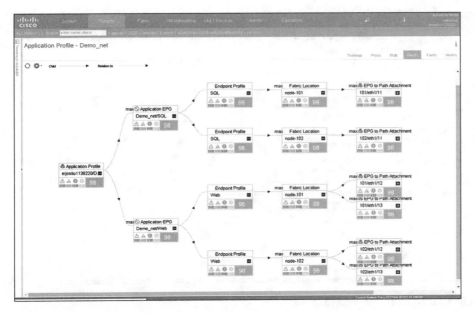

Figure 8-13 *Correlating Applications to Physical Devices*

Correlating this information with the cost of each port, distributing the cost of a port across multiple tenants, making use of it at the same time, and incorporating finance elements such as amortization are all outside the scope of this chapter.

Migrating to an Application-Centric Model

Migrating from a network-centric to an application-centric policy depends on what your target policy looks like: Do you want to incorporate contracts between your EPGs for security reasons? Or do you just want to cluster your EPGs in application profiles with meaningful names? This section assumes you want to achieve all of these and provides a possible path to migrate from the VLAN=EPG=BD model to a more sophisticated network policy that reaps the benefits of Cisco ACI.

Disable Bridge Domain Legacy Mode

The first thing you will probably want to do is break the one-to-one relationship between bridge domains and endpoint groups, in case you had configured your bridge domains in legacy mode. Remember that disabling legacy mode will have an impact on the maximum number of EPGs and bridge domains per ACI leaf switch (3500 in legacy mode and 1750 otherwise, assuming one EPG per each BD).

Figure 8-14 shows how to disable legacy mode for a single BD in the GUI.

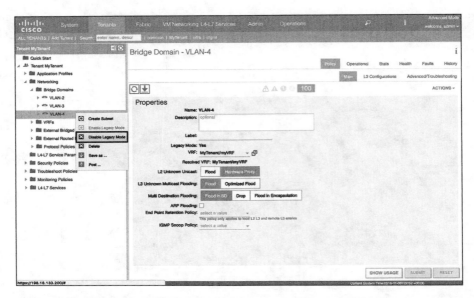

Figure 8-14 *Disabling BD Legacy Mode*

Disable VRF Unenforced Mode

You might want to have the possibility of adding security rules to the network configuration in case you need them. If you configured your VRF in unenforced mode, you will have to change that setting. However, if you just did that, you would start dropping lots of packets, unless you had previously defined contracts for your EPGs.

The vzAny feature comes to the rescue here, because you can define a contract that allows all protocols (for example, using the default filter) that is consumed and provided by all EPGs in your VRF.

But remember we want to have the option to selectively configure more restrictive security policies for certain EPGs, so using the option Preferred Group Member, as the previous section "Any EPG" described, would be a good idea.

The configuration steps might be similar to the following:

Step 1.   Configure all your EPGs as preferred group members.

Step 2.   Configure a contract and a subject that use the default filter (which permits all traffic).

Step 3.   Apply the contract to the VRF both as provided and consumed, in the "EPG Collection for Context" section, marked as "Preferred Group Member."

Step 4.   At this point, you can switch your VRF from unenforced to enforced mode.

Step 4 is rather critical, because if you have forgotten to configure an EPG as a preferred group member, that EPG will not be able to communicate with others (unless you have defined explicit contracts for that EPG). Therefore, you probably want to do this in a maintenance window and then monitor for dropped packets in the Operations panel of your tenant. Refer to Chapter 12 for more details on this process.

Create New Application Profiles and EPGs

At this stage, your EPGs are still called VLAN-2, VLAN-3, and so on. However, now you can define additional EPGs, possibly in new application profiles, that are mapped to the same bridge domains as the existing EPGs. You can decide whether to define new contracts between those EPGs, or configure the new EPGs as preferred group members so that the vzAny contracts in the EPG apply to them as well as to the old, "network-centric" EPGs.

Additionally, make sure you add the same physical and virtual domains to the new EPGs; otherwise, the endpoint migration will not work. You'll probably want to create a table similar to Table 8-1.

Table 8-1 *Example of Network-Centric to App-centric EPG Correspondence Table*

Network-Centric EPG	BD	App-Centric Application Profile	App-Centric EPGs
VLAN-2	VLAN-2	App1-PROD	Web
VLAN-3	VLAN-3	App1-PROD	App
VLAN-4	VLAN-4	App1-PROD	Test
VLAN-5	VLAN-5	App1-TEST	Web, App, Test

In this example, you can see that most EPGs have a one-to-one equivalence to application components, but for VLAN-5 it was found out that three distinct EPGs need to be defined as migration destinations for the endpoints in EPG called VLAN-5.

Move Endpoints to the New EPGs

Now you can start moving endpoints from the old to the new EPGs. Depending on whether those endpoints are physical or virtual, the migration will look slightly different. Remember the EPGs are the same for both virtual and physical workloads; the only difference is whether they are attached to a physical domain, a VMM domain, or both:

- For physical endpoints, you will change the EPG bindings and move them from the old to the new EPG. In order to keep disruption to a minimum, the recommendation here is to run this process through a script or a sequence of REST calls.

- For virtual endpoints, you would define the same VMM domain in the new EPG, which would generate a new port group in your hypervisor. You would then reconfigure all vNICs of virtual machines from the old port group to the new one. This migration will typically just have sub-second downtime for any given VM being migrated.

After no endpoints exist anymore in the old EPGs in the common tenant, you can delete the old EPGs safely.

Fine-Tune Security Rules

Assuming all EPGs are still defined as "Preferred Group Member," they still use the vzAny contracts defined at the VRF level, which probably contains a default filter allowing all traffic.

Especially if the driver to go to an application-centric model is security, you will probably want to define contracts between EPGs more restrictive than that. You can apply new security policies to your EPGs with a simple two-step process:

Step 1.   Define your new contracts and then apply them as consumed or provided on the EPGs you want to modify.

Step 2.   Remove the Preferred Group Member definition from the EPG so that it stops using the vzAny contracts from the VRF level.

Remember that modifying the security policy can have a big impact on production traffic if the security policy defined in the contracts is not correct. Therefore, after removing EPGs from the preferred group member, it is strongly recommended that you verify the logs for dropped packets, as described in other chapters in this book (at the tenant level in the Operations panel).

How to Discover Application Dependencies

In spite of the multiple benefits that an application-centric model brings, a typical objection to these granular network configurations is that no information is readily available that allows one to easily move a network-centric network deployment in this direction.

Network administrators who currently run a legacy network where configuration is strictly mapped to VLANs probably do not even know the applications running on it. Many network administrators haven't configured QoS or ACLs in their networks precisely because of this lack of knowledge. And suddenly they get with Cisco ACI an instrument in which they could very easily implement application-based network policies.

In many organizations, this application knowledge resides with the application team; however, chances are that the application team hasn't bothered in the past with "the network stuff," and as such they don't even know the TCP or UDP ports their applications require, or even which groups of servers need to speak to each other.

Without application knowledge, no application-based policies are possible. Therefore, this type of organization will probably start using Cisco ACI in the network-centric mode described at the beginning of this chapter, while at the same time looking to gain knowledge about the applications running on the network. With this knowledge they will be able to move to an application-centric model, and thus extract all the value of a modern, application-centric network.

Focus on New Applications

The immediate answer to the problem of how to move to an application-centric network is to do it only for newly deployed applications. When a new application is to be deployed, a group of subject matter experts from different areas (application, security, networking) will make sure that all requirements of that application are correctly reflected in IT policies, including ACI policies.

This exercise is not only applicable when rolling out new applications, but when existing applications are to be refreshed and new infrastructure should be deployed. New application releases will normally introduce minor modifications into the application architecture, so it could be a good time to sit down together and discuss whether the new release should be deployed using an application-centric model.

Therefore, some organizations decide to leave the old applications alone (that is, leave the network configured with a network-centric style) because it would be rather difficult to find out reliable data on them. They instead focus on new deployments because it would be easier putting application, security, and network experts together to define the network policy for these new projects.

As you've probably realized, the network-centric and application-centric configuration styles are not mutually exclusive: You could have in the same Cisco ACI fabric one EPG called something like VLAN37, because no application information exists about it, and another EPG called Sharepoint16, where you know exactly what is inside.

Most applications have documentation that explain how they have been architected. This is probably your first information source if you want to learn about the internal components of a certain application, and on which TCP ports each of these components communicate. Application owners should know how to get to that information, by checking with the relevant application vendor if required.

The disadvantage of this approach is that for every application, you need to check on its support pages, making it a rather time-consuming activity. There is an alternative, though: Certain companies (mostly vendors of application-related software such as application delivery controllers and next-generation firewalls) have already made the effort of gathering information related to multiple apps, so optionally you could tap into that knowledge pool and just connect the missing dots, instead of re-creating all that work that has already been done.

This is the goal of an open source tool called ACI Profiler, which you can find in the GitHub repository for Cisco Data Center products (https://github.com/datacenter/profiler). This application is external to the APIC and will create objects such as filters that can be used in contracts between EPGs in your Cisco ACI network policies.

The assumption is that over a period of time, old applications will be replaced by new ones, or at least by new releases, so that within a number of years most of the applications in the data center will have been migrated to an application-centric model.

Migrate Existing Applications

The benefits of application-centric network models can be so appealing that organizations decide to migrate existing applications. Depending on the complexity of the architecture of those applications, the efforts to find out the necessary information might be very significant.

Essentially, the following is the required information you are looking for:

- Different tiers in which an application can be decomposed
- Which server belongs to which application tier
- TCP and UDP port numbers used for inter-tier communication
- Whether the servers inside of each tier should be allowed to speak to each other
- TCP and UDP port numbers that are required to externally access each tier
- TCP and UDP port numbers required to manage and monitor the servers at each tier
- Additional Layer 4-7 services required for the correct operation of the application

As you can see, if your application architecture is fairly complex (for example, some applications are made out of more than 20 components or tiers), this task will be herculean, so you need to compare the efforts of finding out that information to the goal of the task.

You might not need all of the information, though. For example, you could start without the TCP/UDP port information and leave the implementation of security for a later stage by defining contracts that permit all IP-based communication between EPGs, but still reap some of the benefits of the application-centric model, such as better security and application visibility. As you gain more knowledge about your applications, you could refine your contracts as required by your security policies.

The following sections focus on how to tackle the step previous to the migration itself—gathering the information required, sometimes described as the *application dependency mapping* (ADM) process.

Legacy Application Dependency Mapping

Some tools already exist that can inspect traffic and generate some application dependency mappings. Most of these tools do a limited point-in-time analysis and try to generate those mappings with very limited information. And that is because the increasing network bandwidths and new technologies in modern data centers convert application dependency mapping into a "big data" problem.

Let's look at the different approaches that most legacy application dependency mapping tools use in order to collect the information they require. The most common one is using a flow accounting technology such as Cisco NetFlow or sFlow. Switches are configured in order to periodically export the flows that have been seen in the last time interval. However, the numbers of flows in data centers are dramatically increasing due to multiple reasons:

- **Server virtualization and scale-out architectures:** These typically bring along the proliferation of virtual machines. Where in the past a couple of big HTTP servers would handle traffic for an application (or multiple applications), today this is handled by farms consisting of tens of virtual web servers. These farms can be elastically scaled up and down, and have significant operational benefits, but they dramatically increase the number of flows existing in data centers.

- **Microservices architectures:** Two-tier applications based on databases and an application frontend mostly belong to the past. Modern applications are much more modular, and the trend is to reduce these modules to a minimum so that each module can be individually modified, tested, and deployed, thus increasing application agility. For example, companies embracing microservices architectures such as Netflix and Flickr have applications consisting of more than 500 microservices that speak to each other over complex communication matrices.

- **Linux containers:** These are a nascent technology that promises a similar revolution to what server virtualization did in the past. Linux containers are typically associated with microservices architectures, because they can be compared to lightweight virtual machines that are spun up whenever additional resources for a certain microservice are required, and then torn down when that requirement disappears. Obviously, the individual performance of a single Linux container is an implementation decision, but these containers tend to be smaller than the standard virtual machine. In other words, if an application is migrated to a container-based infrastructure, chances are that the number of endpoints required as compared to a VM-based infrastructure is a lot higher.

- **Increasing network bandwidth:** Modern switches and network adapters can communicate over higher-bandwidth links than in the past; speeds of 10Gbps are today common, and 25Gbps seems to be the next frontier. Additionally, modern servers can support higher workloads and are therefore able to fill up those 10Gbps or 25Gbps pipes. This fact does not necessarily increase the number of flows in a data center, but it does have an impact on the number of flows in a single switch, because more workloads are directly attached to it.

As these points illustrate, the increase of flows in the data center has been increasing for the last few years already, and switches (or more accurately, the switches' CPUs in charge of exporting flow information) have not evolved accordingly. As a consequence, flow sampling was born. The *s* in "sFlow" actually means "sampled." Many high-bandwidth data center switches only support exporting sampled flow information, with sampling rates that can vary a great deal, reaching in some cases sampling rates higher than 1000.

That means only one packet every 1000 is processed, in the hope that, statistically, the overall flow statistics will be accurate.

However, hope is not something that we can rely on for application dependency mapping. Sampled NetFlow is a great tool in order to run reports such as Top Talkers (the flows that escape sampling are typically negligible from a bandwidth perspective), but it is not that useful when you need a higher accuracy. For example, for security reasons, flows that escape sampling might be the flows that you are actually most interested in.

If you're relying on sampled NetFlow to run application dependency mapping, chances are that a lot of important communication is left out of the model, leading to application outages when the dependency model is applied to the network in the form of a security policy.

In order to overcome sFlow and NetFlow limitations, some application dependency mapping tools use a completely different technology. Instead of relying on the network devices to extract and send flow information, why not have the whole of the traffic mirrored to an application dependency mapping (ADM) appliance that will then extract the required information?

This approach has multiple deficiencies. The first one is scalability—in other words, the period of time over which ADM appliances can store data. Let's run some numbers to explain this. Think of a standard modern leaf switch such as the Nexus 93180YC-EX, with 48 server-facing 25Gbps ports. Imagine that all ports are utilized at 100% (we could apply a load-correction factor at a later stage). That makes 1.2Tbps full-duplex, or in other words, 2.4Tbps or 300GBps of traffic traversing the switch (consider the traffic to be local to the switch without having to use the uplinks). Now, let's take an average packet size of 600 bytes, to be conservative. That makes 50Mbps traversing the switch: 50 million packets every second. Let's imagine that our ADM appliance only stores the packet headers (say, 40 bytes per packet). We are now at 2GBps. In other words, 2GB are filled every second, which is 172.8TB every day. And that's just a single switch! Suppose that the switch is not 100% utilized, but is only used at 10%. Now we are back down to 17.28TB per day. And now suppose you have 20 switches in your network: That's 345.6TB per day for the whole network.

Obviously, this type of appliance could only store a very short snapshot of the network traffic, and flows happening out of this window (such as for applications that are only run at the end of the quarter or even once every year) would be left out of the application dependency model. Unfortunately, you would only find out after a few weeks, when the finance department cannot close the fiscal year reports because the network security policy is forbidding it.

Cisco Tetration Analytics

Who will try to solve this problem? Cisco has developed from the ground up a solution that utilizes a range of modern technologies in different areas such as distributed computing, analytics, machine learning, and big data, and it is called Tetration Analytics.

The mission of Tetration Analytics is being able to see every single packet that traverses the network and offering actionable application insights in order to answer questions such as the following:

■ Which servers have similar communication patterns and can therefore be grouped into EPGs?

■ Which of these EPGs need to speak to which other EPGs, and on which TCP or UDP ports?

■ Is there any traffic coming from an unusual and maybe suspect source? Or is unusual traffic leaving the data center, which might indicate some sort of data leakage?

■ Is the network under attack right now?

■ Which operating system process on which server actually generated a specific traffic flow? Was this traffic generated by a legitimate application, or has it been generated by some malware?

■ If I change the network security posture, would I be able to repel a specific attack?

■ If I migrate an application to the cloud, should I be migrating other components as well, upon which that application depends?

Note that these are only some of the questions that Tetration Analytics can answer. It's nothing short of the "all-knowing data center oracle." In order to achieve this objective, Tetration Analytics can collect information from two sources:

■ Modern Cisco ACI Nexus 9300 EX series switches are able to analyze bandwidth in real time and send flow information to the Tetration Analytics appliance. Only flow information is sent, as opposed to the full packets. Different from NetFlow and sFlow, this flow information is enriched with additional details such as packet latency and context information (what was going on in the switch at the time that specific flow went through).

■ Software agents in virtual and physical servers, both Windows and Linux, can send traffic as it is generated by the operative system. This telemetry data is also enriched with information such as the process that sent the network packet into the TCP/IP stack of the operating system. The Tetration Analytics software agent is very lightweight and consumes a minimum amount of resources of the machine where it is installed. At the time of this writing, multiple Windows versions are supported, starting with Windows Server 2008, as well as many Linux distributions, such as RHEL, SLES, CentOS, Ubuntu, and Oracle Linux. For more details, refer to the Tetration Analytics data sheet.

Other than the information sources, the analytics appliance absorbing this traffic needs to have enough storage capacity, but still have an affordable cost. Here is where big data technology can help, enabling the use of common off-the-shelf servers, hard disks, and solid state disks, combined into a single, high-capacity, high-performance storage system.

After collecting information and storing it, the next challenge consists of analyzing all that data to extract meaningful and actionable insights out of it. Cisco has developed analytics algorithms, specifically conceived for the analysis of network flow information, that are supported by unassisted learning systems to reduce to a minimum the need for human intervention to eliminate false positives and false negatives from the equation.

The result of the innovations around these three areas (information collection, storage, and analysis) is Cisco Tetration Analytics, a solution that dramatically simplifies zero-trust implementations. It provides visibility into everything that lives in a data center in real time. It uses behavior-based application insight and machine learning to build dynamic policy models and automate enforcement.

For more information on Cisco Tetration Analytics, refer to https://www.cisco.com/go/tetration.

Summary

Most organizations start using ACI in the same way as legacy networks use ports and VLANs, which sometimes is referred to as a "network-centric" ACI deployment. There is nothing wrong with that approach, and those organizations will reap multiple benefits from Cisco ACI that will help to improve the way their networks operate, as Chapter 7 explained. However, moving to an application-centric model can bring yet another set of benefits, and this chapter has focused on those benefits. There are mainly two use cases why organizations move to application-centric ACI deployments:

- **Security:** Cisco ACI can help to dramatically improve data center security, making security pervasive all through the network, and not just centralized in chokepoints such as firewalls.

- **Operations:** Through injecting application-related knowledge into the network configuration, operators will have data that can help them bridge the gap with developers. This use case is very important in organizations that strive for implementing DevOps models.

And last but not least, these different deployment options can coexist with each other: Some applications for which no application knowledge exists might be configured using the network-centric approach, security-critical applications might have a more stringent security policy, and applications where DevOps methodologies are being used might be configured using the application-centric approach.

Chapter 9

Multi-Tenancy

In this chapter, you will learn the following:

- What multi-tenancy means in a network context, both from a data perspective and from a management perspective

- How to migrate to a multi-tenant model in ACI

- How to connect tenants to external resources

- How to provide connectivity between tenants, and how to share resources such as routed external connections

- How to integrate L4-7 network services with multi-tenancy

If this chapter is going to deal with multi-tenancy, it begs for an opening question: What is a tenant? Is it an external customer? Maybe an internal customer? Or is it a division inside of a big organization?

In their 2012 paper "Architectural Concerns in Multi-Tenant SaaS Applications," Krebs, Momm, and Kounev define *tenant* as "a group of users sharing the same view on an application they use." And that's pretty close to the way many enterprises are using Cisco ACI's multi-tenancy today: as a way to define what part of the network a certain group of users have visibility and access to.

That group of users is exactly that—a group. It could be a customer (external or internal), a division, an IT (or non-IT) department other than the network department, and so on. You can decide what a tenant means for the network organization, and there can be multiple answers to this question.

This chapter explores the benefits of network multi-tenancy as implemented in Cisco ACI, as well as offers some examples of how others are using this function so that you can better assess what would be the best multi-tenancy concept for your organization.

The Need for Network Multi-Tenancy

The two aspects of network multi-tenancy are data-plane multi-tenancy and management multi-tenancy, and this chapter consistently refers to both meanings when dealing with the multiple facets of the topic.

Data-Plane Multi-Tenancy

The first aspect of network multi-tenancy is traffic separation, or data-plane multi-tenancy. This is a concept that already exists in traditional networks and is typically achieved through the following two familiar technologies:

- **Virtual local area network (VLAN):** This is network virtualization at Layer 2 (L2). It allows for the use of an L2 switch for multiple user groups (tenants), isolating the traffic belonging to one of those groups from the rest. Essentially, this equates to virtualizing a single switch into multiple logical switches.

- **Virtual routing and forwarding (VRF):** As an evolution of the VLAN concept, VRF represents Layer 3 (L3) network virtualization. In this case, the idea is virtualizing a router so that multiple tenants can share it. These different router partitions should be independent of each other at L3, including different IP address namespaces (which could even overlap with each other), different routing protocol instances, different route tables, and so on.

Multiple designs combine multiple VLANs and VRFs to achieve an L2 and L3 fabric segmentation. There are multiple reasons for this kind of segmentation, such as the following:

- Two companies merging that have overlapping IP address ranges

- Security requirements that demand some environments be completely separated from each other

- Traffic engineering (in other words, making sure traffic between two endpoints flows through specific network points)

Network technologies other than Cisco ACI have been combining data-plane multi-tenancy and management multi-tenancy for decades, and they have proven to be very effective. Since there's no need to reinvent the wheel, Cisco ACI leverages the same concepts in order to achieve network multi-tenancy at the data-plane level (or in other words, traffic segmentation at Layer 2 and 3), but augmented by its centralized management concept: In ACI, creating a new bridge domain (BD) or a new VRF automatically applies to all switches in a fabric, making data-plane multi-tenancy extremely easy to accomplish.

Management Multi-Tenancy

The second aspect of multi-tenancy is multi-tenancy at the management level, and the network industry has struggled with this aspect in the past. To illustrate this, assume that companies A and B merge, and two sets of VLANs and VRFs are created in a data center so that traffic belonging to those two companies does not meld together. Now the question is, how do you give network administrators of company A access to their resources (such as their VLANs and VRFs) but not to the resources of company B? This kind of multi-tenancy has never been present in most network platforms, and it was only achievable through the usage of additional network software.

Multiple applications exist for management multi-tenancy. As described in Chapter 7, "How Life Is Different with ACI," maybe you want to offer dedicated network views to specific groups of people, such as your virtualization admins, or to a certain part of your company. As this chapter will show, you can use security domains for that purpose.

Even if nobody other than the network management team has access to Cisco ACI, multi-tenancy can make the administration of the system easier in some ways. You can place your network and applications into groups (your ACI tenants) so that you can see the overall health scores when faults happen, which helps you quickly identify the affected area of your network (for example, you could have tenants such as Production, Staging, and Test).

If you decide to implement security in your network, as Chapter 8, "Moving to Application Centric-Networking," describes, you will find out that having multiple tenants can make your life a lot easier. For example, when troubleshooting a problem that is related to the security policy implemented by contracts, you can have a look at the logs that relate to a specific tenant, instead of having to browse all contract logs for the entire network. Having a granular separation of your applications and networks in different tenants makes finding information in the GUI easier.

Both data-plane and management multi-tenancy are orthogonal concepts: You could implement both, just one of them, or neither one. Here some examples to clarify the meaning of both concepts:

- If you do not have VRFs in your network today, chances are you will not need them with ACI either. In other words, you do not need data-plane multi-tenancy.

- If you have multiple sets of administrators, and each one cares about different parts of the data center, you will probably want to include tenants in your ACI design. That is to say, you will benefit from management multi-tenancy.

- Even if there is single team of network administrators managing the full data center network, you might want to be able to segment your network into more manageable pieces. Again, management multi-tenancy can provide you a way of achieving this.

Multi-Tenancy in Cisco ACI

As described in the previous section, data-plane multi-tenancy is achieved in Cisco ACI through the use of VLANs and VRFs—exactly the same as in legacy networks. VLANs and VRFs have been associated with network multi-tenancy for decades: With VLANs, you can have multiple groups sharing a Layer 2 infrastructure without interfering with each other, and VRFs achieve the same thing for IP networks.

Again, this is what we have called *data-plane multi-tenancy*. In ACI, you have VRFs to slice Layer 3 networks into multiple domains, and you also have a concept very similar to VLANs: bridge domains. As previous chapters have shown, the concept of a VLAN is slightly different in ACI and can be roughly translated to bridge domains: If two endpoints are in different bridge domains, they will not be able to talk to each other directly over Layer 2, which is exactly the same goal as in VLAN technology. The only way to achieve communication is on Layer 3, where you need to define default gateways in the bridge domains—again, exactly the same as in traditional networks where different VLANs can only be connected to each other through a Layer 3 device.

Those bridge domains need to be associated with the same VRF, though. If you configure different bridge domains and associate them with different VRFs, even configuring default gateways in the bridge domains will not enable Layer 3 configuration between those endpoints (unless inter-VRF communication is explicitly allowed, as later sections in this chapter show).

Now try to step out of the data-plane multi-tenancy concept and into management multi-tenancy. Here the goal isn't to keep packets and routing protocols independent from each other, but rather to have different sets of administrators who have access to different parts of the network. In a way, this is not dissimilar to the application-centricity concept described in Chapter 8.

The concept of a tenant is reflected in Cisco ACI in the object class "tenant" (no surprise there). Tenant objects in ACI are mere containers: folders that can contain other Cisco ACI objects such as application profiles, bridge domains, or EPGs.

Here are two important attributes of these tenant objects we can explore right now:

- Tenants cannot be nested. In other words, you cannot configure a tenant inside of another tenant.

- You always need a tenant to configure most logical constructs in Cisco ACI, such as application profiles, EPGs, VRFs, BDs, and contracts. Organizations that do not need multi-tenancy can just use the default tenant "common," but you need to define ACI constructs inside of one tenant.

Security Domains

Once you define tenants, you can control which network administrators have access to which tenants. You may want some administrators to be able to control all properties on all tenants while other types of administrators can only see and modify certain tenants.

You could have Application Policy Infrastructure Controller (APIC) users associated directly with tenants, but that would create some management challenges. Imagine if you have certain admins who need to access all tenants. Every time you create a new tenant, you should make sure every one of those special admin users is updated so that they can modify the newly created tenant.

This challenge is resolved in Cisco ACI through the use of security domains. A security domain is an intermediate entity between tenants and users. Tenants are assigned to security domains, and security domains are assigned to users. In other words, security domains are subsets of all the tenants in the system, and users have access to all tenants contained in the security domains that have been assigned to them.

In our previous example of the special admins who need to see all the tenants, you have a special security domain called "all," and just by assigning that security domain to a user, you can be sure that user will be able to access all tenants in the system.

Tenants can be assigned to multiple security domains, so you can have multiple overlapping tenant subsets to control user access in a very granular way. One use case where you would want to have overlapping security domains is if you have some hierarchy in your tenants. For example, imagine that companies A and B are merging, and for each company you define a Virtualization tenant and a Storage tenant. In total, you would have four tenants: Virtualization-A, Virtualization-B, Storage-A, and Storage-B. You can use multiple security domains to achieve the following:

- Users with access to all Storage tenants (both A and B)
- Users with access to all infrastructure belonging to company A (both Virtualization and Storage)
- Users with access exclusively to Storage-A

As you can see, the security domain is a very useful logical construct for getting maximum flexibility when describing which APIC user can access the configuration contained in which ACI tenant.

Role-Based Access Control

After you determine that some administrators can access only the tenants under certain security domains, you need to figure out what those users should be able to do in those tenants. Should they be able to see and modify every single attribute there? Or maybe just a subset? This is exactly what role-based access control (RBAC) can achieve. Through roles, you can assign certain users read-only or read-write access to some attributes in a tenant.

RBAC is a critical part of the security posture of a network. Most security policies dictate that IT administrators should only have access to the functions they need in order to do their job. Here's an example from another industry: If you work in the HR department at a bank, you probably do not need to have clearance to enter the money vault. RBAC does the same in IT—its mission is to provide to each administrator only the infrastructure access they need in order to prevent accidental or malicious usage of that infrastructure.

RBAC is not new in network infrastructure, although legacy implementations are typically either too crude or too complicated to implement and maintain. Legacy Cisco IOS devices had 16 privilege levels, and users were allowed to execute commands for which their privilege level had clearance. The main problem was that the assignment of commands to privilege levels was a manual and very error-prone process.

NX-OS introduced the concepts of roles and feature groups, which were aimed at simplifying the old process. Predefined roles such as "network-admin" and "network-operator" were defined, and commands could be assigned to these roles, not individually, but clustered in feature groups.

ACI follows the same architecture that is present in NX-OS. There are some predefined roles in Cisco ACI, such as "fabric-admin," "ops," and "read-all." However, you can certainly create new roles that better match your requirements. Here's a list of the predefined roles you can find in Cisco ACI, in alphabetical order:

- **aaa:** Used for configuring authentication, authorization, accounting, and import/export policies.

- **admin:** Provides full access to all the features of the fabric. The admin privilege can be considered a union of all other privileges. This is the role you want to have if you are the main admin of an ACI system.

- **access-admin:** For configuring access port attributes.

- **fabric-admin:** Allows for configuring fabric-wide attributes and external connectivity.

- **nw-svc-admin:** Users with this role are allowed to configure L4-7 network service insertion and orchestration.

- **nw-svc-params:** This role grants access to the parameters governing the configuration of external L4-7 devices.

- **ops:** Designed to cater to the needs of network operators, this role provides access to monitoring and troubleshooting functionality in ACI.

- **read-all:** For giving full visibility to the system, but no permission to modify any setting.

- **tenant-admin:** Tenant-admins can configure most attributes inside of a tenant, but they cannot change fabric-wide settings that can potentially impact other tenants.

- **tenant-ext-admin:** A subset of the tenant-admin role, this role allows for configuring external connectivity for ACI tenants.

- **vmm-admin:** Grants access to the integration with virtualization environments such as Microsoft Hyper-V, OpenStack, and VMware vSphere.

You can go to the Cisco ACI GUI and verify which privileges are assigned to each of the previous roles. For example, Figure 9-1 shows the privileges assigned to the aaa role (only one privilege, incidentally also called "aaa"). There are 62 privileges, and for each role you can decide whether or not it should be able to see those categories. You can enlarge or diminish the administrative scope of any given role by adding privileges to or removing privileges from the role, respectively.

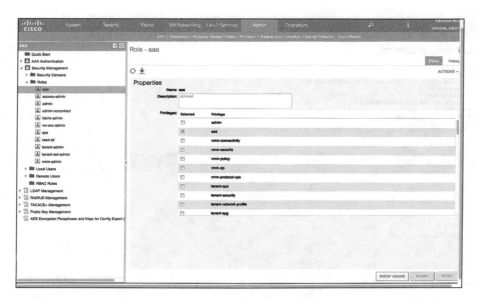

Figure 9-1   *Role aaa and Its Associated Privilege, Also Called "aaa"*

The next question probably is, what does a certain privilege allow and not allow one to do? Privilege names are often self-explanatory, but if you want to know exactly which privileges are allowed to read to or write from a certain object, you can browse Cisco ACI's object model. Chapter 13, "ACI Programmability," describes in more depth how to use the tool Visore, which is embedded in every APIC in order to access a detailed description for each object class in ACI.

For example, assume you are trying to figure out which privilege is allowed to create or modify locally defined users. When having a look at the class (aaa:User) to which locally defined users belong (Chapter 13 will describe how you can find out class names using Visore and the Debug option in the APIC GUI), you can see that both the privileges "aaa" and "admin" can have read and write access to objects belonging to this class, and no other, as Figure 9-2 shows. That is, only users including roles where the privileges "aaa" or "admin" are included are allowed to see or modify locally defined users.

Figure 9-2 shows how Visore displays the attributes of the class aaa:User. Note the "Write Access" and "Read Access" properties at the beginning of the class description refer to the allowed privileges.

When creating a user, you first configure which security domains (that is, which *tenants*) that user is going to be allowed to access. Then, in a second step, you define which roles the user will get assigned for each security domain, and whether the objects contained in those roles will be visible with read-only or with read-write permission.

For example, Figure 9-3 shows the creation of a user that will be able to access two security domains: "Pod3" and "common."

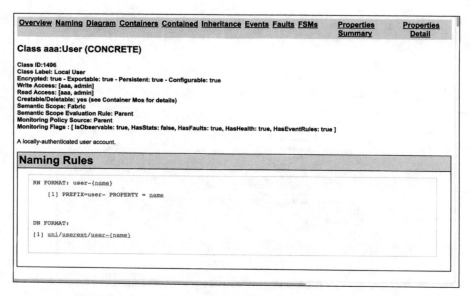

Figure 9-2   *Visore Showing Access Attributes for Object Class aaa:User*

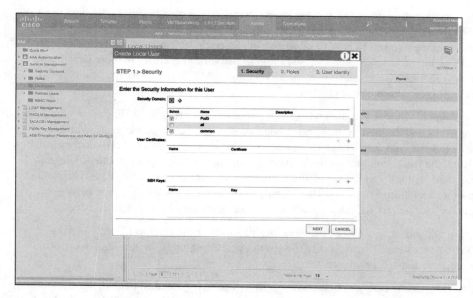

Figure 9-3   *Defining the Security Domains That a New User Will Be Allowed to Access*

You also decide which objects the user will be able to access by assigning roles to that user either in read-only or in read-write mode, as Figure 9-4 illustrates.

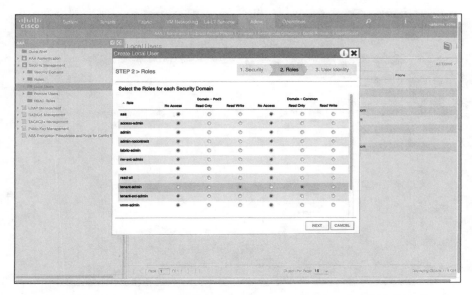

Figure 9-4 *Defining Which Roles the New User Will Have for Each Security Domain*

But what about if none of the predefined roles in Cisco ACI satisfies your requirements? For example, have a look at the role aaa (for authentication, authorization, and accounting). As you saw in Figure 9-1, it has only one privilege associated, which happens to be called "aaa" as well.

But say you want to have a role that includes not only AAA configurations, but something else, such as "tenant-security," for example. You could either modify the existing aaa role or create a new one, so that both privileges are included in the role. Figure 9-5 shows the configuration of a newly created role called "aaa-new."

Physical Domains

You might additionally restrict where a certain tenant can deploy workloads. That is, besides management-plane multi-tenancy (a group of users gets a personalized GUI with just the objects they are allowed to see) and data-plane multi-tenancy (the objects created by two groups of users cannot communicate with each other), the possibility of some physical multi-tenancy exists.

Why would you want to do this? One example might be because you want to partition your network. You may want to have both production and test workloads in your application, and you would like to deploy them in dedicated leaf switches. In this case, you would have specific racks where only production servers are installed, and racks containing only test and development infrastructure.

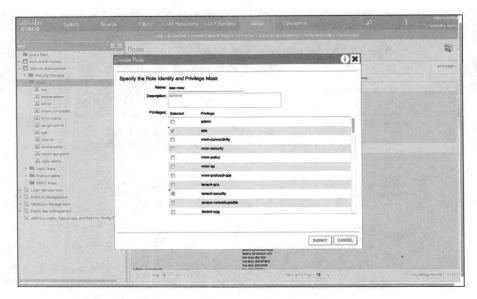

Figure 9-5 *New "aaa-new" Role, Which Includes an Additional Privilege*

Such an approach brings a certain rigidity to the infrastructure (you cannot seamlessly promote a workload from test to production, because it needs to be moved to a different rack), but on the other hand it offers very clean hardware separation. Sticking to the preceding example of production and test separation, here are some advantages of dedicating networking hardware to specific purposes:

■ From a bandwidth perspective, by statically allocating leaf switches to either test or production, you can be completely sure that production workloads are not going to be impacted by test activity.

■ From a scalability perspective, you don't consume hardware resources in your production ACI leaf switches that are used by test workloads. As previous chapters have covered, spine/leaf architectures depend heavily on individual leaf scalability, so making sure that test workloads do not burn resources that production workloads might need in the future can be very interesting.

■ From a security perspective, having dedicated ACI leaf switches for each workload category may be desirable. Note here that having VLAN and VRF separation is a very secure way to isolate workloads, but there might be situations where physical separation is advantageous (having an "air gap" in between, as some people in the industry like to describe it).

As explained in Chapter 1, "You've Purchased ACI. Now What?" Cisco ACI offers an innovative concept to achieve this physical separation of tenants: physical domains. A physical domain is a collection of physical resources, where a certain EPG can be deployed. Part of the EPG configuration consists of specifying on which virtual or physical domains the endpoints that belong to that EPG are allowed to exist.

Physical domains also contain the VLAN pools with the IDs that objects attached to that slice of the infrastructure are allowed to use. If you do not want to restrict the VLAN IDs that a certain tenant can use, you can have big pools containing all possible VLAN IDs.

Otherwise, you might want to allocate, say, VLAN IDs 1 through 2000 to use by production workloads, and IDs 2000 through 4000 to use by test workloads. Remember that you can have many more segments than VLAN IDs, because these IDs are reusable from port to port. For example, you could have, say, VLAN ID 37 on port 11 of a certain switch allocating workloads to the Web EPG, and the same VLAN ID 37 on port 12 of the same switch allocating workloads to the DB EPG. As a consequence, the VLAN pools associated with different physical domains can overlap.

The allocation of EPGs to physical domains is therefore straightforward: You configure the physical domains in the EPG. But how are the individual infrastructure components allocated to physical domains? In Cisco ACI, this is achieved through the use of Attachable Access Entity Profiles (AAEPs). This term might sound very complicated, but the concept behind it is actually quite simple. The next paragraphs describe other possible theoretical options of having implemented the networking model in ACI, and why using AAEPs is the most flexible way of accomplishing the association between infrastructure elements and physical domains.

First of all, Cisco ACI architects needed to define how granular these infrastructure assignments should be. The smallest physical entity in a network is a switch port, so this is how granular physical domains should go. Now the first choice might have been associating each port with a physical domain, but this would complicate port configuration. Every time you configure a port, you need to remember to which physical domain or domains it needs to belong, which would have been clearly inefficient.

The next option would have been having the interface policy groups (roughly equivalent to port profiles in the NX-OS world) directly associated with the physical domains. Port configuration is simplified because you would only need to attach the port to the corresponding interface policy group, and that would already contain the association to the physical domain. However, this model would have had a problem: Modifying the association of the infrastructure to physical domains would be extremely painful because it would involve going through each individual interface policy group and changing the association to physical domains.

Thus, the concept of AAEP was created. It is a sort of "connector" that acts as the glue between interface policy groups and physical or virtual domains. From this perspective, you could look at AAEPs as a way of allocating VLAN pools to Ethernet ports. Figure 9-6 illustrates this concept.

As a consequence of this flexible data model, modifying existing physical domain associations is very easy, because you only need to change the associations at the AAEP level, most of the time without modifying the interface policy groups.

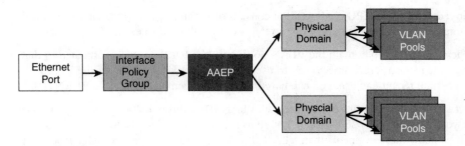

Figure 9-6   *AAEP Used to Associate Ports to Physical Domains*

Coming back to the preceding example, you could define a production physical domain associated with production VLANs 2 through 1999, and a test physical domain associated with VLANs 2000 through 3999 (in Figure 9-7 "PRD" stands for "production" and "TST" stands for "test"). Say Ethernet port 1/1 (where, for example, a VMware hypervisor for production workloads is attached) is associated with a production policy group (in Figure 9-7, "ESX-PRD"). Similarly, Ethernet port 1/2 is bound to the interface policy group "ESX-TST," where only test VLANs are allowed. If an admin tried to use a production VLAN on the test ESX host connected to port 1/2, it would not work because the physical port would not accept that encapsulation as defined by the physical domain relationship.

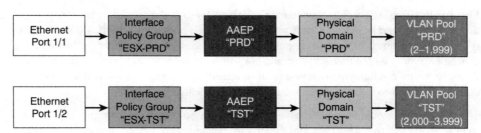

Figure 9-7   *Port Assignment Example for Separating Physical Domains*

After this excursion into what physical domains are, and how you can restrict which VLAN IDs and which infrastructure elements (switch ports) can be associated with an endpoint group (EPG), hopefully you have a better view of how these concepts can be used in order to slice the network (for example, to achieve the goal stated at the beginning of this section: dedicating ports or even whole switches to a specific tenant, where the EPGs in that tenant are associated with physical domains that only contain certain ports or switches).

Logical Bandwidth Protection Through Quality of Service

As the previous section has shown, slicing the network in different physical domains has advantages in the areas of bandwidth allocation, leaf resource scalability, and security.

But what if you are only interested in the bandwidth component? Sticking to the example in the previous section, let's assume that test and production workloads share the same Cisco ACI fabric. One of your primary objectives is probably that regardless of what activity occurs in the test environment, it should not interfere in any case with the performance of production workloads.

To that purpose, you can use different classes of service for each tenant. For example, you could define that your production EPGs (and the contracts between them) are mapped to the QoS policy "Level 1" and test EPGs to "Level 2." You could increase the bandwidth allocation for production traffic (Level 1) to some value higher than the default 20%. Figure 9-8 shows a bandwidth allocation for Level 1 traffic of 40%, while the other two classes get 20%. This means that production traffic will under all circumstances get at least twice as much bandwidth as any of the two other traffic classes.

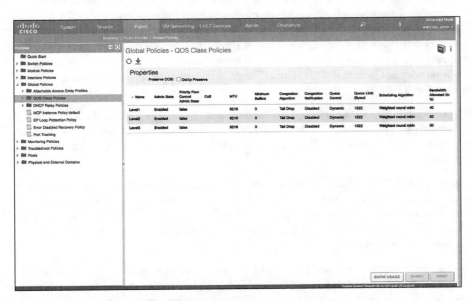

Figure 9-8 *QoS Classes in Cisco ACI*

Note that this approach obviously does not scale for more than three tenants, so it is only valid for a scenario such as test and production separation, Internet and extranet separation, or a company merge where two or three organizations share the same network.

What Is a Tenant? What Is an Application?

As previous sections have shown, tenants are fundamentally folders that can be used to restrict administrative access. Inside of those tenants you can define application profiles, which are again a sort of folder containing EPGs. One frequently asked question is whether to configure the networking policy for two applications using two different application profiles inside of one tenant, or to use two different tenants altogether.

As is oftentimes the case in engineering, the answer is, "it depends." Recall the definition of the word *tenant* at the beginning of this chapter: A tenant is described by a group of users. So what groups of users need to have access to the network for these two applications, and are they interested in the whole of it or just in a subset?

The following sections explore some common use cases that organizations across the globe have followed when implementing Cisco ACI.

Logical Separation for Lines of Business

This is one of the most typical use cases for multi-tenancy. In ACI, you can configure your network using an application-centric model. Suppose you have structured the network configuration for your applications using ACI application profiles (as detailed in the previous chapter). Chances are some of those applications belong to the same organization inside of your company, such as finance, human resources, and engineering. Therefore, why not group, say, all of the finance applications in a Finance tenant to offer a consolidated view?

The term *line of business* might not be the one used in your organization; perhaps the term *division*, *department*, *business unit*, *product line*, *venture*, or just *business* might apply better to your situation. The concept is still the same: an entity that owns distinct applications.

What you get with this tenant separation model is the possibility of giving access to each line of business for the network state around the applications it owns. Using the previous example, administrators interested only in the Finance application could see and modify network information specific to them, without being distracted by events or configurations not relevant to them.

Even for administrators who are not specific to one line of business, it is beneficial being able to segment the network into more manageable pieces. For example, if somebody complains about a problem in a Finance application, you don't want to be looking at configuration that is not relevant to the issue at hand.

Note that in this case we are describing management multi-tenancy, and you might not have requirements for creating multiple VRFs. A popular option when deploying management multi-tenancy is to leave network objects (bridge domains and VRFs) in the common tenant (in other words, having management multi-tenancy but not necessarily data-plane multi-tenancy).

After all, "Networking" could be just considered as yet another line of business; therefore, a frequent ACI design consists of putting all network objects in a single tenant, where only network admins have access. Other administrators who design EPG relationships, contracts, and application profiles will have access to those objects placed in specific tenants, as Figure 9-9 shows.

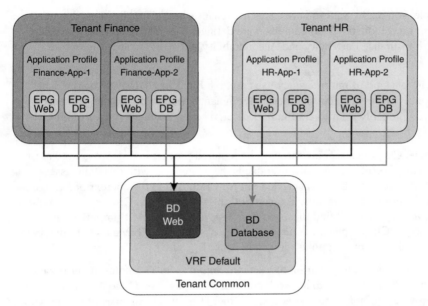

Figure 9-9 *ACI Tenant Design with Network Constructs in the Common Tenant*

Note that this is just an example (albeit a relatively common one) from a tenant design, so you might want to change it based on your own specific needs (for example, moving up the bridge domains to the more specific tenants). Here are some of the benefits of such a design:

- You can have "Finance admins" or "HR admins" who would get access (even write access if needed) to their own specific network policies.

- These administrators would not have privilege to change fabric-wide settings that might impact other tenants.

- Networking-specific information such as subnets, multicast parameters, and VRFs are located in one single tenant (the common tenant) and are accessible only by global network administrators.

- Network admins can concentrate on a specific part of the network when trouble-shooting issues, either in the individual tenants (if the problem is specific to a certain tenant) or in the common tenant (for fabric-wide issues).

Logical Separation for Security or Compliance

Another reason for separating configuration into multiple tenants might be not because the related applications belong to different entities but because they have different security requirements. So you might want to divide your applications in security zones that correspond to tenants.

For example, you might want to have a specific tenant where all applications that need to be Payment Card Industry (PCI) compliant are defined. And maybe another one where your Health Insurance Portability and Accountability Act (HIPAA) applications are located.

Note that in this kind of multi-tenancy use case, the focus lies decisively on the data plane. Applications in different security zones (tenants) need to be isolated from each other, so you probably want to configure dedicated bridge domains and VRFs on each one of them.

At press time, Cisco ACI is going through the required process in order to get the most relevant security certifications. One example is the whitepaper with the audit, assessment, and attestation that Verizon carried out for Cisco ACI in the context of PCI compliance, with very positive results. You can find this whitepaper at Cisco.com. As a quick one-line summary, you will find these words in that document: "ACI simplifies Payment Card Industry (PCI) compliance and reduces the risk of security breaches with dynamic workloads while maintaining policy and compliance."

Another fairly typical interpretation of the word *tenant* is for IT admins in our organization who need limited access to network constructs. In this case, Cisco ACI multi-tenancy provides the ability to give access to other IT groups to the part of the network that supports their processes.

For example, you could define a "VMware" tenant, where you give access to your VMware admins. Here, they can see the state of the network for their "applications." What are the applications relevant to a VMware administrator? Examples include vMotion, VSAN, and Management. In this case, if the VMware admin suspects that something is wrong with the network that impacts vMotion, for example, the APIC will show them whether that is indeed the case. And when the VMware admin logs on to APIC, they will only be allowed to see whatever information is relevant for their "applications."

The case of the virtualization administrator is fairly significant, because it illustrates the next philosophical question that might arise: What is an EPG? Let's focus on vMotion and assume that multiple virtualization clusters exist. Should you define an application profile per cluster, and inside each application profile define an EPG for vMotion? Or should you define a "vMotion" application profile, and inside of it one EPG per cluster?

The overall recommendation is to stick to the meaning of the word *application*. In this case, "vMotion" is closer to the application concept than is "cluster," so the second approach ("vMotion" app profile) would be the preferred one. The implication is that when there is something wrong with vMotion in the Test cluster, the operator will see the following process:

1. Health score of the VMware tenant goes down.

2. Health score of the vMotion application profile goes down.

3. Health score of the Test EPG inside of the vMotion application profile goes down.

This is the model shown in Figure 9-10, where the vSphere admin gets access to the applications and EPGs configured under the tenant "vSphere," so that network issues impacting the vSphere infrastructure can be identified quickly. In the example depicted in Figure 9-10, a fault is slightly impacting the health of vMotion for vSphere cluster 1 (note that these application profiles and EPGs have been statically defined by the network administrator).

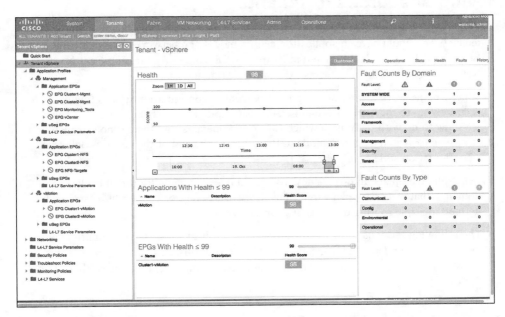

Figure 9-10   *Example of Tenant Defined for vSphere Infrastructure*

Following the other approach, where application profiles actually map to VMware clusters, would be perfectly fine, too. In the case of a problem similar to the preceding example (something goes wrong with vMotion in the Test cluster), here is the order in which operators would be alerted:

1. Health score of the VMware tenant goes down.

2. Health score of the cluster Test application profile goes down.

3. Health score of the vMotion EPG inside of the Test application profile goes down.

As you can see, there is a slight difference in the way that alerts will be reported up the object tree, and depending on how the VMware administrator would like to group infrastructure objects (vMotion vmknics, vSphere clusters, and so on), some other choices might be more adequate.

This example illustrates the abstract character of the concepts *tenant* and *application*. Although you can map ACI tenants to groups of people in your organization, and ACI applications to business applications running in your data center, you could use those

ACI terms in other ways. For example, you can consider these ACI constructs as a 2-level hierarchy folder system for Cisco ACI EPGs (tenants contain applications, applications contain EPGs), offering a summarization layer for all information regarding end points in ACI.

Moving Resources to Tenants

This section assumes that the network has been implemented without any multi-tenancy. You could have an application-centric model or a network-centric one (the BD=EPG=VLAN model discussed in Chapter 8 "Moving to Application-Centric Networking"), but all your objects exist in the common tenant.

Whether a network-centric or an application-centric configuration style is followed is entirely up to the network administrator, as Chapter 8 described. It does not have anything to do with the way in which Cisco ACI operates, and there is no setting anywhere to switch from one mode to the other. At the end of the day, it is only that, a configuration style.

Regarding data-plane multi-tenancy, you could have a single VRF for all bridge domains (that is no data-plane multi-tenancy whatsoever), or you might have already defined multiple routing domains in your data center.

The following sections show the different steps involved in moving to a multi-tenant model, including data- and management-plane separations. Realize that not all steps are required because you might be only interested in implementing one of those two options.

Creating the Logical Tenant Structure

If you want to move resources out of the common tenant, the first thing you need is the target tenant, including the application profiles and EPGs inside, and optionally VRFs and bridge domains. Why you would want to leave VRFs and bridge domains in the common tenant was explained earlier in the section "Logical Separation for Lines of Business."

If you have already decided that the new tenant will belong to a certain security domain, make sure to configure the new tenant accordingly.

Implementing Management Multi-Tenancy

Multi-tenancy at the management plane is relatively easy to achieve (from a migration standpoint) because it only involves creating application profiles and EPGs in another tenant, while leaving the objects responsible for packet forwarding (such as bridge domains, VRFs, and external networks) in the common tenant. As a consequence, it can be achieved essentially without downtime.

A migration to a multi-tenant environment from a data-plane perspective is trickier, as you will see later in this chapter in the "Implementing Data-Plane Multi-Tenancy" section.

Moving EPGs and Contracts

In order to get to a multi-tenant network on the management level, the EPGs will have to shift from the common tenant to a dedicated one. Well, to be completely honest, EPGs and contracts will not actually be moved; instead, new EPGs and contracts will be created in the new tenant. It's the endpoints that will be migrated to the new EPGs.

The first step is obviously creating the new tenant and the new application profile, if they do not already exist. You should map the new EPGs to the same bridge domain as the original EPGs. That bridge domain is still in the common tenant, so any EPG in any other tenant can be associated with it. Do not forget to create contracts governing the communication between the newly created EPGs; otherwise, communication will break. Configure temporary contracts that will allow all communication between the old and the new EPGs (typically endpoints inside of one EPG need to talk to each other, but not necessarily).

As described in the previous chapter, physical and virtual endpoints can be gradually migrated to the new EPGs, with very little impact for the application.

Figure 9-11 shows an example of such a migration, where new EPGs "Web" and "DB" are configured in a new tenant and mapped to the same bridge domains as the old EPGs (under the common tenant). When the endpoint migration is completed, the old Web and DB EPGs can be deleted from the common tenant.

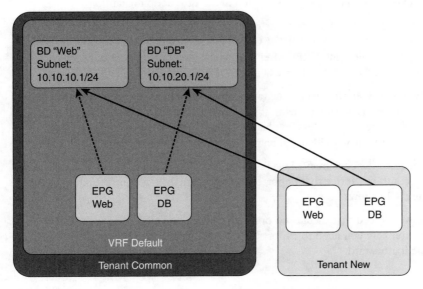

Figure 9-11 *Migration to Management-Plane Multi-Tenancy*

Exporting and Importing Contracts for Inter-Tenant Communication

At this stage, you might have EPGs spread out across multiple tenants, all in the same VRF, and you have implemented contracts inside of those tenants that control how the EPGs communicate to each other. Alternatively, you could have left the contracts in the common tenant, but it is recommended that you move the contracts to the tenant where they are used—mostly for manageability reasons.

However, this implies that EPGs in one tenant do not need to speak to EPGs in a different tenant. If you encounter this situation, you have two options: The first option is "promoting" the contract to the common tenant. Do not forget to define its scope as Global or VRF so that it is interpreted correctly by two EPGs in different tenants, as was explained in Chapter 7.

As mentioned before, you might not want to do this in order to keep your common tenant clean and tidy and to have an application-specific configuration in the tenants. Your second choice is exporting the contract from the tenant containing the provider EPG and importing it into the tenant with the consumer EPG.

For example, imagine you have two tenants, Test and Production, each with Web and Database EPGs. Normally the Test-Web EPG only talks to the Test-DB EPG, and the Production-Web EPG only talks to the Production-DB EPG. Now imagine that you have the requirement to provide services from the Production-DB to the Test-Web EPG.

You have the Test-DB-Services contract in the Test tenant (provided by Test-DB and consumed by Test-Web), and you have the Production-DB-Services contract in the Production tenant. The objective is to consume the Production-DB-Services contract from the Test-Web EPG, which in principle should not be possible (because the Test tenant has no visibility to the contracts located in the Production tenant).

As a first step, you need to make sure the contract Production-DB-Services in the Production tenant has a scope of VRF or Global (in this example, it's VRF, because all EPGs are mapped to the same VRF). After that, you can export the contract by right-clicking on the Contracts folder, as Figure 9-12 illustrates.

In the next window, you can specify the target tenant as well as the name used to make the contract known to the target tenant. It is recommended that you choose the same name for simplicity reasons, unless you have naming conflicts (for example, if you're exporting two contracts with identical names from two different tenants to a third one).

Now you can go to the consumer EPG (Test-Web in the Test tenant, in our example) and consume the contract. Notice that imported contracts are called "contract interfaces" in ACI, as Figure 9-13 shows.

You might have noticed that there is no option to "add a provided contract interface." That's the reason why you need to export the contract from the provider side, so that you can consume it afterward.

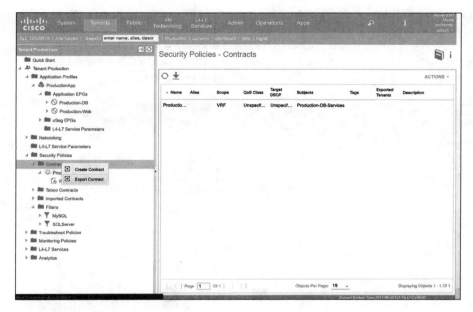

Figure 9-12   *Exporting a Contract*

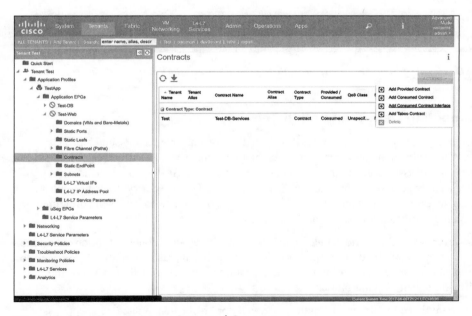

Figure 9-13   *Consuming an Imported Contract*

After consuming the contract interface, the Test-Web EPG can speak both to the Test-DB and to the Production-DB EPGs. If you check the visualization pane for the application profile, you will notice that the imported contract is shown with a different format (a dented circle instead of a standard circle), and that the provider EPG is not shown (and it shouldn't because it's in a different tenant), as Figure 9-14 depicts.

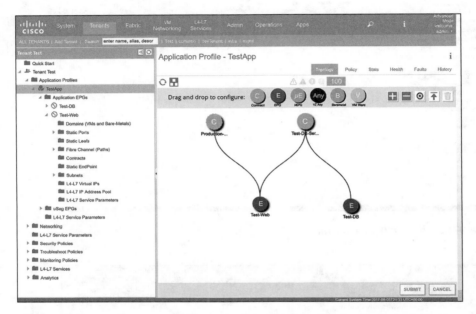

Figure 9-14   *Application Profile with Both a Standard and an Imported Contract*

Implementing Data-Plane Multi-Tenancy

You have your application profiles distributed across multiple tenants, and all EPGs relate to bridge domains are still in the common tenant. The VRFs to which those bridge domains are associated are in the common tenant as well. At this point, chances are you have already achieved your objective: Through the usage of security domains you can grant access to the new tenants to different groups of users, who can even configure certain communication parameters such as contracts and traffic filters.

However, network-centric details such as VRF attributes and subnet definitions in bridge domains must still be done at the common tenant. This might be desirable if you want to keep all network configuration in a single tenant, but the rest distributed across the different tenants in your fabric.

Be aware that a migration to a multi-tenant network from a data-plane perspective is considerably more complex than the management multi-tenancy covered in the previous sections, because it involves moving the endpoint groups to different bridge domains and VRFs, and it will typically be associated with some application downtime.

This section covers a process that can be followed if you want to implement multi-tenancy in the data plane, and additionally in the management plane (which the previous section described). Essentially, we describe how to migrate bridge domains and VRFs from the common tenant to a newly created tenant. You have two main alternative approaches to accomplish this migration:

- Create new bridge domains, VRFs, and external L3 connections in the new tenant, and migrate EPGs from the BDs in the common tenant to the BDs in the new tenant.

- Migrate only bridge domains to the new tenant, while still associated with the VRFs in common, and subsequently migrate the VRFs and external L3 connections.

Both options involve downtime, so make sure to execute them in a maintenance window.

The first approach is the recommended one because it allows for quick and partial fallback of migrations, should something not go according to plan. This is not specific to ACI but instead is a common network design best practice: When performing network migrations, it is usually advisable to have both the old and new environments available so that you can migrate workloads at your own pace.

As just described, the recommended approach for migrating BDs and VRFs from the common tenant into a new tenant is creating a brand-new structure of bridge domains, VRFs, and external Layer 3 networks in the new tenant. You should configure all attributes of the new VRFs and BDs the same way as in the original objects in the common tenant, with one exception: Do not configure the subnets in the new bridge domains to be "advertised externally" just yet, because you would be advertising to external routers the same subnet simultaneously over two different routing adjacencies.

Remember that there's no problem configuring the same IP address in two different bridge domains, if they belong to different VRFs. You would have the structure in Figure 9-15, where endpoints still are in the common tenant.

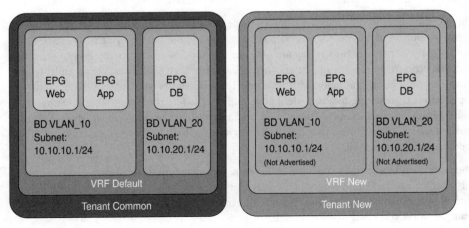

Figure 9-15 *Old and New VRFs and BDs*

You can now move endpoints from the old EPGs to the new ones. Note that until you configure the new subnets to be advertised, the new EPGs will not have connectivity. When you have a critical mass of endpoints in the new EPGs, you could make the routing switch:

1. Configure the subnets in the old BD to *not* be "advertised externally."

2. Configure the subnets in the new BD to be "advertised externally."

At this point, external routers should learn the subnets over the new external routed network in the tenant. Note that any endpoints mapped to BDs and VRFs in the old tenant will lose connectivity. You can now migrate the rest of the endpoints to the new EPGs.

When to Use Dedicated or Shared VRFs

The previous sections have covered how to migrate from a single-tenant concept to a multi-tenant network, divided into two main blocks: data-plane and management-plane multi-tenancy. We described what each one of the approaches involves, but what are the advantages and disadvantages of each one? When should you use each one?

Although control-plane and data-plane multi-tenancy often go hand in hand, it could happen that you will only need one of them. Most likely, you want to have management multi-tenancy in every single case, even if it is only for ease of management. You could argue that in your organization only the network team needs to have access to the network, so no multi-tenancy is required. Even in this case, a single network administration team can benefit from multi-tenancy due to the operational reasons described in this chapter. You are essentially breaking the network down into smaller slices or chunks so that they can be managed in an easier manner. You get tenant-specific fault reporting and dashboards (as you saw in Figure 9-10), you can back up and restore the configuration related to a single tenant without affecting others (as shown by Figure 9-16 and described in Chapter 7), you get tenant-specific statistics, and much, much more.

The question here is not really whether multiple tenants are desirable, but what is the best distribution in tenants for a certain network? Here, the best approach, as usual, is to move slowly. Most networks today are not multi-tenant, so you probably do not want to start with too many tenants in one go. Instead, a better way of moving into a multi-tenant concept would be to gradually introduce new tenants. Maybe start with moving some applications that belong to a well-defined group to a different tenant (like the vSphere-related applications such as vMotion) and begin exploring the operational advantages of multi-tenancy. You will find that the migration into the best multi-tenancy concept will follow a natural evolution.

The next question actually boils down to when data-plane multi-tenancy is required. As this chapter has shown, this data-plane segregation essentially equates to multiple VRFs that allow the use of overlapping IP addresses (hence the title of this section). That is the main question you need to ask yourself.

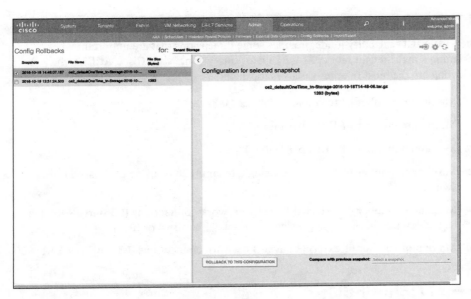

Figure 9-16 *Configuration Rollback Specific to a Single Tenant*

If you need to support overlapping IP addresses today or in the future, you will need to have multiple VRFs. Note that 100 VRFs do not necessarily equate to 100 tenants. You might have tenants for which no IP address range overlapping is required, and they could share a single VRF (which would be in the common tenant). Only those tenants that require overlapping IP addresses would need dedicated VRFs.

But why wouldn't you want to deploy dedicated VRFs for every tenant? You might argue that even if you do not need overlapping IP addresses now, you might need them in the future. The answer is two-fold: complexity and scalability. These concepts are related to each other. By having multiple VRFs in a Cisco ACI fabric, the level of complexity of the network will rise:

■ Two EPGs in different VRFs cannot speak to each other, even when adding contracts. Additional configuration is required, as the later section "Inter-Tenant Connectivity" will show.

■ You would typically configure dedicated external L3 network connectivity per each VRF (even if that is not strictly required), which would increase the number of routing protocol adjacencies you need to maintain.

The previous two facts lead to further scalability limits that you need to take into account, such as number of VRFs and number of external L3 connections, which will be discussed in the next section.

Multi-Tenant Scalability

The Cisco ACI scalability guide provides some dimensions that are important when designing a multi-tenant fabric. At the time of this writing, with Cisco ACI 3.1, the following are the most relevant variables to watch:

- **Maximum number of tenants per fabric:** 3,000

- **Maximum number of VRFs per fabric:** 3,000

- **Maximum number of VRFs per leaf:** 400

- **Maximum number of VRFs in one single tenant:** 128 (if using LSE-based leaf switches)

- **Maximum number of external Layer 3 network connections (L3 outs):** 4400 per leaf, 2,400 per fabric if using a single IP stack (either IPv4 or IPv6)

- **Maximum number of external Layer 3 network connections (L3 outs) per VRF:** 400

External Connectivity

Most likely the endpoints in each tenant will have to be able to speak to the outside world. In environments where no data-plane multi-tenancy is required, this goal is straightforward, because all tenants use the same VRFs and external network connections located in the common tenant.

In configurations with data-plane multi-tenancy (each tenant has its own VRF), having Layer 2 or Layer 3 connectivity to external devices is mostly no different than in single-tenant deployments. However, two options exist to achieve this goal, and you should know when to use which one.

This chapter uses the terms *external routed network* and *L3 out* interchangeably. In the APIC GUI, you find the former term, but most people just use the latter, probably because it is shorter.

The most immediate design is replicating the configuration of a single tenant. If you needed only one external network connection in your common tenant, now you would need one external connection per each tenant having its own VRF. This is the design that Figure 9-17 describes.

This design is very easy to understand and troubleshoot because each tenant is a self-contained entity with its own networking constructs. Because it is identical to what has been discussed in other chapters for single-tenant designs, this section will not cover the details of this implementation.

Another benefit of this design is the high level of traffic separation between tenants, and even the possibility of having dedicated external routers for each tenant. This might be desirable, for example, in the case of two companies merging together within one data center, where each company brings its own routing infrastructure.

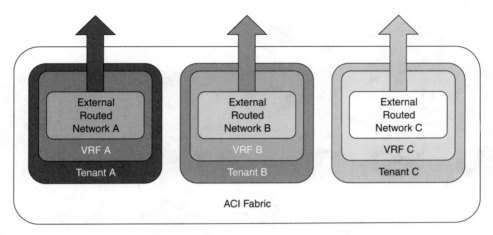

Figure 9-17   *Dedicated External Routed Networks per Tenant*

The main disadvantage of this design is the high number of network adjacencies required, which can put some scalability pressure in the system; plus the administrative burden of configuring and maintaining them.

Therefore, this design is recommended essentially for automated environments (such as service providers). Otherwise, it is probably better for low tenant numbers, and for situations where tenant traffic must be absolutely kept separate from the other tenants.

What if not only Cisco ACI is multi-tenant, but the external network as well? Many organizations have deployed MPLS-based virtual private networks (VPNs) so that a wide area network (WAN) can be used by multiple entities, even allowing the usage of overlapping IP addresses.

Does this sound familiar? It should, because it is exactly the same concept as in Cisco ACI. Consequently, it would make sense coupling the multi-tenancy concept of Cisco ACI with that of the external physical network. As Figure 9-18 shows, the connection between the Multiprotocol Label Switching (MPLS) network and the external world is performed at "provider edge" (PE) routers. These routers on one side connect with the backbone routers (called "provider" or P routers) and on the other side with customer routers (called "customer edge" or CE routers).

PE routers separate different tenants with VRF technology. VPNs are transported over an overlay network between the PE routers, so that P routers do not need to see the customer IP address namespaces.

Using this nomenclature, Cisco ACI would be the CE for the MPLS network (actually, a multi-VRF CE). Assuming that every tenant in Cisco ACI has its own VRF, a corresponding VPN should exist for each tenant in the WAN.

The WAN PE router also has a VRF for every configured tenant, and VRF-specific routing adjacencies can be established with ACI (that is, one or more routing adjacencies per tenant).

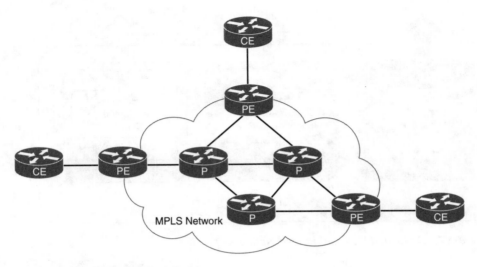

Figure 9-18   *MPLS Router Roles*

These routing adjacencies can use separate physical interfaces, but for cost and scalability reasons, most deployments use one single physical interface and dedicated logical subinterfaces identified by a VLAN tag (that is, a 802.1Q trunk), as Figure 9-19 depicts.

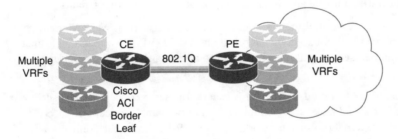

Figure 9-19   *Multiple VRFs from ACI to a PE Router over an 802.1Q Trunk*

As a consequence, for every tenant, you will also need to define a VLAN ID that's used in the subinterfaces on ACI and the external PE routers, so that the routes are handed over from one VRF to the next.

Starting with Cisco ACI 2.0, certain PE routers can be integrated with ACI in a way that no manual configuration of the WAN router with one VRF and one 802.1Q subinterface for each tenant is required. As described in Chapter 6, "External Routing with ACI," with Cisco Nexus 7000 and ASR 9000 and 1000 routers, the configuration of these objects can be done automatically, as new tenants are added to Cisco ACI. This integration greatly simplifies the provisioning of external connectivity for DC tenants.

Shared External Network for Multiple Tenants

Why would you want to share a routed external connection across multiple tenants in the first place? By doing so, you do not need to define dedicated routing adjacencies per tenant. Remember that configuring a routing adjacency involves configuring both the ACI and the external routers (typically ACI is connected to at least two external routers for redundancy purposes). By not having to define additional adjacencies for new tenants, you simplify the deployment process, because no additional interaction with the external routers is required.

Note that through the integration of the external router configuration in ACI, you can alleviate this provisioning overhead, but not every router model is supported. Additionally, by sharing one single routed external connection, you can make more efficient use of the hardware resources of the ACI border leaf switches.

The main disadvantages of this method are the additional complexity involved and the fact that tenant traffic is not completely separated from each other, because multiple tenants come together in the shared external network connection. The most important advantages are the simplified routing design of the data center and the reduced scalability requirements.

In this design, you would have dedicated VRFs in each tenant (tenants B and C in Figure 9-20), plus another VRF in a central tenant (tenant A in Figure 9-20, which would probably be the common tenant in most scenarios). Furthermore, it is in the central tenant where you would configure the external network connection that will be shared across all other tenants.

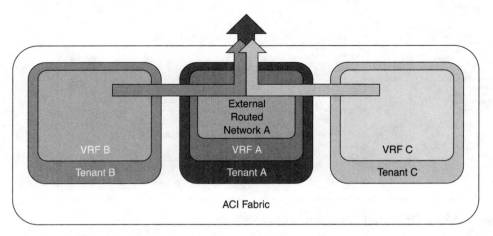

Figure 9-20   *Tenant Design with a Shared L3 Out*

The first thing to consider is how you will be creating the contracts between the external routed network and the EPGs in tenants A, B, and C. You have two choices:

■ The external routed network is the provider. This option requires the smallest configuration effort. You will not need to have the subnets in tenants B and C at the EPG
level (as opposed to the bridge domain level), and if the external routed network is in
the common tenant, you will not need to export any contract.

■ The EPGs are the providers. In this case, the contracts need to be configured
inside of tenants B and C (because imported contracts can only be consumed, not
provided). You need to export the contracts so that they can be consumed by the
external routed network in tenant A. Additionally, subnets in tenants B and C will
have to be defined under the EPG, instead of under the bridge domain.

The recommendation is to have the contracts provided by the external routed network, in
order to minimize the operations required. In any case, the scope of the contract should
be Global, because the contract will be spanning multiple VRFs.

Next, all subnets to be advertised to the outside world in the individual tenants are to be
marked as External (so they can be announced over an external connection) and Shared
(because they will have to be leaked to the VRF in common where the shared external
connection is associated), as illustrated in Figure 9-21. At this point, you will be advertising the tenants' networks to the outside world.

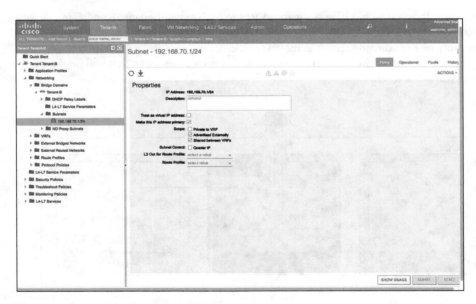

Figure 9-21 *Tenant Configuration to Leak Subnets*

Now you need to get the routes received from the outer world to the tenant. For this
example, we will assume that a default route (0.0.0.0/0) is being received over the external
routed connection. In the external EPG belonging to the external network connection in

common (called "Network" in the GUI, as you have already seen), you would typically have configured **External Subnets for External EPG** in the scope of the subnet, to specify that this route is to be accepted.

Note that you can leak aggregated routes as well, marking the subnet to **Aggregate Shared Routes** in the **Aggregate** section.

At this point, you would have all received routes in the VRF in tenant A, assuming that no ingress route filtering is being performed in the external routed connection (that is, ingress route control enforcement is not enabled), but you would not have those routes in tenants B and C just yet.

In order to leak that default route to the other tenants, you only need to additionally enable **Shared Route Control Subnet** in the subnet scope, as Figure 9-22 shows.

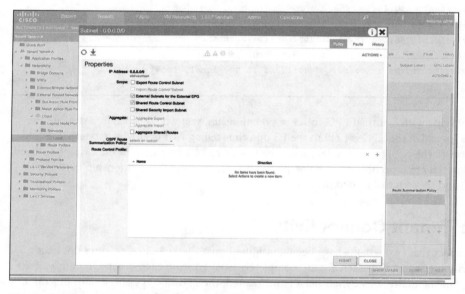

Figure 9-22 *External Routed Network Configuration to Leak the Default Route*

Now you can verify that the route (the default 0.0.0.0/0) is now leaked to the other tenants (for example, with the CLI command **fabric** *leaf_id* **show ip route vrf** *vrf_id*), as demonstrated in Example 9-1.

As the output in Example 9-1 shows, 201 is the ID of a leaf that has endpoints in an EPG in the VRF in tenant B (otherwise the VRF is not deployed), and "Tenant-B:Tenant-B" is the VRF ID (the string before the colon is the tenant name, and the string after the colon is the VRF name). The default route for the VRF in tenant B is reachable over a next hop that is in a different VRF, in tenant A.

Example 9-1   *Verifying That a Route Is Leaked to Other Tenants*

```
apic# fabric 201 show ip route vrf Tenant-B:Tenant-B
-----------------------------------------------------------------
 Node 201 (Leaf201)
-----------------------------------------------------------------
IP Route Table for VRF "Tenant-B:Tenant-B"
'*' denotes best ucast next-hop
'**' denotes best mcast next-hop
'[x/y]' denotes [preference/metric]
'%<string>' in via output denotes VRF <string>
0.0.0.0/0, ubest/mbest: 1/0
    *via 192.168.61.11%Tenant-A:Tenant-A, vlan111, [20/1], 00:00:10, bgp-65100,
     external, tag 65100
192.168.70.0/24, ubest/mbest: 1/0, attached, direct, pervasive
    *via 10.0.0.65%overlay-1, [1/0], 00:19:49, static
192.168.70.1/32, ubest/mbest: 1/0, attached, pervasive
    *via 192.168.70.1, vlan106, [1/0], 01:13:26, local, local
apic#
```

Note that with a normal EPG-to-L3-out relationship, you would typically associate the BD (to which the EPG is tied) to the L3 out, thus telling ACI over which external routed network the public subnets defined in the BD are to be advertised. In the case of a shared L3 out, there is no need for (and no possibility of) creating this relationship between the BD and the external routed network.

Inter-Tenant Connectivity

The fact that two tenants have been configured on a Cisco ACI fabric does not necessarily mean that those tenants are completely isolated from each other. Obviously, if no data-plane multi-tenancy has been implemented, the question is not relevant: In a multi-tenant environment, purely from a management perspective, inter-tenant connectivity is exactly the same as intra-tenant connectivity because you will have a single VRF where all bridge domains belong, possibly under the common tenant.

The following sections cover the case where multiple VRFs have been configured. You have two possibilities to connect two VRFs to each other: inside the Cisco ACI fabric itself, and over an external network device.

Inter-VRF External Connectivity

The first obvious choice when interconnecting two VRFs to each other is through an external IP device such as a router or a firewall, as Figure 9-23 depicts. This design is sometimes known as a "Fusion router" and is quite common in multi-VRF data centers.

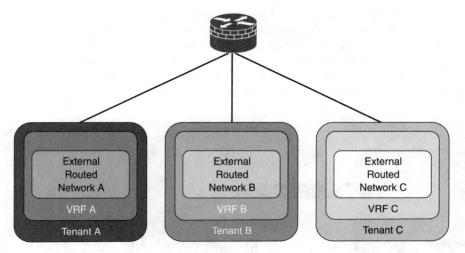

Figure 9-23 *External Router or Firewall Interconnecting VRFs*

The device connecting two or more VRFs to each other typically needs at least the following network functionality:

- **Traffic filtering:** Chances are that tenant traffic separation is motivated by security requirements, so you should only interconnect tenants through a device that provides a high level of security, such as a next-generation firewall.

- **Network address translation:** Because tenants have their own VRF, they can potentially have overlapping IP addresses. In this case, the device interconnecting the tenants should be able to translate addresses in order to work around this overlap.

Each tenant would have its own external L3 network connection and would probably have a default route pointing to the outside (either statically or dynamically over a routing protocol). The external device can connect to the fabric over an 802.1Q trunk and would use IP subinterfaces to peer with the individual VRFs in the Cisco ACI fabric.

EPGs in one tenant that need to speak to other tenants only need to have a valid contract for the external network connection in that tenant. From a tenant perspective, everything that does not belong to the VRF (such as IP addresses from other VRFs) will be classified in the external EPG. Therefore, no contract is required between two EPGs in different tenants that need to communicate to each other, and all filtering required should be done in the external device (or in the contracts between EPGs and external L3 networks).

Inter-VRF Internal Connectivity (Route Leaking)

In case there is a high amount of inter-tenant bandwidth, the requirements for the external router might be too expensive to satisfy in terms of bandwidth. This is one example of a situation in which it would be preferable to achieve the interconnection of two tenants directly inside the Cisco ACI fabric.

Getting Cisco ACI to interconnect two VRFs with each other is also possible without the need of an external routing device, but additional configuration needs to be done (because otherwise VRFs are completely isolated from each other). In essence, it is the same type of configuration that the earlier section "Shared External Network for Multiple Tenants" described, only that routes will not be leaked between an external routed network and an EPG, but between two EPGs, as Figure 9-24 illustrates.

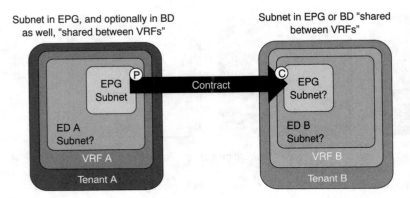

Figure 9-24 *Data Model for Internal Inter-VRF Connectivity*

Essentially, what Cisco ACI needs to do is what the networking industry has dubbed "route leaking." VRFs are considered to be hermetic routing containers, where no single IP information is exposed to other VRFs. However, you can selectively open up fissures to leak specific network prefixes between two VRFs.

In a traditional network, you would do that using the concept of export and import route targets. In Cisco ACI, the object model greatly simplifies this operation, which boils down to two steps: signaling the subnets involved for leaking, and configuring a contract between the EPGs that need to communicate.

In the first place, the subnets of both EPGs need to be marked as **Shared between VRFs** so that Cisco ACI knows that they can be "leaked" to other VRFs. Whether they are marked as **Advertised Externally** or as **Private to VRF** is not relevant for leaking the subnets across tenants (that setting only has an impact for advertising subnets over external routed networks).

As you can see in Figure 9-24, the main construct signaling that routes need to be exchanged between VRFs is a contract, with the usual provider and consumer side. For example, if you have multiple tenants with their own VRFs accessing an area of the network providing common services (such as Active Directory, Domain Name Services, and so on), you would typically configure the provider side in the common services area.

Remember that the contract needs to be created at the provider side (in this example, tenant A) because imported contracts can only be consumed, not provided.

You need to take care of two things: First, at the side providing the contract, the subnet needs to be configured under the EPG instead of the standard configuration under the bridge domain, as Figure 9-25 illustrates. The reason is because when configuring the contract between both EPGs, Cisco ACI will export the subnet configured under the EPG to the consumer VRF in order to have better control over which subnets are leaked to other VRFs and which subnets are not (in case there are multiple subnets configured under the BD). If you already had the subnet defined in the BD, you can just define the same IP address at the EPG level.

On the consumer side, you can have the subnet configured either under the EPG or under the bridge domain—it does not really matter. Therefore, in most situations, you will have it under the bridge domain, which is how it is normally done.

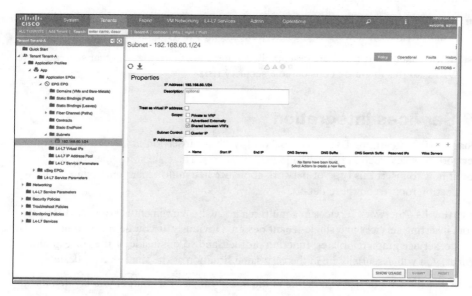

Figure 9-25 *Subnet Marked as* **Shared Between VRFs** *Defined Under the EPG (Provider Side)*

After that, the only thing left to do is to create a contract between both EPGs. However, here we have a small difficulty: If we create the contract, say, in tenant A, how do we make it visible to tenant B? The answer, as you probably have guessed, is through exporting the contract. This way, contracts can be consumed and provided between EPGs, without the need to use the common tenant.

As mentioned before, you need to create the contract in the tenant with the EPG providing that contract. Note that at the consuming side, you need to consume the contract by using the command **Add Consumed Contract Interfaces** in the Contracts section of the EPG. Do not forget to define the contract scope as Global.

And you obviously need to make sure there is no IP address overlap across both VRFs. For example, in the use case involving accessing common services from multiple tenants, you might want to configure your common services with public IP addresses so that they do not collide with the private IP address in use inside the tenants.

Route leaking is a powerful feature that has been used for decades (for example, in many MPLS networks), and it can enable certain use cases that would not be possible without it, such as the "shared services" VRF described later in this chapter. However, you should evaluate your design carefully if you decide to leverage route leaking because it might introduce some potential drawbacks:

- Route leaking is a relatively complex and manual process; make sure your design does not require modifying leaked routes too often.

- If you configure a complex route-leaking configuration, it might make the environment difficult to troubleshoot.

- You can potentially disrupt a network when leaking the wrong routes to a VRF. That is another reason to keep changes to leaked routes to a minimum.

- With leaked routes, you are essentially poking a hole into the wall that separates two VRFs, so this might be considered a security risk.

L4-7 Services Integration

Chapter 10, "Integrating L4-7 Services," deals with the insertion of Layer 4 to Layer 7 network services, such as firewalls and load balancers. There are some specific details about how to insert this type of network appliance in a multi-tenant environment, and this section focuses on these details.

Inserting L4-7 network services in a multi-tenant ACI environment is not very different from inserting services in a single-tenant design. Obviously, if you define all objects (L4-7 device, service graph templates, function profiles, and so on) inside of the corresponding tenant, you will essentially be in the very same situation as the single-tenant design.

Note that the L4-7 device you define in the tenant might be a context you created manually (for an L4-7 device that supports a multicontext configuration such as Cisco ASA), which means you are essentially doing a manual mapping between multi-tenancy at your L4-7 network service appliance and multi-tenancy at ACI.

Exporting L4-7 Devices

Alternatively, instead of configuring the L4-L7 services in the same tenant that is going to consume them, you could centrally define a pool of L4-L7 services that can be consumed by any tenant. For example, you might have some contexts pre-created in your L4-7 device, but you have not decided yet to which tenant you will allocate it. Maybe you just have a pool of firewalling or load-balancing contexts, and they are assigned to the first tenant that asks for them.

As already mentioned, you could wait until a tenant needs L4-7 network services, and only then define the L4-7 device. But you would need to keep separate documentation with the L4-7 devices that you have already provisioned. An alternative would be defining those L4-7 devices in a specific tenant (such as "common"), and only when exporting those L4-7 devices to the tenant that requires the L4-7 functionality.

Note that even if an L4-7 device is defined in "common," you will need to export to the tenant where you want to use it (where the service graph template is created). This is different from other objects such as contracts, where tenants have immediate access to all instances created in "common" without having to explicitly export them.

Multi-Context L4-7 Devices

Some L4-7 devices support multi-context configuration, meaning that they can be virtualized. For example, inside of a physical Cisco ASA firewall, you could have multiple virtual firewalls, also called *firewall contexts*. Each context acts as an independent device, with its own IP addresses, interfaces, routing table, and L4-7 configuration. Sometimes these contexts will have their own management IP address, but not necessarily.

The interfaces assigned to a context are typically virtual interfaces based on a VLAN so that creating new contexts does not mean having to lay additional cabling to the L4-7 devices.

Cisco ACI supports multi-context service integration, as described in Chapter 10. You can therefore have ACI create the new context for the specific tenant you are inserting the service for. For more information about working with multi-context L4-7 network service devices, refer to Chapter 10.

Use Cases for Multi-Tenancy Connectivity

This chapter has described multiple options for configuring multiple tenants in Cisco ACI, and you might be overwhelmed by all the different choices that ACI provides. This section covers multiple use cases and the recommended multi-tenancy option in each case. The list of use cases is not meant to be comprehensive: Chances are you will be confronted with a slightly different design challenge. However, this section's goal is explaining the motivation behind each multi-tenancy design option in Cisco ACI.

ACI as Legacy Network

In other words, you use Cisco ACI as a traditional network that does not support a multi-tenancy concept. You might want to configure your new Cisco ACI fabric in this way if your main goal is reducing complexity and you have no multi-tenancy requirements whatsoever.

Essentially, you would deploy all ACI objects in the common tenant, using the default VRF in that tenant. Otherwise, there is not much to describe here from a multi-tenancy perspective. This design is not particularly recommended, but it is interesting considering that it's the baseline from which most networks are evolving today, and it's the starting point when migrating a legacy network to Cisco ACI.

Granting Network Visibility to Other Departments

If you often need to inform other departments about how the network is performing for them, but you do not need any traffic separation, management-plane multi-tenancy is the way to go. In other words, you can configure multiple tenants as well as use security domains and role-based access control (RBAC) in order to grant read-only visibility to those tenants for specific users. You would not need to have multiple VRFs, so all EPGs would relate to a single VRF (probably in the "common" tenant). This is very close to the design discussed in the section "Logical Separation for Lines of Business," earlier in this chapter.

Figure 9-26 shows an example of such a configuration, where network constructs (bridge domains and VRFs) are defined in the common tenant, and EPGs are defined in separate tenants. Note that this example would allow for separating web servers from databases via contracts, even if they are sharing the same subnet.

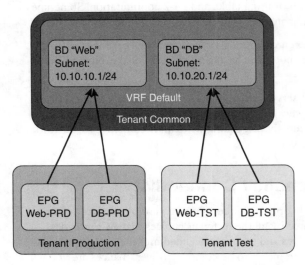

Figure 9-26 *Example with Management-Plane Multi-Tenancy and No Data-Plane Separation*

As mentioned in previous sections, additional network segregation could be implemented by adding separated physical domains for the production and test areas, and configuring different QoS policies for production and test, to make sure that one traffic category will not be able to starve the other one.

Network Shared Across Organizations with Shared Services

There can be multiple reasons why you may end up having multiple organizations sharing the same physical network, such as mergers and acquisitions as well as multiple lines of business with different IT requirements. In this case, you will have a few tenants (not many) that will need a data-plane separation.

You could use different tenants, each with its own VRF, in order to support overlapping IP addresses, and for the sake of simplicity share the external connections to the Internet across all of them. For this purpose, you would configure a shared routed external connection, as described in this chapter. Figure 9-27 shows this design with two organizations, A and B.

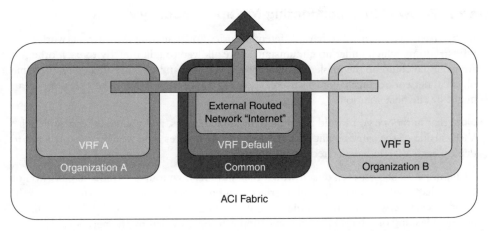

Figure 9-27 *Example Use Case with Two Organizations Sharing an External Routed Network*

Additionally, you could have a "shared services" area in your network (in the common tenant or in another one) from where you would provide, well, shared services to all the other tenants. This is where the configuration of EPG-to-EPG leaking comes into play: The provider EPG would be the one offering the "shared service" (DNS, Active Directory, NTP, and so on), and the consumer offering each of the tenant EPGs that require that service. Figure 9-28 shows this additional use case.

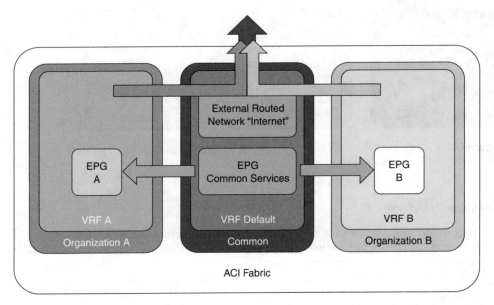

Figure 9-28 *Use Case with Two Organizations Sharing an External Routed Network and Accessing a Common Services Area*

External Firewall Interconnecting Multiple Security Zones

In this use case, you need to have different security zones sharing the same network infrastructure, which under no circumstances are allowed to talk directly to each other. An example could be the implementation of a DMZ area and Intranet area using the same physical network devices. For this use case, using dedicated VRFs for each security area might be the best solution.

Note that in theory you would not require multiple tenants, and you could configure all VRFs inside of the same tenant. For manageability purposes, you would probably want to deploy each VRF in a dedicated tenant, though.

As Figure 9-29 shows, each tenant would then have its own routed external connection or L3 out that would connect to a subinterface or a physical interface in an external firewall. Every packet between tenants would be routed (or dropped) externally by the firewall, so no route leaking or inter-VRF communication is to be provided by the network.

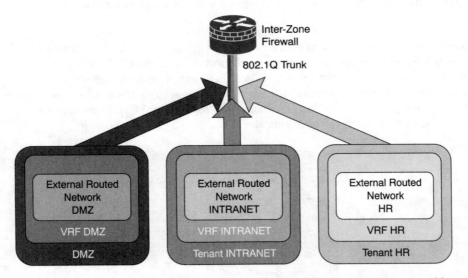

Figure 9-29   *External Firewall Interconnecting Security Zones Represented by Separated VRFs and Tenants*

Service Provider

Very similar to the previous use case from a functional perspective, this use case needs to provide a network for multiple tenants with support for overlapping IP address spaces. However, the number of tenants is probably much higher, and you will likely need to connect those tenants to an MPLS network. Intercommunication between tenants is very unlikely.

In this case, having multiple tenants (each with its own VRF) leveraging the OpFlex-based integration with external routers such as the Nexus 7000 or ASR 9000 (refer to Chapter 6 "External Routing with ACI" for more information) is a very attractive design option that allows for quick, automated onboarding and decommissioning of customers. Figure 9-30 describes this setup.

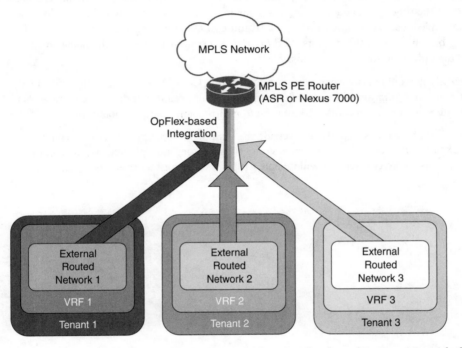

Figure 9-30 *Service Provider Design Including OpFlex-based Integration with the MPLS PE Router*

If the service provider is offering L4-7 services to your customers, integration with multicontext network service devices such as firewalls and load balancers would provide automation for this part of the service, too.

Summary

Administrator multi-tenancy is one of the functions that has been sorely missing in legacy networks. VLANs and VRFs can provide multi-tenancy in the data plane, but Cisco ACI is the first data center network that fully embraces multi-tenancy at all levels, including the management plane.

Cisco ACI has been conceived from the ground up to leverage multi-tenancy technologies, and the APIC supports exposing these technologies accordingly. Combining multi-tenancy with role-based access control, you can define very granularly what admins are allowed (and not allowed) to do: Multi-tenancy defines which Cisco ACI elements administrators can access, and role-based access control which actions they are allowed to perform on those elements.

In short, you can use two types of multi-tenancy in Cisco ACI. On one side, you can use management multi-tenancy, where you separate the network configuration into different tenants (or folders) and later assign administrators who can (or cannot) see those tenants. And on the other side, you can use data-plane multi-tenancy, where workloads belonging to multiple tenants can have overlapping IP addresses, and packets from one tenant will never be sent to the other tenants. And of course, a combination of both management and data-plane multi-tenancy is possible.

Ideally, you would know when you start configuring Cisco ACI whether you want to lay out your configuration in a multi-tenant structure. But even if you don't, there are ways to migrate from a single-tenant configuration to multi-tenant configuration in ACI.

Lastly, you have ways to partially override the data-plane separation between tenants— for example, in order to share external connections across multiple tenants, or to define exceptions where two tenants will be able to speak to each other over Cisco ACI.

Integrating L4-7 Services

Inserting services in application flows that traverse the data center has been a challenge for many years. A combination of physical and virtual hosts, coupled with unpredictable flows, leaves many enterprises with inefficient or complex use of L4-7 resources. Here are some of the challenges enterprises face:

- How to give hosts equal access to services

- How to optimize the traffic flows to the service devices

- How to dynamically add and remove services as applications change

- How to avoid configuration drift across service devices

- How to remove stale configurations from service devices

In this chapter, we examine how ACI can help enterprises solve these concerns through the use of horizontal integration and open APIs, and with the help of ecosystem partners. We cover the following topics:

- Services and ACI

- Ecosystem partners

- Managed versus unmanaged services

- Integrating various types of L4-7 services

Inserting Services

A favorite quote from Joe Onisick in Cisco's ACI business unit is, "For years, network engineers have been like the MacGyvers of networking, using whatever tools they have, like bubble gum and duct tape, to get their application flows to service devices." Although we engineers certainly do not use bubble gum and duct tape, we have all used tools like virtual routing and forwarding (VRF) stitching and/or virtual LAN (VLAN) stitching to try and deliver the application flows where we want them to go. These configurations are very complex, hard to manage, and prone to human error. Many times, enterprises have to invest in larger-than-needed L4-7 service devices, because in order to get some of their traffic inspected, they have to send the majority or all of their traffic to these devices. ACI has features and capabilities to allow enterprises a choice in exactly which traffic they would like to send to an L4-7 device, and it allows all devices equal access to resources.

How We Do It Today

The traditional security policy model for the data center is based on a static network topology (bound to network connections, VLANs, network interfaces, IP addressing, and so on) and manual service chaining. This model requires policy configuration across multiple security devices (firewalls, IPSs, and IDSs), slows application deployment, and is hard to scale because applications are dynamically created, moved, and decommissioned in the data center. Other proposals attempt to take a virtualization-centric approach but fail to address applications not running as virtual machines.

Traditional models require days or weeks to deploy new services for an application. The services are less flexible, operating errors are more likely, and troubleshooting is more difficult. When an application is retired, removing a service device configuration, such as firewall rules, is difficult. The scaling out/down of services based on the load is also not feasible. Because all devices do not have equal access to resources, many times inserting services leads to inefficient traffic patterns through the data center. All of these things, coupled with human error, many times has enterprise engineers asking themselves the following questions:

- Have the VLANs been correctly allocated?

- Did we configure all the VLANs, or is one missing?

- Is the trunk configured properly?

- Could there be a VLAN mismatch between the hypervisor and switch?

- Is there a firewall/load balancer/SSL misconfiguration?

The majority of enterprise firewall deployments for secure inspection can be broken up into three scenarios:

- **Edge services:** The firewall acts as a secure barrier or point of inspection between one network and another.

- **Security zones:** The firewall acts as a secure barrier or point of inspection between different security zones such as production and the DMZ.

- **Application insertion:** The firewall acts as a secure barrier or point of inspection between a single tier or multiple tiers of an application.

Although VLAN and VRF stitching are supported by traditional service insertion models, the Application Policy Infrastructure Controller (APIC) can automate service insertion while acting as a central point of policy control. The APIC policies manage both the network fabric and services appliances. The APIC can configure the network automatically so that traffic flows through the services. The APIC can also automatically configure the services according to the application's requirements, which allows organizations to automate service insertion and eliminate the challenge of managing the complex techniques of traditional service insertion.

Let's examine the ways in which services integrate with an ACI fabric. Following the policy model that we have discussed in previous chapters, the preferred way is to use ACI policies to manage both the network fabric and services appliances such as firewalls, load balancers, and so on. ACI then has the ability to configure the network automatically to redirect or allow traffic to flow through the service devices. In addition, ACI can also automatically configure the service devices according to the application service requirements. This policy, called a *service graph*, is an extension of a contract and can be configured once and implemented many times, as shown in Figure 10-1.

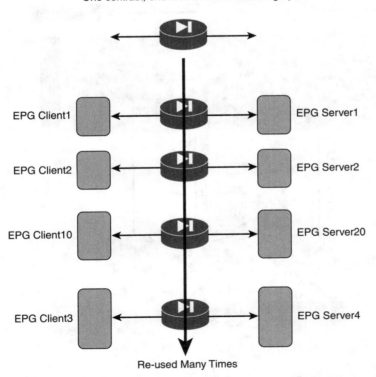

Figure 10-1 *One Graph Template, Many Contracts, and the Same L4-7 Device*

When a service graph is defined, the concept of *functions* is used to specify how traffic should flow between the consumer EPG and the provider EPG, as well as what types of devices are involved in this communication. These functions can be defined as firewall, load balancer, SSL offload, and so on, and APIC will translate these function definitions into selectable elements of a service graph through a technique called *rendering*. Rendering involves the allocation of the fabric resources, such as bridge domains, service device IP addresses, and so on, to ensure the consumer and provider EPGs will have all the necessary resources and configuration to be functional. Figure 10-2 shows an example of this.

Note   A *provider* (for example, a server) is a device (or set of devices) that provides services to other devices. A *consumer* (for example, a client) is a device (or set of devices) that consumes services from a provider. In relation to services, the provider is often thought of as the inside interface or the side facing the services, whereas the outside interface would be the consumer side or the side facing the clients.

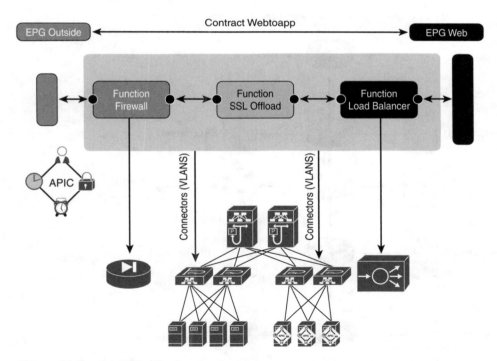

Figure 10-2   *Example of a Service Graph*

After the graph is configured in the APIC, the APIC automatically configures the services according to the service function requirements specified in the service graph. The APIC also automatically configures the network according to the needs of the service function specified in the service graph, which does not require any change in the service device.

A service graph is represented as two or more tiers of an application with the appropriate service function inserted between, as shown in Figure 10-3.

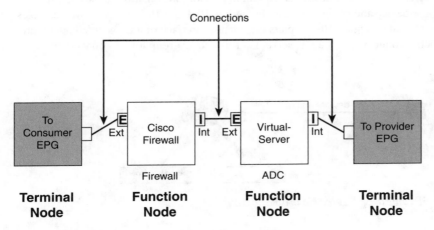

Figure 10-3   *Service Graph, Nodes, and Connectors*

A service appliance (device) performs a service function within the graph. One or more service appliances might be required to render the services required by a graph. One or more service functions can be performed by a single-service device, as shown previously in Figure 10-2 (the ADC device performs SSL offload and load balancing).

This allows the enterprise to create the intent-based policy that incorporates the business needs for a network or application; then ACI can determine which devices from its resource pools can meet the needs of the policy and implement them. This way, devices can be added to the pool when needed or if demand increases, as well as removed from the pool for maintenance or when demand decreases. The definition of your services is not directly tied to a specific device. If you are leveraging non-vendor-specific configurations, you have the potential to move from one vendor's hardware solution to another with ease. For example, if the policy specifies the need for a firewall that inspects or allows traffic on port 443, that firewall could be Checkpoint or Cisco. Either way, ACI knows how to interact with the devices it has available through its service graph and ecosystem partner integrations.

A service graph also provides the following additional operational benefits:

■ **Automatic configuration of VLANs:** Allocates VLANs to be used and configures them on both the L4-7 device and the network

■ **Health score reporting:** Provides information to ACI about the health of the device and of the function

■ **Dynamic endpoint attach:** Provides the ability to add endpoints discovered in the EPG to ACLs or load balancing rules (depends on the vendor)

■ **Traffic redirect:** Redirects specific ports to an L4-7 device

Similar to when we define an application profile, when we define a service graph, ACI collects health information relating to the service graph. This is implemented in different ways by different vendors, but the service graph provides information to ACI about the health of the device and of the function. In Figures 10-4 and 10-5, you see two examples of this functionality. Figure 10-4 depicts the outside interface of a firewall failing. Figure 10-5 depicts two members of a real server load-balancing group losing connectivity.

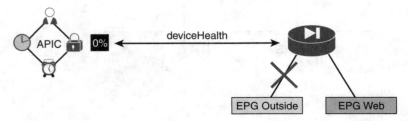

Figure 10-4   *Example of Device Health Reporting*

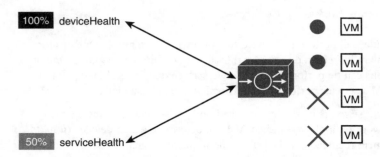

Figure 10-5   *Example of Service Health Reporting*

The ACI fabric tracks every device that is attached to it. A benefit of this function is that ecosystem partners can choose to leverage this information to automatically update the configuration of their service device and reduce operational overhead. Figure 10-6 shows an example pertaining to a load balancer, but this is available for security devices as well.

The Cisco ACI fabric can perform nonstateful load distribution across many destinations. This capability allows organizations to group physical and virtual service devices into service resource pools, which can be further grouped by function or location. These pools can offer high availability by using standard high-availability mechanisms, or they can be used as simple stateful service engines with the load redistributed to the other members if a failure occurs. Either option provides horizontal scale out that far exceeds the current limitations of the equal-cost multipath (ECMP), port channel features, and service appliance clustering, which requires a shared state. When enterprises couple this service resource pooling feature with ACI's service-redirect capabilities, high availability and scale out of resources are taken to a new level.

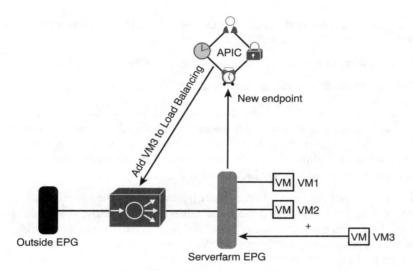

Figure 10-6 *Example of Endpoint Discovery and Automatic Configuration*

Service graph redirect is a recent feature (as of 2.0) that offers many advantages for customers:

- It eliminates the need to make the firewall or load balancer the default gateway.

- It avoids the need for more complex designs using virtual routing and forwarding (VRF) instances to implement L4-7 services.

- It avoids the need to split Layer 2 domains (bridge domains) to insert, for instance, a firewall in the path.

- It allows you to redirect only a subset of the traffic based on the protocol and port.

- It allows you to filter traffic between security zones in the same Layer 2 domain (bridge domain).

- It allows you to scale the performance of the L4-7 device by distributing traffic to multiple devices.

The following design considerations should be taken into account when deploying service redirect:

- Can be enabled for only one node in multinode service graphs.

- Support for both managed node and unmanaged node.

- Works only with GoTo devices. Transparent devices (such as IDS and IPS) are not supported.

- For non-EX leafs, service node cannot be under either the source or destination top of rack leaf switch.

- Service node has to be connected to the ACI fabric via L2; both connectors should be "L3 Adj."

- Endpoint data-plane learning should be disabled on BDs for service node interfaces.

- Both and active and standby service nodes should have the same vMAC.

One difference between the traditional service graph and the redirect option is that in the first case, the contract in the graph allows traffic to go through the L4-7 device, but you have to set up separate bridge domains to have routing or bridging in the fabric forward the traffic to the L4-7 device. With redirect, the contract rule forwards traffic to the firewall regardless of the routing and bridging lookup results.

As mentioned previously, not only is this option easier from a configuration standpoint, but it allows you to scale across multiple devices and redirect only the traffic you would like to send to the L4-7 device based on the protocol and port. Typical use cases include provisioning service appliances that can be pooled, tailored to application profiles, scaled easily, and have reduced exposure to service outages. Policy-based redirect simplifies the deployment of service appliances by enabling the provisioning consumer and provider endpoint groups to be all in the same virtual redirect and forwarding (VRF) instance. Policy-based redirect deployment consists of configuring a route-redirect policy and a cluster-redirect policy, as well as creating a service graph template that uses the route- and cluster-redirect policies. After the service graph template is deployed, use the service appliance by enabling endpoint groups to consume the service graph provider endpoint group. This can be further simplified and automated by using vzAny. While performance requirements may dictate provisioning dedicated service appliances, virtual service appliances can also be deployed easily using PBR. Figure 10-7 shows an example of this.

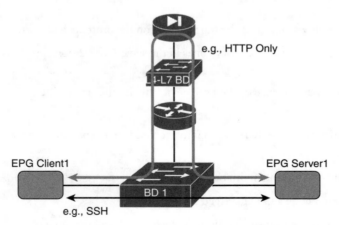

Figure 10-7 *Service Graph Redirect to the Firewall Based on Protocol and Port*

In this use case, you must create two subjects in the contract between EPGs. The first subject permits HTTP traffic, which then gets redirected to the firewall. After the traffic passes through the firewall, it goes to the server endpoint. The second subject permits SSH traffic, which captures traffic that is not redirected by the first subject. This traffic goes directly to the server endpoint.

The order of the subjects in the contracts does not matter because the more specific filter will take precedence. In the second example below, the traffic with port 443 is redirected as follows:

- Contract:
  - **Subject1:** Permit 443 with service graph (PBR)
  - **Subject2:** Permit all without service graph (no PBR)

Symmetric policy-based redirect is also supported in EX hardware. Symmetric policy-based redirect configurations enable scaling out L4-7 device services, as shown in Figure 10-8. This feature allows enterprises to provision a pool of service appliances so that the consumer and provider endpoint groups traffic is policy-based. The traffic is redirected to one of the service nodes in the pool, depending on the source and destination IP equal-cost multipath (ECMP) routing prefix hashing.

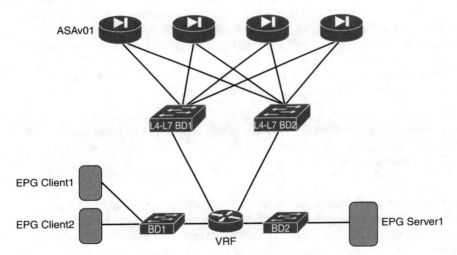

Figure 10-8 *Using Symmetric PBR to Scale Out ASA Virtual Firewalls*

Managed vs. Unmanaged

Once you have decided to integrate services through the use of a service graph, you have three main options available:

- **Network policy mode (or unmanaged mode):** In this mode, Cisco ACI configures only the network portion of the service graph on the Cisco ACI fabric, which means that Cisco ACI doesn't push configurations to the L4-7 devices. This mode does not require a device package (which we will explore shortly), but instead allows a network engineer to get application traffic to the devices more easily. This mode also takes care of all of the ACI fabric side of the configuration. All L4-7 device configurations will be completed by the device administrator.

■ **Service policy mode (or managed mode):** In this mode, Cisco ACI configures the fabric and the L4-7 device (VLANs and device configuration), and the APIC administrator enters the L4-7 device configurations through APIC.

■ **Service manager mode:** In this mode, the firewall or load-balancer administrator defines the L4-7 policy, Cisco ACI configures the fabric and the L4-7 device VLANs, and the APIC administrator associates the L4-7 policy with the networking policy.

ACI L4-7 service integration is available to help streamline service integration in the data center, not add complexity. That being said, if all your enterprise needs is a topology with a perimeter firewall that controls access to the data center, and if this firewall is not decommissioned and provisioned again periodically, you should use the network policy mode deployment.

With the service graph in service policy mode, the configuration of the L4-7 device is part of the configuration of the entire network infrastructure, so you need to consider the security and load-balancing rules at the time that you configure network connectivity for the L4-7 device. This approach is different from that of traditional service insertion where you can configure the security and load-balancing rules at different times before or after you configure network connectivity. In this mode, you will deploy all of these configurations simultaneously. If you need to make changes to the firewall or load balancer, you most likely will have to delete and redeploy the service graph.

Note   Although deleting and redeploying a service graph sounds like a lot of work, remember this system was designed around open APIs and this task can be completed in seconds with programmability.

With the service manager mode (see Figure 10-9), the interactions with the L4-7 device depend on the vendor management tool. Cisco ACI references a policy defined on the L4-7 management tool. This tool may let you make changes to the firewall or load-balancer configurations without the need to redeploy the service graph. Most enterprises are gravitating toward this option. It offers the best of both worlds. Service administrators configure the policies using the tools they are comfortable with, while ACI orchestrates the known-good policy while protecting against human error and configuration drift.

Another option, which is the least-preferred option, is to perform manual service insertion. In Cisco ACI, you also can configure service insertion without a service graph.

To do so, you need to create multiple bridge domains that operate just like VLANs, and you can configure EPGs to connect virtual or physical appliances.

Figure 10-10 shows a simple multinode service insertion design. The configuration consists of multiple bridge domains and EPGs. Bridge Domain 1 has an EPG to which the router and the firewall outside interface connect. Bridge Domain 2 has one EPG to connect the inside interface of the firewalls and the client-side interface of the Application Delivery Controller (ADC) device. Bridge Domain 3 has an EPG for the server-side interface of the ADC device and multiple EPGs for the servers, and the EPGs are connected through contracts.

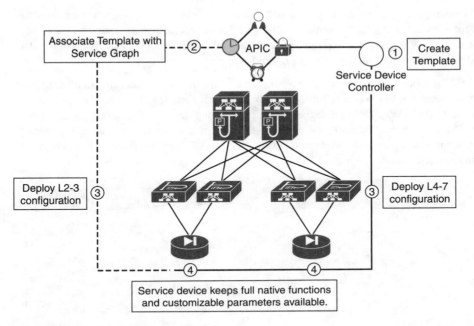

Figure 10-9   *Service Manager Mode*

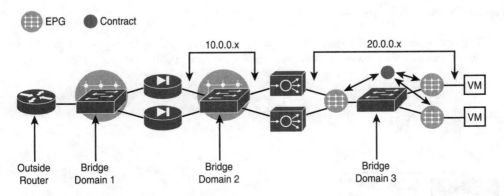

Figure 10-10   *Multinode Service Insertion Design*

ACI can integrate with any vendor's device in manual and or network policy mode. Manual mode, as shown in Figure 10-10, involves stitching things together the same way we have for years and should only be used as a last resort. Network policy mode automates the configuration of the network and allows traffic to flow through devices easily. Service policy mode and service manager mode are where things start to get really interesting. The automation, insertion, and cleanup of devices/policy with health monitoring requires an advanced level of API interaction and integration called a *device package*.

A device package leverages our open API and defines which L4-7 parameters can be configured from the APIC. The vendor of the security or service appliance defines the syntax of these L4-7 parameters, and this syntax reflects the syntax used by the firewall or ADC administrator when the device is configured directly.

The APIC communicates with the firewalls or load balancers to render the graph defined by the user. For Cisco ACI to be able to talk to firewalls and load balancers, it needs to speak to their APIs. The administrator needs to install plug-ins called device packages on the APIC to enable this communication. Installation of device packages can be performed by the infrastructure administrator role using the **L4–L7 Services** menu and the **Packages** sub-menu, as shown in Figure 10-11.

Figure 10-11   *Device Package*

The device package (see Figure 10-12) is a .zip file that includes a description of the device and lists the parameters it is exposing for the APIC configuration.

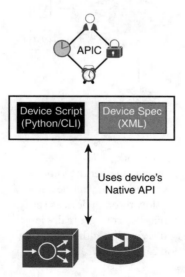

Figure 10-12   *Device Package and Southbound API*

Specifically, a device package includes the scripts that allow Cisco ACI to talk to this device, as shown in Table 10-1.

Table 10-1   *Device Package Contents*

Device specification	An XML file that defines the following: ■ Device properties: 　■ **Model:** Model of the device 　■ **Vendor:** Vendor of the device 　■ **Version:** Software version of the device ■ Functions provided by a device, such as load balancing, content switching, and SSL termination ■ Interfaces and network connectivity information for each function ■ Device configuration parameters ■ Configuration parameters for each function
Device script	A Python script that interacts with the device from the APIC. APIC events are mapped to function calls that are defined in the device script. A device package can contain multiple device scripts. A device script can interface with the device by using REST, SSH, or any similar mechanism.
Function profile	Function parameters with default values that are specified by the vendor. You can configure a function to use these default values.
Device-level configuration parameters	A configuration file that specifies parameters that are required by a device. This configuration can be shared by one or more graphs using a device.

Over time, device packages will need to be maintained and upgraded. It is important to know the following:

■ A device cluster can be managed by only one package at any time.

■ The node in the graph and associated device cluster should point to the same package.

■ A minor version upgrade is considered as the replacement for the existing package for the device.

■ A minor version upgrade is nondisruptive and there should be no impact for existing graphs or device clusters.

■ A new major version is considered a new device package.

■ The existing package is not impacted.

■ The existing graph instances continue to use the previous major version (parallel upgrades and testing are possible).

■ Switching from an old graph/cluster to a new major version package is disruptive and should be scheduled during a maintenance window.

An ecosystem partner's device package is maintained by that third-party vendor (for example, Citrix, F5, Checkpoint, or Palo Alto). Cisco maintains the device packages related to its devices. Likewise, the release of new features and functionality is up to the vendor that owns the package. Certain device packages may have dependencies or functionality tied to particular versions of ACI as well.

Role-based access control (RBAC) is also available to allow enterprises to control access to which users can import or view device packages, as well as who has access to create or export devices and/or policy. Table 10-2 outlines the predefined roles and permissions.

Table 10-2   *RBAC Attribute Privileges*

RBAC Attribute	Privilege
NW-SVC-DEVPKG	Allows an admin to import a package. Only the infra admin can import a package. Tenant admins can only see the packages imported under infra. This gives read-only access to the tenant admin.
NW-SVC-POLICY	Allows a tenant admin to create graph and other related configuration managed objects.
NW-SVC-DEVICE	Allows a tenant admin to create device cluster and other related configuration managed objects.
NW-SVC-DEVSHARE	Allows a tenant to export the device cluster to another tenant.

Note   The credentials are in both the logical device (that is, the cluster configuration) and the concrete device (that is, the physical device configuration), so if you are changing credentials, be sure to change them in both places.

Ecosystem Partners

Cisco ACI has a very mature ecosystem of over 65 partners and growing. ACI is designed as an open architecture using APIs to horizontally integrate with these partners for not only configuration and management use cases but potentially automated response to data center events as well. The ACI ecosystem is designed to help customers use, customize, and extend their existing IT investments with Cisco ACI offerings in the following areas:

- Orchestration, automation, and management

- Configuration and compliance

- Monitoring and diagnostics

- Storage and virtualization

- Traffic flow and analysis
- Security
- Network services

This book will not be able to address all of the possible use cases that may be found in enterprise environments. However, it will focus on some of the more prevalent use cases and configurations to help build a foundational knowledge to move forward with.

Table 10-3 and Table 10-4 provide a few of the ecosystem partner enterprises that commonly integrate with ACI. These ecosystem partners include but are not limited to the vendors listed in Table 10-3.

Table 10-3 *ACI Security Enforcement L4-7 Integration*

Ecosystem Partner	Network Policy	Service Policy	Service Manager
Cisco Security	✓	✓ Cisco ASA	✓ FMC (NGIPS and NGFW)
Palo Alto	✓	X	✓
Check Point	✓	X	✓ vSec
Fortinet	✓	✓	Roadmap FortiManager

Table 10-4 *ACI ADC L4-7 Integration*

Ecosystem Partner	Network Policy	Service Policy	Service Manager
F5	✓	X No longer supported	✓ iWorkflow
Citrix	✓	✓	✓ MAS
Radware	✓	✓	✓ vDirect
A10	✓	✓	✓ aGalaxy
Avi	✓	X	Roadmap Avi Controller

Note Additional ecosystem partner information can be found at https://www.cisco.com/c/en/us/solutions/data-center/data-center-partners/ecosystem-partner-collateral.html.

Before choosing an integration option, enterprises also need to consider how the roles and responsibilities as well as the operational management model for their services may change.

Management Model

The service graph introduces multiple operational models for deploying L4-7 services.

The service graph in network policy mode follows a traditional operational model in which the configuration of L4-7 devices consists of the following steps:

1. The network administrator configures the ports and VLANs to connect the firewall or the load balancer.

2. The firewall administrator configures the ports and VLANs.

3. The firewall administrator configures the ACLs and other components. As shown in Figure 10-13, with the Cisco ACI service graph in network policy mode, the network administrator configures the fabric but not necessarily the firewall.

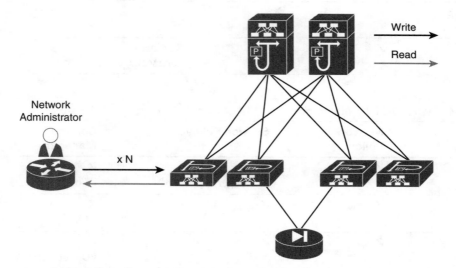

Figure 10-13 *Cisco ACI Service Graph with the Network Policy Mode Deployment Type: The Network Administrator Manages the Fabric but Not the Firewall or Load Balancer*

In addition, with the Cisco ACI service graph in network policy mode, the security administrator administers the firewall through a management tool designed for the L4-7 device (see Figure 10-14).

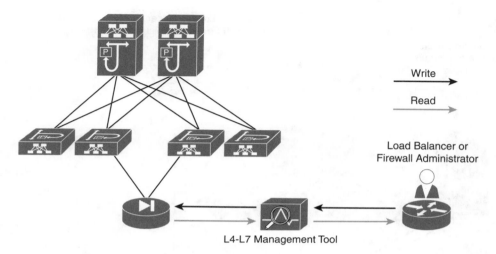

Figure 10-14 *With the Network Policy Mode, the Security Administrator Manages the Firewall Directly or Through a Management Tool*

With the Cisco ACI service graph in service policy mode, the management model changes, as illustrated in Figure 10-15. The network administrator needs to apply the configuration for the network as well as for the firewall through the APIC, and the L4-7 administrator needs to provide the L4-7 configuration to the network administrator. This configuration is then assembled as a function profile.

The APIC then programs both the fabric and the L4-7 device. The L4-7 administrator can read the configuration from the L4-7 management tool but cannot make changes to the configuration directly.

With the Cisco ACI service graph in service manager mode, the L4-7 administrator defines the L4-7 configurations through the L4-7 management tool instead of configuring function profiles with L4-7 parameters. The APIC administrator configures the service graph and references the L4-7 policy defined by the L4-7 administrator. Figure 10-16 illustrates this concept.

Based on the information in this section, you should now understand at a high level the ways in which you can use services with ACI. You should be familiar with these design scenarios:

- Manual service insertion

- Network policy mode (unmanaged, no device package)

- Service policy mode (managed mode, device package)

- Service manager mode (managed mode, device package + third-party OEM device management tool)

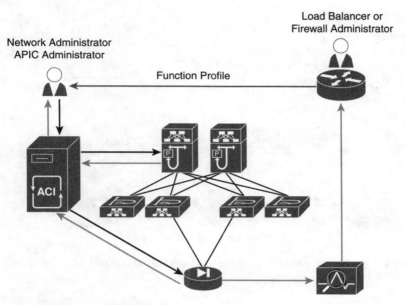

Figure 10-15   *Cisco ACI Operational Model with Service Policy Mode: Network and L4-7 Configuration Are Managed Through APIC*

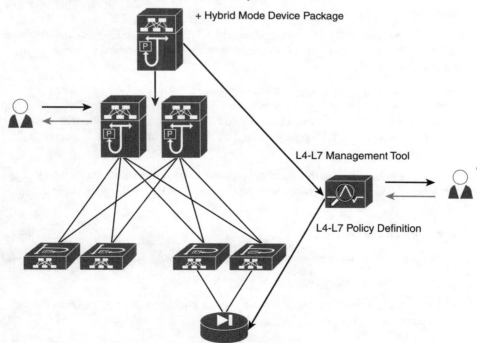

Figure 10-16   *Cisco ACI Operational Model with Service Manager Mode*

We have examined the impact of these modes. We have also examined the management model for each of these scenarios. Figure 10-17 provides a decision tree that summarizes some of the decision points we have discussed earlier in this section. Many enterprises use it as a starting point when they are considering service integration with ACI.

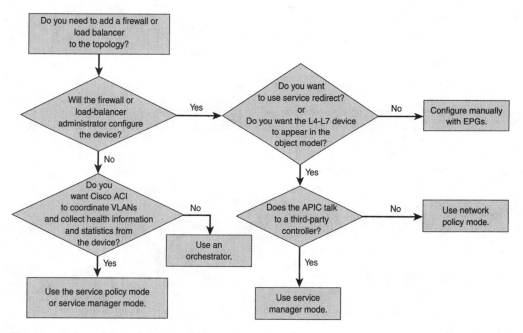

Figure 10-17 *ACI Service Mode Decision Tree*

In the following section, we continue to explore some of the components in managed service integration.

Functional Profiles

With any device, performing manual configuration over and over again can be tedious, so Cisco ACI provides the function profile feature, which allows you to define a collection of L4-7 parameters that you can use when you apply a service graph template. You can create one or many functional profiles. Function profiles can also be prepopulated and provided by the L4-7 device vendor.

When you use the service graph function of Cisco ACI in service policy mode, you enter all the configurations for the fabric and for the service device as part of the same L4-7 configuration process. As a result, you must enter L4-7 parameters that configure the firewall and/or the load balancer. These parameters can be items including but not limited to the following:

- Host Name
- Network Time Protocol Server
- Primary DNS
- Port Channel Configuration

This process can be time consuming, particularly if you want to decommission a device and redeploy it in a different way. As shown in Figure 10-18, the function profile solves this problem.

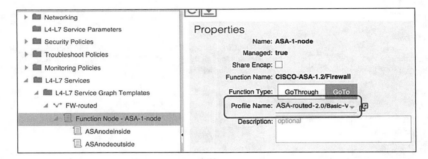

Figure 10-18   *Choosing a Functional Profile for Device Configuration*

With a function profile, you can create a collection of L4-7 configuration parameters that you can use when you apply a service graph template. Functional profiles can be used to define standard policy for L4-7 devices in your environment. You also have the flexibility of being able to keep L4-7 parameters inside certain objects, which allows you to configure a single service graph and then reuse the graph for different tenants or EPGs with a different configuration. L4-7 parameters can be stored under the provider EPG, bridge domain, application profile, or tenant. When a graph is instantiated, the APIC resolves the needed configuration for a service graph by looking up the parameters in various places. Service graph rendering looks for parameters in this order: function profile > AbsNode > EPG > application profile > tenant. By default, L4-7 parameters are placed under the provider EPG if you use the Apply Service Graph Template Wizard.

Note   The bridge domain configuration location is being phased out. Tenant and application profile are the preferred options.

If the tenant contains multiple service graph instances with different provider EPGs, the L4-7 parameters are stored in different places by default. You can place them in one easy-to-find place (under the application profile or tenant). For example, if you use the same ASA service graph on the same ASA appliance for multiple contracts, the L4-7 parameters are placed under the Web1 EPG and the Web2 EPG (see Figure 10-19), which are different APIC GUI locations.

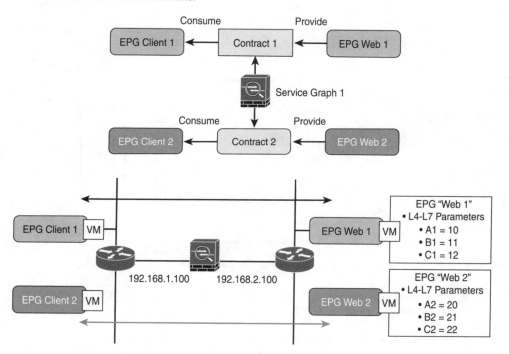

Figure 10-19   *Parameters Under the Provider EPG*

If you want, for management and troubleshooting simplicity, you can place the parameters under the application profile or tenant (see Figure 10-20).

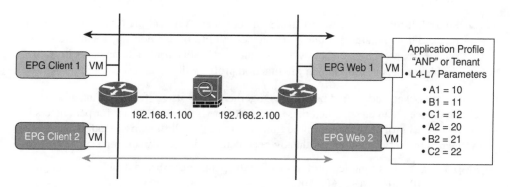

Figure 10-20   *Parameters Under the Provider Application Profile or Tenant*

To further manage parameters and enforce standard policy, each parameter you configure with a functional profile has the ability to be set as Mandatory, Locked, or Shared, as shown in Figure 10-21.

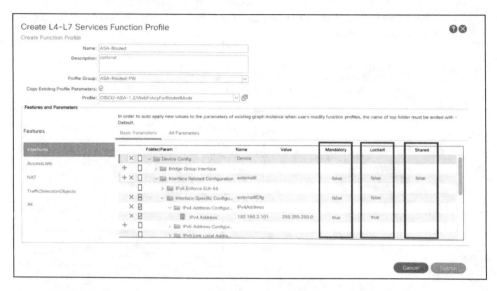

Figure 10-21 *Functional Profile Configuration Parameters*

The setting of these three parameters has the following effect on the final configuration parameters of the device:

- **Mandatory:** When a parameter is set to "true," the configuration item is mandatory. This option is used when the administrator wants to force the user to specify a value or parameter.

- **Locked:** When this is set to "true," the parameter specified in the functional profile will be used instead of the parameter defined at the EPG, BD, application profile, or tenant level.

- **Shared:** If this option is set to "true," the parameter value in the function profile will be used if no parameter value is set under the EPG, bridge domain, application profile, or tenant. If a parameter is defined under the EPG, bridge domain, application profile, or tenant, the value in the function profile will not be used.

Using the Locked and Shared parameters together is very useful for managing and maintaining device parameters. When these two fields are both set to "true" for parameters in the functional profile, a change in the functional profile will flow to the individual device, even when the service graph has already been deployed. Here's an example:

Step 1. Create a function profile that has the parameter "shared=true" (for example, IP address 192.168.1.100).

Step 2. Create a service graph using the function profile.

Step 3. Apply the service graph to a subject in the contract.

IP address 192.168.1.100 is configured on ASA.

Step 4. Change the function profile parameter 192.168.1.100 to 192.168.1.101.

IP address 192.168.1.101 is configured on ASA.

Note Without "shared=true", if a parameter in the function profile is updated, it's not pushed to the concrete device configuration. This feature can be a very powerful tool, but it should be used with care to avoid unintentionally updating production devices by changing a parameter in the functional profile.

Now that we have explored the pieces and parts that allow us to orchestrate services in ACI, let's take a moment to understand the five steps required to implement services in ACI (see Figure 10-22):

Step 1. Define the L4-L7 device or pool.

Step 2. Create a service graph template.

Step 3. Attach the service graph to a contract.

Step 4. Create the device selection policy used to select a service device.

Step 5. Configure the service node with predefined parameters.

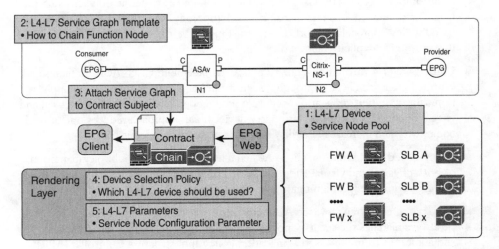

Figure 10-22 *Steps to Insert Services*

The functional profile of a device is also the base configuration of the device, meaning that if you plan to apply a template configuration later on that uses a specific feature, that feature must first be enabled in the functional profile.

Security for All Hosts

The Cisco ACI Security Solution uses a holistic, systems-based approach for addressing security needs for next-generation data center and cloud environments. Unlike alternative overlay-based virtualized network security solutions, which offer limited visibility and scale and require separate management of underlay and overlay network devices and security policies, the Cisco ACI Security Solution uniquely addresses the security needs of the next-generation data center by using an application-centric approach and a common policy-based operations model while helping ensure compliance and reducing the risk of security breaches.

The Cisco ACI Security Solution enables unified security policy lifecycle management with the capability to enforce policies anywhere in the data center across physical and virtual workloads, including containers. It offers complete automation of Layer 4 through 7 security policies and supports a defense-in-depth strategy with broad ecosystem support while enabling deep visibility, automated policy compliance, and accelerated threat detection and mitigation. Cisco ACI is the only approach that focuses on the application by delivering segmentation that is dynamic and application centered.

Here are the main features and benefits of Cisco ACI security covered in this section:

■ **Application-centric policy model:** Cisco ACI provides a higher-level abstraction using endpoint groups (EPGs) and contracts to more easily define policies using the language of applications rather than network topology. The Cisco ACI whitelist-based policy approach supports a zero-trust model by denying traffic between EPGs unless a policy explicitly allows traffic between the EPGs.

■ **Unified Layer 4 through 7 security policy management:** Cisco ACI automates and centrally manages Layer 4 through 7 security policies in the context of an application using a unified application–centric policy model that works across physical and virtual boundaries as well as third-party devices. This approach reduces operational complexity and increases IT agility without compromising security.

■ **Policy-based segmentation:** Cisco ACI enables detailed and flexible segmentation of both physical and virtual endpoints based on group policies, thereby reducing the scope of compliance and mitigating security risks.

■ **Automated compliance:** Cisco ACI helps ensure that the configuration in the fabric always matches the security policy. Cisco APIs can be used to pull the policy and audit logs from the Cisco Application Policy Infrastructure Controller (APIC) and create compliance reports (for example, a PCI compliance report). This feature enables real-time IT risk assessment and reduces the risk of noncompliance for organizations.

- **Integrated Layer 4 security for east-west traffic:** The Cisco ACI fabric includes a built-in distributed Layer 4 stateless firewall to secure east-west traffic between application components and across tenants in the data center (DC).

- **Open security framework:** Cisco ACI offers an open security framework (including APIs and OpFlex protocol) to support advanced service insertion for critical Layer 4 through 7 security services such as intrusion detection systems (IDS) and intrusion prevention systems (IPS), and next-generation firewall services, such as the Cisco Adaptive Security Virtual Appliance (ASAv), the Cisco ASA 5585-X Adaptive Security Appliance, and third-party security devices, in the application flow regardless of their location in the DC. This feature enables a defense-in-depth security strategy and investment protection.

- **Deep visibility and accelerated attack detection:** Cisco ACI gathers time-stamped network traffic data and supports atomic counters to offer real-time network intelligence and deep visibility across physical and virtual network boundaries. This feature enables accelerated attack detection early in the attack cycle.

- **Automated incident response:** Cisco ACI supports automated response to threats identified in the network by enabling integration with security platforms using northbound APIs.

We will continue to examine these benefits in the following sections.

Building an End-to-End Security Solution

In a perfect world, your enterprise's security policies would be enforced from the end user, across the WAN or campus, and into your cloud/DC (private or public), down to the individual server. Cisco has made that world into a reality. The architecture and solution have already been developed and integrated to allow these security dreams to become a reality. We have the capability to define and enforce security policy in the campus and wide area network with Identity Services Engine and APIC-EM (software-defined WAN). Cisco has recently launched further capabilities for intent-based enforcement in its DNA products or software-defined access solution. Cisco ACI has the capability to define and enforce security policy on both physical and virtual workloads (VMware, Microsoft, Red Hat, OpenStack, Kubernetes) in the DC, or in the cloud with its new ACI anywhere announcement. Furthermore, ISE, APIC-EM, and ACI integrations have already been developed so customers can leverage existing intellectual property and share policy between solutions so we can truly have one policy that flows across multiple enforcement platforms.

Through this integration, the security group tags (SGTs) in a TrustSec-enabled network can be converted to endpoint groups (EPGs) in the ACI data center network, and the EPGs from ACI can be converted to SGTs in the enterprise network. Thus, Cisco Identity Service Engine (ISE) enables the sharing of consistent security policy groups between TrustSec and ACI domains. This is shown in Figure 10-23.

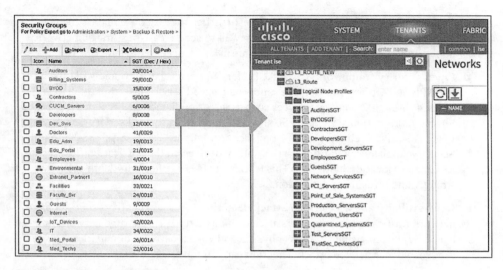

Figure 10-23   *TrustSec Groups Shared Between ISE and ACI*

To enable groups from the ACI domain to be used in the TrustSec domain, ISE will synchronize internal EPGs from the APIC-DC controller and create corresponding security groups in the TrustSec environment. ISE will also synchronize security groups and associated IP-to-security-group mappings with the APIC-DC external endpoints (L3 Out) and subnets configuration. This integration creates an environment where a user (shown as "Auditor" in the figure) logs in to the network, is authenticated based on username and device type, and assigned custom access that is enforced on a hop-by-hop basis from end to end across the architecture. Figure 10-24 shows the resulting architecture.

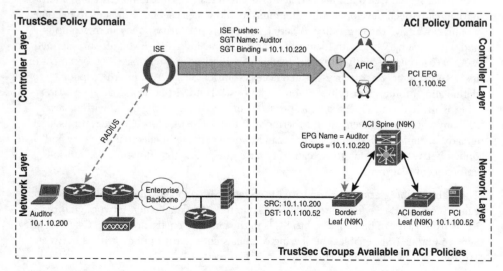

Figure 10-24   *End-to-end Policy Enforcement Campus (ISE) to DC (ACI)*

The final hurdle to getting to this end-to-end security environment is understanding the applications that exist in the data center and how they are used. This knowledge is crucial so that the correct security policies can be can be created, maintained, and enforced with confidence, knowing that there will be no negative effects to your production environment. Tetration Analytics can do all this and more (see Figure 10-25).

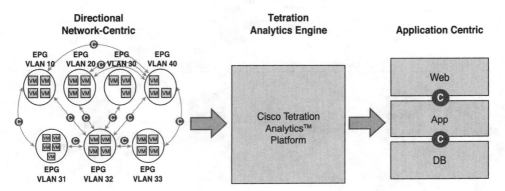

Figure 10-25 *Cisco Tetration Ingests Information from Your Servers and Network and Automatically Creates Whitelist Policy*

Tetration will automatically map your application dependencies through pervasive visibility and machine learning. Tetration consumes information and metadata simultaneously from your servers and network. It uses contextual information from your environment, such as your pre-existing ISE security groups, to build and define intent-based security policies, which you can then take and import into ACI. ISE and ACI will then enforce these policies in each of their domains. All of this is shown in Figure 10-26.

Tetration then becomes a centralized platform to manage, monitor, and update policy. The policies themselves become much easier to manage, because we have the ability to do so with groups or tags instead of port numbers and IP addresses. An enterprise only needs to tag their devices and then create policy based on those tags or groups. In the example in Figure 10-27, we imported the tags from ISE and created policy based on tags named "Contractors and Auditors" and "Production". With one simple rule, "Contractors are denied access to Production," we are able to create a very powerful policy. When this policy is exported from Tetration, the appliance figures out all of the IP addresses and port numbers that need to be included in the rule set so that a security platform such as ACI understands how to enforce the policy. Tetration then tracks the policies to make sure that they have been successfully implemented and are being complied with as intended. If, for some reason, traffic is escaping a policy, Tetration and ACI can help you pinpoint where the misconfiguration is.

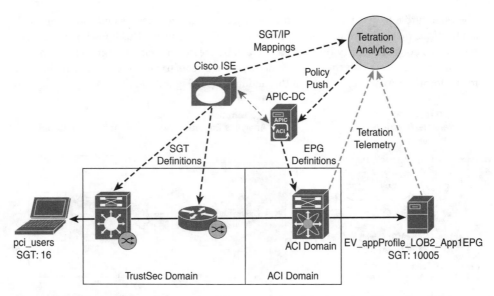

Figure 10-26   *Single Policy Created by Tetration and Shared with ACI and ISE*

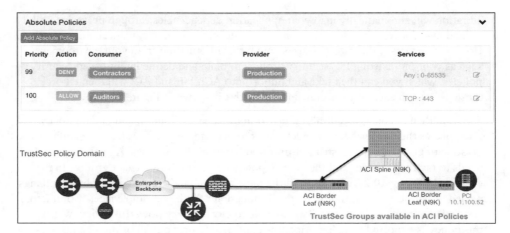

Figure 10-27   *Using Tags or Groups to Create Intent-based Policy, Which Can Be Imported into Security Platforms*

Note   If you would like more in-depth information on ISE+ACI, refer to "Cisco Configuration Guide: TrustSec – ACI Policy Plane Integration" at https://tinyurl.com/ISEplusACI.

Note   If you would like additional information on Tetration, visit www.cisco.com/go/ tetration.

No matter how you have designed your security policies, you have the ultimate choice regarding where, when, and at what level you want your policies enforced. You may choose to enforce L4 security policy in the switching hardware or the hypervisor. You may want application-specific inspections between one tier of an application but not another. You can bring in any service (virtual or physical) from any vendor at any time. In the following sections, we examine specific integration examples of the following device types:

- Firewall

- Load balancer

- IDS/IPS

Each of these device types can be configured in multiple deployment modes. Cisco ACI supports these deployment modes for L4-7 devices with the service graph:

- **Go-to mode (also known as routed mode):** In this mode, the default gateway for the servers is the L4-7 device.

- **Go-to mode with service graph redirect:** In this mode, the default gateway for the servers is the Cisco ACI bridge domain, and traffic is sent to the L4-7 device based on the contract configuration between EPGs. Service graph redirect is the preferred deployment mode for the service graph when Cisco Nexus 9300 EX and FX platform switches are used.

- **Go-through mode (also known as transparent mode or bridged mode):** In this mode, the default gateway for the servers is the client-side bridge domain, and the L4-7 device bridges the client-side bridge domain and the server-side bridge domain.

- **One-arm mode:** In this mode, the default gateway for the servers is the server-side bridge domain, and the L4-7 device is configured for source NAT (SNAT).

- **Routed mode (go-to mode):** The simplest way to deploy a service graph in routed mode is to use NAT on the L4-7 device. Cisco ACI also supports service devices deployed in routed mode with either static or dynamic routing by connecting the L4-7 device to an L3 Out.

Service devices that support routed mode designs integrate with ACI based on these configurations:

- **Routed mode with outside Layer 2 bridge domain:** In this design, the outside of the service graph connects to a Layer 2 bridge domain. The routing to the service device is implemented with an external routing device.

■ **Routed mode with L3 Out and NAT:** In this design, the service graph connects to the outside network through routing provided by the Cisco ACI fabric. This design can be implemented if the service device implements NAT, as in the case of a load balancer or in the case of a firewall that is translating the internal IP addresses.

■ **Routed mode in which the L3 Out interface performs Layer 3 peering with the L4-7 device:** In this design, the L4-7 device doesn't use NAT to translate the addresses of the servers. Therefore, you need to configure static or dynamic routing on the L3 Out interface with the L4-7 device.

■ **Routed mode with policy-based redirect (PBR) to the L4-7 device:** In this design, you don't need L3 Out or NAT on the L4-7 device. The Cisco ACI fabric redirects traffic to the L4-7 device based on contracts.

■ **Routed mode with outside Layer 2 bridge domain:** In this design, the L4-7 service may or may not be configured to translate the IP addresses of the servers, as may be the case with a firewall configuration. In addition, in this design you use an external router to provide the default gateway to the service device.

Regardless of which vendor or which type of integration you are going to use, some preparation work needs to be completed before you can integrate an L4-7 device. These preparation steps are as follows:

Step 1.   Create the necessary physical and virtual domains. These are the VLAN domains that will be used when integrating with the device. Make sure you use physical domains (for physical appliances) or the necessary virtual domain (VMM for virtual appliances), or both. Theses domains will be used in the configurations and should be mapped to the ports where the service devices are going to attach.

Step 2.   Create the necessary fabric access policies. These policies include the best-practice configurations for how the service appliances will physically connect to the ACI leaf.

Step 3.   Use the following basic configuration of device mode for the firewall device:

■ Configure contexts if supported.

■ Transparent/routed.

■ Management IP address and connectivity.

■ Management protocol (Enable: SSH, HTTP, HTTPS).

■ Configure credentials.

Step 4.   Import the device package.

Step 5.   Create the tenant where you will be deploying the service.

Step 6.   Create the VRF where you will be deploying the service.

Step 7.   Create the necessary bridge domains/VRFs.

Here are the most common bridge domain settings for L4-7 devices (see Figure 10-28):

- Do not use IP learning when using PBR.

- Do not use unicast routing in transparent mode.

Step 8.   Create EPGs and contracts.

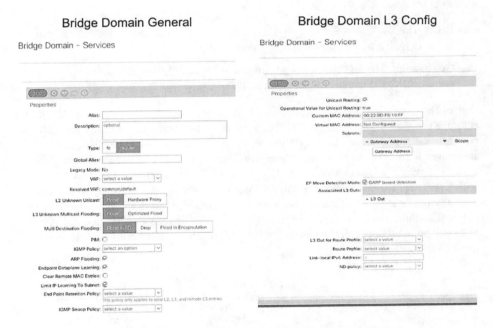

Figure 10-28   *Bridge Domain Configuration Recommendations*

Note   ACI does have multicontext vendor support. Every vendor's implementation is different. For the ASA, you will need to set up multiple contexts before configuration.

Note   If you are using Cisco ASA, then ASAv must be deployed on an ESXi that is participating in a VMware VDS VMM domain.

We will also explore integration examples from multiple vendors such as Cisco, Citrix, and F5.

Integrating Firewalls

The first device integration we will examine in depth is firewall integration. The most common insertion points for a firewall in the fabric are at the perimeter of the fabric, between security zones, or between application tiers where a more granular level of protocol inspection may be needed. Many customers use larger hardware-based firewalls for perimeter applications, and virtual firewalls for inside the fabric. In any case, you will need to decide in which mode the device will be implemented.

For the firewall function, service graph deployment can be configured with one of the following modes:

- **GoTo:** The L4-7 device is a Layer 3 device that routes traffic; the device can be used as the default gateway for servers or the next hop.

- **GoThrough:** The L4-7 device is a transparent Layer 2 device; the next hop or the outside bridge domain provides the default gateway.

One of the easiest and most straightforward configurations of a firewall in the ACI fabric is to use the firewall as the Layer 3 gateway for all of the devices, and to use the ACI fabric for L2 functionality. In this design, as shown in Figure 10-29, the client EPG is associated with BD1, which is configured in L2 mode only. The Web EPG is associated with BD2, which is also configured as L2 only. Both bridge domain 1 and 2 are associated with VRF1, but this association is only in place to satisfy the object model. It does not have any operational significance. The clients and the web servers will have the firewall external and internal interfaces, respectively, configured as their default gateway. A contract will be used between the Client EPG and Web EPG to allow communication and invoke services.

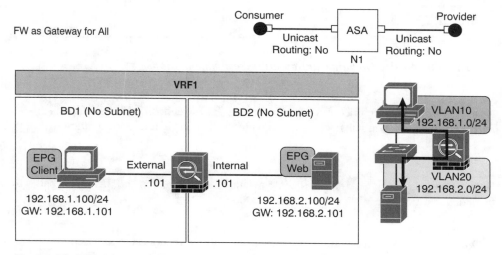

Figure 10-29   *L3 Firewall as the Gateway for All Devices*

In the upper-right part of Figure 10-29, you will notice that Unicast Routing is set to No on the adjacency settings between the firewall and the fabric. They are set to No because the fabric is operating at L2 only and the service device is not peering with the fabric. The graphic on the right of Figure 10-29 shows the logical traffic flow from client to web server.

The second common design option for an L3 firewall that we will examine is to leverage both the firewall and ACI fabric in an L3 capacity. This design requires the devices internal to the firewall to leverage the firewall as the gateway, but allows a much more scalable and operationally efficient design to be leveraged for the devices that are external to the firewall. As shown in Figure 10-30, the firewall can peer with the fabric internally or directly with a specific L3 Out and operate with or without network address translation (NAT). By creating this peering relationship and using routing (the preferred method) or static routes, the fabric is able to determine which devices and subnets exist behind the firewall and route traffic in a bidirectional manner.

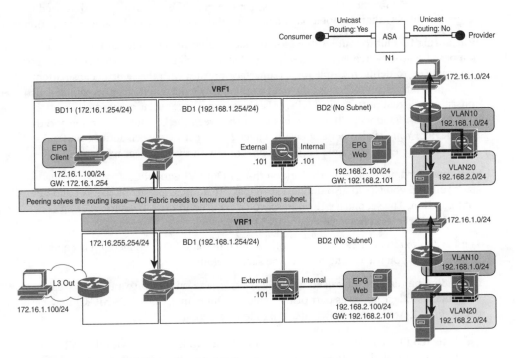

Figure 10-30 *GoTo Firewall with L3 Peering*

In Figure 10-30, multiple bridge domains have been created. In both the top and bottom example, two bridge domains have been created for the inside and outside interface of the firewall. Bridge domain 2 is operating in L2-only mode and is associated with the web clients and the inside interface of the firewall. The devices in the Web EPG are configured to use the firewall as their gateway. The external firewall interface is associated with BD1, which is configured in L3 mode. The ACI fabric will be configured in an L3 Out configuration in relation to the firewall's external interface. The configuration of this L3 Out between the fabric and the firewall will include a routing protocol or static routes so the ACI fabric becomes aware of the subnets that exist behind the firewall. The client devices can then reside outside or inside the fabric in a Client EPG. If the clients are external to the fabric, a contract will be used between the L3 Out and the Web EPG to invoke the firewall and allow traffic to flow between the groups. If the clients are internal to the fabric in a Client EPG, a contract will be used between the Client EPG and the Web EPG to invoke the firewall and allow traffic to flow between the groups. These designs use a single VRF. To reiterate, the association of VRF1 with BD2 only completes the object model and doesn't have operational significance. A contract will be applied between the L3 Out or Client EPG and the Web EPG to invoke the firewall and allow traffic to flow between the EPGs. In the upper-right part of the figure, you will also notice that the consumer adjacency is true or L3 due to the routing adjacency requirement with the fabric.

Part of the L3 Out configuration involves defining an external network (also known as an external EPG) for the purpose of access list filtering. The external network is used to define the subnets that are potentially accessible through the Layer 3 routed connection.

When using L3 Out to route to the L4-7 device, you normally define an L3 Out connection based on the switch virtual interfaces (SVIs) to which the L4-7 device connects. For this you need to define multiple logical interface profiles with the same encapsulation. The logical interface profiles are the path to the L4-7 device interface. The path can also consist of a virtual port channel (vPC). Using the same encapsulation, you are creating an external bridge domain that switches traffic between the L3 Out connection and the L4-7 device. You are also helping ensure Layer 2 adjacency between active-standby L4-7 devices connected to the same L3 Out connection with the same encapsulation.

Static and dynamic routing both work on the L3 Out SVI with vPC. If you are using static routing, you would also define a secondary IP address as part of the SVI and vPC configuration. The secondary IP address would be used in the L4-7 static routing configuration as the next hop (see Figure 10-31).

The Layer 3 external or external network defined in the L3 Out connection is equivalent to an EPG, so you use this to connect the service graph.

Depending on the hardware used for the leaf nodes and on the software release, using more than two leaf nodes as part of the same L3 Out connection in Cisco ACI may have restrictions. Restrictions apply under the following conditions:

- If the L3 Out connection consists of more than two leaf nodes with the SVI in the same encapsulation (VLAN)

- If the border leaf nodes are configured with static routing to the external device

- If the connectivity from the outside device to the fabric is vPC based

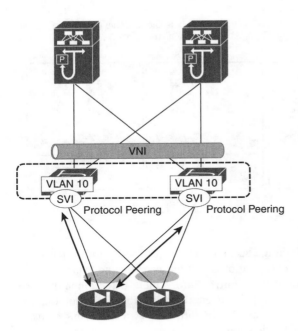

Figure 10-31 *Defining SVIs on an L3 Routed Connection for Service Device*

These restrictions arise because traffic may be routed to an L3 Out connection and then bridged on the external bridge domain to another L3 Out connection. The left side of Figure 10-32 shows a topology that works with both first- and second-generation leaf switches. The right side shows a topology that works with only Cisco Nexus 9300 EX and FX platform switches. In the topology, Cisco ACI is configured for static routing to an external active-standby firewall pair. The L3 Out connection uses the same encapsulation on all the border leaf nodes to allow static routing from any border leaf to the active firewall. The dotted line highlights the border leaf nodes.

Note   First-generation Cisco ACI leaf switches are the Cisco Nexus 9332PQ, 9372PX-E, 9372TX-E, 9372PX, 9372TX, 9396PX, 9396TX, 93120TX, and 93128TX switches.

With topologies consisting of more than two first-generation border leaf switches, the preferred approach is to use dynamic routing and a different VLAN encapsulation per vPC pair on the L3 Out SVI. This approach is preferred because the fabric can route the traffic to the L3 Out connection that has reachability to the external prefix without the need to perform bridging on an outside bridge domain.

Regardless of which hardware is used on the leaf configured for L3 Out, if you are using first-generation leaf switches in the fabric, you also need to consider whether servers are connected to the same leaf configured for L3 Out to an L4-7 device (see Figure 10-33).

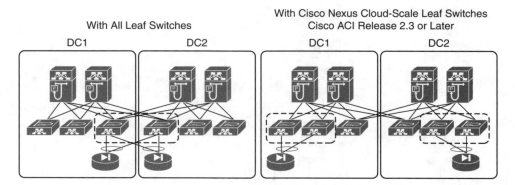

Figure 10-32 *First- and Second-Generation Leaf Switch L3 Connectivity to Service Devices*

The recommendations related to this design take into account the policy for content-addressable memory (CAM) filtering optimization called *ingress filtering*, which is controlled by the configurable option **Policy Control Enforcement Direction** in the VRF configuration. For more information, see the document titled "Cisco Application Centric Infrastructure Release 2.3 Design Guide White Paper" (https://www.cisco.com/c/en/us/solutions/collateral/data-center-virtualization/application-centric-infrastructure/white-paper-c11-737909.html#_Toc478773999).

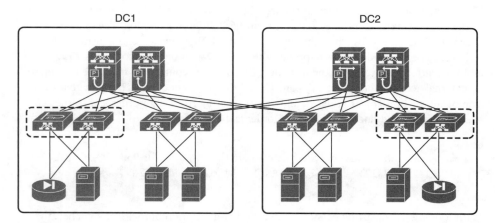

Figure 10-33 *Servers and Service Devices Connected to the Same Leaf Switches*

The following considerations apply to this design:

- Attaching endpoints to border leaf switches is fully supported when the leaf switches are all Cisco Nexus 9300 EX and FX platform switches. You should use Cisco ACI Release 2.2(2e) and you should configure **Fabric > Access Policies > Global Policies > Fabric Wide Setting Policy** by selecting **Disable Remote EP Learn**.

■ If the computing leaf switches (that is, the leaf switches to which the servers are connected) are first-generation leaf switches, you need to consider the following options:

■ If VRF ingress policy is enabled (the default and recommended setting), you need to verify that the software is Cisco ACI Release 2.2(2e) or later. You also should configure the option to disable endpoint learning on the border leaf switches. You can disable remote IP address endpoint learning on the border leaf switch from **Fabric > Access Policies > Global Policies > Fabric Wide Setting Policy** by selecting **Disable Remote EP Learn**.

■ You can also configure the VRF instance for egress policy by selecting the **Policy Control Enforcement Direction** option **Egress** under **Tenants > Networking > VRFs**.

Another deployment model you can use is policy-based redirect (PBR). Unlike previous design options, PBR doesn't require L3 Out for the service node, two VRF instances, or NAT. Using PBR, Cisco ACI fabric can route traffic to the service node based on the source EPG, the destination EPG, and contract filter matching. The bridge domain needs to be configured for routing. The server default gateway and service node (PBR node) gateway must be a Cisco ACI fabric bridge domain subnet (see Figure 10-34).

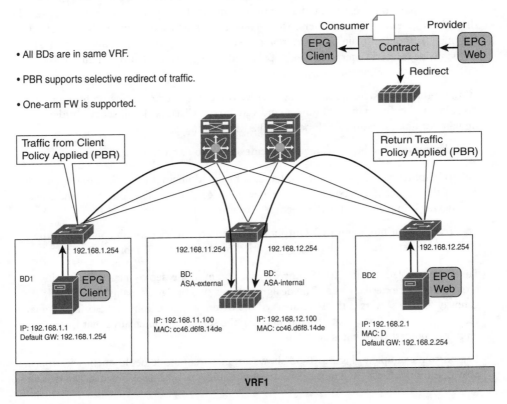

Figure 10-34 *L3 Firewall Design with Policy-based Redirect*

The PBR node has two interfaces: one configured for the consumer side and one configured for the provider side. Both PBR node connectors must be in a bridge domain and must not be in the consumer or provider bridge domain. You therefore need a service bridge domain, and the connectors must be configured for unicast routing. This service bridge domain requirement will be removed in Cisco ACI Release 3.1.

PBR requires a service graph, and the PBR node must be in go-to mode. PBR can be used in a one-arm mode deployment as well.

Note   For one-arm deployments, make sure your firewall allows traffic to be routed in and out the same security zone interface. Here's a non-exhaustive list of firewalls that have this capability at the time of this writing:

- ASA

- Palo Alto

- Checkpoint

Transparent firewall design requires two bridge domains. In transparent mode, the L4-7 device is deployed in pass-through (go-through) mode. The service device doesn't provide the default gateway for the servers. The servers' default gateway is either the subnet on the outside bridge domain or an external router. The routing from the outside (clients) to the inside (servers) interfaces can be provided by the fabric itself (through a VRF instance) or by an external router.

With go-through mode, Cisco ACI doesn't let you configure IP routing on both bridge domains, and even if you configure a hardware proxy, Cisco ACI will set the bridge domain for unknown unicast flooding and ARP flooding.

This chapter divides the transparent mode designs into two categories:

- **Transparent mode with outside Layer 2 bridge domain:** In this design, the outside of the service graph connects to a Layer 2 bridge domain. The routing to the service device is implemented with an external routing device.

- **Transparent mode with L3 Out:** In this design, the service graph connects to the outside network through routing provided by the Cisco ACI fabric.

The top example in Figure 10-35 shows a transparent mode deployment with routing provided by an external router. The design requires two bridge domains. The default gateway for the servers is the IP address of the external router. Tuning the bridge domains for flooding reduction is not possible because the service graph ensures that Layer 2 unknown unicast flooding is enabled.

The bottom example in Figure 10-35 shows a transparent mode deployment with routing provided by the Cisco ACI fabric. This design requires two bridge domains. The default gateway for the servers is the IP address of the subnet of the outside bridge domain. Because IP routing is enabled on BD1, the IP addresses of the endpoints in BD2 are learned as if they were in BD1, and they are associated with the MAC address of the L4-7 device.

Because BD1 has routing enabled, you need to make sure that BD1 learns only the addresses of the subnet that you defined. Thus, you should configure **Limit IP Learning to Subnet** (which was previously called **Subnet Check**). You also need to make sure that a maximum of 1024 IP addresses are learned on this interface (based on the verified scalability limits for Cisco ACI Release 2.3) and that the IP addresses are aged independently by configuring **IP Aging**.

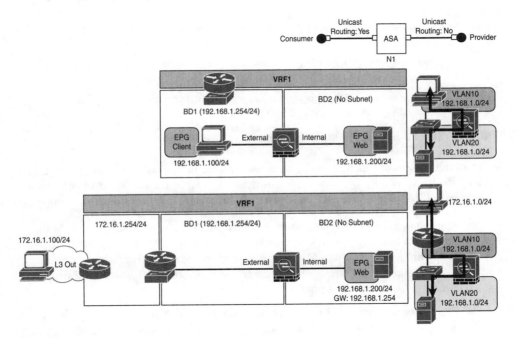

Figure 10-35 *ACI Layer 2 Firewall Design*

Figure 10-36 shows an example of manual insertion of a Layer 3 firewall design. In this design, the service graph has been omitted. Two separate VRFs and BDs with two separate L3 Out connections will be used for this configuration. The L3 Out connections will be used to form neighbor relationships with the firewall and the ACI fabric. The firewall acts as a router between VRFs. ACI will simply send traffic to the FW based on the static or dynamic routing. Traffic will be allowed between the Client EPG and ASA-Ext L3 Out and/or the ASA-Int L3 Out and the Web EPG based on contracts. Traffic will be allowed through the firewall based on its own device-specific configuration.

Non-integrated Route Peering

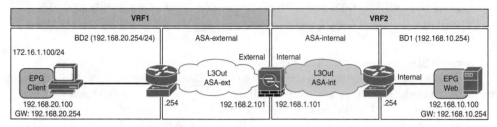

L3 Out EPGs
- One for ASA external interface in VRF1 and one for ASA internal interface in VRF2.

Routing
- FW acts a router between VRF1 and VRF2; both static and dynamic routing are supported.

Contract
- Contracts are applied between Client EPG (Con) and L3Out-ASA-Ext EPG (Prov) in VRF1, and between L3Out-ASA-Int EPG (Con) and Web EPG (Prov) in VRF2.

Figure 10-36 *L3 Firewall Manual Stitching*

In all the designs in which IP routing is enabled on the bridge domain connected to the L4-7 device as with BD1, Cisco ACI learns the IP address of the endpoints of BD2 associated with the L4-7 device MAC address on BD1. Two important considerations apply:

- **Maximum number of IP addresses per MAC address that are supported:** At the time of this writing, Cisco ACI supports a maximum of 1024 IP addresses associated with the same MAC address, so you need to make sure that, with or without NAT, the maximum number of IP addresses learned on BD1 from the L4-7 device interface stays within this limit.

- **Capability for Cisco ACI to age the individual IP addresses:** If Cisco ACI learns multiple IP addresses for the same MAC address, as in the case of BD1, they are considered to refer to the same endpoint. To help ensure that Cisco ACI ages out each NAT IP address individually, you need to enable an option called **IP Aging** under **Fabric > Access Policies > Global Policies > IP Aging Policy.**

In summary, when using designs that require interconnection of multiple bridge domains with IP routing enabled, you should follow these guidelines:

- Enable **Limit IP Learning to Subnet** to avoid learning the endpoint IP addresses of other bridge domains.

- When using an L4-7 go-through design, do not enable routing on both the bridge domains to which the transparent L4-7 device connects.

■ When deploying an L4-7 device in go-to mode, you can enable routing on both bridge domains if you perform NAT on the L4-7 device. With this type of deployment, you should also configure **IP Aging Policy** to age the NAT IP addresses individually.

Service Node Failover

Having a redundancy of service devices improves availability. Each service device vendor has different failover link options and mechanisms. Typical options are as follows:

■ **Dedicated physical interface for failover traffic, such as F5 devices:** The service device has a dedicated physical interface for failover traffic only.

■ **Created failover VLAN and interface, such as Cisco ASA devices:** The service device does not have a dedicated physical interface. Create a failover VLAN or choose interfaces for failover traffic, which typically are created on different physical interfaces, with one for data traffic.

■ **Shared (not dedicated) VLAN and logical interface, such as Citrix devices:** Failover traffic is exchanged over the same VLAN as data traffic.

Typically, use of a dedicated physical interface and a directly cabled pair of failover devices is recommended. If failover interfaces are connected to each service device directly, Cisco Application Centric Infrastructure (ACI) fabric does not need to manage the failover network. If you prefer to have in-band failover traffic within the ACI fabric, create an endpoint group for failover traffic. Figure 10-37 shows this setup.

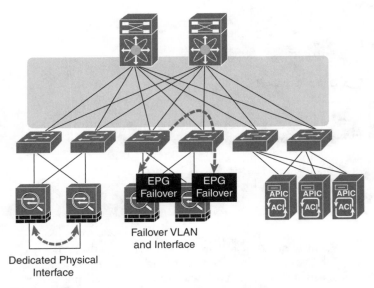

Figure 10-37 *Service Device Failover Network*

If you use a physical appliance and you prefer in-band failover traffic, create an endpoint group for failover using static bindings. This case is similar to the bare-metal endpoint case.

If you use a virtual appliance and you prefer to use out-of-band failover traffic, create a port group manually and use it. If you prefer in-band failover traffic, create an endpoint group for failover using a VMM domain, which is similar to the virtual machine endpoint case.

Deploying Clustering for Physical Appliances (Cisco ASA Cluster)

Cisco ASA clustering allows you to group multiple ASA nodes together as a single logical device to provide high availability and scalability. ASA clustering also can be integrated with Cisco ACI. ASA clustering has two modes: spanned EtherChannel mode (recommended) and individual interface mode. This chapter focuses on the spanned EtherChannel mode because it is the recommended choice.

One member of the cluster is elected as the master switch. The master switch handles the configuration, which is replicated on the slave switches. In spanned EtherChannel mode, all ASA devices in the cluster use the same port channel, and traffic is load-balanced as part of the port channel operation. From the perspective of the Cisco ACI fabric, the cluster is a single logical device connected to the Cisco ACI fabric through one port channel (see Figure 10-38).

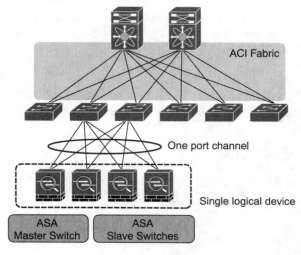

Figure 10-38   *Cisco ASA Clustering*

Note   As of this writing, for spanned EtherChannel mode, ASA devices in the same ASA cluster must be connected to the Cisco ACI fabric through the same vPC or port channel. The reason for this requirement is that Cisco ACI fabric will learn the same endpoint from different port channel interfaces, which may cause endpoint flapping if you use different port channels. Thus, ASA clustering across pods is not supported. The Cisco ACI fabric capabilities will be enhanced to handle this situation in Q2CY18.

For L4-7 device configuration, note that Cisco ASA clustering is supported on physical ASA devices only, not virtual ASA devices. As in the physical appliance example in the previous section, you need to create a virtual context and add it as an L4-7 device on the APIC. However, you need to use the single-node mode, because from the perspective of Cisco ACI, the cluster is one big logical device. The APIC needs to communicate with the master switch to push the configuration to the ASA devices in the cluster.

In an L4-7 device configuration, the device management address is the master management IP address in the virtual context. The cluster management IP address is the master management IP address in the administration context.

Note that ASA clustering must be configured beforehand. Clustering configuration is not supported during L4-7 device creation on the APIC using a device package. To set up ASA clustering, you need separate port channels for the cluster control plane in addition to the spanned EtherChannel for cluster data plane (see Figure 10-39).

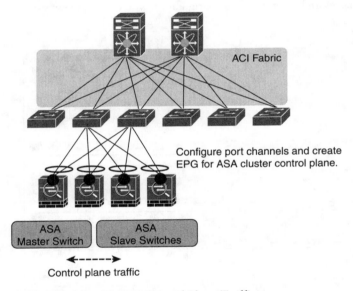

Figure 10-39 *Cluster Control Plane Traffic*

Virtual versus Physical

You have a few differences to take into account when deploying redundant devices in either a physical or virtual format. These differences are noted in the following subsections.

Deploying Redundant Physical Appliances

For a physical ASA device, you typically use multicontext mode. In this case, the failover configuration is in the admin context, which you don't need to configure multiple times for each virtual context, so you can set up failover configuration manually, without using APIC. To set up failover configuration using APIC, you need to register the admin context as an L4-7 device, but it won't be used as the firewall for actual service graph deployment.

Note   You don't have to configure a cluster interface for the failover link and stateful failover link in the L4-7 device. If failover traffic is not within the Cisco ACI fabric (if it is *out of band*), Cisco ACI fabric doesn't have to manage failover traffic. Even though failover traffic is within the Cisco ACI fabric (*in band*), the L4-7 device configuration on the APIC doesn't manage EPG creation for failover traffic. You need to create an EPG for failover traffic.

In this scenario, for each service graph deployment, you need to create a virtual context and add it as an L4-7 device on the APIC. You would then use the APIC to configure failover on the ASA via the **Device Configuration** tab and parameters. While you are configuring the device, you also must configure a secondary management IP address. Otherwise, the APIC can't access the secondary ASA. This is shown in Figure 10-40. It is recommended that you configure this link as a port channel, although this configuration is optional. When you successfully complete the configuration, you can see failover configuration on both ASA devices.

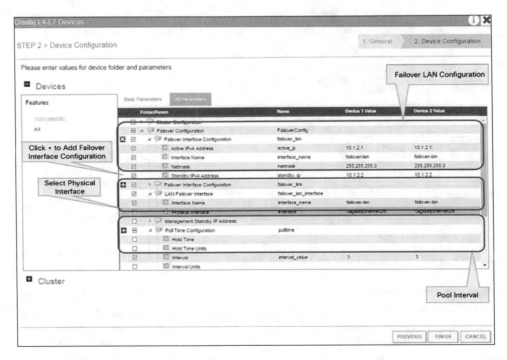

Figure 10-40   *Failover Link Configuration*

Deploying Redundant Virtual Appliances

Regardless of whether you are using in-band or out-of-band failover traffic, you need to create a port group for failover traffic and attach the vNIC to the port group. The device interface and cluster interface for failover traffic should be configured in the L4-7 device.

If your enterprise is using VMM integration, an EPG for the VMM domain for failover traffic (see Figure 10-41) will need to be created, which will create port groups for the EPG. Then you need to configure vNICs for the virtual appliance. An EPG with static bindings can be used if you don't want to use the VMM domain. In this case, you manually create a port group for failover traffic and configure static bindings for the EPG.

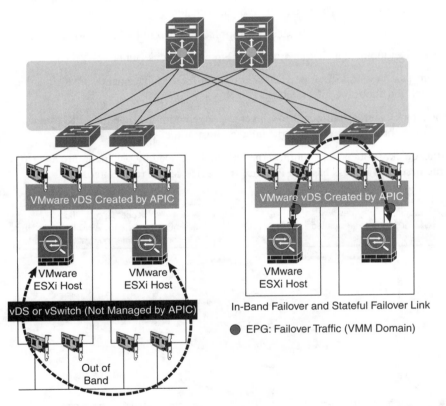

Figure 10-41 *Virtual Appliance Connectivity*

Integrating Security Monitoring

Security threats are escalating every year in terms of sophistication and complexity. ACI has the capability to work hand in hand with your security products to provide a holistic approach to a defense-in-depth strategy. While each device is very powerful on its own, to quote Aristotle, "the whole is greater than the sum of its parts." Using open APIs for integration, enterprises now have the capability to achieve a more proactive approach to security.

ACI integration with Firepower NGIPS (including Advanced Malware Protection) provides security before, during, and after an attack, enabling organizations to dynamically detect and block advanced threats with continuous visibility and control across the full attack continuum. These new security capabilities deliver unprecedented control, visibility, and centralized security automation in the data center.

Figure 10-42 shows an example of this integration, summarized in the steps that follow:

1. Infected endpoint launches an attack that Firepower blocks inline.

2. An intrusion event is generated and sent to Firepower Management Center revealing information about the infected host.

3. The attack event is configured to trigger the remediation module for APIC that uses the northbound API to contain the infected host in the ACI fabric.

4. APIC quickly contains/quarantines the infected workload by placing it into an attribute-based (IP address based) EPG until the device can be remediated.

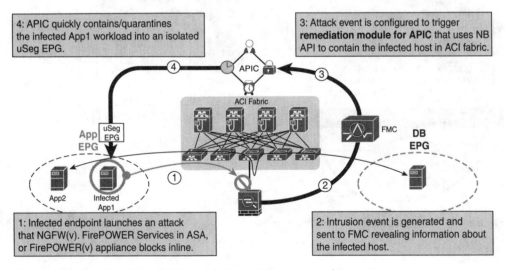

Figure 10-42 *FMC-to-APIC Rapid Threat Detection and Containment*

This out-of-the-box functionality is very powerful. However, it is just the tip of the iceberg regarding what is possible through the use of the API and programmability.

Integrating Intrusion Prevention Systems

As we explored in the previous section, an intrusion prevention system (IPS) is an important part of a defense-in-depth or end-to-end security solution. The following design choices are available when integrating an IPS/IDS (intrusion detection system) with ACI today:

- **Service graph with managed mode:** Cisco has just released a device package for some models and configurations of Firepower Threat Defense. However, for other configurations, as of now there is no device package capable of Layer 1 configuration. Hardware-based Firepower appliances support Layer 1 bypass network modules.

- **Service graph with unmanaged mode:** The IPS/IDS appliance needs to have legs into two different leafs. This is due to the fact that per-port VLAN is not supported with a service graph.

- **Non-integrated mode:** In this mode, a regular EPG is used for the service node legs. The service node legs can be connected to separate leafs or to the same leafs with per-port VLAN functionality enabled. Static binding will be used at the EPG level using the same VLAN encapsulation ID for the service node legs.

The overall design for IPS in L2 and L3 modes is similar to firewall designs referenced earlier in this chapter.

In a Layer 1 configuration mode, the service device doesn't change the VLAN ID. Traffic from both legs of the service node use the same VLAN encapsulation. In order to put devices inline accordingly, the use of two different bridge domains is needed, as shown in Figure 10-43.

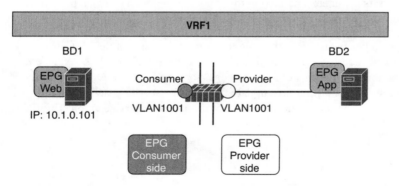

Figure 10-43 *Layer 1 IPS Device Integration*

IPS designs also have special considerations for settings in fabric access policies, specifically in regard to Layer 1 mode. The loop protection features that are available to help you in most cases can work against you in this design. ACI fabric detects loops by default; this configuration will put L1 service device ports in out-of-service status. To avoid this, loop detection on those ports must be disabled. The settings to disable these mechanisms are found here:

- Fabric\Access Policies\Interface Policies\Policies

- MCP, CDP, and LLDP

Also, if the service node legs are connected to the same leaf, then per-port VLAN configuration must be enabled. This configuration can be enabled by creating the following:

- An L2 interface per-port VLAN scope policy that's applied on the interfaces

- Different physical domains with a different VLAN pool (a VLAN encapsulation block contains the same set of VLANs) that's assigned to the IPS provider and consumer EPGs

Cisco has recently released a managed-mode service manager integration for Firepower Threat Defense (FTD). The FTD Fabric Insertion (FI) device package is based on a hybrid model (service manager, in ACI terminology) where the responsibility of the full-device configuration is shared between security and network administrators:

- **Security administrator:** Uses the FMC to predefine a security policy for the new service graph, leaving security zone criteria unset. The new policy rule(s) defines the appropriate access (allowed protocols) and an advanced set of protections such as NGIPS and malware policy, URL filtering, Threat Grid, and more.

- **Network administrator:** Uses the APIC to orchestrate a service graph, insert an FTD device into the ACI fabric, and attach directed traffic to this predefined security policy. Inside the APIC's L4-7 device parameters or function profile, the network administrator sets parameters defined in this guide, including matching a predefined FMC access control policy and rule(s).

When the APIC matches the name of the access control policy rule in the FMC, it simply inserts newly created security zones into the rule(s). If a rule is not found, the APIC creates a new rule by that name, attaches security zones to it, and sets the **Action** to **Deny**. This forces the security administrator to update the new rule(s) criteria and the appropriate set of protections before traffic can be allowed for a given service graph. This is shown in Figure 10-44.

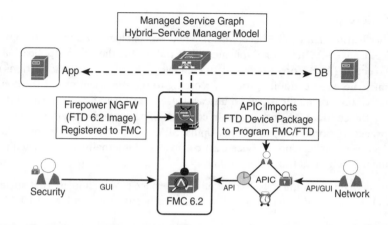

Figure 10-44 *FTD Device Package for ACI*

Table 10-5 outlines the current supported versions of Cisco Firepower Threat Defense.

Table 10-5 *Supported Versions of the Cisco FTD Software*

FTD Device Package Version	Platform	FTD/FMC Version	ACI/APIC Version
1.0.2	Firepower-93xx	6.2.2	2.3(1f) 3.0(1k)
1.0.2	Firepower-41xx	6.2.2	2.3(1f) 3.0(1k)
1.0.2	Firepower-21xx	6.2.2	2.3(1f) 3.0(1k)
1.0.2	vFTD	6.2.2	2.3(1f) 3.0(1k)

Note   Cisco Firepower Threat Defense can have multiple applications, including NGFW and IPS.

Copy Service

Another feature that can be used with IDS and protocol analyzers is ACI Copy Service. Unlike SPAN, which duplicates all of the traffic, the Cisco Application Centric Infrastructure (ACI) Copy Service feature enables selectively copying portions of the traffic between endpoint groups, according to the specifications of the contract. Broadcast, unknown unicast, and multicast (BUM) traffic and control plan traffic not covered by the contract are not copied. In contrast, SPAN copies everything out of endpoint groups, access ports, or uplink ports. Unlike SPAN, Copy Service does not add headers to the copied traffic. Copy Service traffic is managed internally in the switch to minimize the impact on normal traffic forwarding.

Copy Service is configured as part of an L4-7 service graph template that specifies a copy cluster as the destination for the copied traffic, as shown in Figure 10-45.

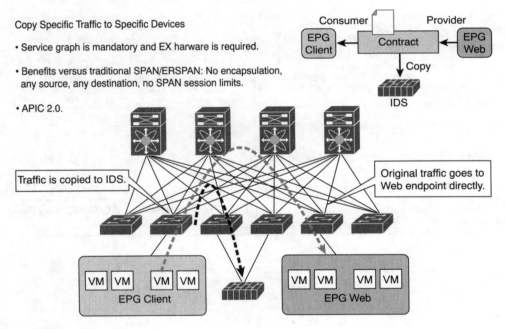

Figure 10-45   *Copy Service*

Copy Service can tap into different hops within a service graph. For example, Copy Service could select traffic between a consumer endpoint group and a firewall provider endpoint group, or between a server load balancer and a firewall. Copy clusters can be shared across tenants.

Copy Service requires you to do the following tasks:

■ Identify the source and destination endpoint groups.

■ Configure the contract that specifies what to copy according to the subject and what is allowed in the contract filter.

- Configure L4-7 copy devices that identify the target devices and specify the ports where they attach.

- Use Copy Service as part of an L4-7 service graph template.

- Configure a device selection policy that specifies which device will receive the traffic from the service graph. When you configure the device selection policy, you specify the contract, service graph, copy cluster, and cluster logical interface that is in the copy device.

The following limitations apply when using the Copy Service feature:

- Copy Service is only supported on the N9K-9300-EX leaf switches.

- For data path traffic that is copied to the local and remote analyzer port, the class of service (CoS) and differentiated services code point (DSCP) values are not preserved in the copied traffic. This is because the contract with the copy action can be hit on either the ingress or egress TOR before or after the actual CoS or DSCP value gets modified.

  When you're policing the data path traffic at a given endpoint ingress direction, the traffic that is copied is the actual incoming traffic before the traffic is policed. This is due to an ASIC limitation in the N9K-93108TC-EX and N9K-93180YC-EX switches.

- Copy Service supports only one device per copy cluster.

- A copy cluster supports only one logical interface.

- You can configure copy analyzers in the consumer endpoint or provider endpoint only in N9K-93108TC-EX and N9K-93180YC-EX switches. Faults are raised if you configure copy analyzers in N9K-93128TX, N9K-9396PX, or N9K-9396TX switches.

Integrating Server Load Balancing and ADC

Leveraging a load balancer in one-arm mode with source network address translation (SNAT) is straightforward. Nothing special needs to be done. A BD/subnet is created for the service device. The load balancer is a go-to device and owns the virtual IP of the servers, so all the inbound traffic is directed to the load-balancing device. When the original source is replaced with the load balancer (SNAT), it ensures the return traffic will come back to the ADC device, as shown in Figure 10-46.

A second option would be to deploy the ADC in one-arm mode using policy redirect. This is useful for design scenarios where the server needs to see the real client IP. In this configuration, the ADC is deployed in its own BD/subnet in go-to mode and owns the VIP. Thus, the incoming traffic is routed directly to the service device. The return traffic is where the policy redirect happens in order to get the traffic back to the ADC device, where it needs to go, as illustrated in Figure 10-47.

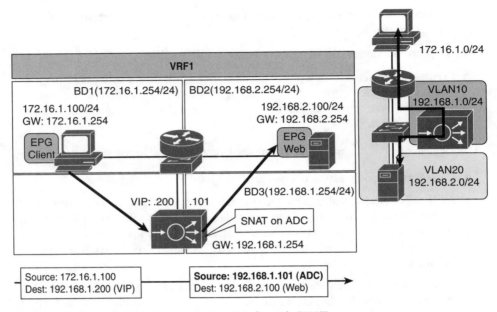

Figure 10-46   *ADC Design: One-Arm Mode with SNAT*

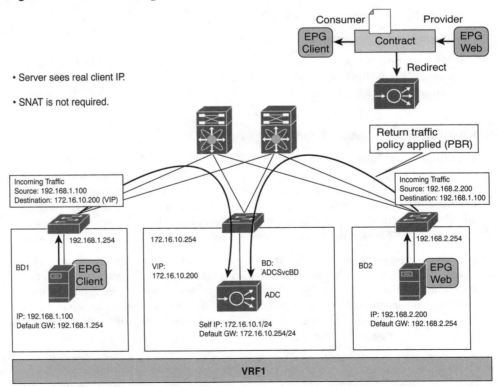

Figure 10-47   *One-Arm ADC with PBR*

Two-arm ADC deployments are similar to the first firewall design we covered, as illustrated in Figure 10-48. The clients and servers use the ADC as the default gateway. Therefore, the two BDs you will need to create for this design can be L2 BDs. This can present a problem when it comes to dynamic endpoint attachment or automatically adding or removing devices from load-balancing groups. If you plan to use this feature with the ADC device, ACI will need to be able to track IP addresses as they are added and removed from the server BD. Layer 3 capabilities will need to be turned on for the BD. **Subnet Configuration** and **Unicast Routing** are required to be enabled on the server BD.

Note If you will be doing any routing with the L3 ADC device in managed mode, L3 Out peering support is required in the device package for a routing exchange with the fabric.

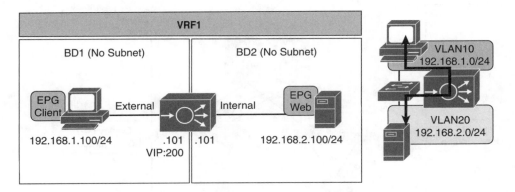

Figure 10-48 *ADC Two-arm Mode*

Manual configuration of the ADC device can be accomplished as well. In these configurations, you will have to configure the network connectivity that ACI does for you in unmanaged or managed mode. Let's take a look at the two configurations we discussed previously:

■ **One-arm Mode with SNAT:**

   ■ A BD with the external VIP subnet(s) will be created and a regular EPG will be associated with the new bridge domain.

   ■ The ADC interface's self IP can be in a different subnet than the VIP subnets.

   ■ An L3 Out can be used when routing configuration is preferred over BD subnet configuration.

   ■ Contracts in the BD configuration will be made between Client/Server and ADC EPGs. Contracts in routing configuration will be configured between the Client and Server EPGs and L3 Outs.

- **Two-arm Mode:**

    - Same rules apply as in one-arm mode for the ADC external interface.

    - If servers are pointing to the fabric as their gateway and SNAT is not allowed, an L3 Out EPG in a separate VRF is required for the ADC internal interface. Otherwise, use a regular EPG in the same VRF as the ADC external interface.

Two of the top ADC vendors in the industry are F5 and Citrix. It's no surprise that these vendors are also ecosystem partners with great integrations with ACI. Both of the integrations from these vendors leverage service manager mode, as shown in Figure 10-49.

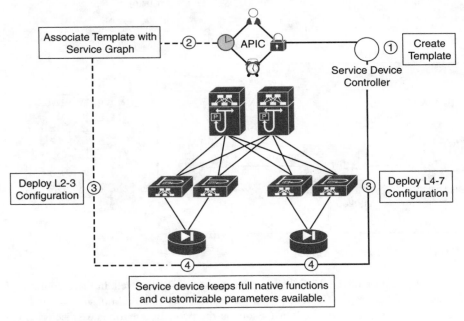

Figure 10-49 *Service Manager Mode*

The Citrix NetScaler hybrid mode solution is supported by a hybrid mode device package (shown in Figure 10-50) and NetScaler Management and Analytics System using a StyleBook. A StyleBook is a configuration template that you can use to create and manage NetScaler configurations for any application. You can create a StyleBook for configuring a specific NetScaler feature, such as load balancing, SSL offload, or content switching. You can design a StyleBook to create configurations for an enterprise application deployment such as Microsoft Exchange or Lync.

You need to upload the hybrid mode device package in the APIC. This package provides all network L2-3 configurable entities from NetScaler. Application parity is mapped by the StyleBook from the NetScaler MAS to the APIC. In other words, the StyleBook acts as a reference between L2-3 and L4-7 configurations for a given application. You must provide a StyleBook name while configuring the network entities from the APIC for NetScaler.

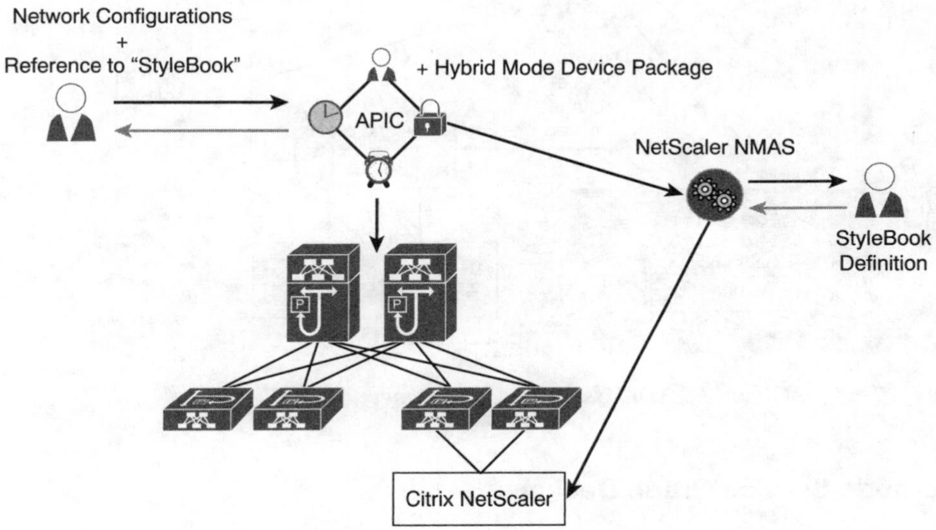

Figure 10-50   *Citrix ADC with NMAS*

Integration between ACI and F5 is similar to the Citrix integration using Device Manager or hybrid mode. The main point of integration for F5 with Cisco ACI is the dynamic F5 Device Package for Cisco APIC. Generated by F5 iWorkflow and based on F5's smart templating technology called iApps, the F5 Device Package is software that provides a single workflow for policy configuration and provisioning. This approach allows multiple variations of the Device Package to be generated based on the L4-7 policy requirements of the application being deployed. The steps are outlined in Figure 10-51.

If a dynamic attachment endpoint is required, unicast routing should be enabled and the subnet should be configured under BD2.

1. Import the iApps template into BIG-IP.
2. iApps is visible to iWorkflow after BIG-IP device discovery.
3. In the iWorkflow catalog, the admin creates the application template based on iApps.
4. iWorkflow creates a custom device package based on the catalog.
5. The admin imports the iWorkflow device package to APIC.
6. When the graph is deployed, APIC sends the iApps configuration to iWorkflow, and iWorkflow deploys application services on BIG-IP.

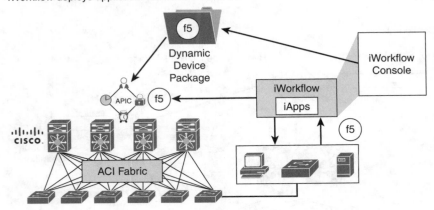

Figure 10-51   *ACI and F5 ADC Using Service Manager*

Two-node Service Graph Designs

A service graph has the capability to include more than one function or node. In this section, we will examine common examples of two-node firewall and ADC designs. You will notice that the configuration options stay the same and how the fabric and devices handle traffic does not change. We are just combining the devices into a single service graph.

The first example we will explore is fairly straightforward (see Figure 10-52). If we combine the firewall in NAT mode with a two-armed ADC using SNAT or the ADC as the gateway, the ACI fabric has everything it needs to deliver the traffic where it needs to go. As we discussed previously, network address translation by the firewall alleviates the need for ACI to know about the subnets behind it. The SNAT-or-ADC-as-gateway configuration allows the traffic to return to the ADC device from the server. This design works very well, assuming the service graph, device adjacencies, BDs, and subnets are configured as we have discussed previously.

If your enterprise would like to avoid NAT on the firewall, route peering can be configured on the external side of the ASA to announce the internal subnets to the fabric, as shown in Figure 10-53. The remainder of the configuration stays the same for the network and ADC device.

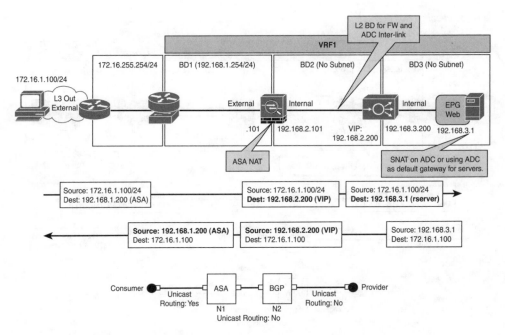

Figure 10-52   *Firewall NAT + Two-arm ADC*

When you combine the popular one-arm ADC mode with a firewall in the same service graph, additional considerations need to be taken into account. These are two designs that work as great as a single graph but don't act as you might think when they are put together. Previously, we used a single VRF or context for all our devices. In this configuration, we need to use two. If we maintained a single VRF, as traffic was returning from the ADC to the firewall, the ACI fabric would bypass the firewall and route the traffic directly to the endpoint. This is because the fabric knows where the endpoint exists and has a direct route to get there. If we split the VRFs, that information (routing domain) is separated. However, if we only do that and leave it, then VRF2 has no route to get to the devices in VRF1, and that configuration would fail as well. This configuration requires an L3 Out with route peering between the ADC and the firewall, so the route to the client network is known in VRF2 as existing through the firewall's internal interface (see Figure 10-54).

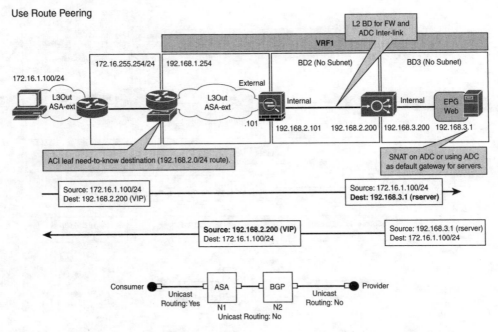

Figure 10-53   *Firewall + Two-arm ADC*

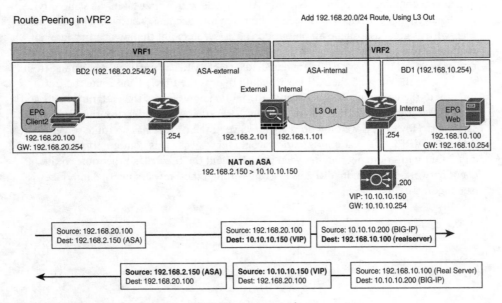

Figure 10-54   *Firewall NAT + ADC One-arm Mode*

If your enterprise prefers not to use NAT on the firewall, an L3 Out with the external interface of the firewall and VRF1 is an option. This configuration is preferred and provides a high level of flexibility for a service graph, including a firewall and a load balancer in one-arm mode. Figure 10-55 shows an example of this design.

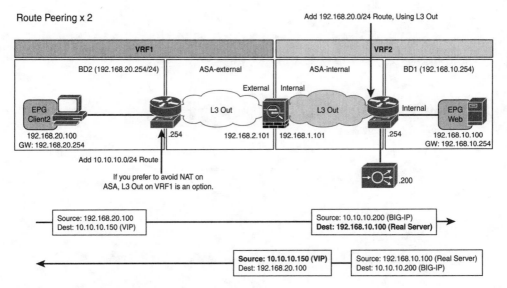

Figure 10-55 *Firewall + ADC One-arm Mode*

Summary

Cisco ACI enables you to automate the provisioning of L4-7 network connectivity and L4-7 configurations in the data center. It also enables you to insert L4-7 devices in the traffic path while keeping the Cisco ACI fabric as the default gateway for the servers.

Cisco ACI can also be used to configure the L4-7 device for the entirety of the configuration or for only the networking portion.

Three operational models are available:

- Network policy mode, for cases where the L4-7 device is managed by a different administrator and Cisco ACI should configure only network connectivity

- Service policy mode, for full automation through the APIC

- Service manager mode, for cases where the APIC administrator defines the networking configuration of the L4-7 device through the APIC while the L4-7 administrator defines the L4-7 policy through a different management tool

These functions can be implemented using the GUI or programmatically in Python and can be automated using the REST API.

Chapter 11

Multi-Site Designs

Terms such as active-active and active-passive are often discussed when data center designs are considered. Enterprises are generally looking for data center solutions that provide or have the capability to provide geographical redundancy for their applications. These statements mean different things to different enterprises. However, more and more IT organizations must provide a data center environment that is continuously available. Customers expect applications to always be available, even if the entire data center experiences a failure. Enterprises also need to be able to place workloads in any data center where computing capacity exists—and they often need to distribute members of the same cluster across multiple data center locations to provide continuous availability in the event of a data center failure. In this chapter, we examine the design scenarios and capabilities that ACI offers to address these needs. In particular, we discuss the following items:

- Multiple fabrics
- Supported designs
- Multiple fabrics
- L2 connectivity
- Multi-Pod
- Multi-Site

Bringing Up a Second Site

Many enterprises start with a single data center and grow into a second, or beyond, over time. Some enterprises start with multiple sites from the beginning. If your IT organization is fortunate enough to have visibility into this intended outcome, a phased migration can be planned with as much reuse of resources as possible. ACI is a very flexible architecture. With the technologies and protocols that are used in ACI, we are able to support several design scenarios, such as the following:

- Stretched fabric (dark fiber, dense wavelength division multiplexing, pseudowire)

- Multiple fabrics with pervasive gateway

- Multi-Pod

- Multi-Site

A huge benefit of ACI is that the tenant and application policy are decoupled from the underlying architecture. Changes can be made to the physical configuration of the underlying fabric with minimal policy reconfiguration. Enterprises have moved from a single fabric to a Multi-Pod fabric, by the addition of or modification of a few of access policies. When this is coupled with the ability to push changes immediately through the use of the API, entire data center configurations have been changed in hours and minutes instead of days, weeks, or months. Application functionality testing is also exponentially reduced because the same policies and contracts were used both before and after the changes, as shown in Figure 11-1.

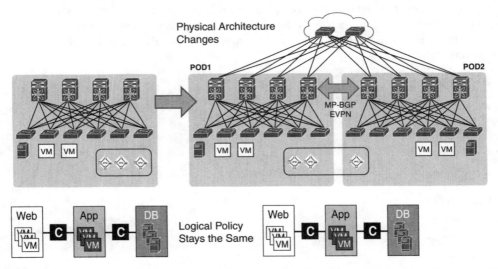

Figure 11-1 *Physical Versus Logical Changes when Bringing up a Second Site with ACI*

ACI understands the policy as defined and implements it across the stateless hardware architecture that is available.

When planning an active-active architecture, you need to consider both active-active data centers and active-active applications. To have active-active applications, you must first have active-active data centers. When you have both, you have the capability to deliver new service levels by providing a continuously available environment.

A continuously available, active-active, flexible environment provides several benefits to the business:

- **Increased uptime:** A fault in a single location does not affect the capability of the application to continue to perform in another location.

- **Disaster avoidance:** Shifting away from disaster recovery and preventing outages from affecting the business in the first place.

- **Easier maintenance:** Taking down a site (or a part of the computing infrastructure at a site) for maintenance should be easier, because virtual or container-based workloads can be migrated to other sites while the business continues to deliver undisrupted service during the migration and while the site is down.

- **Flexible workload placement:** All the computing resources on the sites are treated as a resource pool, allowing automation, orchestration, and cloud management platforms to place workloads anywhere, thus more fully utilizing resources. Affinity rules can be set up on the orchestration platforms so that the workloads are co-located on the same site or forced to exist on different sites.

- **Extremely low recovery time objective (RTO):** A zero or nearly zero RTO reduces or eliminates unacceptable impact on the business of any failure that occurs.

This chapter provides guidance on designing and deploying Application Centric Infrastructure in two or more data centers in an active-active architecture that delivers the benefits in the preceding list.

At its release, ACI supported two architectures, stretched fabric and multiple fabrics, as shown in Figure 11-2.

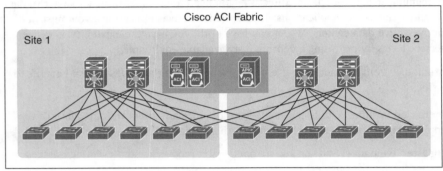

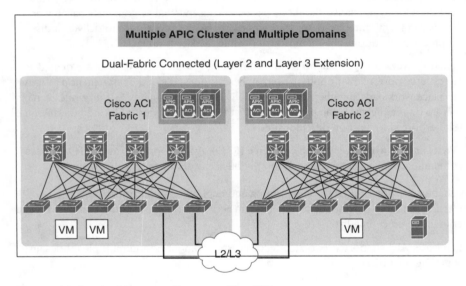

Figure 11-2   *Architectures Supported by ACI*

Stretched Fabric Design

A Cisco ACI stretched fabric is a partially meshed or fully meshed design that connects Cisco ACI leaf and spine switches distributed in separate geographic locations.
The stretched fabric is functionally a single Cisco ACI fabric. The interconnected sites
are one administrative domain and one availability zone with shared fabric control
planes (using Intermediate System to Intermediate System [IS-IS] protocol, Cooperative
Key Server Protocol [COOP], and Multiprotocol Border Gateway Protocol [MP-BGP]).
Administrators can manage the sites as one entity; configuration changes made on any
APIC node are applied to devices across the sites.

The stretched fabric is managed by a single APIC cluster, consisting of three Application Policy Infrastructure Controllers (APICs), with two APICs deployed at one site and the third deployed at the other site. The use of a single APIC cluster stretched across both sites, a shared endpoint database synchronized between spines at both sites, and a shared control plane (IS-IS, COOP, and MP-BGP) defines and characterizes a Cisco ACI stretched fabric deployment.

Currently ACI supports a stretched fabric across up to three locations, as shown in Figure 11-3.

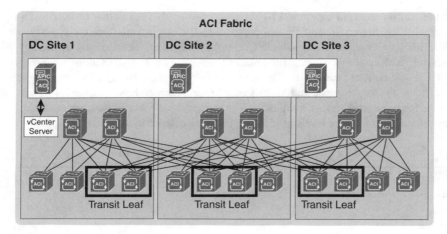

Figure 11-3 *ACI Fabric Support*

At least two leafs at each location will be designated as transit leafs, the purpose of which is to provide connectivity between the locations. The transit leafs allow the sites to be connected to each other without requiring a full mesh.

Site-to-Site Connectivity Options

ACI stretched fabric site-to-site connectivity options include dark fiber, dense wavelength division multiplexing (DWDM), and Ethernet over MPLS (EoMPLS) pseudowire. The following media types, speeds, and distances are supported:

- Dark fiber 40G/40km

- DWDM 40G/800km

- EoMPLS 10G/40G/100G/800km

All configurations require 10ms round trip time (RTT). You can reference Cisco.com for supported optics.

Psuedowire can be used with the Nexus 9K and the ASR9K. The benefit of the pseudowire configuration is the capability to support a stretched fabric when bandwidth is a constraining issue. This design also allows the use of the link for other types of traffic.

However, when there is a low-speed link (for example, a 10G link) or the link is shared among multiple use cases, an appropriate quality of service (QoS) policy must be enabled to ensure the protection of critical control traffic. In an ACI stretched fabric design, the most critical traffic is the traffic among the APIC cluster controllers. Also, the control protocol traffic (such as IS-IS or MP-BGP) also needs to be protected. In this design, enterprises will need to assign this type of traffic to a priority queue so that it is not impacted when congestion occurs on the long-distance Data Center Interconnect (DCI) link. Other types of traffic (such as SPAN) should be assigned to a lower priority to prevent crowding out bandwidth from production data traffic.

The sample configuration in Example 11-1 shows how to apply QoS policy on an ASR9K to protect APIC cluster traffic and control protocol traffic originating from the supervisor of leaf and spine switches. This sample QoS policy identifies the incoming traffic by matching the 802.1p priority value. It then places the APIC cluster traffic, along with traceroute traffic and control protocol traffic, in two priority queues. The QoS policy assigns SPAN traffic to a separate queue and assigns very low guaranteed bandwidth. SPAN traffic can take more bandwidth if it is available. The three classes for user data are optional, and they are mapped to three levels of classes of service offered by the ACI fabric.

Example 11-1   *Example ASR QOS Policy for Psuedowire Architecture*

```
class-map match-any SUP_Traffic
 match mpls experimental topmost 5
 match cos 5
 end-class-map
!
class-map match-any SPAN_Traffic
 match mpls experimental topmost 7 4        <== Span Class + Undefined merged
 match cos 4 7
 end-class-map
!
class-map match-any User_Data_Level_3
 match mpls experimental topmost 1
 match cos 0
 end-class-map
!
class-map match-any User_Data_Level_2
 match mpls experimental topmost 0
 match cos 1
 end-class-map
!
class-map match-any User_Data_Level_1
 match mpls experimental topmost 0
 match cos 2
 end-class-map
!
```

```
class-map match-any APIC+Traceroute_Traffic
 match mpls experimental topmost 3 6
 match cos 3 6
 end-class-map
!
policy-map QoS_Out_to_10G_DCI_Network
 class SUP_Traffic
  priority level 1
  police rate percent 15
 class APIC+Traceroute_Traffic
  priority level 2
  police rate percent 15
 class User_Data_Traffic_3
  bandwidth 500 mbps
  queue-limit 40 kbytes
 class User_Data_Traffic_1
  bandwidth 3200 mbps
  queue-limit 40 kbytes
 class User_Data_Traffic_2
  bandwidth 3200 mbps
  queue-limit 40 kbytes
 class SPAN_Traffic
  bandwidth 100 mbps
  queue-limit 40 kbytes
 class class-default

interface TenGigE0/2/1/0
 description To-ASR9k-4
 cdp
 mtu 9216
 service-policy output QoS_Out_to_10G_DCI_Network
 ipv4 address 5.5.2.1 255.255.255.252
 load-interval 30
```

Stretched ACI Fabric Preserves VM Mobility

The stretched ACI fabric behaves the same way as a singular ACI fabric, supporting full VMM integration. An APIC cluster can interact with a virtual machine manager (VMM) for a given distributed virtual switch (DVS). For example, one VMware vCenter operates across the stretched ACI fabric sites. The ESXi hosts from both sites are managed by the same vCenter, and the DVS is stretched to the two sites. The APIC cluster can register and interact with multiple vCenters when multiple DVSs are involved.

Each leaf provides distributed anycast gateway functions with the same gateway IP and gateway MAC addresses, so workloads (physical or virtual) can be deployed between sites. Live migration is supported in case of virtual workloads. Each leaf switch provides the optimal forwarding path for intra-subnet bridging and inter-subnet routing.

Note Anycast gateway is a distributed and pervasive gateway functionality that allows the leaf closest to an endpoint to perform routing functionality. The subnet default gateway addresses are programmed into all the leafs with endpoints present for that specific subnet and tenant. This also provides redundancy for gateways.

Loss of a Single APIC

The loss of one APIC in either site has no impact on the ACI fabric. With two APIC nodes alive, the cluster still has a quorum (two out of three), and administrators can continue to make configuration changes. There is no configuration data loss due to the APIC node being unavailable. The two APIC nodes retain redundant copies of the APIC database, and the leadership role for the shards of the lost APIC is distributed among the remaining APICs. As is the case with the non-stretched ACI fabric, best practice is to promptly bring the APIC cluster back to full health with all APIC nodes being fully healthy and synchronized.

Split Fabric

When all the connections between the sites are lost, the fabric splits into two fabrics. This scenario is referred to as *split brain* in some documents. In Figure 11-4, the APIC in Site 2 is no longer able to communicate with the rest of cluster.

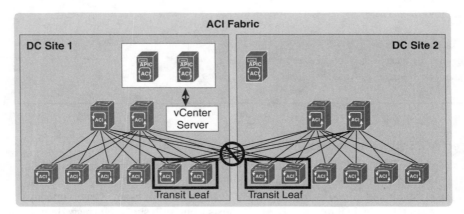

Figure 11-4 *Lost Connectivity Between Sites (Split Brain)*

In this situation, the split fabrics continue to operate independently. Traffic forwarding is not affected. The two fabrics can learn the new endpoints through the data plane. At the site containing the VMM controller (Site 1 in Figure 11-4), endpoints are learned by the control plane as well. Upon learning new endpoints, leaf switches update the spine proxy. Independently of leaf switches, spine switches in each site learn of new endpoints via the Cooperative Key Server Protocol (COOP). After the connections between sites are restored, the spine proxy databases from the two sites merge and all spine switches have complete and identical proxy mapping databases.

The split-fabric site with two APIC nodes (Site 1 in Figure 11-4) has quorum (two working nodes out of a cluster of three). The APIC in Site 1 can execute policy read and write operations to and from the fabric. An administrator can log in to either APIC node in Site 1 and make policy changes. After the link between the two sites recovers, the APIC cluster synchronizes configuration changes across the stretched fabric, pushing configuration changes into the concrete model in all the switches throughout the fabric.

When the connection between two sites is lost, the site with one APIC will be in the minority (Site 2 in Figure 11-4). When a controller is in the minority, it cannot be the leader for any shards. This limits the controller in Site 2 to read-only operations; administrators cannot make any configuration changes through the controller in Site 2. However, the Site 2 fabric still responds to network events such as workload migration, link failure, node failure, and switch reload. When a leaf switch learns a new endpoint, it not only updates the spine proxy via COOP but also sends notifications to the controller so that an administrator can view the up-to-date endpoint information from the single controller in Site 2. Updating endpoint information on the controller is a write operation. While the links between the two sites are lost, leaf switches in Site 2 will try to report the newly learned endpoints to the shard leader (which resides in Site 1 and is not reachable). When the links between the two sites are restored, the learned endpoints will be reported to controller successfully.

In short, the split brain has no impact on the function of the fabric other than the controller in Site 2 is in read-only mode.

Standby APIC

Standby controller is a feature that enables making configuration changes in the case where the site with two APIC nodes become unavailable and need to be restored. Provisioning a standby controller for Site 2 allows the administrator to restore the quorum and provides the ability to make stretched-fabric-wide policy changes while the two APIC nodes at Site 1 are restored. Figure 11-5 shows an example of this design and configuration.

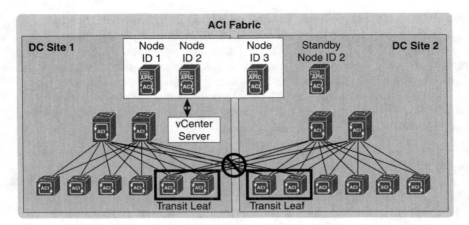

Figure 11-5   *Using a Standby Controller to Enhance Controller Availability*

The benefits of a stretched fabric are as follows:

■ Reduced complexity (it's all just one big fabric).

   ■ Anycast gateway across sites.

   ■ Redundant L3 outside connections can be distributed across locations.

   ■ VMM integration shared across locations.

■ Define policy once for multiple sites.

Here are the potential negatives of a stretched fabric:

■ Policy is defined once for multiple sites, so misconfiguration of a policy can affect multiple DCs.

■ Limited supported connectivity options and hardware platforms.

■ Strict RTT requirements.

Multiple-Fabric Design

In a Cisco ACI multiple-fabric design, each site has its own Cisco ACI fabric, independent from each other, with separate control planes, data planes, and management planes. The sites consist of two (or more) administration domains and two (or more) availability zones with independent control planes (using IS-IS, COOP, and MP-BGP). As a consequence, administrators need to manage the sites individually, and configuration changes made on the APIC at one site are not automatically propagated to the APIC at the other sites. You can deploy an external tool or orchestration system (Cisco Cloud Center or UCS Director) to define policy once and apply it to multiple sites.

A multiple-fabric design has an APIC cluster per site, and each cluster includes three (or more) APICs. The APICs at one site have no direct relationship or communication with the others at other sites. The use of an APIC cluster at each site, independent from other APIC clusters, with an independent endpoint database and independent control plane (using IS-IS, COOP, and MP-BGP) per site, defines a Cisco ACI multiple-fabric design.

In an ACI multiple-fabric design, the fabrics can be interconnected through one of the following DCI options: back-to-back vPC over dark fiber, back-to-back vPC over DWDM, VXLAN or OTV (refer to Figure 11-6).

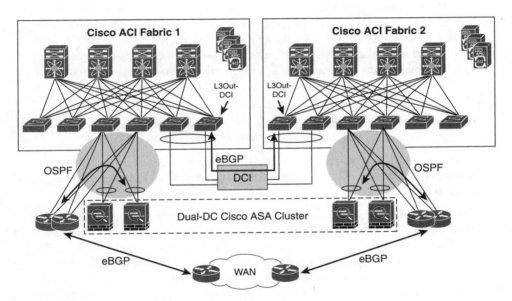

Figure 11-6 *Multiple-Fabric Design*

Each fabric is composed of Cisco Nexus 9000 Series spine and leaf switches, and each site has an APIC cluster consisting of three or more APICs. Between the sites, over the DCI links, Layer 2 is extended by configuring a static endpoint group (EPG) binding that extends an EPG to the other site using the DCI technology. At the remote site, a static binding using the same VLAN ID maps the incoming traffic to the correct EPG.

Note Successful Layer 2 extension between multiple fabrics is dependent on a VLAN = Bridge Domain = EPG design for the extended EPGs. If multiple EPGs of the same bridge domain are extended, this will result in loops between the fabrics.

For Layer 3 connectivity between the sites, exterior BGP (eBGP) peering is established between the border leaf switches. Each Cisco ACI fabric is configured with a unique autonomous system number (ASN). Over this eBGP peering system, IP prefixes relative to subnets that are locally defined at each site are advertised.

For the perimeter firewall, to handle north-south communication (that is, WAN to data center and data center to WAN), a recommended topology is to deploy an active-active ASA cluster, with two Adaptive Security Appliance (ASA) devices at each site. This topology also has been validated using an active-standby firewall design with, for example, the active ASA at Site 1 and the standby ASA at Site 2. On both cases, the firewalls are inserted without a service graph, instead using IP routing with an L3 Out connection between the ACI fabric and the firewalls using Open Shortest Path First (OSPF) as the routing protocol.

The ASA cluster solution is better suited for an active-active architecture, because north-south communication is through the local ASA nodes for IP subnets that are present at only one of the sites. When an ASA cluster is used, the cluster-control-link (CCL) VLAN is extended through the DCI links. For traffic to subnets that exist at both sites, if the traffic entering through Site 1 needs to be sent to a host in Data Center 2, intra-cluster forwarding keeps the flows symmetrical for the IP subnets present at both sites.

The ASA uses the OSPF peering shown in Figure 11-6 between the ASA firewalls and the WAN edge routers to learn about the external networks and to advertise to the WAN edge devices the subnets that exist in the Cisco ACI fabric.

Between the WAN edge routers and the WAN, the reference design uses eBGP because it provides demarcation of the administrative domain and provides the option to manipulate routing policy.

The Cisco ACI dual-fabric design supports multitenancy. In the WAN edge routers, virtual routing and forwarding (VRF) provides logical isolation between the tenants, and within each VRF instance an OSPF neighbor relationship is established with the ASA firewall. In the ASA firewall, multiple contexts (virtual firewalls) are created, one per tenant, so that the tenant separation is preserved. Tenant separation is maintained by creating multiple tenants in the Cisco ACI fabric and extending Layer 3 connectivity to the firewall layer by using per-tenant (VRF) logical connections (L3 Out connections). Per-tenant eBGP sessions are also established between the Cisco ACI fabrics, effectively creating between the fabrics multiple parallel eBGP sessions in a VRF-lite model over the DCI extension.

Note   The ASA firewall design outlined in this section was included because it is a Cisco-validated design. The main concern is around symmetrical versus asymmetrical flows, and how they are handled by firewalls. Firewalls track state and will drop flows when they do not see the entire communication. Symmetric flows are a requirement, unless your firewall vendor has a feature to mitigate this design issue.

Cisco Data Center Interconnect

To meet disaster-avoidance and workload-mobility needs requirements, Layer 2 domains (VLANs) need to be extended across different Cisco ACI fabrics. The simple requirement of routing between sites must also be met.

Unlike with other networking approaches, Cisco ACI allows for the establishment of Layer 3 connectivity over vPC, using a Layer 3 dynamic routing protocol. The solution proposed in this document has been unified to use direct eBGP peering between the Cisco ACI fabrics over a VLAN offered by the DCI. The DCI network between the sites is then a Layer 2–enabled transport, used both to extend Layer 2 connectivity and enable the establishment of route peering.

The following three DCI options are proposed (see Figure 11-7):

■ One very simple option, limited to dual-site deployments, uses vPC. In this case, the border leaf switches of both fabrics are simply connected back to back using either dark fiber or dense wavelength division multiplexing (DWDM) connections.

■ The second option uses the most popular DCI technology: Overlay Transport Virtualization (OTV). It is still uses vPC to connect to the fabric, but it uses a Layer 3 routed connection over the core network.

■ The third option uses VXLAN technology to offer Layer 2 extension services across sites.

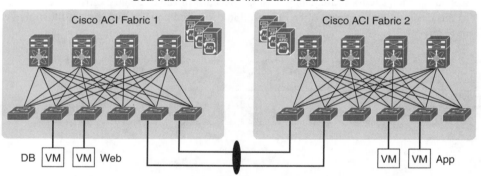

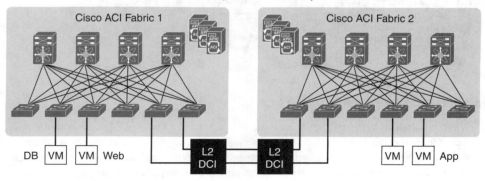

Figure 11-7 *Dual-Fabric Scenarios with vPC and OTV*

Whatever technology is chosen for the interconnection, the DCI function must meet a set of requirements. Remember that the purpose of DCI is to allow transparency between sites with high availability: that is, to allow open Layer 2 and Layer 3 extension while helping ensure that a failure in one data center is not propagated to another data center. To meet this goal, the main technical requirement is the capability to control Layer 2 broadcast, unknown unicast, and multicast flooding at the data-plane level while helping ensure control-plane independence.

Layer 2 extension must be dual-homed for redundancy, but without allowing the creation of end-to-end Layer 2 loops that can lead to traffic storms, which can overflow links and saturate the CPUs of switches and virtual machines. Layer 2 connectivity between sites will be examined in depth in the following sections.

Transit Leaf and L3 Out Considerations

In a stretched fabric, *transit leaf* refers to the leaf switches that provide connectivity between two sites. Transit leaf switches connect to spine switches on both sites. No special requirements or additional configurations are required for transit leaf switches. Any leaf switch can be used as a transit leaf. At least one transit leaf switch must be provisioned for each site for redundancy reasons. Because of the criticality of these resources in this design, they are more often deployed in dedicated pairs at each site, as illustrated in Figure 11-8.

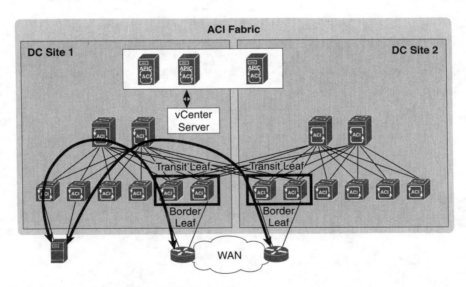

Figure 11-8   *Example of ACI Transit Leaf*

When bandwidth between sites is limited, it is preferable to have WAN connectivity at each site. Although any leaf can be a transit leaf, and a transit leaf can also be a border leaf (as well as provide connectivity for compute or service appliance resources), it is best to separate transit and border leaf functions on separate switches. By doing so, you cause hosts to go through a local border leaf to reach the WAN, which avoids burdening long-distance inter-site links with WAN traffic. Likewise, when a transit leaf switch needs to use a spine switch for proxy purposes, it will distribute traffic between local and remote spine switches.

DCI or Inter-Pod Network Considerations

The Layer 3 network used to connect an ACI fabric or fabrics across multiple locations is a critical resource. Depending on the architecture being used this network can be referred to as a DCI network and or inter-pod network. An inter-pod network is a network used to connect multiple "pods" of ACI. A DCI network is a more generic name given to the underlay network your Data Center Interconnect protocols use for transport. These networks should be architected in a redundant and highly available manner using best practices where applicable as shown in Figure 11-9.

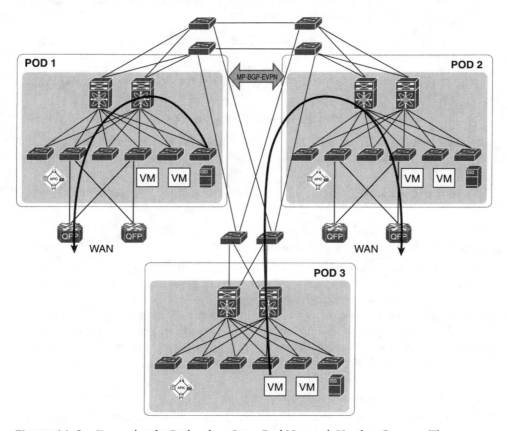

Figure 11-9   *Example of a Redundant Inter-Pod Network Used to Connect Three ACI Pods*

DCI services will be deployed over and leverage these networks as an underlay network. The DCI services or overlay networks such as VXLAN or OTV will have their own requirements for the support of these protocols. Here are three of the main requirements for VXLAN and OTV:

- Large MTU size required to support the encapsulation protocol.

- Multicast support requirements.

    - OTV and VXLAN support options both with and without multicast.

    - Required for inter-pod network (IPN).

- Hardware requirements, depending on the protocol/architecture (for example, OTV is only supported on certain hardware platforms).

Specifically, the inter-pod network, which is responsible for connecting an ACI Multi-Pod network, has the following main requirements:

- Multicast BiDir PIM (needed to handle Layer 2 broadcast, unknown unicast, and multicast traffic)

- The OSPF protocol must be used to peer with the spine nodes and learn VTEP reachability

- Jumbo MTU support (9150B) to handle VXLAN encapsulated traffic

- DHCP-Relay

- 50ms RTT

We will examine specific design considerations for each of these networks in the following sections.

Multiple Fabric Connectivity Options

As we have already discussed, enterprises have multiple connectivity options extending Layer 2 capabilities between sites. Which architecture you choose will depend on a number of factors, such as hardware requirements, physical connectivity, and comfort level with available technologies. vPC and OTV are currently the most widely deployed connectivity options, with VXLAN on the rise. As enterprises become more comfortable with supporting VXLAN and it is more widely deployed, it will become the DCI protocol of choice due to being an open standards–based protocol.

Layer 2 Connectivity Between Sites

Cisco recommends isolating and reducing Layer 2 networks to their smallest scope, usually limiting them to the server access layer. However, in some situations, Layer 2 must be extended beyond the single data center. Layer 2 connectivity is required for server-to-server communication, high availability clusters, networking, and security.

In a very simple approach, two Cisco ACI fabrics can be directly connected back to back. As shown in Figure 11-7, on each side, one pair of border leaf nodes can use a back-to-back vPC connection to extend Layer 2 and Layer 3 connectivity across sites. Unlike traditional vPC deployments on Cisco Nexus platforms, with Cisco ACI you don't need to create a vPC peer link or a peer-keepalive link between the border leaf nodes. Instead, those peerings are established through the fabric.

You can use any number of links to form the back-to-back vPC, but for redundancy reasons, two is the minimum.

This dual-link vPC can use dark fiber. It can also use DWDM, but only if the DWDM transport offers high quality of service. Because the transport in this case is ensured by the Link Aggregation Control Protocol (LACP), you should not rely on a link that offers only three 9s (99.9 percent) or less of resiliency. In general, private DWDM with high availability is good enough.

When using DWDM, you need to keep in mind that loss of signal is not reported. With DWDM, one side may stay up while the other side is down. Cisco ACI allows you to configure Fast LACP to detect such a condition, and the design outlined previously has validated this capability to achieve fast convergence.

Layer 3 Connectivity with DCI

The IP transport option applies when the enterprise-edge device is peering at Layer 3 with the first service provider device. In this case, an overlay needs to be created to logically interconnect the enterprise devices in the different data centers. In current network designs, this is the preferred method of connectivity. With modern-day DCI protocols, you get the stability of a Layer 3 protocol, the connectivity of a Layer 2 protocol, with protections and optimizations built in. We will cover two of the preferred Layer 3 DCI options in the next sections.

OTV as DCI Transport   OTV is a MAC-in-IP technique for supporting Layer 2 VPNs to extend LANs over any transport. The transport can be Layer 2 based, Layer 3 based, IP switched, label switched, or anything else, as long as it can carry IP packets. By using the principles of MAC address routing, OTV provides an overlay that enables Layer 2 connectivity between separate Layer 2 domains while keeping these domains independent and preserving the fault-isolation, resiliency, and load-balancing benefits of an IP-based interconnection.

The core principles on which OTV operates are the use of a control protocol to advertise MAC address reachability information (instead of using data-plane learning) and packet switching of IP encapsulated Layer 2 traffic for data forwarding. OTV can be used to provide connectivity based on MAC address destinations while preserving most of the characteristics of a Layer 3 interconnection.

Before MAC address reachability information can be exchanged, all OTV edge devices must become adjacent to each other from an OTV perspective. This adjacency can be achieved in two ways, depending on the nature of the transport network that interconnects the various sites. If the transport is multicast enabled, a specific multicast group can be used to exchange control protocol messages between the OTV edge devices. If the transport is not multicast enabled, an alternative deployment model is available, starting with Cisco NX-OS Software Release 5.2(1). In this model, one OTV edge device (or more) can be configured as an adjacency server to which all other edge devices register. In this way, the adjacency server can build a full list of the devices that belong to a given overlay.

An edge device forwards Layer 2 frames into and out of a site over the overlay interface. There is only one authoritative edge device (AED) for all MAC unicast and multicast addresses for each given VLAN. The AED role is negotiated, on a per-VLAN basis, among all the OTV edge devices that belong to the same site (that is, that are characterized by the same site ID).

The internal interface facing the Cisco ACI fabric can be a vPC on the OTV edge device side. However, the recommended attachment model uses independent port channels between each AED and the Cisco ACI fabric, as shown in Figure 11-10.

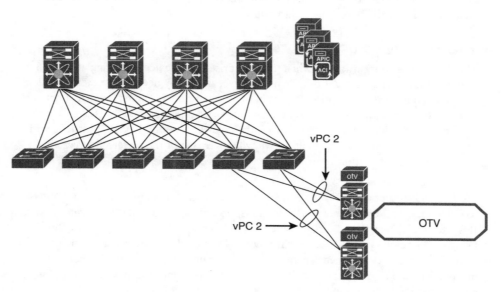

Figure 11-10   *Connectivity Between OTV Devices and the ACI Fabric*

Each OTV device defines a logical interface, called a *join interface*, that is used to encapsulate and decapsulate Layer 2 Ethernet frames that need to be transported to remote sites.

OTV requires a site VLAN, which is assigned on each edge device that connects to the same overlay network. OTV sends local hello messages on the site VLAN to detect other OTV edge devices in the site, and it uses the site VLAN to determine the AED for the OTV-extended VLANs. Because OTV uses IS-IS protocol for this hello, the Cisco ACI fabric must run software release 11.1 or later. This requirement is necessary because previous releases prevented the OTV devices from exchanging IS-IS hello message through the fabric.

Note   An important benefit of the OTV site VLAN is the capability to detect a Layer 2 backdoor that may be created between the two Cisco ACI fabrics. To support this capability, you should use the same site VLAN on both Cisco ACI sites.

One of the main requirements of every LAN extension solution is Layer 2 connectivity between remote sites without compromising the advantages of resiliency, stability, scalability, and so on, obtained by interconnecting sites through a routed transport infrastructure. OTV achieves this goal through four main functions:

- Spanning-tree isolation

- Unknown unicast traffic suppression

- ARP optimization

- Layer 2 broadcast policy control

OTV also offers a simple command-line interface (CLI), or it can easily be set up using a programming language such as Python. Because Ethernet frames are carried across the transport infrastructure after OTV encapsulation, you need to consider the size of the maximum transmission unit (MTU).

Enterprises should increase the MTU size of all the physical interfaces along the path between the source and destination endpoints to account for those additional 50 bytes. An exception can be made when you are using the Cisco ASR 1000 Series Aggregation Services Routers as the OTV platform, because these routers do support packet fragmentation.

In summary, OTV is designed for DCI, and it is still considered the most mature and functionally robust solution for extending multipoint Layer 2 connectivity over a generic IP network. In addition, it offers native functions that allow a stronger DCI connection and increased independence of the fabrics.

VXLAN as DCI Transport   VXLAN, one of many available network virtualization overlay technologies, is an industry-standard protocol and uses underlay IP networks. It extends Layer 2 segments over a Layer 3 infrastructure to build Layer 2 overlay logical networks. It encapsulates Ethernet frames in IP User Data Protocol (UDP) headers and transports the encapsulated packets through the underlay network to the remote VXLAN tunnel endpoints (VTEPs) using the normal IP routing and forwarding mechanism. VXLAN has a 24-bit virtual network identifier (VNI) field that theoretically allows up to 16 million unique Layer 2 segments in the same network. Although the current network software and hardware limitations reduce the usable VNI scale in actual deployments, the VXLAN protocol by design has at least lifted the 4096-VLAN limitation in the traditional IEEE 802.1Q VLAN namespace. VXLAN can solve this dilemma by decoupling Layer 2 domains from the network infrastructure. The infrastructure is built as a Layer 3 fabric that doesn't rely on Spanning Tree Protocol for loop prevention or topology convergence. The Layer 2 domains reside on the overlay, with isolated broadcast and failure domains.

- The VTEP is a switch (physical or virtual) that originates and terminates VXLAN tunnels. The VTEP encapsulates the end-host Layer 2 frames within an IP header to send them across the IP transport network, and it decapsulates VXLAN packets received from the underlay IP network to forward them to local end hosts. The communicating workloads are unaware of the VXLAN function.

- VXLAN is a multipoint technology and can allow the interconnection of multiple sites. In the solution proposed in this document, a VXLAN standalone network simply offers Layer 2 extension services to the Cisco ACI fabrics. This Layer 2 DCI function is used both to stretch Layer 2 broadcast domains (IP subnets) across sites and to establish Layer 3 peering between Cisco ACI fabrics to support routed communication.

- As shown in Figure 11-11, logical back-to-back vPC connections are used between the Cisco ACI border leaf nodes and the local pair of VXLAN DCI devices. Both DCI devices use a peer link between each other and connect to the fabric border leaf nodes using either two or four links. Any edge VLAN is then connected to a VXLAN segment that is transported using one only VNI (also called the VXLAN segment ID).

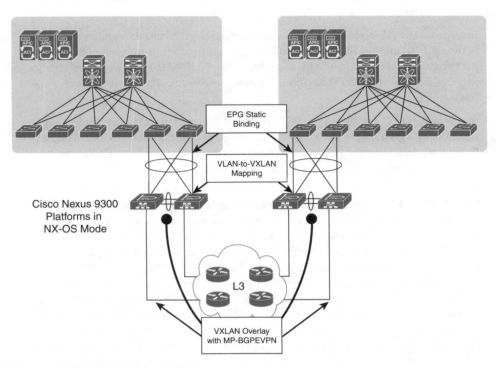

Figure 11-11   *VXLAN as DCI Transport*

The transport network between VTEPs can be a generic IP network. Unicast Layer 2 frames are encapsulated in unicast Layer 3 VXLAN frames sent to the remote VTEP (both remote VXLAN devices advertise themselves in the VXLAN network as a single anycast VTEP logical entity), and the packet is delivered to one of the remote DCI nodes, with load balancing and backup. This backup is managed by the underlay routing protocol at the convergence speed of this protocol. BGP in conjunction with Bidirectional Forwarding Detection (BFD) can be used for fast convergence, but any other routing protocol, such as OSPF or IS-IS, can also be used.

Layer 2 broadcast, unknown unicast, and multicast frames must be delivered across the VXLAN network. Two options are available to transport this multidestination traffic:

- Use multicast in the underlay Layer 3 core network. This is the optimal choice when a high level of Layer 2 multicast traffic is expected across sites.

- Use head-end replication on the source VTEP to avoid any multicast requirement to the core transport network.

VXLAN can also rate-limit broadcast, unknown unicast, and multicast traffic, and as shown previously in Figure 11-11, and should be used in conjunction with ACI storm-control capabilities. VXLAN uses BGP with an Ethernet VPN (EVPN) address family to advertise learned hosts. The BGP design can use edge-to-edge BGP peering, which is the best choice for a dual site, or it can use a route reflector if the network is more complex, in which case internal BGP (iBGP) can be used. VXLAN can provide Layer 2 and Layer 3 DCI functions, both using BGP to advertise the MAC address, IP host address, or subnet connected. As previously mentioned, in this chapter VXLAN is used as a pure Layer 2 DCI, and no Layer 3 option is used. The Layer 3 peering is fabric to fabric in an overlay of VXLAN Layer 2 in a dedicated VLAN. VXLAN is by nature a multipoint technology, so it can offer multisite connection.

One interesting VXLAN option is the capability to perform ARP suppression. Because VXLAN advertises both Layer 2 MAC addresses and Layer 3 IP addresses and masks at the same time, the remote node can reply to ARP locally without the need to flood the ARP request through the system.

Note   ARP suppression in VXLAN fabrics to extend only Layer 2 (and not Layer 3) connectivity is not supported at the time of this writing, so it was not configured in validating this design.

Multi-Pod Architecture

ACI Multi-Pod represents the natural evolution of the original ACI stretched fabric design and allows one to interconnect and centrally manage separate ACI fabrics (see Figure 11-12).

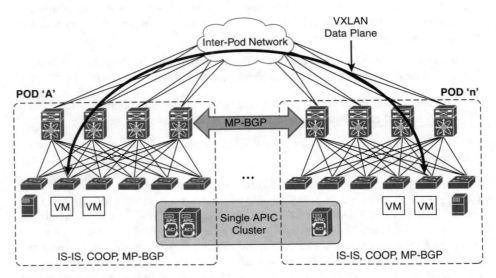

Figure 11-12   *ACI Multi-Pod Solution*

ACI Multi-Pod is part of the "Single APIC Cluster/Single Domain" family of solutions, as a single APIC cluster is deployed to manage all the different ACI fabrics that are interconnected. Those separate ACI fabrics are named "pods," and each of them looks like a regular two-tier spine-leaf fabric. The same APIC cluster can manage several pods, and to increase the resiliency of the solution the various controller nodes that make up the cluster can be deployed across different pods.

The deployment of a single APIC cluster simplifies the management and operational aspects of the solution, as all the interconnected pods essentially function as a single ACI fabric: Created tenants configuration (VRFs, bridge domains, EPGs, and so on) and policies are made available across all the pods, providing a high degree of freedom for connecting endpoints to the fabric. For example, different workloads that are part of the same functional group (EPG), such as web servers, can be connected to (or move across) different pods without you having to worry about provisioning configuration or policy in the new location. At the same time, seamless Layer 2 and Layer 3 connectivity services can be provided between endpoints independently from the physical location where they are connected and without requiring any specific functionality from the network interconnecting the various pods.

Note The previous paragraph refers to the fact that a Multi-Pod design provides the same policy and network resources across pods. The pods look like a single availability zone or fabric to the workload. Any workload mobility would be provided by manually moving a physical device, or by a virtualization vendor such as VMware vMotion or DRS.

Even though the various pods are managed and operated as a single distributed fabric, Multi-Pod offers the capability of increasing failure domain isolation across pods through separation of the fabric control plane protocols. As highlighted in Figure 11-12, different instances of IS-IS, COOP, and MP-BGP protocols run inside each pod, so faults and issues with any of those protocols would be contained in the single pod and not spread across the entire Multi-Pod fabric. This is a property that clearly differentiates Multi-Pod from the stretched fabric approach and makes it the recommended design option going forward.

From a physical perspective, the different pods are interconnected by leveraging an "inter-pod network" (IPN). Each pod connects to the IPN through the spine nodes; the IPN can be as simple as a single Layer 3 device, or as a best practice can be built with a larger Layer 3 network infrastructure.

The IPN must simply provide basic Layer 3 connectivity services, allowing for the establishment across pods of spine-to-spine and leaf-to-leaf VXLAN tunnels. It is the use of the VXLAN overlay technology in the data plane that provides seamless Layer 2 and Layer 3 connectivity services between endpoints, independently from the physical location (pod) where they are connected.

Finally, running a separate instance of the COOP protocol inside each pod implies that information about local endpoints (MAC, IPv4/IPv6 addresses, and their location) is only stored in the COOP database of the local spine nodes. Because ACI Multi-Pod functions as a single fabric, it is key to ensure that the databases implemented in the spine nodes across pods have a consistent view of the endpoints connected to the fabric; this requires the deployment of an overlay control plane running between the spines and used to exchange endpoint reachability information. As shown in Figure 11-12, Multi-Protocol BGP has been chosen for this function. This is due to the flexibility and scalability properties of this protocol and its support of different address families (such as EVPN and VPNv4), thus allowing for the exchange of Layer 2 and Layer 3 information in a true multitenant fashion.

ACI Multi-Pod Use Cases and Supported Topologies

There are two main use cases for the deployment of ACI Multi-Pod, and the substantial difference between the two is the physical location where the different pods are deployed:

- Multiple pods deployed in the same physical data center location
- Multiple pods deployed for geographically dispersed data centers

Figure 11-13 illustrates the scenario where multiple pods are deployed in the same physical data center location.

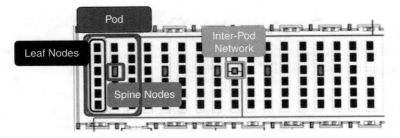

Figure 11-13 *Multiple Pods Deployed in the Same Physical Data Center Location*

The creation of multiple pods could be driven, for example, by the existence of a specific cabling layout already in place inside the data center. In this example, top-of-rack switches are connected to middle-of-row devices (red rack), and the various middle-of-row switches are aggregated by core devices (purple rack). Such cabling layout does not allow for the creation of a typical two-tier leaf-spine topology; the introduction of ACI Multi-Pod permits one to interconnect all the devices in a three-tier topology and centrally manage them as a single fabric.

Another scenario where multiple pods could be deployed in the same physical data center location is when the requirement is for the creation of a very large fabric. In that case, it may be desirable to divide the large fabric into smaller pods to benefit from the failure domain isolation provided by the Multi-Pod approach.

Figure 11-14 shows the most common use case for the deployment of ACI Multi-Pod, where the different pods represent geographically dispersed data centers.

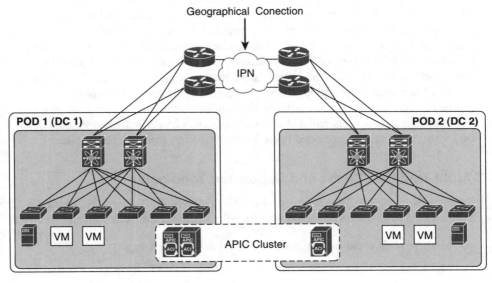

Figure 11-14 *Multiple Pods Across Different Data Center Locations*

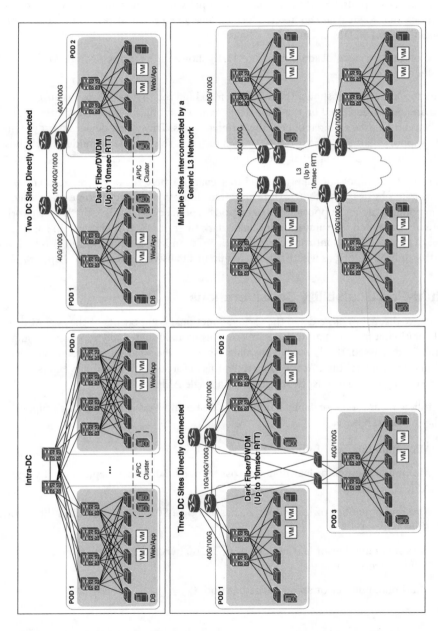

Figure 11-15 *Multi-Pod Supported Topologies*

The deployment of Multi-Pod in this case ensures that one meets the requirement of building active-active data centers, where different application components can be freely deployed across pods. The different data center networks are usually deployed in relative proximity (metro area) and are interconnected leveraging point-to-point links (dark fiber connections or DWDM circuits).

Based on the use cases described, Figure 11-15 shows the supported Multi-Pod topologies.

In the top-left corner is shown the topology matching the first use case. Because the pods are locally deployed (in the same data center location), a pair of centralized IPN devices can be used to interconnect the different pods. Those IPN devices must potentially support a large number of 40G/100G interfaces, so a couple of modular switches are likely to be deployed in that role.

The other three topologies apply instead to scenarios where the pods are represented by separate physical data centers. It is important to notice how at the time of writing, the maximum latency supported between pods is 50 msec RTT. Also, the IPN network is often represented by point-to-point links (dark fiber or DWDM circuits); in specific cases, a generic Layer 3 infrastructure (for example, an MPLS network) can also be leveraged as an IPN, as long as it satisfies the requirements listed earlier in this chapter.

ACI Multi-Pod Scalability Considerations

Before we discuss in more detail the various functional components of the ACI Multi-Pod solution, it is important to reiterate how this model functionally represents a single fabric. As discussed, this is a very appealing aspect of the solution, as it facilitates operating such an infrastructure. At the same time, this enforces some scalability limits because all the deployed nodes must be managed by a single APIC cluster.

The following are some scalability figures for ACI Multi-Pod based on what's supported in the initial 2.0 release:

- **Maximum number of pods:** 4

- **Maximum number of leaf nodes across all pods:** 300 (when deploying a five-node APIC cluster)

- **Maximum number of leaf nodes across all pods:** 80 (when deploying a three-node APIC cluster)

- **Maximum number of leaf nodes per pod:** 200 (when deploying a five-node APIC cluster)

- **Maximum number of spine nodes per pod:** 6

Note   It is recommended that you consult the ACI release notes for updated scalability figures and also for information on other scalability parameters not listed here.

Inter-Pod Connectivity Deployment Considerations

The inter-pod network (IPN) connects the different ACI pods, allowing for the establishment of pod-to-pod communication (also known as east-west traffic). In this case, the IPN basically represents an extension of the ACI fabric underlay infrastructure.

In order to perform those connectivity functions, the IPN must support a few specific functionalities, as described in the following list:

- **Multicast support:** In addition to unicast communication, east-west traffic also comprises Layer 2 multidestination flows belonging to bridge domains that are extended across pods. This type of traffic is usually referred to as *broadcast*, *unknown unicast*, *and multicast* (BUM), and it is exchanged by leveraging VXLAN data-plane encapsulation between leaf nodes.

  Inside a pod (or ACI fabric), BUM traffic is encapsulated into a VXLAN multicast frame, and it is always transmitted to all the local leaf nodes. A unique multicast group is associated with each defined bridge domain (BD) and takes the name of bridge domain group IP–outer (BD GIPo). Once received by the leafs, it is then forwarded to the connected devices that are part of that bridge domain or dropped, depending on the specific bridge domain configuration.

  The same behavior must be achieved for endpoints that are part of the same bridge domain connected to the different pods. In order to flood the BUM traffic across pods, the same multicast used inside the pod is also extended through the IPN network. Those multicast groups should work in BiDir mode and must be dedicated to this function (that is, not used for other purposes, applications, and so on).

  Here are the main reasons for using PIM BiDir mode in the IPN network:

  - **Scalability:** Because BUM traffic can be originated by all the leaf nodes deployed across pods, it would result in the creation of multiple individual (S, G) entries on the IPN devices that may exceed the specific platform capabilities. With PIM BiDir, a single (*, G) entry must be created for a given BD, independent from the overall number of leaf nodes.

  - **No requirement for data-driven multicast state creation:** The (*, G) entries are created in the IPN devices as soon as a BD is activated in the ACI Multi-Pod fabric, independent from the fact there is an actual need to forward BUM traffic for that given BD. This implies that when the need to do so arises, the network will be ready to perform those duties, avoiding longer convergence time for the application caused, for example, in PIM ASM by the data-driven state creation.

  - **Cisco recommended:** It represents Cisco's prescriptive, well-tested, and hence recommended design option.

■ **DHCP relay support:** One of the nice functionalities offered by the ACI Multi-Pod solution is the capability of allowing auto-provisioning of configuration for all the ACI devices deployed in remote pods. This allows those devices to join the Multi-Pod fabric with zero-touch configuration, as it normally happens to ACI nodes that are part of the same fabric (pod). This functionality relies on the capability of the first IPN device connected to the spines of the remote pod to relay DHCP requests generated from a new starting ACI spines toward the APIC node(s) active in the first pod.

■ **OSPF support:** In the initial release of ACI Multi-Pod fabric, OSPFv2 is the only routing protocol (in addition to static routing) supported on the spine interfaces connecting to the IPN devices.

■ **Increased MTU support:** Because VXLAN data-plane traffic is exchanged between pods, the IPN must able to support an increased MTU on its physical connections, in order to avoid the need for fragmentation and reassembly. At the time of writing, the requirement is to increase the supported MTU to 9150B on all the Layer 3 interfaces of the IPN devices.

■ **QoS considerations:** Different nodes of the APIC cluster will normally be deployed across separate pods, and intra-cluster communication can only happen in-band (that is, across the IPN network). As a consequence, it is important to ensure that intra-cluster communication between the APIC nodes is prioritized across the IPN infrastructure. Although this recommendation should always be followed in production deployments, it is worth noting that the APIC offers a built-in resiliency function: If for whatever reason (because of link failure or excessive packet loss) the connection between APIC nodes is lost, the site with quorum will function without problem. The site with the minority of APICs will be read-only. Once the connection is resumed, the database will be synchronized and all functions will be regained.

IPN Control Plane

As previously mentioned, the inter-pod network represents an extension of the ACI infrastructure network, ensuring VXLAN tunnels can be established across pods for allowing endpoints communication.

Inside each ACI pod, IS-IS is the infrastructure routing protocol used by the leaf and spine nodes to peer with each other and exchange IP information for locally defined loopback interfaces (usually referred to as VTEP addresses). During the auto-provisioning process for the nodes belonging to a pod, the APIC assigns one (or more) IP addresses to the loopback interfaces of the leaf and spine nodes that are part of the pod. All those IP addresses are part of an IP pool that is specified during the boot-up process of the first APIC node and takes the name "TEP pool."

In a Multi-Pod deployment, each pod is assigned a separate, non-overlapping TEP pool, as shown in Figure 11-16.

The spines in each pod establish OSPF peering with the directly connected IPN devices to be able to send out the TEP pool prefix for the local pod. As a consequence, the IPN devices install in their routing tables equal-cost routes for the TEP pools valid in the different pods. At the same time, the TEP-Pool prefixes relative to remote pods received by the spines via OSPF are redistributed into the IS-IS process of each pod so that the leaf nodes can install them in their routing table (those routes are part of the "overlay-1" VRF representing the infrastructure VRF).

Note The spines also send a few host route addresses to the IPN, associated with specific loopback addresses defined on the spines. This is required to ensure that traffic destined to those IP addresses can be delivered from the IPN directly to the right spine where they are defined (that is, not following equal-cost paths that may lead to a different spine). No host routes for leaf nodes loopback interfaces should ever be sent into the IPN, which ensures that the routing table of the IPN devices is kept very lean, independent from the total number of deployed leaf nodes.

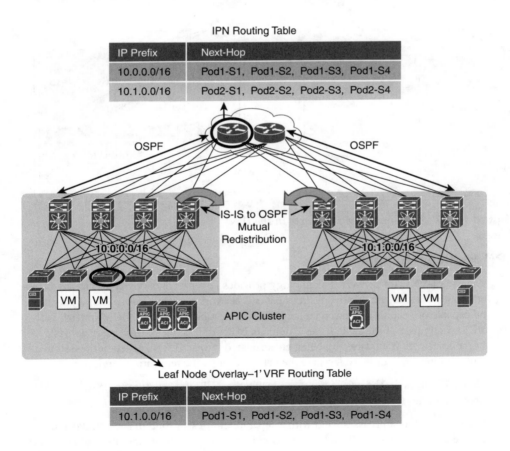

IPN Routing Table

IP Prefix	Next-Hop
10.0.0.0/16	Pod1-S1, Pod1-S2, Pod1-S3, Pod1-S4
10.1.0.0/16	Pod2-S1, Pod2-S2, Pod2-S3, Pod2-S4

Leaf Node 'Overlay–1' VRF Routing Table

IP Prefix	Next-Hop
10.1.0.0/16	Pod1-S1, Pod1-S2, Pod1-S3, Pod1-S4

Figure 11-16 *IPN Control Plane*

The fact that OSPF peering is required between the spines and the IPN devices (at the time of writing, OSPF is the only supported protocol for this function) does not mean that OSPF must be used across the entire IPN infrastructure.

Figure 11-17 highlights this design point; this could be the case when the IPN is a generic Layer 3 infrastructure interconnecting the pods (like an MPLS network, for example) and a separate routing protocol could be used inside that Layer 3 network. Mutual redistribution would then be needed with the process used toward the spines.

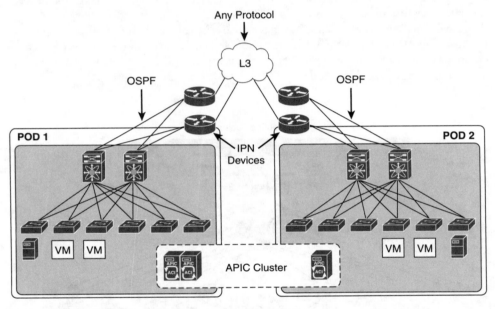

Figure 11-17 *Support of Any Protocol in the IPN*

IPN Multicast Support

The use of VXLAN as overlay technology provides Layer 2 connectivity services between endpoints that may be deployed across Layer 3 network domains. Those endpoints must be capable of sending and receiving Layer 2 multidestination frames (BUM traffic), as they are logically part of the same Layer 2 domain. BUM traffic can be exchanged across Layer 3 network boundaries by being encapsulated into VXLAN packets addressed to a multicast group, in order to leverage the network for traffic replication services.

Figure 11-18 shows the use of multicast inside the ACI infrastructure to deliver multidestination frames to endpoints that are part of the same bridge domain (BD).

Each bridge domain is associated with a separate multicast group (named "GIPo") to ensure granular delivery of multidestination frames only to the endpoints that are part of a given bridge domain.

Note   As shown in Figure 11-18, in order to fully leverage different equal-cost paths for the delivery of multidestination traffic, separate multicast trees are built and used for all the defined BDs.

A similar behavior must be achieved when extending the BD connectivity across pods. This implies the need to extend multicast connectivity through the IPN network, which is the reason why those devices must support PIM BiDir.

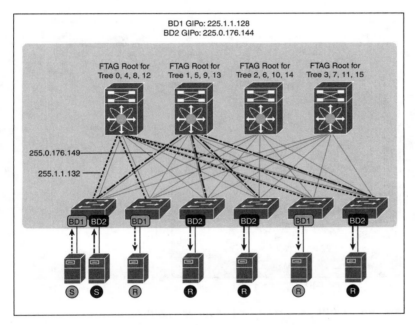

Figure 11-18   *Use of Multicast in the ACI Infrastructure*

Multidestination frames generated by an endpoint that's part of a BD are encapsulated by the leaf node where the endpoint is connected and then need to transit across the IPN network to reach remote endpoints that are part of the same BD. For this to happen, the spines must perform two basic functions:

■ Forward received multicast frames toward the IPN devices to ensure they can be delivered to the remote pods.

■ Send Internet Group Management Protocol (IGMP) Joins toward the IPN network every time a new BD is activated in the local pod, to be able to receive BUM traffic for that BD originated by an endpoint connected to a remote pod.

For each BD, one spine node is elected as the authoritative device to perform both functions described in the preceding list (the IS-IS control plane between the spines is used to perform this election). As shown in Figure 11-19, the elected spine will select a specific physical link connecting to the IPN devices to be used to send out the IGMP Join (hence to receive multicast traffic originated by a remote leaf) and for forwarding multicast traffic originated inside the local pod.

> **Note**   If case of failure of the designated spine, a new one will be elected to take over that role.

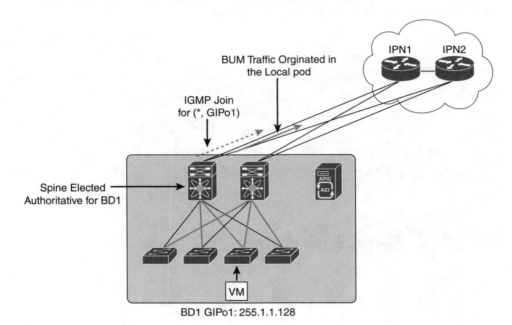

Figure 11-19   *IGMP Join and BUM Forwarding on the Designated Spine*

As a result, the end-to-end BUM forwarding between endpoints that are part of the same BD and connected in separate pods happens as follows (see Figure 11-20):

1. EP1 (belonging to BD1) originates a BUM frame.

2. The frame is encapsulated by the local leaf node and destined to the multicast group GIPo1 associated with BD1. As a consequence, it is sent along one of the multidestination trees assigned to BD1 and reaches all the local spine and leaf nodes where BD1 has been instantiated.

3. Spine 1 is responsible for forwarding BUM traffic for BD1 toward the IPN devices, leveraging the specific link connected to IPN1.

4. The IPN device receives the traffic and performs multicast replication toward all the pods from which it received an IGMP Join for GIPo1. This ensures that BUM traffic is sent only to pods where BD1 is active (that is, there is at least an endpoint actively connected in the BD).

5. The spine that sent the IGMP Join toward the IPN devices receives the multicast traffic and forwards it inside the local pod along one of the multidestination trees associated with BD1. All the leafs where BD1 has been instantiated receive the frame.

6. The leaf where EP2 is connected also receives the stream, decapsulates the packet, and forwards it to EP2.

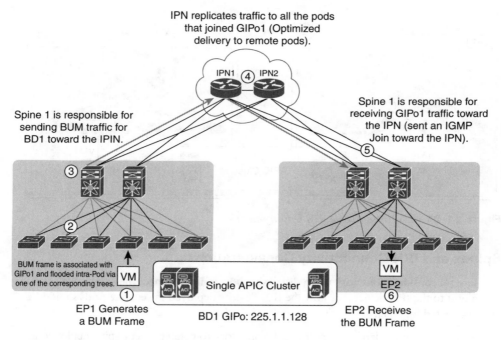

Figure 11-20   *Delivery of BUM Traffic Between Pods*

An important design consideration should be made for the deployment of the rendezvous point (RP) in the IPN network. The role of the RP is important in a PIM BiDir deployment, as all multicast traffic in BiDir groups vectors toward the BiDir RPs, branching off as necessary as it flows upstream and/or downstream. This implies that all the BUM traffic exchanged across pods would be sent through the same IPN device acting as the RP for the 225.0.0.0/15 default range used to assign multicast groups to each defined BD. A possible design choice to balance the workload across different RPs consists in splitting the range and configuring the active RP for each sub-range on separate IPN devices, as shown in the simple example in Figure 11-21.

It is also important to note that when PIM BiDir is deployed, at any given time it is only possible to have an active RP for a given multicast group range (for example, IPN1 is the only active RP handling the 225.0.0.0/17 multicast range). RP redundancy is hence achieved by leveraging the "Phantom RP" configuration, as described at https://supportforums.cisco.com/document/55696/rp-redundancy-pim-bidir-phantom-rp.

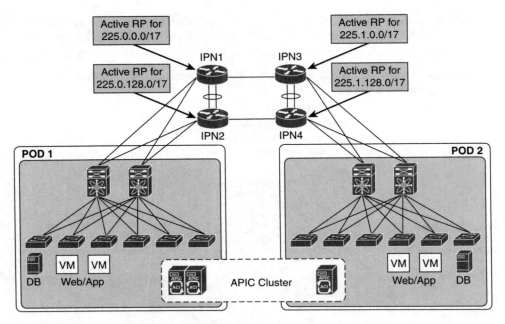

Figure 11-21   *Multiple Active RPs Deployment*

Spines and IPN Connectivity Considerations

Several considerations arise when discussing how to interconnect the spines deployed in a pod to the IPN devices, or how the IPN devices deployed in separate pods should be connected together.

The first point to clarify is that it is not mandatory to connect every spine deployed in a pod to the IPN devices. Figure 11-22 shows a scenario where only two of the four spines are connected to the IPN devices. There are no functional implications for unicast communication across sites, as the local leaf nodes encapsulating traffic to a remote pod would always prefer the paths via the spines that are actively connected to the IPN devices (based on IS-IS routing metric). At the same time, there are no implications either for the BUM traffic that needs to be sent to remote pods, as only the spine nodes that are connected to the IPN devices are considered for being designated as responsible to send/receive traffic for a GIPo (via IS-IS control plane exchange).

Another consideration concerns the option of connecting the spines belonging to separate pods with direct back-to-back links, as shown in Figure 11-23.

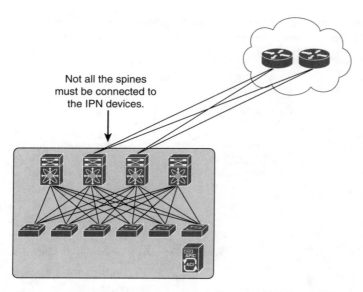

Figure 11-22   *Partial Mesh Connectivity Between Spines and IPN*

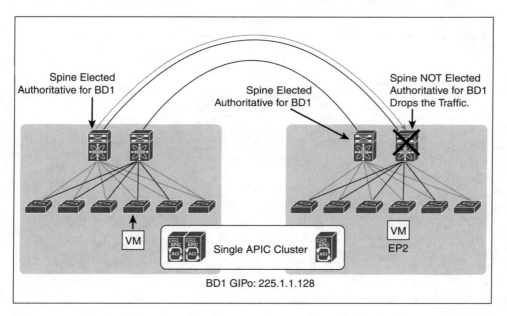

Figure 11-23   *Direct Back-to-Back Links Between Spines in Separate Pods (Not Supported)*

As Figure 11-23 shows, direct connectivity between spines may lead to the impossibility of forwarding BUM traffic across pods, in scenarios where the directly connected spines in separate pods are not both elected as designated for a given BD. As a consequence, the recommendation is to always deploy at least a Layer 3 IPN device (a pair for redundancy) between pods.

It is important to point out that a similar behavior could be achieved when connecting the spines to the IPN devices. Consider, for example, the topologies in Figure 11-24.

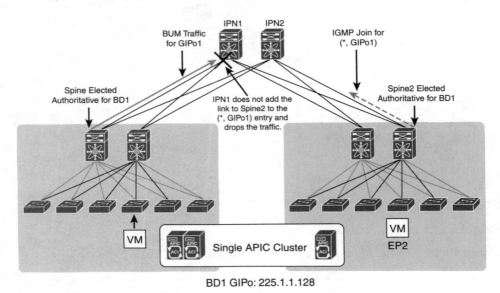

Figure 11-24   *Issues in Sending BUM Traffic across Pods* (**NOT Supported**)

Both scenarios highlight a case where the designated spines in Pod1 and Pod2 (for GIPo1) send the BUM traffic and the IGMP Join to IPN nodes that do not have a valid physical path between them to the destination. As a consequence, the IPN devices won't have proper (*, G) state, and the BUM communication would fail. To avoid this from

happening, the recommendation is to always ensure that there is a physical path interconnecting all the IPN devices, as shown in Figure 11-25.

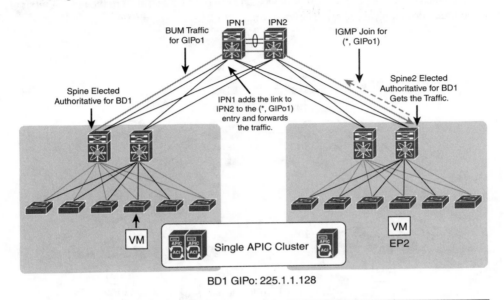

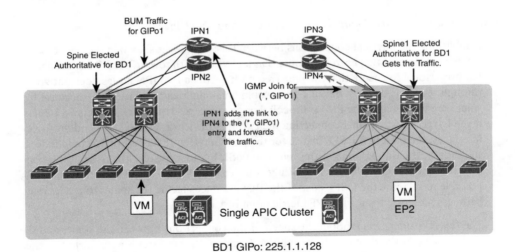

Figure 11-25   *Establishing a Physical Path Between IPN Devices*

Note The full mesh connections in the bottom scenario could be replaced by a Layer 3 port channel connecting the local IPN devices. This would be useful to reduce the number of required geographical links, as shown in Figure 11-26.

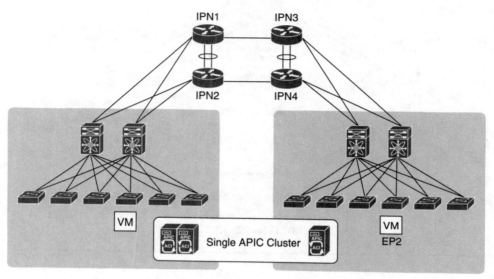

Figure 11-26 *L3 Port Channels Connecting Local IPN Devices*

Establishing the physical connections between IPN devices, as shown in the previous figures, guarantees that each IPN router has a physical path toward the PIM BiDir active RP. It is critical to ensure that the preferred path between two IPN nodes does not go through the spine devices, because that would break multicast connectivity (because the spines are not running the PIM protocol). For example, referring back to Figure 11-26, if the Layer 3 port channel connecting the two IPN devices is created by bundling 10G interfaces, the preferred OSPF metric for the path between IPN1 and IPN2 could indeed steer the traffic through one of the spines in Pod1. In order to solve the issue, it is recommended that you use 40G links to locally connect the IPN devices. Alternatively, it is possible to increase the OSPF cost of the IPN interfaces facing the spines to render that path less preferred from an OSPF metric point of view.

The final consideration is about the speed of the connections between the spines and the IPN devices. At the time of writing, only 40G and 100G interfaces are supported on the spines, which implies the need to support the same speed on the links to the IPN (see Figure 11-27).

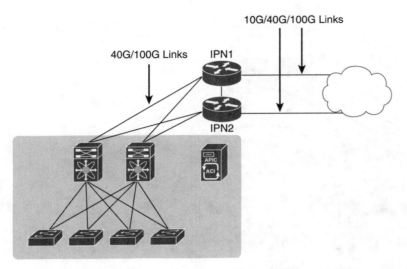

Figure 11-27 *Supported Interface Speed Between Spines and IPN Devices*

The support of Cisco QSFP to SFP or SFP+ Adapter (QSA) Modules on the spine nodes would allow you to start using 10G links for this purpose. Refer to the ACI software release notes to verify support for this connectivity option.

It is also worth note that the links connecting the IPN devices to other remote IPN devices (or to a generic Layer 3 network infrastructure) do not need to be 40G/100G. It is, however, not recommended that you use connection speeds less than 10G in order to avoid traffic congestion across pods that may affect the communication of APIC nodes deployed in separate pods.

Pod Auto-Provisioning

One of the important properties of Cisco ACI is the capability of bringing up a physical fabric in an automatic and dynamic fashion, requiring only minimal interactions from the network administrator. This is a huge leap when compared to the "box-by-box" approach characterizing traditional network deployments.

The use of a common APIC cluster allows ACI to offer similar capabilities to an ACI Multi-Pod deployment. The end goal is adding remote pods to the Multi-Pod fabric with minimal user intervention, as shown in Figure 11-28.

Before we describe the step-by-step procedure, a few initial assumptions are required for having a second pod join the Multi-Pod fabric:

- The first pod (also known as the "seed" pod) has already been set up following the traditional ACI fabric bring-up procedure.

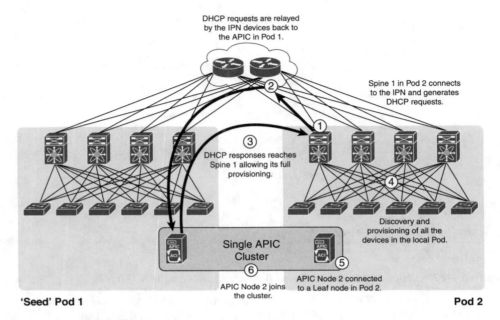

Figure 11-28   *Pod Auto-Provisioning Process*

Note   For more information on how to bring up an ACI fabric from scratch, refer to chapter 3 or this book.

- The "seed" pod and the second pod are physically connected to the IPN devices.

- The IPN devices are properly configured with IP addresses on the interfaces facing the spines, and the OSPF routing protocol is enabled (in addition to the required MTU, DHCP-Relay, and PIM BiDir configuration). This is a Day 0 manual configuration required outside the ACI-specific configuration performed on APIC.

As a result of these assumptions, the IPN devices are peering OSPF with the spines in Pod1 and exchange TEP pool information. The following sequence of steps allows Pod2 to join the Multi-Pod fabric:

1. The first spine in Pod2 boots up and starts sending DHCP requests out of every connected interface. This implies that the DHCP request is also sent toward the IPN devices.

2. The IPN device receiving the DHCP request has been configured to relay that message to the APIC node(s) deployed in Pod1. Note that the spine's serial number is added as a Type Length Value of the DHCP request sent at the previous step, so the receiving APIC can add this information to its Fabric Membership table.

3. Once a user explicitly imports the discovered spine into the APIC Fabric Membership table, the APIC replies back with an IP address to be assigned to the spine's interfaces facing the IPN. Also, the APIC provides information about a boot-strap file (and the TFTP server where to retrieve it, which is the APIC itself) that contains the required spine configuration to set up its VTEP interfaces and OSPF/MP-BGP adjacencies.

Note   In this case, the APIC also functions as the TFTP server.

4. The spine connects to the TFTP server to pull the full configuration.

5. The APIC (TFTP server) replies with the full configuration. At this point, the spine has joined the Multi-Pod fabric and all the policies configured on the APIC are pushed to that device.

Important Note   The spine's joining process described above gets to completion only if at least a leaf node running ACI code is actively connected to that spine. This is usually not a concern, as in real life deployments there is no use for having a remote spine joining the Multi-Pod fabric if there are no active leaf nodes connected to it.

6. The other spine and leaf nodes in Pod2 would now go through the usual process used to join an ACI fabric. At the end of this process, all the devices that are part of Pod2 are up and running, and the pod is fully joined the Multi-Pod fabric.

7. It is now possible to connect an APIC node to the pod. After running its initial boot setup, the APIC node will be able to join the cluster with the node(s) already connected in Pod1. This step is optional because a pod could join and be part of the Multi-Pod fabric even without having an APIC node locally connected. It is also worth noting that all the APIC nodes get an IP address from the TEP pool associated with the "seed" pod (for example, the 10.1.0.0/16 IP subnet). This means that specific host routing information for those IP addresses must be exchanged through the IPN network to allow reachability between APIC nodes deployed across different pods.

APIC Cluster Deployment Considerations

The ACI Multi-Pod fabric brings some interesting considerations concerning the deployment of the APIC cluster managing the solutions. In order to understand better the implications of such model, it is useful to quickly review how the APIC cluster works in the regular single-pod scenario.

As shown in Figure 11-29, a concept known as *data sharding* is supported for data stored in the APIC in order to increase the scalability and resiliency of the deployment.

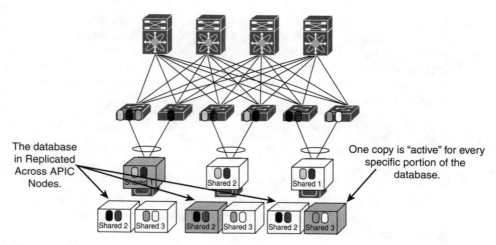

Figure 11-29 *Data Sharding Across APIC Nodes*

The basic idea behind sharding is that the data repository is split into several database units, known as *shards*. Data is placed in a shard, and that shard is then replicated three times, with each copy assigned to a specific APIC appliance. The distribution of shards across clusters of three and five nodes is shown in Figure 11-30.

Note To simplify the discussion, we can consider the example where all the configuration associated with a given tenant is contained in a "shard."

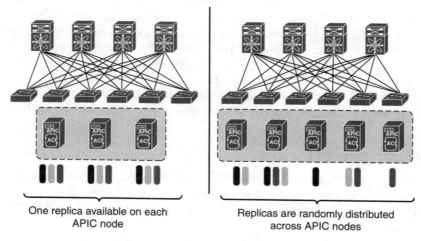

Figure 11-30 *Replicas Distribution Across APIC Nodes*

In the three-node APIC cluster deployment scenario, one replica for each shard is always available on every APIC node, but this is not the case when a five-node cluster is being deployed. This behavior implies that increasing the number of APIC nodes from three to five does not improve the overall resiliency of the cluster, but only allows support for a higher number of leaf nodes. In order to better understand this, let's consider what happens if two APIC nodes fail at the same time.

As shown on the left of Figure 11-31, the third APIC node still has a copy of all the shards. However, because it does not have the quorum anymore (it is the only surviving node of a cluster of three), all the shards are in read-only mode. This means that when an administrator connects to the remaining APIC node, no configuration changes can be applied, although the node can continue to serve read requests.

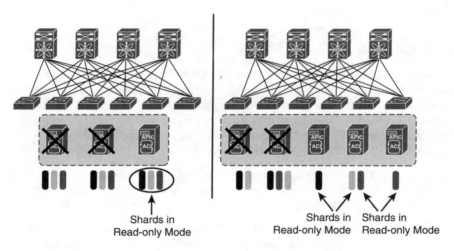

Figure 11-31 *APIC Nodes Failure Scenario*

On the right, the same dual-node failure scenario is displayed when deploying a five-node cluster. In this case, some shards on the remaining APIC nodes will be in read-only mode (that is, the green and orange shards in this example), whereas others will be in full read-write mode (the blue shards). This implies that connecting to one of the three remaining APIC nodes would lead to a nondeterministic behavior across shards, as configuration can be changed for the blue shard but not for the green-orange ones.

Let's now apply the aforementioned considerations to the specific Multi-Pod scenario where the APIC nodes are usually deployed in separate pods. The scenario that requires specific considerations is the one where two pods are part of the Multi-Pod fabric and represent geographically separated DC sites. In this case, two main failure scenarios should be considered:

■ A "split-brain" case where the connectivity between the pods is interrupted (see Figure 11-32).

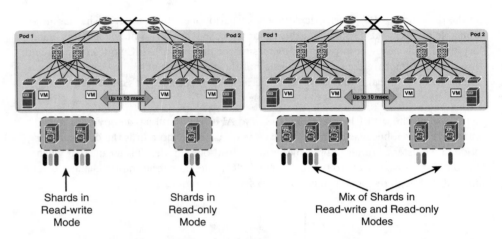

Figure 11-32 *Split-Brain Failure Scenario*

In a three-node cluster scenario, this implies that the shards on the APIC nodes in Pod1 would remain in full read-write mode, allowing a user connected there to make configuration changes. The shards in Pod2 are instead in read-only mode. For the five-node cluster, the same inconsistent behavior previously described (some shards are in read-write mode, some in read-only mode) would be experienced by a user connecting to the APIC nodes in Pod1 or Pod2.

However, once the connectivity issues are solved and the two Pods regain full connectivity, the APIC cluster would come back together, and any change made to the shards in majority mode would be applied to the rejoining APIC nodes as well.

■ The second failure scenario (see Figure 11-33) is one where an entire site goes down because of a disaster (flood, fire, earthquake, and so on). In this case, there is a significant behavioral difference between a three-node and five-node APIC cluster stretched across pods.

In a three-node APIC cluster deployment, the hard failure of Pod1 causes all the shards on the APIC node in Pod2 to go in read-only mode, similar to the left scenario in Figure 11-31. In this case, it is possible (and recommended) that you deploy a standby APIC node in Pod2 in order to promote it to active once Pod1 fails. This ensures the reestablishment of the quorum for the APIC (two nodes out of three would be clustered again).

The specific procedure required to bring up the standby node and have it join the cluster is identical to what is described for the ACI stretched fabric design option in the "Restrictions and Limitations" section of "Cisco ACI Stretched Fabric Design" (http://www.cisco.com/c/en/us/td/docs/switches/datacenter/aci/apic/sw/kb/b_kb-aci-stretched-fabric.html#concept_524263C54D8749F2AD248FAEBA7DAD78). Note that the same applies to the procedure for eventually recovering Pod1.

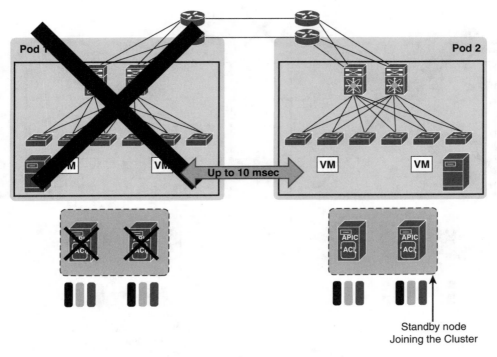

Standby node
Joining the Cluster

Figure 11-33 *Standby APIC Node Joining the Cluster*

It is important to reiterate the point that the standby node should be activated only when Pod1 is affected by a major downtime event. For temporary loss of connectivity between pods (for example, due to long-distance link failures when deploying pods over geographical distance), it is better to rely on the quorum behavior of the APIC cluster. The site with APIC nodes quorum would continue to function without problem, whereas the site with the APIC node in the minority would go into read-only mode. Once the interpod connection is resumed, the APIC database gets synchronized and all functions fully restart in both pods.

In a five-node APIC cluster deployment, the hard failure of the pod with three controllers would leave only two nodes connected to Pod2, as shown in Figure 11-34.

Similar considerations made for the three-node scenario can be applied also here, and the deployment of a standby APIC node in Pod2 would allow re-creating the quorum for the replicas of the shards available in Pod2. However, the main difference is that this failure scenario may lead to the loss of information for the shards that were replicated across the three failed nodes in Pod1 (like the green ones in the example in Figure 11-34).

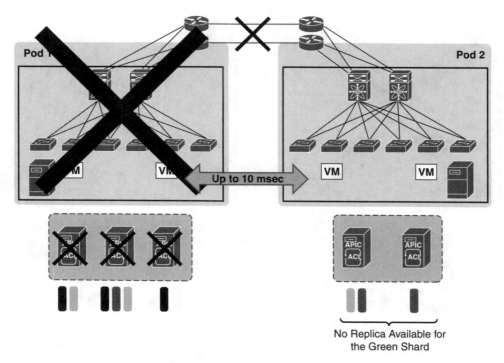

Figure 11-34 *Pod Failure Scenario with a Five-Node APIC Cluster*

A specific fabric-recovery procedure is offered starting with the 2.2 release to recover the lost shard information from a previously taken snapshot. It is mandatory to contact Cisco TAC or Advanced Services for assistance in performing such a procedure.

It is important to notice how this procedure is currently an "all-or-nothing" implementation: The full APIC cluster and fabric state are restored at time t1 based on the info of the snapshot taken at time t0, and this also applies to the shards whose information was still available in Pod2 (that is, the orange and blue shards in Figure 11-34). As a consequence, configuration changes (add/delete) for all the shards are lost for the [t0, t1] window, together with statistics, historical fault records, and audit records. Active faults are instead evaluated again once the APIC cluster is reactivated after the completion of the fabric-recovery procedure.

Note An alternative approach could be deploying four APIC nodes in Pod1 and one in Pod2. This would not protect against the loss of info of some shards after the hard failure of Pod1 (and the consequent need to execute the fabric-recovery procedure); however, it would allow keeping all the shards in full read-write mode in Pod1 when the two pods get isolated or after a hard failure of Pod2.

Based on the preceding considerations, the following recommendations can be made for deploying a two-site Multi-Pod fabric:

- When possible, deploy a three-node APIC cluster with two nodes in Pod1 and one node in Pod2. Add a backup APIC node in Pod2 to handle the "full site failure" scenario.

- If the scalability requirements force the deployment of a five-node cluster, whenever possible follow the guidelines depicted in Figure 11-35.

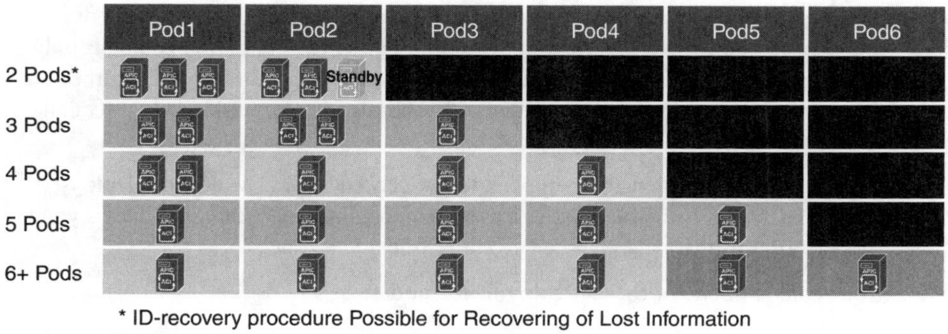

	Pod1	Pod2	Pod3	Pod4	Pod5	Pod6
2 Pods*	APIC APIC APIC	APIC APIC Standby				
3 Pods	APIC APIC	APIC APIC	APIC			
4 Pods	APIC APIC	APIC	APIC	APIC		
5 Pods	APIC	APIC	APIC	APIC	APIC	
6+ Pods	APIC	APIC	APIC	APIC	APIC	APIC

* ID-recovery procedure Possible for Recovering of Lost Information

Figure 11-35 *Deployment Guidance for a 5 Nodes APIC Cluster*

Two things can be immediately noticed when looking at the table in this figure: First, the basic rule of thumb is to avoid deploying three APIC nodes in the same pod, to prevent the potential loss of shard information previously discussed. This recommendation can be followed when deploying three or more pods.

Second, a pod can be part of the Multi-Pod fabric even without having a locally connected APIC cluster. This would be the case when deploying six (or more) pods leveraging a five-node APIC cluster or when deploying four (or more) pods with a three-node APIC cluster.

Reducing the Impact of Configuration Errors with Configuration Zones

The deployment of a single APIC cluster managing all the pods connected to the same ACI Multi-Pod fabric greatly simplifies the operational aspects of the fabric (providing a single point of management and policy definition). As a consequence, and similar to a single-pod ACI deployment, it is possible to make changes that apply to a very large number of leafs and ports, even belonging to separate pods. Although this is one of the great benefit of using ACI—because it makes it possible to manage a very large infrastructure with minimum configuration burden—it may also raises concerns that a specific configuration mistake that involves many ports may have an impact across all the deployed pods.

The first solution built in to the system to help reduce the chances of making such mistakes is a button labeled **Show Usage** that's provided next to each policy configuration. This provides system and infrastructure administrators with information about which elements are affected by the specific configuration change they are going to make.

In addition to this, a new functionality has been introduced in the APIC to limit the spreading of configuration changes only to a subset of the leaf nodes deployed in the fabric. This functionality calls for the creation of "configuration zones," where each zone includes a specific subset of leaf nodes connected to the ACI fabric.

Using configuration zones lets you test the configuration changes on that subset of leafs and servers before applying them to the entire fabric. Configuration zoning is only applied to changes made at the infrastructure level (that is, applied to policies in the "Infra" tenant). This is because a mistake in such a configuration would likely affect all the other tenants deployed on the fabric.

The concept of configuration zones applies very nicely to an ACI Multi-Pod deployment, where each pod could be deployed as a separate zone (the APIC GUI allows you to directly perform this mapping between an entire pod and a zone).

Each zone can be in one of these "deployment" modes:

■ **Disabled:** Any update to a node that's part of a disabled zone will be postponed until the zone deployment mode is changed or the node is removed from the zone.

■ **Enabled:** Any update to a node that's part of an enabled zone will be immediately sent. This is the default behavior. A node not part of any zone is equivalent to a node that's part of a zone set to **Enabled**.

Changes to the infrastructure policies are immediately applied to nodes that are members of a deployment mode–enabled zone. These same changes are queued for the nodes that are members of a zone with the deployment mode disabled.

You could then verify that the configurations are working well on the nodes of the zone with deployment mode enabled, and then change the deployment mode to "triggered" for the zones with deployment mode disabled in order for these changes to be applied on the leafs in this other zone.

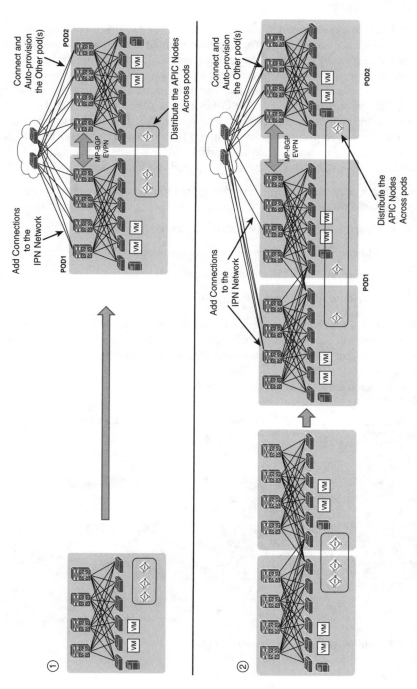

Figure 11-36 *Migration Scenarios: Adding Pods to an Existing ACI*

Migration Strategies

Multi-Pod and the capabilities it provides comprise a very exciting proposition for most customers. As such, many customers have questions about supported architecture and migrations strategies. At press time, the architectures we discuss in this chapter are not mutually exclusive, meaning that enterprises can take advantage of multiple architectures across the environment given that they are running supported configurations and meet the hardware and software requirements. For instance, a site may start as a single fabric. Later the enterprise may choose to expand this fabric into a Multi-Pod architecture by using the original fabric as a seed pod, as shown in Figure 11-36. In another scenario, an enterprise may have a stretch fabric implemented. The stretch fabric is also viewed as a single fabric, and can be used as a seed fabric to build a Multi-Pod solution, as shown in Figure 11-36.

At a very high level, the following steps are required to migrate from a single or stretch fabric to a Multi-Pod design:

Step 1. Bring up and configure IPN according to requirements.

Step 2. Add connections and configure the original pod to IPN.

Step 3. Connect and auto-provision additional pods.

Step 4. Distribute APIC nodes across pods.

Finally, additional capabilities such as ACI WAN integration (shown in Figure 11-37) and Multi-Site (shown in Figure 11-38) can be used, optionally, to provide scalability and path optimization or policy extensibility/consistency, respectively.

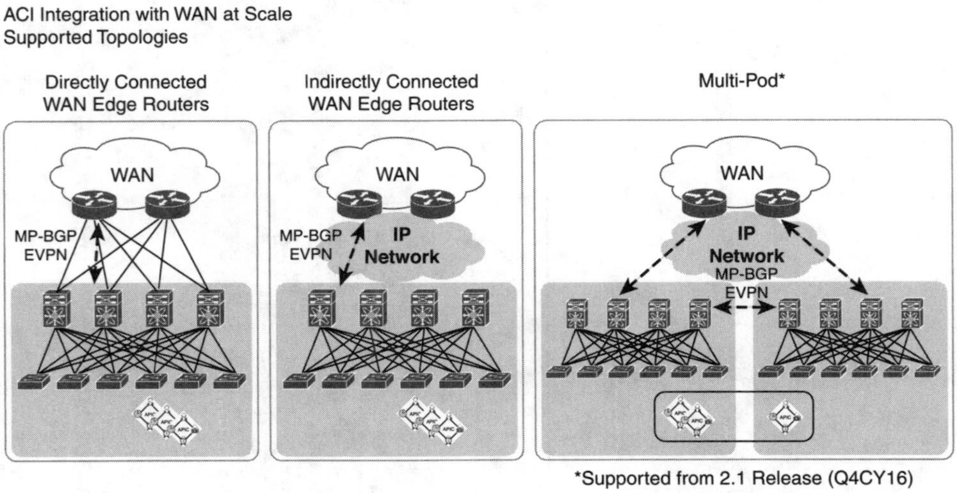

Figure 11-37   *Multi-Pod Integration with WAN*

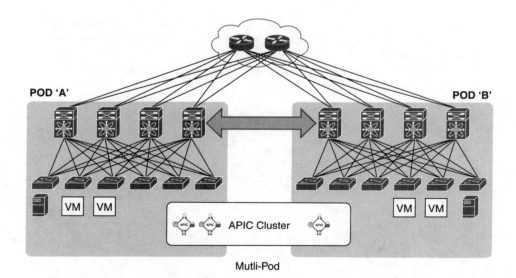

Figure 11-38 *Multi-Pod + Multi-Site*

Multi-Site Architecture

ACI Multi-Site is the easiest DCI solution in the industry. Communication between end-points in separate sites (Layer 2 and/or Layer 3) is enabled simply by creating and pushing a contract between the endpoints' EPGs. The evolution of the dual-fabric option, ACI Multi-Site, has been developed to overcome some of the challenges of the dual-fabric design (see Figure 11-39); for example, the need for policy extensibility and consistency across sites and the lack of a centralized tool for operating and troubleshooting the multiple interconnected fabrics.

ACI Multi-Site Solutions
Current Deployment Option–Multi-Fabric

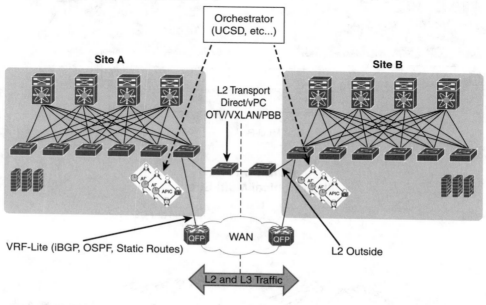

Figure 11-39   *Traditional Dual-Fabric Design*

With ACI Multi-Site, enterprises have the ability to manage multiple fabrics as regions or availability zones. With the addition of licensing and an ACI Multi-Site controller, enterprises have complete control over the following:

- Defining and provisioning policies across sites (scope of changes)

- Provisioning of Day 0 configuration to establish inter-site EVPN control plane

- Data-plane VXLAN encapsulation across sites

- End-to-end policy enforcement

- Multi-Site controllers distributing cross-fabric configuration to multiple APIC clusters

- Monitoring the health-state of the different ACI sites

- Inter-site troubleshooting (post–3.0 release)

Note   All ACI leaf switches (NS, -E, -EX, -FX) support Multi-Site functionality. However, the spine line cards *must* be an EX line card (second generation or newer) with a new FC-E fabric card. First-generation spines (including 9336PQ) are not supported.

The key component to the Multi-Site architecture is the Cisco ACI Multi-Site policy manager. It provides single- pane management, enabling you to monitor the health score state for all the interconnected sites. It also allows you to define, in a centralized place, all the inter-site policies that can then be pushed to the different APIC domains for rendering. It thus provides a high degree of control over when and where to push those policies, hence allowing the tenant change separation that uniquely characterizes the Cisco ACI Multi-Site architecture. Figure 11-40 shows the Multi-Site architecture with the Multi-Site policy manager.

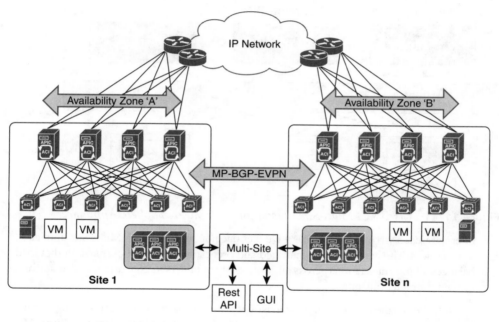

Figure 11-40   *Multi-Site Overview*

The Cisco ACI Multi-Site design uses the out-of-band (OOB) management network to connect to the APIC clusters deployed in different sites. Multi-Site has the capability to support network connections between sites with support for a round trip time of 500 msec to 1 second. It also provides northbound access through Representational State Transfer (REST) APIs or the GUI (HTTPS), which allows you to manage the full lifecycle of networking and tenant policies that need to be stretched across sites.

The Cisco ACI Multi-Site policy manager is not responsible for configuring Cisco ACI site-local polices. This task still remains the responsibility of the APIC cluster at each site.

The policy manager can import the relevant APIC cluster site-local policies and associate them with stretched objects. For example, it can import site-locally defined VMM domains and associate them with stretched EPGs.

The Cisco ACI Multi-Site design is based on a microservices architecture in which three virtual machines are clustered together in an active-active fashion. At the Muti-Site feature release, Multi-Site clusters are packaged in a VMware vSphere virtual appliance, as shown in Figure 11-41.

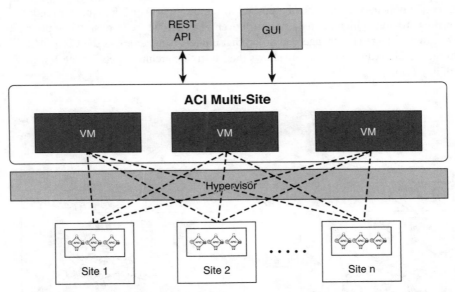

Figure 11-41   *Cisco ACI Multi-Site Cluster for the VMware vSphere Appliance*

Internally, each virtual machine has a Docker daemon installed with Multi-Site application services. Those services are managed and orchestrated by a Docker swarm that load-balances all job transactions across all Multi-Site containers in concurrent active-active fashion for high availability.

A stable data-plane connection must exist between the Cisco ACI Multi-Site cluster virtual machines when they are deployed over a WAN. The virtual machines in a Cisco ACI Multi-Site cluster communicate with each other over a TCP connection, so if any drops occur in the WAN, dropped packets will be retransmitted. Also, be sure to appropriately mark the Differentiated Services Code Point (DSCP) value of virtual machine traffic in a VMware port group. The recommended approach is to mark the DSCP as Expedited Forwarding (EF).

The recommended connection bandwidth between virtual machines in a Cisco ACI Multi-Site cluster is from 300Mbps to 1Gbps. These numbers are based on internal stress testing while adding very large configurations (over maximum scale numbers) and deleting them at high frequency.

APIC Versus Multi-Site Controller Functionalities

It is important to note the different roles that the APICs will play in the infrastructure versus the Multi-Site controller. In short, the Multi-Site controller does not replace the APIC. The APIC maintains its role as controller for a fabric. The Multi-Site controller is responsible for provisioning and managing inter-site tenant and networking policies. The Multi-Site controller then granularly propagates those policies to the multiple APIC clusters across the enterprise based on enterprise policy. Table 11-1 outlines the roles of the APIC and Multi-Site controller.

Table 11-1   *APIC Versus Multi-Site Controller Functionalities*

	APIC	**Multi-Site Controller**
Role/Function	Central point of management and configuration for the fabric. Responsible for all fabric-local functions such as the following: ■ Fabric discovery and bring up ■ Fabric access policies ■ Service graphs ■ Domain creation (VMM, physical, and so on)	Provisioning and managing of "inter-site tenant and networking policies." Does not replace but complements APIC.
Integrations with Other Devices	Integration with third-party services.	Can import and merge configuration from different APIC clusters.
Runtime Data	Maintain runtime data (VTEP address, VNID, Class_ID, GIPo, and so on).	No runtime data, only a configuration repository.
Data Plane/ Control Plane	No participation in the fabric data plane and control plane.	No participation in data plane and control plane.
Troubleshooting/ Visibility	Single-fabric or Multi-Pod visibility and troubleshooting.	End-to-end visibility and troubleshooting.
Scope of Changes	Within a Multi-Pod or single fabric.	Granularity to propagate policies to multiple APIC clusters.

Now that we are familiar with the Multi-Site cluster and what its role is, the following is a list of best practices for deploying a Multi-Site cluster:

■ Connect the Multi-Site cluster to the APICs using the OOB management network.

■ The Multi-Site cluster should never be deployed within a Cisco ACI fabric that it is managing as a site. It should always be deployed outside the Cisco ACI fabric (for example, connected to the OOB network). Otherwise, double failures can occur if the Multi-Site cluster fails or the Cisco ACI fabric fails.

■ Each Multi-Site virtual machine should have a routable IP address, and all three virtual machines must be able to ping each other. This setup is required to form a Docker swarm cluster.

> **Note**   For more information on Docker, see the following link: https://www.docker.com/.

■ Deploy one Multi-Site virtual machine per ESXi host for high availability. The virtual machines will form a cluster among themselves through a Docker swarm.

■ The maximum RTT between the virtual machines in a cluster should be less than 150 ms.

■ The maximum distance from a Multi-Site cluster to a Cisco ACI fabric site can be up to 1 second RTT.

■ A Multi-Site cluster uses the following ports for the internal control plane and data plane, so the underlay network should always ensure that these ports are open (in the case of an ACL configuration of a firewall deployment in the network):

   ■ TCP port 2377 for cluster management communication

   ■ TCP and UDP port 7946 for communication among nodes

   ■ UDP port 4789 for overlay network traffic

   ■ TCP port 443 for Multi-Site policy manager user interface (UI)

   ■ IP 50 Encapsulating Security Protocol (ESP) for encryption

■ IPSec is used to encrypt all intra-Multi-Site cluster control-plane and data-plane traffic to provide security because the virtual machines can be placed up to 150 ms RTT apart.

■ The minimum specifications for Multi-Site virtual machines are ESXi 5.5 or later, four vCPUs, 8GB of RAM, and a 5GB disk.

> **Note**   At press time, Multi-Site scalability numbers are eight sites, 100 leaf nodes per site, 2000 BDs, 2000 EPGs, and 2000 contracts. These numbers will increase with future software versions.

Multi-Site Schema and Templates

The Multi-Site controller essentially becomes the controller of controllers in regard to managing policy across your Multi-Site environment. To manage these policies in a hierarchical manner, a new policy type called a schema was added to the object model. Schemas are the containers for single or multiple templates that are used for defining policies. Templates are the framework for defining and deploying the policies to the sites in a Multi-Site configuration. Figure 11-42 depicts this new policy model.

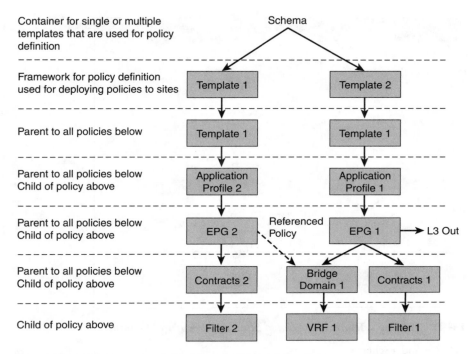

Figure 11-42 *Framework for Cisco ACI Multi-Site Schema and Templates*

Assuming the Multi-Site design is already up and running, an enterprise need only start creating policies and associating them with sites. In-depth step-by-step information on how to do this can be found in the white paper titled "Modeling an Application with Cisco ACI Multi-Site Policy Manager" on the Cisco site (https://www.cisco.com/c/dam/en/us/solutions/collateral/data-center-virtualization/application-centric-infrastructure/white-paper-c11-739481.pdf).

A high-level overview of the steps for configuring a Multi-Site policy using the Multi-Site controller is provided here to give you an idea of the workflow. The steps are as follows:

Step 1.   Create a tenant.

Step 2.   Associate the tenant with one or more sites and specify the security domain (this controls the objects a user can access or interact with).

Figure 11-43 shows the first two steps.

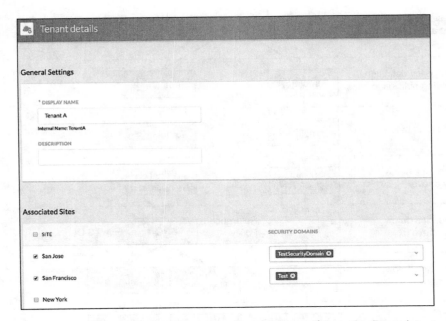

Figure 11-43 *Adding a Tenant, Associated Sites, and Security Domains*

Step 3. Add a schema.

Step 4. Create or rename the default template.

Step 5. Associate the template with a tenant.

Figure 11-44 shows steps 4 and 5.

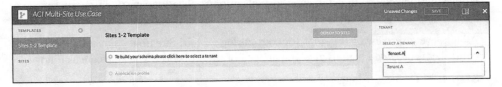

Figure 11-44 *Associating a Template with a Tenant*

Step 6. Associate the template to sites where it should be deployed (as shown in Figure 11-45).

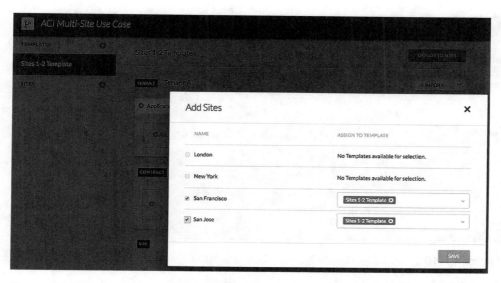

Figure 11-45   *Associating the Template with Sites*

Step 7.   Create an application profile.

Step 8.   Create EPGs.

Step 9.   Associate the EPGs with a domain.

Step 10.   Define bridge domains and the following options (as shown in Figure 11-46):

- **L2 STRETCH:** This flag indicates that the bridge domain should be stretched across both sites, which implies that the associated IP subnet 10.10.1.0/24 will also be available in the two sites.

- **INTERSITE BUM TRAFFIC ALLOW:** This flag indicates that flooding is enabled across the sites for Layer 2 broadcast, unknown unicast, and multicast frames. This capability is required, for example, to allow live migration of endpoints and to deploy inter-site application clusters. If this flag was not set, the same bridge domain and associated IP subnet would still be deployed at the two sites (because the bridge domain is stretched), but the deployment could handle only inter-site "cold" IP mobility scenarios (for example, for disaster-recovery use cases).

- **OPTIMIZE WAN BANDWIDTH:** This flag helps ensure association of a unique multicast group with this bridge domain. This feature optimizes the utilization of WAN bandwidth because it prevents flooding across a site's broadcast, unknown unicast, and multicast frames that define a subnet for BDs that are stretched across sites. If a BD is not stretched, configure it as "site local" by clicking the site and then configuring the BD.

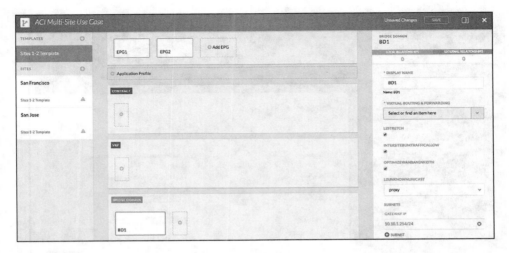

Figure 11-46 *Multi-Site Bridge Domain Configuration*

Step 11. Define a VRF.

Step 12. Create a contract with the appropriate filters and with EPGs selected as consumers and providers, as shown in Figure 11-47.

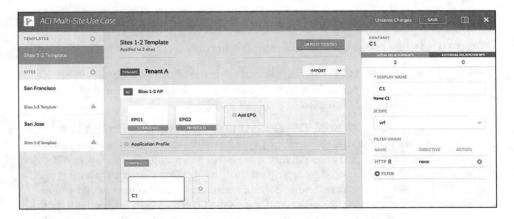

Figure 11-47 *Multisite Contract Configuration*

Step 13. Deploy the template to sites, as shown in Figure 11-48.

Now that we have examined Multi-Site schemas and templates, we will discuss individual use cases in the following section.

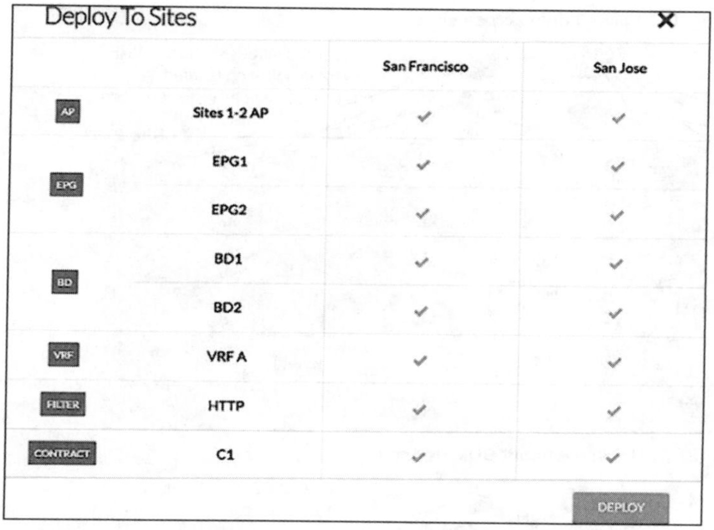

Figure 11-48 *Deploy the Template to Sites*

Multi-Site Use Cases

Multi-Site will have the capabilities to address the following three main use cases, as illustrated in Figure 11-49:

1. L3 connectivity between sites and centralized management of policy

2. IP mobility for disaster recovery (for example, "cold" VM migration)

3. Highly scalable active-active DCs (for example, "hot" VM migration)

In the sections that follow, we will explore each Multi-Site option and the use cases it supports.

Stretched Bridge Domain with Layer 2 Broadcast Extension (Option 3)

This is the most sought-after data center and Cisco ACI Multi-Site use case (active-active data centers), in which a tenant and VRF are stretched between sites. The EPGs in the VRF (with their bridge domains and subnets), as well as their provider and consumer contracts, are also stretched between sites.

In this use case, Layer 2 broadcast flooding is enabled across fabrics. Unknown unicast traffic is forwarded across sites leveraging the Head-End Replication (HER) capabilities of the spine nodes that replicate and send the frames to each remote fabric where the Layer 2 BD has been stretched, as illustrated in Figure 11-50.

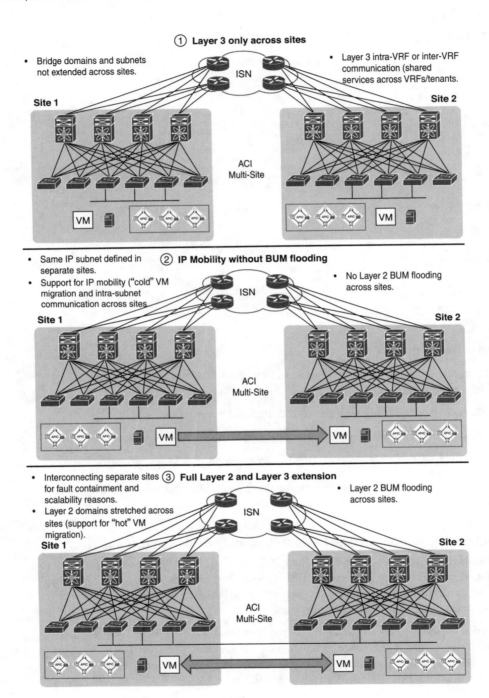

Figure 11-49 *Multi-Site Use Cases*

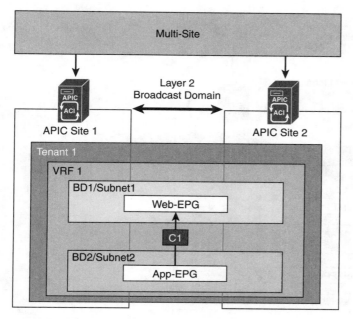

Figure 11-50 *Stretched Bridge Domain with Layer 2 Broadcast Extension*

The specific use cases this design addresses are as follows:

■ The same application hierarchy is deployed on all sites with common policies. This allows for seamlessly deploying workloads belonging to the various EPGs across different fabrics and governing their communication with common and consistent policies.

■ Layer 2 clustering.

■ Live VM migration.

■ Active-active high availability between the sites.

■ Using service graphs to push shared applications between sites is not supported.

Stretched Bridge Domain with No Layer 2 Broadcast Extension (Option 2)

This Cisco ACI Multi-Site use case (active-passive/disaster recovery) is similar to the first use case where a tenant, VRF, and their EPGs (with their bridge domains and subnets) are stretched between sites, as shown in Figure 11-51.

However, in this case, Layer 2 broadcast flooding is localized at each site. Layer 2 broadcast, unknown unicast, and multicast (BUM) traffic is not forwarded across sites over replicated VXLAN tunnels.

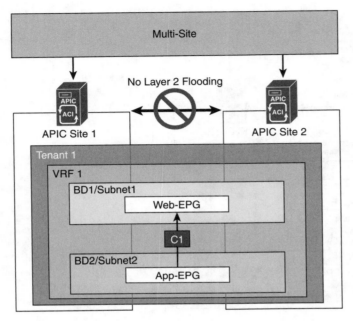

Figure 11-51 *Stretched Bridge Domain with No Layer 2 Broadcast Extension*

Here are the specific use cases this design addresses:

■ Control plane overhead is reduced by keeping Layer 2 flooding local.

■ Inter-site IP mobility for disaster recovery.

■ "Cold" VM migration.

■ Using service graphs to push shared applications between sites is not supported.

Stretched EPG Across Sites (Option 1.1)

This Cisco ACI Multi-Site use case provides endpoint groups (EPGs) stretched across multiple sites. Stretched EPG is defined as an endpoint group that expands across multiple sites where the underlying networking, site local, and bridge domain can be distinct, as shown in Figure 11-52.

This use case allows Layer 3 forwarding to be used among all sites.

Stretched VRF with Inter-Site Contracts (Option 1.2)

This Multi-Site use case provides inter-site communication between endpoints connected to different bridge domains (BDs) that are part of the same stretched VRF, as illustrated in Figure 11-53. VRF stretching is a convenient way to manage EPGs across sites (and the contracts between them).

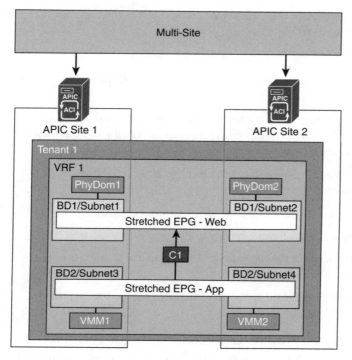

Figure 11-52 *Stretched EPG Across Sites*

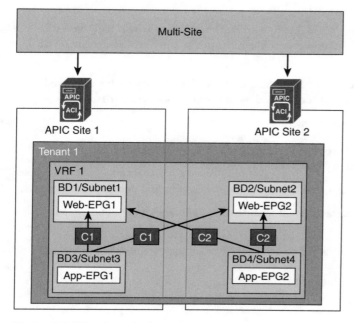

Figure 11-53 *Stretched VRF with Inter-Site Contracts*

In this figure, the App-EPGs provide the C1 and C2 contracts across the sites, and the Web-EPGs consume them across the sites.

This use case has the following benefits:

- The tenant and VRF are stretched across sites, but EPGs and their policies (including subnets) are locally defined.

- Because the VRF is stretched between sites, contracts govern cross-site communication between the EPGs. Contracts can be consistently provided and consumed within a site or across sites.

- Traffic is routed within and between sites (with local subnets) and static routing between sites is supported.

- Separate profiles are used to define and push local and stretched objects.

- No Layer 2 stretching and local Layer 2 broadcast domains.

- "Cold" VM migration, without the capability of preserving the IP address of the migrated endpoints.

- Using service graphs to push shared applications between sites is not supported.

Shared Services with Stretched Provider EPG

In this use case, the Provider EPGs in one group of sites offer shared services, and the EPGs in another group of sites consume the services. All sites have local EPGs and bridge domains, as illustrated in Figure 11-54.

As Figure 11-54 shows, Site 4 and Site 5 (with BigData-EPG, in Tenant BigData/VRF BigData) provide shared data services, and the EPGs in Site 1 to Site 3 (in Tenant 1/VRF 1) consume the services.

In the shared services use case of Multi-Site, at the VRF boundary routes are leaked between VRFs for routing connectivity and by importing contracts across sites.

This use case has the following benefits:

- Shared services enable communications across VRFs and tenants while preserving the isolation and security policies of the tenants.

- A shared service is supported only with non-overlapping and non-duplicate subnets.

- Each group of sites has a different tenant, VRF, and one or more EPGs stretched across it.

- Site groups can be configured to use Layer 2 broadcast extensions or to localize Layer 2 flooding.

- Stretched EPGs share the same bridge domain, but the EPGs have subnets that are configured under the EPG, not under the bridge domain.

- The provider contract must be set to global scope.

- VRF route leaking enables communication across the VRFs.

- Using service graphs to push shared applications between sites is not supported.

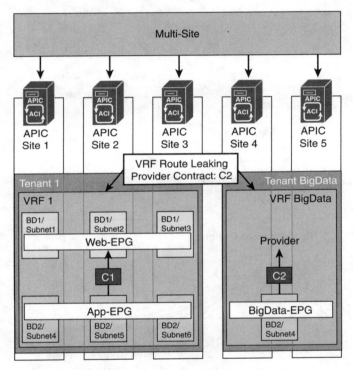

Figure 11-54 *Shared Services with Stretched Provider EPG*

Multi-Site and L3 Out Considerations

Similar to a single-fabric deployment, ACI Multi-Site can connect to an external Layer 3 domain with both traditional L3 Out connections defined on the border leaf nodes and EVPN WAN integration. At press time, the only supported configuration for endpoints wishing to communicate with external networks over a Layer 3 outbound domain is via a L3 Out that is local to the fabric the endpoint is connected to, as shown in Figure 11-55.

Supported Design

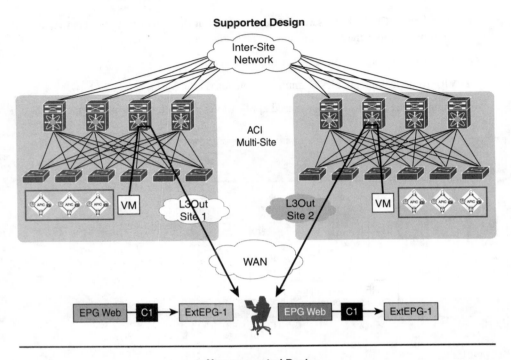

Non-supported Design

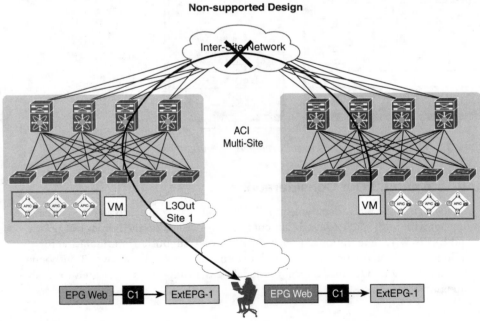

Figure 11-55 *Supported and Non-supported Uses of L3 Out in a Multi-Site Deployment*

Note   This requirement applies to both traditional L3 Out configurations and WAN integration.

In this design, traffic has the opportunity to enter the fabric at Site 1 and be sent to a resource at Site 2, where it is required to exit locally. If this traffic will pass through a firewall, it will normally be dropped due to its stateful nature. Enterprises need to pay attention to the creation of asymmetric traffic paths when stateful devices are being used in their deployment. Finally, as you'll remember from earlier chapters, some devices connect and share information with the fabric over a L3 Out connection. Enterprises need to consider if network devices (mainframe, voice gateways, and so on) are connected to the ACI fabric via L3 Out instances that must be accessible across sites. These devices may have to be deployed in a more distributed manner for the traffic to be able to use a local L3 Out to communicate with them.

Layer 3 Multicast Deployment Options

Earlier chapters examined the multicast support options for non-Multi-Site designs. At press time, there is currently no support for native Layer 3 multicast with ACI Multi-Site. The currently supported options, depicted in Figure 11-56, are as follows:

- Source(s) and receiver(s) part of non-stretched BDs and connected to the same site (top left)

- Source(s) part of a non-stretched BD and receiver(s) outside the fabric (bottom left)

- Source(s) outside the fabric and receiver(s) connected to a non-stretched BD (right side)

Note   Layer 3 multicast configuration is performed at the local APIC level and not on the ACI Multi-Site policy manager.

It is also worth noting, as shown in Figure 11-57, that the source(s) in Site 1 cannot send an L3 multicast stream to receiver(s) in a remote site. This is planned to be supported in a later release.

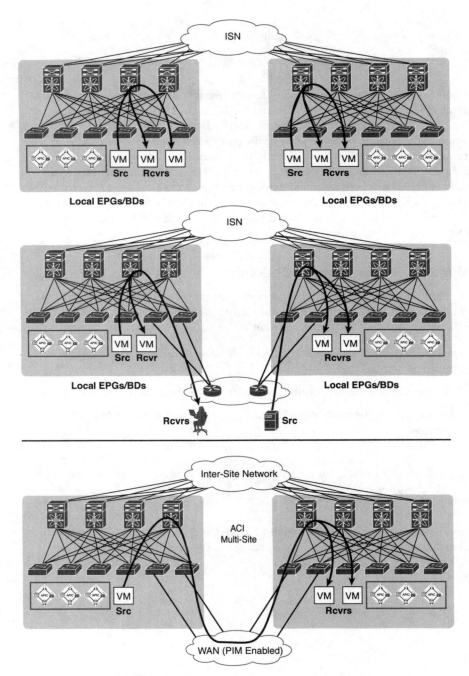

Figure 11-56 *Supported Multicast Designs with Multi-Site*

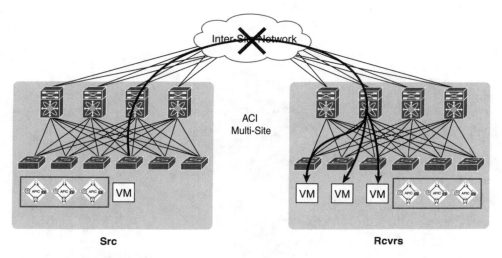

Figure 11-57   *Unsupported Multi-Site Design with Multicast*

Migration of Cisco ACI Fabric to Cisco ACI Multi-Site

In this section, we will explore a common Cisco ACI Multi-Site use case in which a tenant is migrated to or imported from Cisco ACI fabric to Cisco ACI Multi-Site.

This use case is targeted for brownfield-to-greenfield and greenfield-to-greenfield types of deployments. The brownfield-to-brownfield use case is only supported in this release if both Cisco APIC sites are deployed with the same configuration. Other brownfield-to-brownfield use cases will be deployed in a future Cisco ACI Multi-Site release.

The top two examples shown in Figure 11-58 for brownfield configurations reflect two scenarios that are considered for deployments:

■ A single pod ACI fabric is in place already. You can add another site in a Multi-Site configuration.

■ Two ACI fabrics are in place already (each fabric is configured as a single pod), the objects (tenants, VRFs, and EPGs) across sites are initially defined with identical names and policies, and they are connected by leveraging a traditional L2/L3 DCI solution. You can convert this configuration to Multi-Site as explained in the following configuration diagram.

Note   Cisco ACI Multi-Pod migration to Cisco ACI Multi-Site shown as the third option in Figure 11-58 will be supported in a future Cisco ACI Multi-Site release.

Figure 11-58 illustrates the enterprise migration path from existing architectures to Multi-Site architectures.

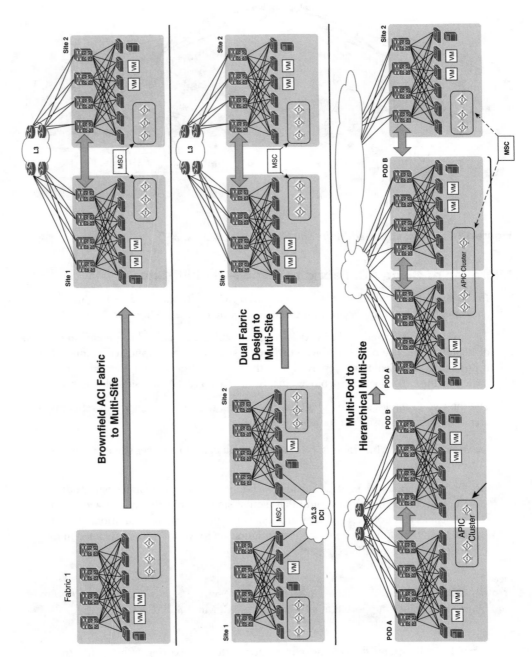

Figure 11-58 *Migration Paths*

Summary

Enterprises can be confident that ACI has an architecture that meets their business requirements and data center needs. ACI started with a single fabric with version 1.0. With version 1.1, ACI had the ability to create geographically stretched single fabrics. To address the concerns about extending a single network fault domain across the entire stretched-fabric topology, Cisco ACI Release 2.0 introduced the Cisco ACI Multi-Pod architecture. The need for complete isolation (at both the network and tenant change domain levels) across separate Cisco ACI networks led to the Cisco ACI Multi-Site architecture, introduced in Cisco ACI Release 3.0.

No matter which design you choose, you will find that ACI is the easiest-to-deploy, the most secure, and the most operationally efficient data center fabric there is, regardless of what type of workloads you support—virtual or physical.

Chapter 12

Troubleshooting and Monitoring

In this chapter, you will learn the following:

■ Use of the Cisco ACI graphical user interface (GUI) and command-line interface (CLI) in order to troubleshoot frequent issues, such as connectivity problems and access control lists (ACLs)

■ New troubleshooting tools available in Cisco ACI that did not exist previously, such as atomic counters, the Endpoint Tracker, and the Traffic Map

■ Improved ways of leveraging existing technologies such as Switched Port Analyzer (SPAN) and traffic counters

■ How to use the Troubleshooting Wizard in Cisco ACI

■ Integration between Cisco ACI and network monitoring tools using both the Simple Network Management Protocol (SNMP) and the REST API

Designing and implementing a solid network are a big part of the job of a network administrator; however, after you build the network, it needs to be monitored, and eventual problems need to be fixed as quickly as possible. The more robust a network is, the fewer problems that appear later. Cisco ACI takes care of part of that job by incorporating state-of-the-art designs and technologies that reduce and minimize problems. Here are some examples:

■ An IP-based fabric is much more robust and flexible than networks that rely on Spanning Tree.

■ ACI by default preserves network resources, deploying network constructs only where required.

■ The spine-leaf architecture can be easily scaled in case bottlenecks are identified.

Nevertheless, problems will appear sooner or later, no matter how robust the network design may be. Previous chapters have described how those problems can be easily identified in the GUI, along with their tenant and application impact, using ACI's integrated health scores and other methods. This chapter focuses on how to monitor the network and how to troubleshoot existing problems once they have been identified.

You Have a Poor Health Score. Now What?

Chapter 7, "How Life Is Different with ACI," described how the different options in Cisco ACI provide a quick view of the state of the network—either of the logical objects (viewed via dashboards) or of the physical ones (shown in the **Fabric** tab of the GUI). Hopefully everything is at 100% health, but eventually problems will arise and some health score will go down.

The standard way in which you observe that the network is not behaving properly is by realizing (or getting alerted) that a certain health score has dropped below 100%. As previous chapters have shown, this approach is more effective than traditional network monitoring, because it immediately provides information about the criticality of the network issue, in terms of which tenant and application are impacted.

Obviously, as described in Chapter 9, "Multi-Tenancy," the more granular your tenant and application structure is, the more accurately the health scores will describe the impact of a certain fault. For example, if you have all your network objects and endpoint groups (EPGs) under the common tenant, the fact that this tenant's health goes down will not tell you a lot about the impacted objects. However, if you have structured your network objects in multiple tenants and applications (as Chapter 9 describes with the example of a tenant for a vSphere infrastructure), Cisco ACI dashboards will show you exactly which tenant is impacted in case of a network outage. This is extremely useful when you're prioritizing troubleshooting activities because the network operators will have the required information needed to focus on the issue impacting the most critical applications.

Another area of the GUI you want to be checking on regularly is the overall Faults panel. As described in Chapter 7, you can see the whole list of issues present in your network in the Faults panel, so it is a very good place to start when troubleshooting a problem. If you consult this view, as shown as example in Figure 12-1, you can quickly verify the overall status of the network, and whether there are any critical faults that might be impacting the proper functioning of the fabric. Actually, it is good practice to check the Faults panel every now and then, especially after performing configurations.

Figure 12-1   *Cisco ACI Faults Panel Showing the Existing Faults in a Fabric*

NX-OS CLI

Network administrators have traditionally relied heavily on the command-line interface (CLI) of network devices for troubleshooting. Although most information is available in the GUI, Cisco ACI offers a CLI for those specialists who prefer it. Whether administrators use the text-based command line or the GUI depends on personal preference, as most information is available both ways.

Cisco ACI's command line shares similarities with other Cisco networking products, including the overall look and feel and most commands. However, at the same time, it is in some aspects different. The main difference is that Cisco ACI's CLI is centralized— network professionals no longer need to connect to every single device in order to extract information out of the network.

The CLI is accessed on the Application Policy Infrastructure Controller (APIC)—an SSH session needs to be established to the APIC's IP address, and the familiar Cisco CLI prompt will be available. Once you connect to the APIC, you can gather interesting information from a central CLI, without having to open multiple SSH windows (as was the case in legacy, device-centric networks).

For example, you might want to find out information about a certain endpoint. This is where the **show endpoints** command comes into play, where you can see details such as its IP address, its MAC address, the switch and port where it is connected, and to which tenant, application, and EPG it belongs, as demonstrated in Example 12-1 (note that your output might be different because the following examples have been modified so that they fit the page's width).

Gone are the days when network administrators need to open multiple windows just to find out where a certain server is connected or to troubleshoot network issues.

You can verify the object model or the health scores for different objects as demonstrated in Example 12-2, which shows how to get the health of a tenant, even if that tenant is physically deployed across multiple switches.

Example 12-1   *Finding Out Where a Specific Host Is Attached to the Fabric*

```
apic# show endpoints ip 192.168.20.11
Dynamic Endpoints:
Tenant      : Pod2
Application : Pod2
AEPg        : EPG1
 End Point MAC     IP Address               Node   Interface       Encap
----------------- ------------------------ ------ --------------- --------
00:50:56:AC:D1:71 192.168.20.11            202    eth102/1/1      vlan-12
Total Dynamic Endpoints: 1
Total Static Endpoints: 0
apic#
```

Example 12-2   *Verifying Tenants' Health Scores*

```
apic# show health tenant
 Score  Change(%)  UpdateTS            Dn
 -----  -----      ------------------- -----------------------------
 100    0          2016-09-19T15:09:29 uni/tn-common/health
                   .324+02:00
 100    0          2016-09-19T15:09:29 uni/tn-SiriusCyber/health
                   .328+02:00
 100    0          2016-09-19T15:09:29 uni/tn-VMware/health
                   .319+02:00
 100    0          2016-09-19T15:01:39 uni/tn-CONTIV-default/health
                   .210+02:00
 99     0          2016-09-19T15:09:29 uni/tn-infra/health
                   .324+02:00
 100    0          2016-09-19T15:10:05 uni/tn-Docker/health
                   .365+02:00
 100    0          2016-09-19T15:09:29 uni/tn-LeisureMech3/health
                   .327+02:00
 100    0          2016-09-19T15:09:29 uni/tn-Pod1/health
                   .326+02:00
 100    0          2016-09-19T15:10:05 uni/tn-ASA_admin/health
                   .366+02:00
```

Chapter 13, "ACI Programmability," explains in more detail the structure and naming conventions of the internal objects in Cisco ACI. For the sake of understanding this example, you need to know that ACI objects get an internal name that is prefixed with a string denoting the class to which those objects belong. For example, the tenant "common" is actually called "tn-common" internally, because the prefix "tn-" means that this object is a tenant. Chapter 13 explains how to find out the string prefix that identifies each object class. For the rest of this chapter, though, you can safely ignore those prefixes.

You can even have a look at the complete configuration, as you would do with any NX-OS switch, using the **show running-configuration** command. As in NX-OS, you can have a look at the full running configuration, or just at a part of it, such as the configuration corresponding to a specific tenant, as demonstrated in Example 12-3.

Example 12-3   *Displaying a Tenant's Configuration*

```
apic# show running-config tenant Pod1
# Command: show running-config tenant Pod1
# Time: Mon Sep 19 15:13:12 2016
  tenant Pod1
    access-list Telnet
      match raw telnet dFromPort 23 dToPort 23 etherT ip prot 6 stateful yes
      exit
    contract EPG1-services
      scope exportable
      export to tenant Pod2 as Pod1-EPG1
      subject EPG1-services
        access-group default both
        exit
      exit
    contract EPG2-services
      subject EPG2-services
        access-group Telnet both
        access-group icmp both log
        exit
      exit
    vrf context Pod1-PN
      exit
    l3out ACI-ISR
      vrf member Pod1-PN
      exit
    bridge-domain Pod1-BD
      vrf member Pod1-PN
      exit
    application Pod1
      epg EPG1
        bridge-domain member Pod1-BD
        contract consumer EPG2-services
        contract provider EPG1-services
        vmware-domain member ACI-vCenter-VDS deploy immediate
          exit
```

```
      exit
   epg EPG2
      bridge-domain member Pod1-BD
      contract provider EPG2-services
      exit
   exit
external-l3 epg Pod1-L3-NW l3out ACI-ISR
   vrf member Pod1-PN
   match ip 0.0.0.0/0
   contract consumer EPG1-services
```

The Cisco ACI CLI offers some interesting ACI-specific tools. One of these tools is the **acidiag** command, which is demonstrated in Example 12-4. This tool can be used for very specific troubleshooting purposes but is outside the scope of this book. One of its most interesting aspects is that it can generate a token with which Cisco Technical Assistance Center (TAC) produces a root password used for logging in to an APIC as the root user. Needless to say, this is not an operation you would perform every day, but probably something that Cisco specialists would help you with in case your ACI environment has some kind of trouble.

Example 12-4 acidiag *Command Output*

```
apic# acidiag
usage: acidiag [-h] [-v]
{preservelogs,bootother,rvreadle,avread,touch,installer,start,crashsuspecttracker,
   reboot,dmestack,platform,version,verifyapic,run,stop,dmecore,fnvread,restart,
   bootcurr,bond0test,rvread,fnvreadex,validateimage,validatenginxconf,linkflap,
   dbgtoken}
              . . .
apic# acidiag dbgtoken
OWDHFZPPDSQZ
```

There are many other examples of useful CLI commands in Cisco ACI, but we will stop with **acidiag** because the main purpose of this section isn't to list Cisco ACI commands but to describe its main architectural difference as compared to legacy networks.

Connecting to the Leaf Switches

If you want to run certain commands in one or more leaf switches, you can do so from the ACI CLI, instead of connecting to each individual leaf. You do this by prefixing the command with the word **fabric** and then the leaf or leaf switches where you want to run it.

For example, if you want to have a look at the traffic counters on the port where the server mentioned in the preceding examples is connected, you could use the command **show interface** prefixed by **fabric 202** (because, as you saw, the server is connected to leaf 202), as demonstrated in Example 12-5.

Example 12-5 *Displaying Traffic Counters on a Specific Port from the ACI Centralized CLI*

```
apic# fabric 202 show interface ethernet 102/1/1
------------------------------------------------------------------
 Node 202 (Leaf202)
------------------------------------------------------------------
Ethernet102/1/1 is up
admin state is up, Dedicated Interface
  Port description is ESX-01
  Hardware: 100/1000/auto Ethernet, address: f029.296a.5682 (bia f029.296a.5682)
  MTU 9000 bytes, BW 1000000 Kbit, DLY 1 usec
  reliability 255/255, txload 1/255, rxload 1/255
  Encapsulation ARPA, medium is broadcast
  Port mode is trunk
  full-duplex, 1000 Mb/s
  FEC (forward-error-correction) : disable-fec
  Beacon is turned off
  Auto-Negotiation is turned off
  Input flow-control is off, output flow-control is off
  Auto-mdix is turned off
  Switchport monitor is off
  EtherType is 0x8100
  EEE (efficient-ethernet) : n/a
  Last link flapped 10w75d
  Last clearing of "show interface" counters 10w75d
  1 interface resets
  30 seconds input rate 3792 bits/sec, 6 packets/sec
  30 seconds output rate 6800 bits/sec, 11 packets/sec
  Load-Interval #2: 5 minute (300 seconds)
    input rate 3792 bps, 5 pps; output rate 7160 bps, 12 pps
  RX
    4360376993 unicast packets  108340 multicast packets  13000840 broadcast packets
    4373486173 input packets  10439463704 bytes
    2084 jumbo packets  0 storm suppression bytes
    0 runts  2084 giants  0 CRC  0 no buffer
    0 input error  0 short frame  0 overrun  0 underrun  0 ignored
    0 watchdog  0 bad etype drop  0 bad proto drop  0 if down drop
    0 input with dribble  0 input discard
    0 Rx pause
  TX
    4328569988 unicast packets  4505014 multicast packets  75985490 broadcast packets
    4409060492 output packets  13099256068 bytes
    507 jumbo packets
    0 output error  0 collision  0 deferred  0 late collision
    0 lost carrier  0 no carrier  0 babble  0 output discard
    0 Tx pause
```

Alternatively, you could verify which interfaces exist in the leaf altogether with the command **show ip interface brief**, as demonstrated in Example 12-6. Just remember that ACI is a multi-VRF network, so you need to specify which VRF you are interested in (or just ask for all of them).

Example 12-6   *Verifying IP Addresses Configured in a Leaf from the ACI Centralized CLI*

```
apic# fabric 203 show ip int brief vrf all
----------------------------------------------------------------
 Node 203 (Leaf203)
----------------------------------------------------------------
IP Interface Status for VRF "overlay-1"(12)
Interface            Address              Interface Status
eth1/49              unassigned           protocol-up/link-up/admin-up
eth1/49.1            unnumbered           protocol-up/link-up/admin-up
                     (lo0)
eth1/50              unassigned           protocol-down/link-down/admin-up
eth1/51              unassigned           protocol-down/link-down/admin-up
eth1/52              unassigned           protocol-down/link-down/admin-up
eth1/53              unassigned           protocol-down/link-down/admin-up
eth1/54              unassigned           protocol-down/link-down/admin-up
vlan11               10.0.0.30/27         protocol-up/link-up/admin-up
lo0                  10.0.96.64/32        protocol-up/link-up/admin-up
lo1023               10.0.0.32/32         protocol-up/link-up/admin-up
IP Interface Status for VRF "black-hole"(3)
Interface            Address              Interface Status
IP Interface Status for VRF "management"(2)
Interface            Address              Interface Status
mgmt0                192.168.0.53/24      protocol-up/link-up/admin-up
IP Interface Status for VRF "SiriusCyber:Sirius-external"(4)
Interface            Address              Interface Status
vlan6                192.168.7.25/29      protocol-up/link-up/admin-up
lo3                  192.168.7.204/32     protocol-up/link-up/admin-up
```

The CLI local to every leaf is very similar to standard NX-OS. As the previous example demonstrates, you can run local leaf commands directly from the APIC with the **fabric** prefix, or you can connect to an individual leaf using the **ssh** command in the APIC CLI, followed by the name or the number of the leaf to which you want to connect. The password is the same as for the APIC. If you don't remember the name of a certain leaf, you can easily have a look at the switch names with **show version**, as demonstrated in Example 12-7.

Example 12-7   *Displaying Versioning Information for All ACI Components*

```
apic# show version
  Role        Id          Name                      Version
  ----------  ----------  ------------------------  --------------------
  controller  1           apic                      2.0(1m)
  leaf        201         Leaf201                   n9000-12.0(1m)
  leaf        202         Leaf202                   n9000-12.0(1m)
  leaf        203         Leaf203                   n9000-12.0(1m)
  spine       301         Spine301                  n9000-12.0(1m)
apic# ssh Leaf201
Password:
Last login: Tue Sep 13 14:50:24 2016 from 192.168.0.50
Cisco Nexus Operating System (NX-OS) Software
TAC support: http://www.cisco.com/tac
Copyright (c) 2002-2016, Cisco Systems, Inc. All rights reserved.
The copyrights to certain works contained in this software are
owned by other third parties and used and distributed under
license. Certain components of this software are licensed under
the GNU General Public License (GPL) version 2.0 or the GNU
Lesser General Public License (LGPL) Version 2.1. A copy of each
such license is available at
http://www.opensource.org/licenses/gpl-2.0.php and
http://www.opensource.org/licenses/lgpl-2.1.php
Leaf201#
```

Again, the point of this section is not to create a command reference for Cisco ACI's CLI, but to help you understand how to use different commands relevant to different trouble-shooting activities, and to demonstrate how the Cisco ACI CLI gives you information about the whole network from a single spot.

Linux Commands

As you probably know, most network operative systems have Linux as the underlying OS, and Cisco ACI is no exception. Both images on the controller and the switches are based on Linux, and Cisco has made this Linux OS available for the network admin. You only need to type those commands from the standard ACI CLI, when you are connected to either an APIC or a switch, as demonstrated in Example 12-8.

Example 12-8   *Linux commands in the ACI CLI*

```
apic# uname -a
Linux apic 3.4.49.0.1insieme-20 #1 SMP Thu Jun 2 21:39:24 PDT 2016 x86_64 x86_64
  x86_64 GNU/Linux
```

You can use SSH to connect to other components of ACI, such as leaf and spine switches, in case you need information that cannot be retrieved over the centralized Cisco ACI CLI, as Example 12-9 shows.

Example 12-9   *Connecting to a Leaf in Order to Run a Command on the Switch Itself*

```
apic# ssh Leaf201
[...]
Leaf201# uname -a
Linux Leaf201 3.4.10.0.0insieme-0 #1 SMP Mon Aug 1 16:18:10 PDT 2016 x86_64 GNU/
   Linux
```

Coming back to the APIC, let's look at some interesting operations you can perform using Linux commands, if you know your way. For example, let's have a look at storage utilization in the controller, as demonstrated in Example 12-10.

Example 12-10   *Displaying Controller Storage Utilization*

```
apic# df -h
Filesystem              Size  Used Avail Use% Mounted on
/dev/dm-1                36G   14G   21G  40% /
tmpfs                   4.0G  203M  3.9G   5% /dev/shm
tmpfs                    32G  4.0K   32G   1% /tmp
/dev/mapper/vg_ifc0_ssd-data
                         36G   14G   21G  40% /data
/dev/mapper/vg_ifc0-firmware
                         36G   13G   21G  38% /firmware
/dev/mapper/vg_ifc0-data2
                        180G  2.3G  168G   2% /data2
apic#
```

Alternatively, you can look at the different IP addresses in the controller (out-of-band, in-band, infrastructure, and so on) with well-known Linux commands such as ifconfig and ip addr. Example 12-11 shows the filtered output of ifconfig.

Example 12-11   *Displaying Controller IP Addresses*

```
apic# ifconfig -a | grep addr
bond0     Link encap:Ethernet   HWaddr F4:4E:05:C0:15:4B
          inet6 addr: fe80::f64e:5ff:fec0:154b/64 Scope:Link
bond0.1019 Link encap:Ethernet   HWaddr F4:4E:05:C0:15:4B
          inet addr:10.13.76.12  Bcast:10.13.76.255  Mask:255.255.255.0
          inet6 addr: fe80::f64e:5ff:fec0:154b/64 Scope:Link
bond0.4093 Link encap:Ethernet   HWaddr F4:4E:05:C0:15:4B
          inet addr:10.0.0.1  Bcast:10.0.0.1  Mask:255.255.255.255
          inet6 addr: fe80::f64e:5ff:fec0:154b/64 Scope:Link
```

```
[...]
oobmgmt    Link encap:Ethernet  HWaddr F0:7F:06:45:5A:94
           inet addr:192.168.0.50  Bcast:192.168.0.255  Mask:255.255.255.0
           inet6 addr: fe80::f27f:6ff:fe45:5a94/64 Scope:Link
[...]
```

As you've probably noticed, you are logged in as admin, not as root (root privilege is protected in Cisco ACI and is normally not needed). However, in certain exceptional situations, root access might be required. In this unlikely situation, Cisco Technical Assistance Center can generate root passwords for your APICs.

Mapping Local Objects to Global Objects

Cisco ACI is a policy-based system: The APIC tells the switches that they should perform a certain operation, but it does not tell them how to do it. You could compare this to an airport control tower, which informs airplane pilots about the next action they need to take (approach the runway, maintain a holding pattern until a slot becomes available, fly at a certain altitude, and so on). However, the control tower will never tell a pilot how to perform these tasks because that is the pilot's job. The pilot knows how to operate the plane, and they are not expecting the tower to tell them how to do their job.

Similarly, the APIC will instruct the switches to perform certain tasks, such as creating a bridge domain (BD) or an EPG, but it will not tell them how to do so. As a consequence, there might be some discrepancies in the way each individual switch decides to implement a task. Therefore, one of the first steps you should take when troubleshooting a certain object is to determine which IDs were locally assigned in each individual switch to the objects that the APIC instructed them to create.

The switches in an ACI fabric not only decide how to create objects but also whether they should be created at all. As Chapter 7 explained in depth, the overall scalability of a spine-leaf fabric design depends on the resources of the leaf switches as well as how efficiently they are used, because most functionality is implemented there. As described in that chapter, in Cisco ACI each leaf switch can decide whether or not to dedicate hardware resources for a certain configuration. For example, if there is no endpoint belonging to a certain tenant connected to a particular switch, programming that switch hardware with the tenant information would be a waste of resources.

In this dynamic environment, where network constructs are dynamically created and torn down depending on what is needed, using a level of indirection for those objects' namespaces can be extremely useful. Indirection is a common resource used in computer systems whereby you refer to something, not by its real name, but by an alias to increase the overall flexibility.

Do not worry if the previous paragraphs do not make a lot of sense just yet; the following sections illustrate this indirection concept with two examples: VLAN IDs and port channels.

VLAN IDs

In order to create a bridge domain or an EPG, switches need to define a VLAN ID to implement it in hardware, since switching Application Specific Integrated Circuits (ASICs) still deal in VLANs, not in bridge domains or EPGs. Leaf switches decide which VLAN ID to assign to each bridge domain and each EPG individually. Therefore, the VLAN IDs allocated to bridge domains and EPGs will most likely be different across the various leaf switches.

But now we come across an interesting problem: Say that APIC has instructed the leaf switches to create a certain bridge domain called "Web," and the switch has picked up VLAN 5 to internally represent that EPG, for example. And right after that, the network administrator creates a static binding in another EPG in a BD called "Database" that expects packets tagged with VLAN 5 coming from a certain interface.

This would result in erroneous behavior because the switch would immediately put all those packets into the BD "Web" instead of in "Database." Cisco ACI resolves this problem very elegantly, by using two different VLAN namespaces: an internal name space and an external namespace.

An approximate comparison would be your phone's address book. When you want to call somebody, you look for their name and press dial. Obviously, the phone will internally translate the name to the number and then will place the call. The interesting thing here is the existence of two namespaces: the one you interact with, containing your contacts' names, and the one used internally by the telephone to actually establish the connection with the actual phone numbers.

In Cisco ACI, there is an external VLAN namespace for the VLANs you have configured (similar to the contacts' names in your phone), but there is also an internal VLAN namespace for the VLAN numbers that the switch uses internally (your contacts' phone numbers).

Now let's come back to our example. As you saw, the Web BD was mapped to the *internal* VLAN 5, and a static binding was configured on another EPG (Database) using VLAN 5. The latter is an *external* VLAN. Both are VLAN 5, but in different namespaces. The obvious conclusion is that to prevent conflicts, in this case, the ACI leaf switch will associate the external VLAN 5 with an internal VLAN different from VLAN 5 (otherwise, there would be a collision in the internal VLAN namespace).

One of the corollaries of the existence of two VLAN namespaces is that the internal VLAN IDs are locally significant to each leaf switch. Therefore, commands that refer to the internal VLAN namespace will only work in single leaf switches.

That's enough theory. Let's look at some output examples. The first thing to look at is which VLAN IDs have been allocated to EPGs and bridge domains. Note that normally you don't have a one-to-one relationship between EPGs and BDs, so each one of these objects will receive a dedicated and unique VLAN ID. This is the reason why the default scalability of the ACI leaf switch is the sum of EPGs and BDs (3500 at press time).

Let's have a look at what a bridge domain and an EPG look like from an APIC's perspective, as demonstrated in Example 12-12. Notice how no VLAN ID is shown, because the

VLAN ID assigned to each BD and to each EPG is locally significant to each leaf switch (in other words, it belongs to the internal VLAN namespace).

Example 12-12 *Showing Information Related to a Bridge Domain (No VLAN Information Is Displayed)*

```
apic# show bridge-domain Web
 Tenant        Interface   MAC Address         MTU       VRF           Options
 ----------    ----------  ------------------  --------  ----------    -----------------
 ------
 MyTenant      Web         00:22:BD:F8:19:FF   inherit   default       Multi
  Destination: bd-flood

  Unicast: proxy                                                       L2 Unknown

  Multicast: flood                                                     L3 Unknown

 yes                                                                   Unicast Routing:

 no                                                                    ARP Flooding:

 no                                                                    PIM Enabled:

  regular                                                              BD Type:
apic# show epg Web
 Tenant        Application  AEPg     Consumed Contracts    Provided Contracts
 ----------    ----------   -------  ------------------    -------------------
 MyTenant      MyApp        Web      DB-Services           Web-Services
```

However, by running a command localized to a specific leaf switch, you can actually check whether the bridge domain or EPG has been deployed, and which internal VLANs have been chosen, as Example 12-13 shows. Remember that EPGs and bridge domains will be deployed in a switch only when there are existing endpoints in that switch, not before.

Example 12-13 *Displaying Internal VLANs in Specific Leaf Switches*

```
apic# fabric 201 show vlan extended
-------------------------------------------------------------------
 Node 201 (Leaf201)
-------------------------------------------------------------------
 VLAN Name                             Status     Ports
 ---- ------------------------------   --------   --------------------------------
 [...]
 5    MyTenant:Web-BD                  active     Eth1/3, Eth1/4,  Eth1/5,
                                                  Eth101/1/1, Eth101/1/4, Po2
 [...]
 74   MyTenant:MyApp:Web               active     Eth101/1/1, Eth101/1/4
```

If you issue the **fabric 201 show vlan extended** command in a different leaf switch, the VLANs would typically be different, because those VLANs belong to the VLAN namespace internal to each individual leaf switch.

Legacy Mode

You can define EPGs to operate in "legacy mode" if your main objective is preserving VLAN resources at the leaf, as Chapter 8 "Moving to Application-Centric Networking" explained. In this case, you force ACI to use the same VLAN ID for both the EPG and BD (obviously, only one EPG is supported in each BD in this mode), thus increasing the leaf scalability regarding BDs and EPGs.

Figure 12-2 shows how to configure a bridge domain in legacy mode, and Figure 12-3 shows the dialog where you need to tell ACI which VLAN encapsulation you want to associate with the bridge domain and its associated EPG. This can be useful to simplify troubleshooting, because the same VLAN ID will be used for the bridge domain and its EPG throughout the entire fabric.

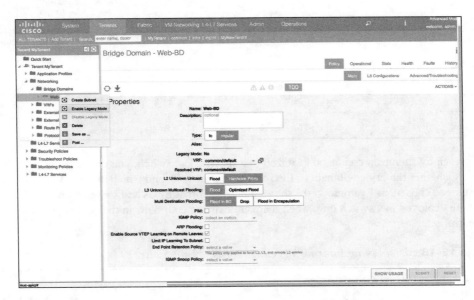

Figure 12-2   *Configuring a Bridge Domain in Legacy Mode*

Port Channels

In the Cisco ACI object model, port channels and virtual port channels (VPCs) are identified by port channel interface policy groups. All throughout the GUI, you refer to port channels using the name of the interface policy group. For example, when you define static port bindings in EPGs to a certain VLAN, you will use that name to create the binding. This means you can use descriptive names like "UCS FI A" and "N7K Production" instead of meaningless numbers such as "Portchannel 5," for example.

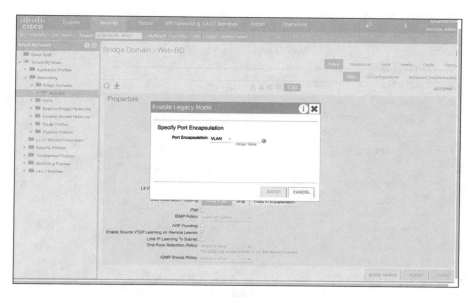

Figure 12-3 *Introducing the VLAN ID for Legacy Mode Configuration*

Nevertheless, when a switch implements those interface policy groups (port channel or virtual port channel), it actually creates numbered port channels interfaces. If you need to retrieve information from the leaf CLI relative to a specific port channel, the first thing you need to know is the number of the port channel you are looking for.

Similar to VLANs, two namespaces exist for port channels as well. In this case, though, it is easier to understand. If you look at Example 12-14, you'll see that UCS-FI-A and iSCSI-b are names used in the GUI to configure a port channel. If we use the address book comparison again, those would be similar to your contacts' names. Each switch will map those names to internal port channel numbers (2 and 7, in these examples), comparable to the actual telephone numbers of your phone contacts.

In the CLI, you need to use the word **extended** in order to see the mapping between both namespaces. The command **show port-channel extended** will display the names of the interface policy groups and the related port channel interfaces that have been created out of them.

Example 12-14   *Displaying Port Channel Mappings*

```
apic# fabric 201 show port-channel extended
-----------------------------------------------------------------
 Node 201 (Leaf201)
-----------------------------------------------------------------
Flags:  D - Down         P - Up in port-channel (members)
        I - Individual   H - Hot-standby (LACP only)
        s - Suspended    r - Module-removed
        S - Switched     R - Routed
        U - Up (port-channel)
        M - Not in use. Min-links not met
        F - Configuration failed
-------------------------------------------------------------------------
Group Port-        BundleGrp             Protocol  Member Ports
      Channel
-------------------------------------------------------------------------
1     Po1(SU)      FEX101                NONE      Eth1/47(P)    Eth1/48(P)
2     Po2(SU)      UCS-FI-B              LACP      Eth1/4(P)
3     Po3(SU)      UCS-FI-A              LACP      Eth1/3(P)
4     Po4(SU)      L2-Cat3560            LACP      Eth1/46(P)
5     Po5(SU)      iSCSI-mgmt            LACP      Eth101/1/9(P)
6     Po6(SU)      iSCSI-a               LACP      Eth101/1/7(P)
7     Po7(SU)      iSCSI-b               LACP      Eth101/1/8(P)
```

Some Useful Leaf Commands

Every network administrator has a list of favorite commands, and you will be able to use most of them in the leaf CLI. Here is a list of some NX-OS commands that can help you find useful information. If you are familiar with Cisco IOS or NX-OS, you will certainly recognize all of them. Note that this section is by no means an exhaustive list of useful troubleshooting commands, because that would be outside the scope of this book. Instead, the goal here is to provide some examples to illustrate how similar the commands in NX-OS and the ACI command-line interfaces are.

- **show interface** *interface-name*: This command gives you generic information about a certain interface, as demonstrated in Example 12-15. As in NX-OS, you can use this command for both physical and logical interfaces.

Example 12-15 *Displaying Interface Information on a Specific Leaf Switch*

```
apic# fabric 201 show interface port-channel 2
----------------------------------------------------------------
Node 201 (Leaf201)
----------------------------------------------------------------
port-channel2 is up
admin state is up
  Hardware: Port-Channel, address: f40f.1bc2.3e8a (bia f40f.1bc2.3e8a)
  MTU 9000 bytes, BW 10000000 Kbit, DLY 1 usec
  reliability 255/255, txload 1/255, rxload 1/255
  Encapsulation ARPA, medium is broadcast
  Port mode is trunk
  full-duplex, 10 Gb/s
  Input flow-control is off, output flow-control is off
  Auto-mdix is turned on
  EtherType is 0x8100
  Members in this channel: eth1/4
  Last clearing of "show interface" counters never
  1 interface resets
  30 seconds input rate 992 bits/sec, 0 packets/sec
  30 seconds output rate 3032 bits/sec, 3 packets/sec
  Load-Interval #2: 5 minute (300 seconds)
    input rate 1840 bps, 0 pps; output rate 4672 bps, 4 pps
  RX
    27275512 unicast packets  508574 multicast packets  5094 broadcast packets
    27789180 input packets  10291351853 bytes
    0 jumbo packets  0 storm suppression bytes
    0 runts  0 giants  0 CRC  0 no buffer
    0 input error  0 short frame  0 overrun  0 underrun  0 ignored
    0 watchdog  0 bad etype drop  0 bad proto drop  0 if down drop
    0 input with dribble  0 input discard
    0 Rx pause
  TX
    7010317 unicast packets  9625817 multicast packets  2330117 broadcast packets
    18966251 output packets  3109169535 bytes
    0 jumbo packets
    0 output error  0 collision  0 deferred  0 late collision
    0 lost carrier  0 no carrier  0 babble  0 output discard
    0 Tx pause
```

- **show interface** *interface-name* **trunk:** This command shows the VLANs configured on an interface, as demonstrated in Example 12-16. Do not forget to map the internal VLAN IDs that this command shows with the command **show vlan extended**.

Example 12-16 *Displaying VLANs Configured on an Interface on a Specific Leaf Switch*

```
apic# fabric 201 show interface port-channel 2 trunk
--------------------------------------------------------------
 Node 201 (Leaf201)
--------------------------------------------------------------
--------------------------------------------------------------------
Port            Native    Status      Port
                Vlan                  Channel
--------------------------------------------------------------------
Po2             vlan-50   trunking    --
--------------------------------------------------------------------
 Port           Vlans Allowed on Trunk
--------------------------------------------------------------------
Po2             2,5-6,8,10,13-17,19-21,23-24,27,30-32,38,41-42,47-50,56-57,60,63-6
                5,107
[...]
```

- **show vrf:** Displays the VRFs configured on a switch, as demonstrated in Example 12-17.

Example 12-17 *Displaying VRFs Deployed on a Specific Leaf Switch*

```
apic# fabric 201 show vrf
------------------------------------------------------------------
 Node 201 (Leaf201)
------------------------------------------------------------------
VRF-Name                 VRF-ID State    Reason
black-hole                    3 Up       --
common:default                8 Up       --
management                    2 Up       --
mgmt:inb                     10 Up       --
MyTenant:MyVRF                7 Up       --
overlay-1                     4 Up       --
```

- **show ip interface brief vrf** *vrf-name*: With this command, you can quickly verify the existing L3 interfaces, as demonstrated in Example 12-18. Note that you should always use the **vrf** option in Cisco ACI (or specify the option **vrf all**). This command can be used to show infrastructure IP addresses in VRF **overlay-1**, out-of-band management IP address in VRF **management**, and in-band management IP addresses in VRF **mgmt:inb**.

- **show ip route vrf** *vrf-name*: This is another command you will probably find yourself checking when dealing with routing adjacencies in ACI, as demonstrated in Example 12-19. Again, it works the same as in any other NX-OS-based switch and can be used not only for tenant VRFs, but for any VRF in the switches.

Example 12-18 *Showing IP Interfaces Deployed on a Specific Leaf Switch*

```
apic# fabric 201 show ip interface brief vrf common:default
----------------------------------------------------------------
 Node 201 (Leaf201)
----------------------------------------------------------------
IP Interface Status for VRF "common:default"(8)
Interface          Address               Interface Status
vlan6              172.16.1.1/24         protocol-up/link-up/admin-up
vlan7              172.16.101.254/24     protocol-up/link-up/admin-up
vlan9              172.16.102.254/24     protocol-up/link-up/admin-up
vlan13             192.168.3.65/27       protocol-up/link-up/admin-up
vlan26             10.13.76.254/24       protocol-up/link-up/admin-up
vlan29             192.168.3.9/29        protocol-up/link-up/admin-up
vlan30             192.168.3.129/28      protocol-up/link-up/admin-up
vlan39             172.16.103.1/24       protocol-up/link-up/admin-up
vlan40             192.168.100.1/24      protocol-up/link-up/admin-up
vlan43             172.18.40.1/24        protocol-up/link-up/admin-up
lo4                192.168.3.3/32        protocol-up/link-up/admin-up
lo10               192.168.3.1/32        protocol-up/link-up/admin-up
```

Example 12-19 *Showing the Routing Table for a VRF on a Specific Leaf Switch*

```
apic# fabric 201 show ip route vrf mgmt:inb
----------------------------------------------------------------
 Node 201 (Leaf201)
----------------------------------------------------------------
IP Route Table for VRF "mgmt:inb"
'*' denotes best ucast next-hop
'**' denotes best mcast next-hop
'[x/y]' denotes [preference/metric]
'%<string>' in via output denotes VRF <string>
192.168.0.0/16, ubest/mbest: 1/0
    *via 192.168.4.11, vlan18, [1/0], 03w27d, static
192.168.4.1/32, ubest/mbest: 2/0, attached, direct
    *via 192.168.4.1, lo6, [1/0], 03w27d, local, local
    *via 192.168.4.1, lo6, [1/0], 03w27d, direct
192.168.4.2/32, ubest/mbest: 1/0
    *via 10.0.96.93%overlay-1, [1/0], 03w27d, bgp-65100, internal, tag 65100
192.168.4.8/29, ubest/mbest: 1/0, attached, direct
    *via 192.168.4.9, vlan18, [1/0], 03w27d, direct
192.168.4.9/32, ubest/mbest: 1/0, attached
    *via 192.168.4.9, vlan18, [1/0], 03w27d, local, local
apic#
```

■ As a final remark, if you want to check the routing table on an APIC, you can use the Linux command for it. Note that you will see two default routes, in case you have configured both out-of-band and in-band management IP addresses (with a better metric for the in-band one), as demonstrated in Example 12-20.

Example 12-20 *Showing the Routing Table on an APIC*

```
apic# netstat -rnve
Kernel IP routing table
Destination       Gateway        Genmask          Flags Metric Ref    Use Iface
0.0.0.0           10.13.76.254   0.0.0.0          UG    0      0        0
bond0.1019
0.0.0.0           192.168.0.1    0.0.0.0          UG    16     0        0 oobmgmt
10.0.0.0          10.0.0.30      255.255.0.0      UG    0      0        0
bond0.4093
10.0.0.30         0.0.0.0        255.255.255.255  UH    0      0        0
bond0.4093
10.0.0.65         10.0.0.30      255.255.255.255  UGH   0      0        0
bond0.4093
10.0.0.66         10.0.0.30      255.255.255.255  UGH   0      0        0
bond0.4093
10.13.76.0        0.0.0.0        255.255.255.0    U     0      0        0
bond0.1019
10.13.76.254      0.0.0.0        255.255.255.255  UH    0      0        0
bond0.1019
169.254.1.0       0.0.0.0        255.255.255.0    U     0      0        0 teplo-1
169.254.254.0     0.0.0.0        255.255.255.0    U     0      0        0 lxcbr0
192.168.0.0       0.0.0.0        255.255.255.0    U     0      0        0 oobmgmt
apic#
```

ping

The **ping** command is one of the most frequently used commands, and you can certainly use it in Cisco ACI's CLI. In the APIC, no VRFs are used, so there is no need to specify one. You can just use the **ping** command as in any standard Linux host.

However, in the leaf switches you will certainly have VRFs. This VRF-awareness is one of the enhancements that the **iping** tool provides, which is accessible at any Cisco ACI leaf switch, as demonstrated in Example 12-21.

Example 12-21 *Using* iping *from a Leaf Switch*

```
apic# ssh Leaf201
Password:
[...]
Leaf201# iping
Vrf context to use [management] : management
Target IP address or Hostname : 192.168.0.1
Repeat count [5] :
Datagram size [56] :
```

```
Timeout in seconds [2] :
Sending interval in seconds [2] :
Extended commands [no] :
Sweep range of sizes [no] :
Sending 5, 56-bytes ICMP Echos to 192.168.0.1 from 192.168.0.51
Timeout is 2 seconds, data pattern is 0xABCD
64 bytes from 192.168.0.1: icmp_seq=0 ttl=255 time=1.044 ms
64 bytes from 192.168.0.1: icmp_seq=1 ttl=255 time=1.149 ms
64 bytes from 192.168.0.1: icmp_seq=2 ttl=255 time=0.955 ms
64 bytes from 192.168.0.1: icmp_seq=3 ttl=255 time=1.029 ms
64 bytes from 192.168.0.1: icmp_seq=4 ttl=255 time=1.029 ms
--- 192.168.0.1 ping statistics ---
5 packets transmitted, 5 packets received, 0.00% packet loss
round-trip min/avg/max = 0.955/1.041/1.149 ms
Leaf201#
```

If you prefer to give the complete **ping** command in one line, that's also possible. You can check how to enter the different attributes with the **-h** flag, as demonstrated in Example 12-22.

Example 12-22 *Using* iping *with Inline Options from a Leaf Switch*

```
Leaf201# iping -h
usage: iping [-dDFLnqRrv] [-V vrf] [-c count] [-i wait] [-p pattern] [-s packetsize]
  [-t timeout] [-S source ip/interface] host
Leaf201# iping -V management 192.168.0.1
PING 192.168.0.1 (192.168.0.1) from 192.168.0.51: 56 data bytes
64 bytes from 192.168.0.1: icmp_seq=0 ttl=255 time=1.083 ms
64 bytes from 192.168.0.1: icmp_seq=1 ttl=255 time=0.975 ms
64 bytes from 192.168.0.1: icmp_seq=2 ttl=255 time=1.026 ms
64 bytes from 192.168.0.1: icmp_seq=3 ttl=255 time=0.985 ms
64 bytes from 192.168.0.1: icmp_seq=4 ttl=255 time=1.015 ms
--- 192.168.0.1 ping statistics ---
5 packets transmitted, 5 packets received, 0.00% packet loss
round-trip min/avg/max = 0.975/1.016/1.083 ms
Leaf201#
```

Finally, a special version of the **iping** utility for IPv6 is called **iping6**, and it's used similarly to the previously described **iping**, as demonstrated in Example 12-23.

Example 12-23   *Using* **iping6** *for IPv6 Connectivity from a Leaf Switch*

```
Leaf201# iping6 -h
iping6_initialize: Entry
iping6_initialize: tsp process lock acquired
iping6_fu_add_icmp_q: Entry
iping6_get_my_tep_ip: tep_ip a00605f
UDP Socket is 41993
iping6_initialize: Done (SUCCESS)
iping6: option requires an argument -- 'h'
usage: iping6 [-dDnqRrv] [-V vrf] [-c count] [-i wait] [-p pattern] [-s packetsize]
  [-t timeout] [-S source interface/IPv6 address] host
Leaf201#
```

Troubleshooting Physical Issues

In any fabric you can have physical problems, ranging from cable issues to power grid outages. Cisco ACI offers multiple possibilities to troubleshoot and fix physical network problems, including traditional and new ways of getting your network topology back to normal.

Troubleshooting Cabling

The first step when troubleshooting physical problems is verifying the fabric topology in the **Fabric** tab of the APIC, as Figure 12-4 illustrates.

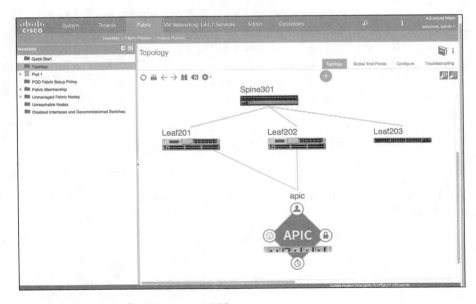

Figure 12-4   *Topology View in APIC*

Note that the topology view will only show the active topology. This means that if, for example, this network should have two spines but one of them has been shut down, only the active one will be displayed, as the next section explains more in detail.

For any cabling problem, faults will be raised with details about the ports involved in the issue, as Figure 12-5 demonstrates.

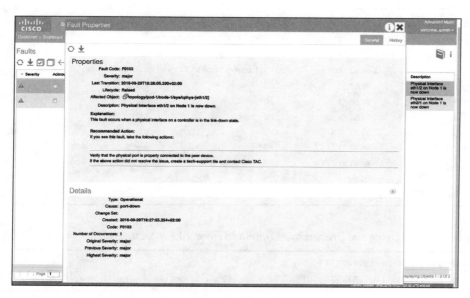

Figure 12-5 *APIC Port Connectivity Fault*

If you prefer to use the CLI to troubleshoot cabling, you can use Layer 2 adjacency protocols such as Link Layer Discovery Protocol (LLDP) and Cisco Discovery Protocol (CDP), the same way that you would do in a non-ACI network. Note that the fabric elements (controller, spines, and leaf switches) speak LLDP by default, but you need to configure the rest of elements, such as Cisco Unified Computing System (UCS) servers and hypervisor hosts, to actively use LLDP, CDP, or both, as demonstrated in Example 12-24.

Finally, there is an improved traceroute tool in the ACI switch software that allows you to check for all paths over which two leaf switches are connected; it is called **itraceroute**. Example 12-25 shows the output from the **itraceroute** command from one leaf to another, where four different paths exist. Note that the IP address that needs to be supplied to the **itraceroute** command is the infrastructure address of the destination leaf (in VRF overlay-1).

Example 12-24   *Showing Neighbor Information for all Leaf Switches Using the Centralized CLI*

```
apic# fabric 201-203 show lldp neighbors
----------------------------------------------------------------
 Node 201 (Leaf201)
----------------------------------------------------------------
Capability codes:
  (R) Router, (B) Bridge, (T) Telephone, (C) DOCSIS Cable Device
  (W) WLAN Access Point, (P) Repeater, (S) Station, (O) Other
Device ID            Local Intf      Hold-time  Capability  Port ID
apic                 Eth1/1          120                    eth2-1
UCS-FI-A             Eth1/3          120         B          Eth1/20
UCS-FI-B             Eth1/4          120         B          Eth1/20
Spine301             Eth1/49         120         BR         Eth1/2
ESX-01               Eth101/1/1      180         B          0050.5653.e331
ESX-02               Eth101/1/4      180         B          0050.565a.480a
Total entries displayed: 6
...
```

Example 12-25   *Using the itraceroute Command from a Leaf Switch*

```
Leaf201# itraceroute 10.0.71.61
Node traceroute to 10.0.71.61, infra VRF overlay-1, from [10.0.71.63], payload 56
  bytes
Path 1
  1: TEP      10.0.71.62  intf  eth1/35  0.016 ms
  2: TEP      10.0.71.61  intf  eth1/98  0.018 ms
Path 2
  1: TEP      10.0.71.62  intf  eth1/33  0.012 ms
  2: TEP      10.0.71.61  intf  eth1/97  0.019 ms
Path 3
  1: TEP      10.0.71.62  intf  eth1/35  0.013 ms
  2: TEP      10.0.71.61  intf  eth1/97  0.014 ms
Path 4
  1: TEP      10.0.71.62  intf  eth1/33  0.014 ms
  2: TEP      10.0.71.61  intf  eth1/98  0.014 ms
```

This command is extremely valuable because it allows you to detect fabric connectivity issues between any two given leaf switches with great ease.

This traceroute capability is called the "Leaf Nodes Traceroute Policy," and it can be leveraged from the ACI GUI under **Troubleshoot Policies** in the **Fabric** tab. Another type of traceroute that's not between switches, but between endpoints, will be described later in this chapter in the "Troubleshooting Wizard" section.

Troubleshooting Switch Outages

The starting point for troubleshooting switch outages is again the network topology in the **Fabric** tab of the GUI. This topology is dynamic and will show the device connectivity that exists at any given time. This means that if a certain switch is not reachable because of a cabling problem or a software upgrade, for example, the following will happen:

- The switch will disappear from the topology. You might expect the switch to appear highlighted somehow, but remember that this topology only shows the current connectivity and has no history of previous states.

- If a switch is not reachable, it will disappear not only from the topology but also from the list of existing nodes. As a consequence, it will not show up in the GUI at all, not even with a zero health score.

So you may be wondering where you find switches that were previously in the topology but are not reachable any more. In the **Fabric** tab there is a section for unreachable nodes that shows you the list of switches that have been acknowledged as part of the fabric but are not reachable at any given point in time. Figure 12-6 shows an example of the **Unreachable Nodes** panel, where one leaf is currently down.

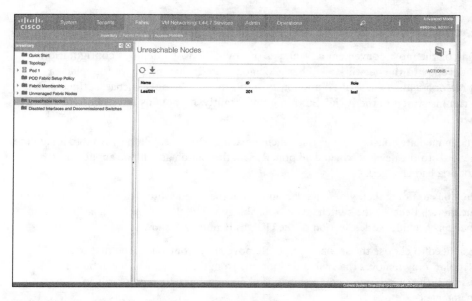

Figure 12-6 *Unreachable Nodes View in APIC*

Additionally, a critical fault is generated about the problem that can be used to notify network operators that a certain network node is currently not reachable in the fabric, as Figure 12-7 shows.

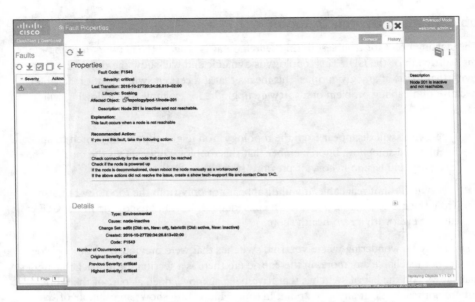

Figure 12-7   *Critical Fault Generated When a Node Is Not Reachable*

Replacing a Fabric Switch

One of the most convenient advantages of how Cisco ACI deploys configuration and policy to the network switches is demonstrated when you have to replace a spine or a leaf. As described previously in this book, the policy (that is, the configuration) is stored in the APIC. But more importantly, it contains references only to the switch IDs.

The immediate consequence is that when replacing hardware, you only need to assign the same ID to the new switch, and all policies will then automatically be applied to it, as if nothing had changed.

Previous to doing that, you must decommission the failed switch (that is, remove it from the fabric). Because the switch is not reachable, you will need to decommission it from the **Unreachable Nodes** section of the GUI, as Figure 12-8 shows.

You need to choose the second option, **Remove from controller.** The first option, **Regular,** only removes the switch temporarily from the fabric, which can be very useful if the switch is not completely out of service, but only temporarily in maintenance.

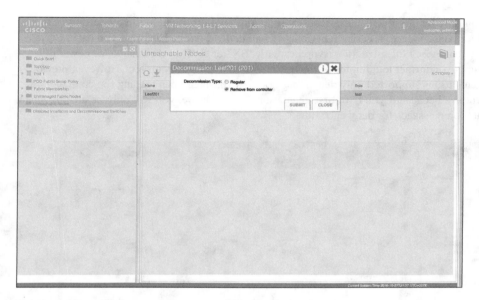

Figure 12-8 *Decommissioning a Failed Switch*

Troubleshooting Contracts

A wrong access list is one of the main reasons why traffic is dropped when it shouldn't be, regardless of whether the object being considered is an access control list in a router, a traffic rule in a firewall, or a contract in Cisco ACI.

The advantage of Cisco ACI is that the contract abstraction makes traffic filtering much easier to troubleshoot. If one server cannot speak to another, you only need to figure out in which EPGs those servers are located, and check the contracts on those EPGs.

Why is this easier than traditional ACL or ruleset troubleshooting? Because this process does not get more complex at scale. Extremely long access control lists make trouble-shooting difficult. However, with the contract abstraction, you just need to look at the EPGs and the contracts between them. If there are hundreds of other EPGs and contracts, you will not even see them.

Therefore, the process could look something like this:

1. Find the involved EPGs, eventually using a tool like the Endpoint Tracker (discussed later in this section).

2. Go to the EPGs and compare the provided and consumed contracts. If the EPGs are in the same tenant, the graphical representation in the application network profile can help to quickly determine the contracts involved, as well as the graphical representation of the contract, as Figure 12-9 illustrates.

3. Go to the contract and have a look at the contract options, subjects, and filters.

As you might remember, Cisco ACI offers security functionality for network traffic without any performance penalty, and that's at very high traffic rates. As you can imagine, this can only be possible if these security functions are performed in the forwarding ASICs. As a consequence, security functionality will depend on the hardware you have. Current switching ACI infrastructure (switches with "EX" or "FX" in their name, or newer) support contract logging for both deny and permit rules in contracts. However, previous generations supported only deny logs. Consider this fact when reading the coming paragraphs, because if you have first-generation ACI hardware, you will only be able to generate log messages for deny entry hits.

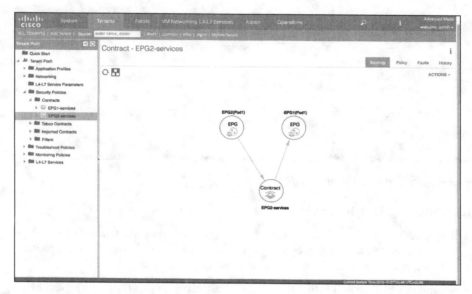

Figure 12-9 *Contract Topology Representation*

Contract logs are a very important component of troubleshooting to determine whether the security policy is doing its job. Suppose, for example, your security policy looks correct, but for some reason the application is still not working. Maybe the application guys have forgotten to tell you about some protocol that the application components need for their correct operation? Looking at the contract logs can give you this information, because you can see exactly which packets have been dropped by your access lists.

Chapter 7 described some of the ways of verifying ACL counters and ACL logs. Typically, the troubleshooting process consists of the following steps:

1. Are packets being dropped at all? You can verify contract hit counters from the Troubleshooting Wizard, for example.

2. If that is the case, then which packets are being dropped? You can refer to the tenant logs for detailed information about allowed and denied traffic. This is especially useful because you will only see logs for the EPGs in this specific tenant, which makes the troubleshooting process much easier, instead of trying to find a "needle in the haystack" if you were to search the global logs (which incidentally you could do, too, if you really wanted to, as Chapter 7 explained).

Figure 12-10 shows an example of the information contained in these logs that allows you to modify the contract policy so that these packets are allowed.

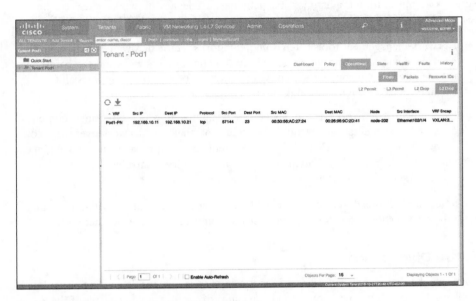

Figure 12-10 *Flow Drop Logs Example*

In addition, you could have a look at the dropped packets, which will provide information like timestamps and the packet length, as Figure 12-11 shows.

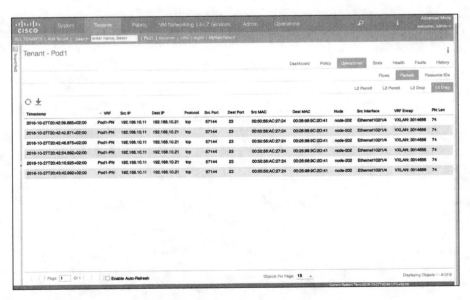

Figure 12-11 *Packet Drop Logs Example*

Troubleshooting Tools in ACI

Network administration is a hard job, partially because legacy networks offer very limited troubleshooting tools. There are various reason for this, such as the following:

- Network management tools often do not support specific hardware functionality in network devices, because integration between controlled devices and the controller is generally loosely coupled. Cisco ACI's controller (APIC) fully supports all functionality in ACI switches through tightly coupled integration.

- Device-centric networks have a device-centric approach, which oftentimes complicates the implementation of troubleshooting tools that need to work over the whole fabric. Opposed to this, Cisco ACI has a system-centric approach, and ACI engineers make intelligent usage of individual device functionality (controller, leaf, spine) in order to deliver overall troubleshooting functions.

The following sections describe some troubleshooting tools, specific to ACI, that can make the troubleshooting process much easier as compared to on legacy networks.

Hardware Diagnostics

Cisco switches have a rich set of instrumentation and telemetry for diagnosing hardware problems. Cisco ACI is no exception, and you can verify at any time the result of those checks, or trigger more exhaustive tests, which will help to perform additional verifications.

Figure 12-12 shows the part of the GUI where the verification check results are visible (in this case, for a top-of-rack switch).

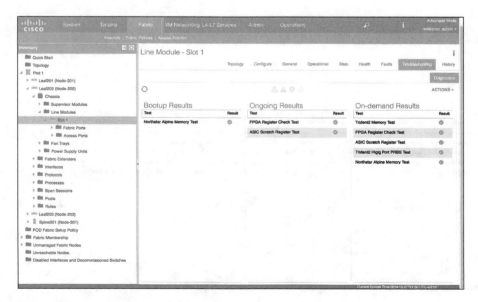

Figure 12-12   *Diagnostics Results*

Note that the on-demand results are only visible after you have configured additional diagnostics to be performed. You can do that using troubleshooting policies, as Figure 12-13 shows (in this case, with full tests for an ACI node).

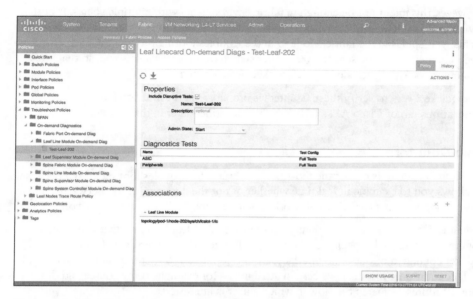

Figure 12-13   *Configuring On-demand Troubleshooting Diagnostics*

Dropped Packets: Counter Synchronization

Have you ever tried to figure out whether the connection between two switches is dropping packets? When you look at one side of the connection, it shows that the interface sent X packets into the cable. At the other side, a different counter in a different switch will show that it received Y packets out of the cable.

Would you expect that X = Y? In legacy networks, you normally don't, because counters across different switches are not synchronized. You can clear the counters in one switch while the other keeps on counting as if nothing happened. Therefore, it is virtually impossible knowing whether or not packets have been dropped.

In Cisco ACI, leaf counters are synchronized. This means that if switch A sends X packets to switch B, you should expect to see the number X on both sides of the connection. In other words, if switch A counters show that it sent 100 packets to switch B, but switch B shows that it received 99 packets, you can safely assume that one packet was dropped along the way.

Not only that, but this synchronization will reset every 30 seconds, and the values will be stored in the controller. This way, you get a history of dropped packets and can determine whether that difference of one packet just happened or occurred a few hours ago.

However, this might not be enough in fabric environments with multiple spines. If both switches A and B are leaf switches, they have multiple ways to reach each other (at least as many as spines in the fabric). To help in the troubleshooting process, ACI leaf switches keep counters of traffic sent to every other switch over every single spine, so that you can quickly see the path along which packets were dropped.

The quickest way to verify these counters is probably via the Traffic Map in the **Operations** tab of Cisco ACI's GUI, which is described later in this chapter.

Atomic Counters

An atomic counter is one of the most useful features for troubleshooting in ACI because it allows you to examine in real time whether or not the communication between any two given endpoints in a Cisco ACI network is being established through the network.

The idea is to have a bank of counters in the Cisco ACI leaf switches that can be configured to count only specific packets. Instead of generic counters, which count every packet coming in or out of an interface, atomic counters will first look at the packet and will count it only if it matches certain attributes—for example, if the source and destination IP addresses match the flow in which a user is interested.

Atomic counters can be configured in the Troubleshoot Policies area inside each tenant. You can define multiple options to define which traffic you want to be counted: between endpoints (EP), between endpoint groups (EPG), between external addresses (Ext), or a combination of the previous three elements.

For example, Figure 12-14 shows how to configure one atomic counter policy to measure all traffic going between two endpoints. Note that many other policy types are possible, such as between EPGs, between an endpoint and an EPG, or with external addresses, to name a few.

Figure 12-15 shows an example of the statistics that can be retrieved out of the atomic counter policy. In this case, a 1-second ping has been initiated, which explains why in every 30-second period there are 30 packets in each direction.

Note that atomic counters can be extremely helpful for proving that the network is not responsible for application performance issues.

Traffic Mirroring: SPAN and Copy Services

SPAN (or Switch Port Analyzer) has been around for the last 20 years and is implemented in most every Cisco Catalyst and Nexus switch. Essentially, it consists of defining criteria in a switch so that the packets matching those criteria are copied, and the mirrored packets are forwarded to another destination.

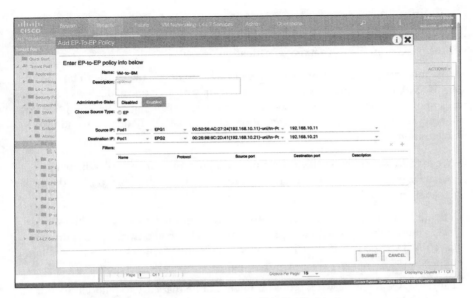

Figure 12-14 *EP-to-EP Atomic Counter Policy Definition*

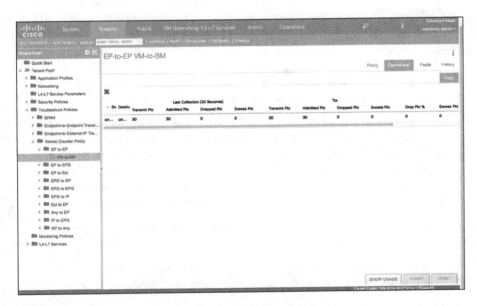

Figure 12-15 *Atomic Counter Operational Statistics*

Depending on what the destination is, multiple SPAN types exist. Standard SPAN sends the copied packets to a local port in the same switch, where typically an analysis appliance (for example, Cisco Network Analysis Module, or NAM) is connected. Remote SPAN (or RSPAN) puts the copied packets in a VLAN so that they can be transported to another switch. This is helpful so that a central analysis appliance can collect packets from every switch. The most flexible option is Encapsulated Remote SPAN (ERSPAN), where the packets are sent to a remote destination over IP.

There are multiple criteria with which you might want to define the traffic to be mirrored. Cisco ACI has a highly sophisticated traffic-mirroring engine and allows for several options in order to send traffic to an analysis appliance. Depending on which option you use in order to mirror traffic, the configuration might look slightly different, and the available options will vary:

- **Access SPAN:** This is the classic port-mirroring functionality available in many switches, but enhanced with additional features such as being able to filter the packets being mirrored.

- **Virtual SPAN:** When investigating network issues involving virtual machines, typically you want to be able to mirror only traffic going to and from those endpoints. Cisco ACI can do that if the Cisco Application Virtual Switch (AVS) is present in the hypervisor.

- **Fabric SPAN:** Some network problems might not be that easy to pinpoint to individual endpoints, so you might want to mirror all traffic. Or maybe you want to send all traffic traversing the network to an appliance for analytics purposes. In this case, you could define fabric ports (that is, the ports connecting leaf switches to spines) as the source for your traffic-mirroring session.

- **Tenant SPAN:** What if the network admin does not care about physical or virtual ports but does care about a certain application? With Cisco ACI, you can define an EPG as the source of a traffic-mirroring session so that all traffic entering or exiting that specific endpoint group will be mirrored.

- **Copy Services:** As part of the ACI 2.0 software version and the EX hardware's new features, Copy Services are available as another option to mirror traffic. Unlike SPAN sessions, Copy Services leverage contracts between EPGs and only mirror traffic that those contracts allow. Again, note that Copy Services are only available on EX-based leaf switches (or newer). Because Copy Services are mainly considered an extension of Cisco ACI Service Insertion, they will not be covered in depth in this section.

Table 12-1 summarizes the different options just described (support for ERSPAN types I and II will be described later in this section).

Whatever traffic-mirroring configuration you do (with the notable exception of Copy Services), the SPAN configuration consists of essentially two parts:

- **SPAN source groups:** Which traffic should be captured

- **SPAN destination groups:** Where the captured traffic should be sent to

Table 12-1 *Traffic Mirroring Options in ACI*

	Source	Destination	Filter	GUI
Access SPAN	Access port	ERSPAN local	Tenant, app, EPG	Fabric/access
Virtual SPAN	VM vNIC	ERSPAN VM vNIC	—	Fabric/access
Fabric SPAN	Fabric port	ERSPAN	BD, VRF	Fabric/fabric
Tenant SPAN	EPG	ERSPAN	—	Tenant
Copy Services	EPG	L4-7 copy device	Contract filter	Contracts, L4-7

SPAN Destination Groups

You start by configuring a destination group, because you will need it when defining the source group (even if the source group window allows you to create a destination group from there).

A destination group can be made out of one or more destinations. If more than one destination is defined, captured traffic will be sent to all of them. Destinations are typically systems that can receive packets and analyze them, such as Cisco Network Access Module (NAM) appliances, or just simple laptops with a traffic analysis application such as Wireshark installed. These appliances can be directly connected to the ACI fabric or accessed via IP.

Depending on the SPAN session type you are configuring, you will be able to define different types of destinations. For example, for Tenant SPAN remote destinations, you need to define the following attributes, as Figure 12-16 shows:

- **Destination EPG (Tenant, ANP, and EPG):** This is where the analysis appliance is connected.

- **Destination IP:** This is the IP address of your analysis appliance, where captured packets will be sent.

- **Source IP:** IP packets need to have a source IP. This IP is typically not relevant (unless you have network filters between the ACI network and your analysis appliance), so you can put a bogus IP here if you want. Note that even if you are capturing on multiple-leaf switches, all packets will come with the same source IP address to the analysis appliance.

You can optionally define other parameters of the IP packets that will transport the captured traffic, such as their **TTL** (time-to-live), **DSCP** (Differentiated Services Code Point), **MTU** (maximum transmit unit), and **Flow ID** (this is an ERSPAN field that can be used in order to separate captures from each other in the analysis appliance).

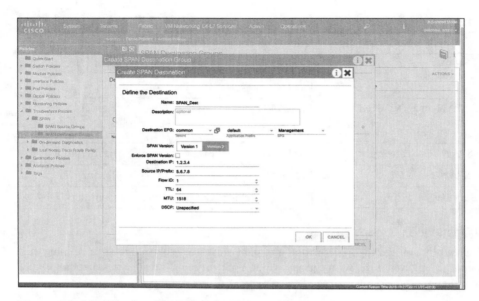

Figure 12-16 *Destination Policy for Tenant SPAN*

ERSPAN Types

You might have noticed in Figure 12-16 the option to specify either Encapsulated Remote Switch Port Analyzer (ERSPAN) version 1 or version 2. The distinction between these two versions of the ERSPAN protocol is very important; otherwise, you might find out that your traffic analyzer is not able to decode the packets received out of a Cisco ACI mirroring session if you send packets encapsulated with the wrong ERSPAN version.

ERSPAN essentially encapsulates packets to be mirrored in IP so that they can be transported to a remote destination. The header used for this encapsulation is Generic Routing Encapsulation (GRE, IETF RFC 1701).

Starting with ERSPAN version 1, an additional header is introduced before applying the GRE encapsulation: the ERSPAN header. This header contains some metadata such as the session ID or the VLAN being mirrored. Figures 12-17 and 12-18 show the different headers of packets encapsulated with ERSPAN versions 1 and 2. Note that ERSPAN versions 1 and 2 are sometimes referred to as types I and II.

As you can see, the ERSPAN header of version 2 (added to the original packet before encapsulating in GRE) carries information such as the Class of Service (CoS).

As an aside, ERSPAN version 3 (or type III) already exists, and it caters to a more flexible header in order to convey other types of metadata that might be relevant for monitoring and troubleshooting. At press time, Cisco ACI does not support ERSPAN version 3.

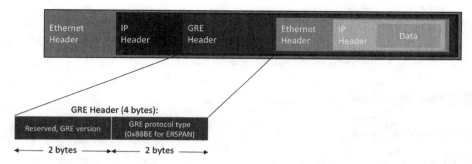

Figure 12-17 *Packet Encapsulation with ERSPAN Version 1, Without ERSPAN Header*

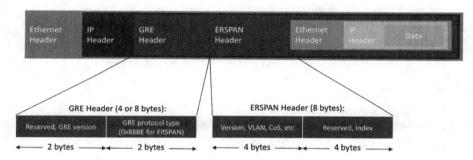

Figure 12-18 *Packet Encapsulation with ERSPAN Version 2, with ERSPAN Header*

Why is this important? Because the application you use to decode the mirrored traffic should be able to understand the format you are using. If your analysis tool expects an ERSPAN header but you are not using one (that is, it expects ERSPAN version 2 but you are sending version 1), it will declare the captured packets invalid.

For example, this is the case with the popular packet capture tool Wireshark. By default, Wireshark will not analyze ERSPAN version 1 packets. However, you can configure it to try to decode ERSPAN packets, even if they appear not to be valid (as would be the case with version 1), as shown by Figure 12-19 (the screenshot shows the Mac OS X version of Wireshark).

You should refer to the analysis tool you are using in order to know the supported ERSPAN types.

So why is it that certain traffic mirroring sessions will only support version 1 or version 2? The reason for this is the need to perform traffic mirroring in hardware due to the high volume of bandwidth potentially being involved and the limited capabilities of some ASICs. In the first generation of Cisco ACI hardware, a combination of ASICs from Broadcom and Cisco was used. Those ASICs had different capabilities in terms of ERSPAN version; the Cisco ASIC already supported the newer type II, but the Broadcom ASICs still only supported version 1. Depending on where traffic needs to be mirrored, a different ASIC might do the traffic encapsulation; for example, Broadcom ASICs control the server-facing leaf ports, and Cisco ASICs control the network-facing leaf uplink ports as well as the spine ports.

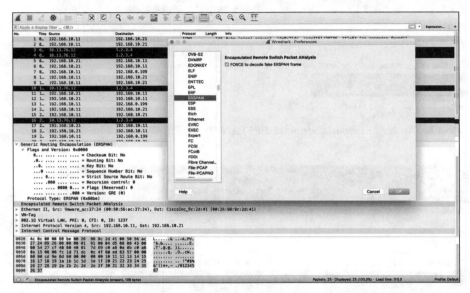

Figure 12-19 *Wireshark Configuration to Force Decoding of ERSPAN Type I Packets*

As a consequence, depending on where you are capturing traffic, the older hardware generation will support either type I or type II, as Table 12-2 describes. Note that this limitation does not exist anymore with hardware of the second generation ("-EX" switches) or later.

Table 12-2 *ERSPAN Destination Types for the First Generation of Cisco ACI Leaf Switch Hardware*

SPAN Type	Destinations Supported in First-Generation Hardware
Access SPAN	ERSPAN version 1 Local
Virtual SPAN	ERSPAN version 1 VM vNIC
Fabric SPAN	ERSPAN version 2
Tenant SPAN	ERSPAN version 1

SPAN Source Groups

You have defined where to send captured traffic, as explained in the previous sections, but which traffic do you want to capture? This is what you need to specify in this section. After entering a name for the source group, you need to tell the APIC whether you will be capturing ingress or egress traffic, or both.

Similar to the destination groups, what sources you can configure depends on what type of SPAN sessions you are using, as described in Table 12-2.

For example, when configuring tenant SPAN, you would define from which EPG you want to mirror traffic, either coming in, going out, or in both directions, as Figure 12-20 illustrates.

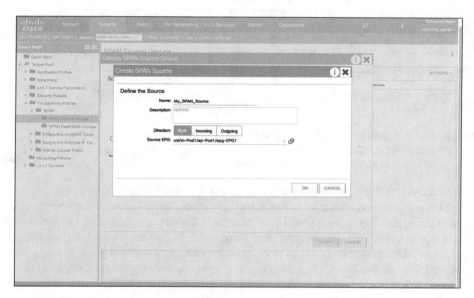

Figure 12-20   *Configuring a Source Group for Tenant SPAN*

Cisco ACI Scalability for SPAN Sessions

Experienced network administrators know that traffic mirroring can potentially consume many hardware resources in a switch; therefore, the number of SPAN sessions supported is limited.

Cisco ACI is no exception, and in the "Verified Scalability Guide for Cisco APIC" at Cisco.com you can verify the maximum number of SPAN sessions that are supported with each ACI software version. For example, in the latest scalability guide at the time of this writing (for Cisco ACI software 3.0), the limits shown in Table 12-3 have been verified.

Table 12-3 *Scalability Limits for SPAN Configuration*

	Maximum per Leaf	Maximum per Fabric
SPAN Sessions	8 unidirectional or 4 bidirectional (for -EX and -FX switches)	N/A
Ports per SPAN Session	No limit	N/A
EPGs per SPAN Session	230 unidirectional or 460 bidirectional (for -EX and -FX switches)	N/A

Nexus Data Broker

What if you want to constantly send traffic to an analysis appliance? You might have multiple reasons to do that:

- The analysis appliance inspects the received traffic and generates NetFlow data (like in the case of the Cisco NetFlow Generation Appliance).

- The analysis appliance needs a continuous data flow in order to inspect packets and generate some data. This generated data might range from statistics about who is using the network to complex anomaly-based security incident detections.

More likely, you will have multiple analysis appliances, each of which is interested in part of the traffic. Maybe your intrusion detection system (IDS) is only interested in traffic going to the web servers, your Cisco NetFlow Generation Appliance is only interested in traffic specific to a tenant, and your laptop with Wireshark is only interested in a specific problem that you happen to be troubleshooting. You could possibly define multiple SPAN sessions in ACI, but there is a limit to doing so, as previous sections have described.

Another way of achieving this goal is by sending the entire traffic to a "SPAN aggregation system" that then distributes the packets to all traffic analysis appliances. However, any specific analysis appliance should only receive traffic in which it is interested.

This "system" must be really scalable, because we are speaking about potentially several terabits per second (Tbps) of traffic. Certain purpose-built switches (sometimes called "matrix switches") have been conceived to solve this challenge. These switches receive traffic and, instead of looking at the destination MAC address in the packets in order to send them forward (as any Ethernet switch would do), they look at other data and compare it with user-defined filters. These filters tell the switch to which analysis appliance (or appliances) every packet needs to be sent.

Normally you would not be able to use commodity Ethernet switches for this task, but Cisco Nexus Data Broker uses OpenFlow technologies to turn a standard Ethernet switch like the Nexus 3000 or the Nexus 9300 into a sort of SPAN aggregation device that achieves the goal described in this section.

You can find more details about this technology at https://www.cisco.com/go/nexusdatabroker.

Troubleshooting Wizard

Cisco ACI offers the previously described mechanisms as well as other mechanisms so that network admins troubleshooting connectivity problems have easy access to all the information relevant to a certain problem from a single screen.

In a non-ACI network, the network administrator would start gathering information about the servers involved in the problem, such as the servers' IP addresses, their MAC addresses, on what switch ports they are connected, what the network design looks like, and whether a firewall or any other Layer 4-7 device is involved.

After the network administrator has gathered the initial information, that's when the real troubleshooting begins: looking at the interface counters, at access control lists in the network or firewalls, etc. Depending on the results of those activities, the troubleshooting might continue in multiple directions.

The following sections offer but a glimpse into the art of network troubleshooting, and they show just how complex it can be. Cisco ACI can help you alleviate the difficulties associated to network troubleshooting by leveraging the concept of centralized management. That is the goal of the Troubleshooting Wizard. This function is called **Visibility & Troubleshooting** and you can find it under the **Operations** tab.

Defining the Troubleshooting Session

After accessing the **Visibility & Troubleshooting** section in the GUI, the first thing you can do is retrieve previously saved troubleshooting sessions or define a new one. In order to create a new troubleshooting session, you need to be familiar with the following parameters (see Figure 12-21):

- You need a name for the session so that you can retrieve it at a later stage.

- You need to know the session type, meaning whether you are troubleshooting a connectivity problem between endpoints that exist in ACI or if one of the endpoints is an external source or destination.

- You need the source and destination MAC or IP addresses. After introducing these addresses, you need to select to which EPG those addresses belong. Bear in mind that because Cisco ACI supports overlapping IP addresses in multiple VRFs, there could be multiple EPGs matching your IP address.

- Alternatively, if an IP address is external to the fabric (for example, the IP address of a client that cannot access a certain application), you are not required to specify the external EPG to which that IP address is assigned. The Troubleshooting Wizard will figure this out using the EPG you select for the other one.

- You need to know how long you want the troubleshooting to look back in time for statistics and logs related to the endpoints involved. The default is 240 minutes; the maximum is 1440 minutes (1 day).

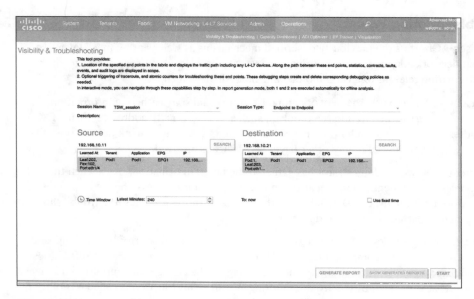

Figure 12-21 *Troubleshooting Wizard Session Definition*

Once those parameters have been defined (or you have loaded them from a previously saved session), you can click the **Start** button. That will take you to the main trouble-shooting window, where you will be able to choose from different panels to explore multiple aspects of the communication, along with the topology with which the end-points are connected to each other. This topology can include Cisco ACI leaf and spine switches, Fabric Extenders, hypervisor information, and even any L4-7 device that has been inserted by ACI into the communication.

Faults in the Troubleshooting Wizard

The top panel, and the one you will see right after starting the session, shows you whether there are any faults in the leaf and spine switches involved in the communication, as Figure 12-22 depicts. You can quickly identify whether there are faults in those devices (you will see an icon indicating the fault severity next to a switch). If there are, have a look at them to verify whether they can be related to the problem you are troubleshooting.

You can click the objects in the diagram (switches, ports, or even virtual machines) in order to see a history of previous faults. This is a great help in order to see the state of the network related to the problem you are looking into.

Notice the information sign inside of both endpoints. You can click it to see a history of when these endpoints have been visible in the network, and on which ports. This can be extremely useful when troubleshooting certain network problems, and it can give you very valuable information, especially about how virtual machines move throughout the data center.

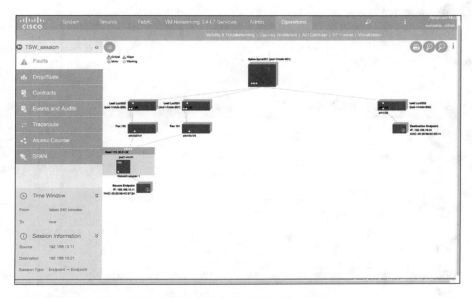

Figure 12-22 *Troubleshooting Wizard's Faults Section*

Statistics in the Troubleshooting Wizard

After you have verified the system faults, the next step is typically checking the interface statistics such as transmitted, received, or dropped packets. You normally want to check for things like unusual traffic spikes in some direction or unusually high amounts of dropped packets.

You can look at the statistics in a table format, which you can configure to show either all values or only nonzero values. You can see all 30-second intervals of the period defined in the troubleshooting session. This is extremely useful because, unlike in legacy switches, it is as if you can go back in time and have a look at interface counters when the problem was actually happening.

Additionally, you get to see exactly how many packets have been transmitted, received, and so on in one 30-second interval. Compare this to a traditional switch, where you need to issue your **show** command every now and then and check for counter increments.

In the network diagram, you can see the switch ports involved in the communication. You can click one of those ports, which will take you to its graphical statistics, as Figure 12-23 shows. Here, you can monitor the counter evolution in real time. You can define which counters you want to have represented in the diagram as well as the interval with which you want to monitor those counters.

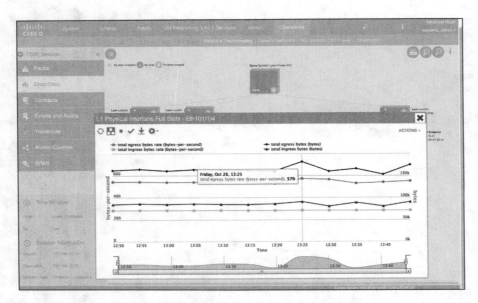

Figure 12-23   *Graphical Representation of Port Statistics*

As you can see in Figure 12-23, you can have two dimensions represented in the diagram, such as bytes per second and packets per second. Those two dimensions will be represented in the vertical axis at the right and left sides of the graph, respectively. Once you have selected to display counters that are measured with two distinct dimensions, only other counters that are measured by one of those two dimensions can be added to the graph.

Contract Information in the Troubleshooting Wizard

One of the most frequent reasons for connectivity problems is that the security policy might be configured to drop certain packets. Therefore, it is very important to be able to quickly verify whether or not that is the case.

The **Contracts** panel of the Troubleshooting Wizard shows the access control lists that Cisco ACI has configured in the fabric. Note that the administrator only defines contracts between EPGs, and ACI will automatically find the right switch ports where the Access Control Lists have been deployed, as shown by Figure 12-24. For more detailed troubleshooting, both directions of the communication (source-to-destination and destination-to-source) are shown, and you can see in real time how many packets have been permitted or dropped by each entry in those access control lists. The permit and drop counters are refreshed every 30 seconds so that you can verify whether packets are still being dropped.

Note the implicit **BD Allow** filter in both directions; this is a special implicit rule in the bridge domain that allows some broadcast, unknown unicast, and multicast packets to go through the network. However, for normal application traffic, you should not see its hit counters increasing.

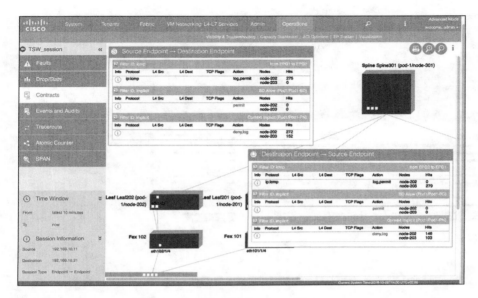

Figure 12-24 *Troubleshooting Wizard Contract View*

As you'll recall from earlier in this chapter, you can see dropped packet logs (and permit logs, if configured on the right hardware) in the tenant view of the APIC.

Events and Audits in the Troubleshooting Wizard

In the troubleshooting session, you can also see changes that have been performed during the time window being investigated. Experience shows that the root cause of many network issues involves changes that have been introduced either manually or automatically in the system. Typically, you would record those changes and events in external applications such as syslog servers and command accounting applications.

However, with Cisco ACI, you do not need to leave your APIC console because that information is just one click away in the **Events and Audits** section of the Troubleshooting Wizard, as shown in Figure 12-25.

You can click a network switch, or even on a port, in order to see which events and changes have taken place during the time window defined as the scope for the troubleshooting session. Figure 12-25 shows an example of clicking the destination port where the destination endpoint is attached. As you can see, it looks like some activity was going on during the minutes preceding the problem.

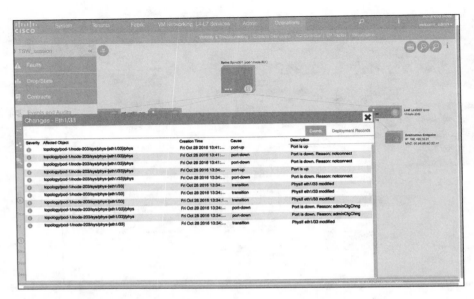

Figure 12-25   *Events and Audits View in the Troubleshooting Wizard*

Traceroute in the Troubleshooting Wizard

Traceroute is a tool that has traditionally been used by network operators to follow the path that packets take over an IP network, leveraging ICMP packets and the TTL (Time-To-Live) field of IP packets. However, the usability of standard IP traceroute is limited in a data center fabric. Consider the following:

- First of all, there is no TTL field in Ethernet for L2 communication.

- In a routed IP flow in ACI, most endpoints are exactly one hop away from each other, because ACI routes the traffic.

- In spine/leaf fabrics, you have multiple paths between any given two endpoints (at least as many as spines), and you need to make sure that you explore all of them.

- Lastly, ICMP packets do not test possible UDP/TCP packet filters that are configured between the endpoints.

To fix these limitations, ACI incorporates a new-and-improved version of the traceroute tool specifically conceived for troubleshooting leaf/spine fabrics. Synthetic traffic is generated in order to verify the fabric operation. The traffic is generated in the leaf switches: The source leaf (that is, the leaf switch where the source endpoint is attached) generates traffic addressed to the destination endpoint, and the destination leaf generates traffic addressed to the source leaf.

This synthetic traffic can be TCP or UDP, on specific destination port numbers (a random source TCP/UDP port number will be picked). This way, you can verify whether ports are opened in the source or destination endpoints, or whether traffic is being dropped by any switch in between because of an access control list. Bear in mind that synthetic traffic might potentially disrupt existing communication, if the source port number matches that of an established TCP/UDP flow. However, given the high amount of possible source port numbers (around 64,000), the probability is rather low.

Furthermore, all paths between the source of the synthetic traffic (the source/destination leaf) and the destination of the traceroute (the destination/source endpoint) are checked, which can be extremely valuable when the connectivity between two endpoints is only partially impaired. Compare this with the traditional traceroute tool, which will typically yield results of a single path on a Layer 2 network, offering little visibility for troubleshooting complex problem scenarios.

After some seconds, the diagram will graphically represent the result of the synthetic probes, either with green (successful) or red (failed) arrows. A green arrow is used to represent each node in the path that responded to the traceroute probes. The beginning of a red arrow represents where the path ends, as that's the last node that responded to the traceroute probes.

A failed traceroute might indicate that traffic is dropped by an access control list (you can verify that in the **Contracts** panel of the Troubleshooting Wizard), or maybe that the TCP/UDP port at the endpoint itself is not open.

Remember that endpoint traceroute tests can be configured from the tenant view in ACI as well, not just from the Troubleshooting Wizard.

Atomic Counters in the Troubleshooting Wizard

Atomic counters can be leveraged using troubleshooting policies, as previous sections in this chapter have explained, as well as directly from within the Troubleshooting Wizard. When the **Atomic Counter** panel is displayed, the wizard will dynamically configure atomic counters that capture the communication between the endpoints defined in the troubleshooting session. Do not panic if the counters do not work immediately; APIC needs around 60 seconds to program the counters, plus an additional 30 seconds to show the first counting interval. Every subsequent 30 seconds, the counters will be refreshed.

Notice in Figure 12-26 how the network is counting every single packet that the source has sent to the destination, as well as in the opposite direction from the destination to the source. This is a very quick way to prove that the network is not dropping traffic between any given pair of servers.

Note that atomic counters are only usable when the source and destination endpoints are located in different leaf switches. The reason is that in the first generation of the Cisco Nexus 9000 hardware, if two endpoints are in the same leaf, the switch will connect them using a fast path in the hardware without going through the Cisco ASIC, where the atomic counter functionality is available.

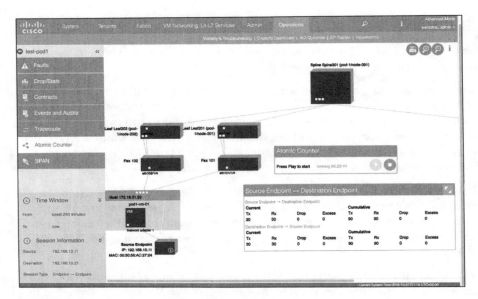

Figure 12-26   *Atomic Counters in the Troubleshooting Wizard*

Configuring SPAN from the Troubleshooting Wizard

If you have not located the cause of the problem yet, the next step is usually capturing traffic and looking at it with some kind of packet analysis tool, watching for anything unusual. You can trigger traffic captures directly from the Troubleshooting Wizard. In this case, it is not required to define any further parameters because all required information has already been entered in the session information (source and destination addresses). The only missing data is where captured packets should be sent. The Troubleshooting Wizard offers four options:

- **EPG:** Use this option if you have a traffic analyzer connected to the ACI fabric.

- **APIC:** Use this option if you are not connected to the network. The traffic capture will be stored in an APIC, and you will be able to download the capture after stopping it. In order to do this, in-band management needs to be configured.

- **Host via APIC:** Use this option if you have a traffic analyzer not directly connected to the ACI fabric, but reachable over the APIC.

- **Predefined Destination Group:** Use this option if you have already defined SPAN destinations in your troubleshooting policies.

Endpoint Tracker

Have you ever wondered where a certain device is connected? Even if you find where it is connected now, where was it connected in the past? These are the questions that the Endpoint Tracker application answers.

This functionality in the ACI GUI has an interesting story that can serve as an example of the way Cisco ACI has evolved. In the first Cisco ACI software versions, there was no tracking functionality for end devices. However, upon customer demand, a very talented Cisco engineer named Michael Smith developed such a function using the ACI Toolkit. As Chapter 13 describes, the ACI Toolkit is a Python software development kit (SDK) that allows you to easily create automation solutions based on the REST API that Cisco ACI provides.

Customer feedback was so overwhelming that Cisco decided to incorporate this tool into the native functionality of the APIC, for a better support experience. Now you can access the Endpoint Tracker under the **Operations** panel.

You need to enter the MAC, IPv4, or IPv6 address of a specific endpoint. In case multiple endpoints match your query (remember, you could have the same IP address across several VRFs, for example), you can choose the EPG where the address you are interested in is located. After doing that, you will see a history of all transitions for that IP address: when it was attached to the network or detached from it, and to which port it was connected.

For example, in Figure 12-27, you can see that the IP address is now being seen in port eth1/4 of FEX 102, but some days ago it was on port 1/4 of FEX 102. Is this correct?

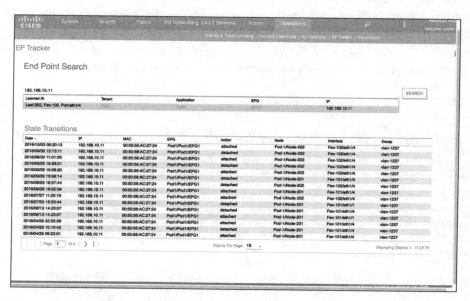

Figure 12-27 *Endpoint Tracking of an IP Address in ACI*

In Figure 12-27, we are looking at the IP address of a bare-metal server, but it could also be that of a virtual machine. Imagine if you have dedicated leaf switches for DMZ and Intranet, and you want to check that a certain critical virtual machine has never been connected to one of the DMZ leaf switches. This is very difficult to do with a traditional network, but it's a walk in the park with the Endpoint Tracker in Cisco ACI.

Alternatively, if you are troubleshooting duplicate IP addresses, this is a quick way of looking at all the endpoints that have been located by the network sharing the same IP address. Otherwise, you need to inspect the ARP tables of your routers, wait for the "bad" IP address to come up, catch its MAC address before the "good" IP takes over, and track the MAC over the fabric to locate the port you need to shut down. The Endpoint Tracker has probably just saved you a good deal of troubleshooting time.

Effectively Using Your Fabric Resources

Spine/leaf networks are extremely scalable. You can scale bandwidth by adding spine switches, and you can scale ports by adding more leaf switches.

Furthermore, in some spine/leaf networks such as Cisco ACI, most functionality is executed at the leaf. In order for the leaf switches not to become a scalability bottleneck, these networks need to be designed so that each leaf only uses the resources it needs. For example, if any given leaf switch does not have an endpoint directly attached that belongs to a certain EPG or bridge domain, there is no need to implement the associated policies. This means that spreading endpoints across multiple leaf switches will increase the overall scalability of the network, because it will decrease the scalability pressure to which each one of the leaf switches is subject.

When should you start to care about resource bottlenecks? How do you identify them with enough time so that you can take the required actions to eliminate them? The following sections describe how to find and solve bandwidth and resource problems in an ACI fabric.

Using Traffic Map to Find Bandwidth Bottlenecks

Traditionally, bandwidth has usually been a scarce resource in data center networks. Oversubscription rates of 50:1 were not that uncommon because of the predominant north-south traffic patterns in legacy applications. However, this pattern has yielded to an overwhelming east-west factor, where those oversubscription rates are no longer acceptable. That is one of the reasons why Cisco Nexus 9000 switches, the foundation for Cisco ACI, work at wire rate. Even if the first 24 server ports were speaking full steam with the last 24 ports, the switch would not drop traffic.

Even though the Nexus 9000 switches work at wire rate, there is an implicit oversubscription in the way the networks are built. For example, if you take a switch with 48 10GbE server ports and six 40GbE uplink ports, that produces a potential oversubscription of 480 to 240 (in other words, 2:1). This is typically more than acceptable, because a good amount of the traffic will be locally switched, and most likely not all servers are going to fill up their pipes at the same time.

Therefore, more aggressive subscription rates of 3:1 and even 6:1 are not unusual. A 6:1 oversubscription with 48 10GbE server ports means that only two 40GbE uplinks are used. Actually, this is a very common starting configuration for Cisco ACI customers.

But once the network goes into production, how do you make sure that your chosen oversubscription rate is still good enough? You can certainly monitor link utilization over SNMP or the REST API to make sure that it does not go over certain thresholds. Once you have identified that there is a bandwidth issue with one of your links, in a traditional network the next action would probably be upgrading the bandwidth.

In ACI, there are a couple of easy steps you can take before doing that, and this is where ACI's Traffic Map comes into play. This graphical tool enables you to see whether the traffic patterns in your network are creating bottlenecks. You can customize the information shown in the Traffic Map; here are some examples:

- Whether to show packets going through all spines, or only packets that traverse a specific spine.

- Whether to show a count of packets sent, received, dropped, or in excess. (In-excess packets usually denote some network inconsistency.)

- Whether to show a cumulative packet count (all packets seen to date) or just the ones seen in the last 30-second period.

The Traffic Map can be extremely useful in better balancing the decision of where to put new hosts in the network. For example, it is obvious from the simple example in Figure 12-28 that the leaf switches with highest traffic amongst them are leaf switches 201 and 202. Therefore, it seems obvious that if new hosts were attached to the fabric, you would ideally want to put them in leaf 203.

Figure 12-28 *Traffic Map of a Fabric with Three Leaf Switches*

Although you could have arrived at the same conclusion by individually monitoring the leaf uplinks, in the case of a big network with potentially up to 200 leaf switches (the maximum leaf count supported at the time of this writing), this kind of graphical visualization greatly simplifies the process of locating bandwidth bottlenecks.

Using Capacity Dashboard to Detect Resource Bottlenecks

Bandwidth is one of the finite resources that should be closely monitored in a network, but by far it's not the only one. Every system has a limited amount of resources that can be leveraged for its functionality, and Cisco ACI is no different.

Cisco has thoroughly tested multiple scenarios that have been documented in Cisco ACI scalability guides, where the maximum supported configuration limits are specified. As you can see in those documents, there is a maximum supported limit for the number of endpoints, EPGs, VRFs, and other objects. The network administrator should maintain a close eye on these parameters, to verify they do not exceed Cisco's supported maximum values.

In order to make this task easier, Cisco ACI includes this capacity verification natively in the APIC controller. Network administrators no longer need to write down the number of configured objects in their network and compare them to a static document in Cisco's website; instead, the system gives out this information—always accurate and up to date—in Cisco ACI Capacity Dashboard.

The Capacity Dashboard reports two kinds of limits in ACI:

- **Fabric limits:** There are some system-wide limits that determine the overall number of network objects supported by the network.

- **Leaf limits:** Each individual leaf has specific limits that are compared to the resources actually provisioned.

Modern systems spread scalability across multiple devices, in what is known as the *scale-out model*, so that each individual component does not determine the scalability of the overall system. Cisco ACI is no different, and the fabric scale is much higher than the individual scale of each leaf.

Legacy networks are mostly *scale-up models*, where the system scalability (such as the maximum number of MAC addresses) is dictated by each individual switch, and the only way of increasing those numbers is changing all switches in the network with more powerful models.

With Cisco ACI's scale-out concept, if any individual leaf is close to exceeding its scalability limits, you can just install additional leaf switches (or replace that specific leaf with a more powerful one, which would be a combination of the scale-out and scale-up models).

As Figure 12-29 shows, Cisco ACI Capacity Dashboard provides information related to both fabric and leaf limits.

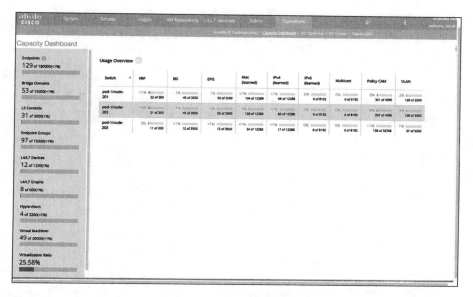

Figure 12-29 *Cisco ACI Capacity Dashboard Showing System-wide and Leaf-wide Limits*

Using ACI Optimizer to Plan for Changes

Looking at the current utilization of hardware resources in Cisco ACI Capacity Dashboard is very useful, but you might want to go one step further. The network should be able to answer the question of whether hardware resources are enough, not only for today's requirements, but for future ones as well.

This is the purpose of ACI Optimizer. You can use this design tool to design what-if scenarios. You can simulate configurations with certain sizes and characteristics, such as the number of tenants, VRFs, bridge domains, or EPGs, and estimate whether a certain hardware would have enough resources to support that configuration.

The creation of a simulation involves four steps:

Step 1.   Create the configuration template.

Step 2.   Create the configuration objects that will exist in the simulation (tenants, bridge domains, EPGs, contracts, and so on).

Step 3.   Create the physical network topology (spines, leaf switches, and FEX devices).

Step 4.   Examine the simulation output.

Step 1 is straightforward; there is no option to provide other than the name you want to assign to your template. Now you can create configuration objects in the **Config** tab, as Figure 12-30 and Figure 12-31 demonstrate.

For example, after you create a new config template in the **Operations** menu of the GUI, you get to add objects to the canvas to simulate a future state of the fabric. Figure 12-30 demonstrates how to add 500 bridge domains, each with 200 endpoints with dual-stack IPv4 and IPv6 deployed across 20 leaf switches.

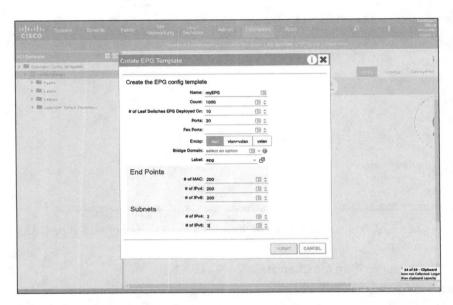

Figure 12-30 *Cisco ACI Optimizer: Creating EPGs*

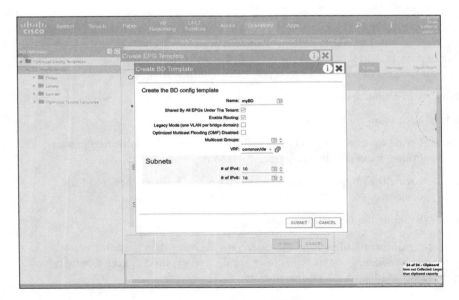

Figure 12-31 *Cisco ACI Optimizer: Creating Bridge Domains*

As you can see from the previous figures, you can simulate in a single step the creation of hundreds of identical objects (in this example, 1000 EPGs). Continue creating the required objects to make your simulation accurate, and when you are satisfied, proceed to the next step of defining the topology.

In the **Topology** tab, you can specify how many spines, leaf switches, and optionally FEX devices your simulated ACI network will consist of. As before, you can create all the devices of any given type in one single go, as Figure 12-32 depicts.

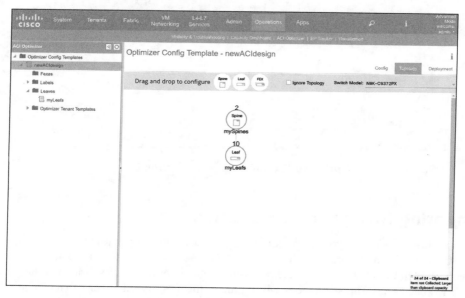

Figure 12-32   *Cisco ACI Optimizer: Creating the Physical Topology*

Lastly, you can proceed to the **Deployment** tab to simulate the results. This information might be extremely valuable, either when designing your fabric for the first time or when deciding how to best evolve a fabric upon new scalability requirements. For example, Figure 12-33 shows the simulation of a setup on 10 leaf switches with a certain number of VRFs, bridge domains, and EPGs. You can see in the foreground the **Issues** window with the two scalability challenges that this setup would encounter, and in the background you can see the detailed analysis with the simulated scenario compared to the maximum scalability limits per leaf and per fabric.

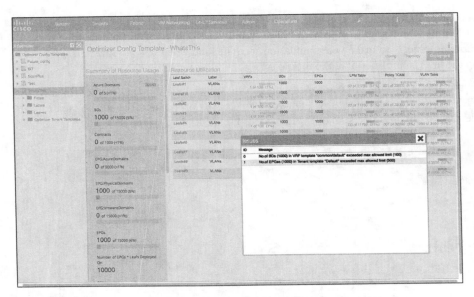

Figure 12-33   *Cisco ACI Optimizer: Examining the Simulation Output*

Monitoring Policies and Statistics

In a traditional network, you would configure the monitoring properties of its elements, switch after switch. As you have already seen, this type of configuration is completely centralized in Cisco ACI, and it is defined using the monitoring policies located in the **Fabric Policies** tab. This section describes some of the most useful policies that can be configured in order to be able to better monitor a Cisco ACI fabric.

SNMP Policies

Data networks have been traditionally monitored using the Simple Network Management Protocol (SNMP). Essentially, this protocol allows a two-way communication:

- A monitoring station can poll the state of certain variables (called *object IDs*, or *OIDs*) on the monitored object.

- The monitored object can asynchronously inform the monitoring station about any anomaly by sending messages called *traps* or *informs*.

Both Cisco ACI switches and controllers can be monitored using SNMP, although as explained in Chapter 13, this might not be the best way to do so. The reason is that the REST API in Cisco ACI offers much more information over a consolidated interface, instead of having to poll individual switches one after the other to get the required information.

At press time, the SNMP Management Information Bases (MIBs) supported by ACI components are detailed in this document: http://www.cisco.com/c/dam/en/us/td/docs/switches/datacenter/aci/apic/sw/1-x/mib/list/mib-support.html.

You can configure SNMP in ACI through the corresponding SNMP policy, which you can find in the **Fabric** tab of the GUI, as Figure 12-34 shows. As you can see, there are a few elements pertinent to this policy:

- **Generic SNMP settings:** SNMP administrative state, contact, and location information.

- **Client Group Policies:** Which IP addresses are allowed to access the system via SNMP (optional).

- **SNMP V3 Users:** It is strongly recommended that you use SNMPv3 because it offers much stronger authentication and encryption than SNMPv2. Here, you can define SNMPv3 users and their authentication.

- **Community Policies:** In case you use version 1 or 2 of SNMP (which, again, is not recommended but could be desirable in some situations such as lab environments), you can configure here the SNMP community strings that will be used as the means of authentication.

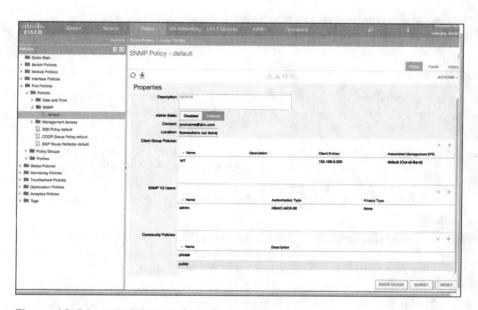

Figure 12-34   *ACI SNMP Policy Example*

The second part of the SNMP configuration is where to send SNMP traps. Figure 12-35 illustrates the configuration of a remote SNMP destination in the **Admin** tab of the GUI.

Figure 12-35 *SNMP Destination*

Next, you need to configure ACI to send SNMP traps to that destination in the monitoring policies.

Syslog Policies

Syslog is configured similar to SNMP, but syslog offers better control over which messages to send out, with which severity, and on which facility. Here are the configuration steps:

Step 1.   Define a syslog destination in the **Admin** tab. Here, you can define whether you want to send the syslog messages to a file in the APIC (/var/log/external/messages), to the console, and/or to an external destination. In the latter case, you can optionally define which facility to use, the minimum severity, and a port number.

Step 2.   Define a syslog source under **Monitoring Policies** in the **Fabric** tab, as Figure 12-36 shows. You can specify which event category and the minimum severity you want to forward to the destination.

Statistics

Statistics monitoring is how traditional networking has been done. Note that Cisco ACI comes out of the box with a default configuration for statistics and threshold alarming. Just to mention one example, a fault will be generated in ACI when there are too many drops in an interface, without having the admin explicitly configuring anything. However, advanced users might want to override the default behavior, and this section explains where to find the main controls that can determine the way in which Cisco ACI handles statistics.

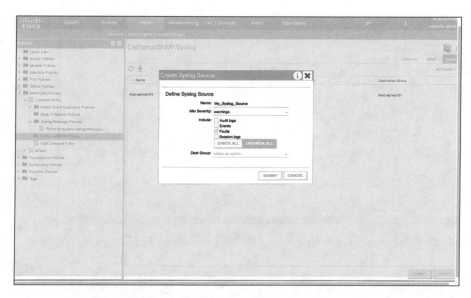

Figure 12-36   *Syslog Source Configuration*

Statistics are controlled by monitoring policies. You can define monitoring policies associated with multiple objects in ACI. For example, you could have different monitoring policies for certain bridge domains, logical objects like EPGs, or physical objects like ports. There is, however, one common monitoring policy that will be used if no specific monitoring policy has been defined for any given object, and it can be found in the **Fabric** tab of the GUI, as Figure 12-37 shows for collection statistics. Other monitoring policies include for which events syslog messages are generated, SNMP and syslog destinations (as the previous sections on SNMP and syslog have discussed), and the fault lifecycle policy.

Monitoring policies define the following:

- How long and how often statistics are collected and retained
- Upon which threshold crossing faults are triggered
- Which statistics are exported

For example, if in the default monitoring policy you select **L1 Physical Interface Configuration** as the monitored object and **Egress Drop Packets** as the statistics type, you will be able to see the default thresholds for packet drops and even modify them, as Figure 12-38 shows.

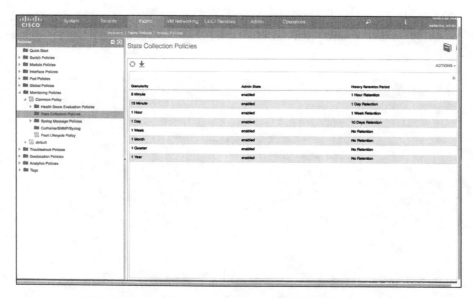

Figure 12-37 *Common Monitoring Policy for the Collection of Statistics*

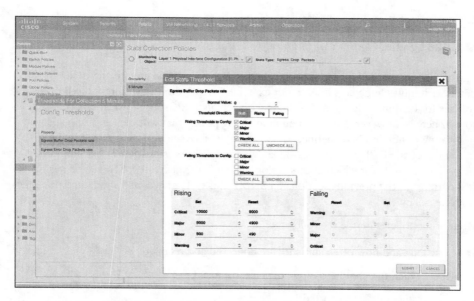

Figure 12-38 *Modifying Statistics Thresholds for Fault Generation*

Third-Party Monitoring Tools with ACI Support

Multiple monitoring tools are available that support the Cisco ACI infrastructure. This section describes a few of these tools. Note that this list is not supposed to be comprehensive; instead, it contains the off-the-shelf monitoring integrations at press time.

IBM Tivoli Netcool

Netcool is the network monitoring component of the IBM Tivoli software family. It communicates with managed objects over so-called "probes" that implement the mechanism with which those managed objects are accessed.

Cisco APIC provides northbound REST APIs through which the IBM Tivoli Netcool/OMNIbus probe for ACI can communicate with the systems it monitors. The probe can acquire JavaScript Object Notification (JSON) events from the REST APIs using the WebSocket protocol. It then converts these events into Netcool/OMNIbus events and sends them to the ObjectServer.

SevOne

SevOne has several monitoring products and solutions for monitoring traditional and modern IP networks, as well as 4G LTE networks and hybrid cloud deployments. SevOne's monitoring solution supports Cisco products and technologies such as IP SLA, NetFlow, StarOS for 4G LTE networks, Cisco Unified Compute System (UCS), and Cisco ACI.

ScienceLogic

ScienceLogic specializes in removing complexity out of IT services management and monitoring, through consolidating multiple tasks into a single monitoring platform.

ScienceLogic's ACI support helps customers in multiple ACI-related tasks: monitoring through easy-to-understand visuals, troubleshooting with root-cause-detection algorithms, and combining non-ACI and ACI network operations into a single pane of glass.

Splunk

Splunk also has a very good understanding of how ACI works, and this is reflected in Splunk Enterprise. Splunk gathers data out of ACI over the REST API, providing real-time visibility of ACI information and events, and correlating them to each other as well as to other IT domains, such as VMware vSphere.

Zenoss

Zenoss for Cisco ACI software delivers application-centric IT operations monitoring for the software-defined data center. Cisco ACI defines tenant and application needs, and

Zenoss software delivers service impact and root-cause analysis unified across the network, computing, virtualization, and storage resources in the infrastructure. Zenoss for Cisco ACI uses the business definitions of tenants, applications, endpoint groups, and contracts to build an end-to-end live model of your data center. The Zenoss live model identifies the specific infrastructure components used by each application and correlates the network health, key performance indicators (KPIs), faults, and events for each ACI tenant and application to identify the root cause of performance and availability problems.

Summary

One of the main advantages of Cisco ACI as network architecture is its centralized management plane. Having a single GUI and a single API from which to monitor and troubleshoot the network is a decisive improvement over legacy network concepts. No longer do network administrators need to log in to individual devices in order to retrieve network status or information.

This single point of management is very useful, for example, when monitoring Cisco ACI from an external tool such as Splunk, Zenoss, or SevOne, to name a few, because this tool can get the state of the full network with just a single API call.

Additionally, Cisco ACI builds on this centralized management plane with tools that make monitoring and troubleshooting easier than ever before. Examples of these tools are improved ping and traceroute versions, the Traffic Map for easy hot spot identification, the Troubleshooting Wizard for easy access to all information related to a problem, and the Capacity Dashboard for a quick verification of the resource consumption in the fabric as a whole, as well as in the individual leaf switches.

All in all, Cisco ACI offers, out of the box, all the monitoring capabilities that most organizations demand from their networks, without them having to incur extra costs for additional tools.

Chapter 13

ACI Programmability

In this chapter, you will learn the following:

- Why network programmability is important

- How to program Cisco ACI over its REST application programming interface (API)

- Multiple tools that help in developing network automation solutions for Cisco ACI, such as Visore, the API Inspector, and Arya

- Software development kits (SDKs) for programming Cisco ACI

- Integration between Cisco ACI and automation tools such as IaaS (Cisco Enterprise Cloud Suite, Microsoft Azure Pack, VMware vRealize) and PaaS (Apprenda)

Why Network Programmability? Save Money, Make Money!

No matter where you go, any IT event you visit nowadays will be full of sessions talking about automating and programming. Why is that? The reasons for this automation frenzy are the very same objectives of any IT organization. To put it bluntly: save money, make money.

In the "save money" camp, automation has become a major target of most organizations due to a very simple reason: IT budgets must be kept to a minimum, while IT complexity and scale are expected to grow. How does one handle more devices, more complex configurations, and more dependencies with the same IT staff? Either they start working overtime, or you give them automation tools with which they can do their job in a shorter amount of time.

But saving time is not the only reason why organizations seek to automate their processes. In particular, when you are dealing with complex IT technologies, manual actions are error-prone. Slight mistakes when typing a command can take whole systems down. Have you ever forgotten to paste the second page of that access control list that you put in a Word document? Or maybe you've pasted the wrong configuration text file in the wrong router. If you have, you know what I am talking about.

But there is a second perspective to automation and programmability: the "make money" part. If an IT organization limits itself to streamlining existing processes, its added value to the organization as a whole will not increase. More CIOs are willing to use IT as an enablement for business generation, and in order to do that, automation is a must.

The first reason is that by streamlining existing processes, IT administrators will have more time to invest in innovating, instead of just focusing on "keeping the lights on." Secondly, only through automation and programmability can you start delivering added value to the organization, whether it is through DevOps initiatives, continuous integration and continuous development, or public/private/hybrid cloud projects.

In this chapter, you see how to approach automation from these two perspectives ("save money, make money"), and we look at multiple examples of how ACI helps to achieve these objectives.

What Is Wrong with Previous Network Automation Concepts?

Is automation something completely new to the network domain? Absolutely not. Networks have been automated since the dawn of Internet; otherwise, operating large network environments would have been impossible. However, the lack of general-purpose application programming interfaces (APIs) has plagued the network industry since its very inception.

Most traditional network automation tools out there focus on the command-line interface (CLI) as a means to automate the network. This means that the automation tool (or script) will connect to a series of devices, and on each one it will run certain commands. Those commands generate a text-based output, and the script will analyze that output either to extract information out of it or to conclude that the previously executed CLI commands ran successfully.

The problem with this approach is that network CLIs have been created to be read by humans. As such, normally no specific care has been taken that they be machine readable. For example, imagine that a certain command gives the output **ok** and another one gives the output **OK**. A human being would without any doubt recognize those two outputs as the same, indicating that whatever ran before was executed successfully.

However, those two strings are completely different for a machine (such as a network automation tool or script), so you now need to enter code so that upper- and lowercase expressions are correctly processed. Add different table formatting across software versions as well as different outputs for the same command across network platforms, and you'll soon realize that with time, these automation tools or scripts are just not maintainable and end up imploding due to the complexity of handling every small variation in strings that are only intended to be read by humans.

This is why network APIs were created, but as you'll see, these are typically limited in one way or the other.

SNMP

The Simple Network Management Protocol, or SNMP, was the first sort of API created specifically in order to more efficiently manage networks. Information is structured in one or many management information bases (MIBs) in variables or object identifiers (OIDs). These variables can be either read (through a "get" operation) or written (yes, you guessed right, through a "set" operation). Additionally, SNMP implements the possibility of devices informing asynchronously when certain events took place, through so-called "traps" or "informs."

The main weakness of SNMP is the fact that it is completely decoupled from the device's operating system (OS), but it runs as an additional application on top. As a consequence, not all device information is available over SNMP. However, MIBs need to be implemented after the fact, which often leads to questions like, "What is the OID to monitor this or that information?" Vendors can decide how shallow or how deep their SNMP implementation will be.

Cisco ACI does support SNMP, although due to inherent inefficiencies in the protocol, Cisco's recommendation is to use the REST API to query any information in the fabric, as was already discussed in Chapter 12, "Troubleshooting and Monitoring."

Network Configuration Protocol and YANG

The Network Configuration Protocol (NETCONF), developed by the Internet Engineering Task Force (IETF), is a more modern attempt at providing APIs in order to manage network devices. As with other IETF projects, NETCONF is openly documented in an RFC. In this case, it was originally described by RFC 4741, which has been replaced by RFC 6241 (https://tools.ietf.org/html/rfc6241).

The core of NETCONF is its Remote Procedure Call (RPC) layer, which uses Extensible Markup Language (XML) to encode both network configuration and the protocol messages.

YANG (Yet Another Next Generation) is a data model that can be used by NETCONF in order to describe network state and operations. YANG is also documented by IETF in RFC 6020 (https://tools.ietf.org/html/rfc6020).

YANG relies on XML constructs, such as XML Path Language (XPath), as a notation for specifying dependencies. However, YANG documents are more "human readable" than XML (YANG documents are actually closer to JSON syntax), and that is one of the reasons for its popularity.

YANG organizes network data hierarchically so that it is easier to process, and it offers a network model mostly consistent across multiple network vendors. Hence, the combo of NETCONF with YANG has attracted much interest as a vendor-neutral way of automating and managing multivendor network environments.

As its very name indicates, NETCONF is network-centric. As such, even if it is success-fully utilized by organizations such as network service providers to achieve network automation, it is not that well known in development communities outside of the network industry. Therefore, its ecosystem is not as broad as other non-network APIs, such as REST.

Programming Interfaces and SDKs

As you have already seen in this book, Cisco ACI offers multiple interfaces for manage-ment and configuration: not one but two graphical user interfaces (basic and advanced), a command-line interface, and a RESTful API (which is the main object of this chapter).

What Is REST?

REST (Representation State Transfer) APIs (sometimes called RESTful) have become the de-facto standard for programming interfaces. Sometimes considered a simplification of SOAP (Simple Object Access Protocol, conceived for the interoperation of web services), RESTful APIs essentially use HTTP (Hypertext Transfer Protocol) verbs like GET, POST, and DELETE to transmit, receive, and delete information, respectively. This information is normally coded using some structured description language like JSON (JavaScript Object Notation) or XML.

Purists will argue that the previous description is inaccurate at best, and they would probably be right, although it does give a good glimpse of what REST is all about. Let's go for the official description for the record, though (and you can keep whichever expla-nation you understand better).

REST is an architectural style consisting of a coordinated set of architectural constraints applied to components, connectors, and data elements, within a distributed hypermedia system. REST ignores the details of component implementation and protocol syntax in order to focus on the roles of components, the constraints upon their interaction with other components, and their interpretation of significant data elements.

REST imposes architectural constraints to whatever architecture follows it:

- Client/server, stateless, cacheable. layered, code on demand (optional), or uniform interface

- Identification of resources, manipulation of resources, self-descriptive, or hyperme-dia as the engine of application state

Here are the HTTP verbs that RESTful implementations reuse:

- GET, POST, PUT, and DELETE

- The PUT and DELETE methods are idempotent methods. The GET method is a safe method (or *nullipotent*), meaning that calling it produces no side-effects. POST is a create method.

What Is a Software Development Kit?

Software Development Kits (SDKs) are "modules" that allow you to use certain objects natively in a programming language. Depending on the programming language, these modules might be called libraries, plug-ins, or something else—but the concept stays the same.

Note that most languages support sending and receiving REST API calls. When doing so, the code is not really aware of what is being sent or received. If, on the contrary, you use an SDK, you will be able to use native constructs inside of your code.

For example, when using the ACI Python SDK (called Cobra), you can use natively created concepts like "Tenant," "EPG" and "Application Profile" inside of your Python code, whereas when sending REST API calls, you are just sending and receiving text, without your code knowing what that text means.

Cisco ACI Programming Interfaces

In this section, we explore how the concepts discussed so far in this chapter are implemented in Cisco ACI.

Cisco ACI REST API

Cisco ACI implements a very rich REST API that allows you to access every single piece of information available in the GUI—actually, even more, because some ACI objects are not completely exposed by the GUI but can be accessed over the REST API.

Compare this with SNMP in the old days, where you always had to ask your network vendor to tell you whether this or that counter was supported in SNMP (and what OID you needed to poll).

Like most RESTful APIs, ACI uses HTTP or HTTPS for transport. It offers the option of using JSON or XML in the payload. ACI uses the HTTP actions GET (to retrieve information) and POST (to run actions). Whenever you send a POST, you need to specify a JSON or XML body in the HTTP request, and this body will describe the action to be executed.

REST API Authentication

ACI's REST API does not use HTTP authentication mechanisms, but it implements authentication as any other POST call. You need to specify a username and password in the body (either in XML or JSON), and the call will return an authentication token if successful.

This authentication token is to be used in subsequent REST API calls as a cookie or HTTP header, without requiring you to send the authentication credentials until that particular token expires.

API Inspector

A critical part of every API is documentation, and you can find plenty of that both online (at Cisco.com) and directly in the APIC GUI itself. However, something that's even better than documentation is when you don't even need to look at it. Let me explain.

If you want to find out if a REST API call does something specific, you would normally look it up in the API reference guide. You can certainly do so with ACI, too, but there is a much better way: using the API Inspector. You can launch this tool from the APIC GUI, and it will open in a new window. If you have ever worked with the macro-recording function of Microsoft Office applications, then you'll know exactly what this tool does. After opening the API Inspector window, you can now do anything you want in the GUI, and the Inspector will reflect whatever API calls are required to accomplish the same task over REST.

The API Inspector offers some controls in its window to define at which level of granularity you want to be logged, to start and stop logging, and to clear the log, among other operations, as illustrated in Figure 13-1.

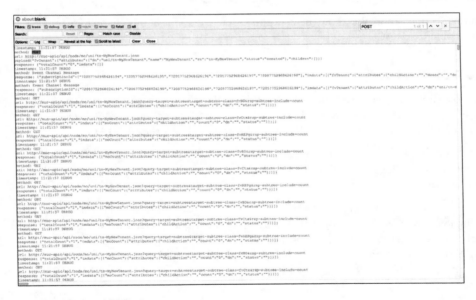

Figure 13-1 *API Inspector*

REST API Clients

A multitude of clients allow you to put your REST API calls to practice. Here are a few popular ones:

- **Postman:** Probably the most widely used REST client, Postman was created as a plug-in for the popular web browser Chrome, and it has evolved into a standalone application. It includes support for variable environments and other useful functionality, which is even greater in its paid version.

- **Paw:** A popular standalone client for the Mac. One of its nicest features is the translation of REST calls into other formats, such as JavaScript and Python (see the following section on more about why this is useful).

- **Poster:** A Firefox extension, Poster hasn't kept up with the functionality of its peer, Postman.

Using REST APIs in Programming Languages

As you have seen in the previous sections, finding out which API calls need to be carried out in order to perform a specific operation is easy. With the API Inspector, it is just a matter of running that task in the GUI and then looking at the Inspector window. But what if you want to create a script or program with that REST call? Most programming languages support using REST calls, from Perl to PHP to Python, to name just a few.

You need to be careful with the cookie, though. As you saw in the section about REST API authentication, you first need to authenticate to API to obtain the authentication token, and then you pass that authentication token in every single subsequent REST request.

Some languages will handle the cookies for you (for example, JavaScript uses the "http-Client" module): If you make an HTTP request and the server returns a cookie (the authentication token in case of Cisco ACI), that cookie is automatically inserted into subsequent requests to the same server. This is also the way most REST clients like Postman, Paw, and Poster behave.

However, other languages like Python (which uses the "requests" module) will not do this for you. You need to extract the authentication token out of the response for a successful authentication attempt and then insert it as an HTTP header in every single REST request.

Cisco ACI Object Model

The secret sauce for ACI's success is undoubtedly its object model. By modeling the complete network configuration in a structured, hierarchical, and object-oriented data model, you'll find it relatively easy to implement additional functions such as the REST API.

Objects are structured in the so-called *management information tree* (MIT), where objects are hierarchically structured in classes. Objects contain both attributes and child objects. This hierarchy makes it easier for applications using the API to explore the state of the network without having to deal with all the network information at once, and to dynamically extract from the network only the information required at any given time.

Classes describe the attributes that their objects will have. Chapter 9, "Multi-Tenancy," provided an example of useful information contained in classes, such as the roles that are allowed to read from and write to the objects belonging to a class.

For example, Figure 13-2 shows a very small subtree of an ACI fabric, where a couple of objects are depicted. This hierarchy can be considered a directory structure—for example, the object containing the configuration for the tenant "common" is actually called "tn-common," and its full name (its Distinguished Name, or DN, in ACI parlor) is "uni/tn-common." Here, "uni" is the big object that contains the whole fabric policy. As you will find out, most configurable objects are placed under the "uni" hierarchy.

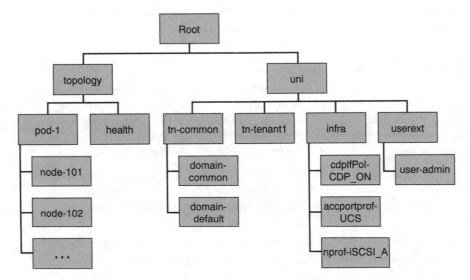

Figure 13-2 *Status Bar in Cisco APIC after Enabling Debug Information*

The next sections describe how you can find out the Distinguished Names of different ACI objects, as well as information regarding the classes they belong to.

Debug Information in the GUI

You might be wondering how you would interact with a specific object in ACI program-matically. The first step is finding out its Distinguished Name, so that you can reference it. In the GUI, you can activate the **Debug** option, so that you can see which object in ACI's MIT you are accessing at any given time. You can do so in the menu at the top-right corner of the GUI, with the command **Show Debug Info**.

A status bar at the very bottom of the GUI will appear (blue in 1.x or 2.x ACI versions, gray in 3.x ACI versions), where you can see some detailed information about the object onscreen, such as its Distinguished Name, as shown in Figure 13-2.

Current Screen:insieme.stromboli.layoutTab [fv:InfoTenant;center:a] [Current Mo:insieme.stromboli.model.def.fvTenant [uni/tn-MyNewTenant]   Current System Time :2016-10-25T11:25 UTC

Figure 13-3 *Status Bar in Cisco APIC after Debug Information Is Enabled*

As you can see in the Figure 13-3, the Debug Status Bar shows different information fields:

■ **Current Screen:** GUI information about which screen the GUI is currently showing. In the example in Figure 13-3, the screen is named *"insieme.stromboli.layoutTab[fv:*

infoTenant:center:a]". You can safely ignore this part of the status bar, it is mostly used by the Cisco ACI GUI developers.

■ **Current Mo:** "Mo" stands for "Managed Object". This is the most interesting piece of information for our purpose, and it is divided in two parts:

 ■ First, the class name of the Managed Object that is selected in the GUI. In the example of Figure 13-3, it is "*insieme.stromboli.model.def.fvTenant*". The class name is the part of the string after the last dot: "*fvTenant*".

 ■ Secondly, the Distinguished Name of the Managed Object that is selected in the GUI, in the example of Figure 13-3 it is "*uni/tn-MyNewTenant*".

The next step is to use this Distinguished Name in ACI's object model browser (also known as *Visore*) to find out more details about it.

Visore

When interacting with Cisco ACI REST API, oftentimes you'll wonder which values are possible for a specific variable, or which variables exist for each object, or what the relationship is between objects belonging to different classes. Again, to find the answers, you could check the online documentation, but you can also get these details from the object model in your APIC.

Each APIC comes with an object model browser called "Visore," which means "viewer" in Italian (probably due to the influence of the many Italian developers who have contributed to the creation of ACI). You can access Visore at https://your_apic_ip_address/visore.html (replace the string "your_apic_ip_address" with the host name or IP address of your APIC), and it offers you some search fields to start browsing. Note that this URL is case-sensitive.

After you have found out the Distinguished Name for a certain object with the Debug Status Bar (see the previous section), you can search for it in the filter query that appears in Visore's home page. For example, if you want to know information about a certain QoS policy in ACI, you would first find out its Distinguished Name using the debug task-bar (for example, **uni/infra/qosinst-default/class-level1** for the Level1 QoS policy), and then you would look it up in Visore, as Figure 13-4 shows.

After you have located an object (for example, by entering the Distinguished Name that you got using the Debug functionality of the GUI), you have several options you can explore (note that not all options will be available for every object):

■ **Show the parent object:** Click the green < sign next to the object's Distinguished Name.

■ **Show the children object:** Click the green > sign next to the object's Distinguished Name.

■ **Show object-related statistics:** Click the black bars next to the object's Distinguished Name.

- **Show object-related faults:** Click the red exclamation mark next to the object's Distinguished Name.

- **Show information of the class to which the object belongs:** Click the question mark next to the object's class name (in the example, above **qosClass**).

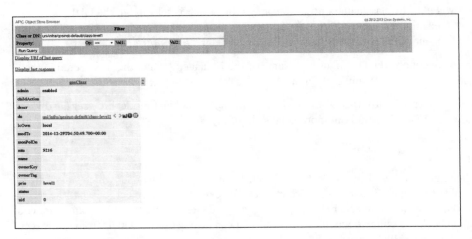

Figure 13-4   *Finding a Specific ACI Object in Cisco ACI Visore*

This last link is very useful because it will show valuable information for interacting with the object model, such as class-related information (see Figure 13-5).

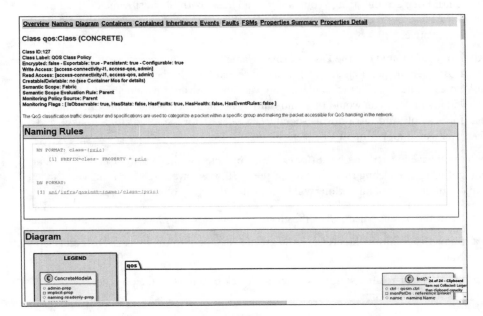

Figure 13-5   *Attributes for the Class* **qos**, *Extracted from Visore*

Here are some of the class attributes you can see in Figure 13-5 that are especially interesting:

- **The class prefix ("class-" in this example):** In ACI, all objects are prefixed by a string, so that when you look at the name, you can know to which class they belong. For example, the QoS class **level1** is actually called **class-level1**. This is the reason why the common tenant is called "tn-common," because the prefix for tenant objects is "tn-."

- **Distinguished Name format ("uni/infra/qosinst-{name}/class-{prio}" in this example):** This field tells you about the hierarchy of the object in the management information tree.

- **Write and read access:** As you learned in Chapter 9, these attributes show which ACI roles have read or write access to objects that belong to this class.

Another use of Visore is to find out which values can be entered for a specific property of an object. For example, if you want to know the maximum length of the description of a static binding (by the way, this is an example of an object that exists in the data model, and it cannot be set from the GUI), you can go to any object belonging to **fvRsPathAtt** and click the question mark next to the class name.

This will show you exhaustive documentation about that particular class, including all its attributes. Clicking the **Description** property will take you to the place in that page where the syntax and maximum length of that specific property are described (which, as you can see, can go up to 32 characters), as illustrated later in this section in Figure 13-8. Now you know why the GUI will throw an error if you try to define a description field over 32 characters.

If you scroll further down the web page with information related to the class, you will find valuable information such as a diagram showing the relationships between objects belonging to that class and other classes (depicted in Figure 13-6).

- Finally, after the description diagram, you get to see the different properties of the object, with links that will take you to detailed sections with information such as the syntax rules for those properties. In the example shown in Figure 13-7, you can see the rules for the description field such as the maximum and minimum length and the allowed characters.

Now let's have a look at a practical example. Imagine that you would like to find out the switch ports where a certain VLAN encapsulation is configured using EPG static bindings. To achieve that, you could follow these steps:

- First, you need to find the class name for EPG static bindings (or EPG static ports, as they are called in newer ACI versions). You can go to any static binding of any EPG in the APIC GUI, and find the class name in the Debug Status Bar. For example, if the Status Bar reads something like "*Current Mo: insieme.stromboli.model.def. fvRsPathAtt[uni/tn-myTenant/ap-myApp/epg-myEPG/temporaryRn1]*", the class name is "*fvRsPathAtt*" (see the previous section for more details about how to interpret the Debug Status Bar output).

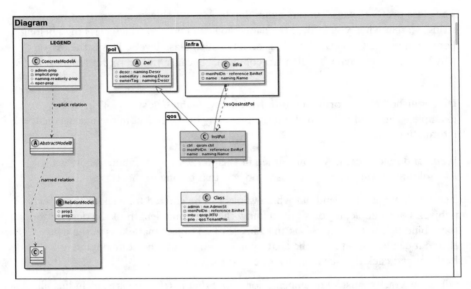

Figure 13-6   *Relationship Diagram for the Class* qos, *Extracted from Visore*

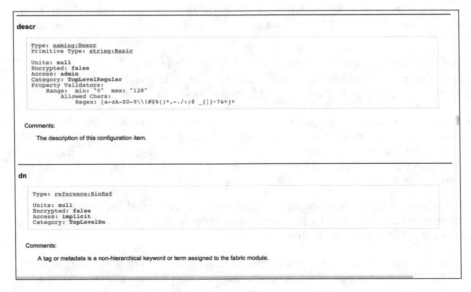

Figure 13-7   *Detailed Description of an Object Property*

- Now that you know the class name, you need to find out how the VLAN is encoded inside of objects that belong to that class. You can search for objects that belong to the class "fvRsPathAtt" in Visore, just by entering "fvRsPathAtt" in the "Class or DN" text box and clicking on the button "Run Query". If the GUI asks you whether you wish to find all objects that belong to that class, click on "OK". Now click on the name of any one of the objects on the screen to see its properties. You will see that they have an attribute called "**encap**" where the VLAN ID is specified.

- At this point, you have all you need: You know that you want to look for objects of the class **fvRsPathhAtt** with a certain value in their property **encap**. You can now run that search, as Figure 13-8 shows.

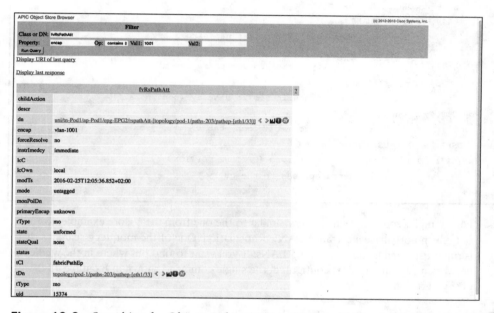

Figure 13-8   *Searching for Objects Belonging to a Certain Class with Specific Properties in Visore (in This Case, VLAN Encapsulation)*

A more detailed description of ACI's object model and the viewer Visore are outside the scope of this book, but the previous example illustrates one of the most frequent use cases of Visore.

moquery

There is a command-line version of Visore called **moquery**, which is short for *Managed Object Query*. **moquery** accepts multiple parameters in order to search the object model with different criteria. Example 13-1 shows the options this command takes.

Example 13-1 *Command Output for* **moquery**

```
apic# moquery -h
usage: Command line cousin to visore [-h] [-i HOST] [-p PORT] [-d DN]
                                      [-c KLASS] [-f FILTER] [-a ATTRS]
                                      [-o OUTPUT] [-u USER]
                                      [-x [OPTIONS [OPTIONS ...]]]
optional arguments:
  -h, --help            show this help message and exit
  -i HOST, --host HOST  Hostname or ip of apic
  -p PORT, --port PORT  REST server port
  -d DN, --dn DN        dn of the mo
  -c KLASS, --klass KLASS
                        comma separated class names to query
  -f FILTER, --filter FILTER
                        property filter to accept/reject mos
  -a ATTRS, --attrs ATTRS
                        type of attributes to display (config, all)
  -o OUTPUT, --output OUTPUT
                        Display format (block, table, xml, json)
  -u USER, --user USER  User name
  -x [OPTIONS [OPTIONS ...]], --options [OPTIONS [OPTIONS ...]]
                        Extra options to the query
apic#
```

For example, you could run a query similar to the one from the Visore example, to find out which ports have a certain VLAN encapsulation. One of the **moquery** searches that is run most often is the search for VLANs. If you want to find out where in the whole network a certain VLAN is configured, the single command shown in Example 13-2 will give you the answer.

Example 13-2 *Determining VLAN Configuration Location*

```
apic# moquery -c fvRsPathAtt -f 'fv.RsPathAtt.encap == "vlan-1001"' | grep tDn
dn            : topology/pod-1/paths-203/pathep-[eth1/33]
apic#
```

Essentially, here we are instructing **moquery** to find all objects of the class **fvRsPathAtt**, but to display only the objects where the **encap** property equals "**vlan-1001**". Finally, we are only interested in the lines containing "Distinguished Name." With a single command we can see that this VLAN has been configured on port 1/33 in leaf 203.

As you are probably thinking, this is not the easiest command to use, but with some practice you can do some really flexible queries of Cisco ACI's object model. As is the case with Visore, a more advanced description of **moquery** is outside this book's scope.

Cisco ACI Software Development Kits

As you know by now, software development kits (SDKs) offer a way of interacting native-ly with ACI's object model from inside your favorite programming language. SDKs, as well as many other tools related to Cisco ACI and other Cisco Data Center products, can be found on the Internet. More specifically, Cisco uses GitHub as an open development and versioning platform, where everybody can see the source code and even contribute to it. You will find most of the open-source elements quoted in this chapter in the GitHub repository https://github.com/datacenter.

Let's have a look at the different options ACI has to offer in this area.

Python SDK: Cobra

Python is a language that has gained massive popularity in the last few years due to fac-tors such as its ease of use and its modularity. It is object-oriented and provides very flex-ible and easy-to-use data structures like dictionaries.

The Python SDK for ACI is called "Cobra." This is the first SDK described in this book for a particular reason: It is the only one officially maintained by Cisco. In other words, for every new ACI version, a new revision of this SDK will be released supporting the new functionality, which you can download directly from your ACI controller without the need for Internet connectivity. The URL to download the two files required for the Python SDK installation is http[s]://<APIC address>/cobra/_downloads/ (with <APIC address> being the IP address or DNS name of your APIC).

One of the most interesting aspects of this SDK is the existence of a tool to dynamically generate code. This tool is called Arya (APIC REST Python Adapter), and it can be down-loaded from the GitHub repository at https://github.com/datacenter. This tool provides Python code that leverages the ACI Python SDK to implement a certain configuration, taking as input the desired configuration in JSON format.

You can obtain a JSON-formatted configuration for most objects in Cisco ACI directly from the GUI, using the **Save As** function that displays when you click the object's name, as Figure 13-9 shows.

When you select **Save As**, there are a couple of options you should understand in order to make sure your saved configuration contains all the items you want. Figure 13-10 sum-marizes the recommendations to originate JSON files that can be fed to Arya:

- **Content:** Selecting **All Properties** will include in the JSON any file transient infor-mation that is not configuration related, such as counters or operational state. **Only Configuration** is the recommended option because it will only include configura-tion-related properties.

- **Scope:** Here you can select whether you want to save configuration related exclu-sively to the object you clicked (**Self**) or you want to include configuration related to all its children (**Subtree**). The recommendation is **Subtree**; otherwise, you will have an incomplete configuration.

■ **Export format:** No additional explanation is required here. Just know that Arya only accepts JSON format and not XML. So if you are planning to feed the configuration to Arya, you should select **JSON**.

Figure 13-9 *Right-click the* **Save As** *function in the ACI GUI to Save the JSON Configuration for a Tenant*

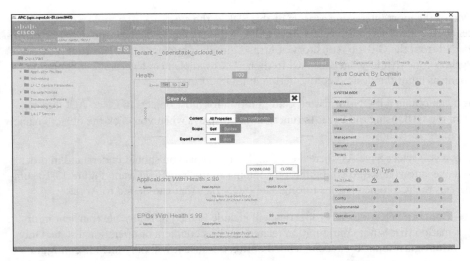

Figure 13-10 *Select the Right Options to Save the Complete Configuration Tree*

When you feed this JSON-formatted configuration information to Arya, it will generate Python code that you can start using immediately so that you can build network automation solutions extremely quickly.

Simplified Python SDK: ACI Toolkit

As you might have realized from reading the previous chapters, some networking configurations require a very rich data structure, and that is reflected by ACI's object model. However, for many daily tasks, we could do with a simpler model, and that is exactly the mission that the ACI toolkit tries to fulfill. The ACI toolkit consists of three elements:

- A simplified version of ACI's object model

- A Python SDK to interact with that simplified model

- Multiple sample applications that leverage the simplified Python SDK

With the simplified Python SDK toolkit, you can quickly develop automation scripts that leverage the most frequently used networking configurations in ACI. Be aware that for more sophisticated designs, you will have to fall back to the standard Python SDK.

Ruby SDK

Ruby is a dynamic, reflective, object-oriented, general-purpose programming language. It was designed and developed in the mid-1990s by Yukihiro "Matz" Matsumoto in Japan.

According to its creator, Ruby was influenced by Perl, Smalltalk, Eiffel, Ada, and Lisp. It supports multiple programming paradigms, including functional, object-oriented, and imperative. It also has a dynamic type system and automatic memory management.

The Ruby SDK comes with a sample application in the form of an ACI dashboard that leverages it. You can find it in GitHub under https://github.com/datacenter/acirb.

PowerShell SDK

PowerShell is becoming very popular in Microsoft environments because it is embedded in modern Windows OSs for desktops and servers, and therefore it's prevalent in many data centers.

Although there is an ACI snap-in for PowerShell, at the time of this writing, it was pretty old and did not work well with recent ACI versions, so it is not recommended that you use it. If you wish to use Powershell to interact with ACI, your best bet is leveraging native REST API calls with commands (or "cmdlets" in Powershell speech) such as "Invoke-WebRequest".

Where to Find Automation and Programmability Examples

The first rule when coding is not to create anything that somebody else has already created. It's better to "steal with pride," as I call it, than to reinvent the wheel. To that purpose, you can find lots of code examples using multiple programming languages at these sites:

- **Cisco Developer Network for ACI:** https://acidev.cisco.com

- **GitHub repository:** https://github.com/datacenter

Developing and Testing Your Code Without an ACI Fabric at Hand

Ideally, you want to test your automation solutions against a real ACI fabric. This way, you can make sure your tests are as close as it gets to production deployments. For developers who might not have an ACI fabric at hand, there are some alternatives.

Cisco DevNet

Cisco DevNet (Cisco Developer Network) is a great resource for programmability tasks, not only for Cisco ACI but for any other Cisco technologies. You can access the DevNet portal from any browser with Internet connectivity via the URL https://developer. cisco.com. From here, you can navigate to pages dedicated to different products, including Cisco ACI, that will offer multiple resources. Alternatively, you might want to bookmark this other URL that takes you directly to the ACI DevNet page: https://developer.cisco.com/site/aci. Figure 13-11 shows this DevNet page.

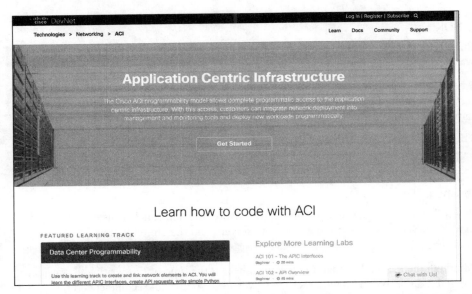

Figure 13-11 *DevNet Portal for Cisco ACI (the Current Appearance of the Web Site Might Deviate from This Screenshot)*

Figure 13-11 shows just the first section, "Learn how to code with ACI." If you browse further down this page, you will find these other ones:

- Find sample code and scripts
- See what others have built with ACI
- See what others are saying
- Test your code in an ACI sandbox

This last option is extremely interesting because it provides an always-on Cisco APIC simulator that you can connect to in order to verify your code.

dCloud

dCloud is a virtual lab environment where Cisco partners and customers can get training on multiple Cisco solutions. The dCloud is publicly available at https://dcloud.cisco.com.

As shown in Figure 13-12, dCloud is a modern, simplified web portal. In the catalog section, you can easily browse for different categories of labs and demos, or you can search for anything you might be interested in (for example, searching the string "aci" will give you all ACI-related labs and demos). When you find the lab you are looking for, you can schedule it either immediately or for a later use.

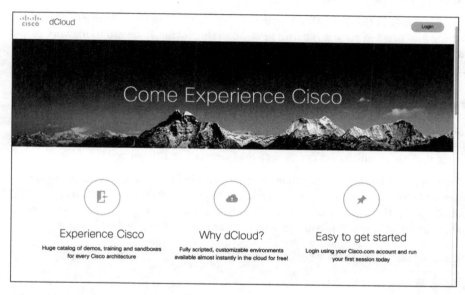

Figure 13-12   *Cisco dCloud Web portal*

Once you have reserved a certain lab for your particular use, you have two ways you can access the lab environment:

- Through a Remote Desktop client embedded in your web browser
- Through an SSL tunnel with the Cisco AnyConnect VPN client

The second option with the SSL tunnel has the advantage of putting your laptop in the lab environment network, so you will be able to test your scripts or automation solutions against the APIC in dCloud.

Cisco ACI Simulator

In some situations, you will find that dCloud is not enough. For example, if you want to test integration with a device that does not support the installation of Cisco AnyConnect client.

In this case, testing against an ACI emulator might be a good replacement for having an ACI fabric. The ACI emulator is a physical appliance where a complete ACI fabric (including APICs and ACI leaf and spine switches) is simulated.

Note that this simulation does not include packet forwarding, so you will not be able to test data-plane-related events.

Increasing Operational Efficiency Through Network Automation

Now that you have the theoretical foundation, we are ready to start. As usual, when entering into new territory, it is better to do so in small steps. In regard to network automation, the first step is probably the automation of recurring operative tasks, which can help network administrators to free up their time (in other words, "save money").

Offering Visibility to the Network

One of the most important objectives of ACI is to democratize the network (that is, offer ways for non-networking personnel to interact with it). In other words, the objective is to change the way in which data center networks are used and consumed.

For example, if you step into the shoes of a storage administrator, the systems they are responsible for heavily rely on the network, but traditionally they have had very limited visibility to it. As Chapter 9 described, ACI can expose the state of the network relevant for storage applications in an easy-to-understand manner, as Figure 13-13 shows.

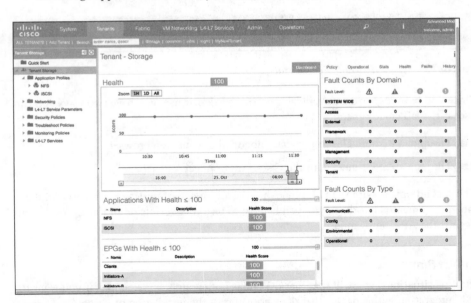

Figure 13-13 *A Sample Out-of-the-Box ACI Dashboard for a Storage Admin Showing the Network Health of the NFS and iSCSI Protocols*

In additional to the dashboards included in the APIC, nothing prevents you from developing new dashboards that leverage Cisco ACI's API. At the end of the day, that is exactly what the ACI GUI is doing!

It is also exactly what the Ruby-based dashboard in GitHub (https://github.com/data-center/acirb) does. Including a Ruby SDK, this dashboard leverages the dashing.io framework (https://dashing.io) to poll ACI for certain information and show the results in a mosaic-like layout, where adding or removing individual widgets is very easy, as shown in Figure 13-14.

Figure 13-14 *Ruby-based ACI Dashboard*

Another example that testifies to the flexibility of ACI is the Mac OS X desktop, which you can find in GitHub at https://github.com/erjosito/ACIHealth.wdgt. Mac OS X desktop widgets are essentially HTML pages that include Cascading Style Sheet (CSS) formatting and JavaScript code. This code has some specific widget-related functionality available (for example, executing some system script). The ACI Mac OS X widget leverages this functionality and calls Python scripts in the background that get information such as tenant health, switch health, and the most critical alerts in the system, as illustrated in Figure 13-15.

Externalizing Network Configuration

You have just seen the benefits of granting visibility to the fabric to non-network administrators, so why not take this a step further?

If you think about it, when it comes to routine changes, the network admin does not provide any added value. If the only thing the network admin does is to translate human language to network configuration, there is probably a better solution available.

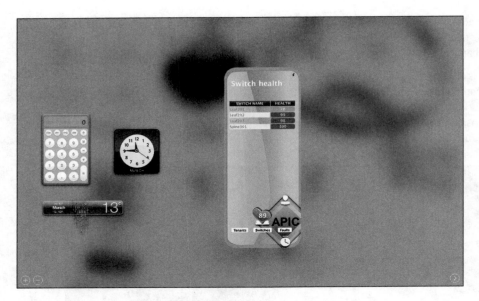

Figure 13-15   *ACI Mac OS X Desktop Widget*

Let me tell you a situation I was involved with. In this certain company, network admin Jane was responsible for user connectivity to the campus network, and the Windows admin Dave was responsible for the OS installed on the users' computers. Whenever a user had a connectivity problem, Dave would try to figure out whether there was an issue with the OS configuration: wrong proxy settings, wrong IP address, or wrong default gateway. If everything was okay, he would call Jane to verify the switch port settings.

And that's where the problems started. User connectivity was not Jane's only job, and she had better things to do, such as designing the new Multiprotocol Label Switching (MPLS) company network. However, whenever Dave called, she had to drop everything in order to troubleshoot the issue. They needed to work out together whether the configuration in the network switch matched the configuration in Windows (VLAN and speed/duplex settings). It was even worse when Jane was not at her desk, because then Dave could not carry on with troubleshooting, and the unhappy user without connectivity would complain to both Jane and Dave's bosses.

What was the solution? Jane implemented a database (at the time using Microsoft Access, but that's not important) that not only showed Dave how specific ports were configured, but correlated that information to cable labels and room numbers so that Dave could easily find which port he should be checking out. Additionally, the database allowed Dave to do some basic switch port configuration (enable, disable, change VLAN, change speed/duplex settings, and so on) so that he could fix problems quicker without having to call Jane every time.

As a result, everybody was happier. Jane had more time for her MPLS project. Dave was able to fix problems more quickly, so he also had more time for other stuff. And more importantly, user satisfaction increased because their issues were resolved faster.

Whenever you see any process inefficiency, chances are that automation (and a bit of good will) can help you fix it.

Externalizing Switch Port Configuration

One area where network administrators add little to no value is in the physical configuration of ports. Typically, servers will be cabled by persons in the hardware or server teams. They normally know which server is connected to which port, and how that connection has been configured at the server side, including port speed, port duplex, whether it is a dual connection, whether it is active/active or active/standby, and whether it uses channeling protocols like Link Aggregation Control Protocol (LACP) or neighbor detection protocols like Cisco Discovery Protocol (CDP) or Link Layer Discovery Protocol (LLDP).

The person responsible for the server configuration will likely put all that information into their documentation and then open a change request so that the network administrator configures the switch ports accordingly. This manual process, as you can imagine, is quite prone to errors as well as generates unneeded delay in the process to bring servers into production.

So why not give the server admins the ability to configure the switch port themselves? This way, they do not need to send their parameters to the network folks. And more importantly, in order to make the process as seamless as possible, what about enabling this port configuration directly from the documentation tool that the server administrator uses? What's more, we could even add the network automation functionality to that tool.

This is the concept behind the module for Visual Basic for Applications (VBA) and the sample spreadsheet at https://github.com/erjosito/VBA-ACI. If the server administrator documents server connectivity in Excel, why not add a button in that very same spreadsheet?

This module has been developed and tested with Microsoft Excel for Mac 2011 and 2015, and it requires importing two additional libraries:

- **VBA-Web:** To send HTTP requests (and therefore REST calls)

- **VBA-JSON:** To interpret programmatically the data returned by APIC (for example, to extract the authentication cookie from the login response)

Other than that, the ACI functionality has been entirely developed using REST calls and the API Inspector (described earlier in this chapter).

Externalizing Security Configuration

Another area where many organizations suffer headaches is the management of firewall rulesets. These have grown too complex, and part of the reason is due to the suboptimal processes we have been discussing in previous sections. For example, the application owners need to tell the security admins which ports or which application protocols need to be allowed by the firewall.

With ACI, you can configure L2-4 packet filters in the fabric in the form of contracts, as you have seen in previous chapters. You can obviously modify these contracts over the API, so it would be conceivable to give the application owner a self-service portal from which to configure these contracts (possibly with baseline rules, dictated by the security administrator, that cannot be overruled).

Furthermore, if you insert a firewall in ACI using L4-7 service graphs, you can configure that firewall over ACI's API, as you will see in the following section. Doing so makes it possible to use ACI's API and tools like the API Inspector to configure the firewall.

However, in this particular case, using native REST calls captured with the API Inspector and ported over to Python, for example, with the Paw client, is not the most efficient solution to the problem. You can certainly do it, but you need to build a very big string dynamically as the payload to the REST request.

This is a perfect example of a situation where an SDK is better suited for the problem, and here we have the perfect use case for using Cobra:

1. You can download the JSON configuration for the provider EPG where the service graph has been inserted, because this is where the L4-7 attributes are stored. Use the **Save As** function in the GUI by right-clicking the EPG.

2. You can edit the JSON file to remove everything you are not interested in, such as other EPG configuration aspects (physical/virtual domains, static bindings, and so on), and leave the L4-7 parameters.

3. Supply the modified JSON file to Arya, which will generate the required Python code to create all attributes.

4. Modify the dynamically generated code to fit your purpose.

Horizontal Automation Integrations

In modern data centers you typically have some kind of orchestrator that, as the name implies, automates operations across multiple devices in order to achieve a particular common goal. It can speak to the network, the physical compute, the virtual compute, the storage, L4-7 device, or any other device required to provide that service, as Figure 13-16 shows.

As you can see in this diagram, the orchestrated elements do not need to know each other because the orchestrator will make sure the discrete configurations deployed to these devices are consistent with each other.

However, sometimes horizontal integration can alleviate the functionality pressure in a central orchestrator. In other words, if the orchestrated devices are aware of each other, the job of the orchestrator turns out to be easier, as Figure 13-17 illustrates.

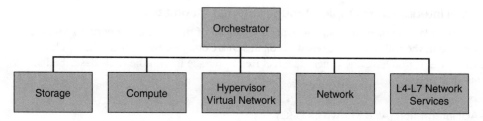

Figure 13-16 *General Automation Implementation Centralized in the Orchestrator*

This is exactly the case described in the previous section, where ACI took care of the firewall configuration, so the orchestrator (our Python script) didn't even bother to speak to the firewall. ACI did all the heavy lifting, thus simplifying the number of APIs (or Python modules, in this case) we had to load.

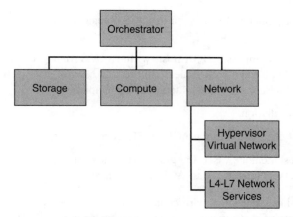

Figure 13-17 *ACI Integrations Greatly Simplify the Job of the Orchestrator*

Horizontal Integration Examples Embedded in the Product

Embedded in ACI are multiple examples of horizontal integrations, where you need to decide whether the additional functionality of ACI can reduce the complexity in the IT automation layer.

Here are some examples of this type of integration:

- **VMM integration:** By configuring the virtual switch in vSphere, Hyper-V, or OpenStack, ACI eliminates the need for an orchestrator to do so.

- **L4-7 integration:** Similarly, in managed service graphs, ACI will configure the L4-7 device—be it a firewall, a load balancer, or anything else.

Horizontal Integration Example Through External Automation

It is possible to implement some external integration of this kind using network automation, and in the following sections we look at some examples. By no means is this list exhaustive; if you have any other idea, feel free to pursue it with the tools described in this chapter.

UCS-ACI Integration (Also Known as B2G)

This integration, also known as Better Together (B2G) scripts, has the objective of simplifying deployments that include both Cisco ACI and Unified Compute Systems (UCS), Cisco's physical compute platform.

It supports both B-Series (blade form factor) and C-Series (rack mount form factor) servers, and it covers multiple use cases or "stories," as they are called in the product, including the following:

- Auto-formation of a virtual port channel (vPC) between the UCS domain and the peer ACI leaf nodes.

- VMM (VMware vSphere) domain encompassing ESX hosts within a UCS Manager (UCSM) domain (VLAN or VXLAN backed with vShield). In the VLAN case, VLANs are created in the Fabric Interconnects and added to vNIC templates.

- UCSM blade server bare-metal installation.

- Auto-matching of the UCS SPAN destination to the ACI leaf SPAN source instance.

- Auto-formation of linkages from standalone Cisco Integrated Management Controller–managed UCS rack servers (connected to ACI leaf switches).

This script is sitting on a Linux virtual machine (VM) with connectivity to both APIs from Cisco ACI and Cisco UCS. It listens for events on one side, and when something happens, it performs some actions on the other side. This is a great example of automation using the rich APIs of these products.

The advantage for the user is that both ACI and UCS move synchronously in the same direction, without the need for an orchestrator. You could certainly implement these functions in an orchestrator, but it would generally be more difficult than just downloading the ACI-UCS integration scripts.

Other Ideas

The previous section explained the concept of ACI-UCS integration: code living somewhere outside the APIC that reads and writes configuration information to ACI upon certain events. The idea is to disseminate information as it happens, taking it directly from the source to whomever might be interested in it. Here are some other examples using the endpoint intelligence:

■ **Firewall object groups automatic configuration:** If your teams have spent some time defining applications and endpoint groups (EPGs), and ACI has the information about which MAC addresses and IP addresses belong to each EPG, you might as well leverage this information somewhere else (for example, at firewalls). Some firewall vendors are thinking about extracting the EPG and related endpoints out of ACI and creating object groups that can be then leveraged to build the firewall ruleset. Note that a similar functionality is available in certain device packages for managed service graphs, but in some cases this simpler integration might be desirable (for example, where the device package does not support it, or where the firewall topology is not supported by a service graph).

■ **Application Delivery Controller (ADC) server pool automatic configuration:** Here's a similar use case, but with your favorite load balancer ("Application Delivery Controller" is a fancy word for "Load Balancer" commonly used in the industry). If the network already knows when servers come and go, why not use this information in order to automatically adapt the server pool that your ADC uses to load-balance traffic? Again, notice that device packages like the ones for F5 BigIP/BigIQ and Citrix NetScaler support the Dynamic Endpoint Attach functionality, but in some other cases this integration might be advantageous.

■ **Verification of IP/MAC address:** In recent ACI versions, IP-based and MAC-based EPGs are possible, but additional security checks might be carried out when endpoints attach to the network. For example, you might need to check that the IP address is registered with a corporate Active Directory server or that the logged-in user belongs to a certain group.

If you wonder how to implement this kind of functionality, you can have a look at the ACI Toolkit application Endpoint Tracker. This Python script subscribes to an ACI fabric for endpoint events, and upon the attachment or detachment of an endpoint to/from the fabric, it will perform a certain action.

The action that Endpoint Tracker runs is updating a MySQL database, but you can easily replace that with something different (update an object group in a firewall, update the server pool in a load balancer, or perform some verifications against an external information source).

You can find an application that follows this principle to implement a sort of MAC authentication (where authorized MACs and their EPGs are specified in an external JSON file) at https://github.com/erjosito/aci_mac_auth. This application obviously does not scale well (for that the MAC addresses should be stored at a minimum in a database, not in a text file), but it illustrates the concept.

About this topic, note that Cisco ACI later introduced native support for MAC-based EPGs. This is yet another example of functions introduced by the Cisco ACI user community and later incorporated to the product itself.

This is yet another example of taking advantage of coding examples in GitHub and https://acidev.cisco.com. However, instead of starting from scratch to achieve our goal, we have taken something roughly similar and customized it for our own purposes.

Automating the Generation of Network Documentation

Who likes documenting network designs and implementations? However, this is a critical task for the correct operation of network environments, as we all know. Still, most network administrators are not precisely thrilled at the idea of creating detailed Visio diagrams and lengthy design documents that need to be updated with every network change.

The idea of dynamically generating documentation out of a network configuration is certainly not new; however, until the advent of Cisco ACI, it has been very difficult to achieve, mainly for two reasons:

■ Multiple configuration files had to be analyzed simultaneously, because configuration was local to each device.

■ The configuration was in a human-readable, unstructured text format, which is difficult for machines to parse.

As we already know, Cisco ACI has solved both problems, so now it is certainly feasible to look at the network configuration of the entire fabric or a certain tenant and to extract the information relevant for a certain audience and put it in a specific format.

Such tasks could include, for example, updating wiki pages for network operators with network connectivity details, creating Word documents for the security department that focus on the contracts and security details of a certain tenant, or extracting information for the organization configuration management database (CMDB) or configuration management system (CMS).

There are multiple ways to do this. Using an example from GitHub (https://github.com/erjosito/stuff/blob/master/json2doc.py), you can see how to use two Python libraries (pydot for image generation, and pydoc for Word document generation) in order to create a human-readable document with text and pictures out of the configuration of a tenant.

The focus here is not on the Python modules but rather on how the code can easily load the whole configuration into a Python dictionary and then parse that dictionary, looking for certain structures: provided and consumed contracts, VRF belongings, and so on.

Enabling Additional Business Models Through Network Automation

As we discussed at the beginning of the chapter, automation often has the dual goal of saving costs and enabling new business models—what we summarized with the phrase "save money, make money." In that part of the chapter, we focused on the operational cost saving; in this one, we will move to the second part: making money.

Essentially, the automation concepts are the same as in the "save money" discussion, but you can use them to provide additional business benefits to your organization besides enabling IT and business initiatives that might provide the required competitive edge.

You may be wondering whether this is possible at all. Can IT evolve from a cost center to a value-creating organization? It is certainly no small feat, but one that many CIOs across many verticals pursue today. Henk Kolk, Chief Architect at ING, put it this way in his speech at the Docker conference in December 2014:

- Speed is market share.

- The bank is IT, and IT is the bank.

These two statements deserve an explanation because they are not intuitive. The first one implies that in order to gain market share, a good product or service is not enough: You need to be the first to the market. Otherwise, you will be overtaken, and by the time you have made your product available, the market is gone.

The second statement is very interesting too. Although financial institutions have traditionally heavily relied on IT, few would make such a dramatic statement identifying IT as their core business ("the bank is IT, IT is the bank"). That is, if IT runs well the business will run well, but if a company has a poor IT its business will suffer. The implications of this statement are far reaching—from the eternal decision as to whether or not to outsource, to the resources that are granted to the IT organization.

Is Mr. Kolk too far off here? He is not alone in the industry. Many leaders think that IT will have a decisive role when saying which enterprises survive and which ones don't. Some even have the idea of creating investment funds that include enterprises with healthy IT practices, with the conviction that these are the ones that will outperform their competitors.

One way or the other, expectations for the IT organization are increasing exponentially, and new tools are required to satisfy them.

Agile Application Deployment and DevOps

This increased pressure on IT to move swiftly is not exclusive to the infrastructure. Actually, we might say that the infrastructure teams have been the last ones to feel it, because in Development departments, this movement already started some years ago.

There are many names to describe it—agile, lean IT, fast IT, and probably many more—but all of them essentially state that applications must be developed quicker, taking into account customer feedback from the beginning, and the Operations team must support this faster application churn.

It is this last phrase that has motivated the surge of the DevOps movement. Making application development faster does not bring much, if the Quality Assurance (QA) folks and the Operations people take ages to test and deploy the new shiny piece of code.

Therefore, the objective is improving the processes going back and forth between Development and QA, and between QA and Operations. Smaller teams take ownership of reduced application components, but they control the whole process, from code inception to installation in production. This way, frictions are avoided because people writing the code will make it easy to test (or even write the automated tests) and easy to deploy.

Continuous Deployment and Continuous Integration

At this point, the terms *continuous development* (CD) and *continuous integration* (CI) come into the picture. These are processes and technologies that are rooted in the process optimization techniques Toyota introduced in the last century for car manufacturing, but adapted to IT.

The idea is simple: The whole process after code development should be automated. After a developer commits a new version of their code to the software repository (for example, GitHub), automated tests will be carried out against the new version (for example, with Jenkins). These tests verify, among other things, that the new code is syntactically correct, that it does what it should do, and that it does not break previous functionality. If these tests are successful, this new version might be automatically put into production without any human intervention.

While most organizations are hesitant to implement this kind of velocity, others have taken it to heart and are able to deploy multiple code versions per day. Compare this to organizations that update their product version only every 3 to 6 months. And reflect on what it means in terms of competitiveness—recall the statement "speed is market share" from a previous section.

It is this last step that concerns us from an infrastructure operations perspective. Although the developer might have tested the application on their own laptop, or maybe in the public cloud, we might want to deploy it in our own premises. If the application requires modifying the network configuration (creating a new segment or opening a new TCP port), the network must be automated the same way as everything else in the development chain. And here's where Cisco ACI shines when compared to legacy network architectures.

Linux Containers and Microservices Architectures

You saw in a previous chapter that not only does Cisco ACI integrate with hypervisors such as those from VMware, Microsoft, and OpenStack, but with Linux container frameworks such as Docker, Kubernetes, and Red Hat Openshift too. In the light of this section, it is easy to understand why customers demand that integration.

The application development evolution toward ever-increasing speed is dictating a transformation in the internal architecture of applications. The need to deploy new code very rapidly demands that applications be extremely modular so that each individual module can be safely "upgraded" without affecting the rest.

Additionally, a new way of packaging the application is required so that the developer can program the application using their MacBook, perform tests in the public cloud, and deploy on the premises.

In the midst of this perfect storm, container technologies have risen, and with them has come the advent of microservices architectures. Applications are decomposed into tens, if not hundreds, of components, and all of them can be scaled independently from each other.

The network assumes the role of the message bus between these components, and being able to secure and monitor communications across microservices will be paramount in the future.

Configuration Management Tools

CD/CI and DevOps have brought a brave new generation of IT tools and concepts that help to make app development more agile. A very interesting concept is "Infrastructure as Code." The idea is that infrastructure can be described with a text file (like source code) that can be versioned and stored along with the application programs. This way, whenever the application is tested, its infrastructure requirements are equally validated, and production deployments happen in exactly the same manner as the tests that have been carried out.

These Infrastructure as Code tools are generically called by the industry *configuration management tools*. Essentially, they allow you to define in a text file how an IT component should be configured, and some central component will make sure that the IT component is actually configured as it should be.

These configuration management tools have been focused on the Linux OS during the last few years, but this focus is slowly enlarging to encompass other elements of the infrastructure such as the network. Therefore, many customers would like to manage their networks with the same tools they use to control the configuration of their Linux servers. Here are two examples of configuration management tools that offer support for Cisco ACI fabrics:

- **Ansible:** Agentless configuration tools such Ansible map nicely to devices where installing third-party software agents is not possible. This is the case with Cisco ACI, where its REST API and Python SDK offer the ideal basis on which to develop Ansible modules, such as this one: https://github.com/jedelman8/aci-ansible.

- **Puppet:** Although a prominent example of agent-based configuration management tools, Puppet offers additionally a way to interact with entities where agents cannot be installed, such as Cisco ACI. You can find an example of a Puppet module that uses the Ruby SDK to interact with Cisco ACI: https://acidev.cisco.com/public/codeshop/puppet-for-aci/.

Private Cloud and IaaS

Most organizations have traditionally deployed their applications in their own data centers. Public cloud is becoming more and more popular, and many IT departments are successfully implementing a hybrid cloud strategy where some applications are run on-premises (private cloud), but others are run in the public cloud. As a consequence, private and public clouds are constantly compared to each other in order to choose the best platform for applications.

When considering whether a certain application should be deployed on premises or in the public cloud, a question is often overlooked by IT operations: the development department needs. Application developers are not primarily interested in economics or security (factors which would often speak for a deployment on premises), but in speed and ease of use (characteristics where public clouds excel). If the private cloud is too slow, or too difficult to use, developers will quickly turn to a public cloud provider like Amazon Web Services, Google Cloud Platform, or Microsoft Azure.

There are many definitions of what private cloud is and isn't, and what Infrastructure-as-a-Service (IaaS) is and isn't, but no matter what your definition is, certain aspects are common to every project:

- Infrastructure that needs to be automated

- An orchestrator in charge of performing that automation

- A self-service portal that makes processes consumable

Different vendors have different suites that typically include the orchestration and self-service portal capabilities. Cisco ACI does not intend to lock customers into a specific orchestration stack but rather, thanks to its API flexibility, aims to integrate with whichever cloud stack the customer has in place (obviously including Cisco's software).

Integration with Cisco Enterprise Cloud Suite

Cisco's offering for private cloud and Infrastructure as a Service (IaaS) is the Cisco Enterprise Cloud Suite. This is essentially a bundle of multiple products, of which the following stand out for this functionality:

- **Cisco UCS Director:** An IT orchestration tool that supports virtual and physical compute, storage, and network elements, including Cisco and other infrastructure vendors such as HP, IBM, and Brocade. It includes a basic self-service portal that is often used internally for very IT-centric processes.

- **Cisco Cloud Center:** A multicloud orchestration tool that enables application deployment across a variety of multiple private and public clouds. More details can be found later in this chapter in the section "Hybrid Cloud."

- **Cisco Prime Services Catalog:** A more comprehensive self-service portal and process orchestrator that can be leveraged to offer a process that may contain IT elements (provided by UCS Director) or other non-IT elements delivered by other systems in an organization.

Obviously, the main integration point in this architecture is between Cisco ACI and Cisco UCS Director. Cisco UCS Director needs to know how to configure ACI in order to deploy the required workflows. To that purpose, Cisco UCS Director contains a comprehensive list of predefined tasks that the administrator can combine on a graphical canvas with drag-and-drop to compose workflows, as illustrated in Figure 13-18. At the time of this writing, Cisco UCS Director comes with 203 predefined tasks that can automate many network operations on Cisco ACI without the need for any coding.

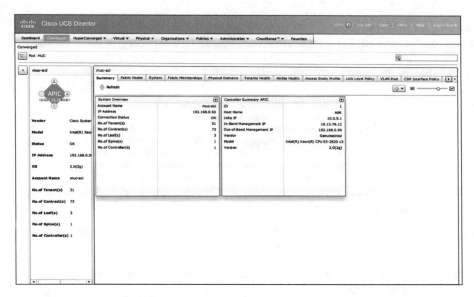

Figure 13-18   *Cisco UCS Director Dashboard for a Cisco ACI-based Pod*

Although unlikely, it could happen that the administrator wants UCS Director to configure a feature in ACI that is not included in those predefined tasks. To that purpose, defining additional tasks is extremely easy in UCS Director to cover that functionality gap. The way those tasks are defined is with JavaScript code that would send two REST API calls to ACI: the first one with the authentication, and the second one with the actual action the task should perform.

As you can imagine, ACI tools like the API Inspector are extremely valuable when creating additional tasks so that you can identify the REST API parameters for the action you are trying to automate. Once you have the JSON code you want to provision, it is possible to automatically generate files that contain UCS Director custom tasks (including their associated rollback tasks) and can be directly included in the tool. For example, you can find a script that generates UCS Director custom tasks out of ACI JSON or XML configuration here: https://github.com/erjosito/request.

Cisco UCS Director workflows can either be accessed through its user self-service portal or can be exported to Cisco Prime Services Catalog so that they can be integrated into higher-level service orchestration processes. This two-phase implementation of private clouds makes it very easy for organizations to achieve quick, tangible results and benefits out of private cloud projects.

Integration with VMware vRealize Suite

VMware's proposal for automation in the data center is the vRealize suite. There are multiple products in this suite, but the most important ones for private cloud and IaaS are vRealize Automation and vRealize Orchestrator.

Cisco ACI integrates seamlessly with the vRealize suite. Through this integration, vRealize Automation (vRA) blueprints leverage vRealize Orchestrator (vRO) workflows that provide the required integration with Cisco ACI. Here are some of the functionalities that these blueprints and workflows provide:

- The creation of endpoint groups (EPGs)

- The creation of VMs and port groups in vSphere vCenter

- Placing VMs in the previously created EPGs

- Creating security policy in the form of Cisco ACI contracts

- Inserting L4-7 services such as firewalls or load balancers in the data flow, including the configuration of those devices

- Providing external connectivity to the deployed workflows through the use of Cisco ACI external L3 network connections

Figure 13-19 depicts the architecture of how different components of the VMware vRealize and vSphere suites integrate with Cisco ACI.

In order to achieve this goal, the integration between Cisco ACI and VMware vRealize supports two main modes of network connectivity, as illustrated by Figure 13-20:

- **Virtual private cloud (VPC):** In this mode, data-plane multi-tenancy is implemented through the allocation of dedicated VRFs in each tenant, thus providing overlapping IP address ranges across tenants. A shared external L3 network connection is used to provide communication with the outside world.

- **Shared infrastructure:** When no data-plane multi-tenancy is required (see Chapter 9 for more details), all workloads are deployed on a single ACI VRF, and security is provided over the contract-based separation of EPGs. Management-plane multi-tenancy is still offered because the EPGs are placed in dedicated tenants. The main advantage of this mode is its simplicity and scalability.

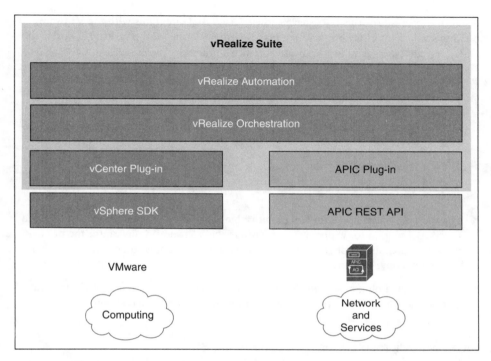

Figure 13-19   *Architecture of the Integration Between Cisco ACI and VMware vRealize*

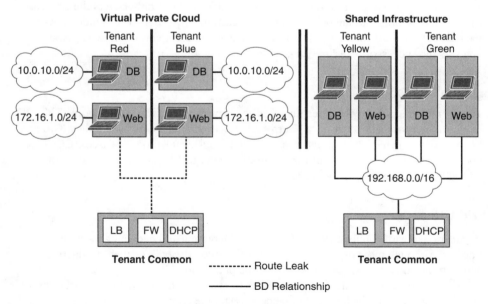

Figure 13-20   *Two Modes of Operation: VPC and Shared Infrastructure*

As multiple sections of this book have shown, Cisco ACI integrates with the VMware software stack at multiple levels, which makes Cisco ACI the ideal physical network and overlay for customers who use VMware software in their organizations:

- Cisco ACI vSphere VMM integration automates the creation of network constructs in vCenter, either using the native vSphere Distributed Virtual Switch (DVS) or the Cisco-provided Application Virtual Switch (AVS) for additional functionality, thus releasing the VMware administrators of the burden of managing the network component of server virtualization.

- These virtual network capabilities include modern security functionality such as micro-segmentation or integration with external L4-7 network services devices like firewalls and load balancers.

- For VMware specialists who feel comfortable with network administration tasks, the Cisco ACI plug-in for vSphere vCenter offers the VMware administrator the possibility of managing all physical and virtual network attributes straight from vCenter, without needing to learn how to use a new user interface (UI).

- The Cisco ACI plug-in for vRealize grants a seamless integration into VMware's automation stack for customers who implement it, as this section has shown.

Integration with Microsoft Azure Pack and Azure Stack

As covered in Chapter 4, "Integration of Virtualization Technologies with ACI", one of the hypervisors with which Cisco ACI integrates is Microsoft Hyper-V. This cooperation between Microsoft and Cisco is far-reaching, and not only covers the creation of logical networks, but encompasses the integration with Microsoft Windows Azure Pack as well. Realize that Microsoft has introduced an architecture known as Azure Stack as the successor to Azure Pack.

Integration with OpenStack

The overall integration with OpenStack has already been discussed in this book. This integration encompasses not only Neutron plug-ins and the group-based policy (GBP), but also how OpenStack Heat, its orchestration module, can automate Cisco ACI. For additional information about this integration, refer to Chapter 4, "Integration of Virtualization Technologies with ACI".

Hybrid Cloud

As mentioned earlier, public cloud offerings are increasing and becoming more and more popular. Although most organizations decide to deploy the bulk of their production applications on premises, the economics of the public cloud is certainly appealing for certain scenarios, such as development and test environments for existing applications, or new applications for which customer demand is still uncertain.

Probably the most decisive advantage of Cisco ACI is its object model and policy-based character. This makes it relatively simple to describe generically the security and network requirements for a specific workload, and if that workload is to be deployed on ACI, to translate those requirements into ACI policy.

Cisco CloudCenter (formerly known as CliQr CloudCenter) is a part of the Cisco Enterprise Cloud Suite, and it allows for the modeling of applications so that they can be deployed in multiple infrastructure environments and integrate with Cisco UCS Director for private cloud deployments. Once it has been defined what tiers an application is made out of, what software components must exist in each tier, and how these tiers relate to each other, CloudCenter is able to translate those models to Cisco ACI logical objects for a deployment in a private cloud, or to AWS, Google, Azure, or any other cloud model for public cloud environments.

Note that Cisco CloudCenter will not move virtual machines between private and public clouds, but will deploy the new workloads directly onto the target cloud, making the deployment process extremely efficient.

With this integration, the deployment of both existing and new applications can be streamlined, because new application instances can be provisioned, decommissioned, or scaled up and down with the push of a button.

Cisco CloudCenter abstracts the complexity of the underlying infrastructure from the application owner so that application architects just need to define the networking and security requirements of their applications, and Cisco CloudCenter will translate those to Cisco ACI policies.

Therefore, the concept of "model once, deploy many times" is extended to the application, including the network, because both Cisco ACI and CloudCenter heavily rely on policies in order to describe network infrastructure and application stacks, respectively. These policies can be easily accessed and represented in Cisco CloudCenter via its GUI, where both the infrastructure operator and the application owner will be able to easily visualize the dependencies between application components and the infrastructure.

Although Cisco CloudCenter supports deploying an application to multiple clouds, only through Cisco ACI's rich security policies can an organization offer the safest environment so that applications run in a scalable, flexible, and secure way.

Platform as a Service

The ultimate goal of a DC is providing applications. As a consequence, in addition to just providing infrastructure upon the click of a button, some organizations have added to their infrastructure offerings some elements that make it easier for application developers to build applications.

There are multiple definitions of Infrastructure as a Service (IaaS) and Platform as a Service (PaaS), but most of them agree on the following critical aspects:

- IaaS is similar to virtualization, in the sense that IaaS users are not relieved of infrastructure-related tasks, such as compute and memory sizing, operative system maintenance, application installation, hardware lifecycle, and so on.

- PaaS, on the other hand, offers a level of abstraction by trying to relieve the PaaS user from infrastructure-related tasks.

- A technology used by many PaaS platforms in the industry to achieve this objective is the Linux/Windows container (such as Docker), which abstracts the infrastructure from the applications running on top of it. Container orchestrator frameworks (such as Docker Swarm, Mesosphere DC/OS, and Kubernetes) offer additional abstraction levels that take care of high availability and application scaling.

ACI Integration with Apprenda

Apprenda is a Platform as a Service product mainly oriented for enterprises, one of whose most important attributes is the possibility of migrating existing applications to a cloud-oriented architecture, even if those applications have not been designed to be operated in a cloud-like fashion.

Apprenda offers multiple benefits for both the developer and the operator, including separate portals for those two user groups. Developers can use all the benefits of a modern Platform as a Service so that they do not need to bother with infrastructure and can deploy their application in containers that can be instanced in a wide variety of environments.

At the same time, operators can define attributes that will control how those applications are deployed—for example, policies that dictate that test environments be deployed in a public cloud and that security-critical applications be deployed in owned data centers with strict security rules.

This is where Apprenda's integration with Cisco ACI comes into play, with which Apprenda can deploy containers in a private cloud with the richness of the security measures offered by Cisco ACI. Application components can be secured with a high level of granularity, and Cisco ACI will offer to the IT operations team all kinds of monitoring and telemetry data that allows for the efficient management of the application lifecycle.

Mantl and Shipped

One of the main objectives of PaaS is liberating the developers from the burden of infrastructure management, and at the same time offering an environment where application microservices can be deployed in the form of containers. One of the most popular forms of application containers is Linux containers, because they can be instantiated in any Linux-based operating system. Although far from being the only Linux container engine nowadays, the company Docker is considered by many to be the leader when it comes to this technology.

However, in order to have a flexible infrastructure in which to provision Linux containers, developers need much more than a container engine:

- First of all, a way to group multiple OS instances (physical servers or virtual machines) into a single resource cluster is of paramount importance.

- Second, some logic needs to manage those resources and decide where to deploy new Linux containers.

- Third, once those containers are deployed, they need to be discovered and possibly added to load-balancing schemes.

- All of the containers need to be monitored to ensure the correct functioning of the application, and maybe scaled up or down depending on the application load at any given point in time.

As the previous paragraphs make obvious, any developer who actually wants to get away from managing infrastructure would be reluctant to embark on such a project, only to create an environment in which to deploy an application yet to be developed. This is where Mantl (an open-source project that anybody can download from https://github.com/ciscocloud/mantl) comes to the game: It's a "bundle" of all those elements required for a container-based IaaS environment. At the time of this writing, Mantl consists of the following elements (for an updated component list, refer to https://docs.mantl.io):

- Calico

- Chronos

- Collectd

- Consul

- Distributive

- dnsmasq

- Docker

- ELK

- etcd

- GlusterFS

- Haproxy

- Kubernetes

- Logstash

- Marathon

- Mesos

- Traefik

- ZooKeeper

- logrotate

- Nginx

- Vault

It is outside the scope of this chapter to describe each of these elements, but one of them is more important for the network admin than the rest: Calico. Project Calico (https://www.projectcalico.org/) is one of the existing ways to interconnect containers with each other, using the Border Gateway Protocol (BGP) in order to advertise the reachability of network containers in one host to the rest of the network, and thus avoid utilizing overlay technologies like VXLAN.

In the future, Mantl will support additional networking stacks for containers such as Contiv, with which the integration of Mantl stacks in an ACI infrastructure will be seamless.

Once a developer team has implemented Mantl as an IaaS layer, they can start to actually work on the application. In order to support them in this task, Cisco has created a continuous integration / continuous development (CI/CD) framework called Shipped (https://ciscoshipped.io), which enables application development on a container-based infrastructure such as Mantl (it should be noted that other IaaS platforms are supported by Shipped, too).

Cisco ACI App Center

This, the last section in this chapter, shortly describes one of the latest additions to the programmability features of Cisco ACI: the Cisco ACI App Center. It essentially provides a sort of "App Store" to the ACI administrator for downloading prepackaged automation solutions that leverage the rich Cisco ACI API and integration ecosystem. These apps are installed in the APICs so that you do not need an additional infrastructure to host them.

The Cisco ACI App Center is integrated into the ACI GUI and can be accessed through the **Apps** panel, as Figure 13-21 demonstrates.

If you want to download one of the prepackaged apps, just click the **Download an ACI App** section, and a new browser tab will open, taking you to the Cisco ACI App Center, as shown in Figure 13-22.

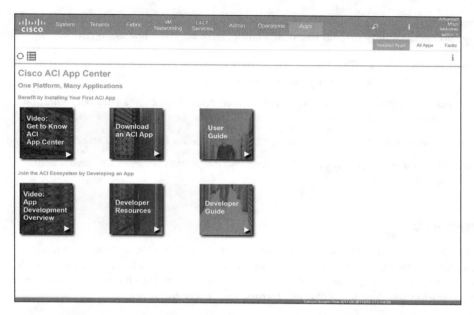

Figure 13-21   *Accessing Cisco ACI App Center*

Figure 13-22   *Cisco ACI App Center Repository*

Here, you can browse multiple automation solutions that greatly enhance the functionality and manageability of your Cisco ACI fabric. Here are just a few examples:

- **Contract Viewer:** Tool used to graphically represent contracts between EPGs as well as to visualize the traffic flowing between them

- **Fault Analytics:** Tool used to analyze and correlate fault events with configuration changes

- **Splunk Connector:** Tool used to send log information from ACI to Splunk Indexer

- **Tetration Analytics:** Tool used for seamless integration between Cisco ACI and Cisco Tetration

Summary

This chapter has described different approaches that show how to introduce network automation with Cisco Application Centric Infrastructure, which is much easier than with legacy network architectures. Which network automation approach is the right one for an organization will depend on multiple factors, such as the following:

- The goal to be achieved, such as DevOps, IaaS, PaaS, or hybrid cloud

- How the network is to be consumed (in other words, what level of access the network users should have)

- The level of programming language expertise

- What automation tools are already deployed

This chapter has demonstrated multiple automation approaches with Cisco ACI—from very network-centric use cases like configuring switch ports from an external application such as Microsoft Excel, to more development-centric models such as PaaS deployments.

Whichever automation strategy is chosen by an organization, Cisco ACI provides the platform on which incorporating network automation into the overall concept is most efficient, thanks to the architecture of Cisco ACI:

- Centralized network automation (one single API for the whole network)

- A modern, RESTful API

- Software development kits for languages such as Python and Ruby

- Development tools that include automatic code generation and API call discovery

- Out-of-the-box integration with many orchestration platforms

Index

Numbers

E

H

I

O

W